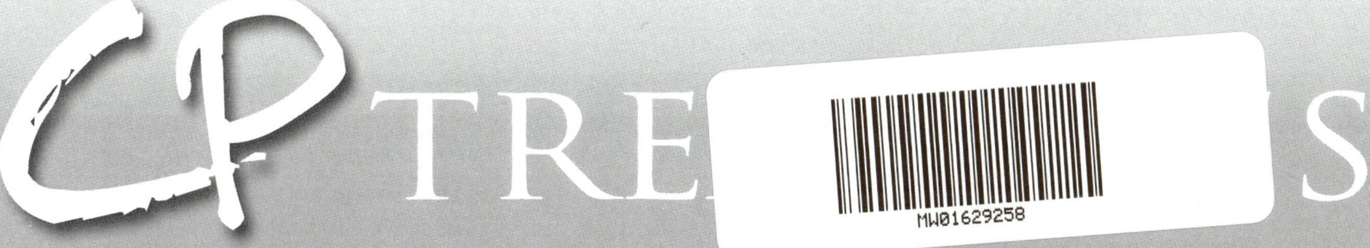

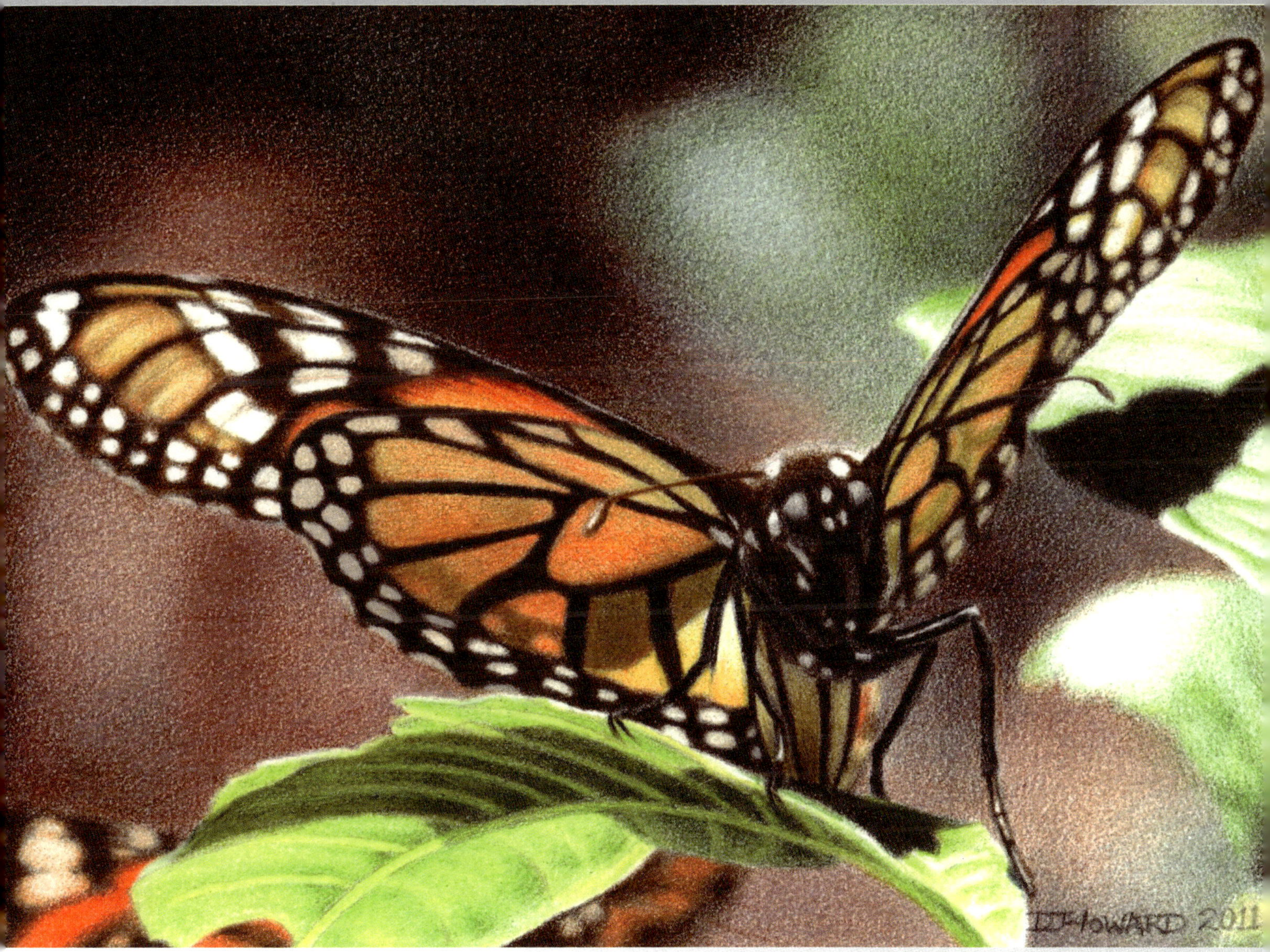

COLORED PENCIL MASTERWORKS
FROM AROUND THE GLOBE

edited by **Ann Kullberg**

www.annkullberg.com

INTRODUCTION

I remember, as if it were this morning, the first time I saw a small colored pencil drawing, hanging in a distant relative's home in 1987. I was transfixed. How could this be done with *colored pencils?* Thus began my love affair with this unassuming medium. In the 25 years since, I have watched in amazement as colored pencil art blossomed first in the US, mostly due to the Colored Pencil Society of America (CPSA) and then, gradually, across the globe. What a thrill. What a thrill to see all the many varied techniques and surfaces and styles emerge from out of the sharpened points of colored pencils.

In *CP Treasures* we have a feast. A feast prepared all over the world – Australia, India, Sweden, Japan, Ireland, the US, Spain, Canada, New Zealand, Denmark, and England. The artists who have graciously agreed to be featured in this book have reached a level of mastery that every one of us can envy and marvel at. Such a banquet of stunning images. They generously share with us the main course: their beautiful artwork. As a side dish, they offer us what drives them, what guides them, what inspires them; giving us the "why" of their art. Then for dessert, we're served their technical expertise in insightful instruction, tips and advice. As with any perfect meal, hopefully you lean back from the table satisfied...but looking forward to the next one, too! With any luck, we will be served another feast again next year, and for many years to come, from an every broadening scope of masterful colored pencil artists around the world.

It has been an honor to bring together in one book the treasures of so many talented artists, chronicling this moment in time in colored pencil art. I hope you too, will be transfixed by the breadth and depth of the beautiful artwork contained within these pages.

Ann Kullberg
Founder and Editor in Chief: CP Magazine

First published in the United States of America by:

Ann Kullberg
31313 31 Ave SW
Federal Way, WA 98023
USA
www.annkullberg.com

ISBN 978-0-9850610-0-5
10 9 8 7 6 5 4 3 2 1

Manufactured in the US by
hp Magcloud

Art on Cover: *Good Vibrations* - Adolfo Fernandez Rodriguez

Art of Back Cover: *Fluctuat Nec Mergitur* - Tanja Gant

PRODUCTION EDITED BY: Ann Kullberg

DESIGNED BY: Augusto Meneses

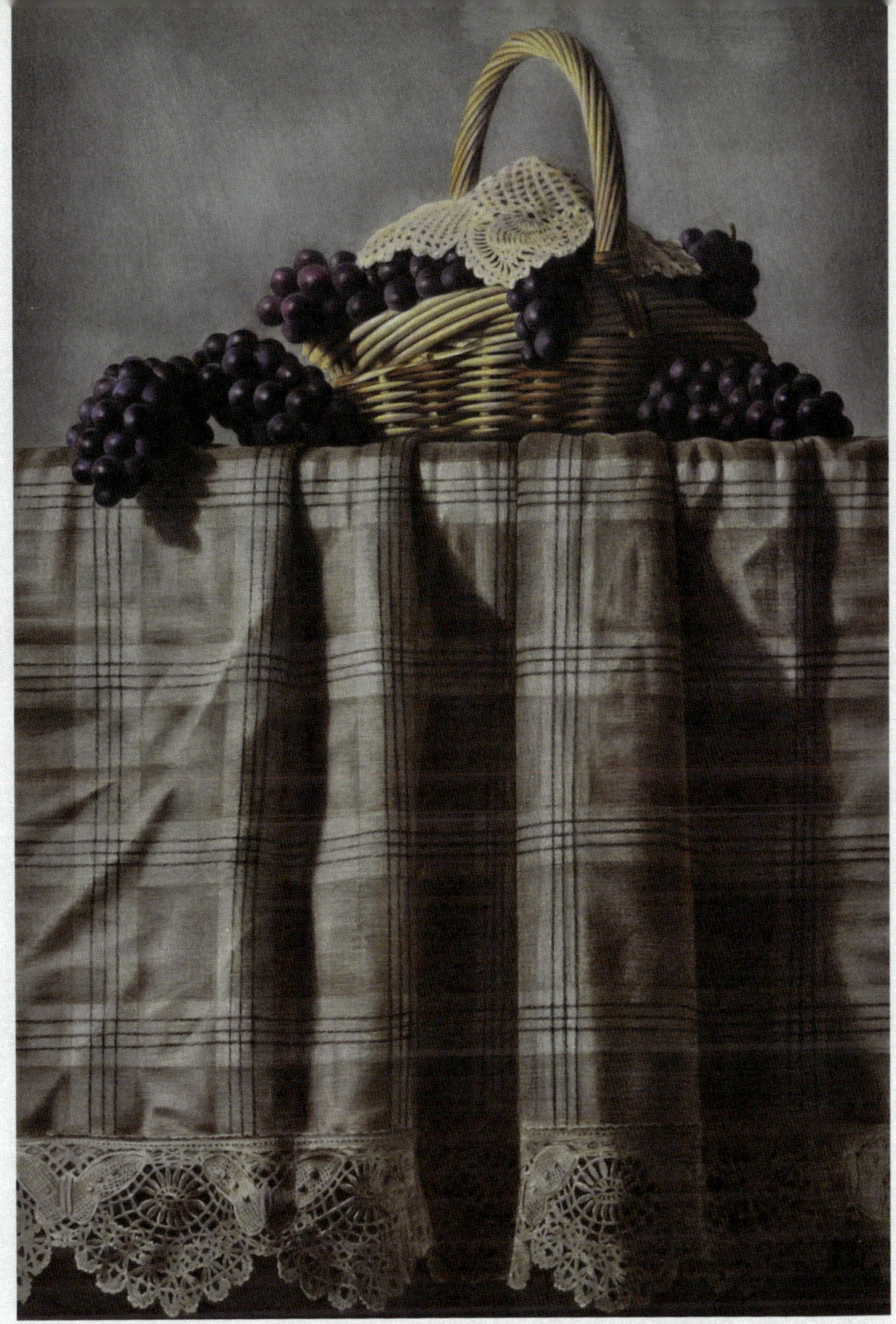

Grapes in a Basket

SHINJI HARADA | JAPAN
http://www.color-pencil.jp

1 For me, drawing a picture is to face myself. I use a motif to draw the world that I want to express. I make new discoveries when I stare at myself in the world of loneliness. One piece of a picture joins one person to another person. Therefore I continue drawing it. The next door is open again by continuing. Then I realize that one's past helps define oneself. Sometimes I have an overwhelming desire to draw the present. I have loved colored pencils since childhood. I give thanks for this encounter with art lovers.

TECHNIQUE AND TIPS
Mitsubishi Polycolor, Holbein Artist's colored pencil | Arches | 26.7" x 18.8"

"Light and expression of the shadows"that I value by work production most. I would like to draw eternal time into my own work. I use a hard colored pencil and the soft colored pencil in addition. Since I give a first coat with a hard colored pencil,then repaint a soft colored pencil. It is to show a deep feeling in a color. I don't use the eraser as much as possible, because it is since the surface of paper collapses. When I draw a still-life picture, I put the real thing and an image together. I paint the whole my work in gray first. It is to let you unify overall colors. I paint the top in a real color.

JANIE GILDOW | UNITED STATES
http://www.janiegildow.com

2 Light, shadow, and color fascinate me and I'm a detail-oriented realist. When I saw these blossoms in the early morning light, I couldn't wait to render them in colored pencil. The blooms only last a few hours, so I treasure their "capture in time."

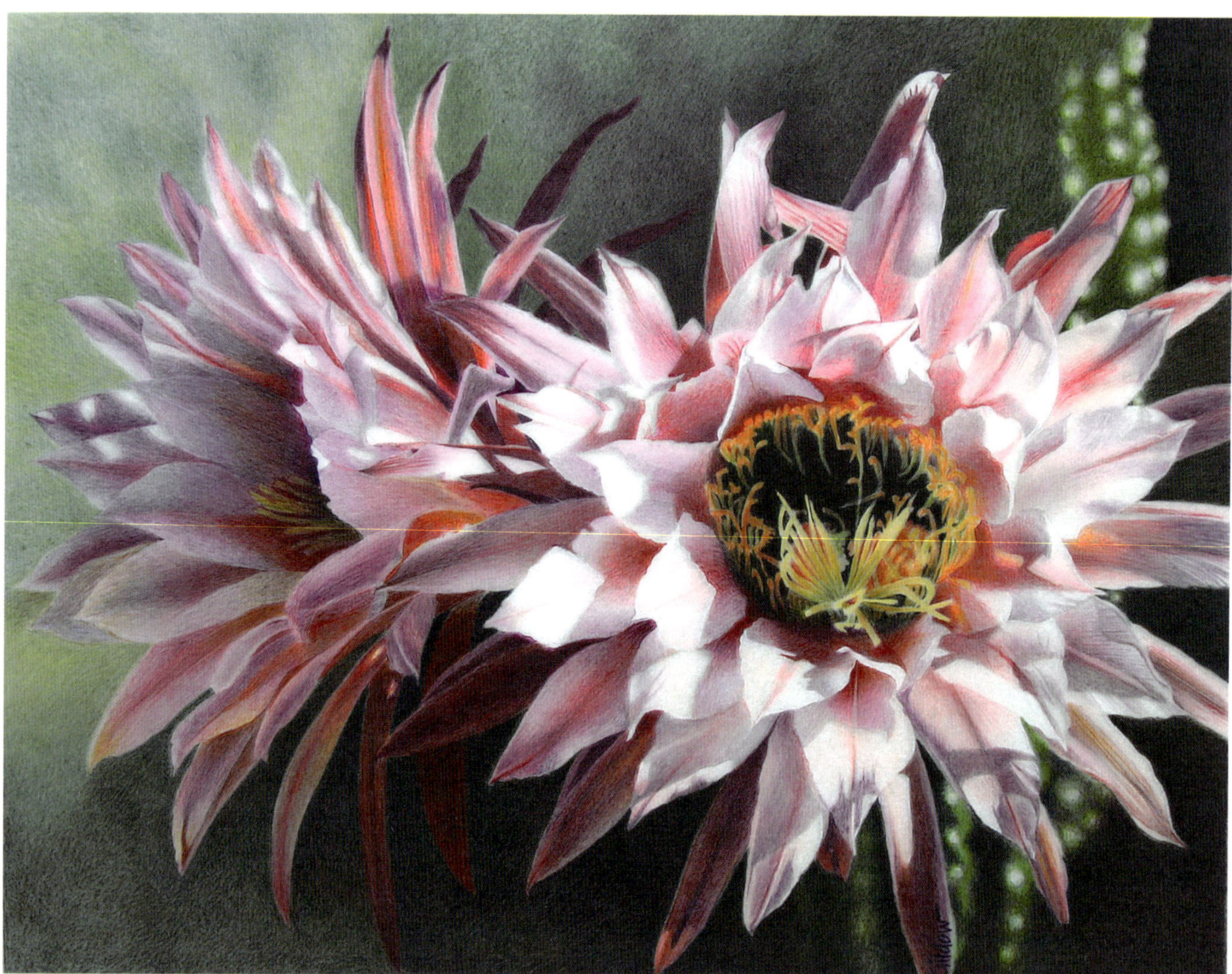

Desert Duo II

TECHNIQUE AND TIPS
Caran d'Ache Pablo, Faber-Castell Polychromos, Prismacolor | Herculene drafting film | 8" x 10"

I firmly believe that the most important elements of successful colored pencil are application (the three aspects of which are: point, pressure, and stroke), composition, creativity/originality, and technical ability, but all the technique and technical ability in the world won't make up for weak or bad composition. I begin with an idea and a subject, then carefully work with its composition before transferring my sketch to good paper. My application technique consists of light-to-medium pressure layering to build contour and color; if I need to burnish, I burnish only as a final step. I look for the magic in the interplay of light, shadow and color and then do my best to instill that magic in my work.

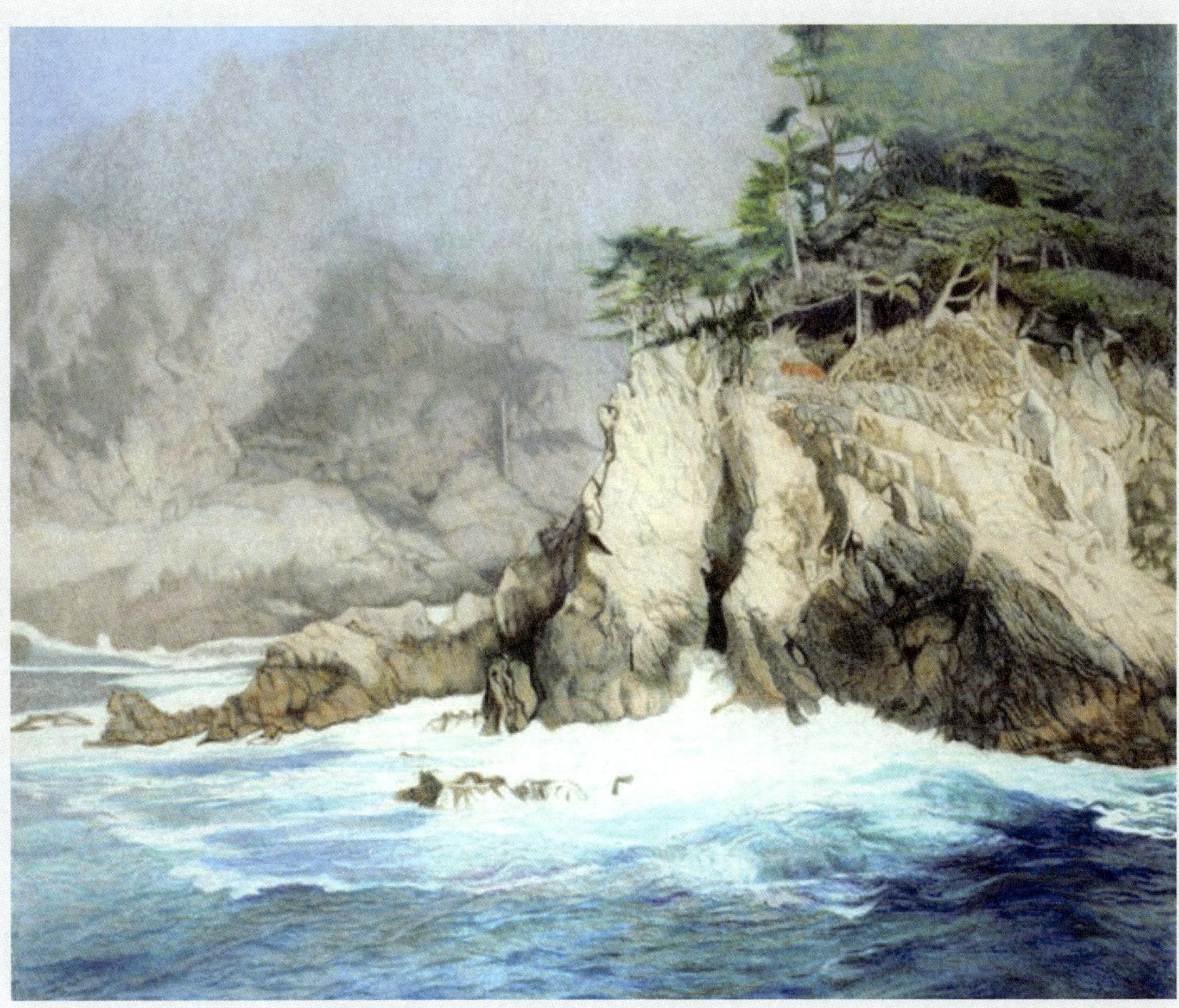

Cypress Cove in the Mist

BARBARA ROGERS, CPSA | United States
http://barbararogersfineart.com

3 Cypress Cove in the Mist is one in a continuing series of seascapes of the Big Sur, Monterey coastline of California. I fell in love with this area many years ago, and began drawing it as a way to keep the place close to me during the times I couldn't be there. After retiring a few years ago I began traveling there off season with a professional grade camera and, boy, what a difference this made!

This particular work is special to me because it depicts the mist that sometimes settles along the shoreline, softening and obscuring some of the rocks and highlighting others. I feel that I made a small leap with this work as I taught myself to create the effect of mist or fog. *(Sometimes wax bloom can be a good thing!)*

TECHNIQUE AND TIPS
Prismacolor and Prismacolor lightfast | Rising Museum Board | 14.5" x 16.5"

In doing landscapes take time to really LOOK at what you want to depict. With observation you will gradually be able to see the wide variety of colors in any given area. Often the color variety is subtle, but it is there. With observation you will be able to see what I call color families in any given scene, and with practice you will be able to select and weave many different colors together into a vibrant whole.

Also, to build rich color use many layers of different colors.

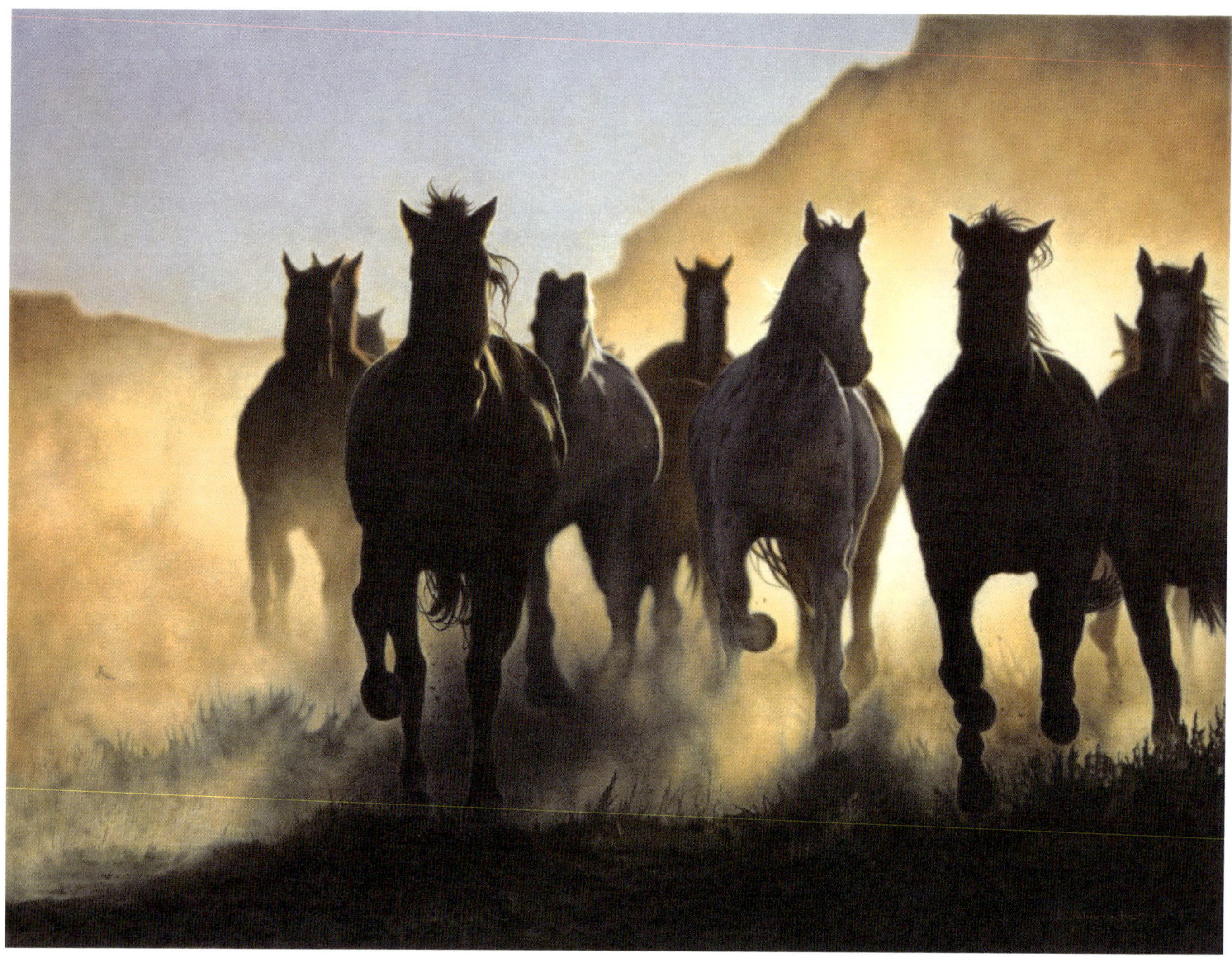

Dust and Thunder

LYNDA SCHUMACHER | UNITED STATES
http://www.lyndaschumacher.com

4 "Dust and Thunder" was initially inspired by my general passion for horses, and in many ways was a pivotal piece for me. I was challenged and energized by the sense of movement and implied sound, the way the dust and late-day lighting obsured forms throughout the image, and the fact that the rather ambiguous nature of the subjects was a tremendous diversion from my tendency to choose close-up subjects with a large amount of detail.

The execution of this work also provided the opportunity to exercise rules of effective composition in ways I had not done before. I attempted to lead and hold the viewer's eye through the use of value, contrast, the control of hard versus soft edges, and the use of light. In general, "Dust and Thunder" required me to stretch myself as an artist in a manner I had not even come close to experiencing previously -- and the amount of learning I received as a result of pushing through my frustration and self-doubt has been invaluable.

TECHNIQUE AND TIPS

Caran D'ache Pablo, Faber-Castell Polychromos, Prismacolor | Uart Sanded Pastel Paper | 18" x 24"

Initially I tend to lay in a base coat of solid colors to clarify the forms and their placement. Depending on what the finished color scheme will be, I sometimes will produce a grisaille of the image, done in only shades of gray. The entire base coat is brushed out using stiff oil painting brushes, a practice I employ often in between layers or to achieve certain textures. I then begin applying subsequent layers of color, gradually increasing the contrast of values and the detail of the textures.

I prefer to work on (Uart) sanded pastel paper as its surface lends itself well to the inherent nature of the textures of my subjects, and the level of tooth it provides holds up well under numerous layers of colored pencil. In addition, I alternate between working light-to-dark and dark-to-light -- and both of these techniques are managed nicely on this surface.

CHRISTI TOMPKINS | UNITED STATES
http://www.christitompkins.com

5 One of my most treasured family traditions is family game night. We tend to get caught up in the daily grind and forget to take time for family, and "Time Slips Away" is a reminder to spend time with the ones you love before it's too late. I usually prefer to draw live subjects, but in this case, I loved the interaction of the game pieces. They took on human qualities, and captured my attention as I drew them.

Time Slips Away

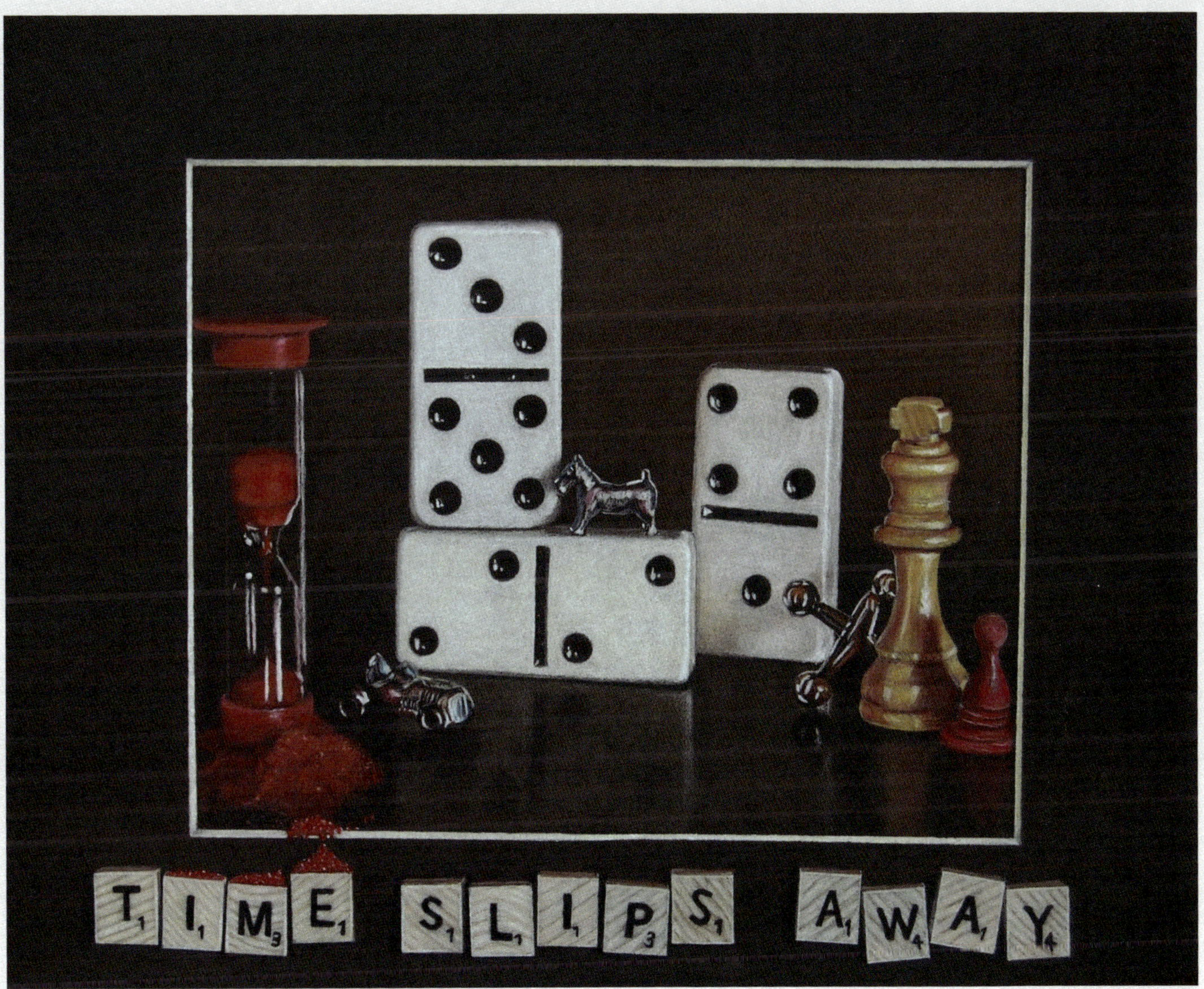

TECHNIQUE AND TIPS
Prismacolor | Black Stonehenge | 14" x 11"

For an artist with limited time, I recommend working on black or colored paper. It seems to take less time to fill the tooth, and you don't have to worry about those little white flecks showing through. The trick with black paper is to start with an underpainting using a white or cream pencil. Bring up your values, and then go back and add your color. This helps to achieve brighter colors. Otherwise, many colors seem to sink in to the black paper, and I think this is the reason why many artists shy away from working on black.

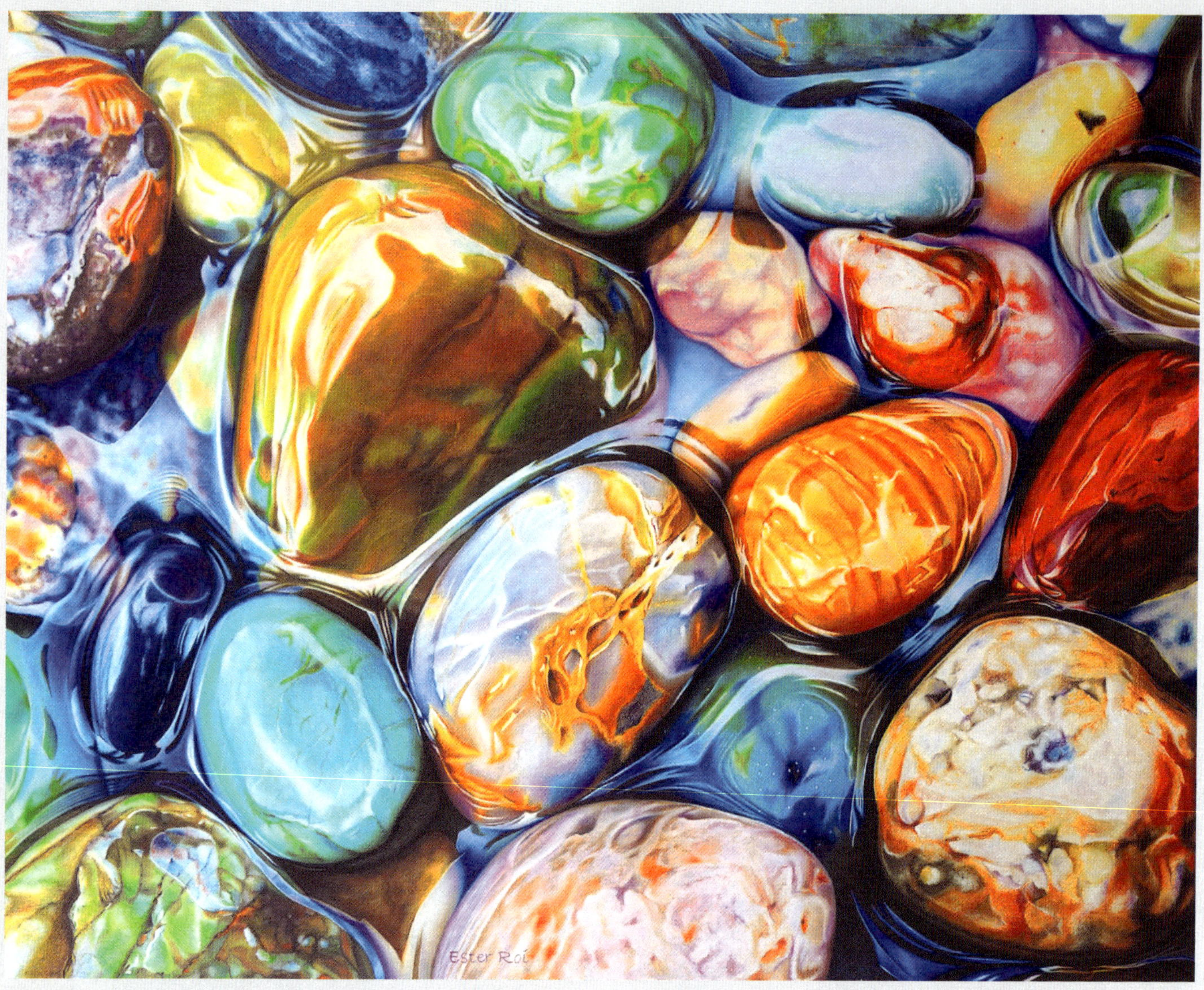

Social Network

ESTER ROI, CPSA | United States
http://esterroi.com

6 In the last several years I have been painting flowers and rocks and their interaction with water. I study them above water, below and in-between, and observe how their visual characteristics change and relate to each other.

I relish the contrast between a solid rock above the surface and its restless reflection below; the realistic depiction of a floating daisy versus its abstract, refracted counterpart. I marvel at how a flower can take on a new identity when floating below the surface and I strive to capture its ever-changing shape.

Water transforms everything it touches: hard lines become soft, warm colors cool, solid shapes break down into parts. Realism evolves into abstraction and the ordinary becomes extraordinary. The interplay among these realms is an endless source of inspiration for me.

TECHNIQUE AND TIPS

Prismacolor Premier and Caran d'Ache Luminance | Art Spectrum Colourfix Paper | 22" x 28"

I have always loved the burnished look in my colored pencil artwork. My goal is to achieve a highly pigmented and saturated surface that is almost indistinguishable from a painting. The secret behind my technique is that I apply heat during the process. Heat makes wax-based colored pencils like Prismacolor Premier or Caran d'Ache Luminance a more malleable and forgiving medium. *(continued on page 77)*

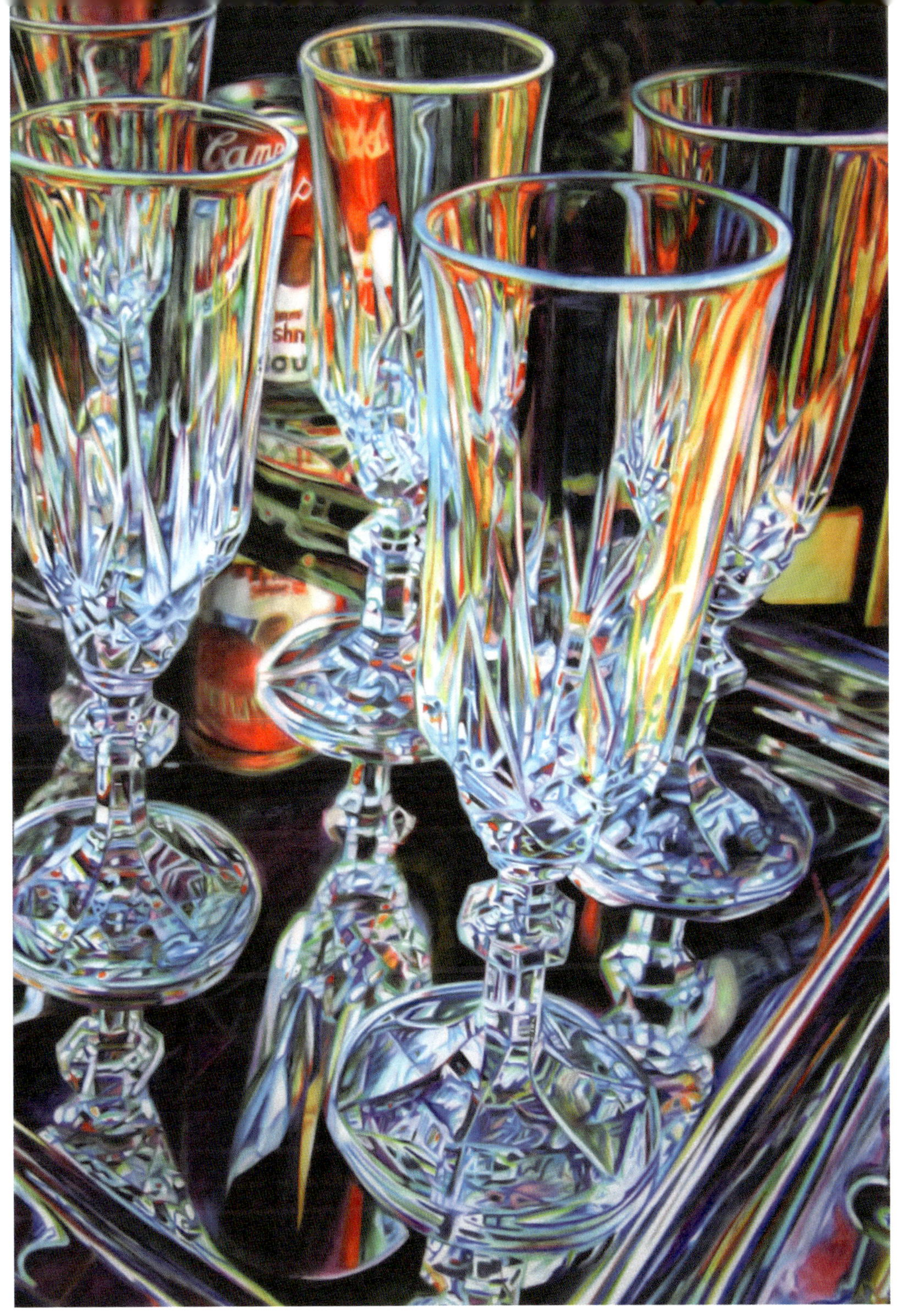

A Toast to Pop, Crystal #23

CAROL SCOTT | United States

7 In the past my work has been driven by concept with a colorist point of view. The Crystal Series begun in the summer of 2008 is about sight and the prismatic affect of color and movement. Although the work is very literal - there is an abstract quality. Looking through a form and how it changes as it goes through the structure multiplies the layers of reality. *(continued on page 77)*

TECHNIQUE AND TIPS
Prismacolor | clay board | 36" x 24"

Take lots of photos of the same subject without a flash. Use a computer to adjust the image as dictated by your personal vision. Copy the image as a soft line drawing on your surface. Work the surface as a puzzle, one small piece at a time.

RANJINI VENKATACHARI, CPSA | UNITED STATES
ranjinivenkatachari@gmail.com

8 Inspired by the finer nuances of simple everyday subjects, I embody my work with a variety of moods by using expressive color and dramatic lighting. Although I prefer to work in a realistic style, I like my art to be a passionate interpretation, rather than a replication of what I see.

My nature of rendering still-life is always evolving. My style varies from traditional ones; those inspired by the Dutch masters to contemporary; those with minimal subjects. "Primary colors" is part of my abstract-realism series where I composed a contemporary setup with a focus on color and paper. I have always been attracted to paper, purely because of its simplicity. The way light interacts with the folds and creases creates a dramatic sophistication that greatly inspires me. Each set-up I compose with a piece of paper brings about a new facet of its nature which always gets me thinking, what's next?

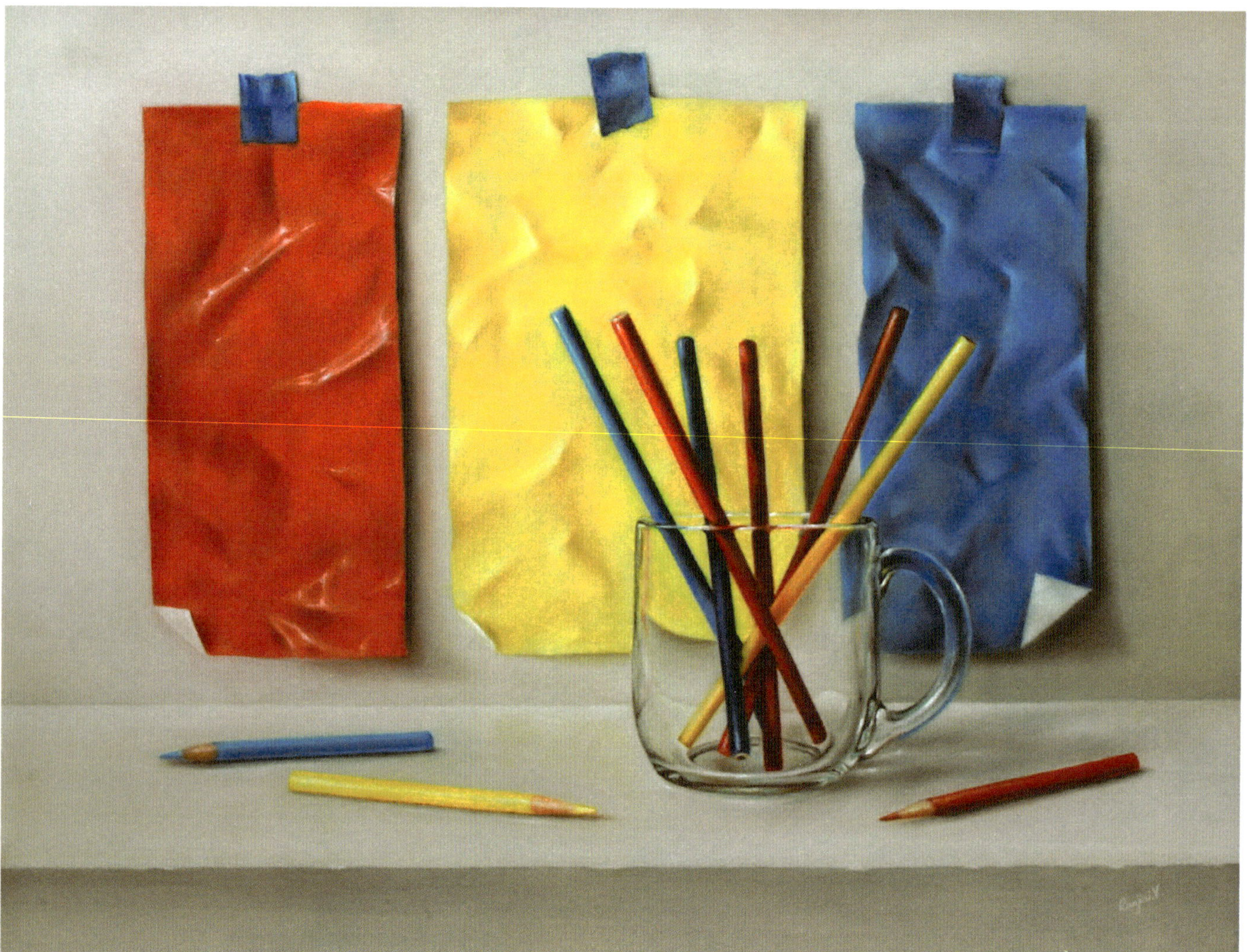

Primary Colors

TECHNIQUE AND TIPS
Neocolor II and Prismacolors | Ampersand pastelbord | 18" X 24"

I work mostly from photographs for my still-life. I make preliminary drawings in small size format to develop my palette and lighting. My preferred support is the Ampersand pastelbord. I love to work on this surface because it can handle several layers of colored pencils and can also be framed without glass just like an oil painting. I first block my colors using Neocolor II water soluble crayon and let it dry overnight. After it is completely dry, I add several layers of colored pencils and blend them with a dry bristle brush. Once the painting is completed, I coat it with fixative, varnish & UV spray and frame it without glass.

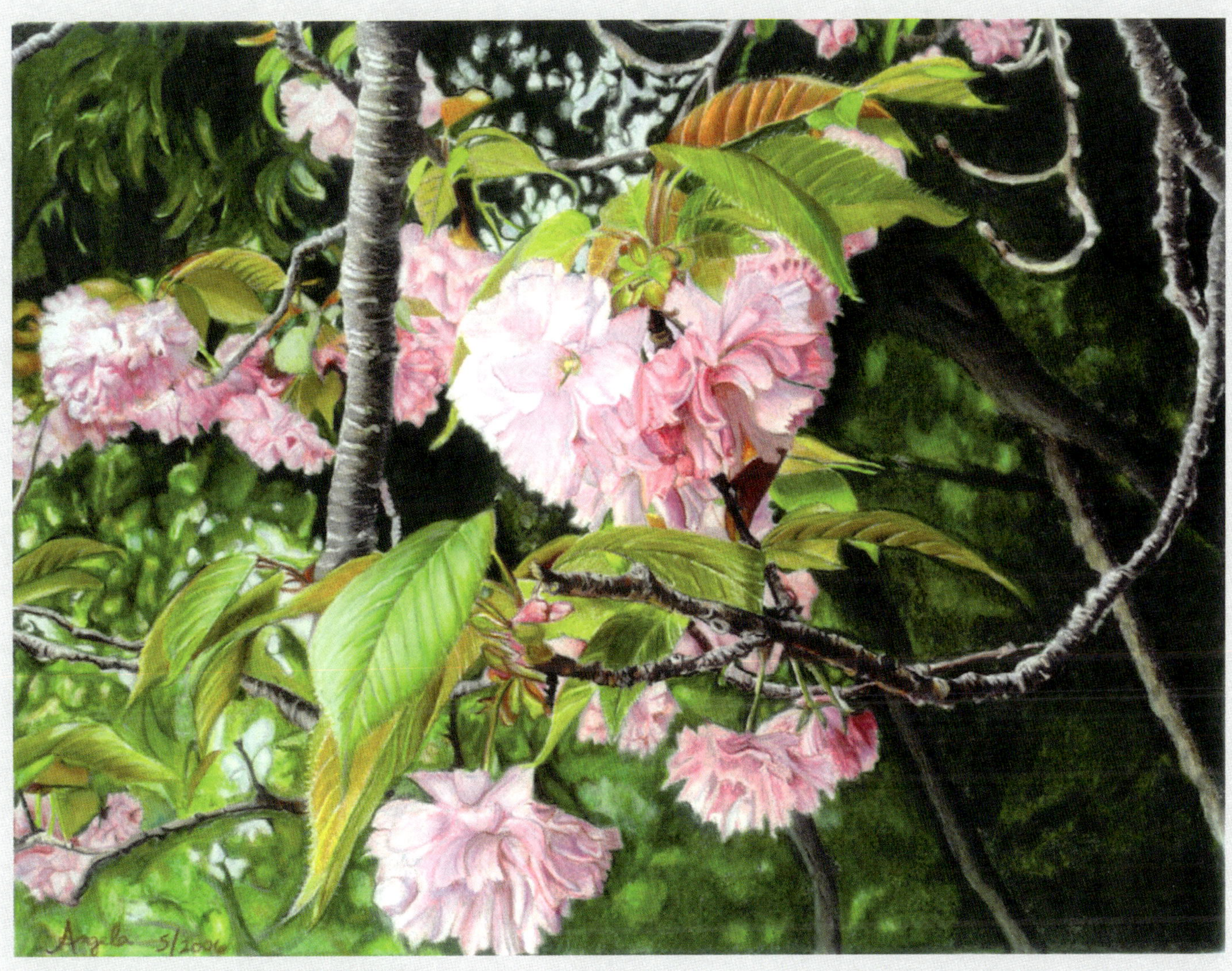

Ohanami, Isahaya

ANGELA BARTLETT | JAPAN
http://www.artgalleryangela.com/

9 I live in Japan and find Japanese gardens to be a great source of inspiration. There is something blooming every month of the year - camellias, plum trees, cherry blossoms and so on, the gardens themselves an art form that date back hundreds of years to the earliest Buddhist temples. There are many beautiful floral paintings in the ancient Buddhist temples here, and floral art continues to be an important part of the culture in the present day. So I have not only the inspiration of the beautiful things growing all around and in every season, but a rich body of work of artists from a great cultural tradition to admire as well. *(continued on page 78)*

TECHNIQUE AND TIPS
Prismacolor | Stonehenge | 8" x 10.5"

I work from photos, and I think it is very important to start with a good photo. You might have to take scores of pictures of a subject, or even more, and get only one to work with. The light and clarity are important. I think it is also nice to have a bit of a challenge. I like to have something in each picture that makes me think, "How am I going to do that?" That means I don't succeed with every picture, but if I have learned something new, then I feel happy about that. *(continued on page 78)*

DONNA CAPUTO, CPSA | UNITED STATES

10 My inspiration for "Wallflower" was this beautiful hydrangea flower which sat all by itself on the bush in front of my home. The colors intrigued me as well as the intricacies of the petals and I got great joy just exploring all of the facets of the bloom.

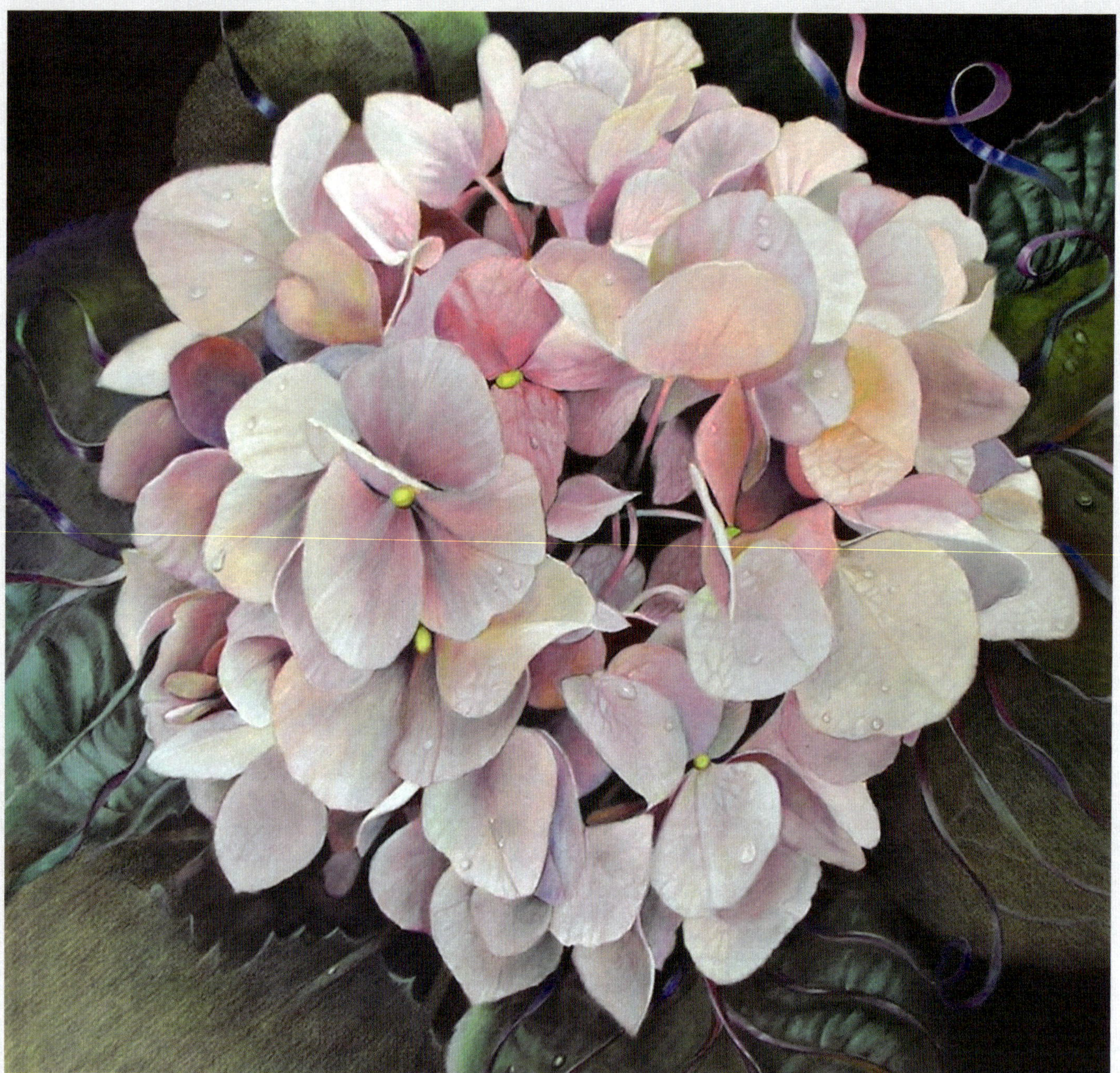

Wallflower

TECHNIQUE AND TIPS
Prismacolor | Windberg | 27" x 27"

Pay particular attention to values. It is the first thing that attracts me to a subject and the most important to me in a finished painting. The second most important thing is, what does the composition say to you. Is it telling a story? Is there an air of mystery about it? Would it draw a viewer in? And lastly, is to have fun with your art. Creativity is a happy and exciting thing.

TONI JAMES, CPSA |
UNITED STATES
http://www.tonijames.blogspot.com

11 My daughter Robyn had come to visit the day I had purchased some vintage furs at an estate sale. I figured eventually I would use as props. I had no idea I'd be using them the same day! As Robyn was having fun hamming it up, I grabbed my Nikon and started shooting. I was thrilled with the images I captured that day. "Vintage Beauty" is the first portrait from that shoot. This piece was a challenge due to the small size, and but also a study in softness and light. I wanted her beautiful eyes and the soft expression to draw your attention and enhance the beauty of the vintage furs.

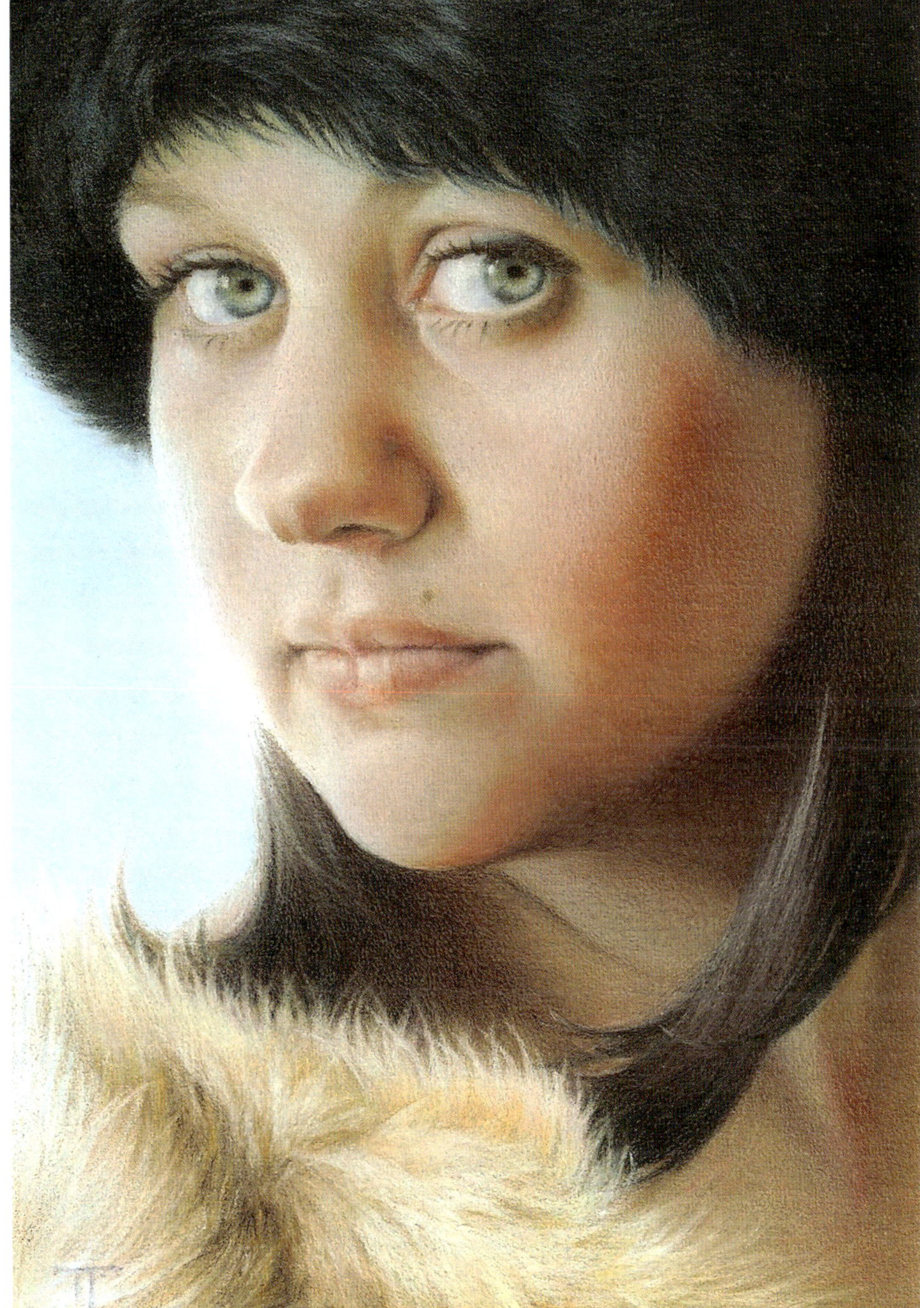

Vintage Beauty

TECHNIQUE AND TIPS
Prismacolor Pencils | Uart 600 | 4" x 6"

I prefer my resource images to be taken in a softer light, without flash. Overcast days are great, as are large areas of shadow, say, next to a building. I work with both a color and grayscale resource image on my easel. Because I'm looking for shapes and blocks of values, I generally work from the grayscale. The fun thing about working from overcast grayscale image is that you can use any color at all, as long as the values stay true! It certainly frees up the creativity. Working on an upright easel and mahl stick made such a big difference in my work, not to mention my shoulders neck and back. Whether I'm sitting down or standing up, I can work longer, more comfortably and more efficiently. I encourage everyone having back/shoulder/neck pain from long hours drawing to try it!

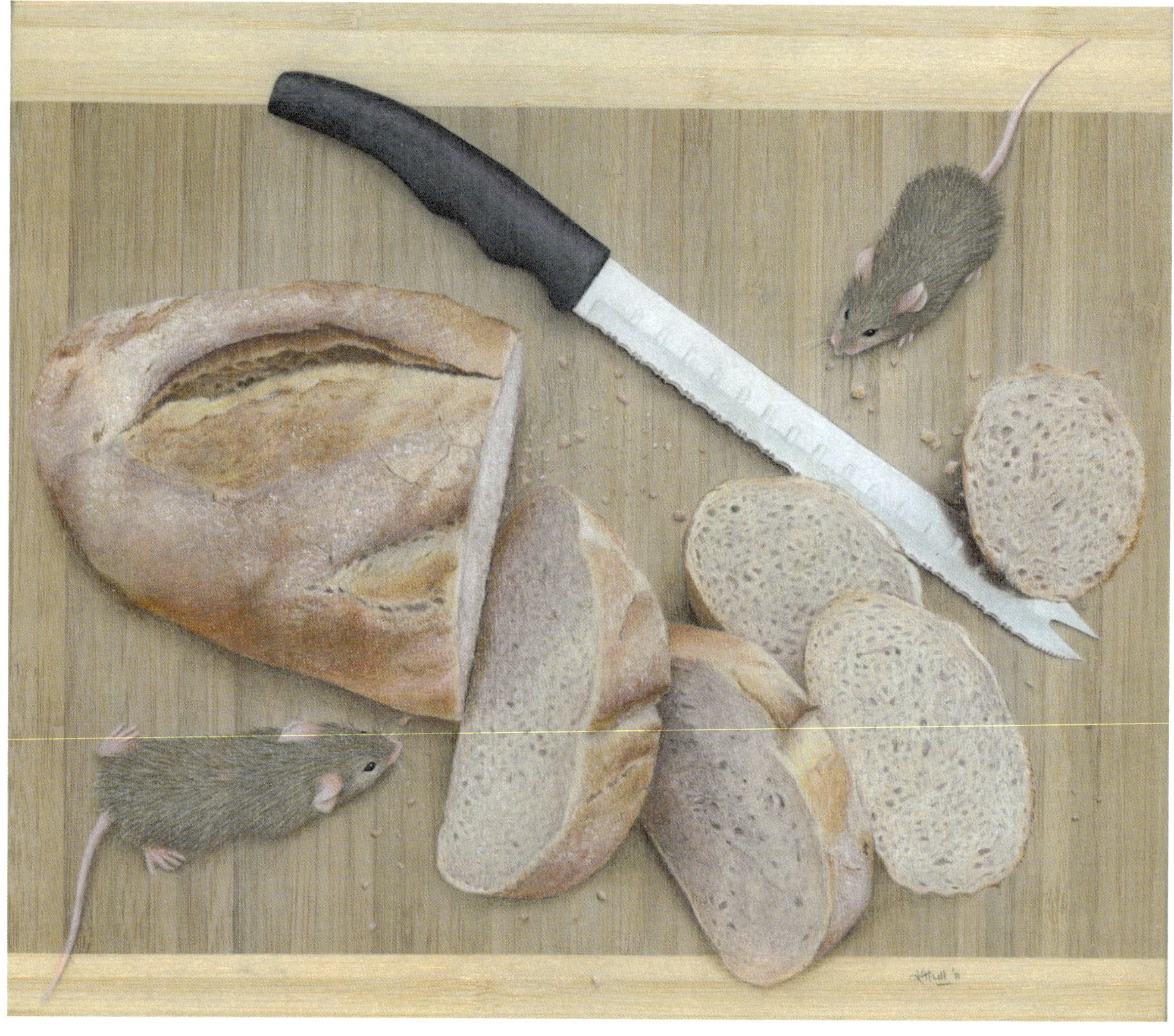

The Uninvited Guests

KAREN HULL | Australia
http://www.miniatureartbykhull.com

12 I love experimenting with coloured pencils on a range of different and unusual surfaces which deceive people into believing the artwork has been painted. I have also always had a fascination for Trompe L'Oeil art, which tricks the viewer into believing they are seeing something that is real and apparently 3D. When working with coloured pencils on bamboo to create extreme realism, the challenge was to try to minimize the texture that showed through from the bamboo grain. *(continued on page 76)*

TECHNIQUE AND TIPS
Faber Castell Polychromos, Derwent Drawing Pencils, Prismacolor Verithins | Bamboo Breadboard | 12" x 12"

I have a range of techniques when working with coloured pencils, which depend very much on the surface that I am using at the time.

Before drawing on the bamboo bread board, I sealed the wood, underpainted the areas to be drawn with white acrylic paint, and then gave the entire surface a coat of Colourfix clear primer, which gives a nice tooth for the coloured pencils to adhere to. *(continued on page 76)*

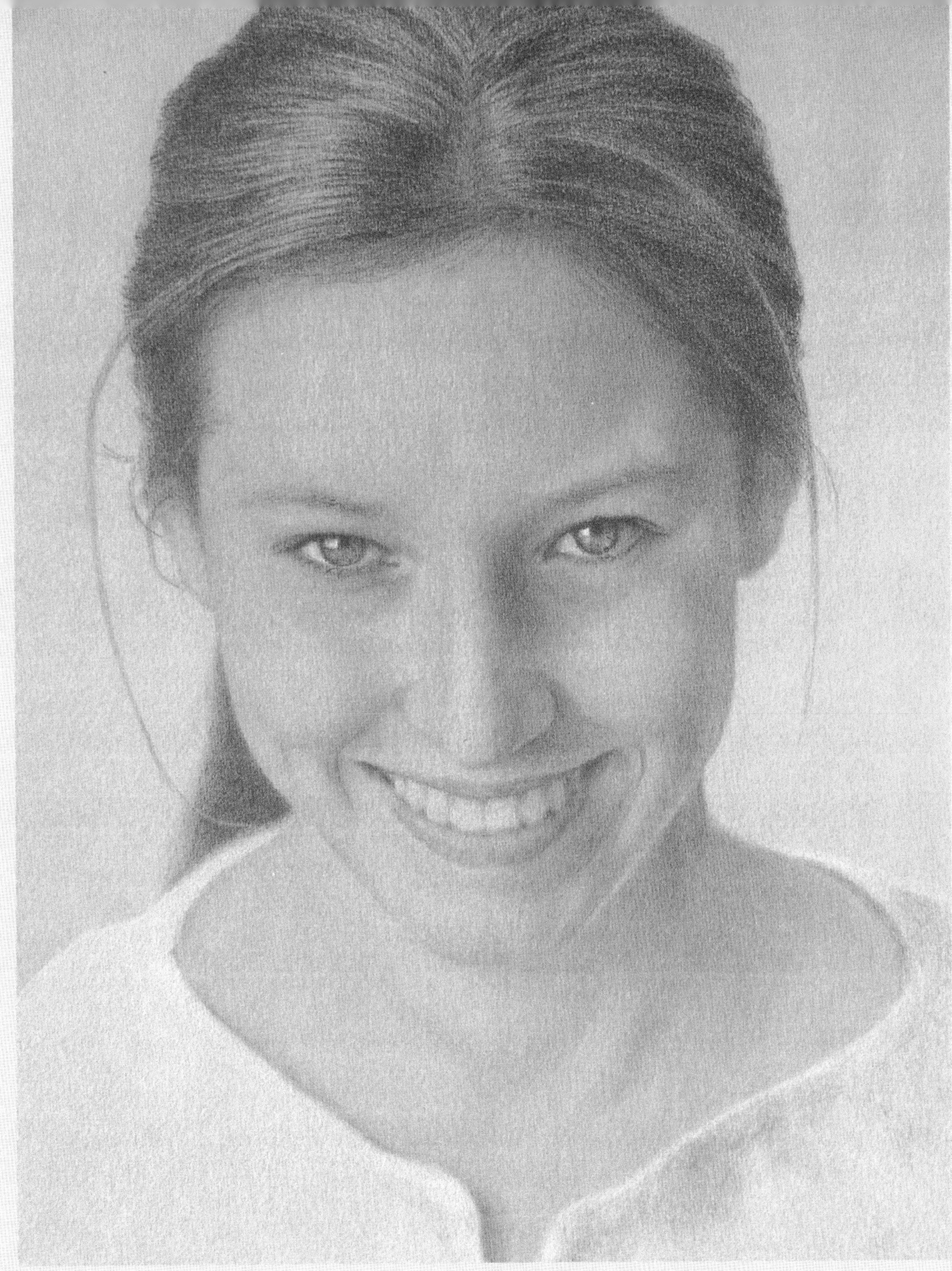

Julianna

HOLLY MAHLA | United States

13 Talk about fearful, my first colored pencil portrait was postage stamp size on a brown paper grocery bag. When I then braved more realistic sizes and surfaces, I still clung to the faces I knew well; my daughter, my son, close friends. I think that is probably the easiest way to gain confidence though, and I finally ventured into doing portraits of 'strangers'. *(continued on page 76)*

TECHNIQUE AND TIPS

Prismacolor | Mi-Teintes paper | 8″ x 10″

Some years ago, I was asked to do a portrait that flat out overwhelmed me. Too much visual information for me to handle. So I "reduced it down" by using only three pencils. *(continued on page 76)*

Oriental Poppy

ANN SWAN | ENGLAND
http://www.annswan.co.uk

14 These stunning poppies always flower in my garden every May and I have been itching to draw them ever since we took over the garden five years ago. But as I usually exhibit at 'The Chelsea Flower Show' in May I have so far be unable to do so. Finally, last year, I retired from Chelsea so I have been able to achieve my ambition and draw them. I love the way the stems curve under the weight of the huge flowers and I particularly wanted to include the amazing seed pods and hairy buds as they have so much character and are often overshadowed by the flamboyant scarlet flowers.

As a botanical artist I often find myself drawn the the underdog, the cabbage rather than the rose, the gnarled bark rather than the ripe fruits as I feel they are overlooked as it's always the showy flowers that grab our attention. I also love the shapes and textures found in the plant world which gives me the opportunity to really push the medium using different techniques of resist, embossing, underpainting, layering and lifting.

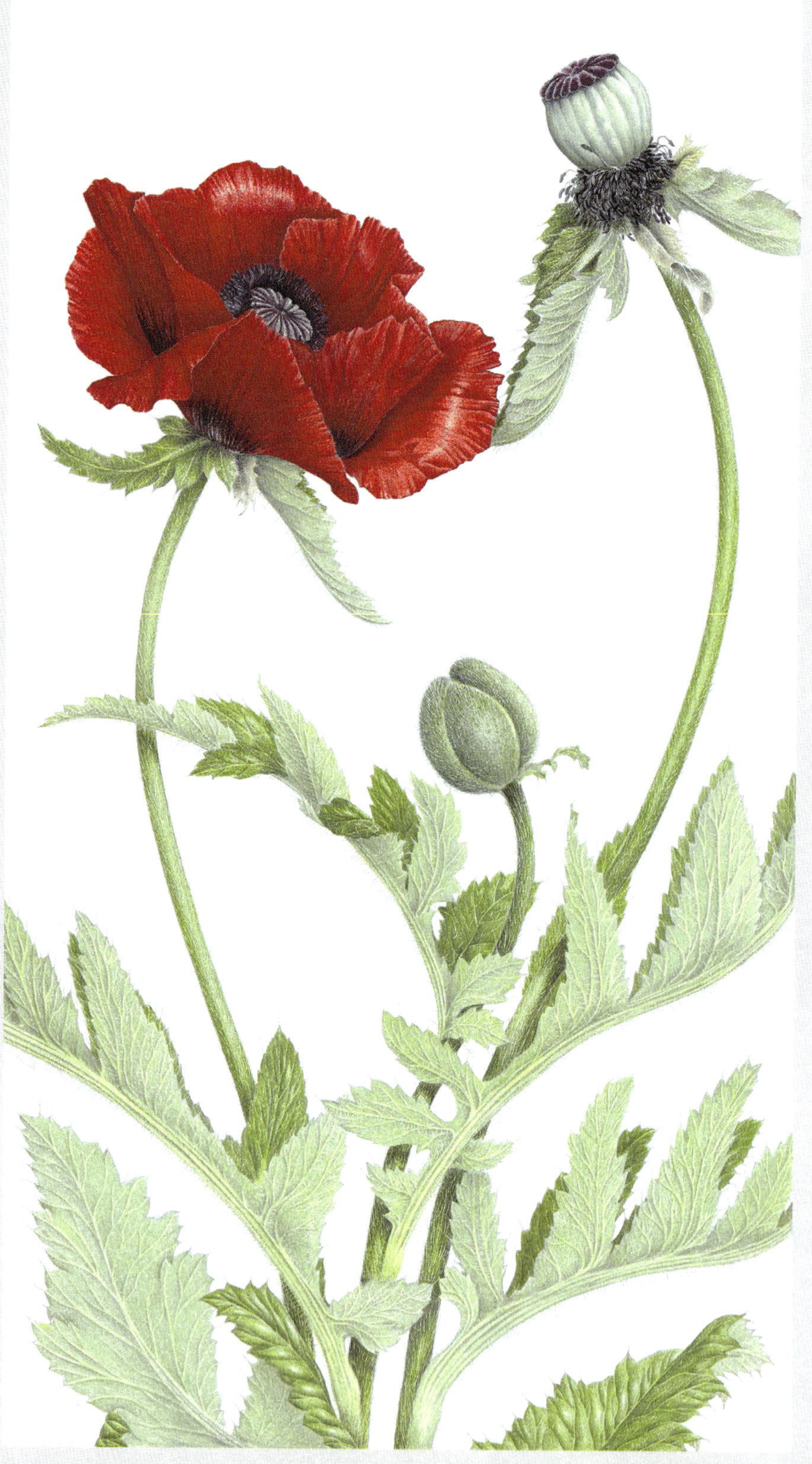

TECHNIQUE AND TIPS
Faber-Castell, Prismacolor and Luminance | Fabriano 5 Classico | 21" x 12"

To achieve the vibrancy of the reds on the flower petals I use a basic mix of Faber-Castell but always add some Prismacolor and Luminance reds to the mix to give the red that extra punch. The hairy buds, stems and leaves can easily, if somewhat painstakingly, be effected by embossing with a Pergamano 0.5 fine stylus. But to achieve the effect of the white hairs standing out from the leaves, stems and bud I have used a neat trick of embossing with the fine stylus and then lightly underlining the embossed line with a 0.3 mechanical pencil to give the impression of a shadow under a white hair. Hopefully it works!

DENISE HOWARD | UNITED STATES
http://www.DeniseJHowardArt.com

15 In February 2011 I fulfilled a lifelong dream by visiting the area of Mexico where the hundreds of millions of monarch butterflies from all over North America east of the Rockies overwinter. It was an incredible experience. I came away wanting to immortalize some of the individuals that had flown those thousands of miles on papery wings, so I started a series of drawings. This is #5, looking right at you with sunlight shining through her wings, turning her into a little stained-glass window.

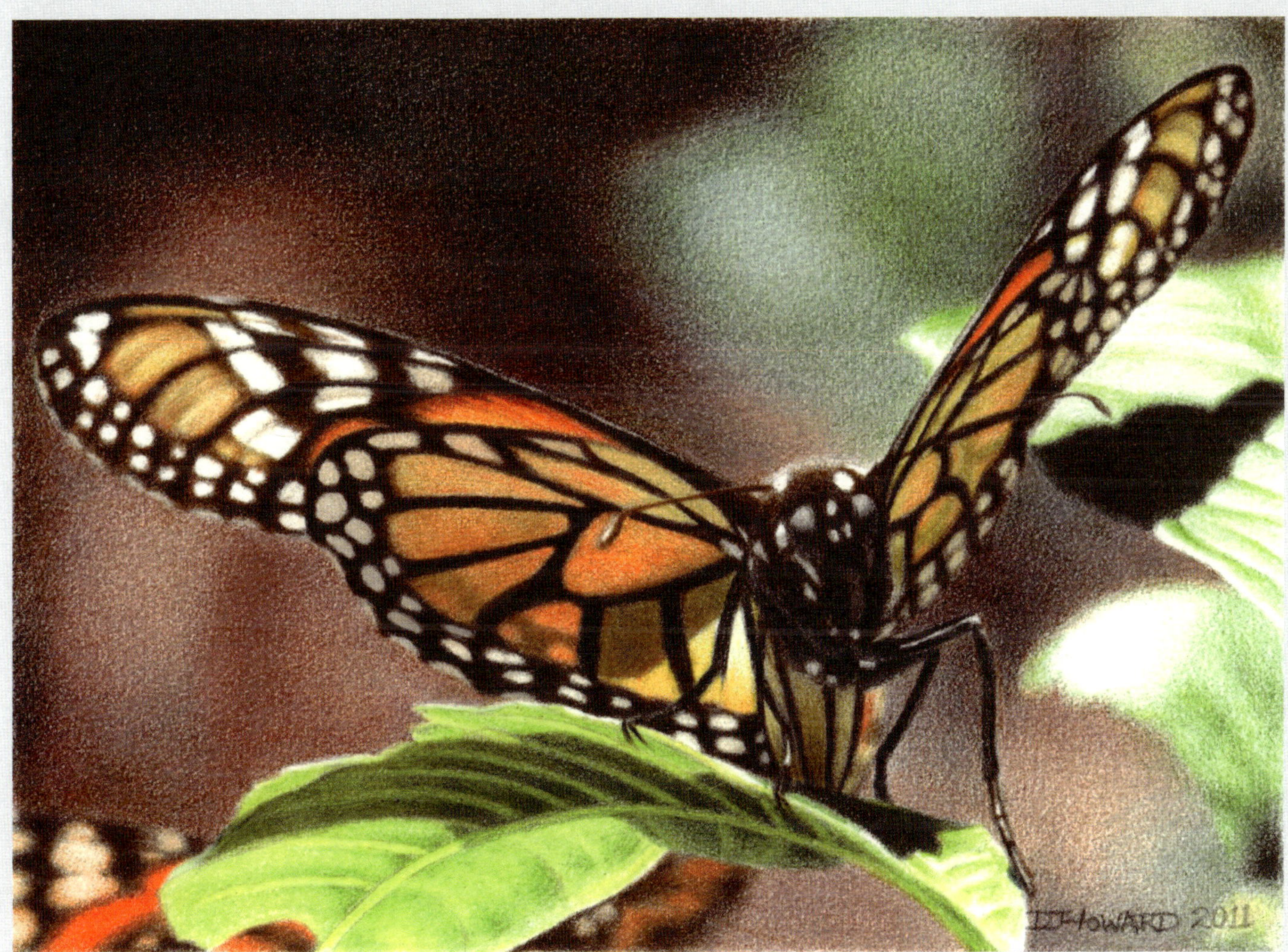

Monarch #5

TECHNIQUE AND TIPS
Prismacolor | Stonehenge paper | 5" x 7"

Rendering blurred backgrounds are a challenge for many people, so I often get compliments on this one. I think it's because once they've finished the subject itself, they just want to get the rest over with so they get sloppy. I've seen many otherwise beautiful drawings ruined by poor backgrounds. I spend at least as much time drawing a background as I do my subject. Take the time to see the colors, forms and values in a background and render them just as carefully. After all, your subject doesn't exist independent of its world!

JANIE PIRIE, UKCPS | ENGLAND
http://janiepirie.co.uk

16 It was just another day of shopping for fruit and vegetables. This cabbage caught my eye as it was so perfectly round. When I arrived home and was unpacking I suddenly thought what a challenge it would be to draw it. I pushed back some of the outer leaves and placed it on a table outside. The sun shone through the top leaves and the colors were utterly magical. That was it! My pencil was out and the drawing began. In all the picture took about 180 hours to complete but I enjoyed every minute of the time spent on this piece. There were so many shades of green, yellow/green, grey/green, blue/green and even creamy/green. Each leaf was an exciting challenge and it was a joy to watch the whole cabbage came to life on my paper. I sprayed the cabbage each day with a fine water mist and kept it in a stay-fresh bag in the fridge every night. It kept well for three weeks and by then I had worked on almost every area. I bought another cabbage just to make sure I maintained my colors on the outer, right-hand leaves. I hope I've shown that something as ordinary as a cabbage can, when looked at through an artist's eye, be a thing of beauty. *(continued on page 76)*

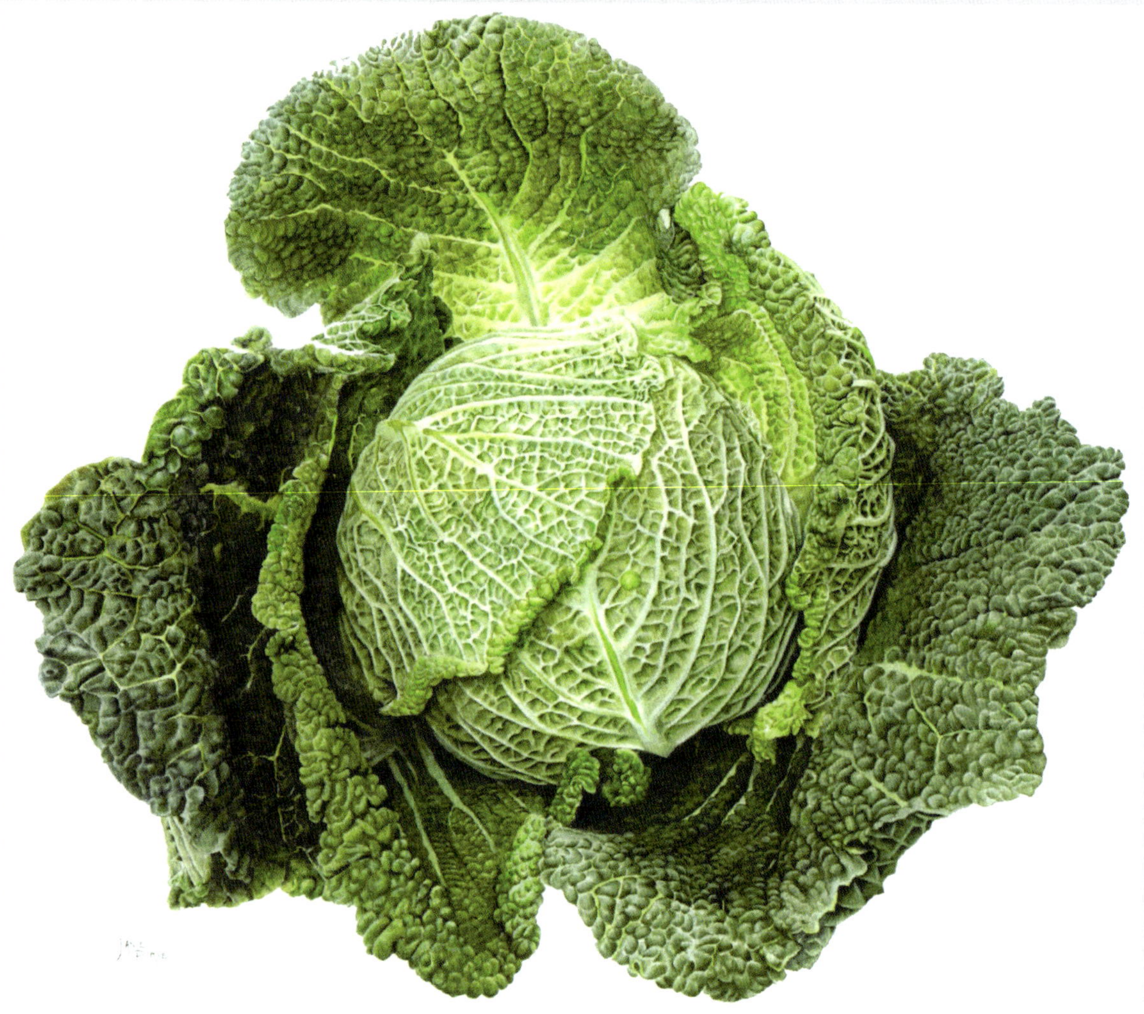

The Majestic Savoy

TECHNIQUE AND TIPS
Prismacolor and F-B Polychromos | Fabriano 5 | 13" x 13"

The drawing must be accurate and this is something I do go on about. Choose colors carefully and keep looking at what you are drawing - don't just get an idea of it in your head and then color away without constantly comparing your work with the subject. GO SLOWLY! If the first layer of color is applied badly then the rest will be messy. So, take care to lay down a really soft layer, making sure the pigment from the pencil has successfully covered the paper surface without any pressure - because too much pressure at the outset will flatten the 'tooth' and make subsequent layers more difficult to apply. Build up your layers slowly and carefully and if you think you've made a mistake don't wait and see if you can cover it - remove it immediately otherwise the whole piece can go wrong. Never hurry to finish your work - it will be complete eventually - and will look better for an unhurried and thoughtful approach.

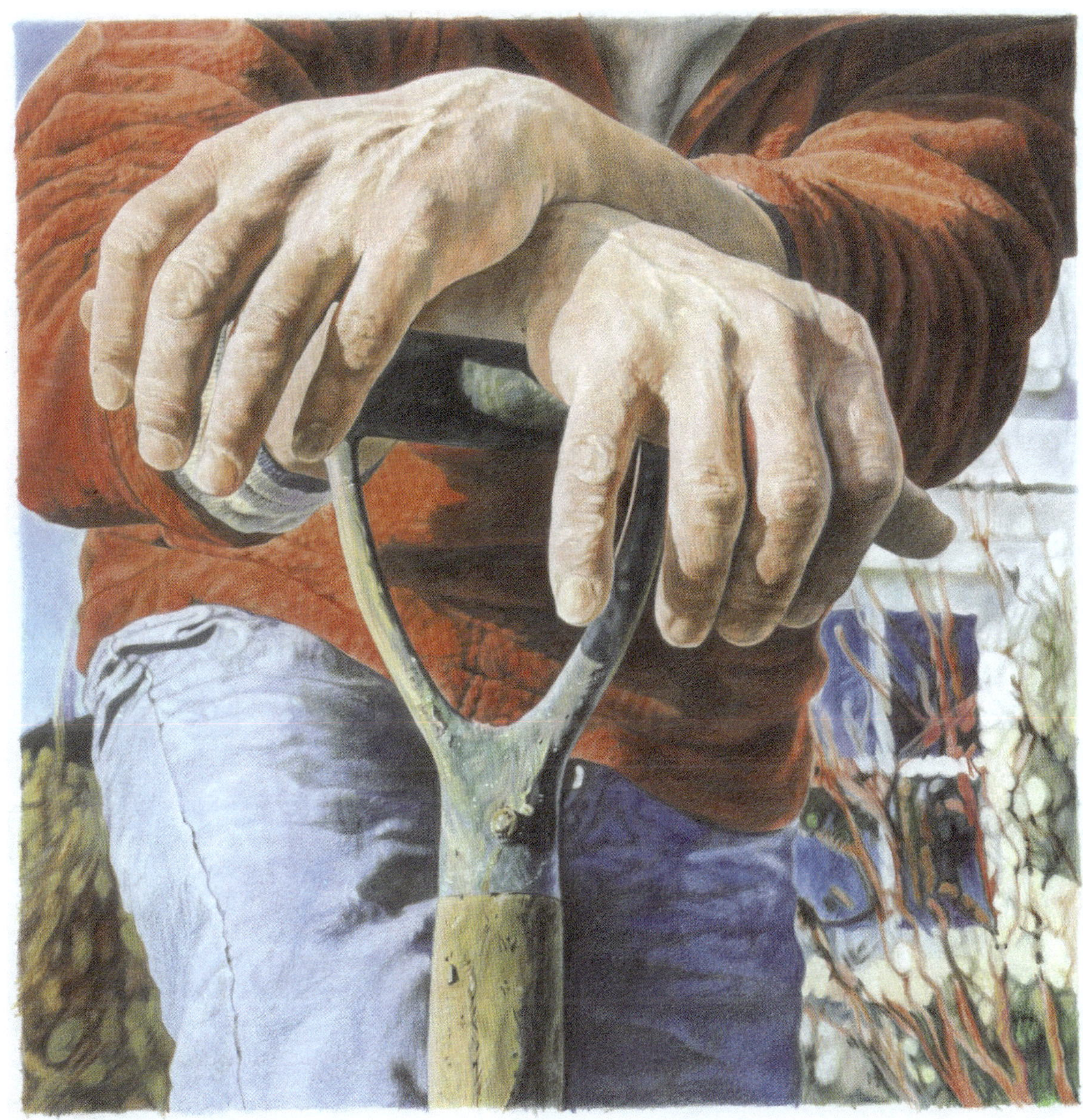

Himself

JULIE DOUGLAS | Ireland
http://juliedouglas.co.uk

17 I love drawing people and animals more than anything else, and always, always the thing that inspires me is light. The difference between something being worth drawing and something not, is always the way that light is hitting it. The depth of shadows, the brights of highlights, nuances of colors reflected and bounced across the image all rely on the magic touch of light. If I am working from a photograph, the vast majority of them are taken outside. I did a portrait of a famous musician, who sat outside my studio and we chatted while it was cloudy, but the second the sun peeped out I interrupted him shouting 'Play! PLAY NOW! And he dutifully did, so I could get a shot of the movement, along with the light. *(continued on page 76)*

TECHNIQUE AND TIPS
Caran d'Ache Prismalo 1 and Caran d'Ache Luminance | Bristol Board by Canson | 9.75" x 9.75"

I always draw everything out as a line drawing first, including every change in tone, light, color, in great detail. It may take 20 or more hours to do this stage - and it is always a good indicator to me how long the color stage will take. I am always eager to start the color, and with faces I begin with the eyes, and flesh areas, then I work as if the color is pouring over the page bit by bit (meaning that I don't jump across the page from one spot to another, instead the color spreads carefully and consistently from the starting point, out). *(continued on page 76)*

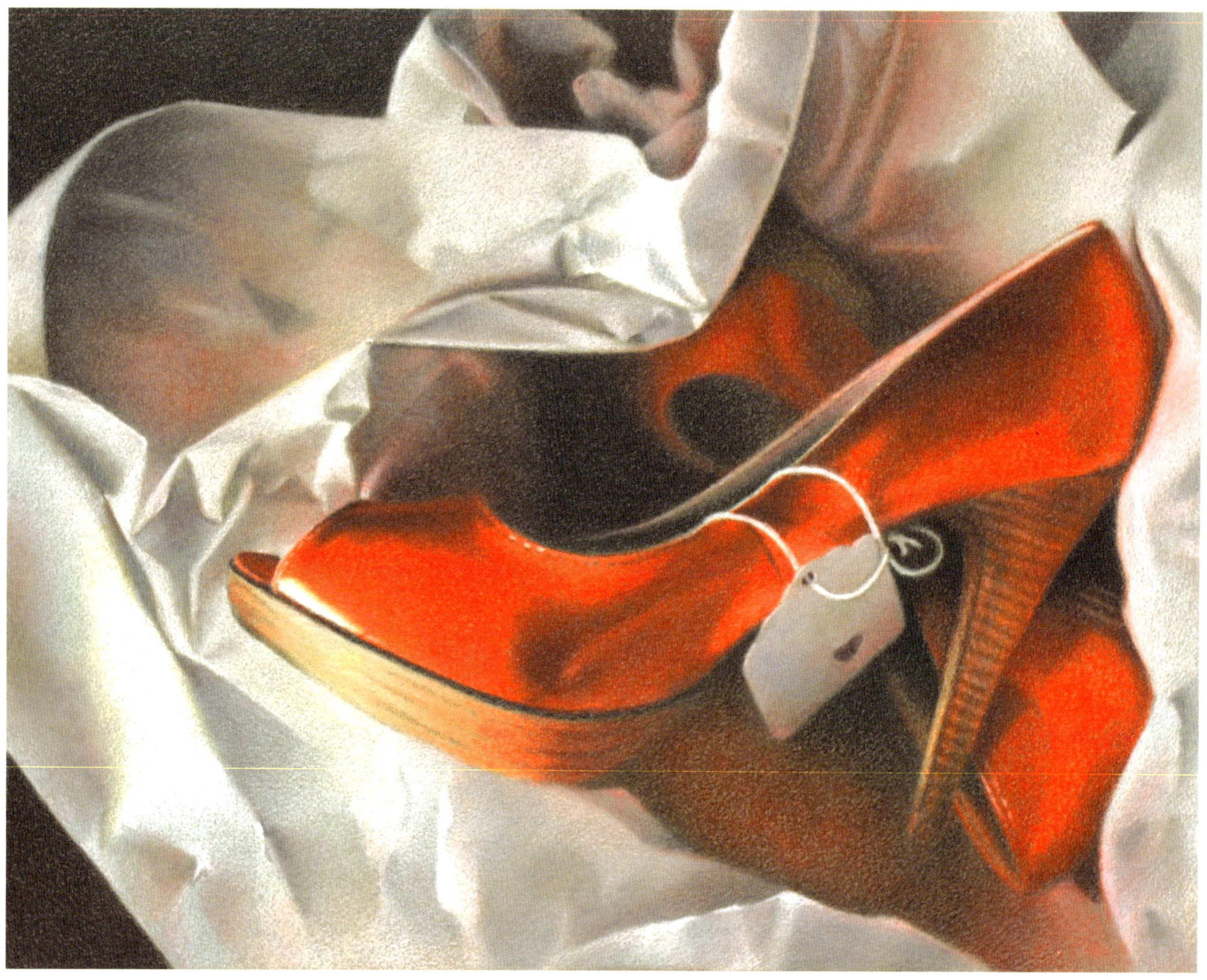

Night's Agents

NICOLE CAULFIELD, CPSA | United States
http://www.nicolecaulfieldfineart.com

18 I like to create illusions of 3-D space - whether it is an actual object like an apple or cup, or if it is space like the the depth of a box or the shadows inhabiting that space. Its feels like I am doing a magic trick. So with this drawing I knew I wanted to draw these shiny red pumps, but it took me a while to come up with the rest of the idea. I thought about putting them in a box with a side light to create shadows in the box, but then remembered that often shoes are in the box with tissue paper. I did a whole series on paper showing crumpled bags in various ways and loved trying to get the paper to look like its valleys and folds were coming out at you. The crumpled, abstract nature of the paper turned out to be the perfect environment for the slick shiny shoes.

TECHNIQUE AND TIPS
Derwent Coloursoft and Prismacolor | Tan Ampersand Pastelbord | 11" x 14"

I work on a sanded surface which makes the colors go on brighter and faster, but it is also a tinted surface. For this piece, the board was tan colored. When you work on a colored surface you have to be aware of if and how much white is in a color. If a color has no white in it, it will sink into the tinted surface. The more white a pencil has in it, the more it will sit on top of the colored surface and stand out. I find that I have to use pencils with white in them even in places that I think of as dark on the value scale - even shadows.

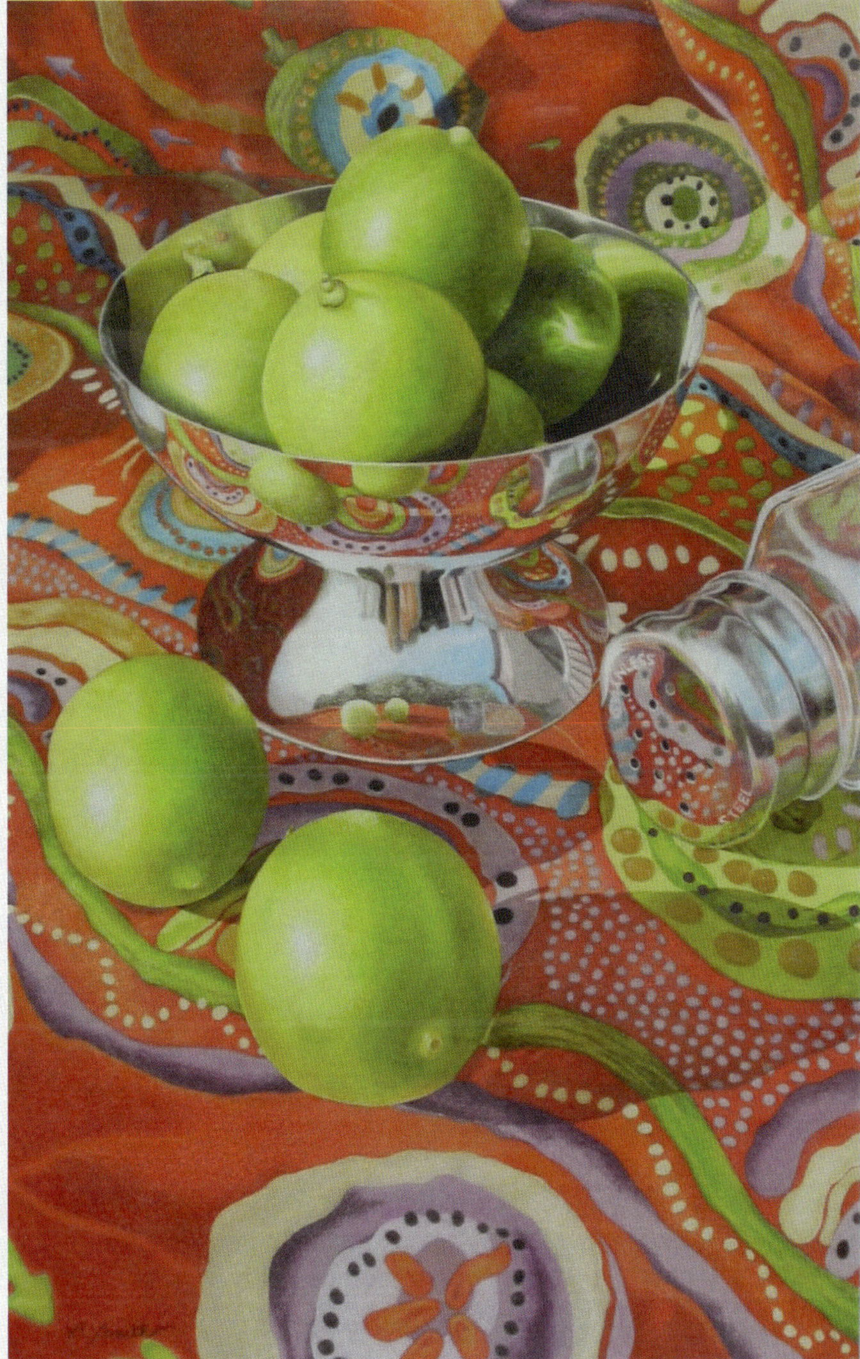

SHERRY SMITH | United States

http://www.sherrysmithart.com

19 I have come to realize that although my work is realistic in nature, it is not about the subject matter as much as it is about my emotional response to color and pattern and light and dark. Bright colors and shapes lift my spirits and bring me a sense of joy. I haunt flea markets and thrift stores to collect reflective objects to highlight the yards and yards of brightly patterned fabrics that are the inspiration for my still life works. It is then a mad dash to gather all of these components and head out to the deck where the sun can bathe everything in its natural warm glow. I take as many as 50 photos of each set up to ensure that the composition is just right. Where the shadows fall upon the fabric are just as important to me as the objects they are cast by!

Key Lime Fiesta

TECHNIQUE AND TIPS

Prismacolor | Strathmore Bristol vellum | 19″ x 30″

After a light drawing with a #2 pencil is in place, the color will then be layered very lightly at first and then slowly more and more opaque layers are added until they all blend into a wonderfully colorful and bright finished piece. Patience is a key element when working layers in colored pencil. The soft blending that occurs upon layering cannot be reproduced with a paint brush.

A large piece may take 6 to 8 weeks to finish, and half-way through I will wonder what ever possessed me to work so large, but the rewards are very well worth the time spent!

JONATHAN NEWEY, UKCPS | England

http://www.jonathannewey.com

20 In 2011 I visited London Zoo to see the Mountain Gorillas. Their enclosure has a glass wall on one side and whilst I was there one of the males was leaning up against the glass chewing on a piece of broccoli giving me an opportunity to take some close up photographs. It also gave me a chance to look into the eyes of one of the most majestic and rarest creatures on earth. His thoughtful gaze transfixed me for a while until he decided he had had enough of his broccoli and wandered over to have a drink of water from a nearby bucket! When I got home I transferred the photos to my computer, zoomed in and cropped the face to concentrate on the reflections in his eyes. The whole drawing took about 40 hours to complete. This is the second complete picture this size I have done working on black Stonehenge paper.

In His Eyes

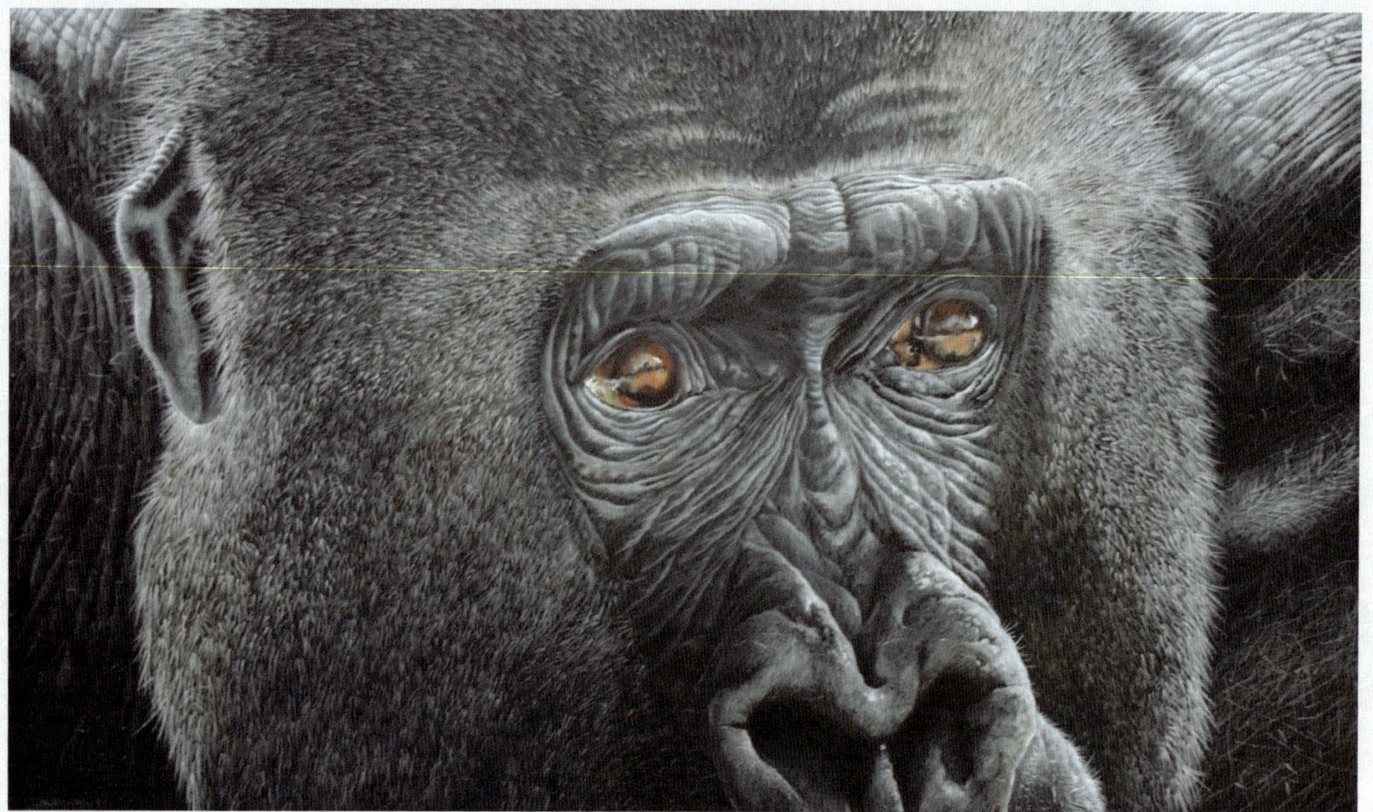

TECHNIQUE AND TIPS

Prismacolor | Black Rising Stonehenge | 13" X 22"

When working on white paper I would normally work from light to dark, sometimes using up to 12 layers of pencil in conjunction with a blender pencil. When I first started working on black paper I found that I could not use the blender pencil as it left a warm grey mark so I had to change my drawing style slightly to compensate. The hair on the Gorillas head was done using 4 different greys from dark through to light. The face was done using a variety of greys, both warm and cool. Because I could not use the blender pencil to smooth the colours together I used each successive grey to smooth the previous layer.

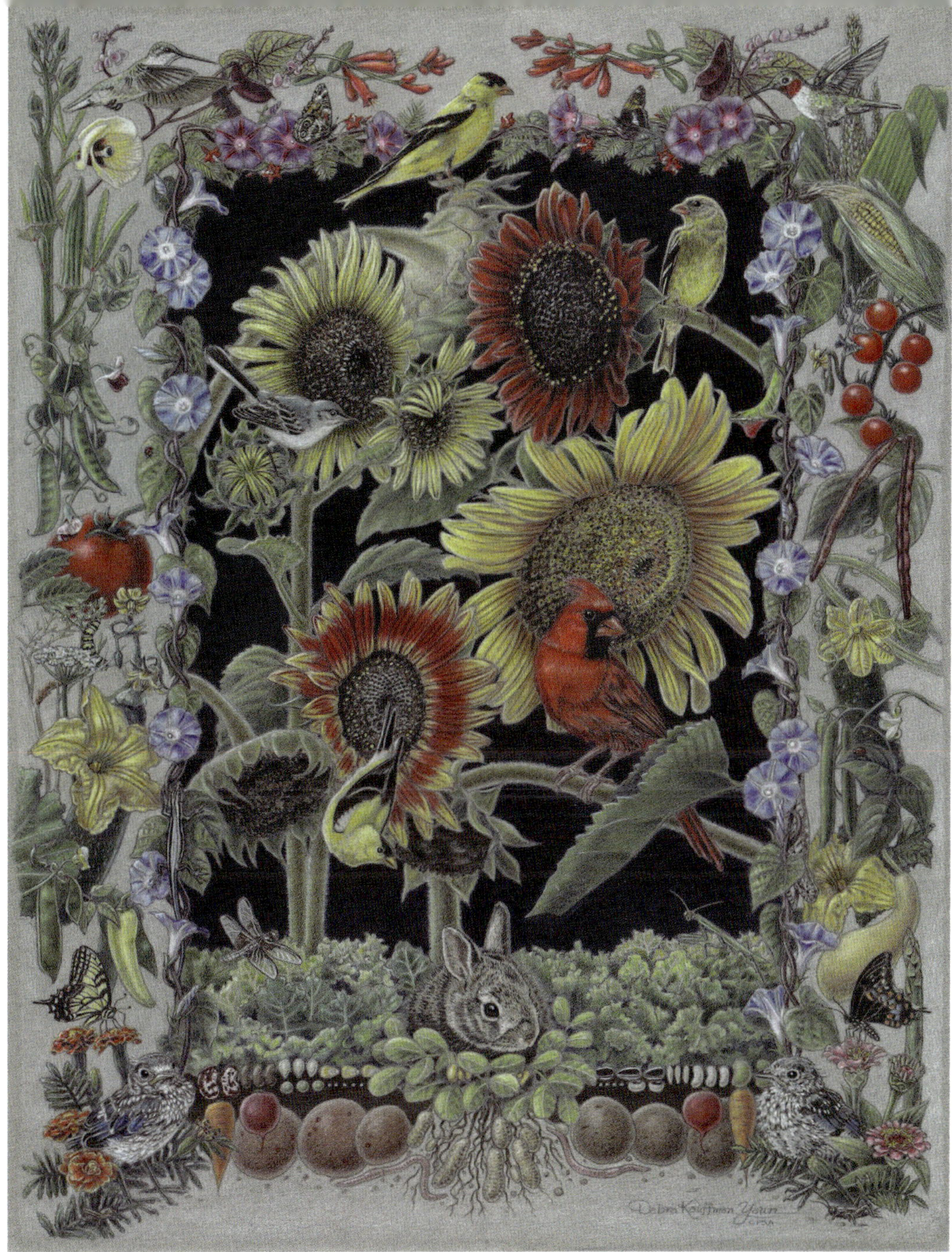

My Garden Tapestry

DEBRA YAUN, CPSA | UNITED STATES
http://debrayaun.com

21 My Garden Tapestry is the second in a series of what I call my Tapestry drawings. Presently there are four completed works. My inspiration for the series came from a simple flower design rug that I purchased. I wanted a way to combine some of the many photos that I am always taking and the tapestry idea came to me. One of the problems with this idea is that it is very time consuming. *(continued on page 77)*

TECHNIQUE AND TIPS
19" x 25" | Prismacolor | Canson Mi Teintes Stone Grey

I use a firm stroke for feathers, hair and for most textured things but layer several colors for smoother areas like a flower petal. A circular stroke is used for filling in backgrounds mostly. Sometimes a stiff brush is used to blend a smooth area and especially for backgrounds, a brush can save time. A blending pencil is great for smoothing details and sharpening edges of objects that are closest to the viewer.

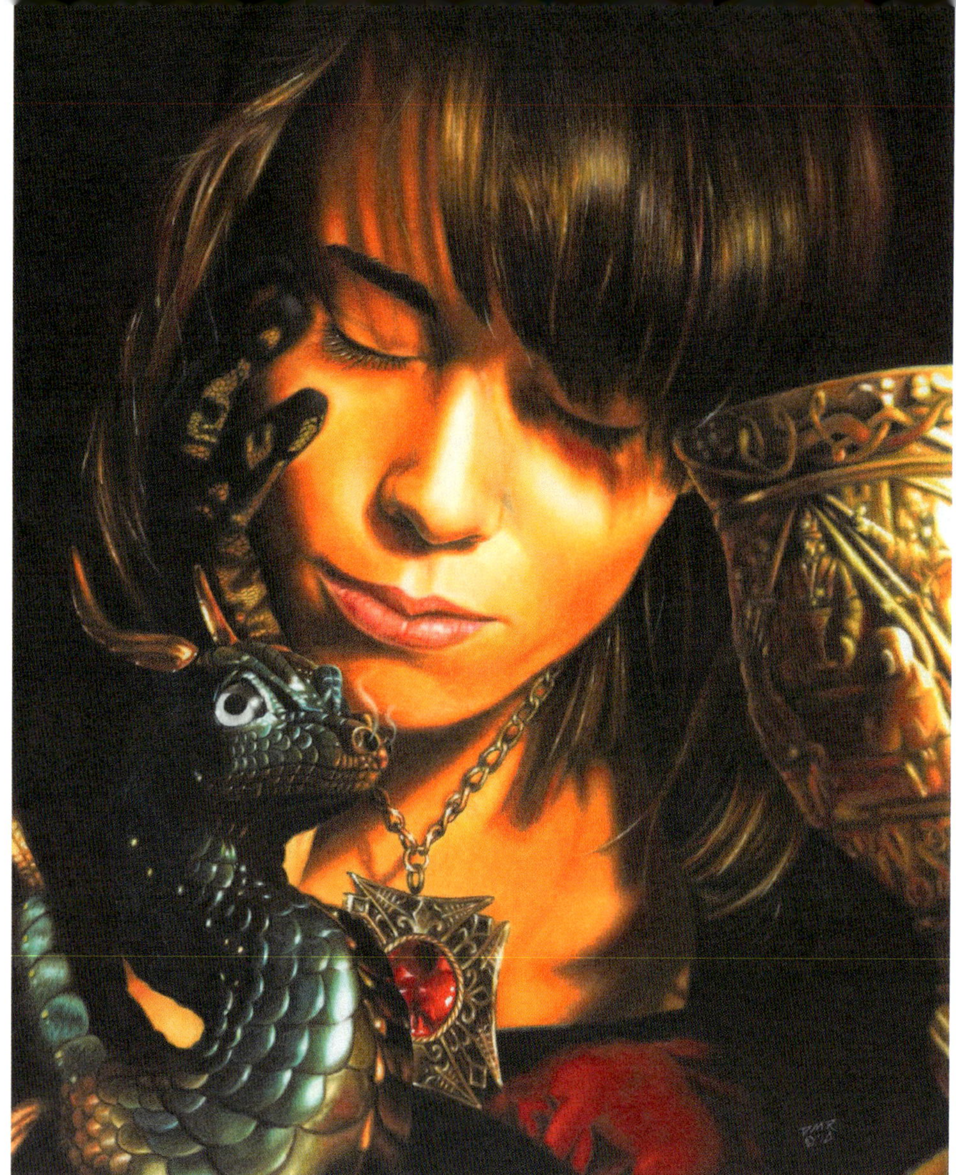

Casting a Spell on You

DEAN ROGERS | UNITED STATES
http://www.cheetahspirit.deviantart.com

22 One thing I've come to enjoy immensely is to recreate a fantasy – to discover that special "something" that someone has always wanted to be, figure out how to achieve it, and put all the parts together – be it a costume, a theme, a setting, a pose, or even a mood. Sometimes it's hard work. But it gives me great pleasure to think that I've made a dream come true, or made someone feel a little more special and a little more beautiful. This is what fantasy art is all about to me.

TECHNIQUE AND TIPS
Prismacolor | 400 series Bristol vellum 4 ply | 22" x 18"

Since my goal is to create extremely realistic portraits that appear to "come to life", I rely extensively on photography. That being the case, having good photo reference can't be stressed enough! Good lighting, contrast, depth of field, and knowing the best pose for your model are all very important! Then comes composition - finding the most interesting way to crop your choice photo, and deciding how to alter the little details to accentuate the final image. I use a thick vellum paper and put down a heavy first layer, followed by several more layers - some with heavy pressure, some with light pressure. I try to match my base color as close as I can with the first layer, and go darker from there - but sometimes I will add light details on top of dark backgrounds. There are no absolute rules for me- I don't like to say always and never!

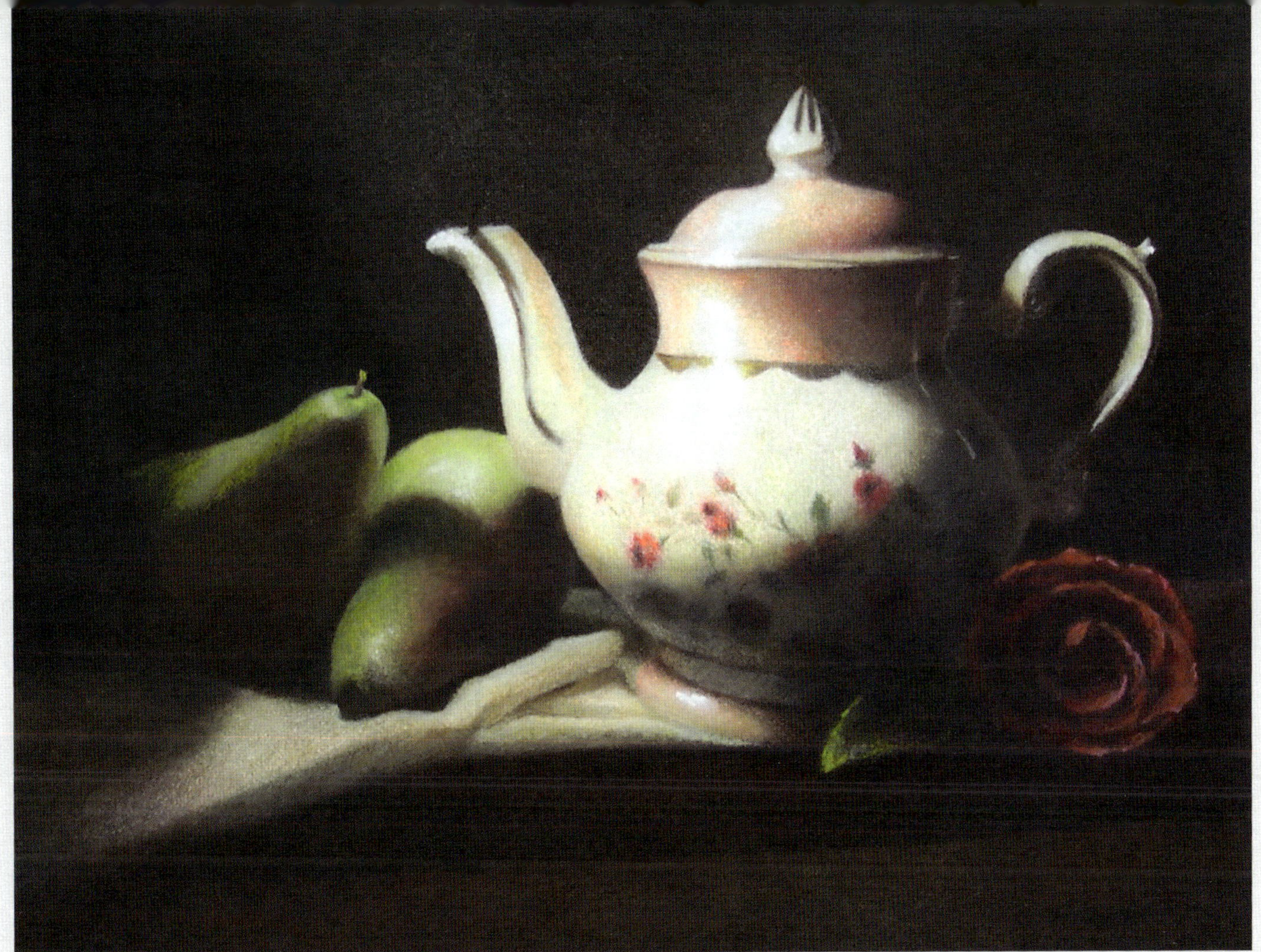

Vintage Teapot

CYNTHIA HAASE | United States
http://www.cynthiahaase.com

23 I love drama! Not in my life but in my art...

For several years I studied with master pastelist, Deborah Bays, who instilled in me the love of dramatic lighting. She taught me to think of setting up a still life as designing a theater stage, and to use lighting and composition to create a mood. "Vintage Teapot" was the first colored pencil piece I created using those concepts. This could be a scene from an opera!

I love nostalgia, and being of Scots ancestry I love a good sense of melancholy. I'm drawn to the old masters' aesthetics and most of my paintings will be on the dark side. But a good, comforting dark...without the dark one can't appreciate the light.

Whether painting in oils, pastels, or colored pencil I strive to use a passage of light, a soft edge, or a splash of color to convey a feeling...a sense of the dramatic or mysterious. When I hear "looks like an old master" or " reminds me of my grandma's table" I know I have conveyed that feeling and it motivates me to keep painting.

TECHNIQUE AND TIPS
Coloursoft by Derwent, Prismacolor, Inktense | Colourfix by ArtSpectrum | 9" x 12"

I set up the still life for "Vintage Teapot" in a black box lit classically from the left side with warm incandescent light. My can lamp was attached to a pole so I could move the light around for the maximum effect, which is much easier than moving the objects. Sometimes the focus in a painting is on a shape of light rather than the objects themselves.

Once I was satisfied with the lighting I began the underpainting, the purpose being to design a structure of dark and light so that it forms an abstract shape, connecting the darks. To speed up the creation of my dark structures I used a dark value Inktense pencil to block in my shapes, then applied water to the watersoluble Inktense. From there it was a matter of applying layers of color to achieve the desired effect. I used a stencil brush to move colors around and to soften edges between similar value shapes. For me the soft edges allow the viewer's eye to move easily through the composition, and also give form to the round shapes. A touch of soft pastel was used to intensify the highlights and further add to the form of the objects.

SHEILA THEODORATOS, CPSA, CPX | United States

24 One of the functions of the brain's Reticular Activating System (RAS) is to act as a filter, a problem solver. We have the ability to tune into what is important and tune out what is not. When something becomes important to us, our brain revs up awareness and starts finding connections.

Creative ideas sometime seem to come from "out of the blue". They can also be coaxed by providing them structured parameters or a framework on which to play or build.

I cropped my reference photo for "Clean Water: Liquid Gold" but the lower third was murky and unusable. Hmmm. What to draw? I posed questions to my imagination. What do I want my picture to convey? What is of value here? my RAS came to the rescue!

A long ago hypothetical conversation about the greatest wealth came to mind. My father had said, " They can have the diamonds, gold and oil. Just give me the world's fresh water rights."

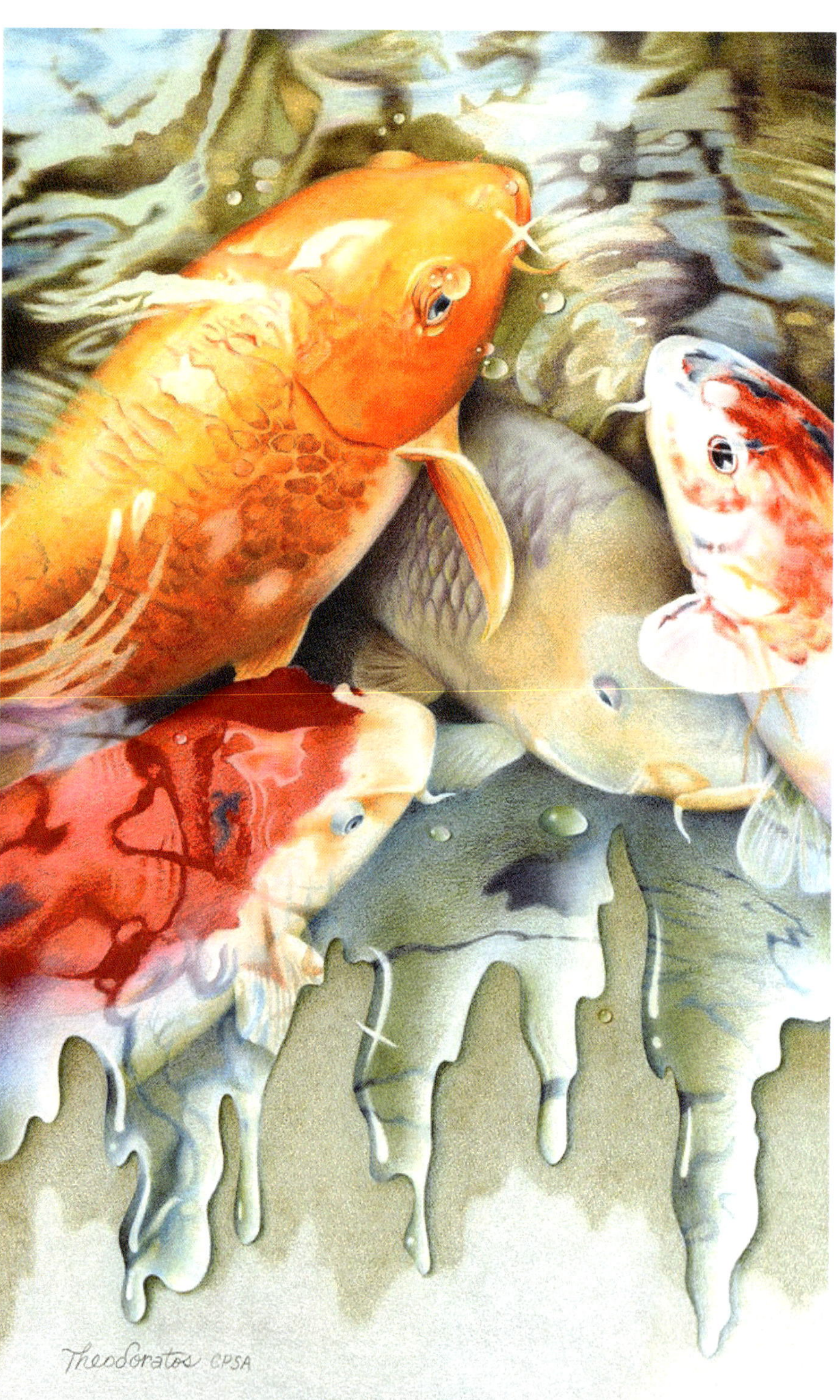

Clean Water: Liquid Gold

TECHNIQUE AND TIPS
Prismacolor & Polychromos | Stonehenge (white) | 18.5" X 11.5"

When using a photo or life study, I remember it is just a reference, a tool to manipulate. I feel free to alter, embellish, add or eliminate any element for the sake of the artwork. I love Canson Vidalon Vellum to work out my initial sketches - seeking a pleasing, flowing compositional story or metaphor that has personal meaning to me.

After choosing a palette of lightfast pencils, I record notes and work out trial blends and textures in my sketchbook. Using a #2 graphite pencil, I lightly transfer my sketch to Stonehenge via my light table. For protection, the paper is taped onto a foam core board. Rolling sticky tack (poster mount putty) over the drawing removes excess graphite that might "muddy" colored pencil. To relieve back strain and reduce visual distortion, I work on a slanted table. At this point, I LOVE to continue amid other working artists.

(continued on page 77)

New Moon

ALLAN SERVOSS, CPSA | United States

25 Sometimes just a sidelong glance while driving or walking down a road will provide me with the essence of a drawing. More often than not, it takes place in the studio when I have nothing specific in mind and the act of applying color to the surface seems to open my mind and eye to possibilities. I may actually change ideas several times while working. My guiding thought is usually composition and mood. I try to place in the drawing only what is necessary: nothing more nothing less. In "New Moon" the centered tree and foreground provide a setting for a barely seen new moon. The red tree is a foil for the complementary green of the corn, and the entire foreground is a foil for the large (almost) empty sky. The "centeredness" of the tree works to provide a sense of calm to the entire scene.

TECHNIQUE AND TIPS
Polychromos | Strathmore 500 Illustration Board | 22" x22"

I work simply and directly making up the image as I go along. I seldom use reference material such as photos or sketches although I believe sketching to be a most valuable skill. If I do a preliminary drawing, it is only the most cursory to allow me as much freedom as possible. A very light pressure is used, layering the color gradually using the texture and whiteness of the surface to give the image transparency and delicateness. Occasionally a bit of burnishing is used, applying color in such a way that the surface texture is covered (usually in very dark areas) towards the completion of a piece. Any detail work is saved for last. Throughout the entire process, the thoughtful placement of shapes, how they guide the eye and relate to each other is the guiding principle.

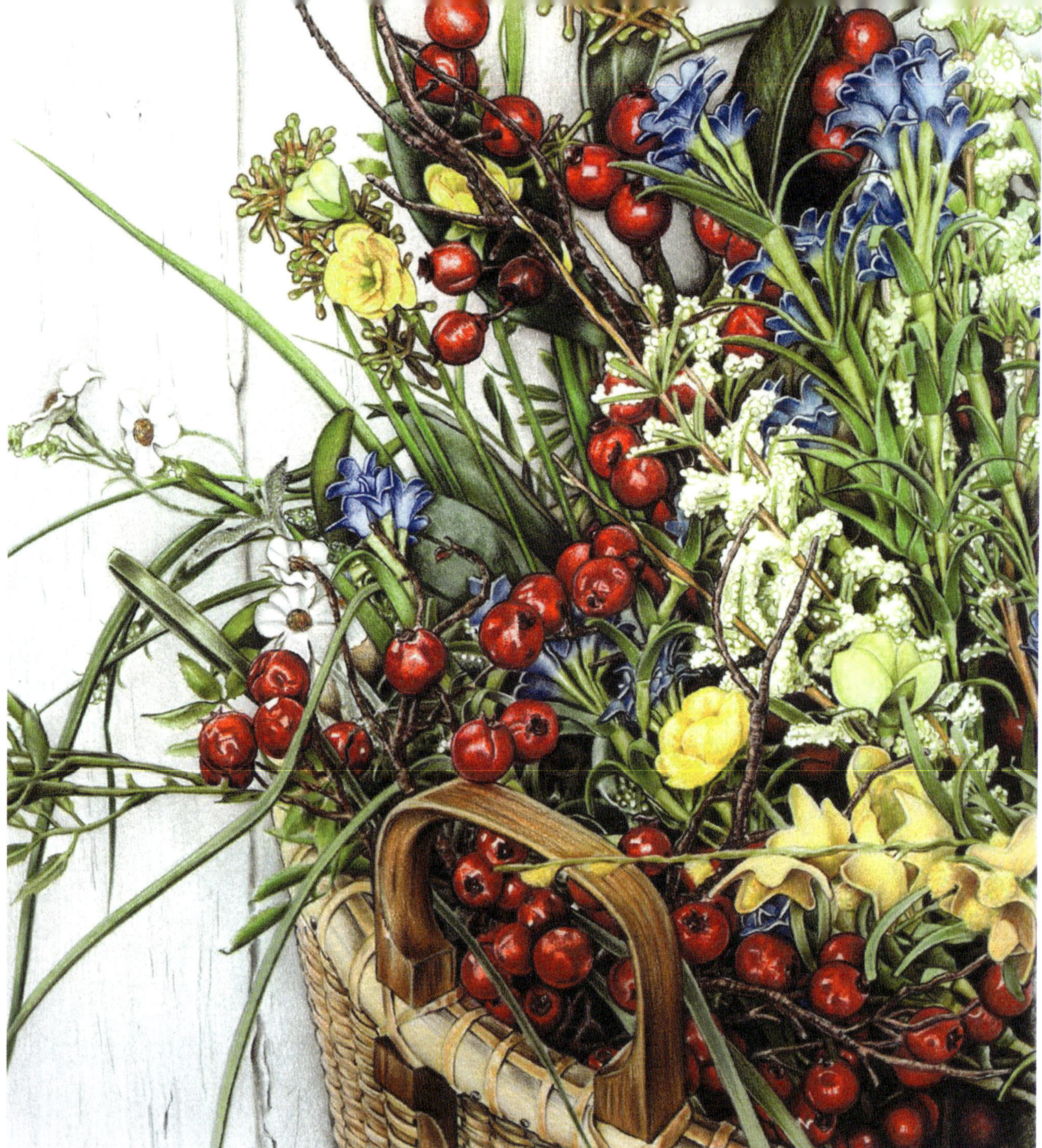

For Barbara

SUSAN TAIT PORCARO, CPSA | UNITED STATES
http://www.2lipsartdesign.com

26 I always admired the works in oil of the old masters and creating in a similar style using colored pencil has been incredibly challenging, yet, ultimately most rewarding. My fascination lies with light, line and color. I tend to lean towards intricate, detailed pieces which allow me to completely immerse myself although sometimes, when I start a complicated piece, I wonder what on earth I was thinking! :)

TECHNIQUE AND TIPS
Prismacolor, Lyra, Polychromos | Stonehenge | 19" x 15"

Hone your drawing skills. To create photorealistic artwork, in any medium, practice all the time, even if its just a doodle on a notepad. Understand the shapes of everything you draw, how the shadows, mid-tones and highlights are all shapes in themselves, which leads me to how you draw them: don't be afraid to get really dark in the shadows and keep highlights light. Draw every day - trust me, if its in your blood to do this and you don't, you get really cranky! :D

SUSAN BROOKS, CPSA | UNITED STATES
http://www.SusanBrooksFineArt.com

27 Artists can quickly grasp the artistic elements such as line, value, texture.... but it has been said that "one can study color for the rest of our lives". As artists continue to work over the years, they find their own color choices changing, morphing and growing in directions that they may never have thought about. This is simply due to observance and awareness by one's own artistic eye.

It has been often said that yellow is one of the most challenging colors to work with. And when working with this hue, value and temperature are particularly important, as well as Chervil's law of simultaneous contrast.

Then there is the genre of landscapes itself, where the artist must learn to capture moments or places that reach the soul. Roll all of this into your work and one produces a unique piece that takes the audieince on a visual journey.

Cypress Creek - a study in yellow

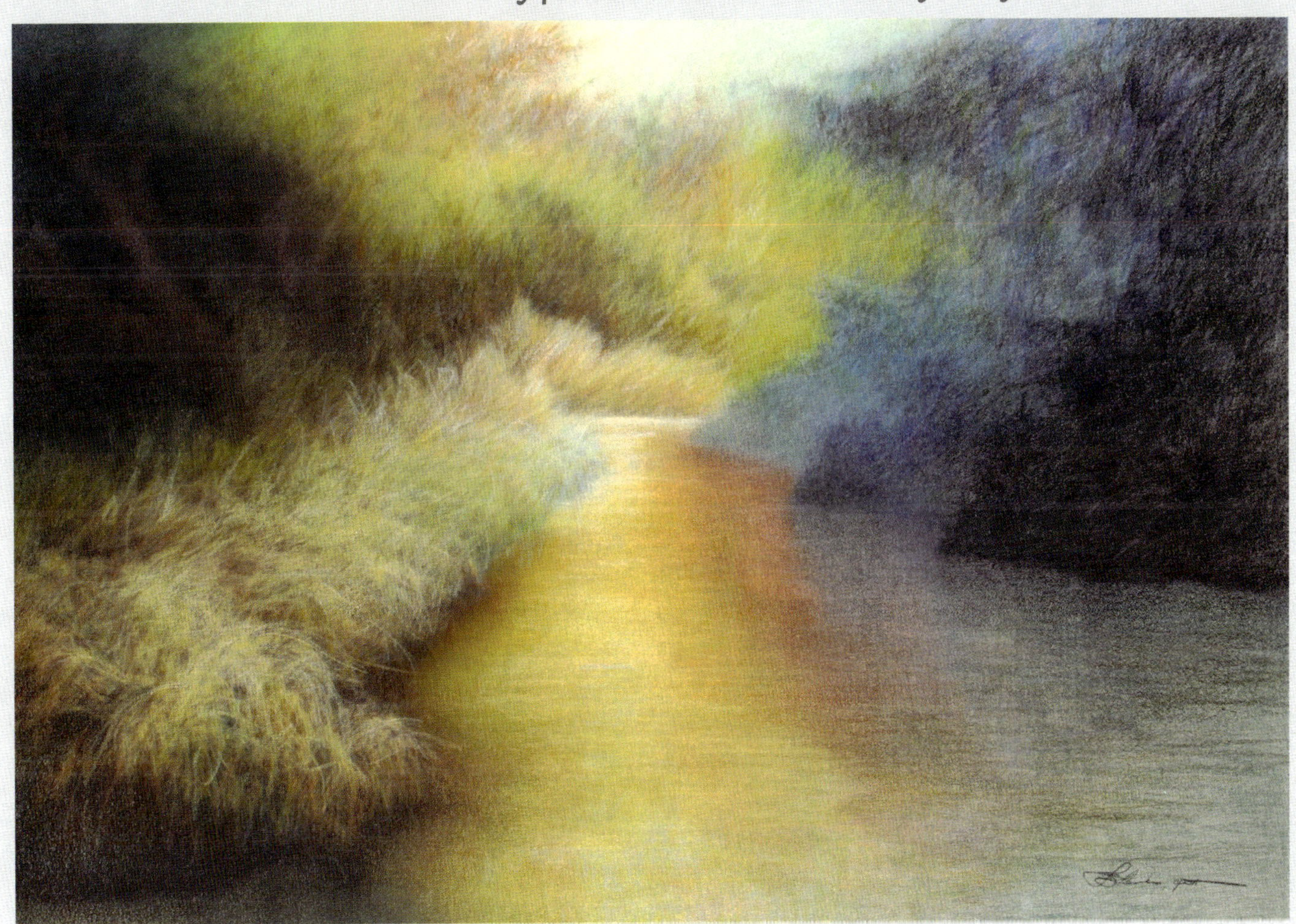

TECHNIQUE AND TIPS
Faber Castell, Caran d'ache, Derwent, Lyra, Prismacolor, Bruynzeel | Art Specturm's Sanded Pastel Paper in Rose Grey | 17" x 26"

Every semester I start students, no matter how advanced with the Grisaille Method. Students must first learn how to 1) deepen a particular hue, 2) how to "scumble" and 3) "how blend" strokes so that the color appears seamless.

They also must learn which "universal darkeners" they can use to create value as well as temperature changes.

They must also develop a "touch". A light one that blends but covers all at once. This is the foundation of colored pencil and whether one is just starting out, or has been working in the medium for many years, there is always a set of circumstances in each piece of artwork that will bring you right back to this very basic exercise.

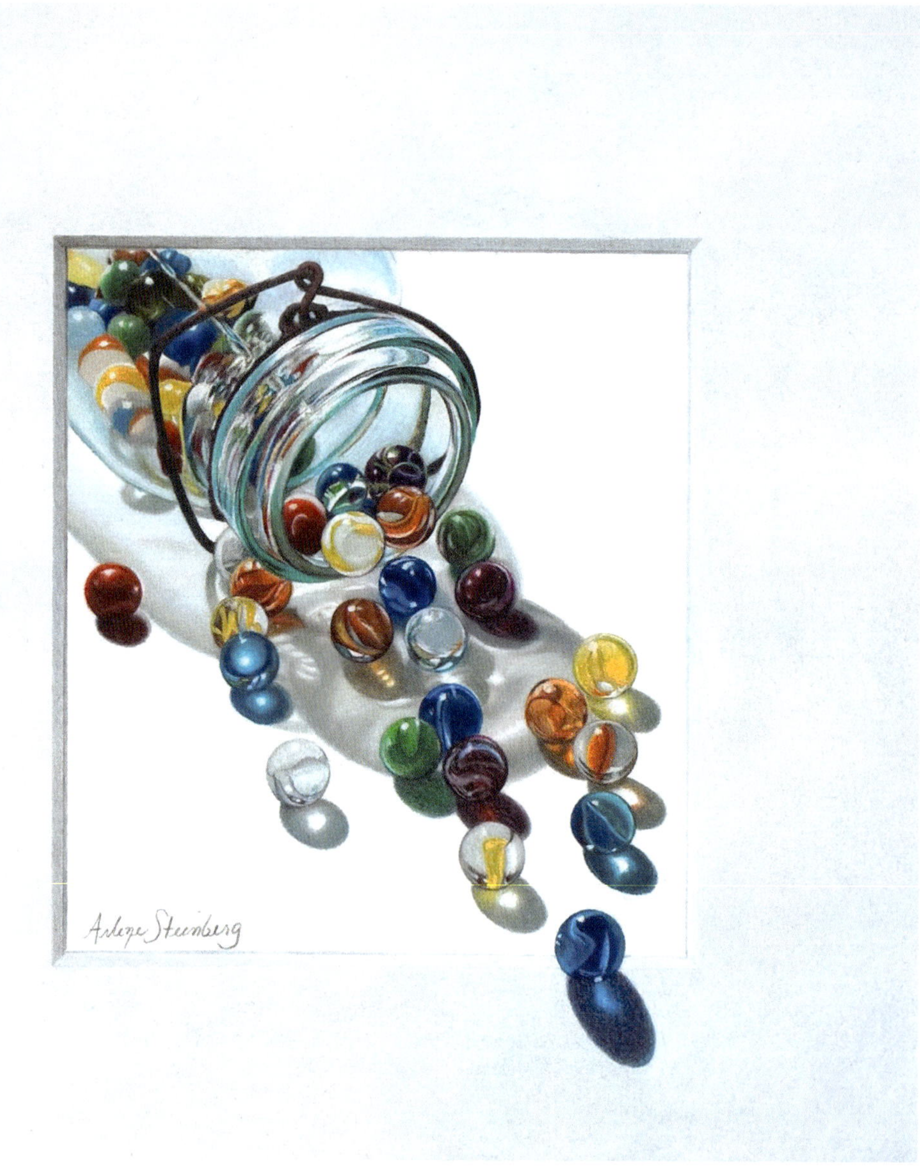

Collected Memories

ARLENE STEINBERG, CPSA | UNITED STATES
http://www.arlenesteinberg.com

28 While I love drawing still lifes and florals, I find myself continually drawn to creating trompe l'oeil drawings. Trompe l'oeil is French for "trick the eye" and describes a painting that deceives the viewer into thinking that the objects in it are real, not merely represented. Trompe l'oeil's intention is to deceive the viewer; to make the objects appear to come forward off the painted surface. I just love the detail work required to create an optical illusion of an image that looks as if it's real. I find myself getting caught up in the tiny details that define a small object. *(continued on page 76)*

TECHNIQUE AND TIPS
Prismacolor, Inktense | Stonehenge paper | 13" x 12.5"

There are several techniques to make a trompe l'oeil drawing believable. Trompe l'oeil needs to be drawn from the eye level and position of the viewer. All objects must be the same size as in life and look believable from a foot away from the picture surface. The objects shouldn't have too much depth to them. *(continued on page 76)*

PAMELA BELCHER, CPSA | United States
http://www.pamelabelcher.com

29 Water and rocks are endlessly fascinating to me. I have done four "water totems" so far. My main source images have been rocks in a tiny stream halfway down the Grand Canyon. For this piece it was water ripples in a crystal clear stream in the magical Hoh Rain Forest in Washington State. Instead of working from the top left horizontally down to the lower right, I worked from the center out, and decided when to stop. This was a fun proposition and presented me with a new challenge.

Water Totem: The Protector

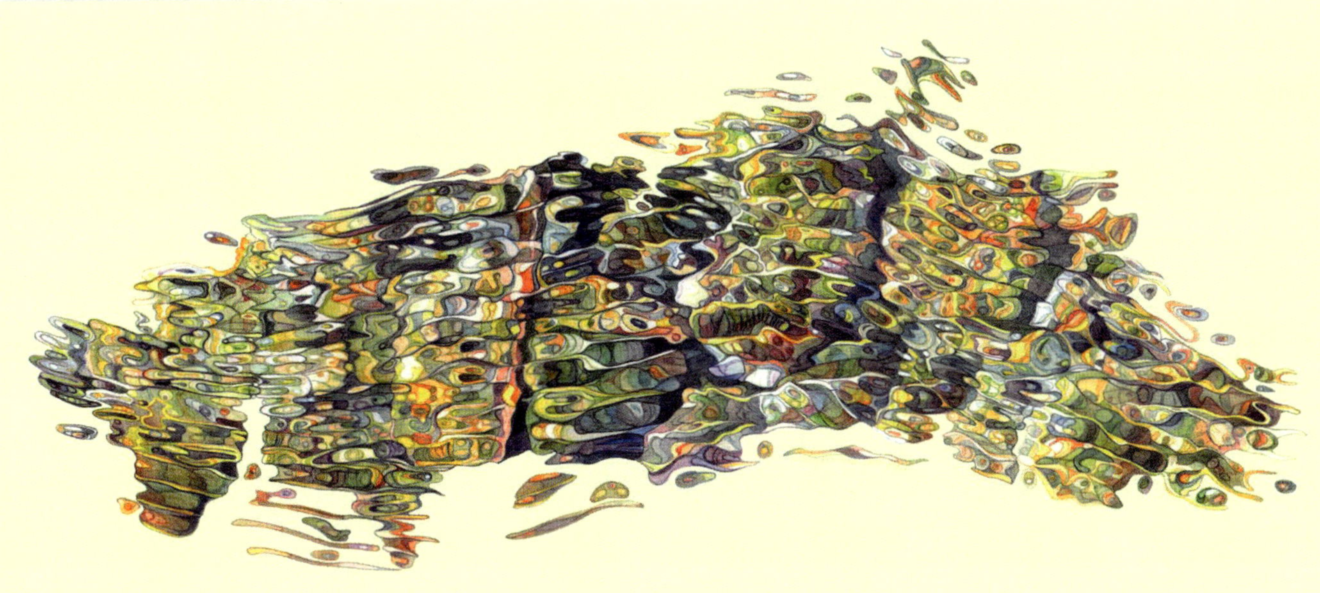

TECHNIQUE AND TIPS
Prismacolor, Polychromos, Pablos | Stonehenge | 12" x 22"

Keep your interest alive by trying new twists and turns on your technique, approach or presentation. I've been doing cp for a long time and have noticed several of my colleagues changing mediums because they became bored. I have avoided this by challenging myself in different ways and therefore remain totally committed to cp and all it can do.

GEMMA GYLLING, CPSA | UNITED STATES
http://www.glassgems.net

30 I am a wildlife artist who wants to share the wonder of nature through my art. I have always been fascinated by animals, particularly wildlife.

I came across this little guy while in South Africa on an photo safari. He was so cute playing with his siblings and his Mother, then finally he flopped down and fell asleep. I took so many pictures of him I'm sure I will be creating more artwork from those photos.

I can't imagine anything else that is as beautiful as nature and the story it is trying to tell us. Animals speak to us in a very special way, it never ceases to surprise me just how beautiful, fascinating and wondrous they really are. I strive to not only create wildlife art but to portray the true spirit of those animals.

A Lion Sleeps Tonight

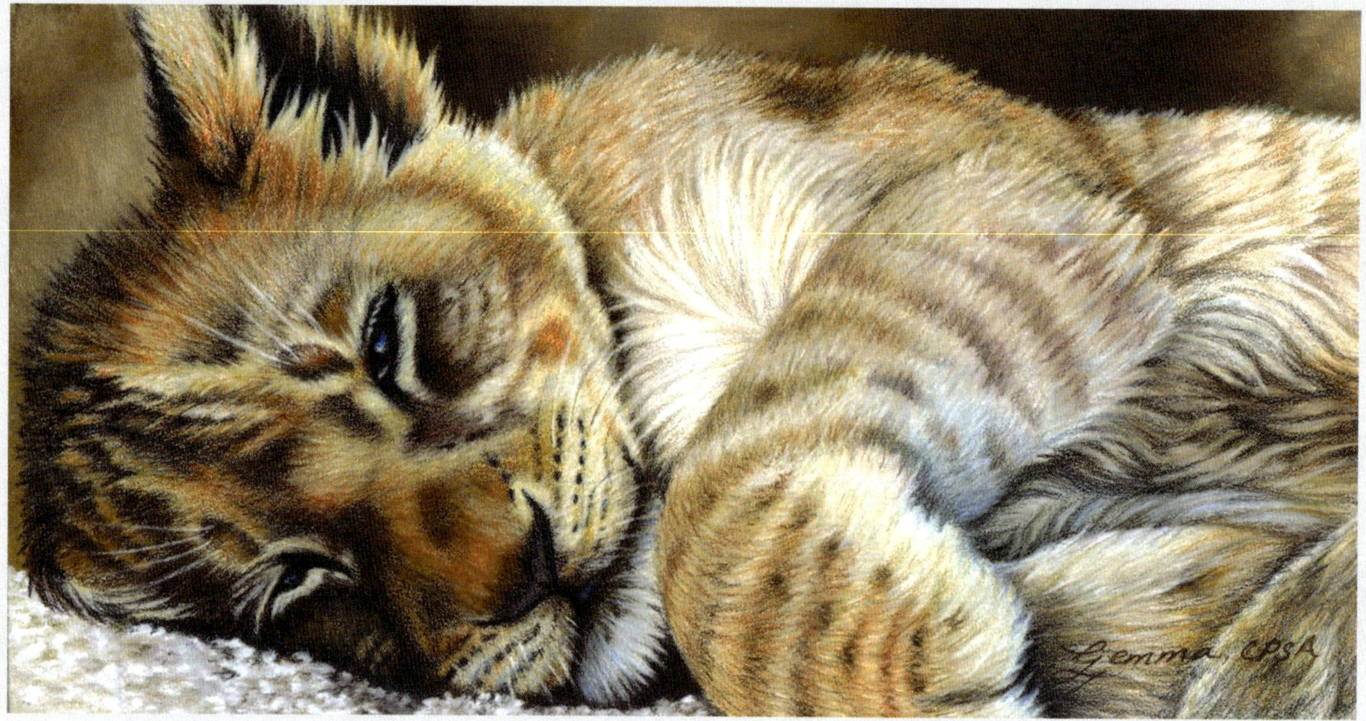

TECHNIQUE AND TIPS
Prismacolor & Derwent Coloursoft | Tan Pastelbord | 6" x 12"

When working on the Pastelbord surface I lay down several layers of colored pencil and then use a stiff bristle brush to blend the pencil down into the pastelbord. I will often times do this over again several times until I get the look I want. To create that realistic fur look I use several different colors of pencil, sometimes as many as 5 different colors. I will rotate between those colors over and over again until I feel it's the look I am trying to achieve. I also occasionally use solvents, especially when I am trying to achieve the out of focus background such as the one in this piece. If I could give a person just one piece of advise when drawing with colored pencil it would be to take your time and be patient.

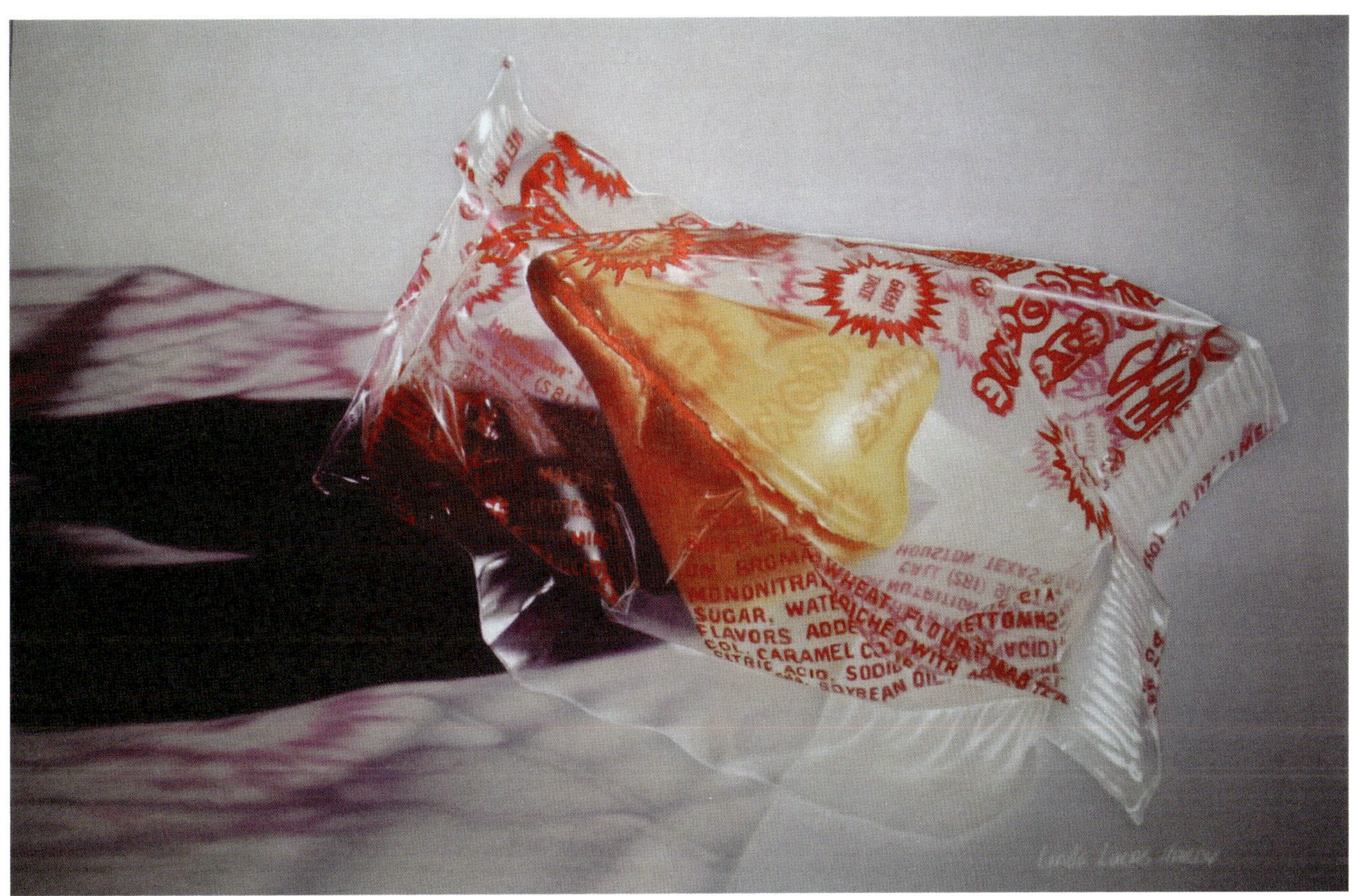

Light Crisp Tasty - Fortune Inside

LINDA LUCAS HARDY, CPSA, CPX | United States
http://www.lindahardy.com

31 This was a very fun piece to do however it came with unsuspected challenges. I chose it because I loved how the shadows from the lettering fell across the cookie. The shadows gave it depth as well as an unusual focal point. Unlike many of my pieces however this one was predominately light, which meant I had to complete the cast shadow first. As you well know colored pencil pigment tends to float across the paper but saturating the area, working on sand paper and blending with a dry brush meant I had to be especially thoughtful in my approach. Once the cast shadow was completed I spent several hours cleaning the paper with sticky tack then used an eraser. Once clean I started laying in the background. *(continued on page 78)*

Technique and Tips
Prismacolor | 800 Uart Sandpaper | 14" x 22"

In order to be successful with my method of "dry brush" blending a small, fairly stiff hog bristle brush is required and Prismacolor Premier colored pencils. The reason I prefer Prismacolor pencils is because they have more wax than most of the other brands. The pigment in the oil based brands tends to be harder and less blendable. I've also noticed that the oil-based pigments do not adhere as well when applied to sandpaper. For me, that creates another problem because I blend the pigment with a brush. The wax-based pigment will blend whereas the other pigments tend to sweep off the sand paper.

(continued on page 78)

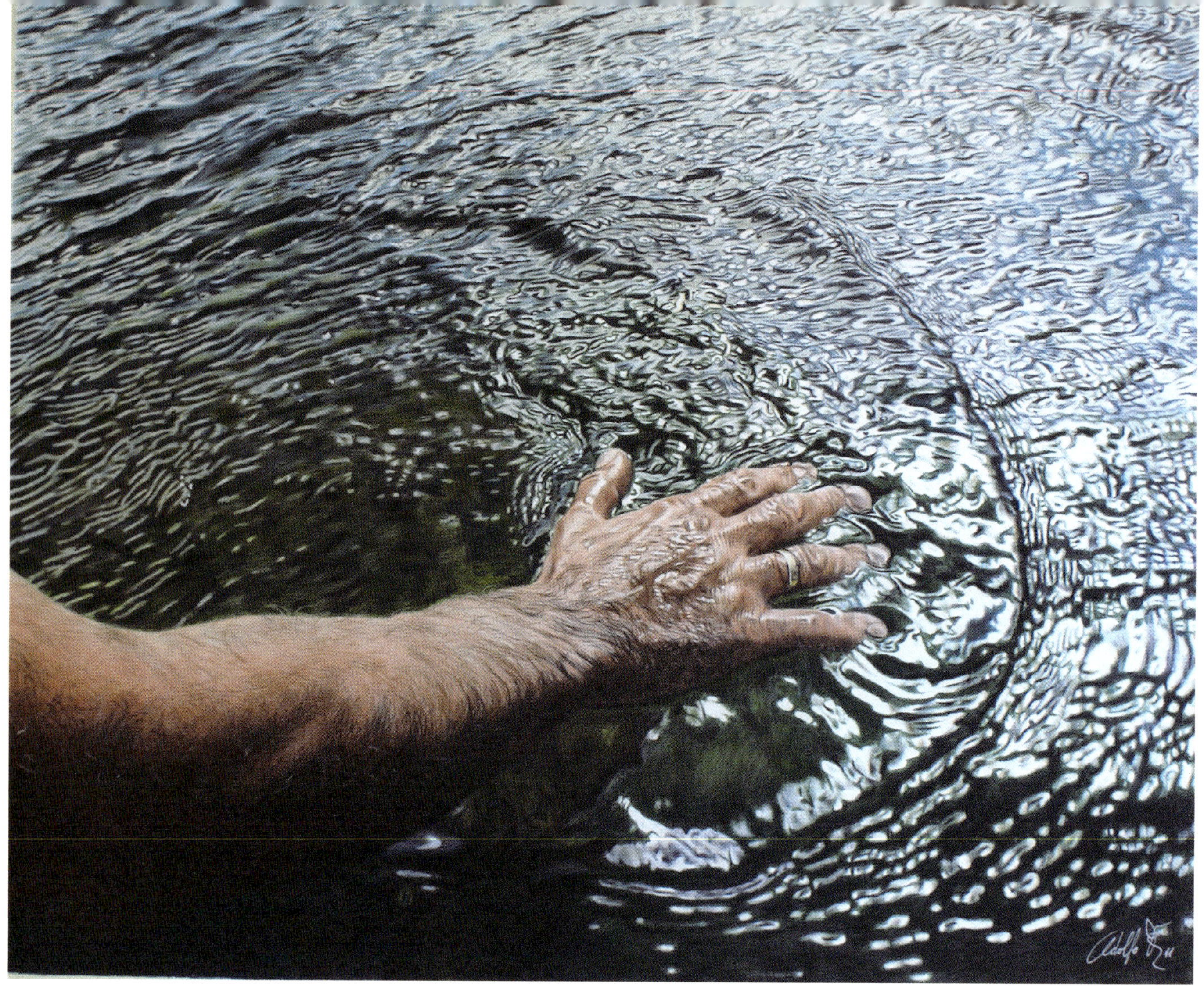

"Buenas Vibraciones"

ADOLFO FERNÁNDEZ RODRÍGUEZ | Spain

http://www.artistasdelatierra.com/artistas/afrpainter/galeria.html

32 Interchange of sensations between the man and the matter that you gave origin, between the Queen of creation and "the element "which gave essence and form ".

I started to paint in order to decorate my house but it became a necessity in a short time. I paint while working in my business. Locked in my store, I've done all my paintings that I have shown in 2011. I paint about my life and what surrounds me - about the details, about the color, about the wonders that surround us... in all of them I can find the hand of God. 'The language of the hands' and how we can express our feelings through them is perhaps the theme I am best at when I paint. . "The language of the hands" and how we can express our feelings through them, perhaps this is the theme that I encounter the most when I paint. *(continued on page 77)*

TECHNIQUE AND TIPS

Faber-Castell Albrech Dürer | Papel de acuarela GVARRO 360 grs/m | 25" x 31 "

To sum up my technique, I would say that the painting with a pencil is a painting of 'pressure'. The best results are obtained exercising certain pressure up to the point which paper cannot receive any more color. With watercolor paper, thick and soft, smooth and white (it has to be a pure target, since this color will be the origin of the subsequent mixtures). We can paint a work with three pencils if we know how to mix them properly. I realized this factor in my first painting. *(continued on page 77)*

TRAVIS BAILEY | UNITED STATES
http://www.baileyartwork.com

33 The inspiration for this drawing comes from a mausoleum next to the lawns where my grandmother is buried in Long Beach, California. The columns, bench, and floor is based on the interior of the mausoleum with the rest of the drawing being my own additions. The top and bottom portion is scripture that relates to death and passing on.

Chambers of Heaven

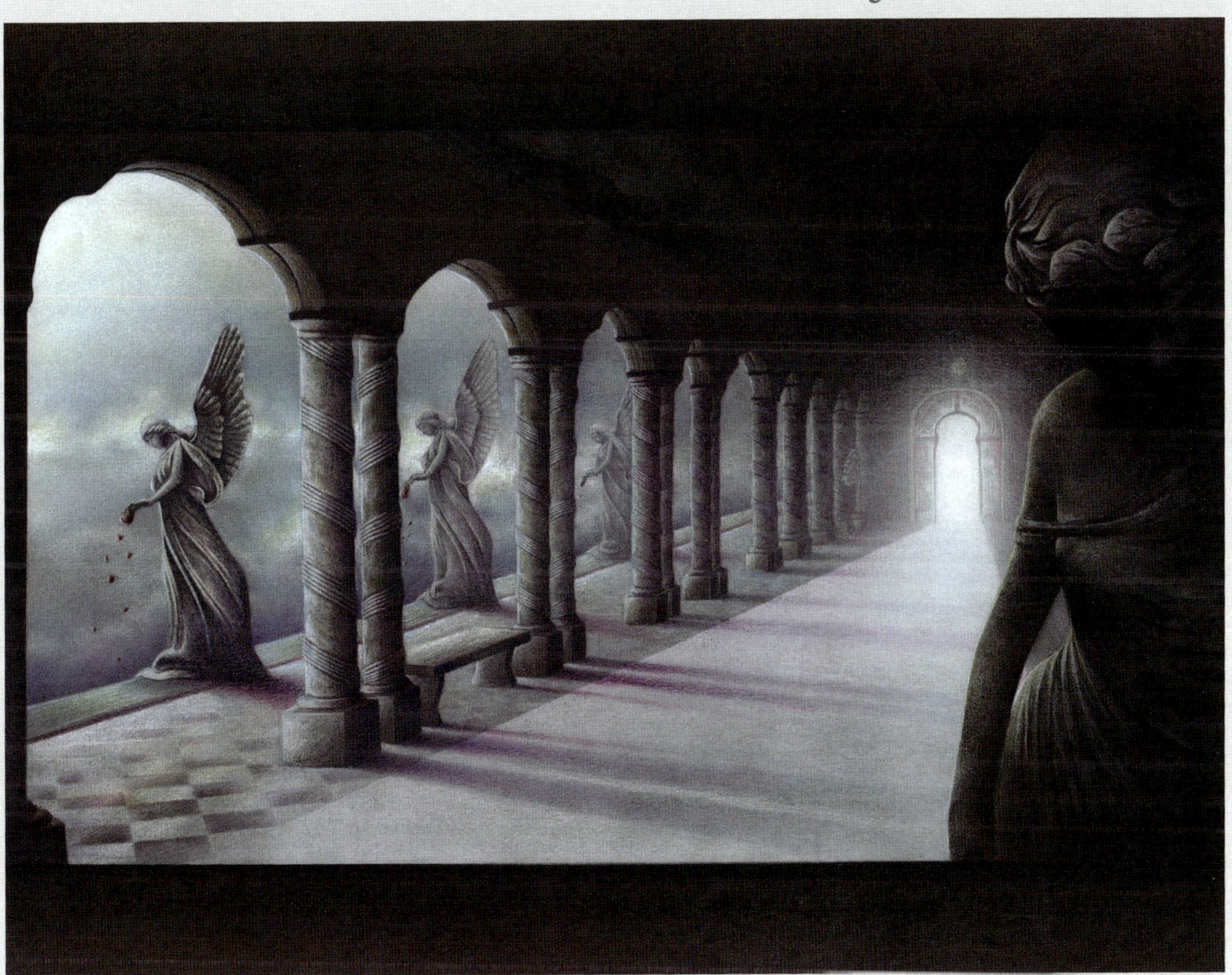

TECHNIQUE AND TIPS
Prismacolor | Tobacco colored Canson Mi-Teintes | 16″ X 20″

My basic technique is fairly common to colored pencils. I keep the pencil sharp and use plenty of layers. I lighten or darken an area with other colors rather than a darker shade of the color I'm going for. I avoid having a block of a single color. In areas that might appear to be one color if you look closely you'll see various other colors. I don't use black pencils. I don't finish a certain area of a drawing and then move on, I constantly work the entire drawing until it's all finished at the same time. I keep my drawings taped to boards so that it's easy to lean the drawing against a wall and observe the drawing from a few feet away since its easy with pencils to become too focused on details rather than the overall drawing.

AMY LINDENBERGER, CPSA | **UNITED STATES**
http://amylindenberger.com

34 Much of my work is inspired by people and events of the American Civil War era. That doesn't mean my colored pencil paintings are always straightforward historical illustrations, however; often I prefer symbolism rather than a literal presentation for my ideas. Each new work I create I strive to make successful on three different levels: 1) my reaction to or interpretation of a factual, historical person or event, 2) relevant and informed by my personal experience, and 3) representative of a larger, universal truth.

While the specific individual who inspired Transformation/Liberation has a story too complex to detail here, the basic theme of the piece is the shared human experience of undergoing a major life adjustment in response to stressful events. The specific meanings of the various symbols and compositional elements I leave up to the viewer to ponder.

Transformation/Liberation

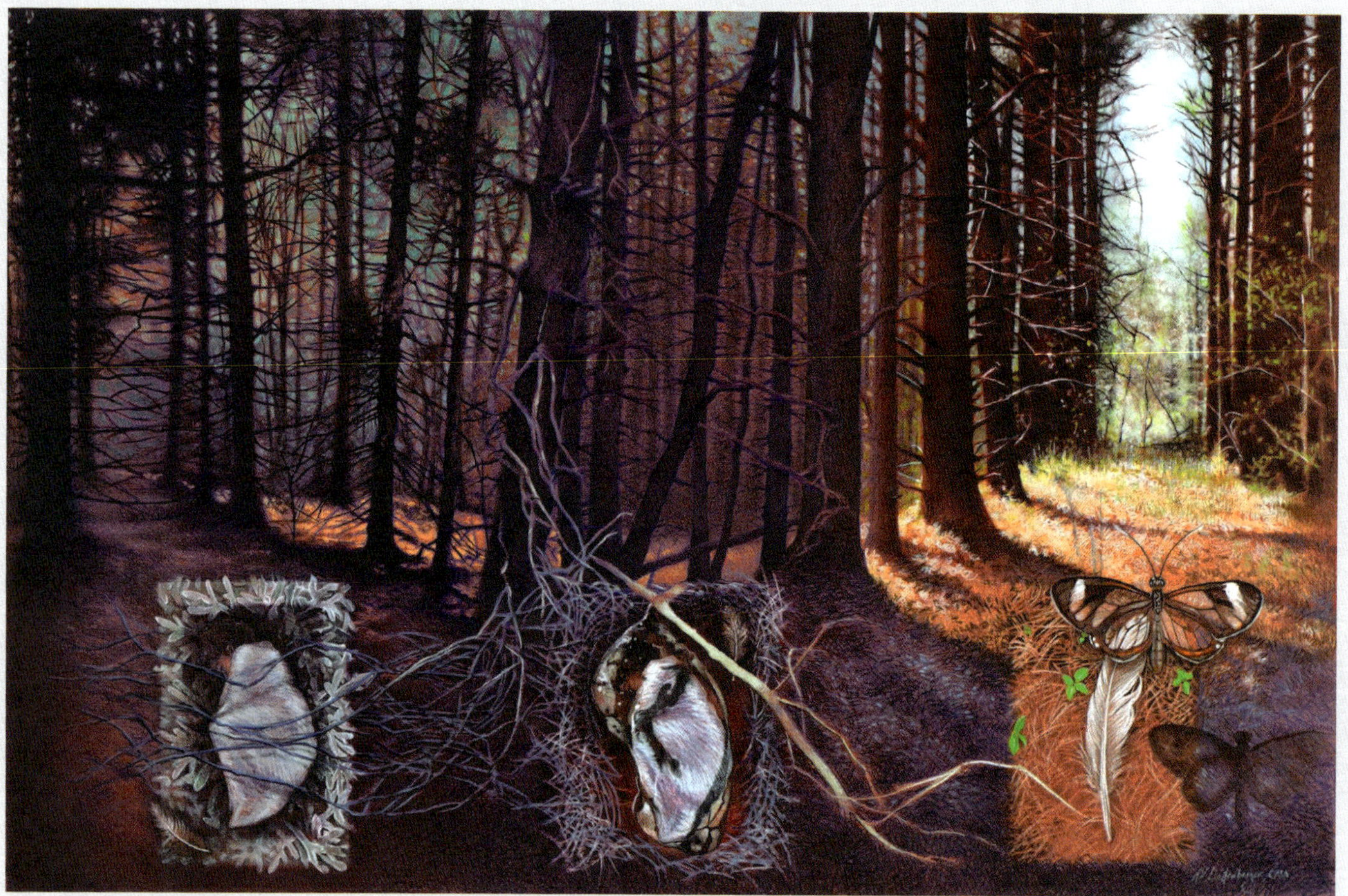

TECHNIQUE AND TIPS

Prismacolor | Crescent Acid-Free Rag Mat Board, color: Taos | 18 x 28

I'm a firm believer in the concept of using a medium in a way that will showcase its strengths. To me, colored pencil's beauty lies in its ability to create beautifully rich, transparent layers of color in addition to extreme detail, so my working methods involve applying the pencil with a very sharp point, never more than light to medium pressure, using short – often circular -- strokes. Colored pencil builds slowly, but I prefer to think of it as a meditative process that allows me the freedom to make color adjustments as the drawing progresses. To really get the most of the medium, however, the artist needs to strive to develop the patience necessary to allow the pencil to work its magic. I use multiple transparent layers to create colors with depth and richness, rather than applying one or two layers with a heavy hand -- something which can serve to make the color look flat and overworked.

Beyond technique, I want to stress one over-riding idea: embrace the subject matter you're passionate about and the concepts that hold the most meaning for you. These are the things that make your art truly unique, in a way that mere technique can't possibly accomplish.

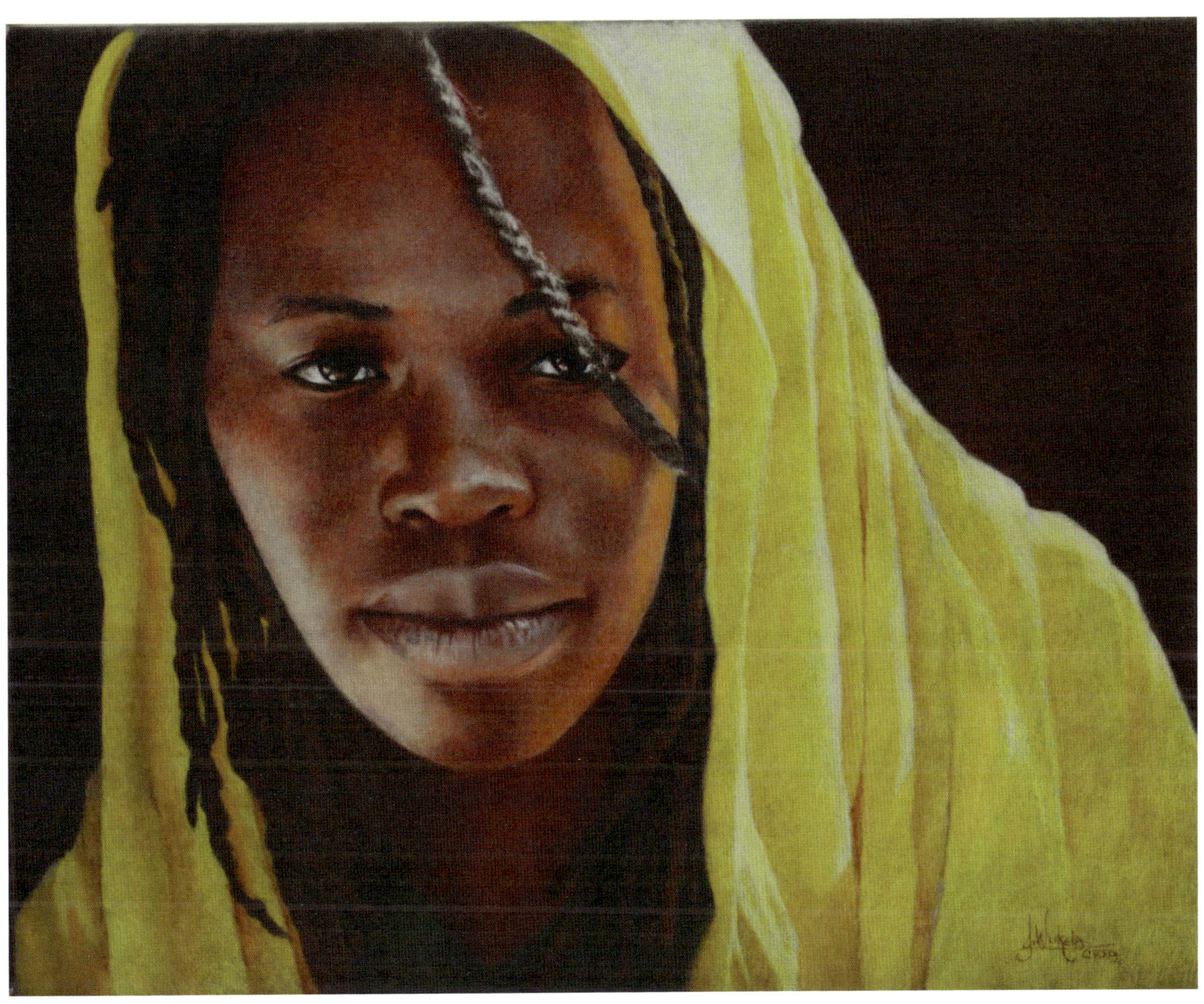

Shadai III

JACLYN WUKELA, CPSA | UNITED STATES
http://Lyndaenglishstudio.net

35 I love faces. I love drawing and painting faces, so I am always on the look out for interesting faces. Sometimes I am on a real SEARCH for a great face, as I was in Freeport, the Bahamas, where I found Shadai. She was working in her booth at the International Market and she had a great face.

Those photos have made me a better artist. In this one, Shadai III, she looked out with those eyes and told me who she was. She challenged me to tell you and I think I did. Who wouldn't want to do that work?

TECHNIQUE AND TIPS
Prismacolor | Ampersand Pastelbord | 16" X 20"

I do colored pencil the hard way; but I believe the best way. I divide areas into layers of value, to which I assign a color sequence. These layers are done in little circles with a very light touch and a sharp pencil point.

The best tip I have right now is to use an IPad to view reference photos. The IPad allows us to enlarge areas of the photo to different magnifications. This is very helpful in seeing detail and subtlety, especially in skin tones.

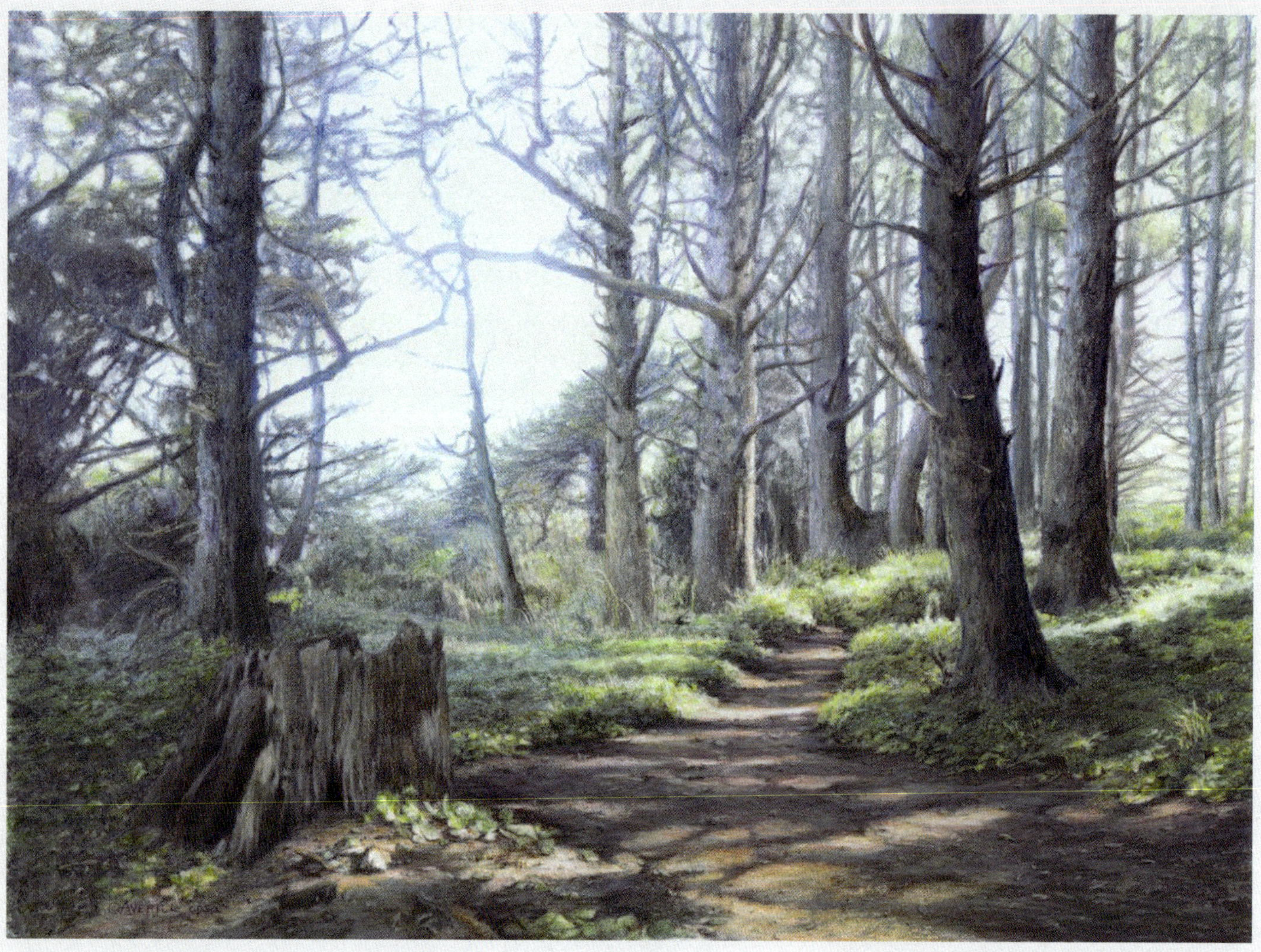

Kindred Spirits

PAT AVERILL | UNITED STATES
http://pataverill.com

36 I find comfort in the simple beauty surrounding me...light, shadow, softness, and color. Driving down the road I'm drawn to the light on grasses, and when I'm near the ocean, the constant motion of waves or foam patterns draw me into the scene.

In this picture, I was searching for a better view of a beach cove, and along the path I saw this close-knit group of Sitka Spruce trees. They seemed to have their arms outstretched in a kind of spirited way, and it grabbed my attention. As I worked on this piece, I became emotionally involved in how the scene related to life in general, and pretty soon it felt like my hands were instinctively creating while I was off in another zone.

TECHNIQUE AND TIPS
Prismacolor, Lyra, Luminance | Stonehenge | 12" x 16.25"

I like the added drama of taking reference photos about 1/2 to 1 hour before/after sunrise/sunset. Natural lighting is best, since you can see highlights and shadows in subtle complementary colors. With my reference photo at hand, I start by plotting a few lines to show placement of the basic design. If the line drawing is too detailed, my creative forces become stifled. I try to focus on the big picture first, and save the details for last! When I'm ready to add color, I lay down a few basic colors with varying pencil pressure to create a more detailed sketch. Once content, I build color layers and pay close attention to the edges. A simple trick that helps make color and value choices easy is to use value viewers. Take 2 small squares of black paper and punch a hole in each. Put one over the photo and one over the art to compare the color and value under the holes.

TANJA GANT | United States

37

There was a time when all I did was draw cartoon characters and dream of making my own comic books, but then I drew a face and there was no going back. Faces and human form still fascinate me, with all their complexity. The subject of my drawing Fluctuat Nec Mergitur ("He who rises with the wave is not swallowed by it") is Galen, my stepson. The title was meant as a metaphor describing a boy of 16 who was trying to figure out who he was and who he wanted to become. The inspiration for this drawing came from Galen's tattoo that depicts the same motto. The challenging part was creating the background that enhanced the composition without taking the focus off the subject. I had fun creating a work of art that tells a story and hope to tell many more.

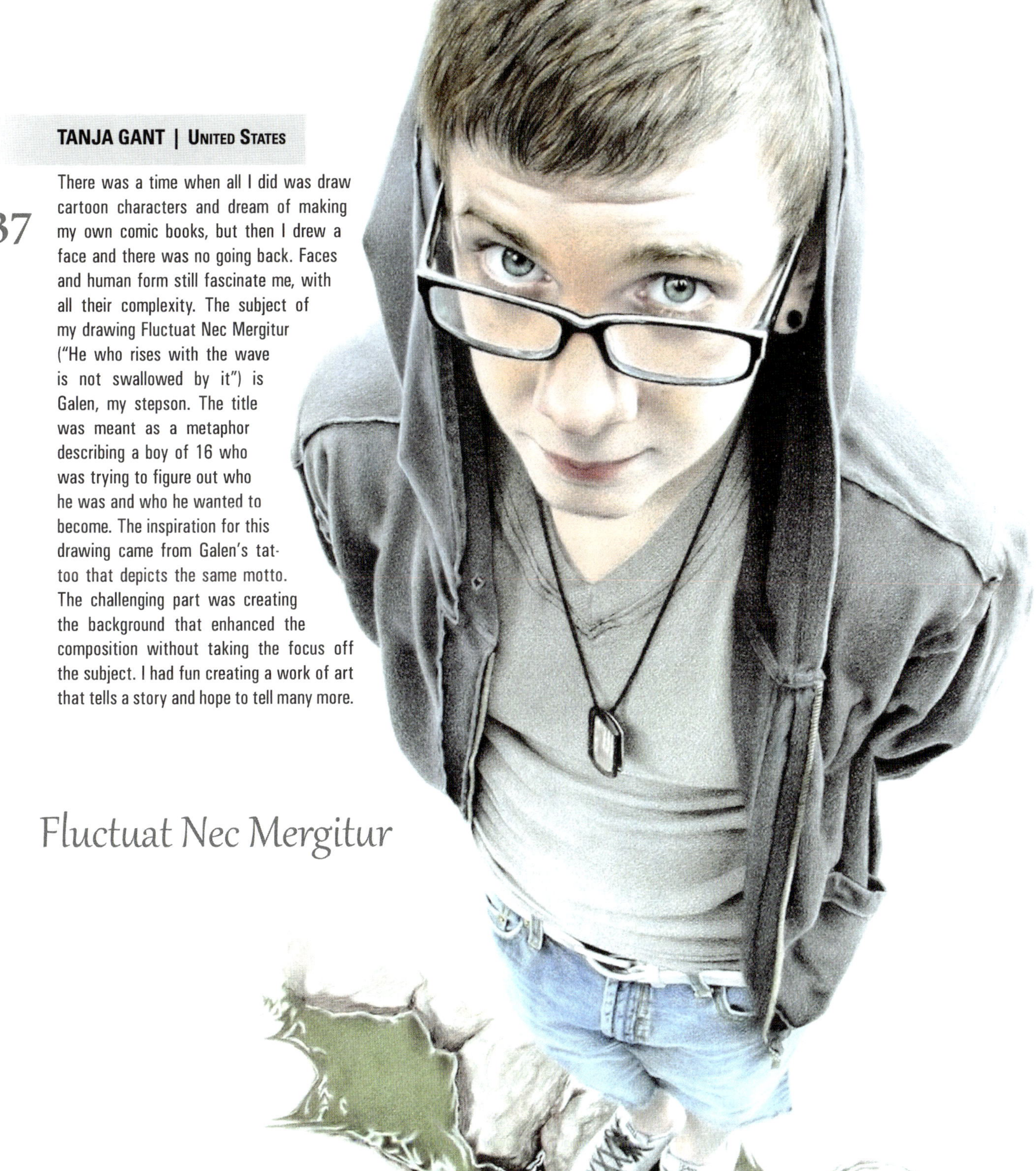

Fluctuat Nec Mergitur

TECHNIQUE AND TIPS

Prismacolor | Strathmore Bristol paper | 25" x 17"

For this drawing I used Prismacolor colored pencils. I started with a simple pencil outline and worked, as I always do, from light to dark. I check and recheck the proportions to make sure everything is where it's supposed to be before I start applying color. I pick out all the colors beforehand but always end up changing them or adding new ones. Light touch, choosing the right colors and many, many layers is essential but what's even more important is establishing the right values. High contrast is what makes a good drawing.

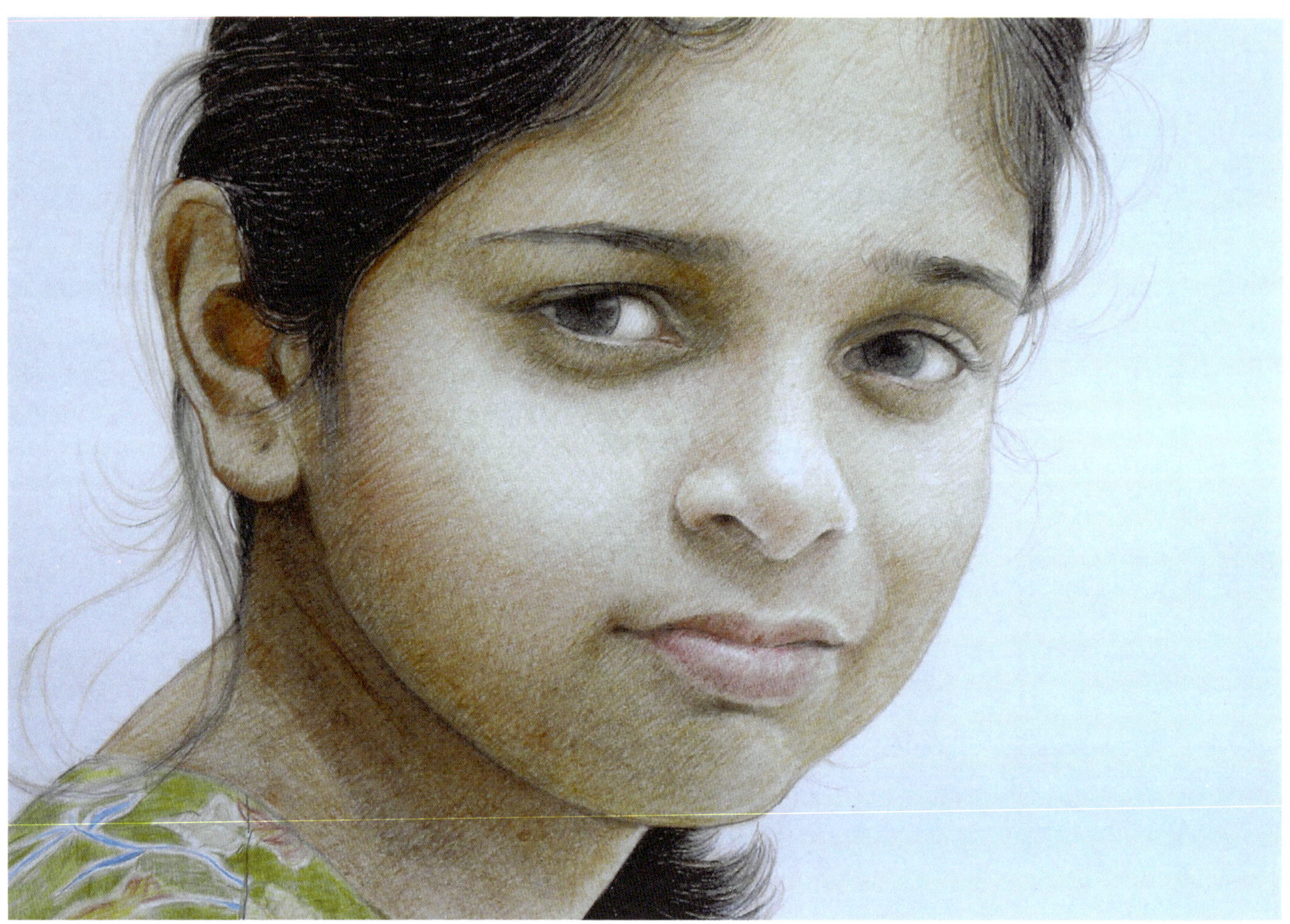

Gaze Celestial

SUNIL JOSHI | INDIA
gpuls@neo.rr.com | http://laurenepuls.com/artwork

38 Being Indian, my sketching style has evolved with the art material available here. I use mainly cross hatching and directional lines to make portraits. I avoid making portraits just similar to reference photograph. For me maintaining likeness and capturing expression is key. I feel that lines and cross hatching have a beauty of their own which are to be retained in the portrait and not done away with by heavy burnishing. I generally choose photos with good contrast and sharp facial features (not necessarily pretty). Making large background and details of ornaments and cloths wear me out.

TECHNIQUE AND TIPS
Faber Castlle and Lyra Skin Tones | Executive Bond Paper (Made in Indai) 13" x 9.5"

Initially do not bother about getting accurate resemblance to reference photo. Just practice making portraits, likeness and perfection will slowly come, on its own. Avoid photos taken in poor light. Start with graphite and then graduate to CP.

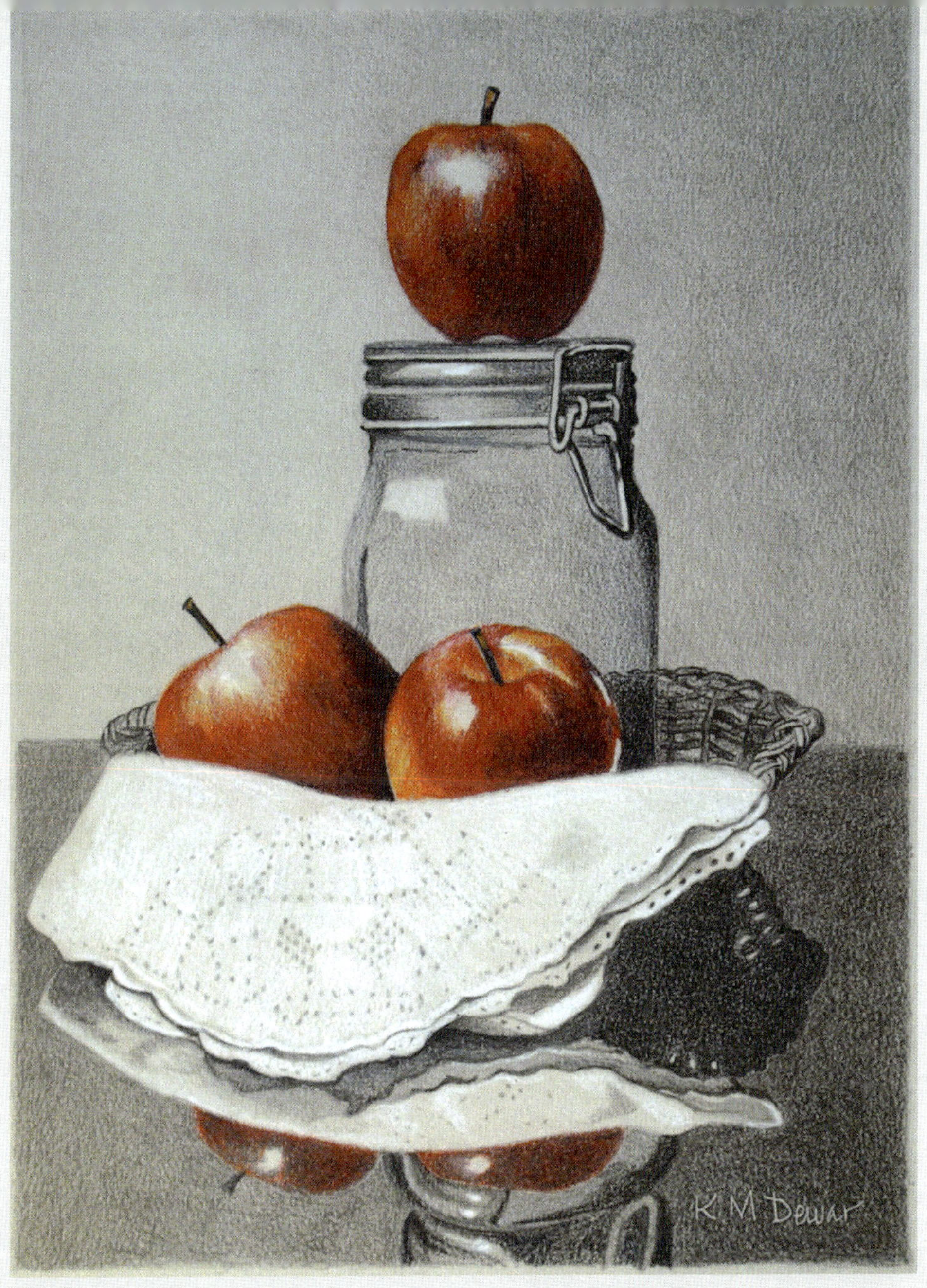

Balancing Act

KAY DEWAR, CPSA | United States
http://kaydewar.com

39 I have loved the textures derived from working with colored pencil on paper since I first tried it many years ago. In combining fabric, glass, and shiny objects the various texture representations are what give the composition life and interest. My French Grey series was created for the purpose of challenging myself to study values and colors. In my work the shadows and reflections are every bit as important to me as the actual objects being depicted.

TECHNIQUE AND TIPS
Prismacolor | Stonehenge | 9.25 x 6.75

In teaching my French Grey technique, the first thing that I stress is taking time to determine the best composition. Since color is only used in limited areas, planning the overall balance of the composition must be decided before beginning the drawing. Also, the careful and even application of the pencil medium is an important element of my technique. The pencil is applied evenly and with little evidence of the directional stroke.

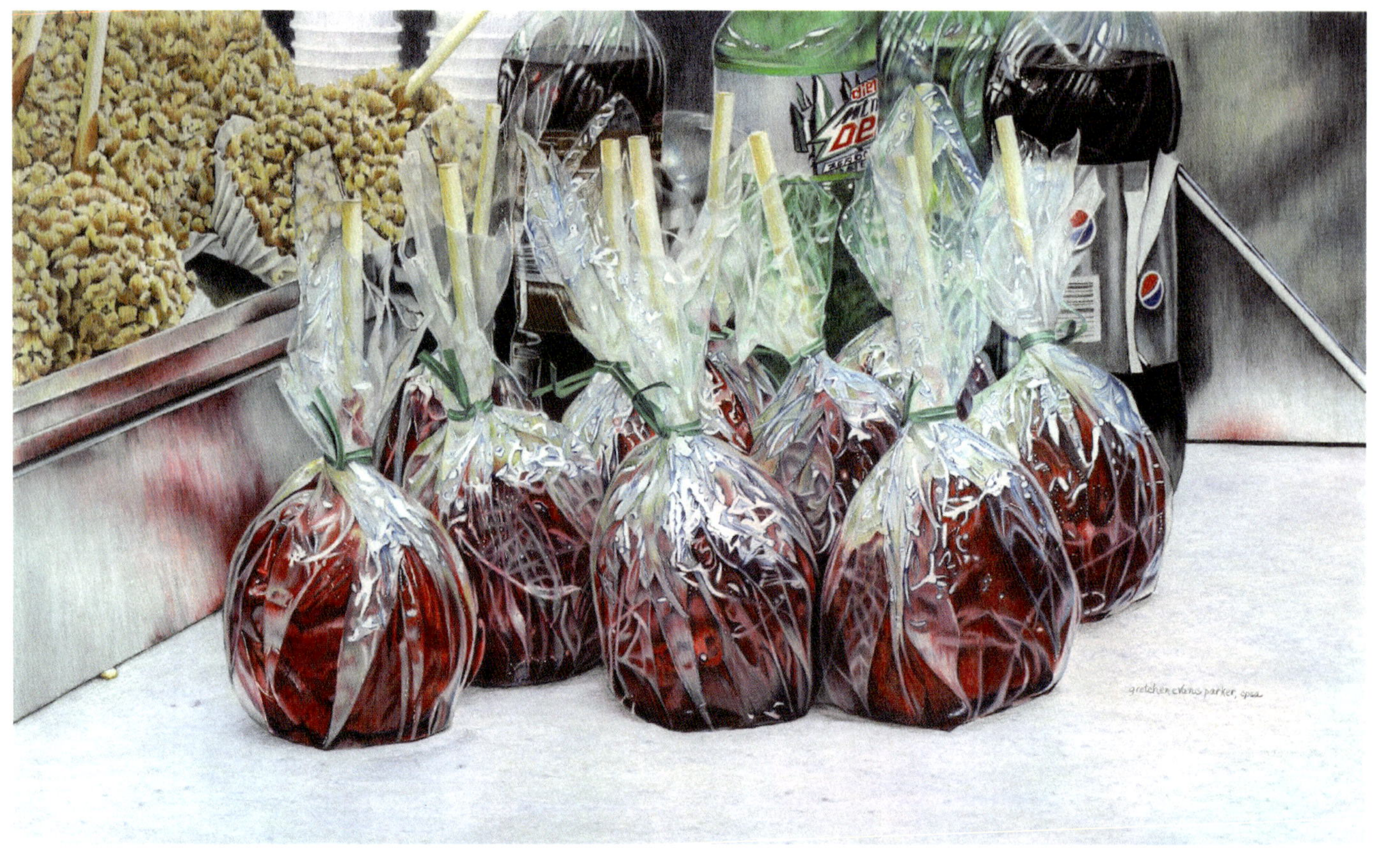

Fair Food

GRETCHEN PARKER | United States
http://www.gretchenevansparker.com

40 I LOVE color. For years graphite was my medium. Learning to work in color seemed so intimidating. Now I wonder what took me so long!

I carry a small camera with me at all times. You never know when a wonderful subject is going to cross your path. The reference photo for this work was shot at our South Carolina State Fair. Those apples take me back to my childhood when we sold candy apples at school.

I look for drama in my reference photos. Lots of light and shadow, whether it is a portrait or a still life, can often promise intrigue in the finished piece. My goal in every painting is realism. Taking on a challenges like the transparency of cellophane or making glass glow with sunshine keeps me returning to my drawing board. When doing a portrait my goal is to express the personality of the person or creature looking out from the paper. If my work jogs a memory or engenders emotion I feel the piece has been successful.

TECHNIQUE AND TIPS
Prismacolor | Stonehenge | 13.5" x 21.5"

I stand at a drafting table with a slanted surface while working so I can step back every few minutes to assess my progress. If I don't move away from the work frequently, the small sections I have finished continue to look like puzzle pieces. By constantly changing my perspective the work begins to blend together and make sense to my eye. I often take my work to another room and stand it up where I can look at it perpendicularly. It resets the way my brain sees what has been done. I can feel an actual click in my body when I know it's right.

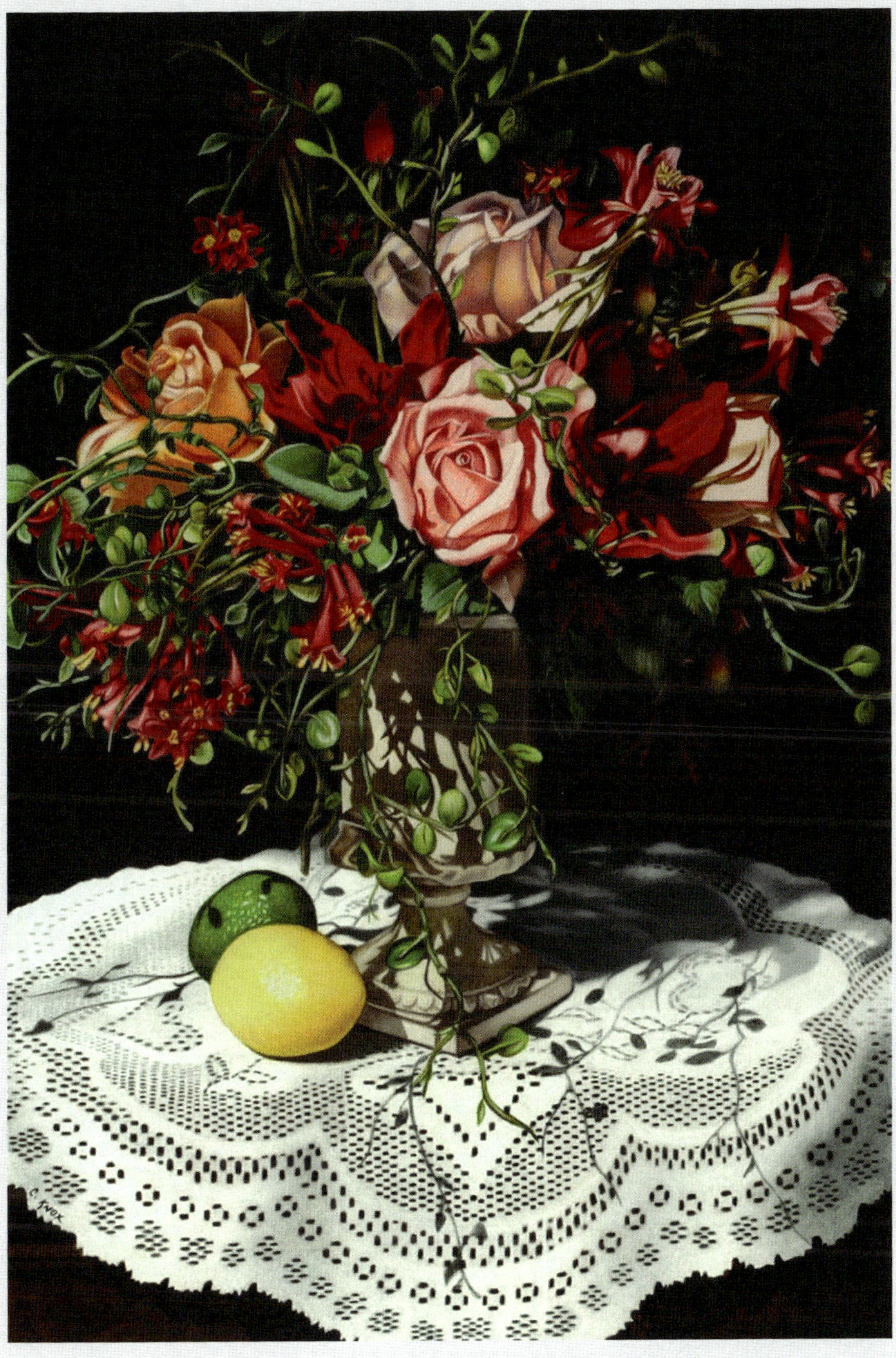

CYNTHIA KNOX, CPSA | UNITED STATES

http://www.cynthiaknox.com

41 This piece was the culmination of all things difficult for me in creating art with colored pencils. There is a lot going on with those flowers, texture of the fruit, and extreme detail in the lace. I wanted a challenge, and believe me, I got it with this still life! However, the satisfaction of being able to figure out the hard stuff was all worth it. I enjoy learning new things with each project I embark upon.

Scentsation

TECHNIQUE AND TIPS

Prismacolor | Strathmore Smooth Bristol | 16″ x 11″

I would say that my style is extreme realism, and my favorite technique is burnishing. Detailed oil paintings have always appealed to me, and when I learned that this look can be accomplished with colored pencils, I was thrilled! The many layers of application and increased pencil pressure blend all colors together and bring them to a high gloss. This combined with a great amount of detail is what I strive for. I'm learning which colors blend best together and currently favor Prismacolor's rich reds.

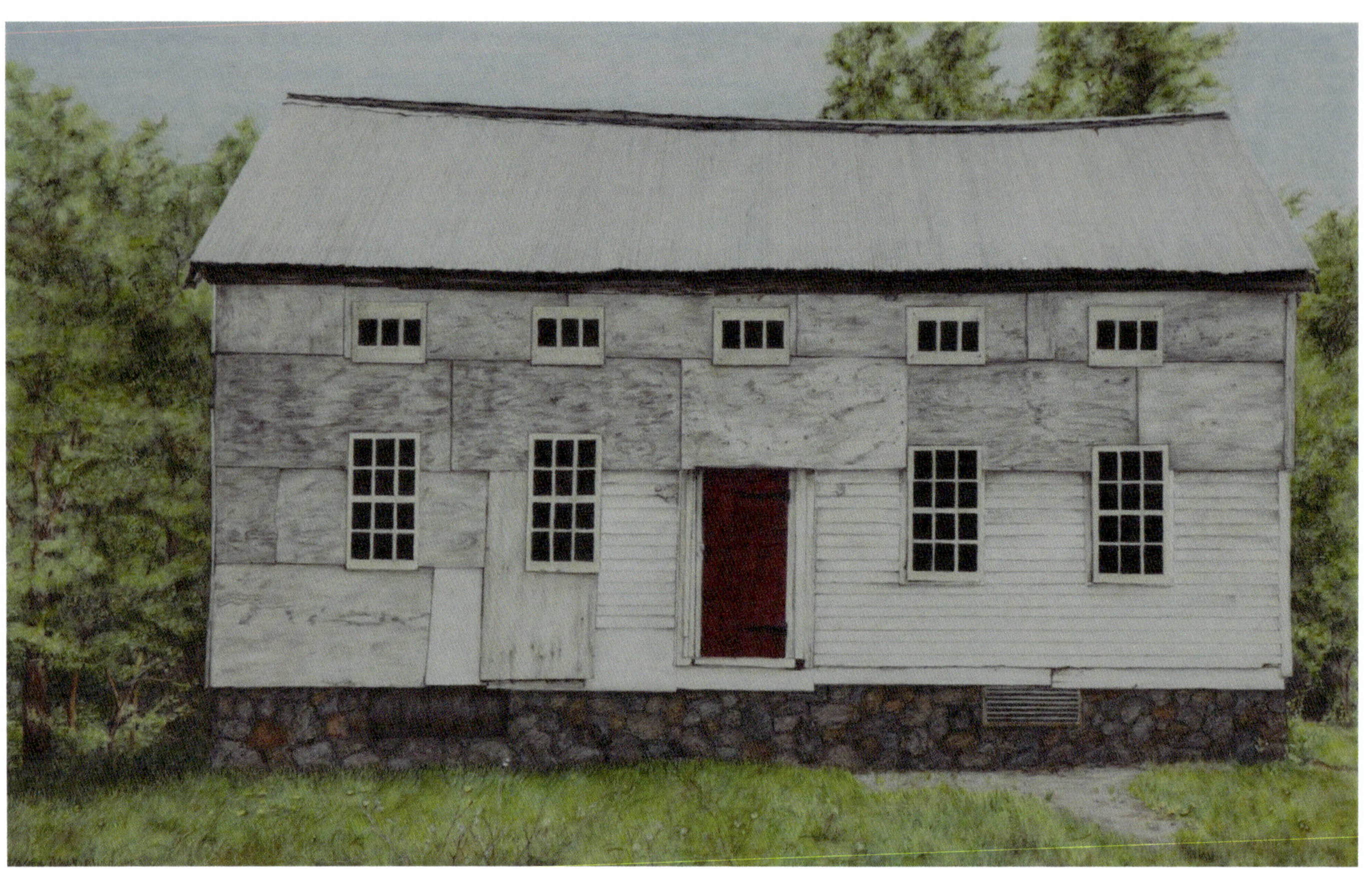

Ward-Ryerson-Patterson House in Summer

PAULA MADAWICK, CPSA | UNITED STATES

42 For me just drawing another old house is not enough. This house sits near a well-traveled road. Drivers zoom by barely giving it a glance. Hikers on their way to woodland trails walk by it. They both see an old house. I see a contemporary installation. Yes, it is an old house but it was moved to its location and it is not quite what it seems. The welcoming red front door is nailed shut, the hinges are painted on and there are no front steps. The windows are not glass but trompe l'oeil, painted on size specific panels overlapping large sheets of painted plywood. The corrugated tin roof hides cedar shingles. I feel there is no inside to this house. It is impenetrable on all sides. This drawing of one side of the Ward-Ryerson-Patterson House depicts summer. I am drawing the four different sides of the house, each represents a season.

TECHNIQUE AND TIPS

Caran D'Ache, Derwent, Faber Castell and Prismacolor | 40 Hot Press Arches Watercolor paper | 12 1/2" x 20 1/2"

I make art; my medium is colored pencil. That's my best tip; the art is first, the medium is second. Don't loose sight of the "art factor." I would rather look at a great idea rendered moderately well than a commonplace idea rendered exquisitely.

Technical tip - work the whole picture building up from base colors and values. And, water-soluble colored pencils are the best!

EILEEN NISTLER, CPSA | United States
http://EileenNistler.com

43 I used to buy up deals at yard sales and flea markets and then have a big auction at my home. It was fairly lucrative but a lot of work. The Silver was from one of those collections prior to the big sale. I polished and set up silver in various vignettes and used some silver from my personal collection. Then I photographed and photographed using natural sunlight for lighting. From those photographs came The Silver. This was a rather tedious painting. It took me three times longer than other paintings of the same size. I think it was worth it! This painting also includes some graphite pencils.

The Silver

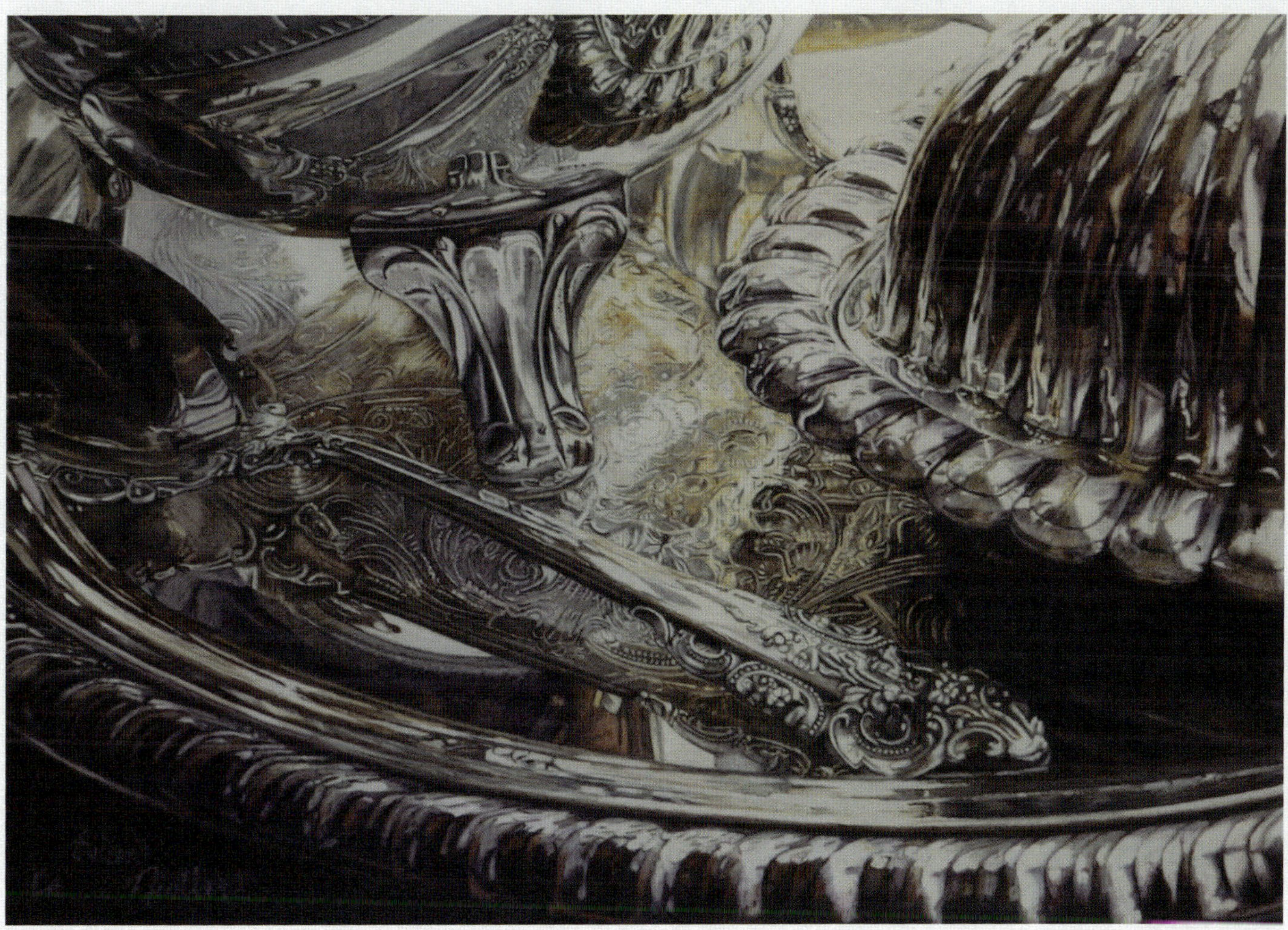

TECHNIQUE AND TIPS
Prismacolor and Derwent Coloursoft | Beige Stonehenge | 10" x 14"

I sketch the final design on a large sheet of paper and overlay that over my paper. I tape a cardboard frame around the final design and hinge it to the top of my board. The cardboard keeps everything in the exact same place throughout the process. I have everything figured out on the design before I cut my paper. I cut the paper the size of the design plus 2 1/2" on all sides (Mat size) so that it doesn't slip when traveling framed. I then work left to right top to bottom finishing each section before moving on. I do this so I don't drag my hand across my finished area. I usually add white and dark to the mostly finished piece to further emphasize whatever I feel needs a little more push. I spray all of my paintings with archival varnish.

LIZ GUZYNSKI | United States

44 Like a lot of other CP artists, I came at the medium sideways, without formal artistic training, but with an intense need for pattern and beauty and depth that seemed lacking in ordinary life.

When I started studying and working with plants more seriously a couple of years ago, my artistic focus moved out of the human part of nature and into chlorophyll-based reality in a big way! Plants are responsible for, in addition to the air we breathe, the most complex inter- and intraspecies relationships on the planet. As far as I am concerned, they have powers of cognition, adaptation, partnership and perhaps even emotion that rival anything else going on.

In my work, I'm growing profoundly interested in how to represent the world from a non-human point of view; to show that there are needs and dependencies and agendas being played out every moment. *(continued on page 78)*

September Hydrangeas

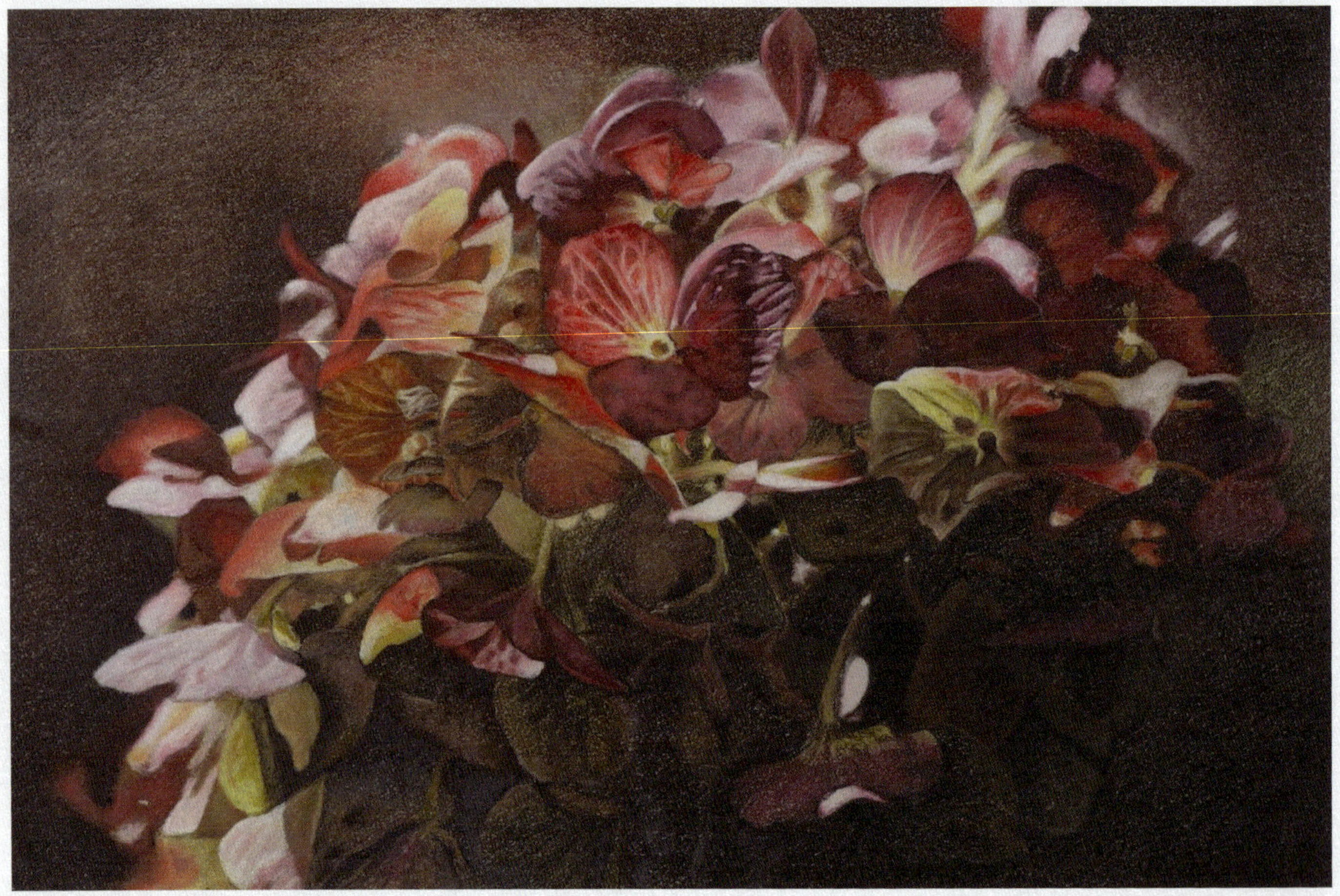

Technique and Tips
Prismacolor, NeoArt, Lyra | Wallis pastel paper, Belgian mist color | 11" x 17"

Following my larger artistic inspirations, my technique involves a lot of emotion. Sometimes I try to be a "good" classical colored pencil artist, and lay down dozens of ethereal layers. But honestly, most of the the time, I am so powerfully in love with my subject that I start pushing rich complex colors into the surface as fast as I can.

I love working on Wallis pastel paper, which is a heavily (but evenly!) sanded surface. There's no point in being gentle with the stuff! You MUST grind a ton of pigment into the gritty surface before you can even think about details. I often start with Neo- color and Neo-Art crayons because you can dissolve them with water and then move the opaque tints around in a painterly fashion. Pencils on top of this under-painting allow me to "sneak up" on the details and subtleties on the subject while maintaining the basic structure. Finally, I adore the freedom to work light over dark. (I have been known to use a palette knife to mash the final highlights and details into place.)

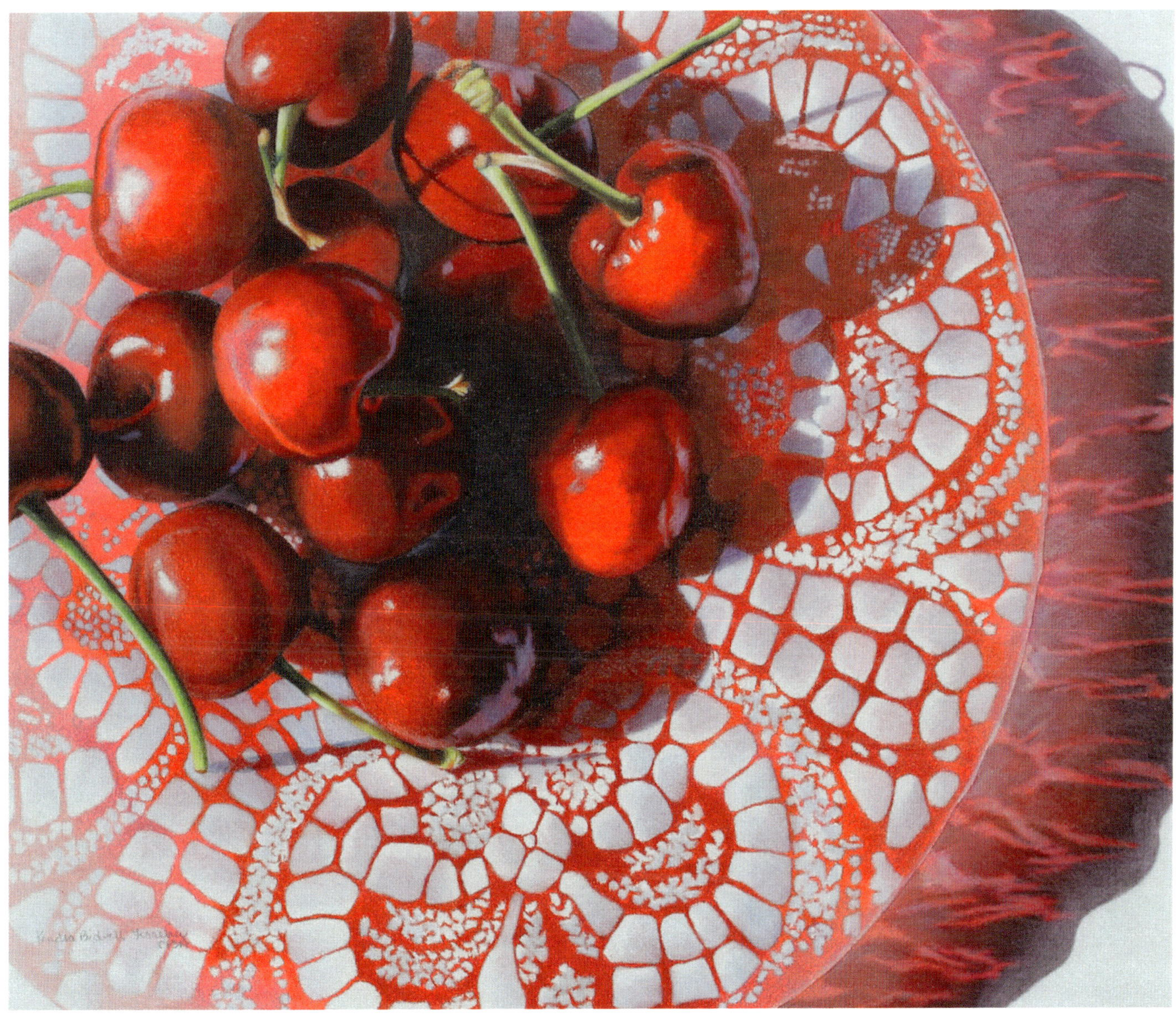

Splendor

KENDRA BIDWELL FERREIRA. CPSA | UNITED STATES
http://kjfdesign.com

45 I am attracted to brightly colored still life subjects which I like to draw larger than life size. I like to draw from a still life set up, however lighting changes so quickly (and live objects don't last) so I also work from my own reference photos. I was captivated by the sunlight shining through this translucent glass plate and wondered if I could capture it's luminance as well as shiny deep reds of the cherries. My goal for this piece was also to render the cherries and the intricate pattern on the plate in different ways so they wouldn't compete with each other and the cherries, my focal point, would stand out.

TECHNIQUE AND TIPS
Prismacolor, Derwent Coloursoft, Lyra Rembrandt, Caran d'Arche Luminance, Verithin | Rtistx board | 14" x 17"

Much of my recent colored pencil work has been done on different types of boards and varnished rather than framed under glass. I am always experimenting with new surfaces and new ways of finishing the piece with varnishes. It is very important to me to be sure all materials that I use are archival. Often with the sanded surfaces, I use solvent with the colored pencils. I apply a layer of pencil and then brush it smooth with a flat soft brush and odorless mineral spirits after which I apply more colored pencil and smooth it again with the brush. With this method, I find I can achieve rich color without any of the surface texture showing through. In this piece, Splendor, I also used a burnishing method on the plate with harder pencils over the soft pencils.

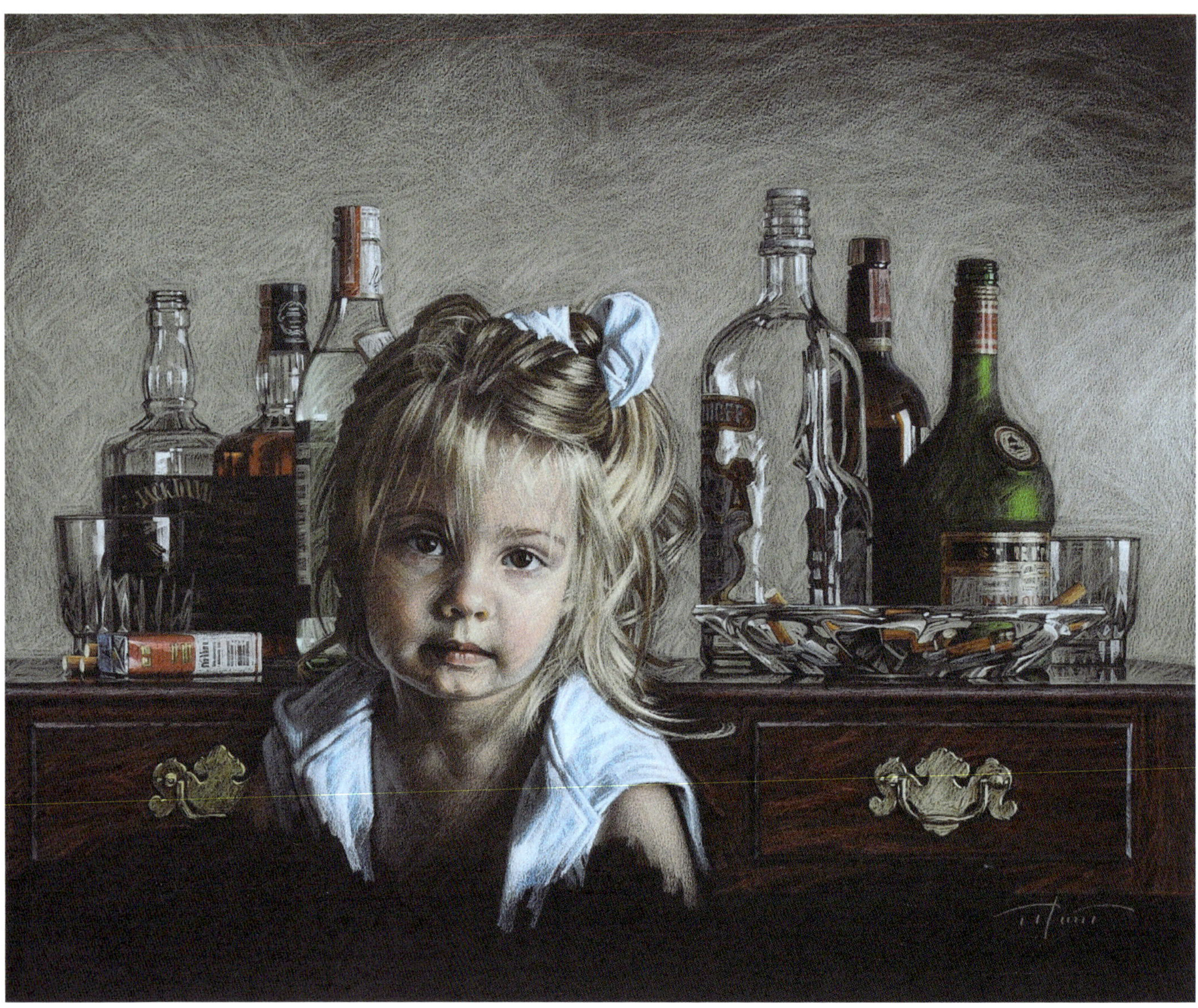

Dawn's Early Light

TOMMY HUNT | United States
http://www.tommyhunt.com

46 'Dawn's Early Light' was inspired by an unfortunate automobile accident involving my granddaughter, Shannen, and her mother. Her mother, under the influence of alcohol, was driving them home one night when an accident occurred. Both were ok, thank goodness, but it pointed out how dangerous our actions can be, not only to ourselves but to others, and particularly our children. In this drawing I envisioned the mother waking up to the concerned look from her child. Some ideas take time to develop. This one came to me in one flash - bingo.

TECHNIQUE AND TIPS
Prismacolor | unknown - paper discontinued | 16" x 20"

Make sure you keep your eye on the foundation of your picture - composition/design, drawing, values and color. Without a solid foundation it is easy to lose your foundation in the details. No amount of detail or special effects will help you. Keep it as simple as much as you can for as long as you can. When you begin looking at complicated reference images, whether live models or photos, you need to squint to help you establish this foundation. Squinting in the early stages, and occasionally throughout the process, will simplify the amount of information you're seeing. Squinting will tell you your values and whether or not the edges of your objects are hard, soft or lost. I generally work on black paper because I like working dark to light. I start by transferring a fairly detailed line drawing onto my paper surface and then working in the darkest values, the darkest colors, first. Over these I'll add lighter and lighter colors, finishing off with the whites. I stay as loose as I can for as long as I can, saving the tight, 'it's just like this', stuff for last.

DONNA SLADE, CPSA | UNITED STATES
http://www.donnasladeart.com

47 My paintings are not a photographic moment in time but represent a unique artistic interpretation through observation. I seek to provide a place for the viewer to find curiosity and appreciation for the process of creation. Emotion, communication and nourishment are all reasons why I am passionate about the art making process.

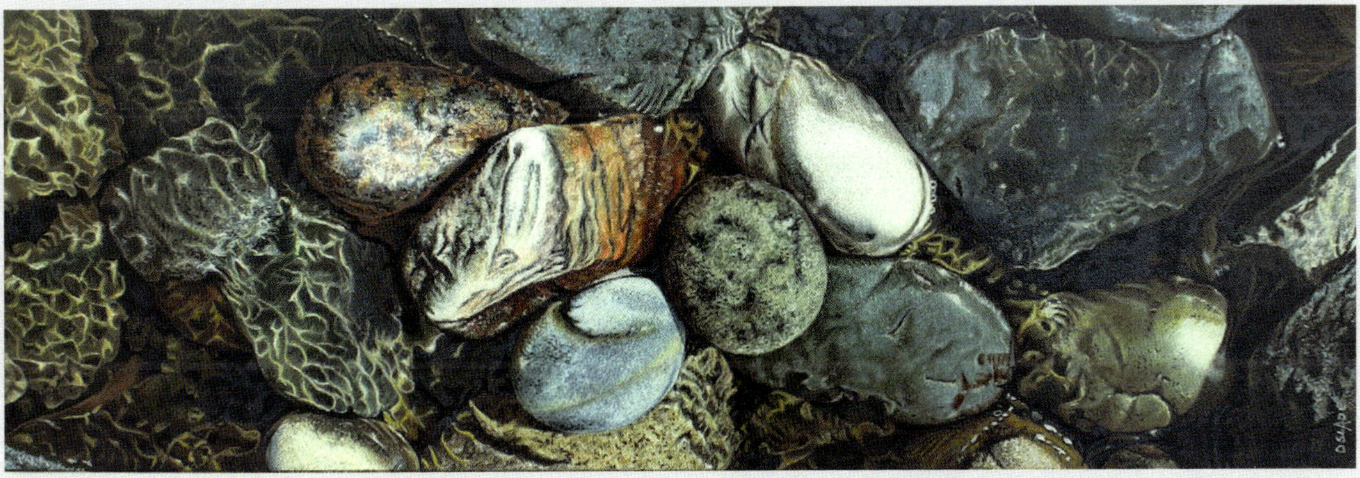

Maine Stream

TECHNIQUE AND TIPS
Prismacolor | Ampersand Pastelbord | 8″ x 16″

My colored pencil paintings are imagined, planned and executed in a representational, realistic style. I love the challenge of creating detail in the light and dark values with each individual stroke and cross-hatching mark. I can very lightly apply eight to ten different colors to build bold but yet sensitive color values, work from dark to light blending my colors to create a soft, feathered look, letting the characteristics of the paper come through to achieve the textured effect that has become the hallmark of my work.

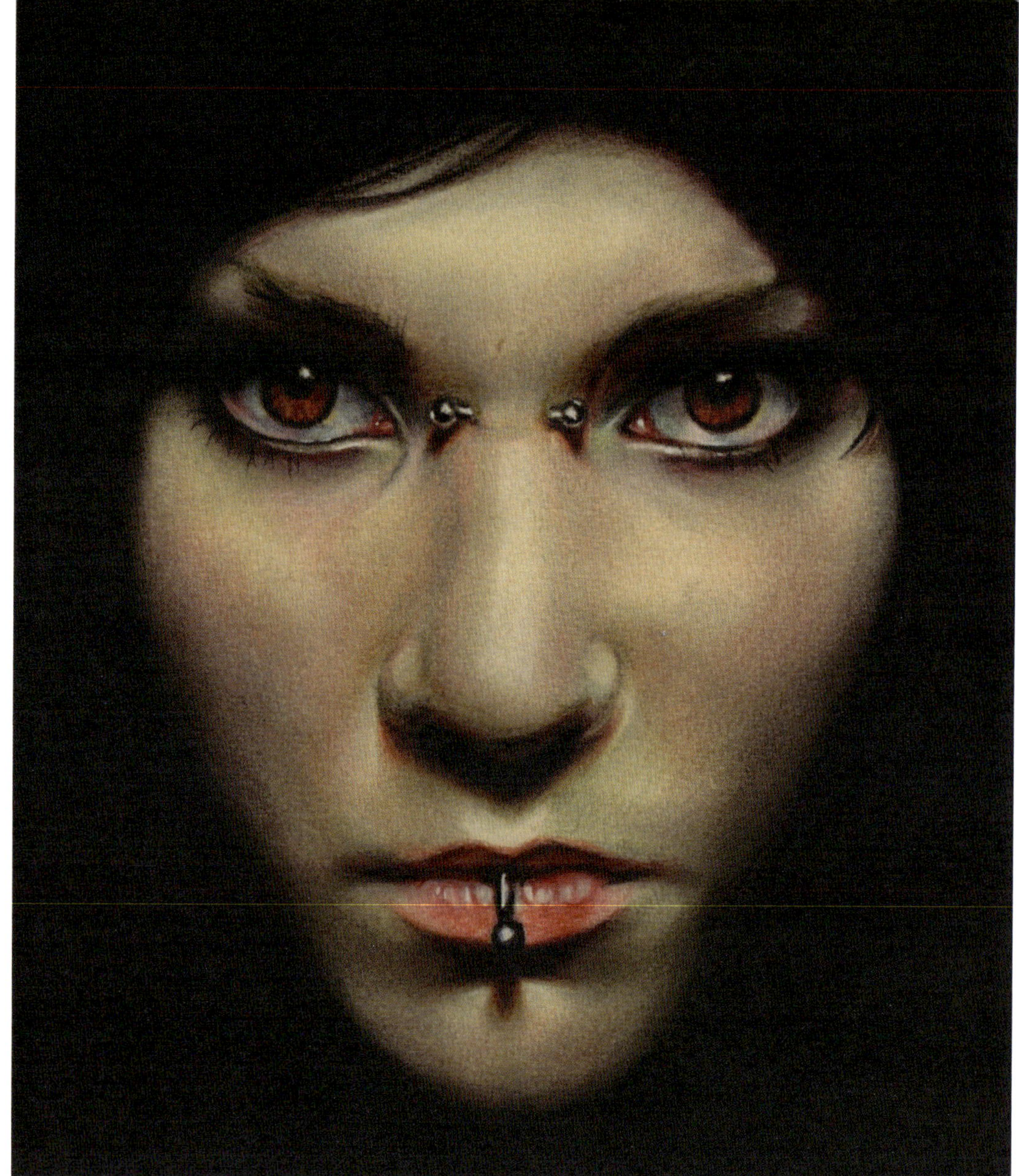

Melu

BRIAN SCOTT | ENGLAND
http://briscott.deviantart.com

48 I wanted to make colored pencils not look like colored pencils, i.e. stiff pencil marks. I try to enhance the drawings by exaggerating light, shade and color, and I try different colors on the face - not just pink. I spend most time on the eyes as in life that's the first thing you look at. The eyes draw you in. Emotion flows through the eye, and I try to catch that.

I love doing hair. Drawing to me is like being in a time machine; once you get zoned in you don't hear the music and 5 or 6 hours pass in a blink . I would draw all day every day if I could. I draw because I love it. If people like my drawings, that's a bonus.

TECHNIQUE AND TIPS
Faber Castell Polychromos | Medium surface cartridge paper (Heavy Weight) | 11″ x 8″

I like my pencils very sharp. I put the colors down lightly and blend with a soft cloth. For the dark backgrounds, I use Faber Castell Pitt oil black pencil then go over it with a little turpentine on a brush to smooth it out. Sometimes for the hair I've laid down the colors I think are in the hair, then I've gone over it with Pitt oil black pencil, then a little turpentine with a brush. I let it dry then with a pencil eraser, I draw in the strands of hair and the bottom color comes through.

Spend time on your drawing. Don't rush. Once you think you've finished, lay it aside for a few days. When you go back to it you see things you might have missed.

SHEILA SCANNELLI, CPSA | United States

49 Shiny, rough, grainy, bumby, smooth, cracked, wavy, silky, fuzzy, glassy......I could go on and on about TEXTURE! This is one of the main elements that I strive to incorporate into my colored pencil drawings. Wood, brick, stone, glass, metal...the types of objects that draw my attention. I am constantly looking for that strange or onusual object that I can zoom down into the details that make up it's surface qualities.

I often drive my husband crazy while he is waiting for me to get just the right shot of a new found object that has grabbed my attention. It dosen't matter if I'm on vacation 1,000 miles away or in my own back yard--you never know when you'll find that next piece of inspiration.

The White Tag

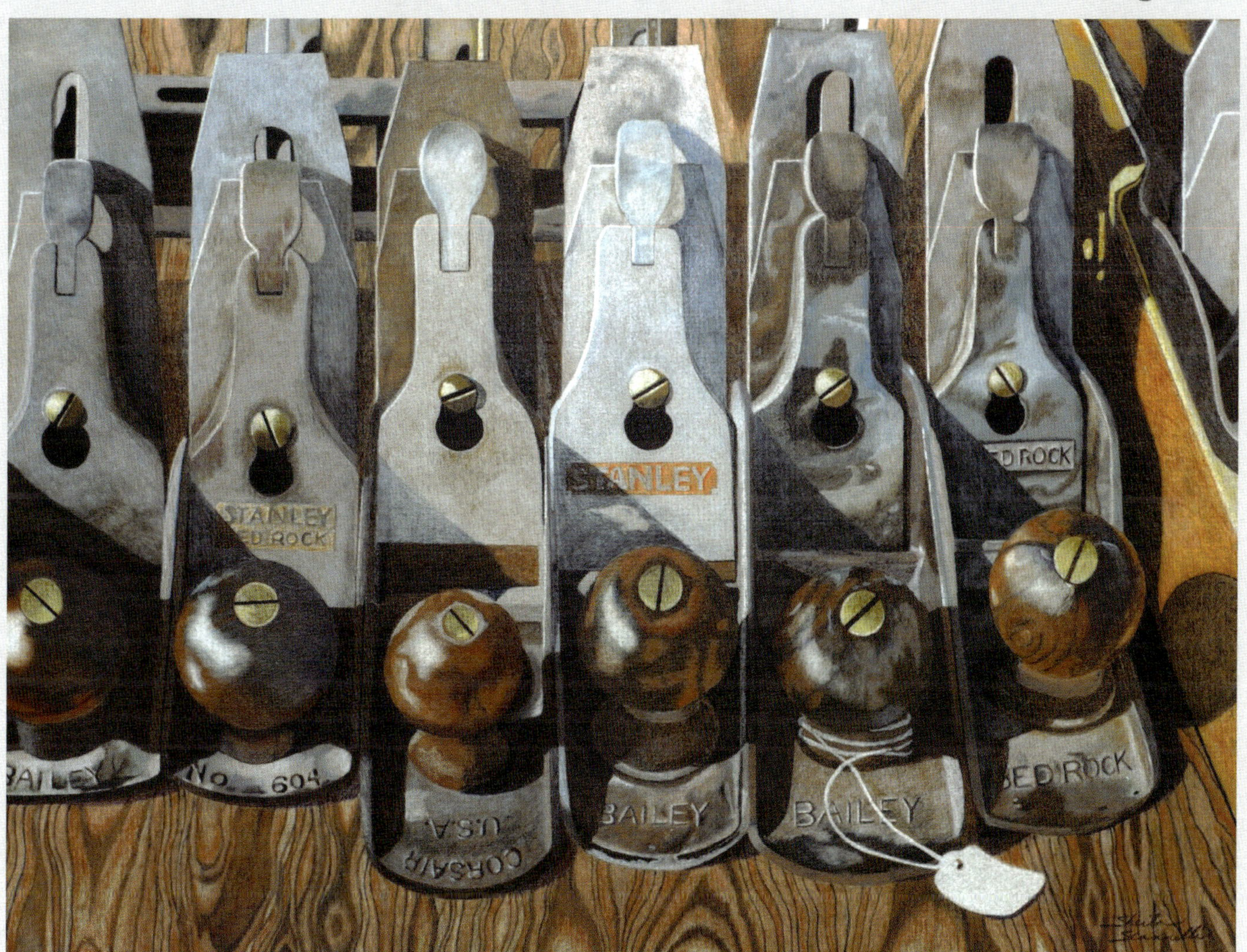

TECHNIQUE AND TIPS
Prismacolor | Mat Board | 23" x 29"

Up close and personnal. This is the way most of my drawings start. When taking photos I often start with an overall view of the scene or item. Then I zoom in on specific areas within the composition. This way I have various aspects that I can pick from when I decide which photos to use as reference.

SANDY PHIFER, CPSA |
United States
http://www.sandyphifer.com

50 I strive for drama in my artwork, either by using bold colors or by using dramatic contrasts. My subject might be a plant, a critter, or a bottle of wine, but it needs to have some dramatic element to spark my interest.

The shiny, sparkling surfaces and reflected light against the intensely dark background adds drama to "A Bottle of Blush". Creating "sparkle" and "shine" on a piece of paper by contrasting light against dark is what appealed to me as an artist and was my inspiration for painting this scene.

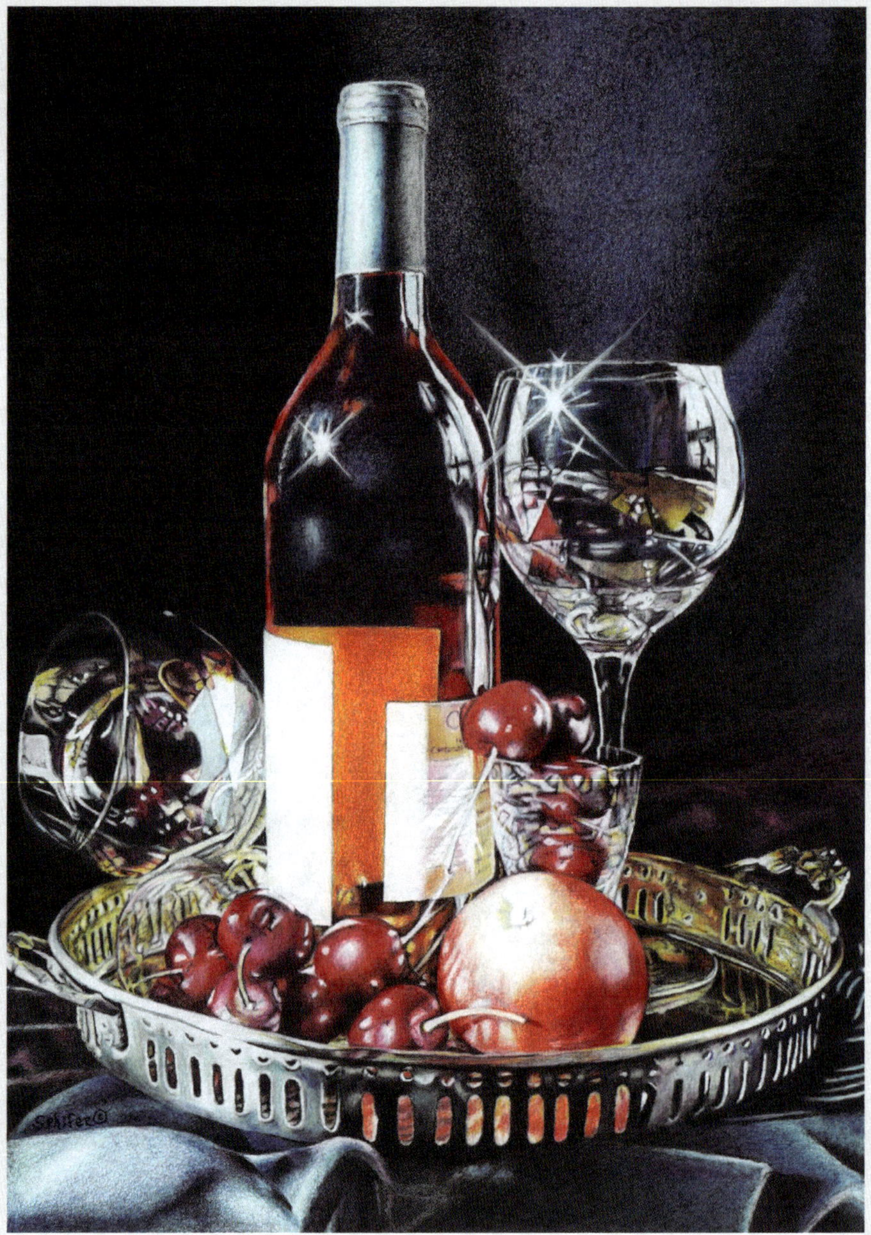

A Bottle of Blush

TECHNIQUE AND TIPS
Prismacolor | Bristol Vellum Paper | 14" x 10"

I always begin a piece by laying in washes of light color first and adding thin layers of darker colors on top of the lighter washes. This creates glowing colors that appear to have depth. My darkest colors, like the background in "A Bottle of Blush", might have 6 or 8 layers, from indigo or dahlia purple, to black. Bright colors, like those seen in the apple, might start with a layer of cream, end with a layer of black cherry, and have 15 or more layers of color in between. I almost always burnish, sometimes burnishing every few layers as I build up color, enabling me to create a very smooth surface with an even texture. Sharpening edges and adding details is my last step. Sometimes I create special textures by not burnishing the final layer of pencil, as in the lighter areas of fabric in "A Bottle of Blush".

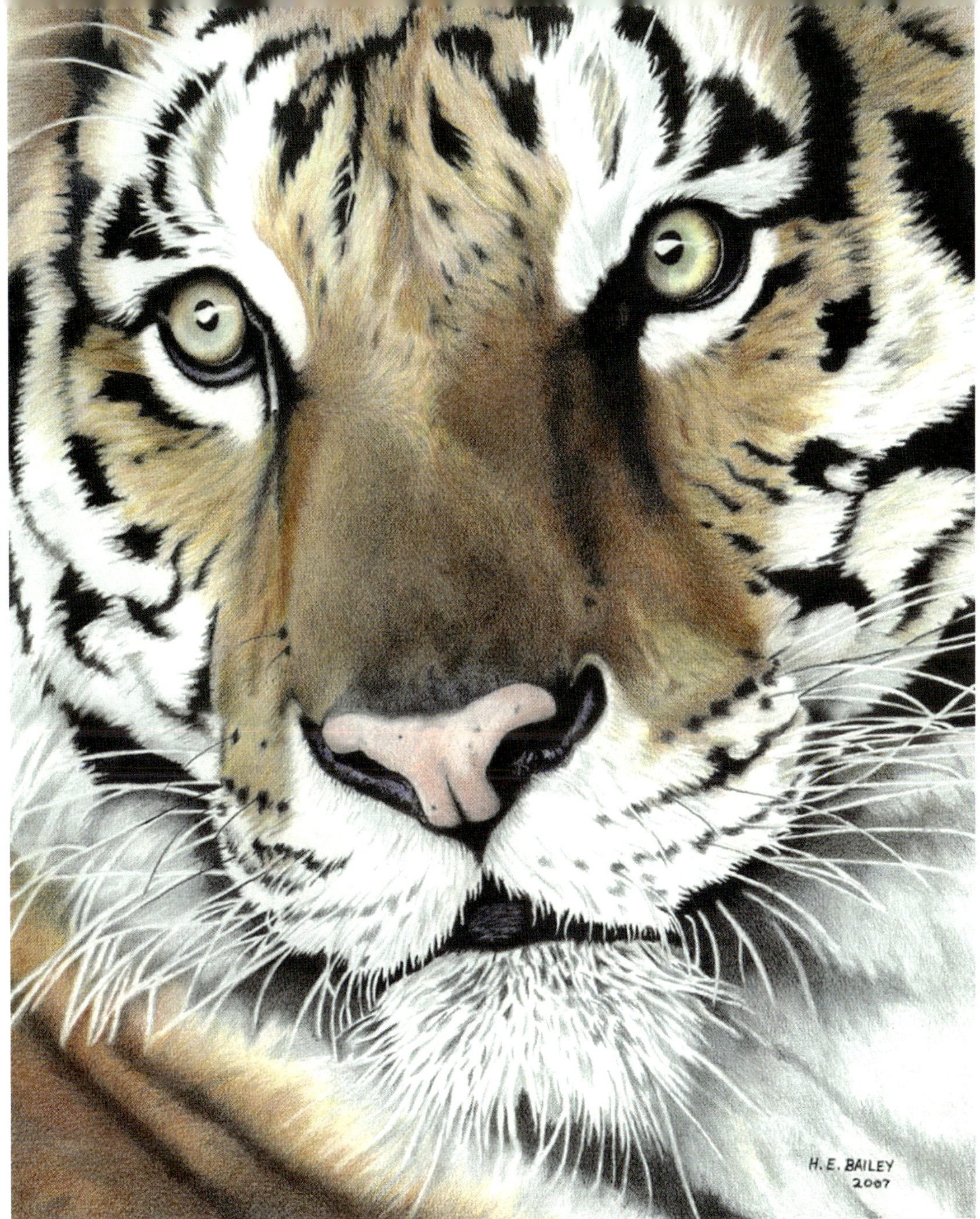

Eric's Legacy

HELEN BAILEY | UNITED STATES
http://www.helenbaileyart.com

51 Animals have always called to me to try to show the "life" of the animal in a drawing - a 2 dimensional piece of art. A photo shows a flat, still image but a drawing can envision the life that animates the soul of this tiger or any other animal I portray. I want to improve with each drawing, knowing that one life time will not be enough time to complete every drawing that I have in my head. When something calls to me, I never lose the excitement that I feel when I start on the next drawing.

TECHNIQUE AND TIPS
Prismacolor | Canson Mi Tientes paper | 30" x 26"

I usually start with large photos so that I can see the features clearly. I like to work in fairly large sizes so the eyes can be drawn with clarity and I have to draw the eyes first. That's when the animal comes to life within the paper. My technique uses many layers built slowly with a light touch. Layered colors that show through each other give the rounded effect that look life-long. I usually start with a mid-tone, adding dark areas next and leaving the lightest areas for the last.

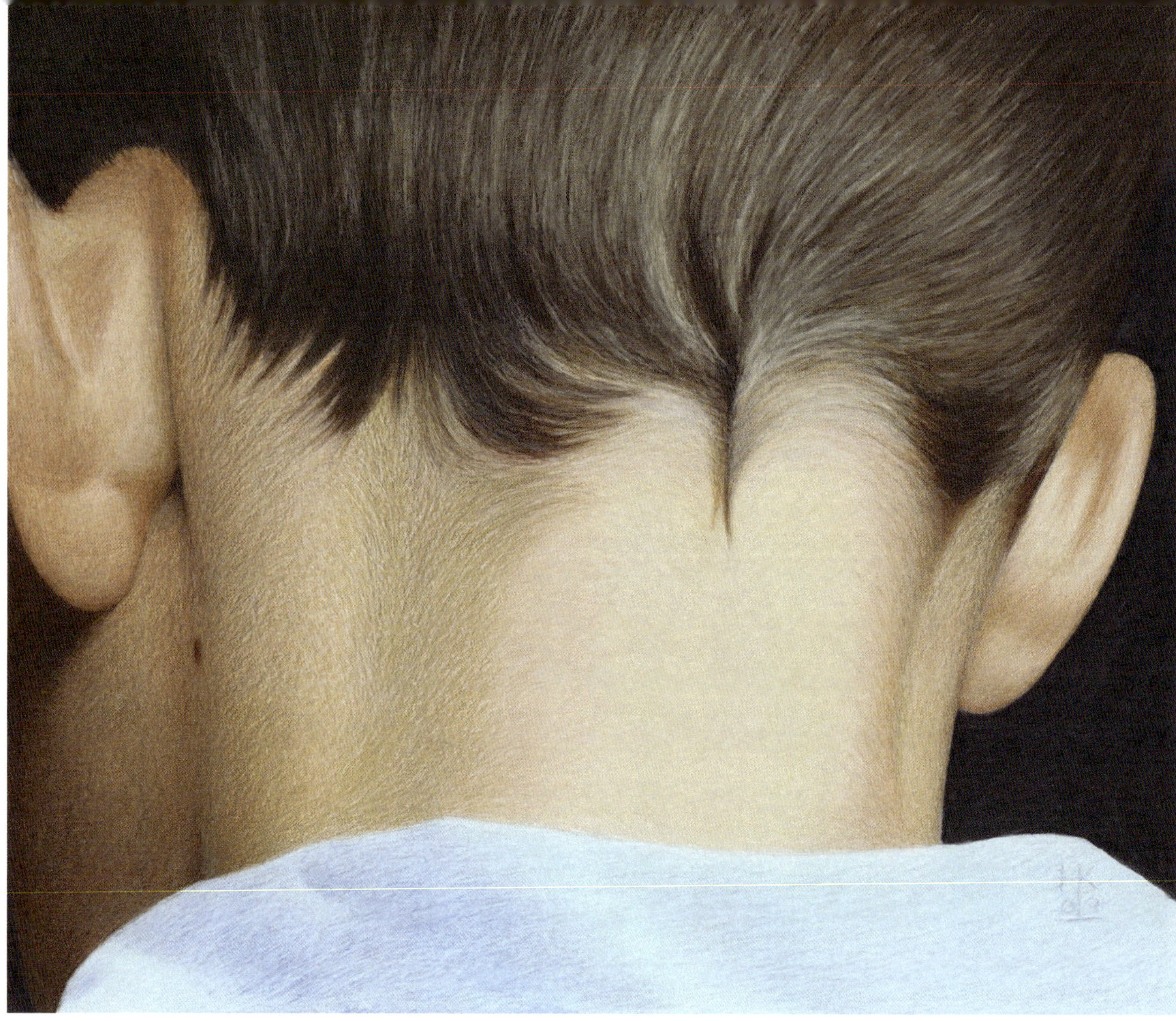

Nolen's Nape

HEIDI J. KLIPPERT LINDBERG | UNITED STATES

52 My challenge is always to strive to bring out the very essence of my subjects--to make them appear sculptural and tactile using glowing color to create depth and movement, so they look almost alive! When I do portraits I must capture the person's spirit or the picture doesn't work. And, as much as I love architecture and design, I've discovered the only subjects that interest me are ones that are, or have been, alive. Ordinary doesn't interest me which is why I also strive to capture my subjects from unusual angles.

TECHNIQUE AND TIPS
Prismacolor | 8-ply mat board | 8" x 12 1/2"

I use a fine-textured 8-ply white matte board because it accepts color deeply, creates fine clean edges, takes a lot of abuse from my extremely heavy pressure, and can be scraped with a razor blade when I need to correct errant color. My technique obliterates the surface texture, even with skin color (a real challenge!), so that no white paper shows. I never use tinted or black paper because it changes the applied color quality and I want "pure" color. I don't want any pencil lines in evidence (though sometimes I can't avoid them)--just smooth color even when it's mixed heavily on the board. I work light to dark so that no shreds of color get mixed in with the light areas. A light layered touch doesn't work for me because I mix my colors directly on the board and grind them together. As I press color into the surface I have the sense that I'm "feeling" the image I'm trying to create.

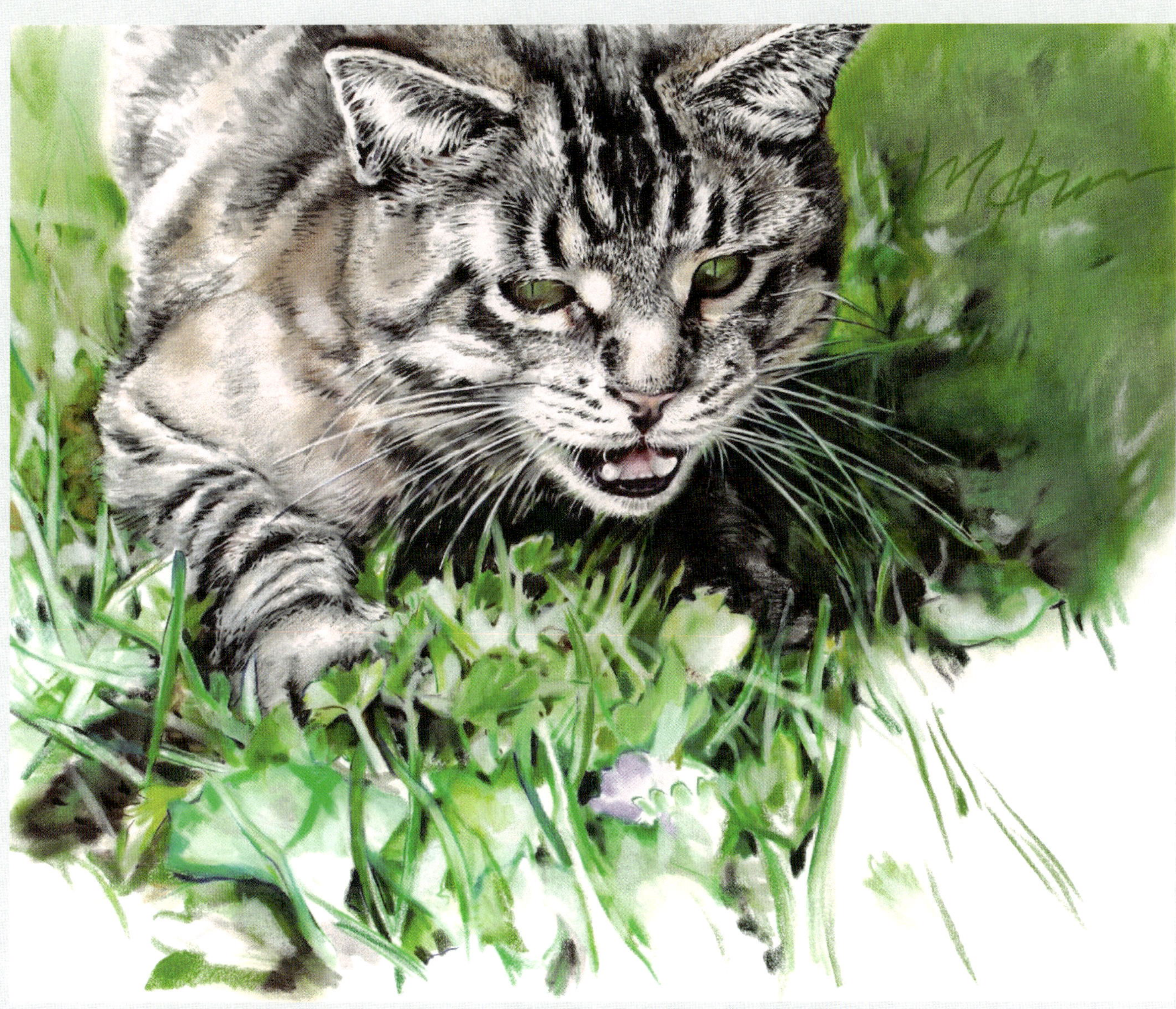

Cleese's Teeth

MARGI HOPKINS | UNITED STATES
http://pepperportraits.com

53 This is Cleese, named after Monty Python's John Cleese. He is a Domestic Shorthair Tabby cat. You might say a common house cat. But even a common house cat like Cleese, is far from boring. And to a small mouse or cricket, the house cat is far from sweet. This house cat is on the hunt.

In human portraiture the artist primarily uses facial expression to convey personality and mood. This is because humans communicate with their faces. *(continued on page 76)*

TECHNIQUE AND TIPS
Prismacolor | 4 ply 100% rag mat board | 22" x17"

Nothing takes me 5 minutes! Because I thrive on challenge and my portraits take a long time to create, I find it less intimidating to know the 10 phases:

1. Inspiration (fun)
2. Layout (grunt)
3. Getting started (fun)

(continued on page 76)

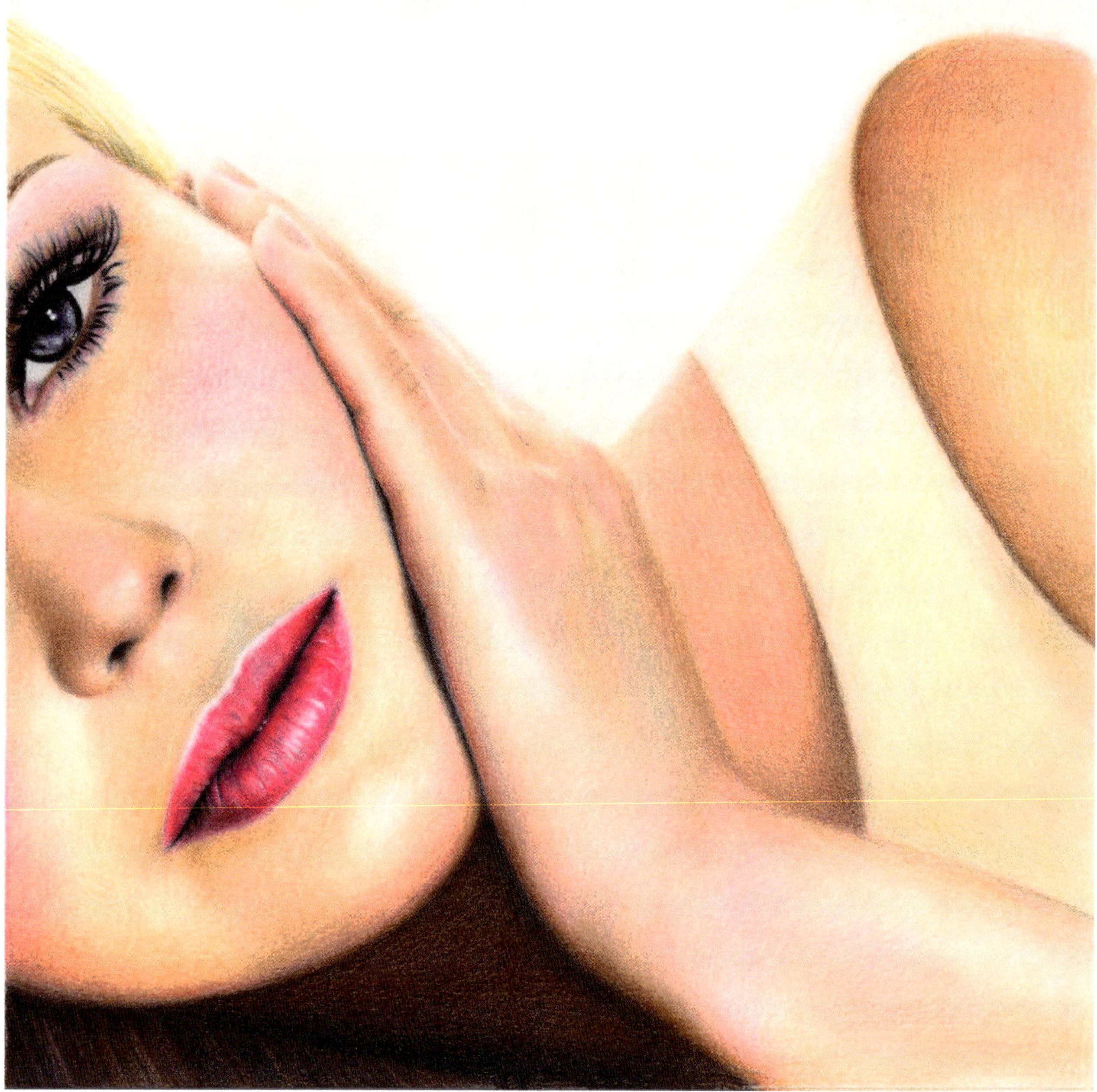

Dreaming of You

SARKIS SARKISSIAN | SWEDEN
http://sikoian.deviantart.com

54 "The objective I had for this drawing was to showcase the softness and the beauty of a woman dreaming of the person that she's looking at. The challenging part of the drawing was to get the soft look and combining the colors together to create the warm tones which further expresses the mood for the drawing."

TECHNIQUE AND TIPS
Faber Castell colored pencils | Aquarelle paper | 8.3" x 11.7"

My tip for portraits is always to make sure the lighting is correct. The contrast in a portrait is equally important for me as the lighting is. I pay a lot of attention to the colors and their cohesion aswell as the position of the model and last but not least the expression of the model. I start a colored pencil drawing often by making a simple sketch preparing for the actual drawing. I start by making the oulines lightly with a pencil and then I go on applying multiple layers of colors until I get the desired tone. *(continued on page 76)*

JEWEL MATHIESON | NEW ZEALAND
http://www.petportrait.co.nz

55 I'm inspired by the unique individual personalities that dogs show through their subtle facial expressions and body language. I am driven to try to capture that essence and portray their character and soul in my drawings. I want people to see more than just a dog. I want them to feel like they know the animal they are looking at.

TECHNIQUE AND TIPS
Faber Castell Polychromos | Bockingford Sketching Paper | 5.8" x 8.3"

I have a very realistic and finely detailed style. My technique incorporates a lot of layering and thousands of tiny pencil strokes with an extremely sharp point to replicate the individual hairs. This gives my fur a very softly blended look.

Oscar - Fox Terrier

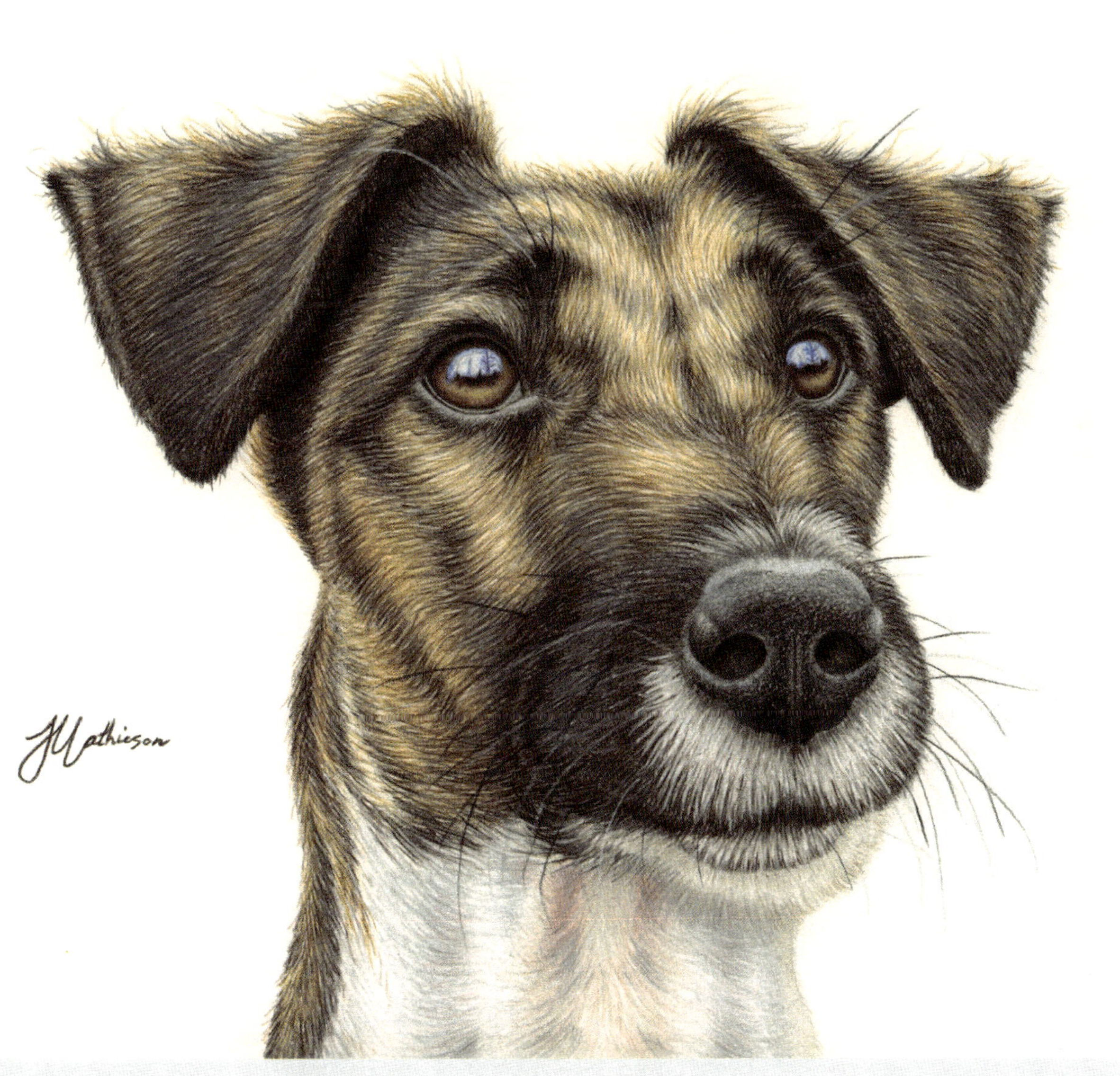

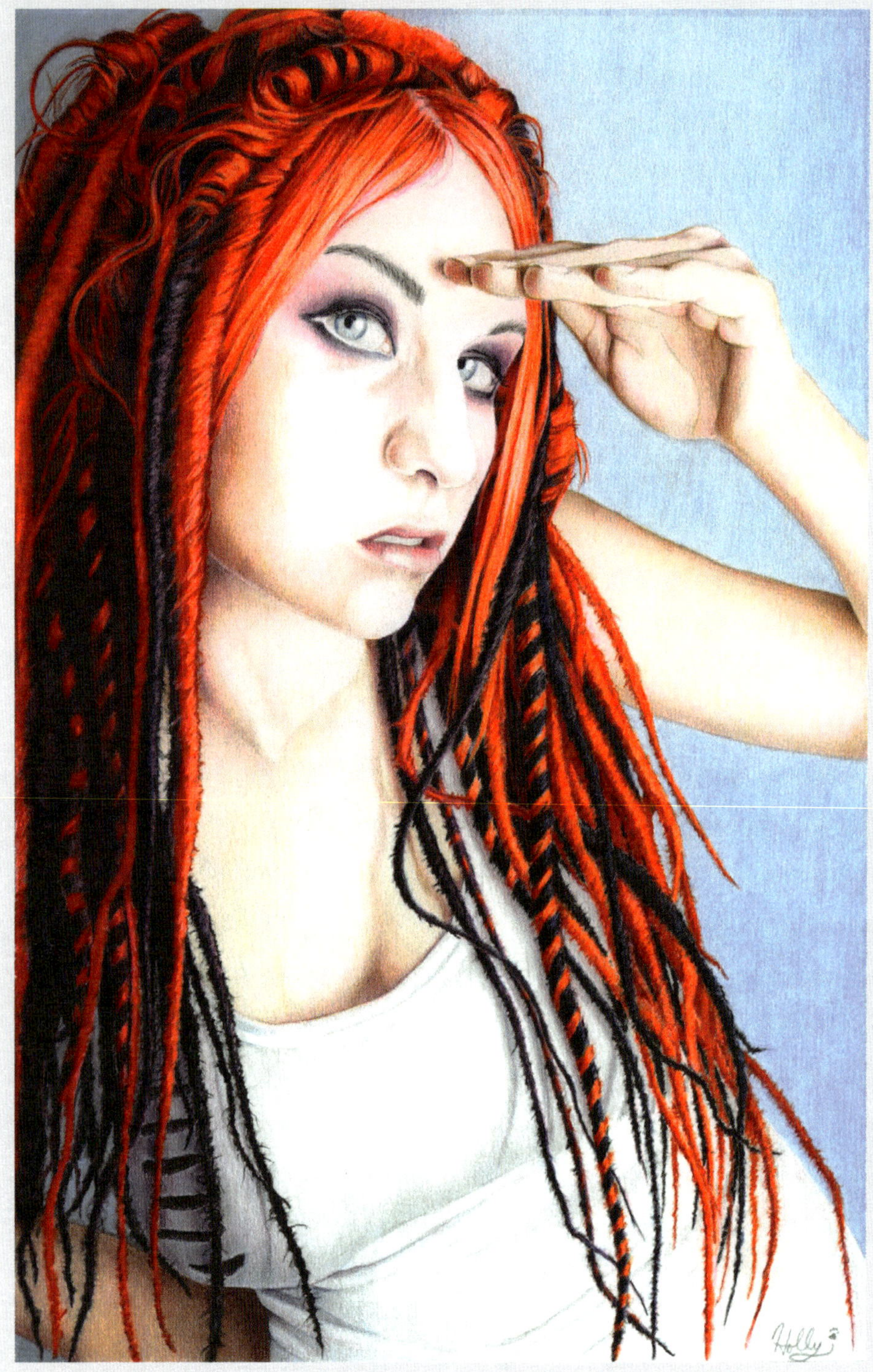

HOLLY SINISCAL | UNITED STATES
http://www.hollyarts1.com

56 "Dredful" is a portrait of my daughter Abby, who's individual style and quirky personality makes for a constant challenge to capture her in that moment when you see more then her superficiality.

Dredful

TECHNIQUE AND TIPS
Prismacolor | Stonehenge | 14 1/2" x 9 1/2"

Get all your images well researched, more than one, go over them and pick out the ones that appeals visually the most. I wind up with several and combine the best attributes, a look here, a hand there, the flow of composition, lighting. Color saturation! Use photoshop to amp up the saturation of the color and use the art filters to inspire a different perspective on the idea. Don't ignore the unloved neon pencils as a base color and colorless blenders to burnish them all together for a painterly effect.

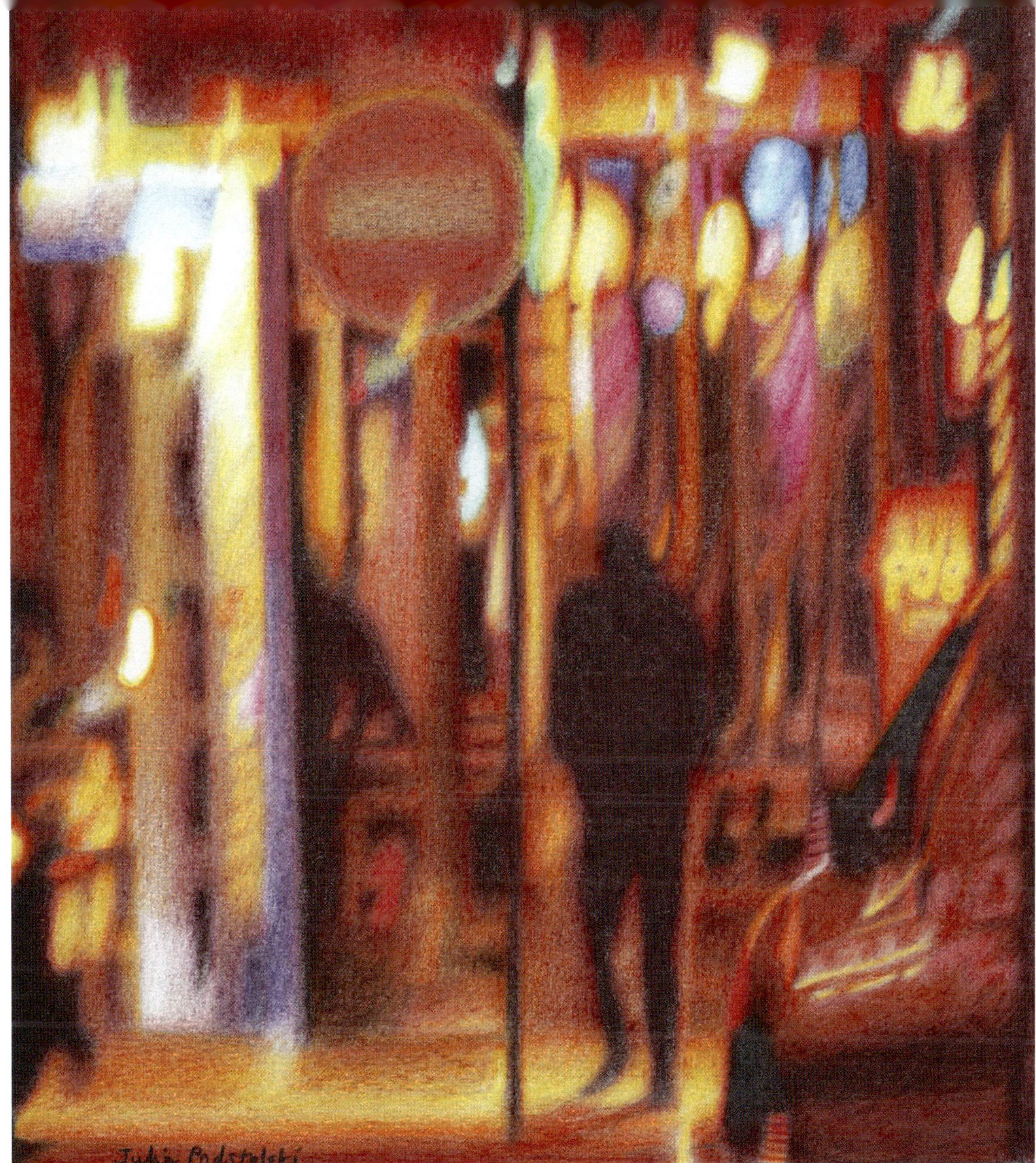

Scarlet Pigalle

JULIE PODSTOLSKI | AUSTRALIA

57 I spent December 2010 in Paris doing what any other artist would do; getting inspired! I explored the city, gathering material with my camera. Since then I have been building a collection of Paris drawings for my next exhibition.

Regal, majestic, ultra-cool, elegant are some of the characteristics of Paris which I hope I have captured in the drawings.

"Scarlet Pigalle" captures a part of Paris which is a red-light district *(hence the word 'Scarlet' in my title).* This drawing has a brooding quality but at the same time it is a bit exciting *(because it is, after all, Paris).* This drawing is part realist and part abstract. I am focused on light in my Paris drawings. In this case the light is brash unapologetic neon, reducing any passing humans to mere insignificant shadows.

TECHNIQUE AND TIPS

Holbein Artist's Pencils, Faber-Castell Polychromos, Caran d'Ache Luminance 6901 | Pescia 300mg hot-pressed printmaking paper | 9.25" x 10.25"

To work with colored pencils it helps to understand color theory as pencil work is essentially the layering of colors. I recommend the classic book "The Art of Color" by Johannes Itten (originally published in USA in 1961 and still in print). I do not use solvents or fixatives when I work with pencils. Therefore I am a person who draws with pencils, as opposed to someone who 'paints' with them. Pencil strokes, dots and dashes (all manner of marks) can clearly be made out on the paper. Sometimes the paper is allowed to show through the layers of pencil, letting paper and pencils breathe together.

I have read that pencils should always be sharp however I enjoy employing the blunt pencil to good effect. The colored pencil I almost never touch is white (as the white you see is simply untouched paper).

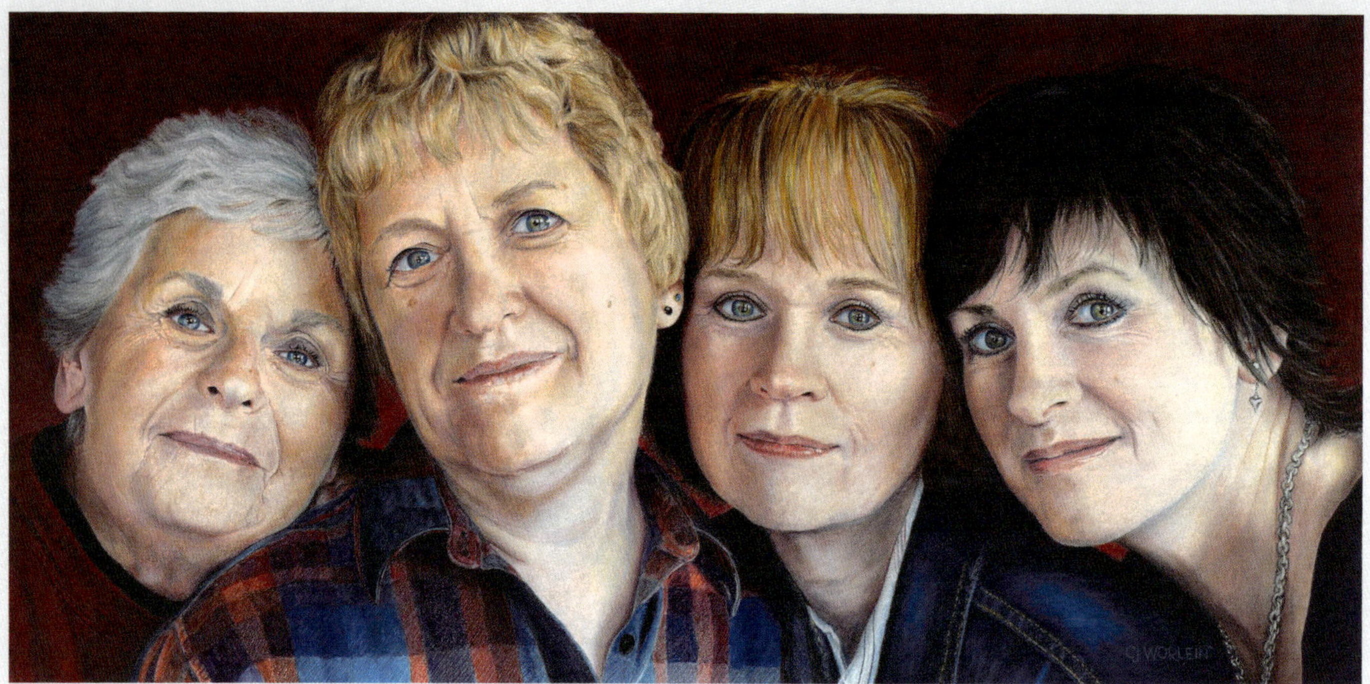

The Sisters

CJ WORLEIN | United States
http://www.cjworleinportraits.com

58 Creating portraits is my passion and focus as an artist. "The Sisters" is a very personal piece, because it's of my own siblings and me. Three of us literally and figuratively stand behind and beside our fourth sister during a difficult time for her. My goal as a portrait artist is to go beyond creating good likenesses. I want to capture that intangible thing we call personality or spirit...the essence that makes us each who we are. I always start with the eyes, and until they seem to be looking back at me, I won't move on. Everything else builds from and supports them.

TECHNIQUE AND TIPS
Prismacolor, Caran d'Ache, Derwent, Faber-Castell, and other brands | Crescent Cold Press Illustration Board #310 | 14 3/8" x 29 3/4"

If I have a technique, it's that I use several techniques, learned from taking many workshops, reading books, and studying artwork from the best colored pencil artists. But before technique, I think it's important to gain a solid understanding of composition and to be a student of the human figure. Look closely at real people, not just photographs of them. Recognize all the subtle hues on a hand or face. Notice every intricacy of an eye. Finally, I would advise against emulating too closely the style of any one artist. I believe in learning from as many other artists as possible, but always with the idea of gaining the tools you need to help you create your own unique style.

DIANNA SOISSON | UNITED STATES
http://www.diannasartcorner.com

59 My passion for art comes from within. As I create these works of art, I bond with them. They are my children with whom every stroke of the pencil I give another breath of life. Through my art I develop a relationship that is so strong, it completely envelops me with its innocence and beauty. I not only want to see the deep passionate colors of the water and the sky's reflections but I want to hear the running current and feel the warmth of the reflections.

As with children, I care for my art and tend to its every need. When children are young, parents nurture and protect them. As I begin, I am very shielding, not allowing myself to make a single stroke on the paper until I have mentally prepared myself for the journey that lies ahead. A child changes your life just as my painting changes mine.

Raising children reveals so many things about ourselves we didn't know and my painting does the same for me. Parents grow with children and I grow with my paintings. Each painting provides me with a newfound understanding of life.

The hardest part as a parent is letting go. With the completion of each work I feel that I am one step closer to fulfilling my dream. As with any dream, once you reach it, there is another waiting to be born. My paintings have filled me with joy, pleasure and satisfaction; it is not a feeling that can be described, it must be felt with the soul. I want to share my children with the world; I want them to draw you into their story, their energy, and their passion. Only then has my real dream come true.

Beyond All Boundaries

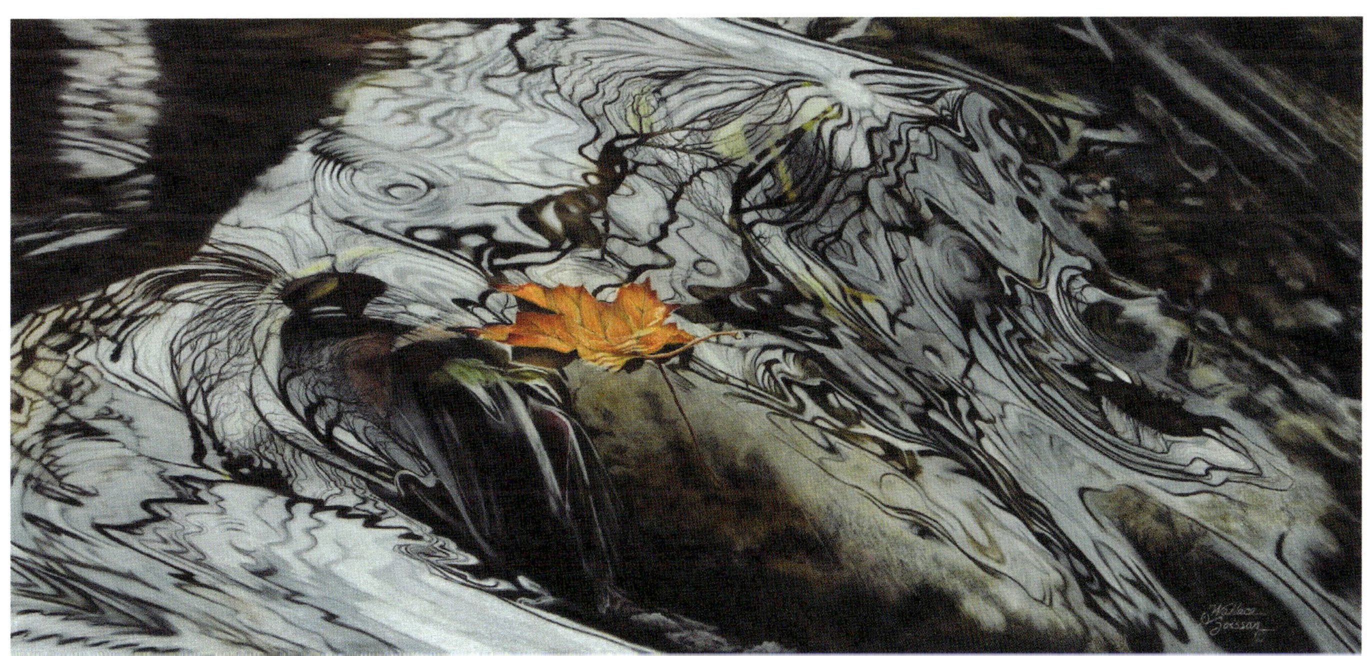

TECHNIQUE AND TIPS
Prismacolors | UArt | 13" x 30"

My water scenes are always photographed on a sunny day where I can get the strongest lighting possible for my contrast. I always remind myself that water and reflections are just shapes of light and dark so as I do not get anxious about "getting it right". Realizing that it's only shapes allows me some freedom in altering colors and employing my own personality into the creation. In order to create the depth of the water I always remember to apply several layers of color and burnish. The technique for making the water appear smooth is blending the shapes together seamlessly either with a light touch of solvent or a colorless blender.

VIRGINIA CARROLL | United States

http://www.virginiacarroll.com

60 I love the view from my porch across the valley to the Santa Catalina Mountains in Tucson, AZ. It is a view that continues to crop up in my work. This particular drawing was done from a scene I captured one late afternoon during the winter and after we had had a rare snow the night before. The colors were so intense and the shadows so deep, it provided a wonderful contrast in light and dark, not to mention the lovely, roiling clouds above the mountains. This piece was done using a heated board called the Icarus Board and incorporated the use of a product called Neocolor II as a compliment to the Colored Pencil work. The dimensions of this work are 9" X 20."

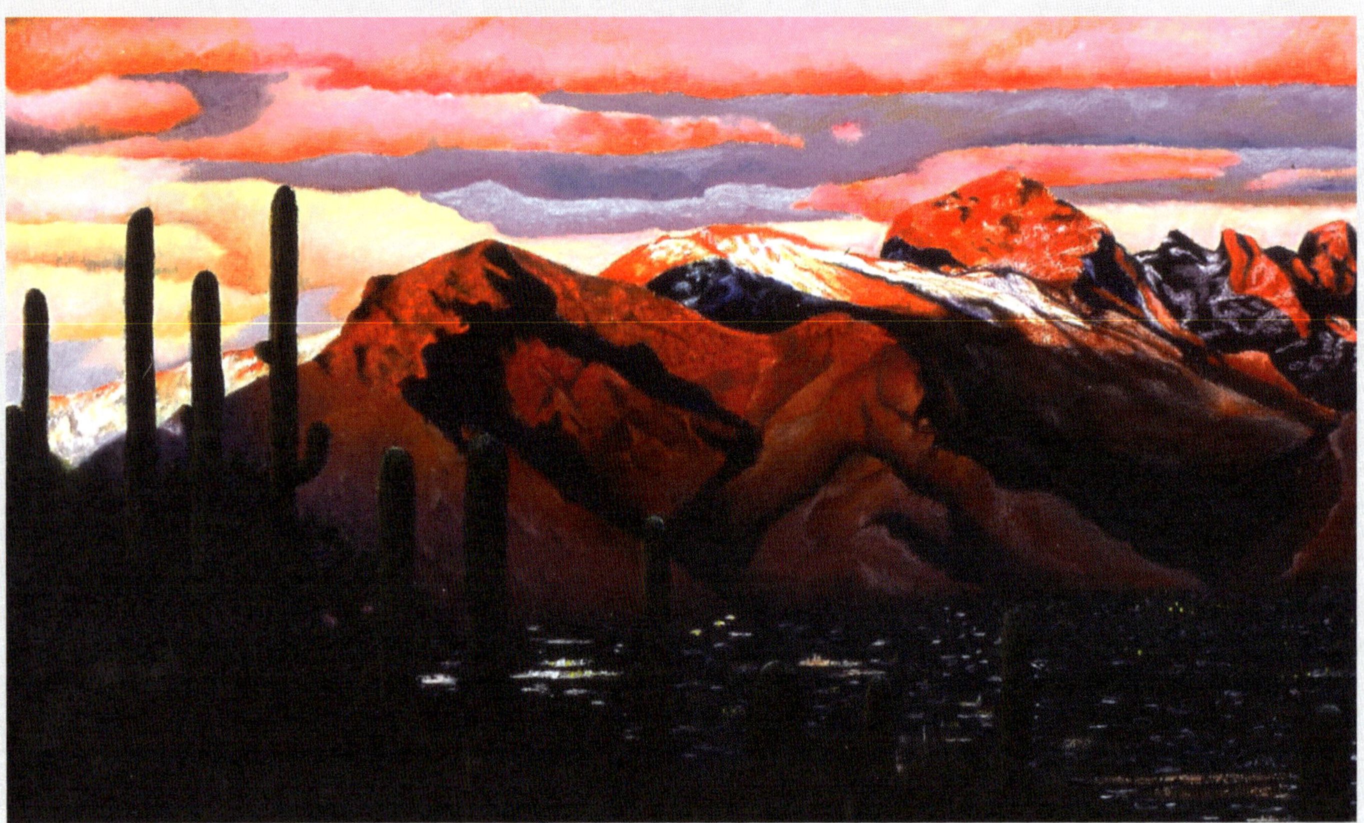

Catalina Winter Sunset

TECHNIQUE AND TIPS

Prismacolor and Caran d'Ache Pablos | UArt 500 grit | 20.5" x 13"

I always tell beginning artists that they must learn to SEE what they are looking at. So many try to draw their paradigm of the subject matter rather than the reality of it. That way they miss the nuances of the subject. One should forget that they are drawing a specific object and concentrate on drawing light, dark and shapes of color. I also recommend that artists experiment with newly discovered materials and techniques.....that's the way we grow as artists.

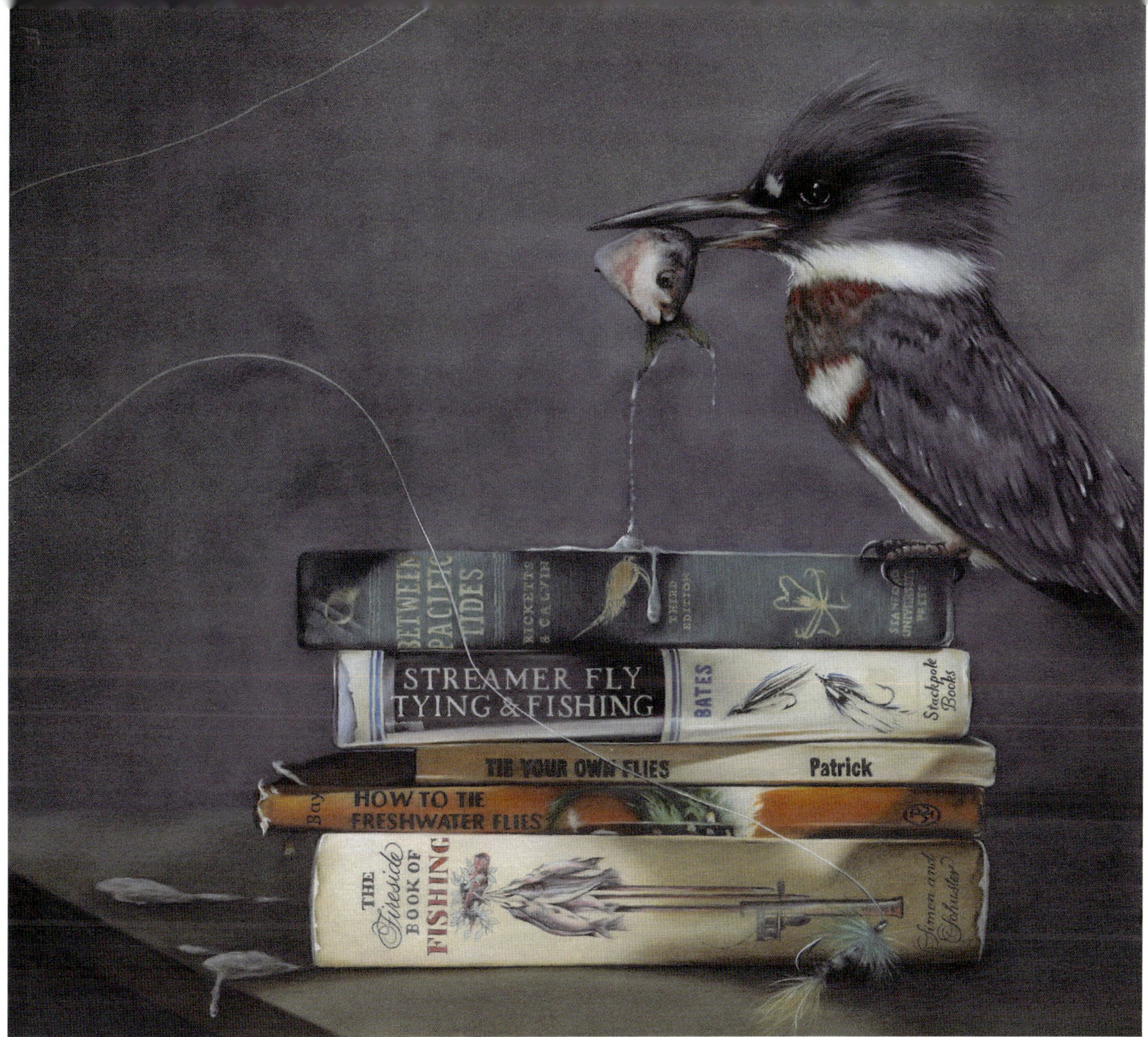

Tying One On

EILEEN SORG, CPSA | UNITED STATES
http://www.twodogstudio.com

61 My work is a visual representation of the stories in my head. I enjoy collecting old objects and weaving a tale around them. Birds are the main conduit for these stories but insects, amphibians, and mammals are also frequent players. The story is really the subject matter of my work, supported by a solid structure of composition and light.

TECHNIQUE AND TIPS
Prismacolor, Derwent | Arches Hot Press 140# | 14x13

I have found that the white of the paper can be very distracting to my eye so the biggest goal I have is to remove this obstacle as soon as possible. I use either water soluble pencils or wax pencils to lay in the large shapes of darks and lights in my drawing and then hit them with water or solvent to really drive the pigment in to the paper. This creates an underpainting much like what an oil painter would use to tint their canvas before moving into the actual painting process. This beginning step allows me to really see my composition and how it holds together without getting bogged down in the details too soon and provides an excellent base for the many layers of pencil to come.

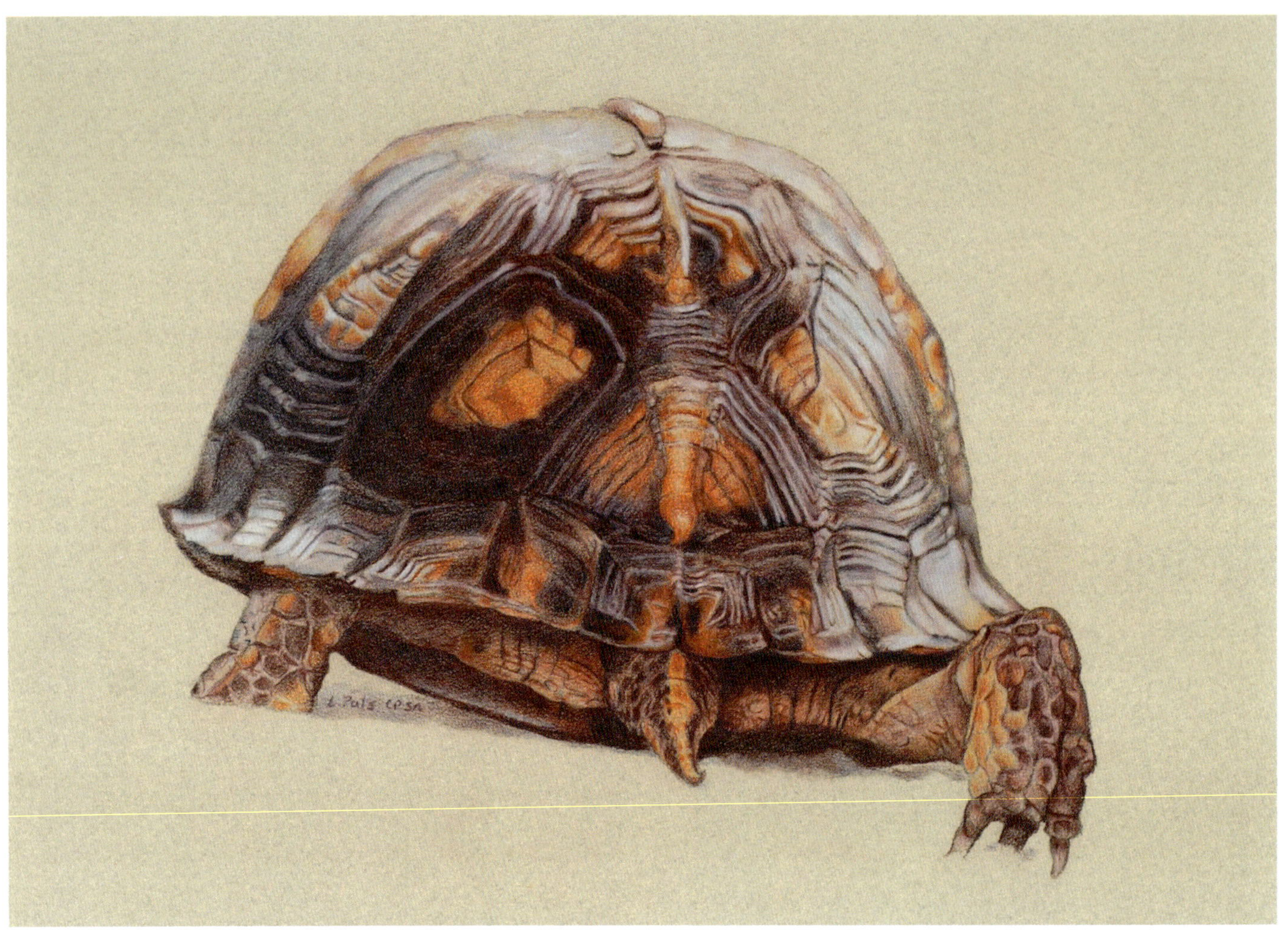

Trudgin' Turtle

LAURENE PULS, CPSA | UNITED STATES
http://laurenepuls.com/artwork

62 My artwork's subjects must have a heartbeat. . .either in nature or in a fantasy setting. Since childhood, I have had a passion for turtles. I believe that my success in getting into shows is based on my emotional connection to these creatures. Whether a pond turtle, a box turtle, a tortoise, or a sea turtle, these animals all represent different aspects of my life and dreams. While drawing turtles, I explore and focus on parts of my inner life.

The challenge in drawing turtles is finding different ways to present them. Since they are in a rigid shell with 6 appendages, there aren't many ways in which they can be posed. In this picture, I drew a turtle walking away. First of all because it is a "different" presentation; and second, the piece was an experiment with colors to use on the shell in light and shadow. Another challenge is relating the emotion that I have for the animals to the viewer since, for the most part, others do not share my perspective of these reptiles.

My goal is to begin presenting box turtles as they are surviving in the environment today. Modernization is not something that is in the best interest of these animals.

TECHNIQUE AND TIPS
Prismacolor | mat board | 8" x 10"

I prefer working in dry pencil using a light-to-dark layering technique. Although this may be the most tedious way to produce a drawing, I think the outcome of this approach speaks for itself. I use Prismacolor pencils for everything but portraits of people. I use Fabrio Uno Hot Press Watercolor Paper when I am drawing a picture with a background and colored archival matboard when I'm not covering the whole surface.

WENDY THOMPSON, CPSA | UNITED STATES
http://www.wthompsonart.com

63 This feather was laying on the beach in some rocks and, thinking it quite intriguing, I took some photos and then brought the leaves home to do a painting. I actually had two false starts when I began working, having difficulty connecting with the feather on those beach rocks. For some reason it just didn't feel right. On the third try, I decided to put the feather in fresh water instead of on the beach, and it worked! A lot of my work is nature oriented with water, rocks and leaves, and working on Feather Light helped me see that my true connection with nature is with the fresh water ponds and creeks of the woods.

Feather Light

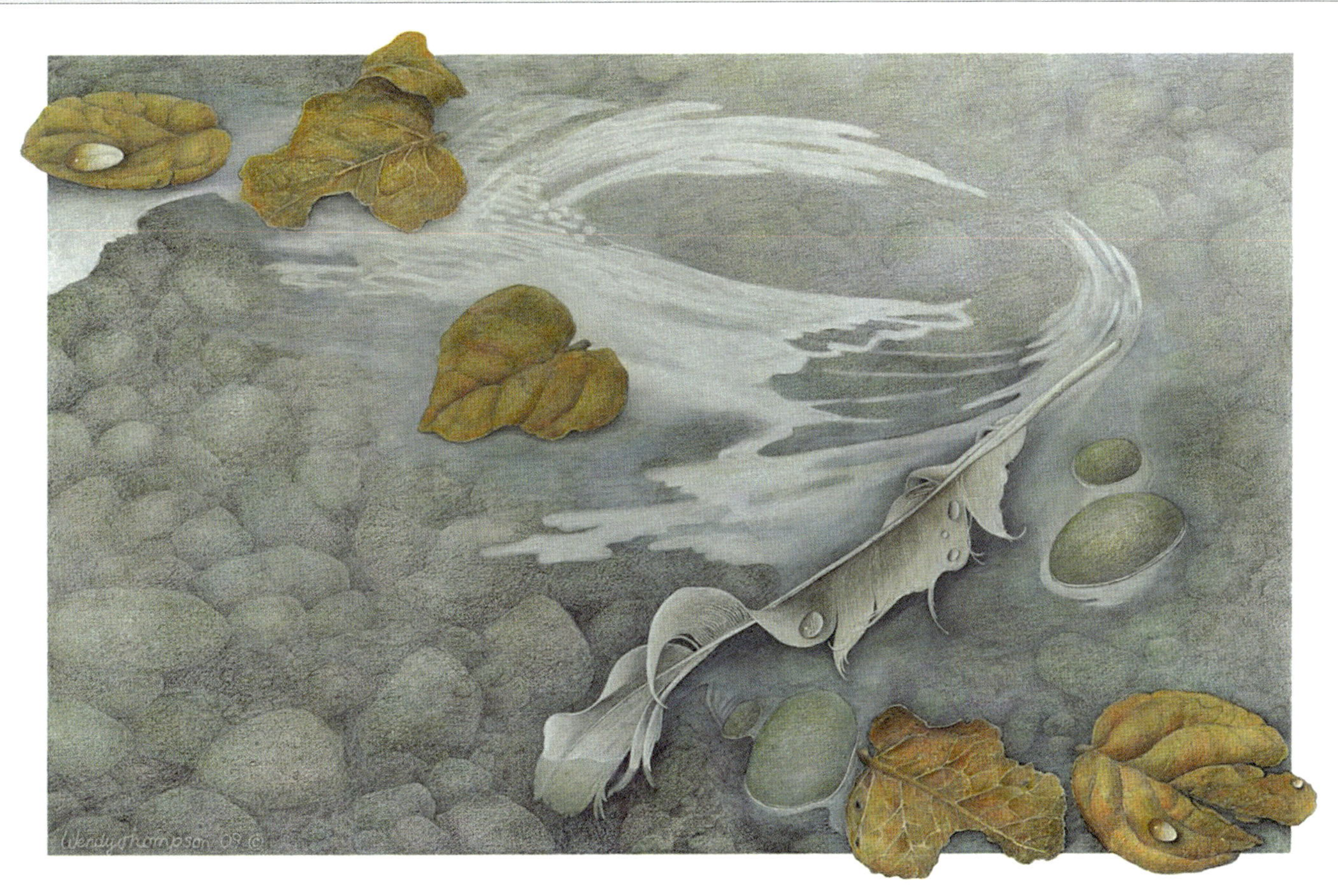

TECHNIQUE AND TIPS
Prismacolor, Lyra, Derwent, Verithin | Strathmore 500 heavy weight vellum board | 13" x 20"

For correct detail, I rely on reference books and my photos, along with the actual bugs, feathers and leaves that clutter my studio. After initial layout on working surface, I begin in sections with a very sharp point, building a base with three or more layers of color. If it's a bird or critter with eyes, I do the eyes first, as this helps me connect with the work. I use a stylus for the whites of the eyes and veins of leaves and feathers. When I'm comfortable the colors are pulling together I begin heavier layering, sometimes burnishing with white, cream or French Grey 10. Before I consider a piece finished, I 'push' the detail and fine tune the edges. Sometimes just a simple additional line under or around something pushes it and makes it really pop out with detail. And, of great importance, I try to pace myself and take breaks to not be so hard on my hands.

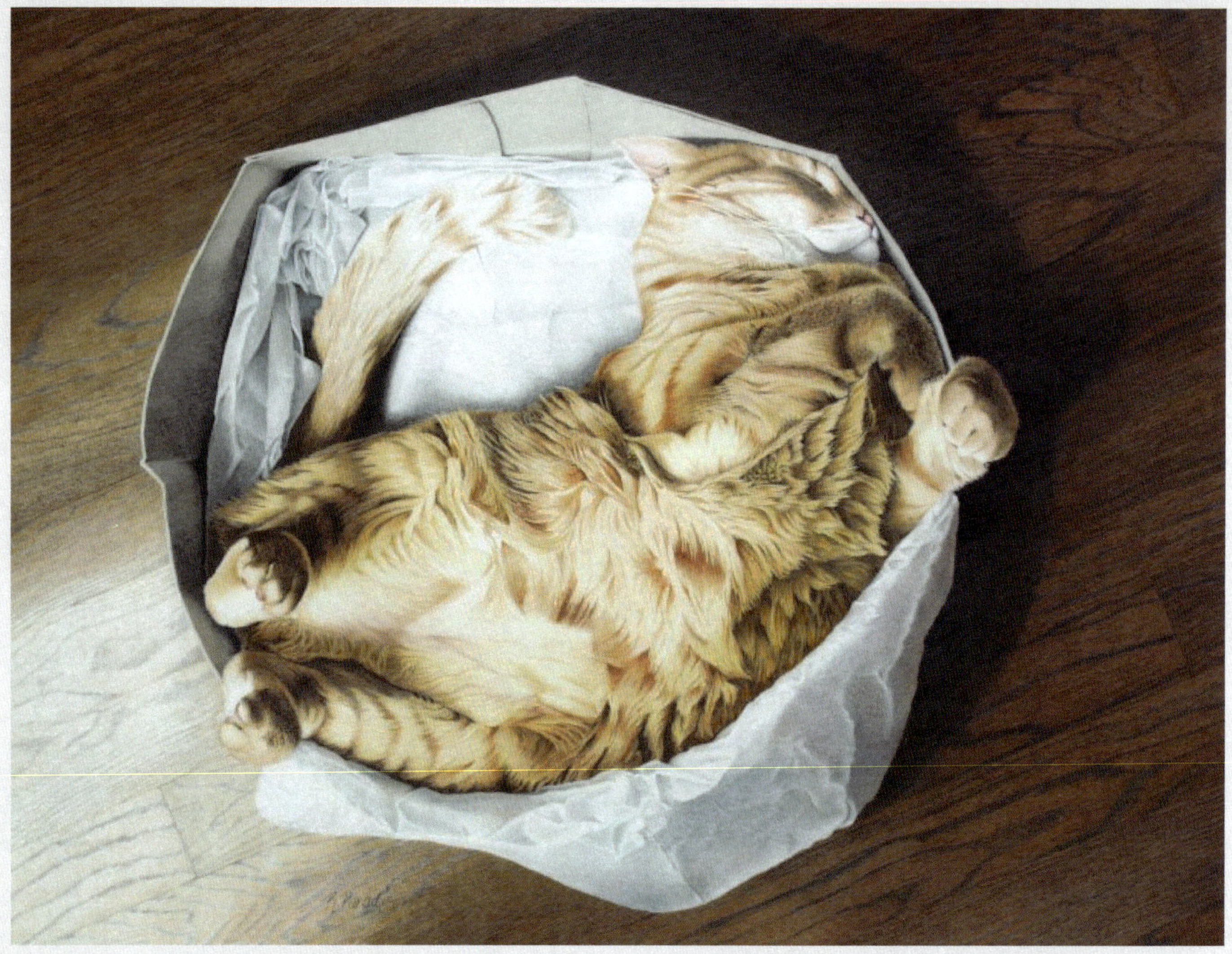

Christmas Afternoon

RITA PARADIS, CPSA | UNITED STATES

64 Textures draw me and then I draw textures. I am enthralled by their variations and see each new texture as a challenge to be reproduced in colored pencil. This image with its warmth and glow and its soft textures was a delight to paint; aside from that, it is my favorite cat, engaged in his favorite occupation, and in his favorite place. I added the crumpled tissue to create a fourth texture. My very favorite part to draw was the cardboard box. But then again, I think it was the tissue paper ... no, the fur. But I had the best time painting the floor.

TECHNIQUE AND TIPS

Pablo, Polychromos, Prismacolor | Stonehenge | 18" x 24"

I achieve my results by layering, layering, and more layering. I use extremely sharp pencils, multiple passages, and many, many colors. I find that the more color I use in making a color, the richer the final color becomes. My work is not burnished, as I usually do not use heavy pressure; rather it is complex and dense. In creating darks, I under-paint with the complimentary color. This gives a wonderful depth to the dark passages. The addition of surprise color is another tool I use. If I feel an area is somewhat flat, I will lift bits of the pigment with museum putty and infuse a bit of surprise color or colors into the lifted spots. I like to use bright colors. If I find my color is too bright, it can easily be toned down but a toned down color is difficult to make bright.

I work from my own photographs taken in strong sunlight. About half-way through a colored pencil painting, I put the photograph away and work from memory and imagination.

SHARON FRANK MAZGAJ | UNITED STATES
http://www.acorn.net/cpsadc101/mazgaj.htm

65 I "inherit" all the old things my parents, in-laws and grandparents deem "too nice" to throw or just give away. Consequently, I have a lot of pottery, dolls & other miscellaneous old things that have little dollar value, but great family heirloom value.

Among these things is a collection of blown glass ornaments. Every year I display them in an old wooden box at Christmas time. One year, as I was packing decorations away, I thought it was interesting the way the light was shining on all those shiny orbs. I rearranged them several times and snapped some photos. *(continued on page 78)*

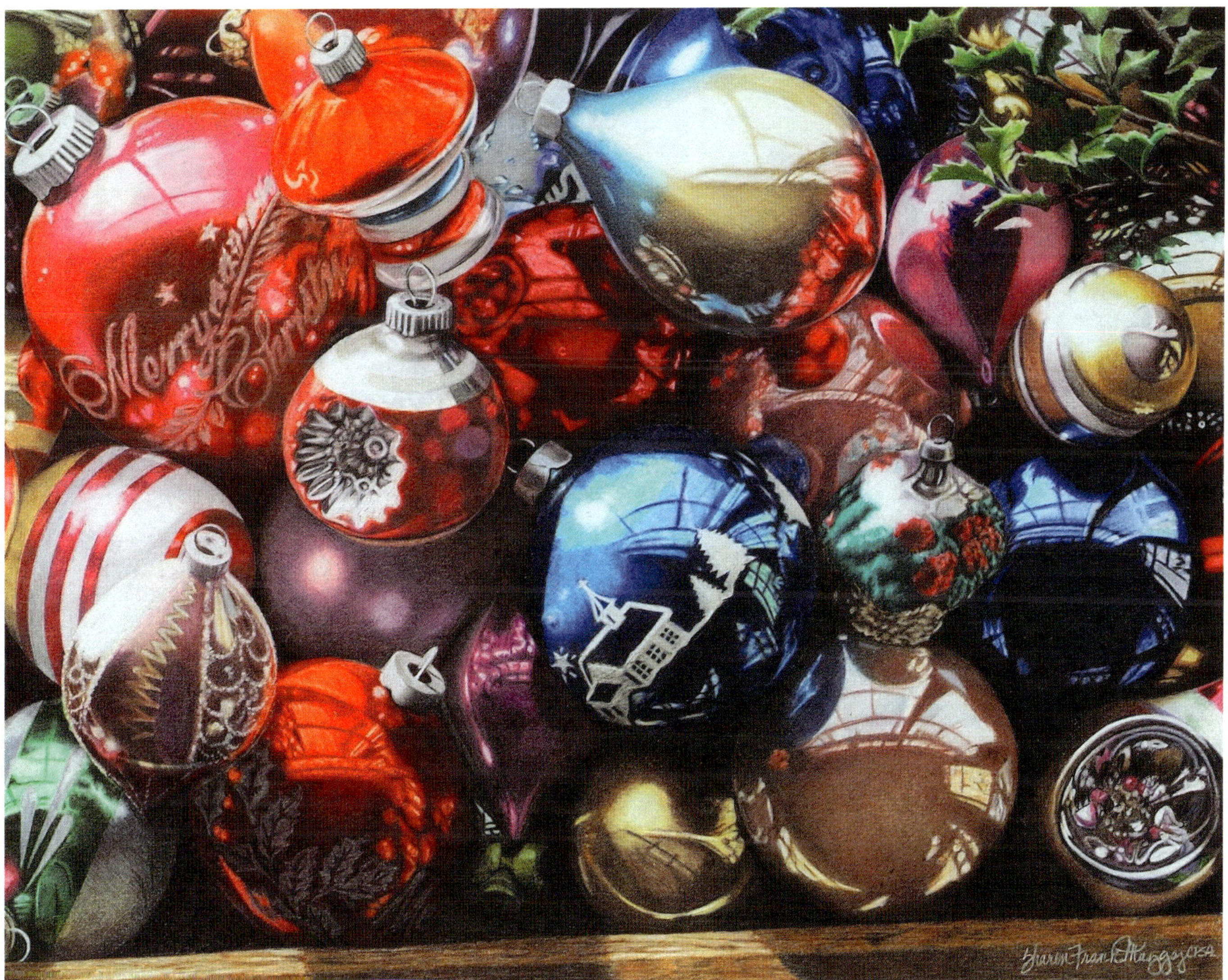

"Vintage Ornaments"

TECHNIQUE AND TIPS
Prismacolor | Illustration Board | 14" x 18"

When setting up a still life, the first thing I consider is the composition. If the composition isn't powerful, the end result will not be successful. I always work with natural light, usually arranging my objects near a window with strong sunlight coming through. I usually take around 30-50 photos of the same basic grouping, tweeking and switching out items as I consider what is interesting. When choosing my objects, I incorporate several different textures. *(continued on page 78)*

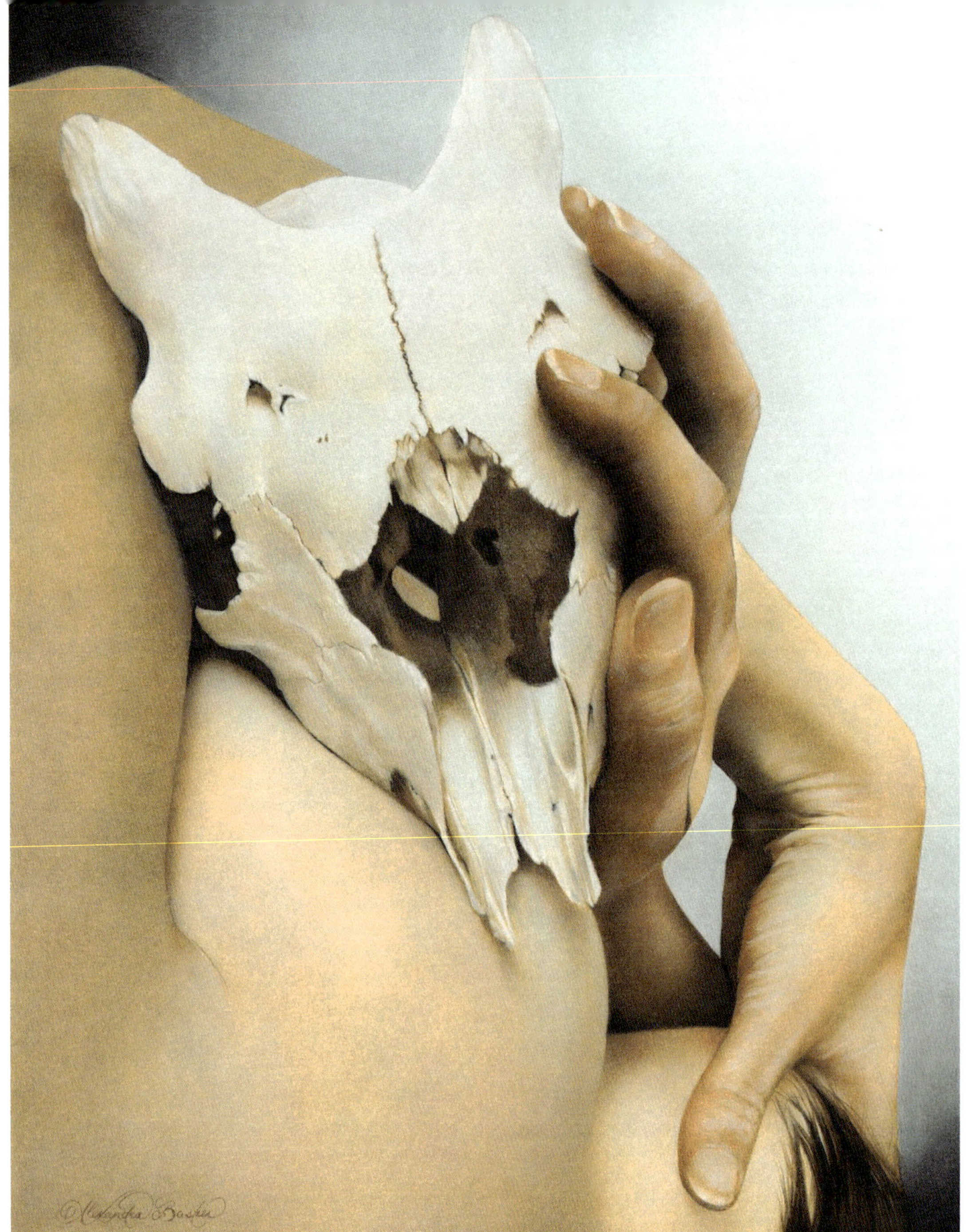

Maternal Instinct

Alexandra Bastien | Canada
http://www.alexandrabastien.com

The artwork "Maternal Instinct" is part of an exhibition project, entitled "Taming the beast". This series of drawings represent a whole new way to create artworks for me. I wanted to expose some situations experienced by women.

Women hide pains inside them that they are sometimes not even aware of.. This profound discontentment can stain their whole life and become an obstacle to their happiness. How can we help raise women's awareness to their own suffering so they can better live with it and learn to break free of it? This is the starting point of the project «Taming the Beast».

(continued on page 77)

TECHNIQUE AND TIPS

Prismacolor Premier, some Faber Castell Polychromos, Derwent Studio | Illustration Board | 14" x 19"

My coloring pencil technique includes the application of twenty to fifty superimposed coloured layers. I apply lighter to darker colors to be able to burnish them up to the very first ones. *(continued on page 77)*

WINIFRED STORKAN STONE, CPSA | UNITED STATES
http://www.winifredstorkanstone.com

67 This drawing is taken from a photo I took in which the light fell on the berries in an unusual and luminescent way. I wanted to capture that effect as well as the out of focus circular areas in the background. In order to unify the parts of this picture I found that I needed to apply a light coat of lemon yellow to the background. As an artist, I want to share the beauty I see in such scenes with others. One artistic goal I have is to be more expressionistic and less literal in my interpretation of a subject.

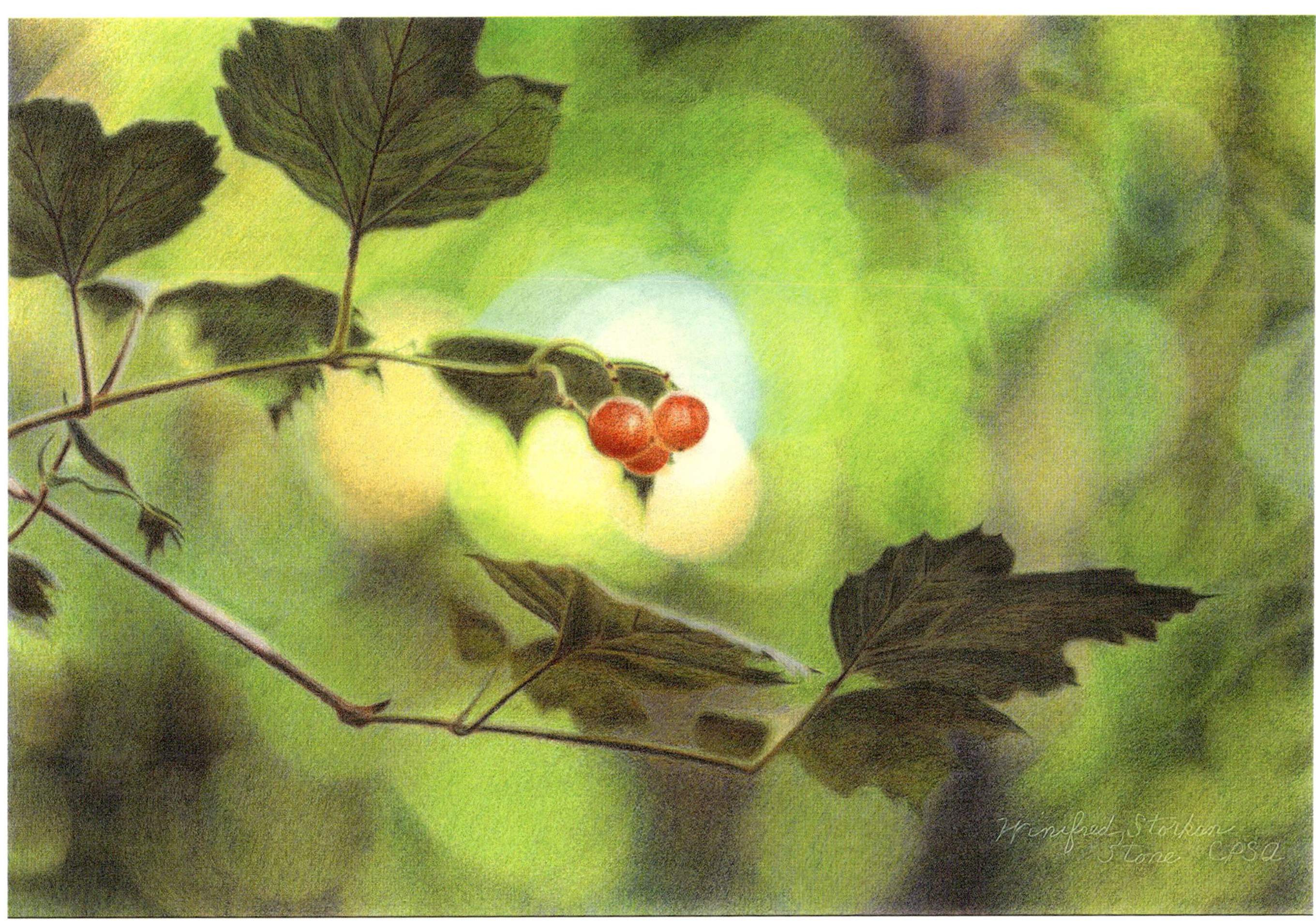

Leaves and Berries

TECHNIQUE AND TIPS
Prismacolor | Strathmore 400 Bristol | 8.5" x 12.75"

I always start with light colors and layer to darker colors. I also use a light touch with my pencils so that I can apply as many layers as possible. I have learned to do small color sketches ahead of time because it saves making major corrections on my drawing later on. Once I have several layers on the paper and am satisfied with the colors, I burnish them with a stiff brush. The room in which I work has both incandescent and GE Reveal 100 lighting, which gives a pretty good mix of natural lighting.

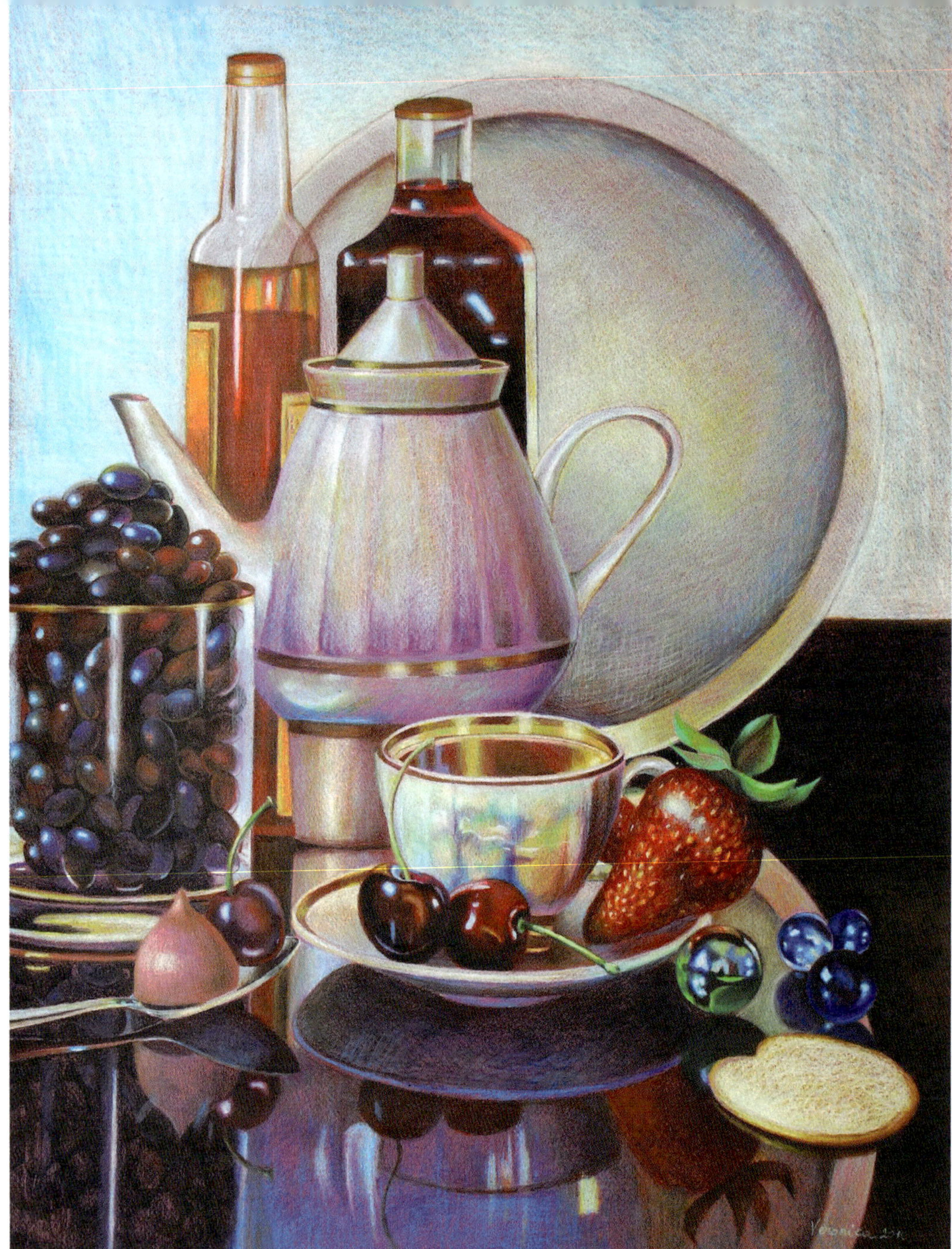

Still life with cherries, chocolate and strawberries

VERONICA WINTERS | UNITED STATES
http://www.veronicasart.com

My colored pencil artwork focuses on capturing different lighting conditions and textures in various objects. These are focused observational studies. I also complete full-scale drawings in colored pencils for my surreal artwork later done in oils. Drawings help me develop paintings and can be either beautiful renderings of light or finished thoughtful pieces.

TECHNIQUE AND TIPS
Prismacolor Premier | Mi-T paper | 25″ x19″

I would encourage shading any area with at least two colors to create vibrant hues. I would suggest keeping colored pencils sharp when drawing and graphite outlines very light.

Also, it's important to leave highlights free of any color if you draw on white paper.

HANS ANDERSEN | Denmark

http://www.tegnebordet.dk/index.php?vis=brugergalleri.php&id=31633&visning=

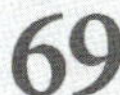

69 I have been inspired by the birds in my garden, and wanted to draw them, so I did.

Bullfinch

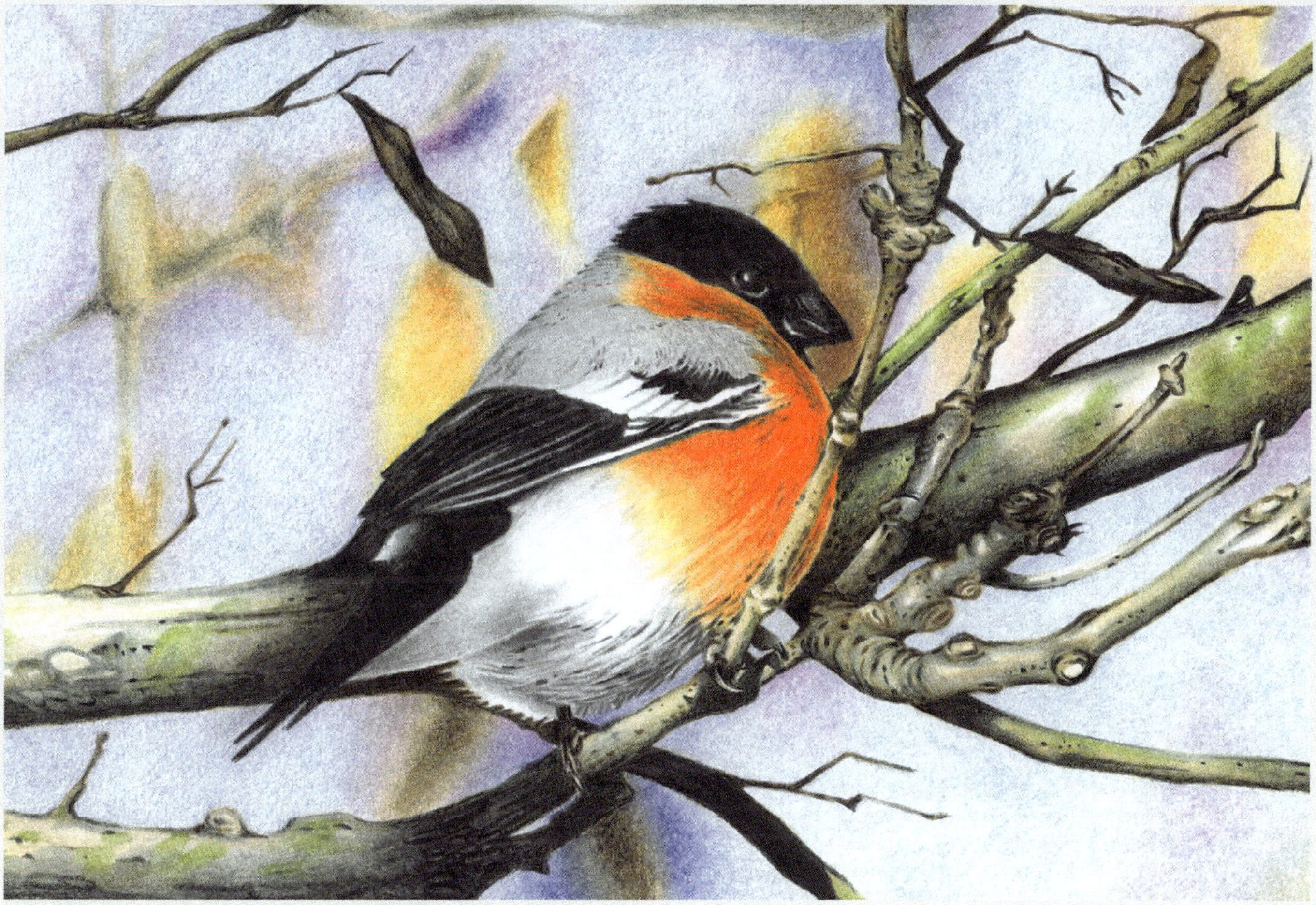

TECHNIQUE AND TIPS

Derwent Watercolor / Brunzeel CP | Winsor & Newton. 100lbs, medium | 200mm X 290 mm

I use my crayons with very light hand, and preferably in a circular motion. After breaking my paints with turpentine, so they flow well together. Turpentine dissolves no paper so it can be repeated many times.

DENA WHITENER, CPSA | UNITED STATES

70 I have had these marbles since my childhood. Just could not part with them. The colors and designs intrigued me as a child and still do. Every one is different; some are opaque and most are transparent. And I still remember my favorite one. They truely were my childhood jewels.

They took on another life when a light shined through them. I liked the challenge of drawing the shadows the marble created.

Juvie Jewels

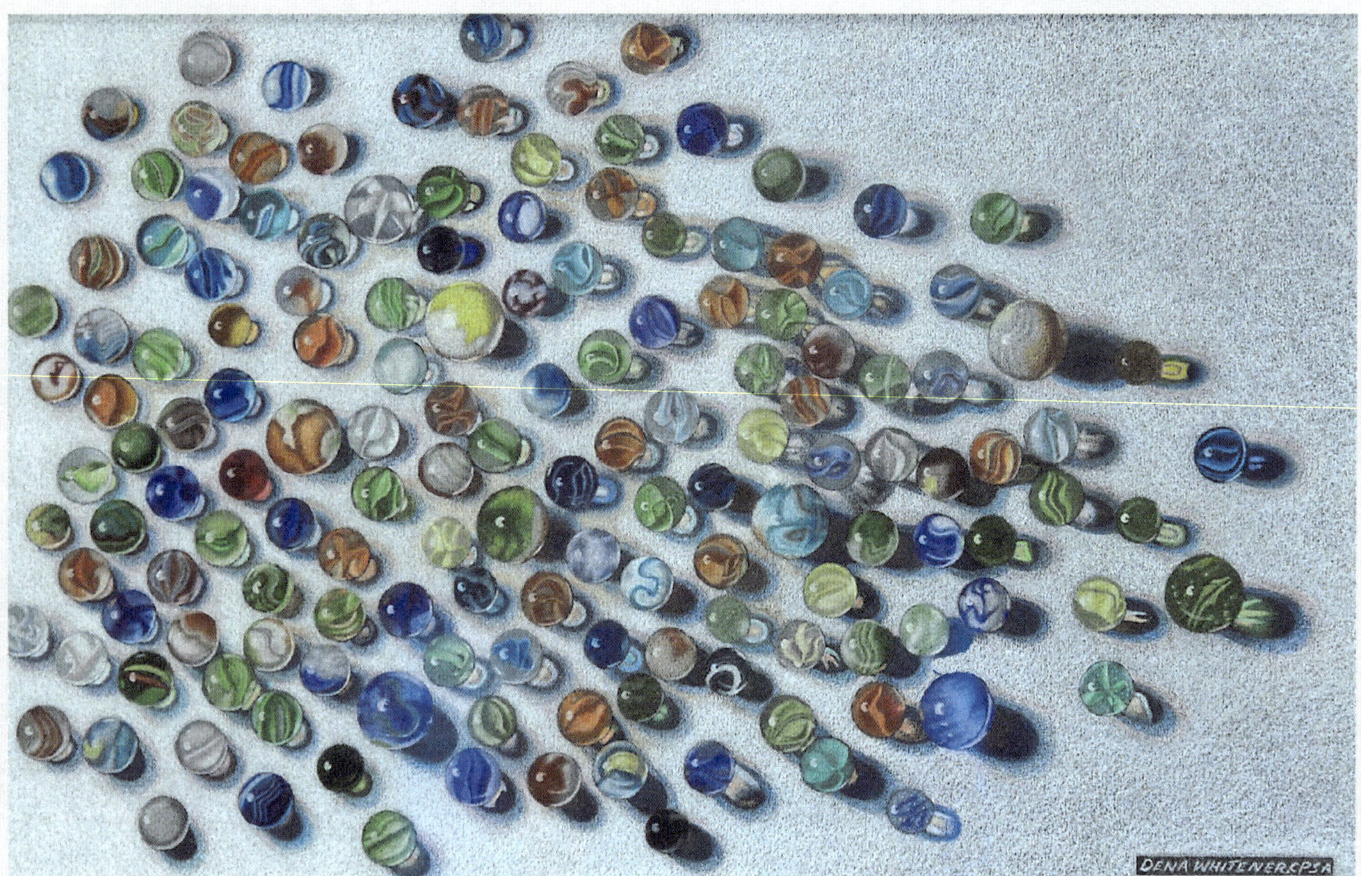

TECHNIQUE AND TIPS

100% Prismacolor | Canson Mi-Teintes black | 9 1/2" x 15 3/4"

I work from life. I glued the marbles to a white board. The board was then placed vertically in front of me. The light was secured in a fixed location and I made very sure this wasn't moved during the time the drawing took.

My studio was darkened so that there was only the one light source.

I used a very light touch as I put down the colors layer after layer. Since this was done on black paper, the background was burnished in areas.

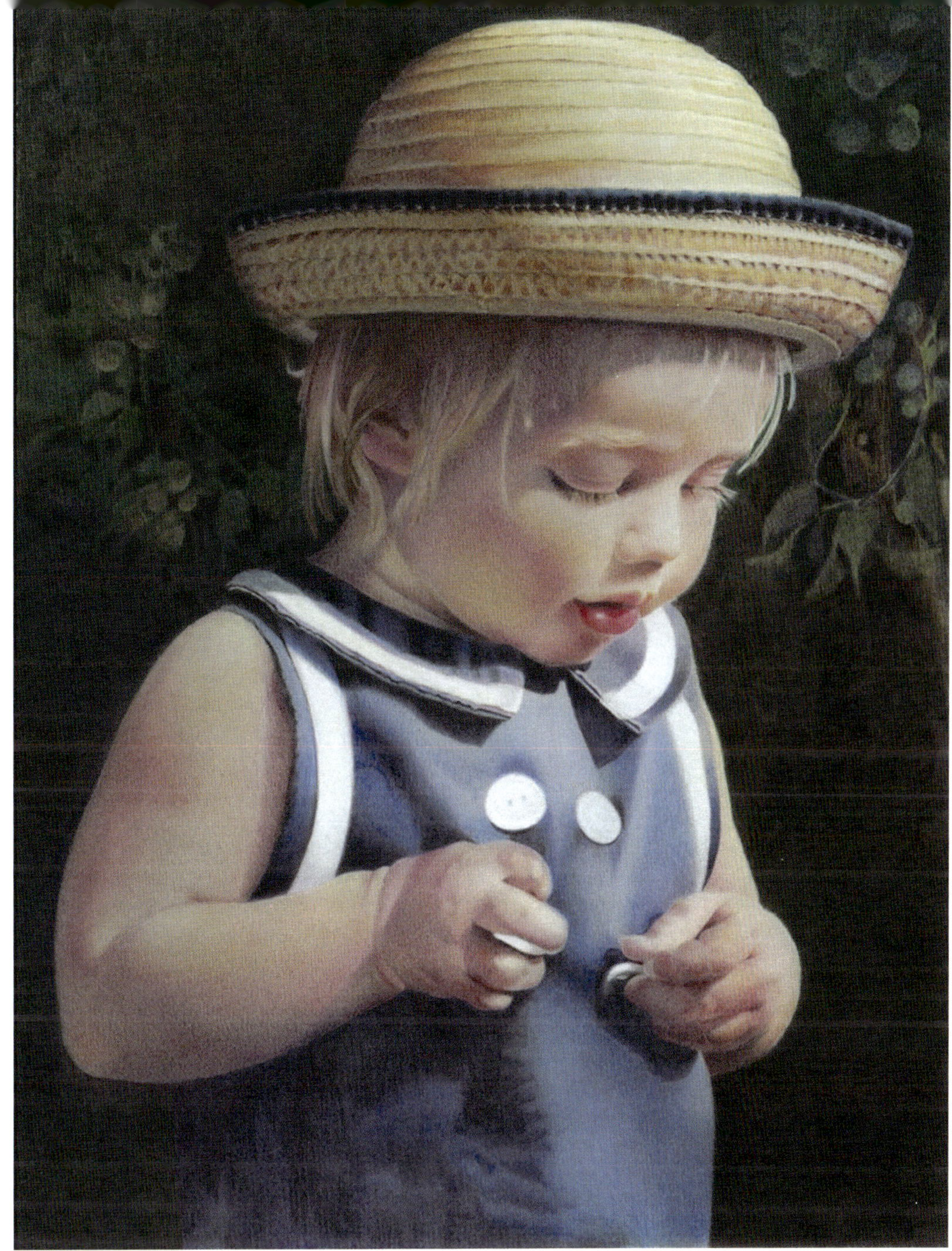

Discovery

CATHERINE WARD, CPSA | UNITED STATES
http://cathy-ward.com

71 Inspirational moment? What I appreciated about this moment was the child's careful examination of the object of her curiosity, the buttons. I believe times like this are indicative of a lifetime of exploration. The purpose of this drawing was to afford the viewer the opportunity to consider a moment in time. The importance of curiosity and all that curiosity embraces is a worthwhile moment. As I approach the world visually, worth whileness continues to dominate my choices for drawing. While looking at 60 or more photographs for this child's portrait I was drawn to the one that could tell me most about who she is.

TECHNIQUE AND TIPS
Prismacolor | Strathmore Bristol 400 | 23" x 17"

Technique for me is continuously evolving. Beginning with the slow process of layer upon layer of colored pencil most often relying on a vertical stroke I build the portrait from light to dark. What continues to keep my process an evolution is a weekly four hour long pose with a model. While I use photographs to complete my colored pencil drawings, it is the study in the studio with a live model that keeps me working to fill forms as I complete a colored pencil portrait.

KAREN HULL... FROM PAGE 16

Much of my work is photorealistic, but it can be so much fun trying to take that realism to the next level, adding some quirkiness or a twist which leaves the viewer wondering.

Mice and little critters always feature heavily in my art, and this probably stems right back to early childhood, when I first fell in love with Beatrix Potter's illustrations. Anthromorphizing animals is another of my loves and has now lead me down the path of doing Children's Picture Book illustrating, which was a lifelong goal realized. I have tried drawing and painting animals in a range of different mediums, but always come back to the coloured pencils, because for me, no other medium enables the artist to do fur as easily or realistically as the coloured pencils do.

- -

The Prismacolor Verithins are invaluable for creating fine detail, even on textured surfaces. The key is to keep the pencil point very sharp and to press quite firmly into the surface. I tend to use short sharp stabbing, or pushing motions with the pencil tip. This is the best way I find to fill in all the crevices on a textured surface.

When doing fur, again I keep the pencil point as sharp as possible and I add in each hair, alternating colours and following the contours of the body. Many artists might find this tedious, but if you are like me and enjoy doing fur, it becomes a form of relaxing meditation.

I find the Derwent drawing pencils are fabulous for blending and smudging colours around and it was these pencils I used predominantly for giving the texture to the loaf of bread in The Uninvited Guests.

The most important tip I have when working with coloured pencils is don't be afraid to experiment and most of all have fun and enjoy the process

JANIE PIRIE... FROM PAGE 20

I will never get bored with colored pencils - they are a wonderful medium. I like to draw really fine detail in my work so pencils are perfect for my style. My students are always amazed at what can be achieved with them.

I have worked on botanical subjects for the past six years as I have a very large garden full of wonderful subjects just waiting to be captured on paper but I'm now working on a portrait - just for a change! However, I will always work with plants, fruit and vegetables as they are so beautiful.

I have a Gold Medal from the Royal Horticultural Society for my botanical work and several Certificates of Botanical Merit from the Society of Botanical Artists, of which I am a full member.

HOLLY MAHLA... FROM PAGE 17

It then became a matter of learning as much as possible about the subjects, including how the they wished themselves to be portrayed, even if that meant straying a bit from reality! By giving away portraits in the beginning, I quickly had art up on friends' walls, and friends of friends became interested. (The only tricky part is when your artistic gift doesn't go up on the wall . . . then you have to pretend not to notice.)

- -

I haven't mastered the technique of the old masters for sure, but it's so enjoyable that I've used it many times since. This portrait was done using white, chocolate and terra cotta. The range of colors you can achieve is surprising, depending upon which are layered on top of which, and the pressure applied. By cutting it down to three pencils, I was able to focus on the forms and contours. I use very light pressure for most of the layers. For me, tiny, tiny circles work best, covering the paper completely, and keeping pencil points insanely sharp.

ARLENE STEINBERG... FROM PAGE 32

I have done several still life drawings of marbles and decided this time to play around to see if I could create the illusion of marbles spilling out of a jar, and falling off of a mat. In this drawing, I wanted the marbles to still be the main focus which is why I decided the background and the drawn mat would be white.

The first challenge was to photograph the marbles at an angle so they would look as if they were starting to fall. Once I had the photo and had it cropped to emphasize the marbles spilling out of the jar, I then had to figure out how to correctly show the one marble falling off the drawing. I did this by keeping my light source the same, and holding a marble up against a real mat. Then it was just a matter of creating the different shadow the marble cast onto the "mat".

- -

This is so the human eye can't detect any real depth to the objects. Values are the key to successful trompe l'oeil drawing. Rendering of shadows is very important. Don't be afraid to use dramatic lighting to create shadows under the objects to help fool the eye into believing there is depth.

I depict shadows in my drawings by first laying down a value under painting. I use complementary colors to create my shadows and build up lots of very light layers till I have a value that matches the value in my photo. For example, to create the shadows under the red marbles, I used Prismacolor's Dark Green pencil and under the orange shadows, I used Prismacolor's Slate Grey and Indigo Blue pencils. I will then start adding color, working from the darkest colors to the lightest colors, building up layers using a very light touch. My students once counted how many layers I added and they came up with 28 layers.

SARKIS SARKISSIAN... FROM PAGE 58

I blend a lot of pencils together with paper tissues and stumps which gives the drawing a softer look - A technique that is very well suited for skin textures. I usually build my drawings starting from the eyes and moving towards the rest that's because I consider the eyes are one of the most important parameters in a good portrait.

JULIE DOUGLAS... FROM PAGE 21

Being light-reliant means that I am prepared to stop what I am doing at any moment, and get back to that place where I saw the sheep yesterday as I know that the light will be right at this time again today.. Or turning the car round because I just spotted some wonderful light in a field, or taking a table of objects outside right NOW with the subject arranged, to catch that shaft of warm light. It makes for a spontaneous life, punctuated with amusing experiences - I'll never forget nervously creeping through the snow with my camera trying to follow three very grumpy geese who were hissing violently at me, while my friend was in hoots of laughter, safely on the other side of the hedge!

With people, I usually start with the flesh - this is where the most subtleties are, and this is where I hold my breath the most while I'm working. But if there is a particular area that I REALLY want to draw, I won't do that first, I save it until well into the piece, something to look forward to. My challenge is Composition - being brave enough to crop something out, for the benefit of a stronger image.

This drawing is all about the light, the warm early-evening light of an Irish summer.

- -

I complete each area as I go along, as opposed to doing light areas all over the artwork and revisiting them. I don't use any graphite apart from the initial line drawing, which I rub out with a clean putty rubber as I go along. The process is slow, intensive and deliciously absorbing. I use many layers to give a richness to the color, and I keep the pencil sharp all the time. I don't smudge, I just Draw.

MARGI HOPKINS... FROM PAGE 57

A slight twitch in the mouth can make all the difference. We pick this up because we understand the nuances. But with animals, the artist must understand how a species communicates in order to capture the essence. For instance, Horses are herd animals. They have eyes on either side of the head to be on the look out for prey as well as keep in touch with the herd. In studying horses you find that much is told by the ears, the posture of the head and the position of the tail. When composing a portrait of a horse you have to think about what gives the horse its personality. What expression will offer a window into the essence of this particular horse? It is difficult to show both the eyes unless you are looking at the forehead. So, as an artist trying to tell the whole story with one picture, what pose do you choose?

With dogs, much depends on the breed, the size even the hair coat; but because they are similar to humans in their facial expressiveness and we are so tightly bonded with them, we think we understand these expressions. "He smiles because he's happy," an anthropomorphic assumption that I like to challenge. This is why even my headshots are not simple. If I were another dog, what would I perceive by this show of teeth? Understanding animal behavior is key.

Here in Cleese's Teeth I left the background loose and gesture like. The painting moves from abstract to high realism as the viewer's eye is pulled toward Cleese's eyes and slightly open mouth. You are his prey.

- -

4. Loving the little corner you just spent four hours on too much to continue on to the next stage.(terrifying)

5. Ruining whatever you loved about the little corner by going on to the rest of the portrait. (nauseating)

6. Pushing through the fear until you get all you can down on the surface.(grunt)

7. Its not quite there. It may never be "there," so you walk around the canvas a few days, tweaking until you are pretty sure you might be there.(grunt)

8. Finish and sign the thing for Goodness sakes.(terrifying)

9. Walk around the piece a few more days until you figure out what's bothering you.(Ah-ha)

10. Seal and photograph.(relief)

SHEILA THEODORATOS... FROM PAGE 28

Until this point, I usually work solo in the studio. Sometimes, it is best to be alone to focus - especially as I think and feel through the conceptual process and prepare my composition. But once the sketch is transferred to Stonehenge and ready for colored pencil, I am soooo ready to at that point to start drawing while among other artists!

One small super dark section on the artwork is applied first. This acts as a gauge to keep overall values rich - avoiding a washed out look.

With sharpened pencils, and a light touch, I apply lightest dry washes all over the drawing, while preserving the white of the paper for highlights.

Gradually, with slightly increasing pressure, layer upon layer is added. For corrections, I use sticky tack, an electric eraser, and/or low-tack friskit film. Between drawing sessions, or to travel, I cover the art with a sheet of Glassine. I choose not to spray fixative on finished artwork that will be framed under glass, since I have found it darkens or discolors the work.

CAROL SCOTT... FROM PAGE 11

Crystal is a reflective surface, which can also distort images seen through or in the crystal, increasing the optical possibilities, a cross between Impressionism and Op Art. I am showing you how to see the magical affects of color and movement. I am exploring perception, seeing beauty. In Crystal #23, I am acknowledging the art of the past, as a Post Modernist toast to Andy Warhol.

I hold a M.F.A. from the University of New Orleans where I was a sculpture major, a painting minor and inducted into Phi Kappa Phi. I teach Art as an Associate Professor at Our Lady of Holy Cross College and show my work at Jean Bragg Gallery in New Orleans. In the 19th Annual Colored Pencil Society of America International Exhibition I received the Outstanding Recognition Award.

ALEXANDRA BASTIEN... FROM PAGE 70

Who has not at least once had to face suffering, whether inside or outside the self? Who has not experienced some form of psychological or physical abuse? Who has not suffered ill treatment, criticism or pressure inflicted by themselves or by someone else? I named this suffering "the Beast". I chose the symbolic images of a woman body and an animal skull to embody the partners in this transformative process. My works depict the dynamic interaction between the marred feminine body and the denatured animal skull. All of this is projected on a minimalist background, which evokes calm and purity.

«Maternal Instinct» speaks of the loss of a person I deeply loved. The subject expressed the willingness to continue to mother something that no longer exists. My work process is an invitation to stop feeding the Beast, exorcise it, get it out of us and let it rest in peace. The Beast is no longer the enemy. To tame the Beast is to recognize it as such and accept to confine it to the past. To reduce the Beast to the state of a skeleton is to leave behind survival and embrace life!

- -

This process allows the wax and the pigment in the coloured pencils to react with the working surface, producing interesting glaze effects, both subtle and profound. I prefer to draw with tight, small streaks and applying light pressure. This way it is possible to readjust the lines and colors easily.

This process required hundreds of hours of work on each piece I draw. I believe it is important to work on a clean surface with professional quality papers and pencils in order to maximise the medium's potential and the pleasure we can draw from it. I love to draw on illustration board and I always transfer my sketches with a copy paper to avoid damaging the surface of my board. I often replace my pencil sharpener so my pencil may always be well cut and sharp.

DEBRA YAUN... FROM PAGE 25

I have to go through many hundreds of photos to select the ones that will work together in the right composition, as well as tell the story I am trying to convey. Also, many hours in are spent laying the properly sized elements out. I draw each subject on a piece of tracing paper and it becomes a puzzle trying to make everything work together.

This piece shows things I grow in my organic garden and the many birds, bugs, etc. that I have observed there also enjoying my garden. You will see not only the vegetables but also the flowers of the plant plus a few extra blooms that add to the beauty of the garden.

ESTER ROI... FROM PAGE 10

For large drawings I usually work on sanded pastel paper like Colourfix; for smaller ones I use Stonehenge paper. I follow three main steps. First I build a quick underlayer of pigment to block-in the main colors and shapes (without heat). Then I begin applying heat to burnish and blend the colors. Here I focus on building enough pigment so that the white of the paper is completely obliterated. Colors are applied over each other or side-by-side and easily blended with a paper stump. Lastly, without heat, I strengthen the highlights, clean up the edges and polish the whole drawing.

The main tool I use to create my art is the Icarus Drawing Board™ that I invented, a portable, electric drawing board for wax-based drawing media.

ADOLFO FERNÁNDEZ RODRÍGUEZ... FROM PAGE 36

I also like Nature, faces, architecture, sculpture, our pasts, as themes for my work. I am self-taught and began painting from scratch 40 years ago – "I paint to be happy". I admire painters like Diego de Silva and Velázquez and Maria Fortuny who allowed me to learn their fabulous work. But Miguel Angel Buonarotti is 'the artist' before whom we all must bow our heads...

- -

I have not forgotten it although now I have a case with 120 colors. I work from light to dark, always preserving the white for glare and light effects. Only pencil, paper and eraser (eraser is very important, not to correct mistakes but because it is 'pencil magic' for certain textures and effects) and nothing more. I am opposed to mixing media, with the use of water, inks and any pigment with the exception of the necessary fixative spray that I always apply to my finished paintings.

ANGELA BARTLETT... FROM PAGE 13

I myself find colored pencil art a way to record happy memories here, and while I'm working, I like to remember the day that I took the photo I'm working from. The word "Ohanami" in the name of this picture is the Japanese word for cherry blossom viewing, a tradition that marks the beginning of spring. When I look at this picture, I remember a hike I did with friends and family long ago. I took this picture right as we stepped out of the woods. This particular species of cherry blossom blooms a bit later than its more famous cousin, and marks the end of cherry blossom season.

I made this painting as a gift for someone here who was always very helpful and kind as well as infinitely patient with my Japanese. I was also thinking of her as I worked, hoping she would like the painting! The Japanese change the pictures hung in their homes with the season. Every spring, my friend reminds me that she has hung my my cherry blossom picture in her home and tells me how much her family enjoys seeing it.

- -

I think you get the best effects with colored pencils by putting in a lot of layers. That means it is a slow, cautious process. I don't like to feel that I have to hurry through it. I like the slowness of it. Sometimes it is hard to figure out what colors to use; at those times I pull out my value viewer and try to separate that portion of the picture from the rest of it.

I really like bright colors, and don't like to leave my pictures too airy. So I stop every few layers and blend with a tortillon. A little summertime heat always helped this process in the past, so I have found using the Icarus board to be a great blending tool since it was invented. I also think an important step is to stand back on a regular basis and see how the picture is progressing as a whole. I ask myself, "What could be better?"

SHARON FRANK MAZGAJ... FROM PAGE 69

The drawing was somewhat of a puzzle; each ornament was reflecting not only the light and the window, but also the other shapes and colors of the ornaments around it. I loved how the shape of each ornament created sort of a fun house mirror effect. The interesting thing about this drawing was I could make out what each reflection was, with the exception of a small triangular shape on the top of every ornament. As I worked on the piece I experienced an "Ah Ha" moment when it dawned on me that the triangle was ME; when taking the photos, I had stood on a chair so that I was looking down on the box. I decided the shape was distracting and unnecessary, and left it out. When I tell that story to people they are always amazed that I could NOT draw something that was in the photo.

- -

I like to mix transparent or shiny objects like glass or metal with cloth or lace, for example. I like any thing with a reflection. I love the play of light and shadow, and I really get excited about reflected color in the shadows of objects.

I use primarily Prismacolor pencils and like to work on illustration board, as it stands up to the wear and tear of working on a piece for 40-60 hours, which actually translates to weeks or months of working on a colored pencil piece!

I never draw exactly what is in the reference photo. I "fuzz out" back ground items, exaggerate colors and shadows. My goal is to enhance the image, never copy it religiously.

LINDA LUCAS HARDY... FROM PAGE 35

When that was done I re-cleaned the area where the cookie lay. I won't even get into what I faced as I formed the letters, they were just hard work, but that wasn't the main challenge. That was realized once I was nearly finished. As I studied the piece from a distance I discovered, to my horror, it was out of balance. The picture seemed to be too heavy on one side. I let it rest for several days then had an idea. I darkened the background and some of the areas inside the cookie on the opposite side, much more than what my reference photos showed, but it solved my problem.

- -

With this method of blending it's important to get enough pigment on the paper or it will not work. In other words, the paper has to be fairly saturated. The brush can only pick up a little bit of color so it's basically just smearing it around. I'm often asked if more color can be added after blending. In some cases, yes, but only if a limited palette is used. Since the colors flatten once they are blended, making one color, that color does not exist. It's like mixing paint. If several colors are put together and mixed, they no longer are individual colors. They become one unique color. Therefore it would be difficult at best to be able to replicate the color "blending" makes.

LIZ GUZYNSKI... FROM PAGE 48

And to think about how dependent people are on these relationships that they mostly don't even know about. Thus, I try to infuse my botanical and wildlife pictures with all the elements we traditionally bring to portrait painting -- emotion, drama, conflict.

I'm also currently very interested in combining my nature work with pattern -- partly because the squirrelly part of my personality loves to draw repetitive doodles and squiggles, and partly because I think that people use pattern as a way to understand and approach complexity in the natural world. Going forward, I hope to produce paintings that use historical patterns to invite them into intimate and alien worlds right beneath our noses.

INDEX

About the Editor

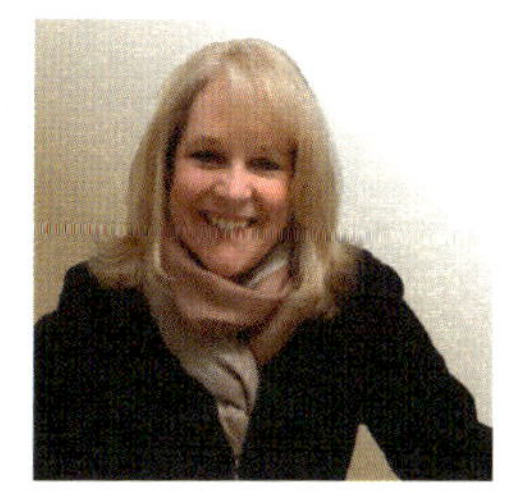

Ann Kullberg began using colored pencil in 1987 and hasn't looked back since. Her sheer love of the medium has led her to write books, found the first monthly colored pencil magazine, create instructional materials and hold hundreds of portrait workshops throughout the US, Canada, Japan, the UK, and on cruises. Ann lives in Seattle, where, in spite of the gloomy skies, she stays sunny by ballroom dancing, eating Indian or Thai food whenever possible, and by interacting daily with her favorite people – *colored pencil artists!*

Ann is the author of the following North Light books:

Colored Pencil Portraits Step by Step
Capturing Soft Realism in Colored Pencil
Colored Pencil Secrets to Success

Also Founder and Editor in Chief of **CP Magazine: Ann Kullberg's Magazine for Colored Pencil Artists**
www.annkullberg.com

Made in the USA
San Bernardino, CA
23 March 2013

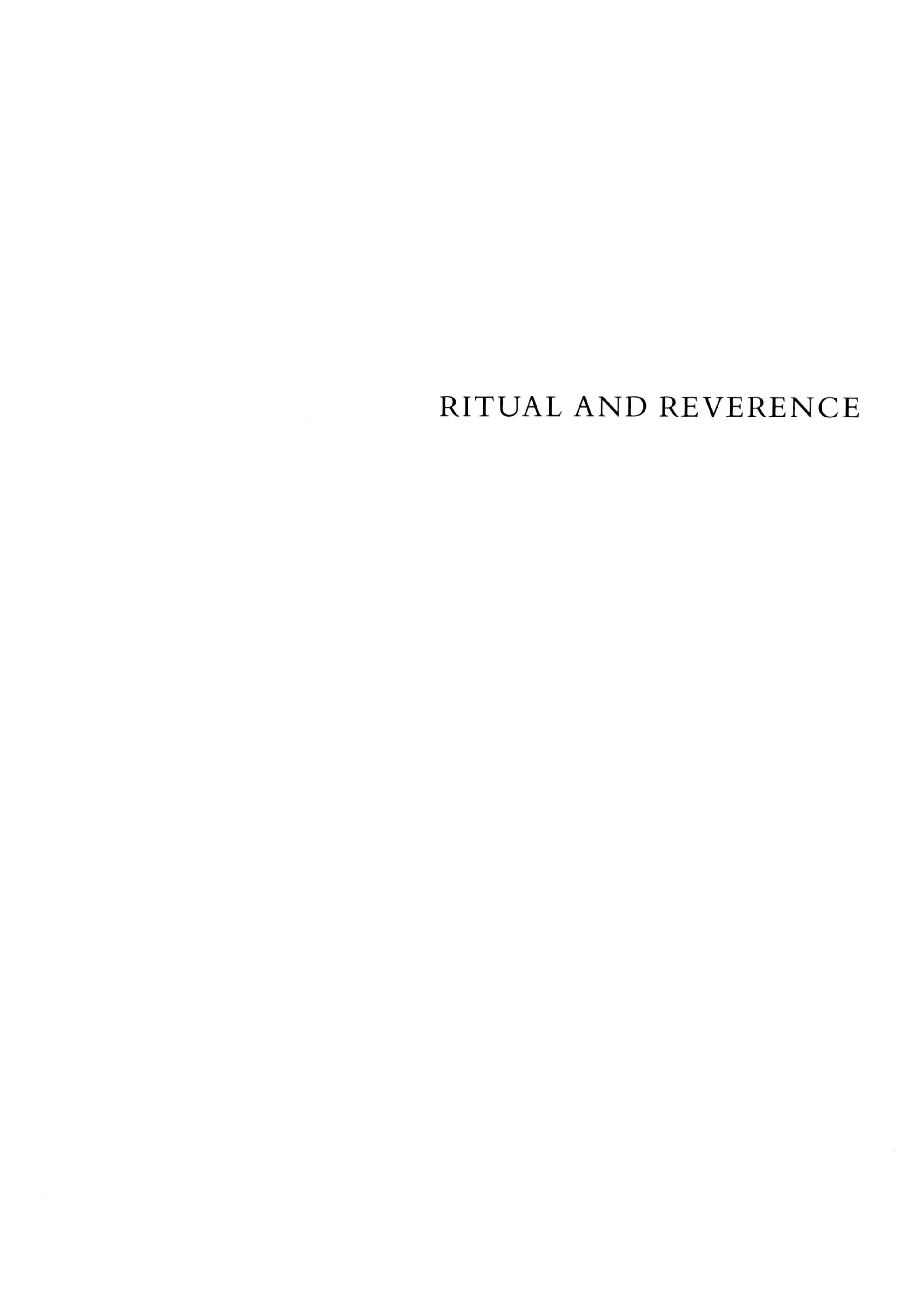

RITUAL AND REVERENCE

RITUAL AND REVERENCE
Chinese Art at The University of Chicago

Catalogue by Robert J. Poor,
Edward L. Shaughnessy,
and Harrie A. Vanderstappen SVD,
with an Introduction by
Richard A. Born

Edited by Harrie A. Vanderstappen SVD,
Richard A. Born, and Sue Taylor

The David and Alfred Smart Gallery, The University of Chicago 1989

Published as the catalogue of the exhibition *Ritual and Reverence: Chinese Art at The University of Chicago*, organized from the permanent collection of The David and Alfred Smart Gallery and shown at the Smart Gallery from 10 October through 3 December 1989.

The exhibition and catalogue were supported by a major grant from the National Endowment for the Arts. Additional funding has been provided by the Prince Charitable Trusts and the Illinois Arts Council, a state agency, and the National Endowment for the Arts. Indirect support has been received from the Institute for Museum Services, a federal agency offering general operating support to the nation's museums.

Cover: Shang dynasty, *Jue*, bronze ritual wine vessel, cat. no. 14.

Library of Congress Catalogue Card Number 89-051202
ISBN 0-935573-10-0

CONTENTS

FOREWORD

Through the study collections of the University of Chicago one can follow innumerable trails into the history of many of its most significant scholarly programs. For nearly one hundred years, Chicago faculty have regarded objects for research and teaching as essential to the university's work; not surprisingly, they have actively shaped its exemplary collections. *Ritual and Reverence: Chinese Art at The University of Chicago* illustrates this relationship, for the exhibition depends overwhelmingly on two faculty contributions: the donation by Herrlee G. Creel, Martin A. Ryerson Distinguished Service Professor Emeritus in the Departments of History and of East Asian Languages and Civilizations, and his wife of their personal collection of ancient bronze vessels, Shang oracle bones and related bronze-age material; and the inspired leadership of Father Harrie A. Vanderstappen, Professor in the Departments of Art and of East Asian Languages and Civilizations, in seeking numerous gifts of Ming and Qing dynasty paintings and funds to acquire them. Among the donors who aided Professor Vanderstappen, Mr. and Mrs. Gaylord Donnelley and Jeannette Shambaugh Elliott deserve special mention. Their continuing generosity and support over the years have been truly remarkable and the museum's collection of Chinese painting would have been much the poorer without them. Others whose gracious contributions have enhanced the collections of paintings and artifacts include Richard and Mali Edmonds, Mr. and Mrs. Isaac S. Goldman, Mitchell Hutchinson, Professor Warren G. Moon, Geraldine Schmitt-Poor and Dr. Robert J. Poor, and a good friend of the Smart Gallery who wishes to remain anonymous.

Most of the works of art pictured in the following pages will be familiar to generations of students who were first beguiled by the study of Chinese art and history in their courses with Professors Creel and Vanderstappen. But these same works of art are virtually unknown to many others. It was Smart Gallery Curator, Richard A. Born, who first saw the need to exhibit and publish these significant collections, and he has set the project on a high plane with his extraordinary degree of personal devotion and curatorial knowledge. Mr. Born brought together three distinguished experts to elucidate various aspects of the Smart Gallery's Chinese holdings: in addition to Professor Vanderstappen, Robert J. Poor, Professor in the Departments of Art History and of East Asian Studies, and the Center for Ancient Studies, University of Minnesota (who studied with both Professors Creel and Vanderstappen), and Edward L. Shaughnessy, Professor in the Department of East Asian Languages and Civilizations, University of Chicago. The breadth of learning and scholarly insight of these eminent teachers is readily evident in the catalogue text. Much less visible is the great personal warmth and collegial spirit each brought to his work with the others. All were aided by the meticulous editorship of Gallery Visiting Associate Curator, Sue Taylor, whose gentle questioning always leaves both the writer and the written better than before. The exhibition would not have been possible without the combined efforts of Smart Gallery staff members Rudy Bernal, Preparator; Mary E. Braun, Registrar; Julianne Gorny, Public Information Officer; and Glen Lafferty, Administrative Assistant. They are to be saluted for their respective, highly professional contributions. Support for the exhibition and catalogue is gratefully acknowledged from the National Endowment for the Arts, a federal agency, the Prince Charitable Trusts, and the Illinois Arts Council, a state agency, and indirect costs were underwritten in part by a grant from the Institute of Museum Services.

Three generations of teachers and their students have contributed to the making of *Ritual and Reverence*. The teachers among us have been poignantly reminded that it is through our students we share our discoveries with the future. The creation of this book is directed toward serving the timeless, continuing needs of students for many generations to come, and thus it is an expression of faith in the delicate relationship that holds teachers and students in the special orbit of learning. May this book aid in the transmission of knowledge from this generation to those that follow, and in so doing serve to remind each of the need to protect the great but fragile promise of our students.

Jeffrey Abt, *Acting Director*

INTRODUCTION

Initiating the fifteenth anniversary of the David and Alfred Smart Gallery, *Ritual and Reverence: Chinese Art at The University of Chicago* consists entirely of works from the permanent collection of the Smart Gallery. The exhibition is not exhaustive but surveys two concentrations that distinguish the museum's holdings: the material culture of the Shang and Zhou dynasties of bronze-age China, and traditions of painting practiced during China's last two dynasties, beginning with a Ming hanging scroll made around 1500 and concluding with a late Qing handscroll dated by inscription to 1824. Amazingly, with the exceptions of a gift and a loan from 1976, the ancient Chinese collection was nonexistent until three years ago, and this is the premiere presentation of ninety-five works given by Professor and Mrs. Herrlee G. Creel. Although Ming and Qing paintings have been on view intermittently since the opening of the museum, this is the most comprehensive display mounted to date from the group of over thirty scrolls, and includes several recent acquisitions not previously on public view.

Ritual and Reverence, however, is not the first exhibition of Chinese art at the University of Chicago. In 1941, for example, the Renaissance Society at The University of Chicago, an affiliate exhibition gallery on the campus since 1915, presented *Ancient Chinese Paintings from the Collection of Mr. Giovanni Del Drago* in celebration of the university's fiftieth anniversary.[1] Arranged by Ludwig Bachhofer, Professor of Far Eastern art in the Department of Art, the exhibition was possibly the earliest manifestation of the research and teaching interests of the East Asian art faculty set forth in the public forum of the art gallery at the university. Thirty years later, the Renaissance Society again mounted an exhibition of Chinese painting, this time focusing on art since 1945.[2] A prescient evaluation of work that only in the last decade has begun to receive widespread scholarly attention, the show was curated by Jeannette Shambaugh Elliott, an advocate and patron of the Chinese painting study collection since the founding of the Smart Gallery. During its first fifteen years, the Gallery has organized or hosted several exhibitions devoted to aspects of Chinese art,[3] but this is the first drawn from its own collection.

The display and collecting of Chinese art and antiquities at the University of Chicago began in the first decade of the university's existence. Dedicated in December 1893 as a natural history museum, the Walker Museum probably exhibited East Asian artifacts as early as 1894.[4] This material was apparently transferred to the Haskell Oriental Museum after it opened in 1896.[5] Devoted to the study of the oriental roots of the Jewish and Christian religions, the museum was seen from the outset as a teaching institution; its collections were gathered for investigation and instruction in accordance with the system of departmental museums envisioned for the university by 1892 and outlined in the 1904 report by the Board of Libraries, Laboratories and Museums, one of the five original Divisions of the university.[6] Photographs, reports, and remnants of the Haskell Oriental Museum's East Asian holdings—the Middle Eastern collections having been transferred to the Oriental Institute when its building was completed in 1931—indicate that acquisitions centered on Japanese Shinto and Buddhist art and artifacts of the Edo and Meiji periods, from the eighteenth through the late-nineteenth centuries, and on Indian and Tibetan painting, sculpture, and cultic objects. Aside from a comprehensive numismatic survey "illustrating the development of coinage from the earliest days in China almost down to the present,"[7] the few documented Chinese works, including the donations of D. C. Graham between 1918 and 1931, are mainly late Qing and best categorized as folk-tradition devotional statuary and memorabilia.

The research and travel of the sinologist Herrlee Glessner Creel is central to the establishment of the study collection of Chinese antiquities at the Smart Gallery. Three years after the award of his Ph.D. from the University of Chicago in 1929, Professor Creel was furthering his studies in Beijing (Peking). Among his associates in China were staff members of the Institute of History and Philology of Academia Sinica, including Dong Zuobin (Tung Tso-pin), who was in charge of archaeological excavations at present-day Anyang when Professor Creel periodically visited the site, identified as the last capital of the peripatetic Shang court. The research campaigns conducted at

Anyang between 1928 and 1936 yielded an immense body of scientifically excavated material, including ceremonial vessels in bronze, weaponry, domestic articles, and inscribed oracle bones, providing the data for nothing less than the complete rethinking of our conception of China's Bronze Age.

It was at this moment, when material evidence was replacing the quasi-legendary status of the Three Dynasties—Xia, Shang, and Zhou—that Professor Creel was, as he recounts in a recent article in *Early China*, a colleague at the informal "seminar" dinners of "historians, archaeologists, paleographers, art specialists, textual critics, even an occasional poet. . . . in Peking [who] were groping toward, and molding, a totally new history."[8] Professor Creel's return to the University of Chicago in 1936 to establish a department of Chinese studies coincided with the publication of his *Birth of China*, the first comprehensive study in English systematically to detail the sweeping revisionist history of prehistoric and early dynastic China.[9] While in China, Professor Creel had informally acquired a group of bronze-age objects, through gift or purchase as opportunity offered.[10] Eventually numbering over one hundred items, these included Shang bronze ritual vessels, bronze weaponry of the Shang and Zhou dynasties, domestic articles in bone, ceramic, shell, and stone, and a precious collection of late-Shang oracle bones ritually inscribed as part of the cycle of royal divination practiced at Anyang. Professor Creel considered these examples of documentary and archaeological interest rather than for display, certain that he did not have the resources to secure "museum pieces." Back in Chicago, he stored this material in his office in the Oriental Institute building, the first home of the Department of Oriental Languages and Literature. His teaching included a class on Chinese history from the Paleolithic Era through the Republic, and subsequently, sequential courses on early, middle, and later Chinese history; they included sessions devoted to discussions of his bronze-age artifacts.[11]

In 1986, Professor and Mrs. Creel donated this historically significant and internally cohesive study collection in its entirety to the Smart Gallery (cat. nos. 3–9, 11 and 13–99), and the transfer of the objects from the vaults of the Oriental Institute Museum, where they had been stored for many years, immediately established a research strength at the Gallery otherwise impossible to duplicate today. Previously, this formative era in Chinese civilization was evoked in the Smart Gallery collection by a single Shang *ding* bronze ritual cooking vessel (cat. no. 12), the gift of Mr. and Mrs. Isaac S. Goldman in 1976, and the anonymous long-term loan of a late Shang-Western Zhou earthenware *li* tripod cooking vessel (cat. no. 10)—which has been generously given to the museum on the occasion of this exhibition. Each complements pieces collected by Professor Creel and, in turn, is placed in context by the Creel donation. For example, a comparison between the Goldman and Creel *ding* (cat. nos. 12 and 13) demonstrates the changes in typology and decor that define the so-called transitional and classic forms of this ceremonial vessel in Shang art. Or again, the *li* is the only complete bronze-age earthenware vessel in the collection, otherwise consisting of Shang gray- and redware shards, an interesting study group in itself because of the diverse techniques and patterns of surface decoration represented (cat. nos. 3–9). Furthermore, the *li* and the unpretentious terracotta mold fragment for a bronze ritual vessel (cat. no. 11) introduce the complex topic of the formal and technical relationships between the ceramic and bronze industries during the Shang period. The recent gifts by Geraldine Schmitt-Poor and Dr. Robert J. Poor of neolithic pottery (cat. nos. 1 and 2) represent the first examples in the collection of the distinctive slip-painted and hand-built earthenware tradition preceding the unpainted Shang gray- and redware vessels with their incised, combed, and cord-paddled ornament.

Mention must be made of a few important works that lie outside the chronological purview of the present exhibition. The single later example of Chinese metalwork in the Creel gift, a mirror decorated with the "lion-and-grapevine" motif, is a superb document of the sophisticated and cosmopolitan culture of Tang China and is contemporaneous with a terracotta tomb guardian figure,[12] a routine apotropaic burial figurine exceptional for its fine painting and partial gilding, which is the gift of Gaylord Donnelley, who has on many occasions enhanced the museum's holdings of Chinese and Japanese paintings and *ukiyo-e* prints. The superior glazed earthenwares and porcelains of China—a high point in the world history of the arts of the kiln—are represented by a few Liao, Song, and Ming vessels and several representatives of the eighteenth- and nineteenth-century Export Ware trade. Useful in teaching as isolated exemplars of a complex tradition, they are important in the context of the museum's Western decorative arts holdings because of their seminal influence on the *chinoiserie* fashion in English and Continental tin-glazed earthenware of the seventeenth- and eighteenth-centuries and especially for their stimulation of the nascent European porcelain industry around 1725 to 1750. Chinese ceramics have entered the collection sporadically as individual gifts, beginning with the 1973 bequest of Joseph Halle Schaffner in memory of his mother Sara H. Schaffner, and continuing with generous contributions from Mrs. Chauncey Borland, Dr. Maurice Cottle, Kelvyn G. Lilley, Mrs. Cora Passin, and the Smart Gallery Vienna Tour, 1985.

Development of a study collection of Chinese painting began three years prior to the groundbreaking for the university's fine arts museum in 1971. The guiding force was Father Harrie A. Vanderstappen, Professor in the Departments of Art and of East Asian Languages and Civilizations. In 1968, Professor Vanderstappen proposed the acquisition of a "solid study collection" of Ming and Qing paintings from the collection of Victoria Contag, author of the standard reference on the subject of artists' and collectors' seals.[13] Assembled in Shanghai between 1925 and 1935, and on deposit at the Nelson-Atkins Museum of Art in Kansas City since the forties, the Nü Wa Chai Collection, as it was called, was on the art market after sales to Avery Brundage in San Francisco and to Stanford University. Professor Vanderstappen wrote:

> The group is representative of all trends in later Chinese paintings. . . . [and] give[s] a good cross-section of. . . . the movements to be found in the last four hundred years. This includes the various techniques and materials such as color, ink, paper and silk and the various formats of Chinese paintings. More important, the works represent the traditional aspects as well as some of the "off-beat" trends of Chinese art during this period. The emphasis in China on the refinements of old traditions can be seen in this collection. . . . Academic works exist next to more informal work done by gentlemen who have insisted throughout Chinese history that the practice of the creative arts was part of their cultural heritage. This group of paintings, valuable and very attractive in themselves, would form a good core for our museum study collection in oriental art.[14]

The last sentence refers to the announcement in October 1967 of a major grant from the Smart Family Foundation for the construction and equipping of the university's first art museum. Already in 1966, in response to a request from the Dean of Humanities, the art department faculty had prepared guidelines for a gallery, noting that "there would be, in the first place, space for the more or less permanent display of works of art carefully chosen to provide direct experience with the artistic expression of our cultural heritage."[15] But, as recalled by President Edward H. Levi at the groundbreaking of the Cochrane-Woods Art Center on 29 October 1971, the dream of the university having its own collection of "original works of art, ancient and modern," had been expressed as early as 1904 by the classicist Frank Tarbell.[16]

Professor Vanderstappen cited in his proposal the need for students of Chinese painting to acquire the kind of connoisseurship possible only through prolonged and undisturbed scrutiny of the original. Such study requires much closer handling than is usual in public or private collections, but is of course normal for the university museum study room. Eventually, through the generosity of an anonymous donor, twelve scrolls were acquired for the Smart Gallery from the Nü Wa Chai Collection, which had itself been gathered by a scholar whose own research was predicated on such firsthand examination. Through the beneficence of Mr. and Mrs. Gaylord Donnelley, eight additional hanging scrolls were acquired by Professor Vanderstappen during a trip to Japan in late 1971. Consequently, with the formal opening of the Smart Gallery three years later, the Founding Director, Professor Edward A. Maser, was able to write that half the space allocated to the display of the permanent collection was devoted to the art of the Far East.[17] Photographs of the installation in late 1974 show the Chinese painting collection as the focus of the East Asian holdings. The sixteen hanging scrolls and handscrolls exhibited represented the core of the study collection assembled by Professor Vanderstappen. The noteworthy exception was the loan of the important handscroll by the late-Ming professional painter Lan Ying, given to the museum in 1987 by Jeannette Shambaugh Elliott in honor of Professor Vanderstappen (cat. no. 108). Along with the intriguing seventeenth-century hanging scroll, probably executed in the finger painting technique, by the little-known Zhu Qizhen (cat.no. 111), this major gift is the latest expression of the donor's longstanding interest in the development of a teaching collection of later Chinese painting at the University of Chicago.

During the past fifteen years, the collection has been increased and refined through the efforts of Professor Vanderstappen and the generosity of friends of the museum. Notable gifts include the Orthodox School landscape painting by the eighteenth-century court official Zhang Pengzhong (cat. no. 115) donated by the collector Mitchell Hutchinson, a former Chicagoan now residing in Honolulu,[18] and the evocative orchid handscroll painted by Yun Xiang in 1824 (cat.no. 121). Given in behalf of one of his mentors, Professor Vanderstappen, by the classicist Professor Warren G. Moon of the University of Wisconsin-Madison, the work testifies to the rich heritage of women painters in Chinese art. The austere plum blossom hanging scroll by Tong Yu (cat. no. 117) from Richard and Mali Edmonds of Berkhamstead, Hertfordshire, England, is the earliest representation in the collection of this quintessential subject in scholar-amateur or literati painting and is different in style and conception from the luxuriant prunus painting by Zhu Xuan from the Nü Wa Chai Collection (cat. no. 120). Among the pieces in the reserve study collection, special mention is appropriate for gifts from Miss Ruth McCollum, Mr. and Mrs. Bertold Regensteiner, Mr. and Mrs. Frank Schubel, and Miss Margaret Walbank, as well as an anonymous donor.

As befits a university study collection, in addition to the entries by Professor Vanderstappen, the catalogue consists of contributions by former and present students, who are listed at the beginning of the painting section of the catalogue. Some are revised graduate papers that demonstrate the complex investigation possible from the physical evidence of the work itself—signatures, seals, colophons, support, medium, and so forth—and the placing of these discrete elements into literary, cultural, and political perspective. Other entries have been written especially for this catalogue by current graduate students and alumni of the Department of Art. The contribution by Anne Burkus, Assistant Professor of oriental art in the Department of Art and the College, publishes for the first time original research in her dissertation that touched upon the today little-known seventeenth-century artist Sun Di (cat. no. 110).

Professor Qiu Xigui of Beijing University is gratefully acknowledged for his sound advice on the periodization of the late-Shang oracle-bone inscriptions. Mr. Wen-Pai Fai in the East Asian Collection of the university's Joseph Regenstein Library is thanked for his help in the difficult process of deciphering and verifying some of the characters of the seals and inscriptions on the Ming and Qing paintings.

It is important to recognize another group who have advanced the planning and execution of this project. The graduate student interns at the Smart Gallery have provided support for all stages of the exhibition and catalogue: Stephanie D'Alessandro,

Tom Fahsbender, Kathleen Gibbons, Kaki Strause, and Melissa Wolfe. Projects such as this further the original goal of the museum to provide experiential museological practice for students of the university. In addition, while engaged in a research project at the Smart Gallery, Julie Thuras, a graduate student of oriental art in the Department of Art, has recovered much of the history of the East Asian collections formerly in the Haskell Oriental Museum. Finally, Mr. Cai Fangpei, a graduate student in the Departments of East Asian Languages and Civilizations, has assisted Professor Edward L. Shaughnessy in the preparation of the thorough and expert transcriptions of the inscriptions on the oracle bones from the Creel collection.

The accretion of single objects or groups of objects into a particular research strength is not unusual in the development of museum collections, and is well represented by the Gallery's acquisition history. But what is exceptional in the case of the Smart Gallery is the quality and cohesiveness of the assembled material and the formation of these research concentrations through remarkable private support in the absence of endowed purchase funds. The Smart Gallery and the audience it serves owe a great debt of gratitude to all the donors and contributors who have made the present exhibition and catalogue a reality and a model for future scholarly endeavors.

Richard A. Born

NOTES

1. The exhibition was held in the galleries of the Renaissance Society in Goodspeed Hall from 28 September to 25 October 1941. See Ludwig Bachhofer, *A Catalogue of Ancient Chinese Paintings from the Collection of Mr. Giovanni Del Grado* (exh. cat.) (Chicago: Renaissance Society at The University of Chicago, 1941). Earlier, when located in room 45 of the Classics Building, the Renaissance Society presented an exhibition of fifteen paintings from the Tang through Yuan periods on loan from the famous oriental art dealer, C. T. Loo. Entitled *Exhibition of Chinese Paintings of the T'ang, Sung, and Yüan Periods*, the show opened on 7 March 1926 and was accompanied by a checklist with introductory remarks by Edward F. Rothschild, an instructor in western and oriental art in the university's art department; a copy of the brochure is among the papers of the Renaissance Society donated to the Archives of American Art, Smithsonian Institution (a microfilm of the document, roll 2400, is on file in the Society's administrative office).

2. *Chinese Painting at Mid-Century* was presented at the Renaissance Society from 4 May to 12 June 1971, accompanied by an illustrated brochure with an introduction and artists' biographies by Jeannette Shambaugh Elliott.

3. Of particular note is *Hsieh Shih-ch'ên: A Ming Dynasty Painter Reinterprets the Past*, organized in 1978 by the museum's first curator, Katharine Lee Keefe, and based on the dissertation of a graduate in the Department of Art, Mary S. Lawton (one of the contributors to the present catalogue). In 1982, the Smart Gallery presented a traveling exhibition from the Honolulu Academy of Arts, *Poetry on the Wind: The Art of Chinese Folding Fans from the Ming and Ch'ing Dynasties*, which focused on a special category of Chinese painting unrepresented as yet in the collection. Other exhibitions have examined the influence of Chinese art: in 1985, then director John Carswell organized *Blue and White: Chinese Porcelain and Its Impact on the Western World*, and in 1987 the museum mounted *Japanese Quest for a New Vision: The Impact of Visiting Chinese Painters, 1600–1900*, featuring Japanese and related Chinese paintings from the Hutchinson Collection at the Spencer Museum of Art, University of Kansas.

4. In February 1894, the curator of the Walker Museum, Frederick Starr, published a "Circular Regarding Collections of Religious Objects," in which he discussed a loan to the museum of Shinto and Japanese Buddhist objects collected by Edmund Buckley. A checklist of the Shinto material was provided. An annotated copy of the brochure is in the files of the Smart Gallery.

5. See, for example, the lower of two photographs of Haskell Oriental Museum galleries as they appeared in 1898, in Jean F. Block, *The Uses of Gothic: Planning and Building the Campus of the University of Chicago, 1892–1932* (exh. cat.) (Chicago: University of Chicago Library, 1983), 41. Several of the Japanese works can be identified from among objects or original labels of the Haskell Oriental Museum transferred from Swift Hall to the Smart Gallery in 1988.

6. On the history of the Division of Libraries, Laboratories and Museums, and the creation of an administrative board, see Thomas Wakefield Goodspeed, *A History of The University of Chicago: The First Quarter Century* (1916; reprint, Chicago and London: University of Chicago Press, 1972), 135–136, 153, and 366. A copy of the report, dated 5 April 1904, by the committee of the Board of Libraries, Laboratories and Museums is in the university's Department of Special Collections in the Joseph Regenstein Library. A full account of the history of pedagogical museums at the university prior to the opening of the Smart Gallery is in preparation by the Gallery's Acting Director, Jeffrey Abt, for the forthcoming handbook of the collection, to be published by the museum in 1990.

7. Goodspeed, *History*, 492.

8. Herrlee Glessner Creel, "On the Birth of *The Birth of China*," *Early China* 11–12 (1985–87):3–4.

9. Creel, *The Birth of China: A Survey of the Formative Period of Chinese Civilization* (London: Jonathan Cape, 1936; New York: John Day, 1937, Frederick Ungar Publishing Co., 1954, 1964).

10. Information regarding the formation of the Creel collection was kindly provided by Professor Creel in interviews with the author during May and June 1989.

11. The extent and intensity of institutional and private collecting of ancient bronzes between 1920 and 1960 in Chicago is remarkable. For example, the Lucy Maud Buckingham Collection at The Art Institute of Chicago was begun in 1925 and essentially formed by 1946 when it was published for the first time; see Charles Fabens Kelley and Ch'en Meng-chia, *Chinese Bronzes from the Buckingham Collection* (Chicago: Art Institute of Chicago, 1946). The Field Museum of Natural History was acquiring Shang, Zhou, and Han bronzes. Among private collectors, Avery Brundage was enlarging and refining his superb and extensive collection, today in the Asian Art Museum of San Francisco; see René-Yvon Lefebvre d'Argencé, *Bronze Vessels of Ancient China in the Avery Brundage Collection* (San Francisco: Asian Art Museum of San Francisco, 1977). In the decades after World War II, Mr. and Mrs. James Alsdorf assembled a formidable collection of Chinese art in all media, from the Shang dynasty to the modern period; see Jack V. Sewell, "The Alsdorf Collection," in Arts Club of Chicago, *Chinese Art from the Collection of James W. and Marilynn Alsdorf* (exh. cat.) (Chicago: Arts Club of Chicago, 1970), unpaginated. Also, beginning in 1949, Mr. and Mrs. Robert B. Mayer, otherwise known for their collection of contemporary art (major examples of which have formed The Robert B. Mayer Memorial Loan Collection at the Smart Gallery since 1975) avidly collected oriental art, eventually numbering over 750 examples, including several ancient Chinese bronze ritual vessels and weapons. The Creel collection was, it seems, the only bronze-age material directly linked to formal research and teaching, despite the rich assemblage of works in Chicago.

12. The Tang sculpture will be published in the forthcoming handbook of the collection, cited in n. 6 above, with an entry by Professor Harrie Vanderstappen.

13. Victoria Contag and Wang Chi-ch'üan, *Seals of Chinese Painters and Collectors of the Ming and Ch'ing Periods* (Shanghai: Commercial Press, 1940; rev. ed., Hong Kong: Hong Kong University Press, 1966).

14. Professor Vanderstappen's original memorandum, dated 21 May 1968, is located in the documentary files of the museum's permanent collection.

15. Excerpted from an unpublished letter, dated 5 October 1968, from the Acting Chairman of the Department of Art, Robert L. Scranton, to the Dean of the Division of Humanities, Robert Streeter. On 20 February 1969, the Department of Art approved the recommendations of their steering committee, that "the principal function of the gallery is education—teaching and research. In addition to a permanent collection, there should be temporary exhibitions." (Memorandum from Scranton to Streeter, 23 March 1971.)

16. President Levi's remarks are reproduced in their entirety in the brochure printed on the occasion of the groundbreaking ceremonies of the Cochrane-Woods Art Center complex, comprised of the Department of Art, the Vera and A. D. Elden Sculpture Garden (named in 1988), and the Smart Gallery. A copy is on file at the Gallery.

17. Edward A. Maser, "An Introduction to the Smart Gallery," *The David and Alfred Smart Gallery, The University of Chicago, 1974* (Chicago: David and Alfred Smart Gallery, 1974), unpaginated.

18. On the Hutchinson collection, see Tseng Yu-ho Ecke, *Wen-jen Hua: Chinese Painting from the Collection of Mr. and Mrs. Mitchell Hutchinson* (exh. cat.) (Honolulu: Honolulu Academy of Arts, 1988).

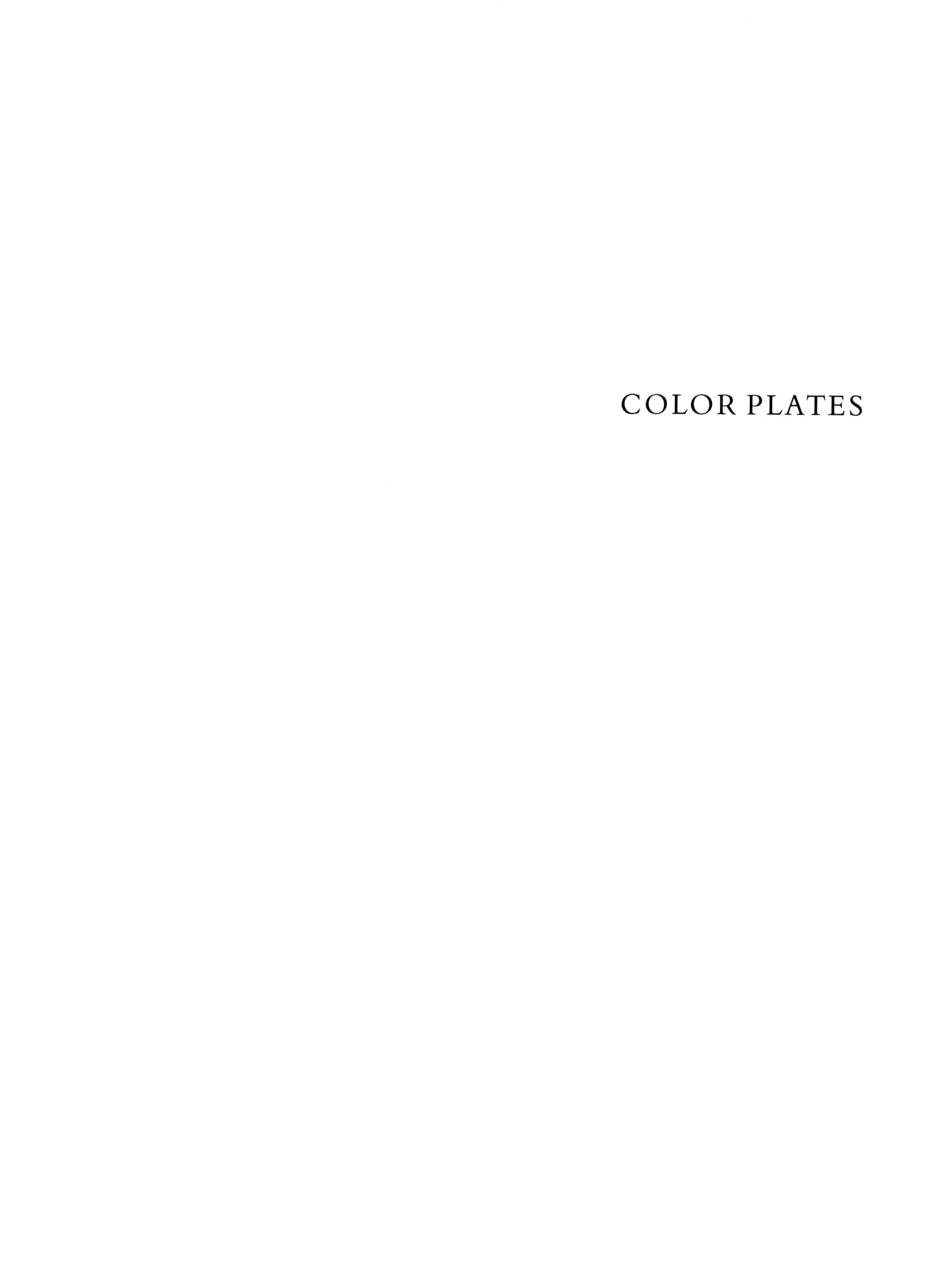

COLOR PLATES

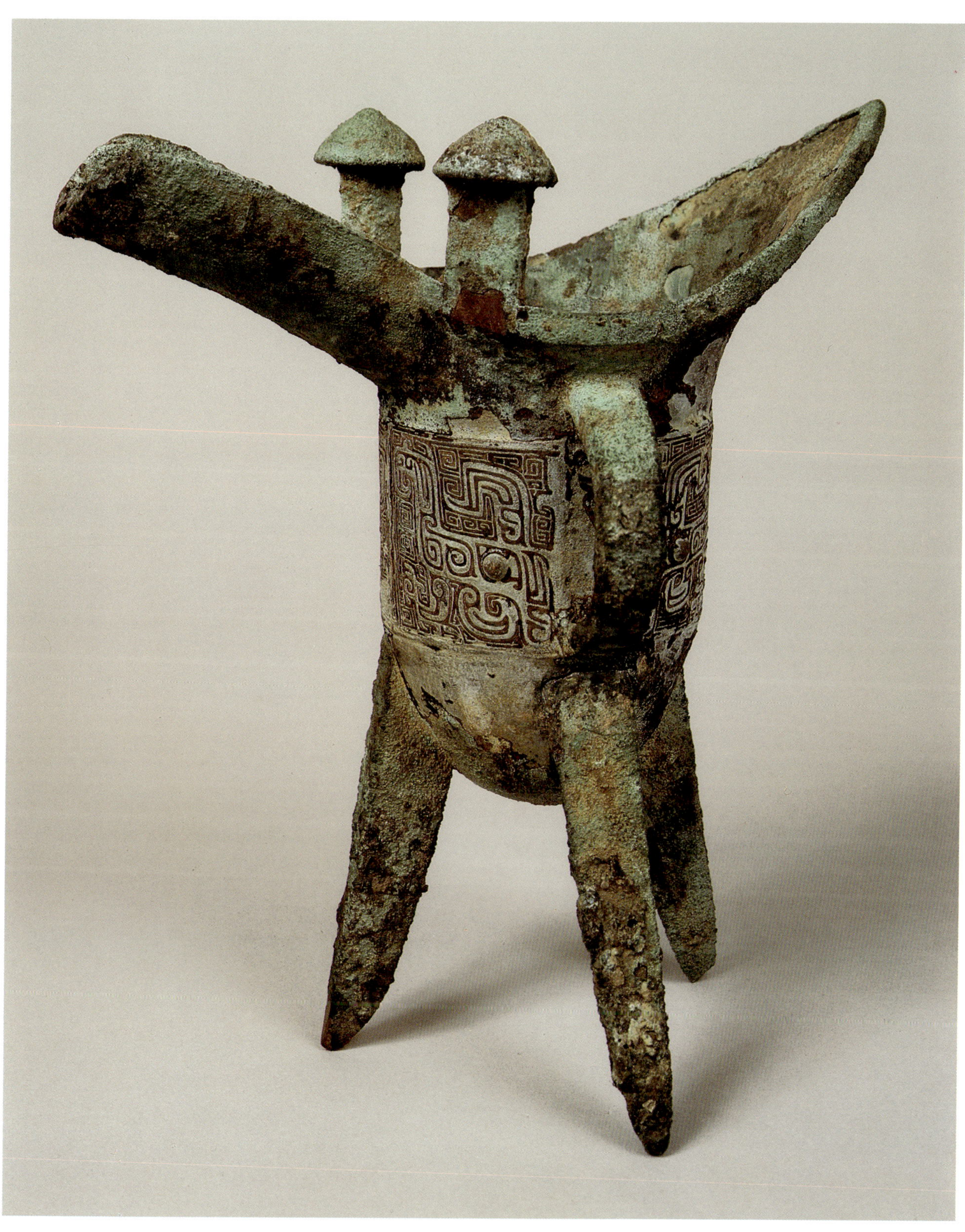

Plate I. Shang dynasty, *Jue*, bronze ritual wine vessel, cat. no. 14.

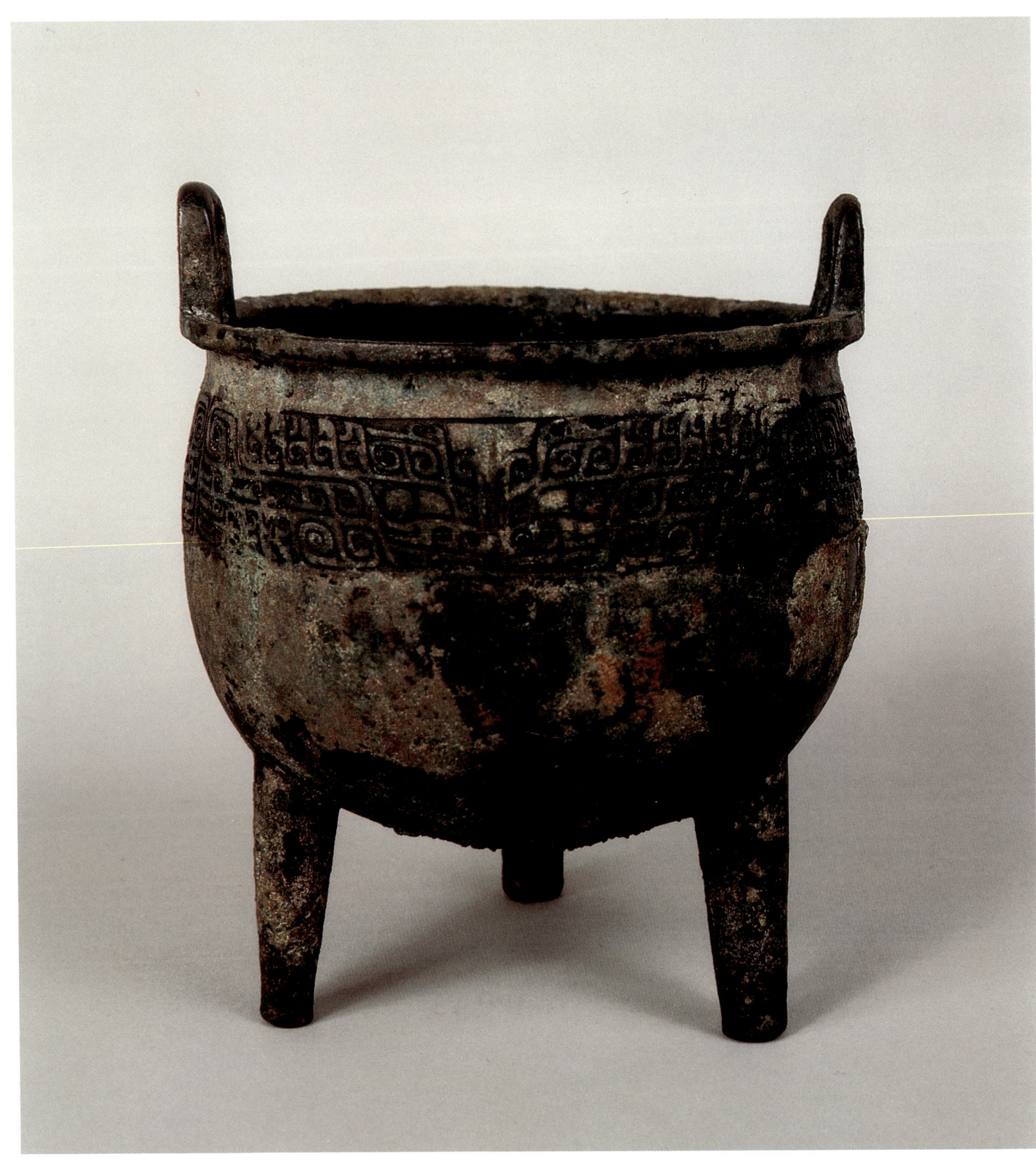

Plate II. Shang dynasty, *Ding*, bronze ritual cooking vessel, cat. no. 12.

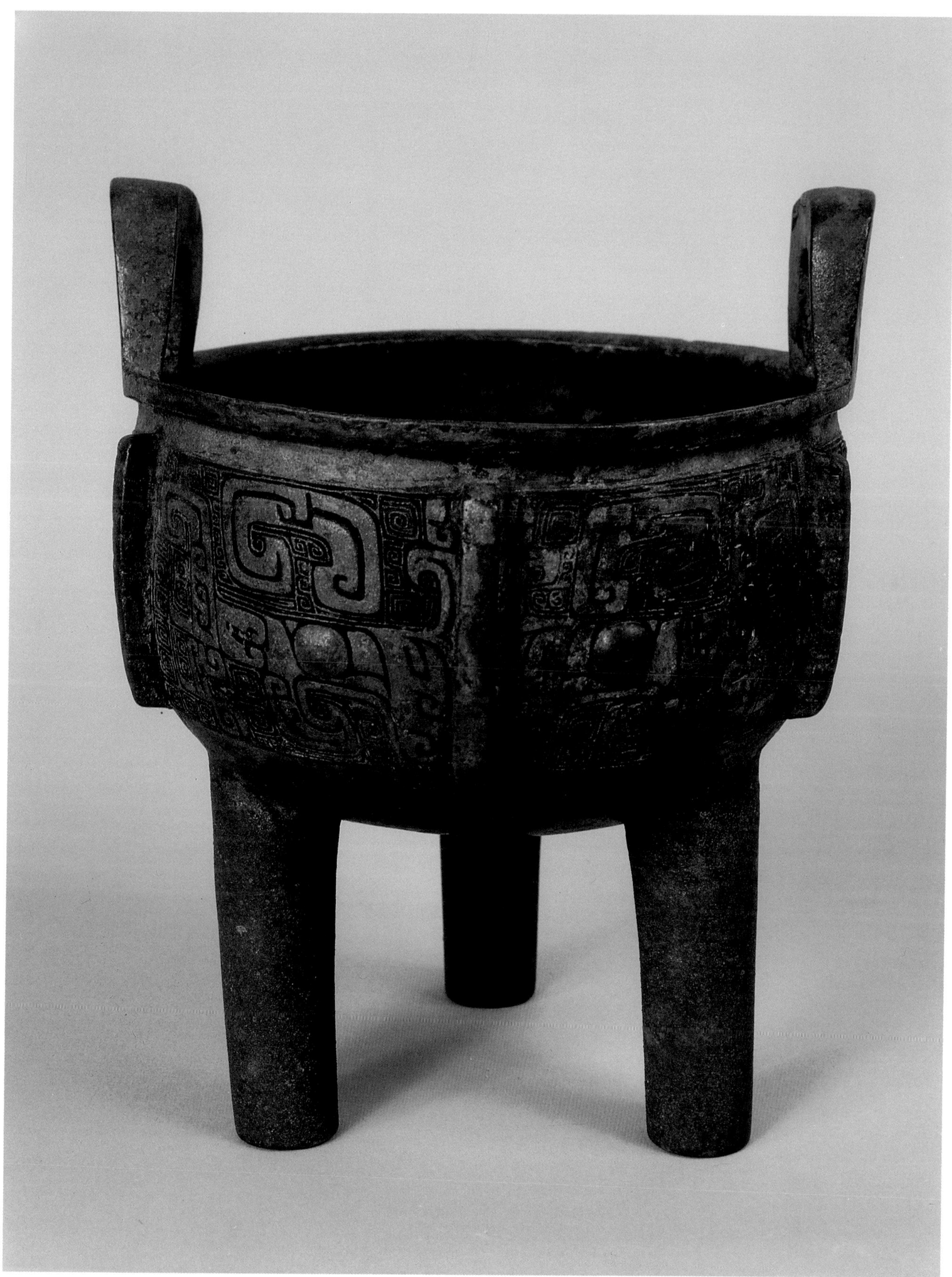

Plate III. Shang dynasty, *Ding*, bronze ritual cooking vessel, cat. no. 13.

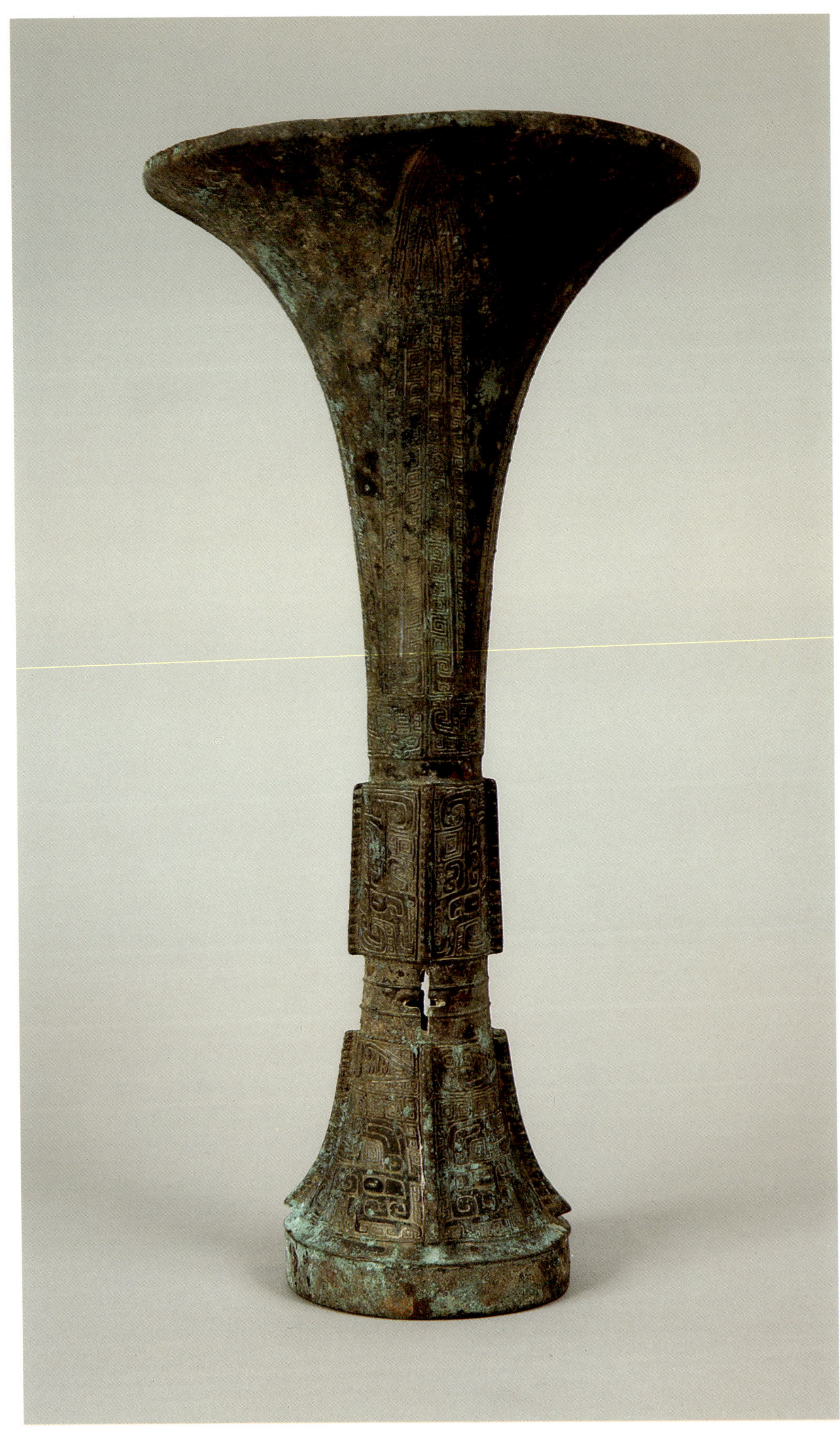

Plate IV. Shang dynasty, *Gu*, bronze ritual wine beaker, cat. no. 15.

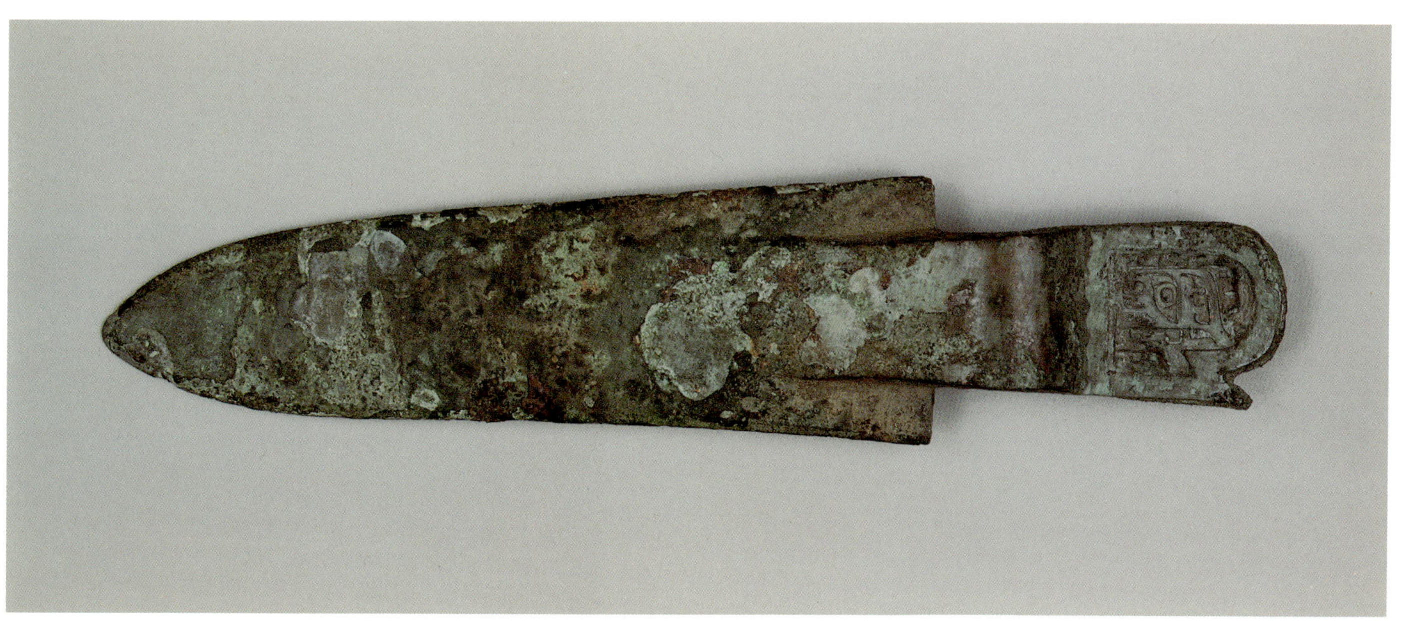

Plate V. Shang dynasty, *Ge*, bronze socketed dagger-axe, cat. no. 17.

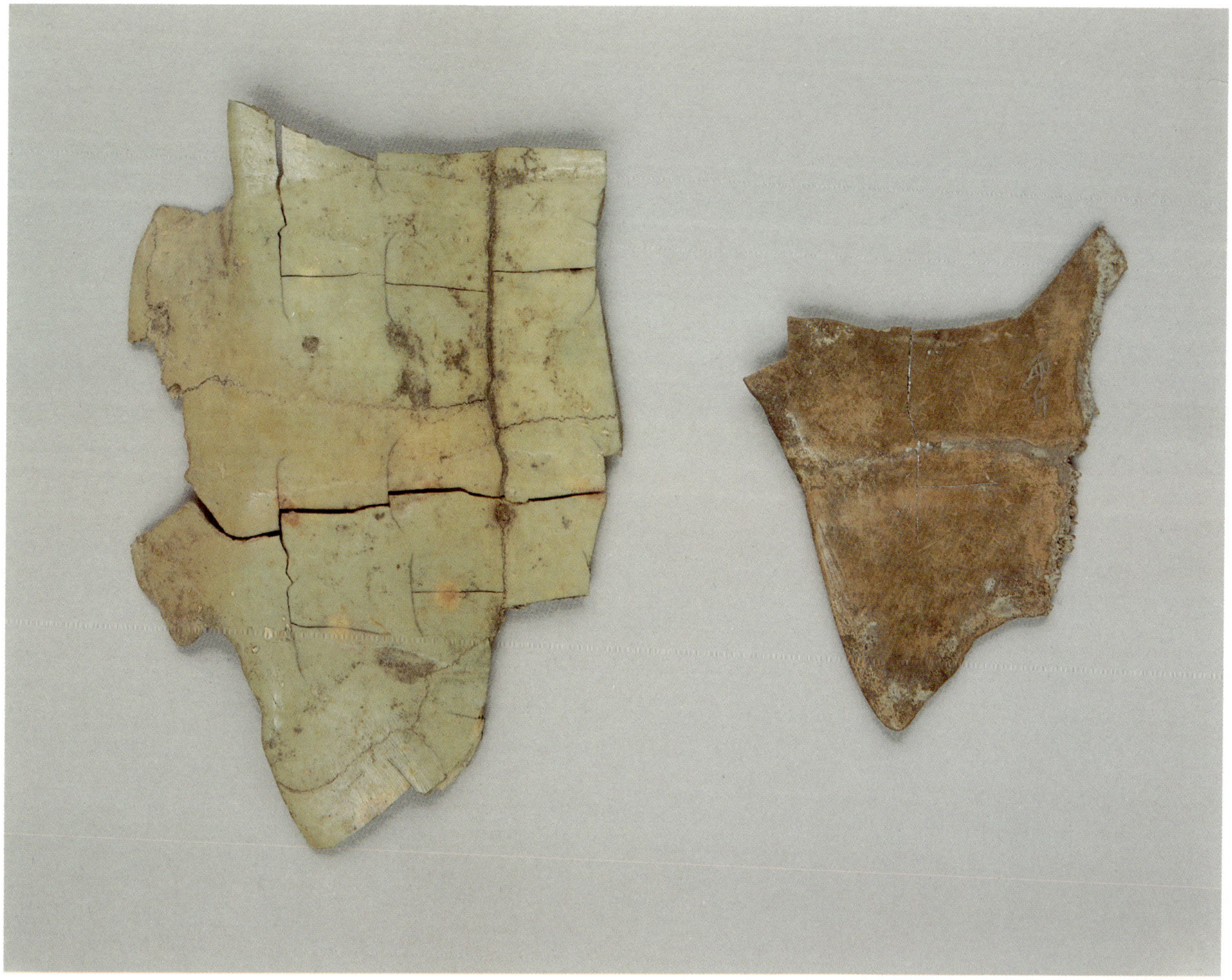

Plate VI. Late Shang dynasty, *Oracle Plastron* (uninscribed) and *Oracle Plastron* (inscribed), cat. nos. 60 and 61, respectively.

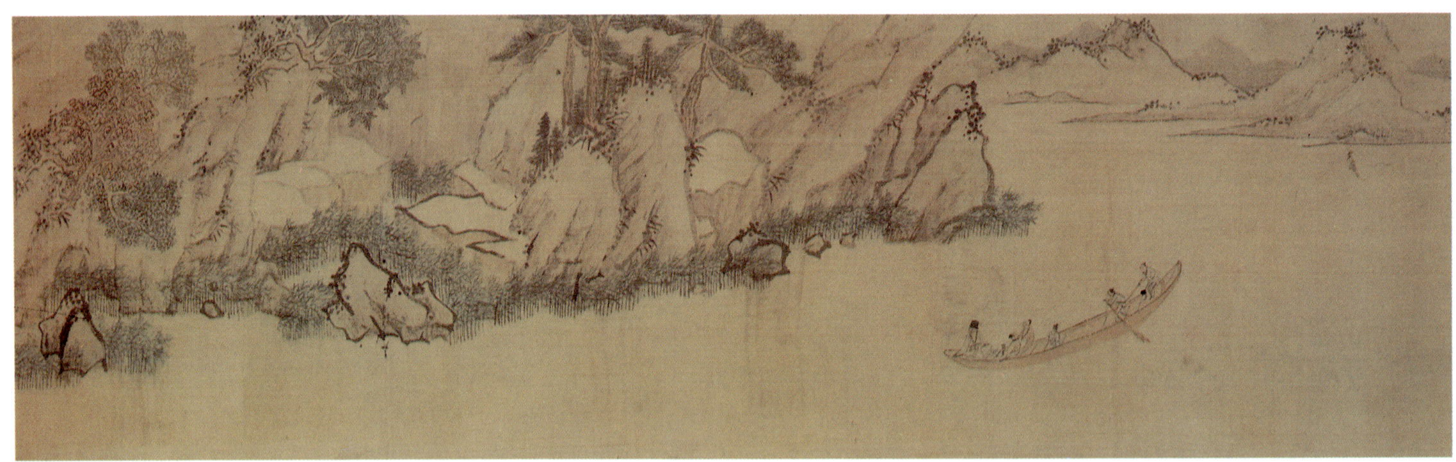

Plate VII. Qian Gu, *The Red Cliff*, 1575, handscroll (detail), cat. no. 103.

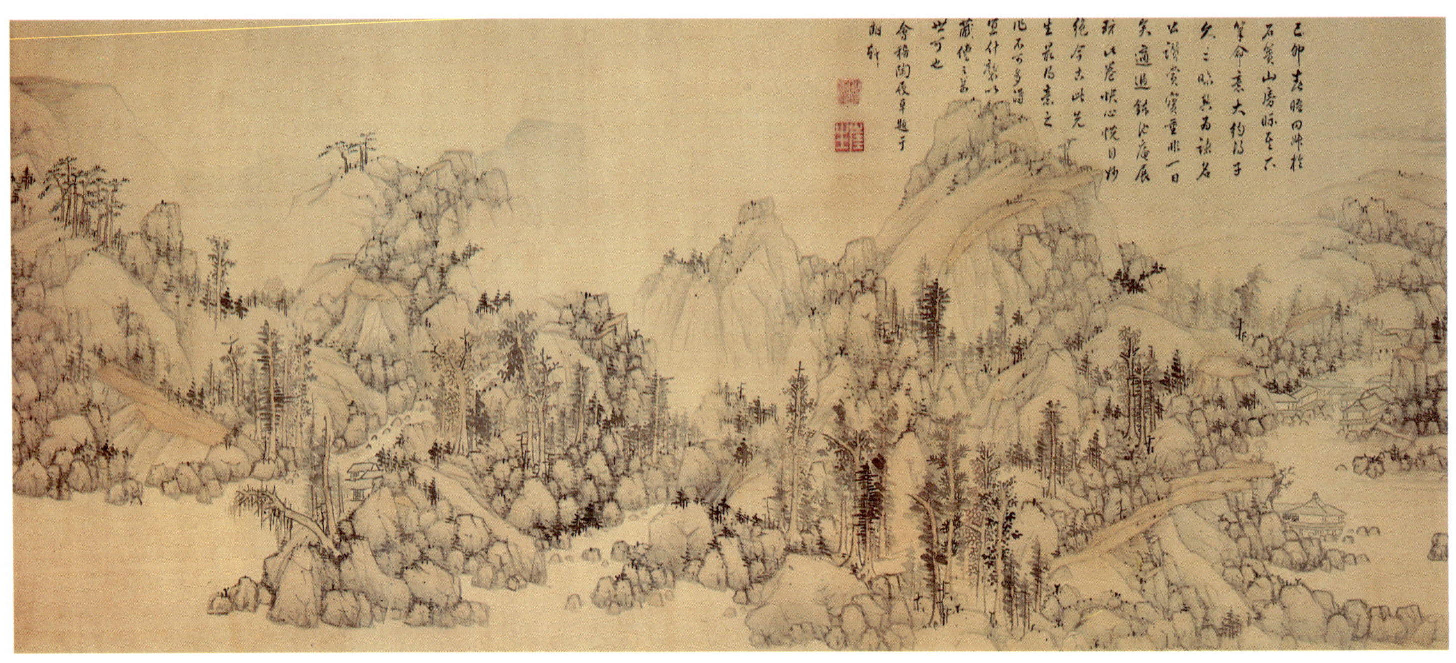

Plate VIII. Lan Ying, *Landscape (after Huang Gongwang)*, circa 1637–38, handscroll (detail), cat. no. 108.

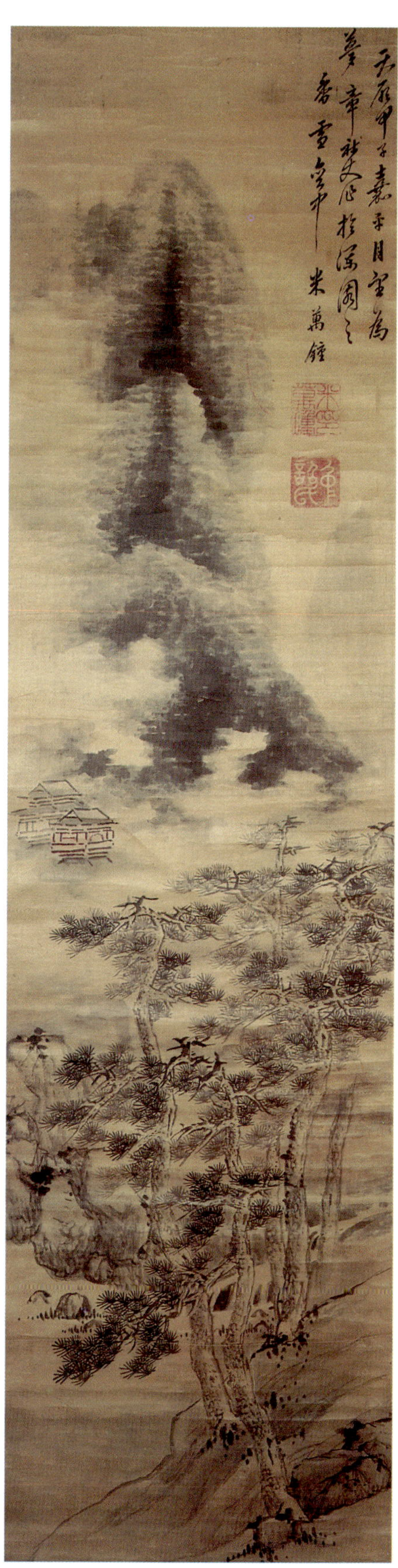

Plate IX. Mi Wanzhong, *Among Fragrant Snowy Mountains by Lan Garden*, 1621, hanging scroll, cat. no. 106.

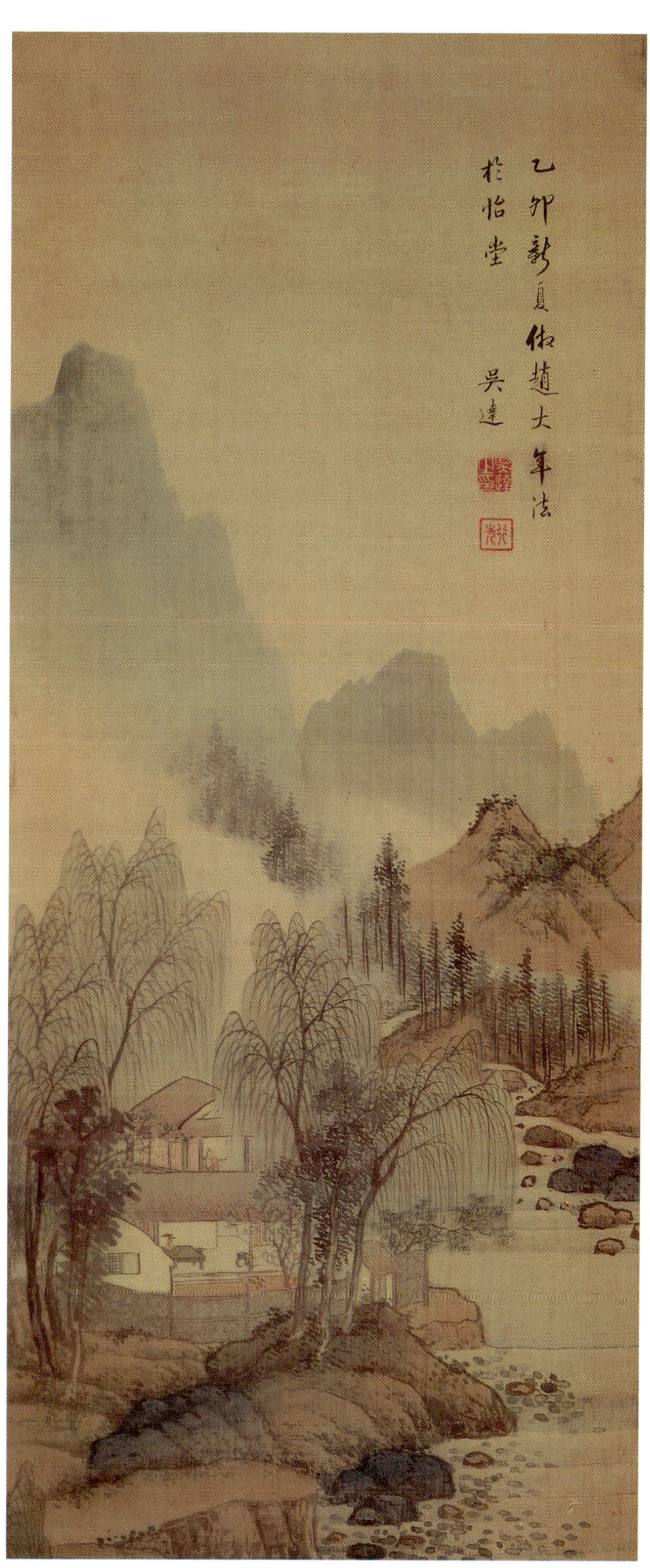

Plate X. Wu Da, *Summer Pavilion (after Zhao Danian)*, 1675, hanging scroll, cat. no. 112.

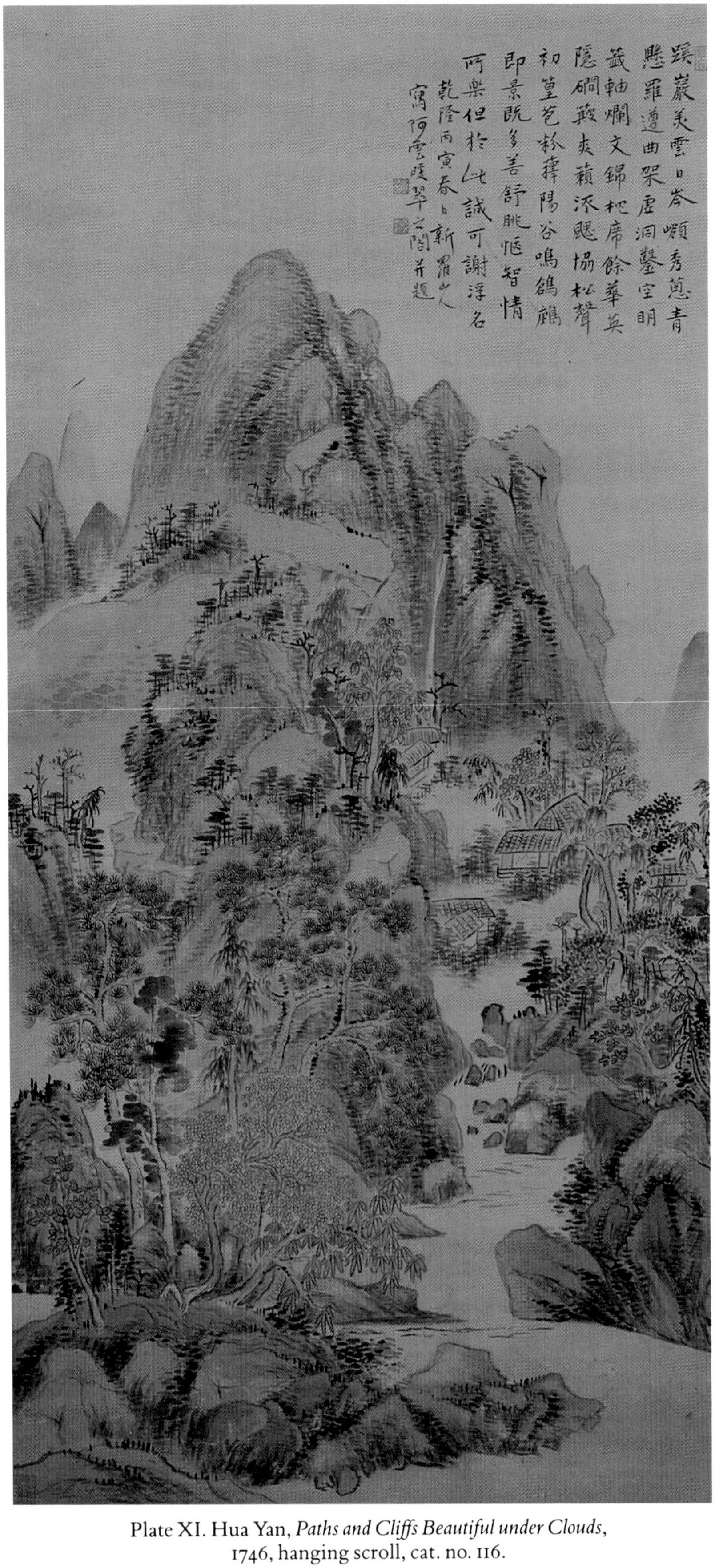

Plate XI. Hua Yan, *Paths and Cliffs Beautiful under Clouds*, 1746, hanging scroll, cat. no. 116.

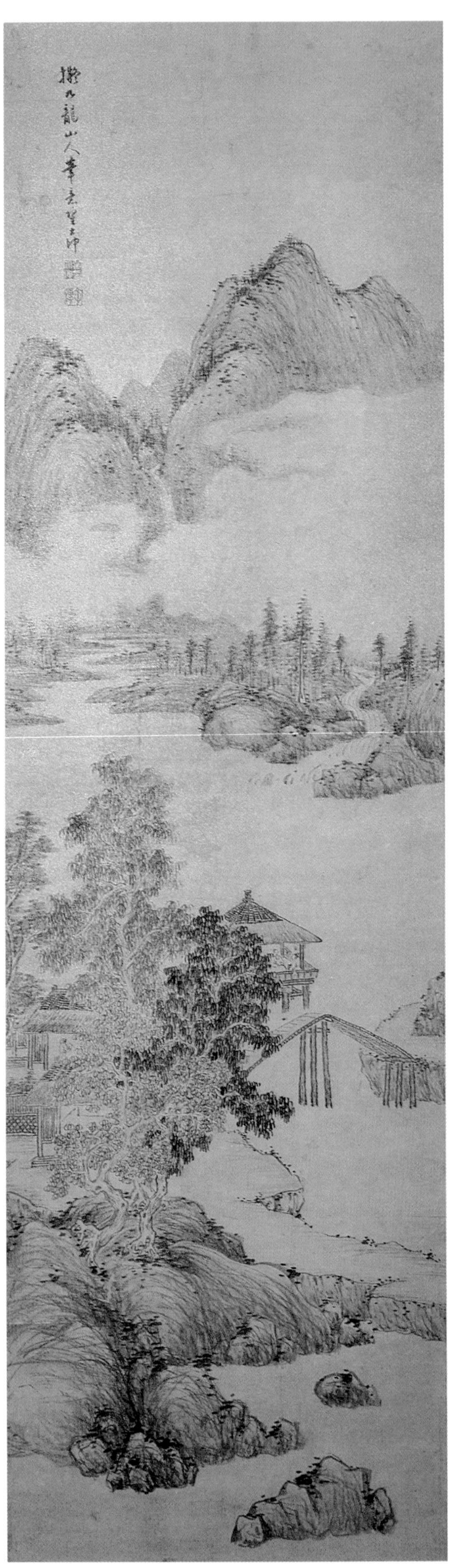

Plate XII. Zhai Dakun, *Landscape (after Wang Fu)*, circa 1790–1800, hanging scroll, cat. no. 118.

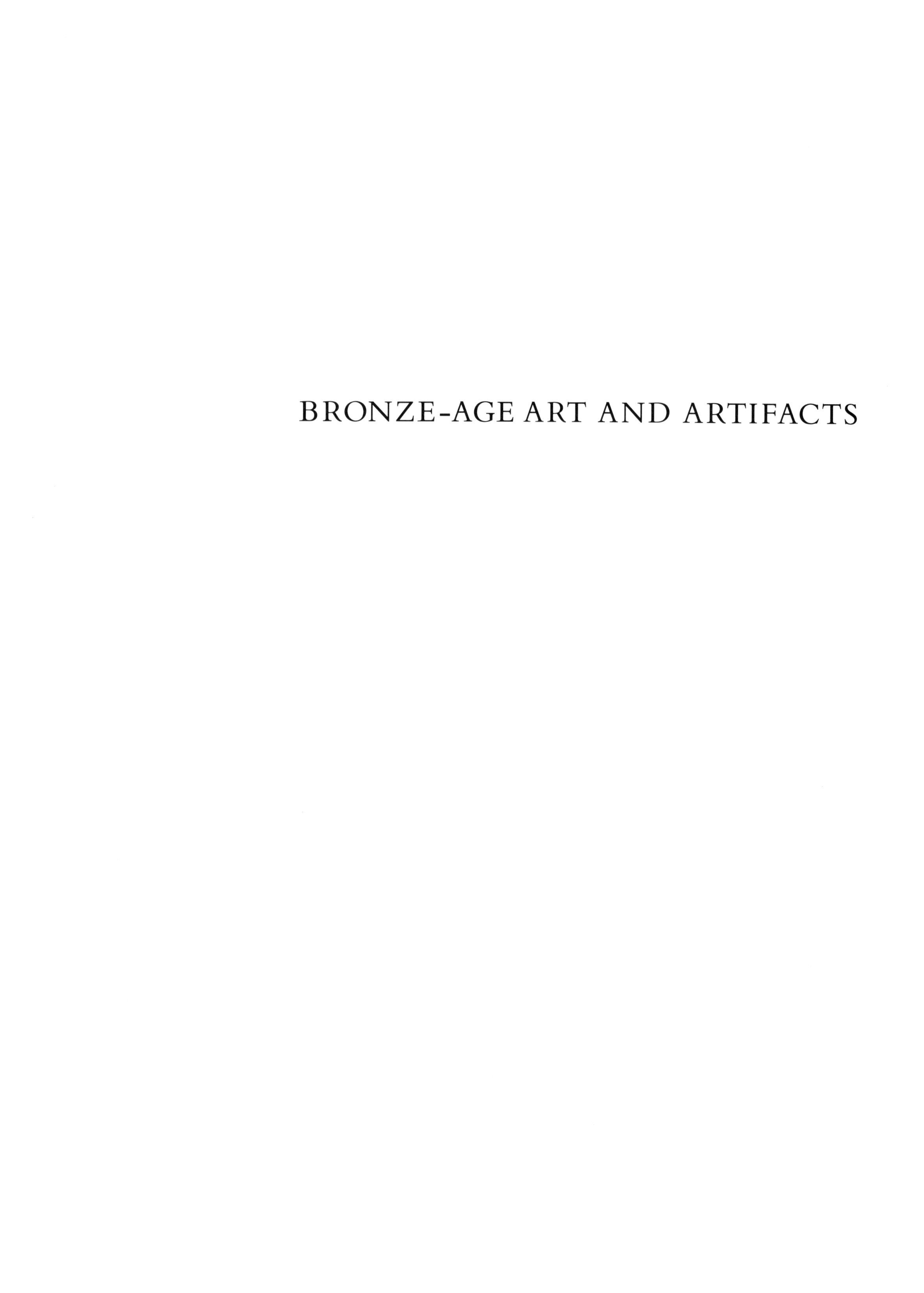

BRONZE-AGE ART AND ARTIFACTS

CHINESE ANTIQUITIES IN THE SMART GALLERY COLLECTION

Robert J. Poor

In traditional histories of ancient China, antiquity was divided into an era of Three Sovereigns and Five Monarchs, followed by the time of the Three Dynasties — the Xia, Shang, and Zhou. The mythology of the earliest period is peopled by fabulous beings whose legendary accomplishments include the discovery of fire, the taming of the turbulent waters of the Chinese flood plain, and the invention of sophisticated arts such as weaving or writing — in short, the basic stuff of civilization. And most of the triumphs outlined in these myths did come to pass in that remote period of Chinese history, the era we understand as the Old, Middle, and New Stone Ages.

Of course, very little is known about the Old Stone Age in China. Judging by the stone tools that give the era its name, however, we see in China the same progress from the crude choppers of the Paleolithic era to the fine points and other specialized implements characteristic of the Neolithic age. In this respect, the Chinese experience falls within a universal framework. And, even though nothing like the elaborately painted caves at Altamira and Lascaux have as yet been discovered in East Asia, there are certain features of neolithic civilization in China that reveal a special local flavor. First and foremost is the prevalence of objects made of jade. Although jade, or more properly hardstones like jadeite or nephrite, is almost synonymous with China, the material was actually scarce there and was regularly imported from sources far removed from the places where it was worked and used. The most unusual jade artifact of the period is a flat disk with a hole in the center, called a *bi* (see cat. no. 57). Despite this object's simple shape, it must have been quite challenging to make. Some *bi* are very large, almost a foot in diameter, yet they are only a fraction of an inch thick. It is difficult to imagine how a slice of the extremely hard stone was removed from the original boulder and then ground to such a thin dimension without the use of modern tools or abrasives. It seems obvious that this object, which is found in grave deposits, must have had some special meaning. Whatever its enigmatic symbolism might have been, whether it referred to heaven, or woman, or the sun, the *bi* is the oldest and most enduring Chinese art motif. The small jade disk sold in jewelry stores today is the direct descendant of this ancient ornament.

Other kinds of jade artifacts, both ornaments and tools, are also found in tombs, but the most commonly discovered objects are pottery food vessels. The regular occurrence of food vessels among grave deposits is a second telltale trait of Chinese neolithic culture and, as with the use of jade, an early expression of an enduring cultural preference. For, as we shall see, the association of food vessels with burial rites is a prominent feature not just of the Neolithic era but of the Bronze Age as well. Moreover, the offering of food sacrifices in the worship of ancestors persists even in modern times. But whereas jade was difficult to obtain and hard to work, the stoneware pottery used throughout China in the Neolithic era did not require any exotic materials. Local soils, which provided the basic building material for the adobe-like dwellings common in late-neolithic sites such as the fifth-millennium settlement at Banbo, could also be used to make cooking pots, storage jars, or serving dishes. The neolithic potters exercised the greatest skill in preparing and manipulating the clay and most especially in firing the pots to give them durability. The differences in color, surface texture, or decoration from one vessel to another are functions of the process, time, or place of manufacture of the vessel and often of its intended use.

The neolithic pots that belong to the Smart Gallery, the earliest Chinese objects in the collection, illustrate various aspects of the type of pottery made during the period called Yangshao (cat. nos. 1, 2). The phase is named after the village where the European sinologist J. G. Anderson first discovered some broken pieces of painted pottery which led to the identification of a prehistoric era of Chinese civilization. Among neolithic pots, the rougher plain wares were strictly utilitarian. Very coarse wares were suitable for cooking; the particles of gravel left in the clay helped transmit heat. Somewhat smoother wares, made from more refined clay, were used for serving- and eating-bowls. The finest clay, purged of all extraneous particles, was used to make vessels for collecting and storing liquids. All three types of vessels were found in the tomb of an adolescent boy at the Banbo site. The pots found in this burial represent a kind of neolithic survival kit and, along with the jade ornaments the boy wore on his body, they are a partial indication of what being civilized meant in neolithic China.

Preparation of the raw material was only one step in the process of creating a neolithic pot. Once the clay was ready it was roughly shaped into coils or slabs and then hand built into an appropriate functional shape: water vessels had narrow mouths and grain vessels wide mouths, or vessels might be given legs to stand over a fire. All of this was done without the use of the high-speed potter's wheel, which is not necessarily the disadvantage we might imagine. Since the vessels were hand built, it was possible to break up the manufacturing process into stages. As a result, no shape is more complicated than its single parts. In the case of a typical open-mouth bowl, the lower body was fashioned as an open cone, a bowl without a bottom, which was then joined to another open cone of the same general shape by wetting the edges of the two pieces and sticking them together, a process called "luting" (see cat. no. 2). The potter could then reach into this open sphere and attach a preformed lip or mouth, using the same technique. Small handles, made of little rolls of clay, were passed through small cuts in the side walls and flattened on the inside like rivet heads. Lastly, the potter attached the preformed bottom by reaching in from above or, in the case of narrow-mouthed vessels, by smoothing the joint on the outside. Final touches included trimming any rough edges on the exterior and, if the vessel was to be painted, dipping the top half in a liquified mix of the same clay from which the pot was made, thus providing a smooth surface free of blemishes. This manufacturing process sounds very much like modern assembly-line procedures and, indeed, there is a great similarity between ancient and modern ways of fashioning objects. The obvious advantage of the technique was, and is still today, that no shape is more complicated than its separate parts. Yet there is a hidden feature of this process—a tendency towards standardization, a certain sameness among objects made in this way. But at its best, the process, which may be called sectionalism, results in a style of great clarity and architectonic vigor.

Something of the same disciplined vitality seen in the shapes of these vessels is evident in the painted designs that appear on the late-neolithic painted wares from cemeteries at the Banshan or Machang sites in western China (cat. nos. 1, 2). The decoration on these vessels is almost always limited to the upper half of the piece, a conventional arrangement characteristic of most examples of painted Yangshao pottery. As a result, the decoration seems consciously coordinated to the shape of the vessel in a way that enhances both of the key aspects of vessel design, the decoration itself and its relation to the structure of the piece. In the example of many of the funerary vessels from Banshan and Machang, the lower edge of the decorative field comes just below the broadest part of the pot, which is precisely where the handles are placed. Thus the overall shape, decor, and disposition of parts work in concert to form a harmonious whole. Even the simplest designs, incised lines, or impressed patterns conform to these design principles, which seems related to the more general notion of sectionalism that pervades the construction of these neolithic wares.

There is an invisible technical aspect of the Yangshao ceramic industry which is of great importance; it concerns the control of fire and the heat produced in the kiln. The walls of these vessels are usually thin and the pieces resound sharply when struck, both signs of high-temperature firing. The paint used to decorate these vessels had to be fired within a very narrow firing range: a kiln atmosphere that was either too hot or too cold resulted in murky colors in the decoration or in fugitive paint that flaked off. As the Yangshao potters developed ever better furnace technology and grew more skillful in the control of heat, they were approaching the outer edges of the soon-to-be-formed technology of the age of metals.

The next step towards the new age was taken in the last phase of Chinese neolithic culture, during the so-called Longshan or Longshanoid era. A very small percentage of the pottery vessels made at that time have a lustrous black finish and walls that are incredibly thin, sometimes no more than a few millimeters thick. Such thin walls are only possible because the clay was prepared with great care and the pots were thrown on a wheel. That does not entirely explain, however, the new repertoire of shapes that becomes common in this period. There are more vessels that look like beakers with long spouts, stem cups, sharp-rimmed compotes, or even ordinary cups which resemble the tin cup used today. The black color is the result of an innovative refinement in the firing process. By controlling the amount of oxygen in the firing atmosphere and introducing a fuel such as green wood that would give off a dense, black, carbon-rich smoke at the suitable moment, the potters were able to effect a transformation of the clay body. The same clay material that yielded the grayish-brown or red wares still common at this time could also produce a fabric that was black throughout and capable of being burnished to a lustrous surface.

This is an extraordinary accomplishment. The discovery of this firing technique borders on the wonders of alchemy. For now the decoration is not the result of applying pigment to the surface of a vessel and then firing it, but the natural outcome of the firing process itself. The metamorphosis from dull clay to glossy black fabric occurs within the furnace, unseen and unwitnessed. This is not so different from what happens in the transformation from stony ore to molten mineral and, finally, to a new material, metal. Perhaps it is not coincidental that Longshanoid vessels are so thin and sometimes resemble objects made of sheet metal. Although there is much disagreement about the origins of the Bronze Age in China, it is certain that the kiln masters of the Longshanoid culture were laying the groundwork for the bronze technology that was soon to come. Some would say that they might have been imitating vessels beaten from chunks of natural copper ore.[1] This is not an overly ambitious claim. For the famous black pottery represents but one of many great accomplishments achieved during the Longshanoid epoch, including what looks like the beginnings of a written language and the custom of consulting oracles by the practice of scapulamancy. These are but two of the myriad features that demonstrate the continuity of Chinese culture in this ancient period. The technology that produced the objects that give the Bronze Age its name is another. For it is clear that the basic procedures of the early metal workers are derived from the practices developed first by the kiln masters of the late-neolithic period. Indeed, it may have been the descendants of master potters who became the foundry masters in the new age.

A realignment of skilled ceramicists away from pottery enterprises to the newly emerging metal industry would help to explain the decline in distinguished examples of pottery in the early historic period. The real ceramic wonders of the early Bronze Age are the crucibles that held the molten metal as it came from the furnace, the furnace itself, and the exceptionally fine mold sections that determined the final appearance of a bronze object. One fragment of a high-fired pottery mold, the damaged survivor of the fury of the furnace, is now in the Smart Gallery collection (cat. no. 11). It is the physical reminder of the important role played by ceramicists in the Bronze Age—at least in its mature stage of development. For little is known about the production of the earliest bronze vessels, and they present a bit of a puzzle. That is because the earliest vessels yet discovered are cast quite thin, which is, surprisingly, much more difficult than casting a thick vessel. In fact, these early bronze pieces look like ungainly versions of the Longshan blackwares and, like the earlier pottery specimens, resemble vessels hammered from sheet metal. If they were not imitating some other material, then why was the metal cast so thin? Whatever the reason for casting the metal in this way, it is a considerable technical feat, all the more incongruous because of the awkward appearance of these vessels. The combination of a difficult technique, which makes sense only as an attempt to imitate some other form, and the suggestion of sheet-metal prototypes for the Longshanoid blackware of the preceding epoch, constitutes a powerful argument for a development as yet undocumented in China, but known from other parts of the world.

The ideal sequence in a universal history of metallurgy would begin with the chance discovery of an outcropping of native copper, which was then hammered into a desired shape. Presumably this accidental discovery of copper led to an active quest for ore deposits and the mining of the useful minerals. The next step represents a quantum leap in metal technology: different ores, usually copper and tin, were alloyed to form a material that does not occur in nature, namely, bronze. The assumption of a single common source for the first uses of metal is a natural conclusion of this theoretical scheme. It is true that metal was employed in other parts of the world thousands of years before it was produced in China. Yet, as I wrote some years ago, "priority does not prove contact," and there is little similarity between the metal objects cast in China and those made in the lands in the ancient Near East that supposedly provided knowledge of metallurgy to the Chinese.[2] Lacking any definitive evidence of contact between cultures, one is left with the argument of "ideational diffusion," the notion that the idea of the use of metal reached China from elsewhere and that this stimulus was enough to trigger the beginnings of the Bronze Age in China. It is equally difficult to prove or to refute this argument; scholarly opinion on the matter seems to change with every generation.[3] In my opinion, the early endeavors of Chinese bronze makers exemplify an emerging tradition, something that looks newly formed and not particularly dependent on the art or science of other cultures.

One of the most remarkable aspects of the Chinese Bronze Age is the extraordinary effort given to the manufacture of metal food vessels. Some of these vessels are huge, weighing many hundreds of pounds, and are often decorated in the most elaborate manner. It is difficult to imagine how one might cook meat in a pot that stands shoulder high, with side walls several inches thick, or why there is such an array of rich ornament on a utensil that would be exposed to fire and cooking smoke. These are clearly not just utilitarian pots; rather, these vessels had a ceremonial function. If they were used in any practical way at all it was as serving dishes in the periodic sacrifices to ancestors or other spirits. It may seem odd that ritual vessels of this sort were frequently deposited in graves. Yet, that is the case and the practice is understandable, for it is no more than an extension of the age-old custom of putting food vessels in the grave. In the Bronze Age, something beyond a sentimental concern for a loved one might have been intended: the deceased apparently retained the ability to affect the affairs of the living and an offering of this sort might have been meant to insure their good will.

Because of the excellence of Shang dynasty bronze castings, it was assumed, until recent times, that these bronzes had been made using the lost-wax technique.[4] This was the way in which the best work had always been done in other parts of the world, but it is not the case in China. Piece-molds for making vessels were found at Anyang, the site of the last capital of the Shang dynasty located in north-central China, as early as 1935, and many more mold fragments, as well as the ruins of some foundries, have been discovered since then. The European model for successful bronze technology simply did not prevail in China. This is not so unusual as it may seem, for there is an obvious element of continuity between the Chinese technique employing piece-molds to cast bronze vessels and the method of constructing neolithic pots in sections. There was a certain way of making a thing in ancient China and the method of manufacture did not change because of the introduction of some new material. A pot was still a pot, whether of clay or metal. The real puzzle is how the ancient bronze masters were able to attain such excellent results.

While there was continuity in technological procedures and in the inclusion of food vessels as a part of the customary grave furniture, there is something very unconventional about the decoration on the bronze vessels made in the latter years of the Shang dynasty. Animal decor, which occurred rarely in neolithic designs, became the favored theme in the art of the Shang, emerging within the first half of the dynasty. This is true whether an object was made of wood, stone, or metal and whether it was painted, carved, or cast. Why the change away from the geometric patterns so common during the many centuries of the Yangshao era? Certainly not because the people whom we call the Shang were some foreign ethnic group newly immigrated to China. All studies show that they were the same racial stock as their neolithic predecessors. The decoration on the earliest bronze vessels, which can be dated to the closing years of the Xia dynasty or the very beginning of the Shang dynasty, are made up of rudimentary geometric patterns which provided the raw material for the animal decor that was to come. It is possible to trace the steps that led to the birth of a coherent Shang artistic style.

One of the earliest vessels yet discovered, a wine beaker of the type called a *jue*, provides a crucial clue (it is the piece with the fantastically thin side walls previously described).[5] At the pinched waist of this vessel, there is a scarcely discernible row of small raised dots. The pattern is so undistinguished that it can be easily overlooked, but the disciplined arrangement of the dots within the raised borders of a rectangle exhibits an embryonic sense of order. This is a deliberate design, one that has been positioned at the critical juncture of the body where there is a sudden change in the contour of the vessel. Other early vessels employ simple geometric patterns placed with equal sensitivity to the harmonious relation of decoration and shape. These simple forms, small dots, zigzags, and the like, are the most basic elements of design which, to quote Susanne K. Langer's wonderful phrase, "are the motifs that motivate towards representation."[6] A decade ago, I described the process that led from geometric ornament to quasi-representational images on ancient Chinese bronzes: "In Shang art we do not deal with the usual process of abstraction, that is, moving from a realistic form to one which is less so, but rather with the creation of conventionalized forms which drew increasingly on visual phenomena, akin in an extended time frame to the creation of a structured motif from an aimless sketch on a scrap of paper."[7] In the case of Shang dynasty art, it appears that the juxtaposition of small dots or other circular forms had an obvious "symbolic potential" (Gombrich's term) and this simple device gave birth to a powerful convention.[8] Two dots could suggest eyes. The addition of a vertical bar between them provided the beginnings of a mask. Eventually a whole creature, conventionally called a *taotie*, or even whole groups of animals, usually of a fabulous kind, appeared on the surface of every object of any importance, including ritual bronzes. These are creatures drawn not from nature but from the rich resources of the human imagination.

The creation of the full-fledged animal conceit, the animal mask that appears on so many Shang bronzes, did not happen overnight. The first designs found on vessels representative of the Erlitou Culture or Erligang phase of Shang art consist of nothing more than a few thread- or ribbonlike lines arranged on either side of a pair of eyes. It is characteristic of vessels executed in this tenuous manner that the decoration is not simply ambiguous, it is also sparse. Only narrow bands of ornament are used, and they cover just a small percentage of the surface of the piece (cat. no. 12). Decoration of this meager kind usually occurs on vessels associated with type-sites that predate the settlement at Anyang. The few vessels of this sort found in the so-called royal cemetery at Anyang itself look decidedly old-fashioned next to those in the classic Anyang style (see cat. no. 14). These later Anyang pieces are richly ornamented, with decoration covering more of the surface of the vessel. Of course, the dominant theme is still the animal mask. But other kinds of creatures, some as fabulous as the *taotie* and a few that are more naturalistic, appear with increasing frequency in the Yin phase of Shang art. There were other significant changes in the manner of decorating vessels. Designs became easier to read, set against a network of thin, meanderlike lines which provided a background for the smooth forms of the animal motifs. One becomes more aware of the symbolic decoration, which was further emphasized by being cast in heavy relief (see cat. no. 13). The *taotie* and the dragon continued to lead the pack of mythological creatures that erupted from the imagination of the Shang bronze masters. These classic motifs were complemented by a contingent of animals that include the snake, bird, cicada, tortoise, rabbit, elephant, oxen, tiger, deer, owl, and, rarest of all, a few human beings (cat. no. 15).

The compositions on these bronzes, and on many of the jade or bone carvings (see cat. no. 46) and stone sculptures of the period, are as rich and varied as those produced many centuries later by the Amerindian Haida, which they greatly resemble.[9] But, unlike the Haida, no living informants survive to explain the ancient Shang traditions. Although our common experience of art teaches us that an object often has some special religious or political as well as aesthetic purpose, some would claim that Shang art is without content.[10] Yet, an appreciation of just the features of design does not explain an art, like that of the Shang, which resonates with a sense of meaning. We cannot know today the significance of those ancient symbols, but they must have had meaning to those who ornamented the surface of every Shang object of importance with animal conceits which I have described not as "pure designs but pure images."[11]

The late Ludwig Bachhofer summed up the historical process that culminated in the mature Shang bronze style: "Its types, its motives, its forms, and its means of representation were developed in many centuries of hard and incessant work."[12] Any assumption, however, that Shang art evolved at a steady pace, reaching its climax only near the end of the dynasty, is incorrect. The evidence from Tomb 5 at Anyang, identified with Lady Fu Hao, a consort of King Wu Ding, indicates that the major developments of Shang art had already been achieved by the early Anyang period, in the latter half of the thirteenth century B.C. Periodic renovation of existing styles led to the creation of distinctive artistic manners, which, though apparently incompatible stylistically, may have existed side by side. It is possible that the process of evolution was not gradual but episodic.[13]

What forces could have prompted these bursts of creativity? Bronze in antiquity, like jade, was more than just another material for making things. The plain bronze object which seems so common to us may have been quite precious when it was made; the artistic motifs that enhanced its appearance also contributed to its meaning. The finished piece had a certain mystique stemming from the human and material resources that went into its manufacture and from the political authority that commanded its production. Surely, a mighty king like Wu Ding, who was active in extending the power of the Shang, was not unaware of the propaganda potential of art and its unique ability to appeal to several levels of the imagination. It is probably no coincidence that art and writing blossomed during his reign. The hundreds of vessels found in the tomb of Fu Hao are as much an expression of power as of reverence. Wu Ding must have recognized this, for there was an artistic explosion during his reign that was unparalleled in all of Shang history. Indeed, it looks as though the enormous production of vessels made in that time exhausted Shang resources. The vessels made in the aftermath are often just attenuated versions of mid-Shang styles or archaistic pieces which may represent efforts to perpetuate the ancient styles. The circle had closed on the first great cycle of Chinese bronze-age art.

NOTES

1. The debate regarding a wrought-metal phase of Chinese culture, preceding the casting of metal, is far from over. The so-called "universal" patterns of development, which form the theoretical basis for assuming such a period of metalworking in China, are derived from Western-oriented evidence. Yet, the Chinese did not always follow the same line of development as the West. In the field of metallurgy, we need only comment on the history of iron technology. The Chinese reversed the sequence of forging iron and then casting it. They were mass producing cast-iron objects centuries before this was done anywhere else in the world. However, there is still the matter of the visual evidence. The extraordinary thinness of some Longshan wares and the occurrence of ornaments that look like rivets placed exactly where one would expect to find this kind of fastener on metal vessels suggest the imitation of wrought-metal objects. Within the Bronze Age, the rolled lips or crimped rims on some very early cast vessels seem related to a hand-wrought tradition rather than to piece-mold casting. The most recent, and most adamant rebuttal of the wrought-metal argument came from Noel Barnard, "Further Evidence to Support the Hypothesis of Indigenous Origins of Metallurgy in Ancient China," in *The Origins of Chinese Civilization*, ed. David N. Keightley (Berkeley, Calif., Los Angeles, and London: University of California Press, 1983), 237–278; for further discussion, see Ursula Martius Franklin, "On Bronze and Other Metals in Early China," in the same volume, 279–296.

2. Robert J. Poor, *Ancient Chinese Bronzes* (New York: Intercultural Arts, 1968), 1.

3. Although metal was used at an earlier date in the ancient Near East than in China, there is no real evidence of the interchange of ideas or artifacts between these two regions. The more compelling comparisons, between Chinese chariot technology or weapons and those made in areas to the northwest, which illustrate later influences on Chinese culture, do not resolve the question of the origins of metallurgy in China. For an incisive summary of the evidence regarding the early use of copper and bronze-casting in general in China see Ma Chengyuan, "The Splendor of Ancient Chinese Bronzes," in Wen Fong, ed., *The Great Bronze Age of China: An Exhibition from the People's Republic of China* (exh. cat.) (New York: Metropolitan Museum of Art, 1980), 1–3; see also Ma Chengyuan, *Ancient Chinese Bronzes*, ed. Hsio-yen Shih (Hong Kong, Oxford, and New York: Oxford University Press, 1986), 1–5. A classic study of Chinese weaponry with emphasis on foreign connections remains Max Loehr, *Chinese Bronze Age Weapons: The Werner Jannings Collection in the Chinese National Palace Museum, Peking* (Ann Arbor, Mich.: University of Michigan Press, 1956). For a comprehensive discussion of the chariot and Western prototypes of the Chinese model, see Edward L. Shaughnessy, "Historical Perspectives on the Introduction of the Chariot into China," *Harvard Journal of Asiatic Studies* 48, no. 1 (June 1988): 189–238.

4. See below, cat. no. 15, n. 1.

5. Robert W. Bagley, "The Beginnings of the Bronze Age: The Erlitou Culture Period," in Wen Fong, ed., *Great Bronze Age*, 74, figs. 17–18, pl. 1, provides a very fine photograph of the early *jue* from Erlitou.

6. Susanne K. Langer, *Feeling and Form* (New York: Charles Scribner's Sons, 1953), 69.

7. Poor, *Ancient Chinese Bronzes, Ceramics and Jade in the Collection of the Honolulu Academy of Arts* (Honolulu: Honolulu Academy of Arts, 1979), 16.

8. Ernst H. Gombrich, *The Sense of Order* (Oxford: Phaidon Press, 1979), 243–247.

9. See Poor, "The Master of the 'Metropolis'-Emblem Gu," *Archives of Asian Art* 41 (1988): 77, n. 21, wherein I discuss the use of templates by the Haida people to construct their traditional designs. In 1936, Herrlee Glessner Creel noted important structural similarities between Northwest Coast Indian art and that of the Shang. Specifically, he commented on "the manner in which animals are combined; . . . the tendency to use isolated eyes as decorative motifs," and "the technique of representing an animal as if it were split and laid flat in two joined halves. . . ." See Creel, *The Birth of China* (New York: Frederick Ungar Publishing Co., 1964), 122.

10. Loehr, *Ritual Vessels of Bronze Age China* (exh. cat.) (New York: Asia Society, 1968), 12–13, and again in an unpublished paper delivered on the occasion of *The Great Bronze Age of China* exhibition at the Metropolitan Museum of Art in New York in 1980, questioned the role of content in Shang decor, which he saw rather as pure design. Bagley, a former student of Loehr, restated the position in the catalogue to that exhibition, *Great Bronze Age*, 101. An alternative view was expressed by Ma Chengyuan in an introductory chapter of the same catalogue, "Splendor of Chinese Bronzes," 6, and finally, Wen Fong, editor of the catalogue, provided a masterly discussion of these and other methodological issues in "The Study of Chinese Bronze Age Arts: Methods and Approaches," 28–29.

11. Poor, *Honolulu Academy*, 16.

12. Ludwig Bachhofer, *A Short History of Chinese Art* (New York: Pantheon, 1946), 35.

13. I recently discussed these issues in "An Episodic Mode of Evolution," a paper delivered to the American Oriental Society, New Orleans, March 1989.

SHANG CEREMONIAL BRONZES AND THEIR DECOR

Harrie A. Vanderstappen

The study of ancient China has been revolutionized in recent decades by excavations uncovering artifacts, inscriptions, city walls, foundations, and other documents and cultural relics. Numerous publications have appeared both in China and the West covering various aspects of this massive information on early Chinese society and its complex cultural traditions. It seems almost quaint to think of the time some thirty years ago when scholars, blissfully unaware of what was to come, were publishing what then seemed the last word on the arts of ancient China. Yet it is worth reflecting on some of those writings, despite the vast progress that has been made. We are still struggling with vocabulary which was then and is now inadequate to deal with the information in front of us.

I specifically refer to the writings on the imagery of Chinese ceremonial bronze vessels. In this introduction, I propose some ways of looking at this imagery which have suggested themselves to me during thirty years of teaching at the University of Chicago. These observations were sparked by my interest in the fascinating altercation between image making and references to reality on the one hand, and the tenacity and discrete changes in the patterns dominating this imagery on the other.

A generation of scholarship has passed since Bernhard Karlgren published his studies on the grammar of the decor on Chinese ceremonial bronzes. He once characterized that decor as a "curious mechanization" with a tendency to fall into one of those clichés that became standard "word forms," the *formantia* of early bronze decor.[1] In the early 1950s, he listed some of these clichés as C, T, and S spirals, and illustrated thirteen examples of what he called the conventional cliché of the quill.[2] No description can really cover all these variants, but their common characteristics are a single or double spiral and some form of a triangle. In one of his last publications, in 1959, Karlgren concluded that "late-Yin [Shang] art was not the product of free artistic, creative power, it was already sophisticated and conventionalized in an amazing degree. The artist was severely bound by all kinds of conventional norms and rules."[3]

Karlgren arrived at this observation through his emphasis on statistical analysis. Using *ding* and *liding* vessels[4] for his investigations, he noted that certain elements of the decor always went together, and that these did not mix with other similar sets. Moreover, he believed he had proven "that the great bronze art of late Yin (and early Chou [Zhou]) was not, after some simple and primitive antecedents, a first and great efflorescence, in which the artists worked with a full freedom, creating ever new types and motifs, unhampered by rules and conventions." On the contrary, he characterized the art as bound by a "straightjacket of scores of conventional rules which restricted the latitude of variation in a most astounding way."[5] And again he emphasized that this highly sophisticated art required richly equipped, dynamic antecedents. Instead of the "primitive types like those of Cheng-chou [Zhengzhou]," he postulated a freer high bronze art of vessel types and motifs not bound by conventional rules. He ended with a rhetorical question: Are these types of high bronze art vessels still to be found, "at present buried many fathoms deep under the silt in the vicinity of the Yellow River?"[6]

One senses an emotional tone in Karlgren's conclusions, drawn after a lifelong study of early Chinese language, culture, and art. In part at least, this tone may have been a reaction to Max Loehr's publication of the sequence of five bronze-age styles several years earlier.[7] Karlgren quoted Loehr's contention that "a style cannot be approached by way of statistics; large numbers cannot tell us more about a style than does *one* example, thoroughly analyzed and understood."[8] Finding this a "foolish pronouncement," Karlgren referred to Loehr in a mocking tone as "a confident art historian [who] has even seen fit to establish six (6!) successive 'styles' in An-yang."[9] Loehr indeed viewed the development of bronze decor in ancient China in sequential stages: from decorative patterns, barely if at all connected with identifiable imagery, he saw a gradual separation between, on the one hand, elements such as eyes and features which can be linked to masks and theriomorphic body forms, and, on the other hand, variously patterned backgrounds for these animal motifs. The end result, according to Loehr's formulation, is an emergence of plastic theriomorphic elements from a graphically patterned background.

More than forty years ago, in a study of early Chinese ceremonial vessels in clay and bronze, Ludwig Bachhofer had introduced the white clay amphora of the Freer Gallery with the observation that "at this time the friezes around the neck, shoulders and the foot were filled with a decor of a radically different, namely, a theriomorphous character."[10] He called this stage the third in his scheme of four main phases in a changing system of decor. The two earlier stages he described as moving from angular volutes and meanders, evenly covering the vessel in a restless manner, to large continuous patterns of meanders and volutes folding into each other in a complicated way. The T, with the ends of the crossbar sharply bent, is part of this second stage. Finally, Bachhofer described the fourth stage in which the smooth bands of decoration are part of theriomorphous forms around one or two eyes. Bachhofer set these four groups cautiously apart from each other by small but significant variations in what he considered a progressive development of decor on white pottery.[11]

Loehr applied the principles of Bachhofer's developmental scheme for clay vessels in a modified form to bronze vessels, identifying a sequence of five styles of decor.[12] This system has gained wide acceptance,[13] but, even granting overlaps and progressive and retrogressive steps in the process, Loehr's sequence is seriously challenged by the contents of Tomb 5 of Fu Hao.[14] Among the many bronze vessels found in the tomb, there is clear evidence establishing the contemporaneity of Loehr's styles III through V—instead of a chronological developmental sequence.[15] The sequences suggested by Virginia Kane, though she correctly assumed that relief style (uninscribed) appeared in Wu Ding's times, would also need readjustment.[16] If one follows the stages of development suggested by Thorp in accordance with the sequence devised by the Anyang Work Team, Tomb 5 should then be placed within the Yinxu II period, roughly 1200–1150 B.C.[17] Following the principles for an orderly transition of style sequences suggested by Loehr, we would expect to find vessels with decor that prepare for those found in Tomb 5. That is a very difficult proposition.

Earlier, in a lengthy and very informative discussion of various aspects of the development of Shang culture and its relationship to ritual vessels, Robert L. Thorp addressed this problem.[18] He suggested a transitional phase between the Zhengzhou finds and those of Tomb 5, thereby trying to ease the discomfort of the Tomb 5 "culture shock." Still, it remains true that styles III through V appear together at the time of Tomb 5 and this proves that the original meaning of Loehr's sequence is not viable. A chronological development is essential in Loehr's arguments and if that is absent in categories III through V, then his individual categories are reduced to an arbitrary list of coexistent patterns. Attempts by various authors, mentioned above, to reconcile the bronze vessels of Tomb 5 with the sequence of styles suggested by Loehr do justice neither to Chinese bronze decor in the early twelfth century B.C. nor to Loehr's own arguments which he presented in 1953.

For the earliest phases in the development of bronze decor, one can see that Loehr's observations have to some degree maintained a broad validity. He carefully observed the patterns of the decor and kept his conclusions clearly within the boundaries of the evidence he gathered. He limited the ideas of a sequential development strictly to degrees of contrast between what he called theriomorphic indications and patterns without reference to images, eventually separating the theriomorph from a patterned background. But even in his style V, in which theriomorphic parts are plastically set off from their background, he scrupulously avoids the words "realism" or "real animal." Still, in the gradual development from the unspecifiable to the clear separation between background and vaguely identifiable nature image, there is an implied growth from the inanimate to something that exhibits close parallels with an observed living reality. How are we then to identify the imagery on Chinese ritual bronzes? This question inevitably arises and it has to do with the problem of when to identify something as eye or mask and body and eventually as bird, cicada, serpent, etc.[19] All problems one faces by the insistence on Loehr's sequence of styles arise from the presumption—albeit unspoken—that things progress towards clarity, readability, and greater readiness for an identity. Loehr's terminology, however, is very cautious and, as I mentioned earlier, he does not in any way suggest that Shang artists were moving towards the portrayal of a physical world.

The importance of his system lies in the realization, similar to Bachhofer's with regard to pottery, that patterns are the true bearers of the world of decor in Chinese bronzes. In the next few pages, I want to show that these patterns were not only the carriers of ornament in early bronze vessel decor, but that they remain the crucial language of communication throughout Shang and Western Zhou. In fact, with modifications, they predominate into the middle of the first millennium B.C. I think that the patterns were, in other words, not only the principal vehicle of meaningful ritual communication, they also had primacy over all other aspects of the decor, including all manner of imagery. I do not look for the differentiation between patterns and image and thereby slowly break down the ritual of the pattern in favor of a study of recognizable imagery. Instead, I plan to show some of the ways in which the pattern itself develops and asserts its consistent authority.

If this sounds as if I am returning to the ideas of Karlgren, it is only partially true. Karlgren never believed in the autonomy of "word forms" and *formantia*; he considered these to be derived from earlier representational forms. Loehr went the opposite way, going from pattern to readable image. But there is some truth in what Karlgren observed about complete "restrictive rules" and an "achieved art perfected in all its conventions."[20] Homogeneity in the art of the bronze maker has also been noted, of course, by many others.[21] It is remarkable to see how difficult it is within this seeming homogeneity to distinguish a group of vessels different from all others and to discover that the difference has to be expressed in fractions of millimeters. Neverthe-

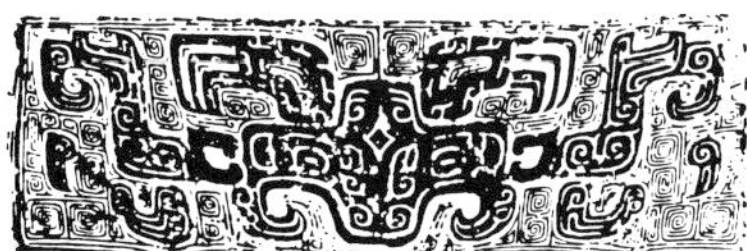

Fig. 1. *Ding* vessel, detail.
Fu Hao tomb, no. 804.

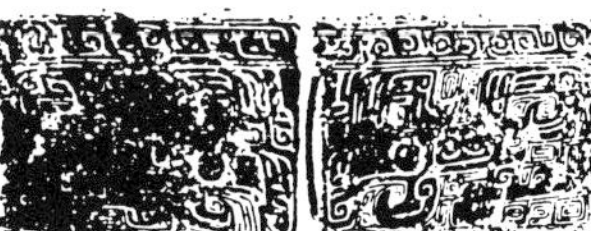

Fig. 2. *Gui* vessel, detail.
Fu Hao tomb, no. 833.

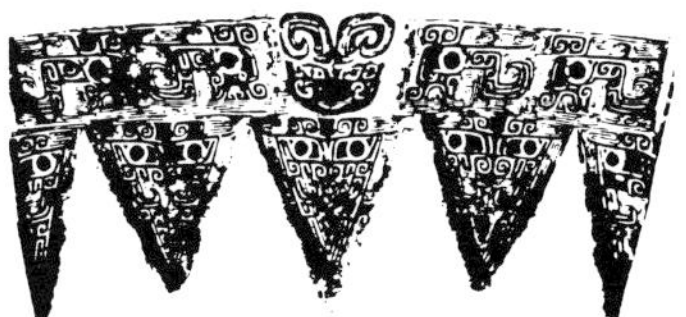

Fig. 3. *Gui* vessel, detail.
Fu Hao tomb, no. 848.

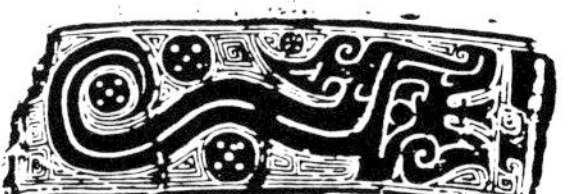

Fig. 4. *Xian* vessel, detail.
Fu Hao tomb, no. 769.

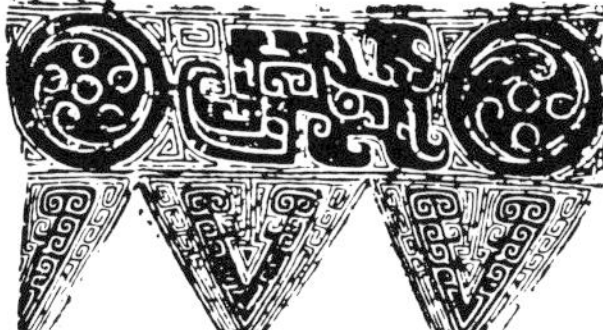

Fig. 5. *Xian* vessel, detail.
Fu Hao tomb, no. 790.

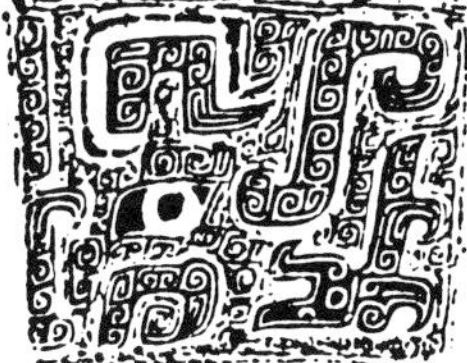

Fig. 6. *Jia* vessel, detail.
Fu Hao tomb, no. 781.

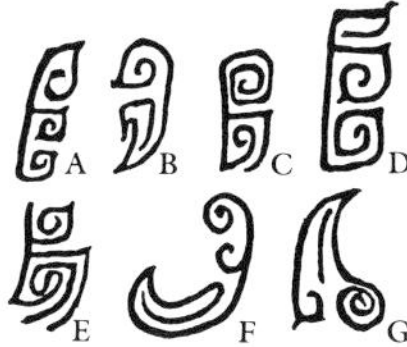

Fig. 7. Tracings by the author from the decor of figure 6.

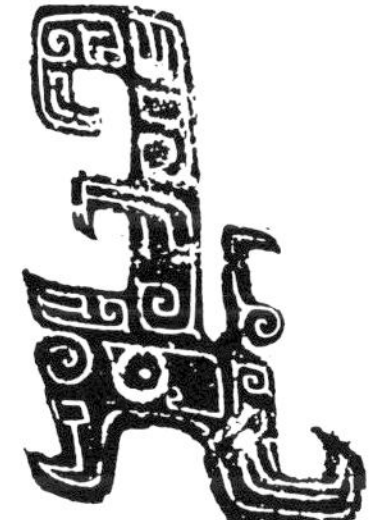

Fig. 8. *Pou* vessel, detail.
Fu Hao tomb, no. 778.

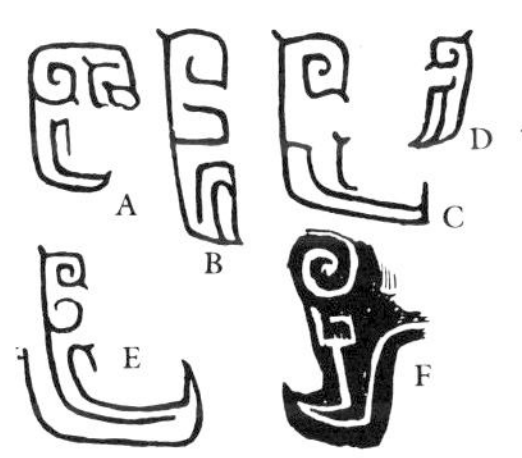

Fig. 9. Tracings by the author from the decor of figure 8.

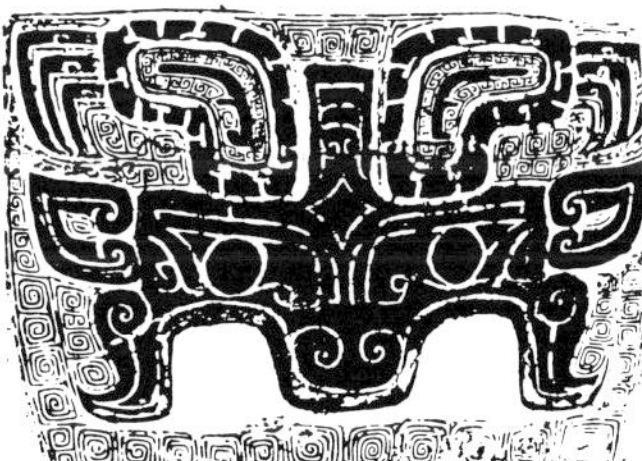

Fig. 10. *Ou fang yi* vessel, detail.
Fu Hao tomb, no. 791.

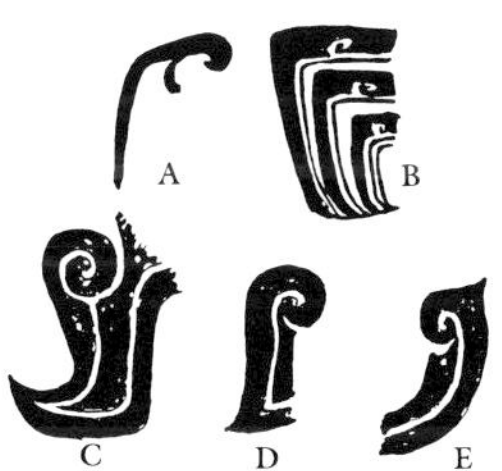

Fig. 11. Tracings by the author from the decor of figure 10.

less, in an excellent paper, Robert Poor has successfully established a group of vessels that show a very slight but consistent variant from all others.[22] His analysis demonstrates the tenacity of certain patterns and the fixed principles underlying these patterns; it also suggests that changes should occur only in minimal steps, and that what appears to be a change may not be significant at all but simply a modification in the same pattern. There is a gritty kind of persistence in the way in which the decor on ritual bronzes is executed. All manner of materials—from bronze, to bone, jade, and stone—is subject to the same regulated pictorial devices. This is not to say that the shapes of vessels, their usage and grouping into functional assemblages,[23] their methods of casting and place of origin, and especially their inscriptions, are not obviously of major importance. It nevertheless remains true that all vessels, irrespective of shape, provenance, and other matters of documentary interest, share a basic identity of decor. It is on this premise that the following remarks are made.

I wish to begin with the graphic aspect of the decor. Instead of following the usual terminology, I treat all decor as basically graphic; that is, I pay no attention to style differentiations based exclusively on distinctions between decor that is level with the body of the vessel and that which is raised from the body in plastic layers. Almost from the beginning, these two modes of decor appear together on bronze vessels. The knobs, for example, identified as eyes, appear as raised decor in very early vessels which are otherwise in the level mode. Entire masks in raised decor on handles, shoulders, and sometimes in the friezes, freely coexist in early and later vessels with level decor on the rest of the vessel.

My main reason, however, for treating all decor as graphic lies in the structural similarities of all decor whether in the level or raised mode. To demonstrate this similarity, I refer to the decor of several vessels from the Fu Hao tomb, illustrated in rubbings shown in figures 1 through 11. Among these, only figures 2 through 5 and figure 8 are taken from decor level with the wall of the vessel. All others are from decor applied, at least in part, in layers of relief. In every instance, the decor is characterized by patterns combining spirals with triangles, most commonly referred to as quills, in conjunction with hooks and curls, all in various degrees of size and density of application. From the overall appearance it is clear that this decor does not alter its character if it is applied on various layers of relief. To demonstrate this essential point further, I am illustrating three pairs of decor in figures 6 through 11. Figures 7, 9, and 11 are tracings of parts of the motifs shown in figures 6, 8, and 10. In doing this, I observe that all parts that make up the motif in figure 7 are variants of the same combination of spirals and triangles in figure 9. These may be shown turning left or right, they may extend, elongate, or sometimes duplicate a part, but they all adhere strictly to the same system of symbols. Those in 7C and 7E are variants from parts in the decor that do not belong to the theri-

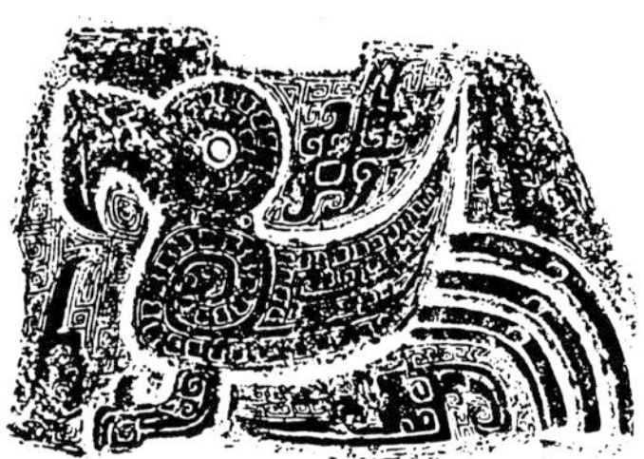

Fig. 12. *Ou fang yi* vessel, detail. Fu Hao tomb, no. 791.

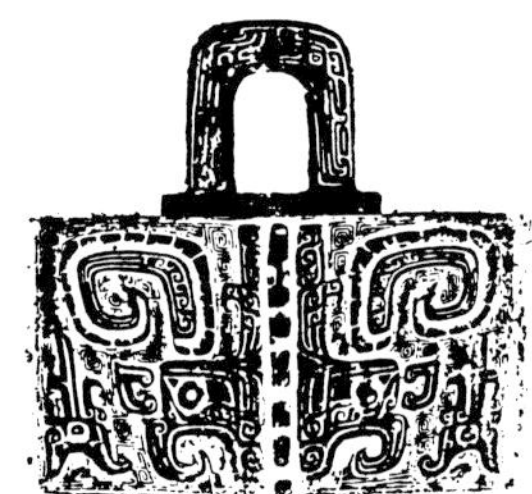

Fig. 13. Square *ding* vessel, detail. Fu Hao tomb, no. 813.

omorphic patterns. Even though figures 6 and 8 seem so different in appearance on the bronzes and in the rubbings, it is essential to realize that the vocabulary of their constituents is identical; the difference is only a result of a change from density and contraction of graphics to a more broadly spaced modality. It is a matter of slower or faster pace within the same rhythmic proportions.

In all these illustrations, we find the same patterns, proportions, manipulations of standard parts of the image, and graphic texture. This leaves little room for interpretation other than a conclusion that these examples of bronze decor share a close-knit family origin. They are variants of each other and should be treated not as steps indicating a change in style over time, but simply as modifications of the same visual components. This analysis is not only true of figures 6 and 8 but extends equally to figure 10, though this image may seem even more different than were the preceding examples. The patterns can appear in black on white as well as in white on black (from engraved part to surface and vice versa.) That means that figure 11E is but a very slight variant of, for instance, figure 7B, and the same is true for figures 11A and 7F. These same patterns in different functions can be seen in the forehead shield in figure 13. Moreover, only a small change leads from figures 11A and 7F to 11B and to the tail of the bird image in figure 12. Similarly, figure 11C is a close parallel to 9F, and they are essentially the same as the linear counterpart in 7G and but a variation of 7B. In addition, it should be noted that level and raised modes are freely mixed in these illustrations.

The patterns are consistent in all these details (figs. 1 through 13) from vessels found in the Fu Hao tomb. A glance at the tail-body part of the *taotie* (dragon or ogre mask) in figure 1 or its horn and leg(?) shows that they derive from the same visual vocabulary as those shown in the tracings. The leg of the bird image is made up of the same configuration and the head of the bird is but a variant of the mouth corners shown in figures 9F and 11C. The same comments can be made about the images in figures 3 through 5. The main reason for all this attention to detail and somewhat tedious and repetitious presentation is to establish reasons for calling all this decor graphic. Whether or not the patterns appear level with the surface of the vessel or in raised bands, the decor is linear and dimensionally the same throughout.

To illustrate the dominance and longevity in bronze vessel decor of these graphic patterns, I have chosen twenty-six rubbings of details of Shang and Zhou decor, figures 14 through 39. The captions indicate their varied provenance and date. All manner of vessel and variety of decor is represented. A visual cross reference between these illustrations and those of the Fu Hao tomb in figures 1 through 11 confirms the consistency of the patterns from the time of Erligang till well into and beyond the middle of the first millennium B.C.

In figures 14 through 27, fourteen variations of a spiral-triangle combination appear in a most vigorous and ingenious uniformity. The pattern of figure 14 holds the key to nearly all subsequent image-making vocabulary.[24] This pattern reads equally well in black or white (surface and groove or ridge). The sequences of spirals and pointed angles (triangles) repeat and alternate with each other, advancing and returning with continued surprises in density and rhythmic variations. It is, in other words, a condensed visual resource for an ever-renewable articulation of the realities of the world of powers that make up early Chinese ritual imagery.

Its startling counterpart in figure 15 survives in Western Zhou. In this much later version, the parts are separate, they have an even and more readily repeatable identity. They subdivide into smaller elements, some of which belong to a main body while others are relegated to frillings of adjunct hooks and curls. Generally, the pattern appears in the simplest permutations, illustrated in figures 16, 18, and 19, and is a representative form in early Zhou times. An early version from Erligang is portrayed in figure 17. Adaptations of the same pattern can be seen in figures 20 through 27. Figure 20 is from Erligang; figure 21, a Western Zhou derivation. Figures 22 and 23 are from the upper part of an early Western Zhou mask and a Shang Yinxu II mask respectively. Figure 26 is a Western Zhou bird claw form, which I have set off against its suggested source and parallels in figures 25 and 27 from Erligang and figure 24 from Shang Yinxu II.

The point to be made is how the basic original idea of a graph, complex as it may seem especially in its richer early appearances, survives throughout Shang and well into Zhou times. It does not depend on the imagery identified as *taotie*, bird, *kui*-dragon, cicada, etc., which comes and goes during that same period. Instead, the pattern seems to assume the role of an anonymous life force, constantly ready to accommodate and give new vitality to the images that emerge.

Additional suggestions for graphic predominance of decor might be made from the illustrations in figures 28 through 39, which indicate how a single form of spiral-triangle combination generates a sequence of animal-mask mouth patterns from Erligang times into the Warring States period. Again, in this choice I have not differentiated between level and raised decor. A survey of these illustrations shows how the same pattern serves for mouth, beak, or combination mouth corner, nose, snout, or trunk. These few select examples can be multiplied in innumerable combinations as rich and varied and as pervasive

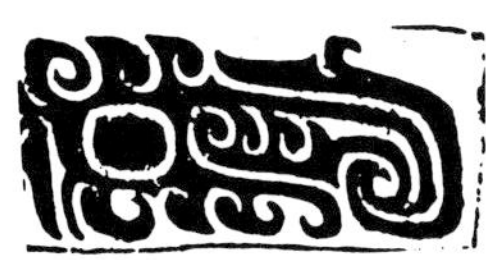
Fig. 14. *Jia* vessel, detail. Erligang.

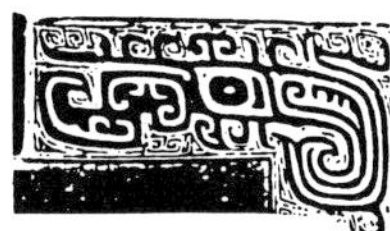
Fig. 15. *Li fang ding* vessel, detail. Western Zhou.

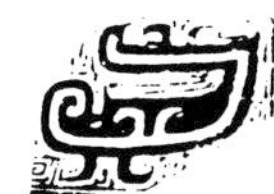
Fig. 16. *Li fang ding* vessel, detail. Western Zhou.

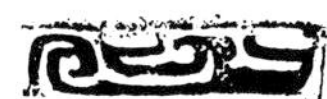
Fig. 17. *Ding* vessel, detail. Erligang.

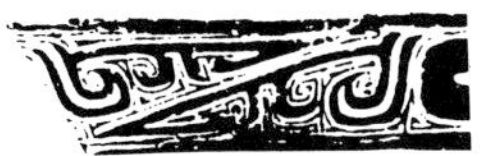
Fig. 18. *Li fang ding* vessel, detail. Western Zhou.

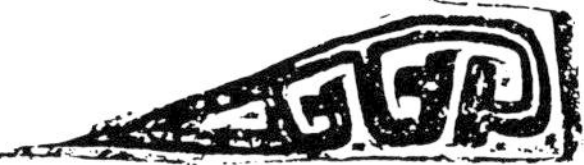
Fig. 19. *Li* vessel, detail. Late Western Zhou, ninth century B.C.

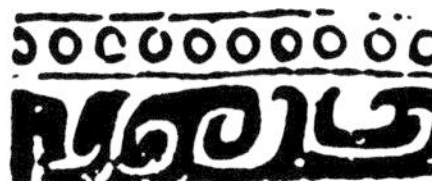
Fig. 20. *Jia* vessel, detail. Erligang.

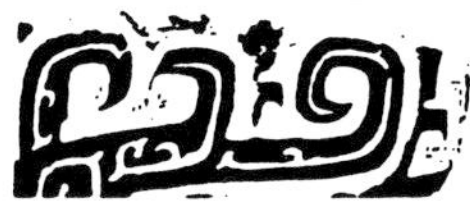
Fig. 21. *Guang* vessel, detail. Western Zhou, circa 970 B.C.

Fig. 22. *Bo*-type bell, detail. Late Western Zhou, ninth century B.C.

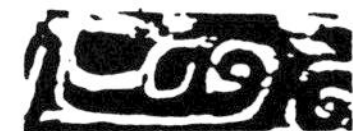
Fig. 23. *Li* vessel, detail. Erligang.

Fig. 24. *Zun* vessel, detail. Yinxu II.

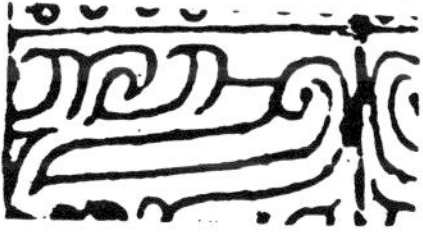
Fig. 25. *Jia* vessel, detail. Erligang.

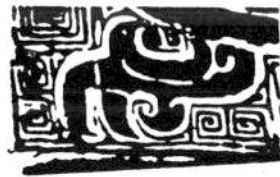
Fig. 26. *You* vessel, detail. Early Western Zhou, tenth century B.C.

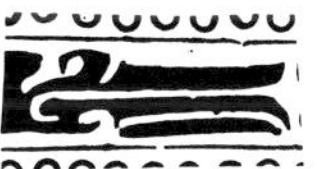
Fig. 27. *Li* vessel, detail. Erligang.

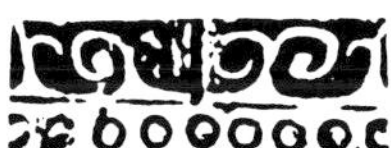
Fig. 28. *Jia* vessel, detail. Erligang.

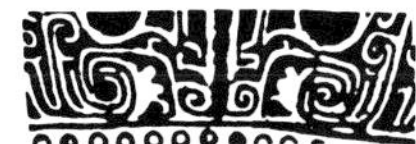
Fig. 29. *Zun* vessel, detail. Yinxu II.

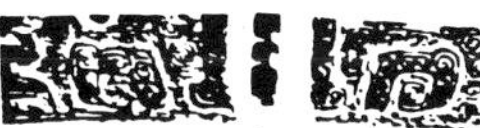
Fig. 30. *Jia* vessel, detail. Fu Hao tomb, no. 781.

Fig. 31. *Hou tu mu jia* vessel, detail. Fu Hao tomb, no. 857.

Fig. 32. *Gui* vessel, detail. Xiaotun, Tomb 82 M1. Yinxu IV.

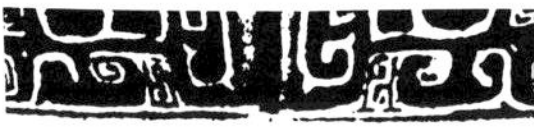
Fig. 33. *Fuyi ding* vessel, detail. Tomb GM284. Yinxu III-IV.

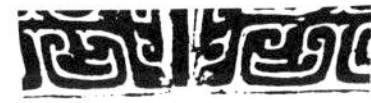
Fig. 34. *Ding* vessel, detail. Early Western Zhou.

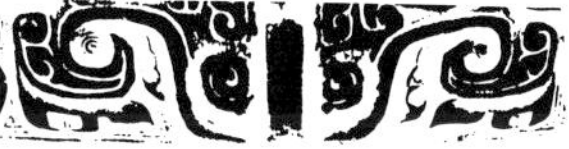
Fig. 35. *Guang* vessel, detail. Early Western Zhou, circa 970 B.C.

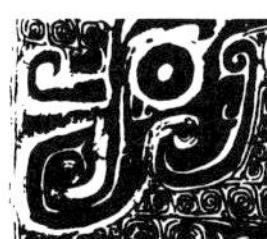
Fig. 36. *Gui* vessel, detail. Early Western Zhou, tenth century B.C.

Fig. 37. *You* vessel, detail. Tomb HGH10. Yinxu IV.

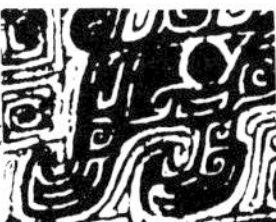
Fig. 38. *Hu* vessel, detail. Fu Hao tomb, no. 863. Yinxu II.

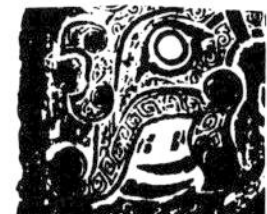
Fig. 39. *Ge* halberd, detail. Circa 300 B.C.

as the pattern itself.[25] Illustrated in figures 28 through 31 are samples from Erligang and from the Fu Hao tomb, therefore dating to Shang Yinxu II or earlier. Figure 32, in level decor except for knobs and handles, is later, from Yinxu IV,[26] and is seemingly problematic; but a comparison with figure 34 of early Western Zhou shows a very similar spacing in the graphics, and the date is confirmed by its provenance. Figure 33 is from tomb GM284, similar to tomb GM1573 and therefore dated to Yinxu III–IV. In turn, figures 33 and 34 are comparable to figure 37, from tomb HGH10 with a suggested date to Yinxu IV. The liveliest execution of the four heads in figures 36 through 39 is that in figure 38, which comes from the Fu Hao tomb. The densely dynamic interactions and clear articulation of parts is typical of this stage of the decor, whereas the widely spaced and sweeping elegance of patterns in figures 36 and 37 is typical of late Yin style forms. The components of the visual vocabulary in these later images exhibit a greater self-emphasis, weakening their service to dynamic imagery. In the last example, figure 39, there is a tendency to repeat even spaces and nearly identical spirals and comma (spiral-triangle) patterns, resembling a maze used in mid-Zhou

Fig. 40. *Jia* vessel, detail.
Erligang.

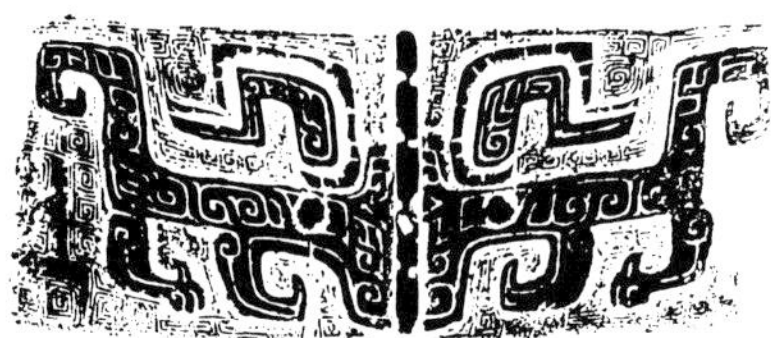

Fig. 41. *Ding* vessel, detail.
Fu Hao tomb, no. 804.

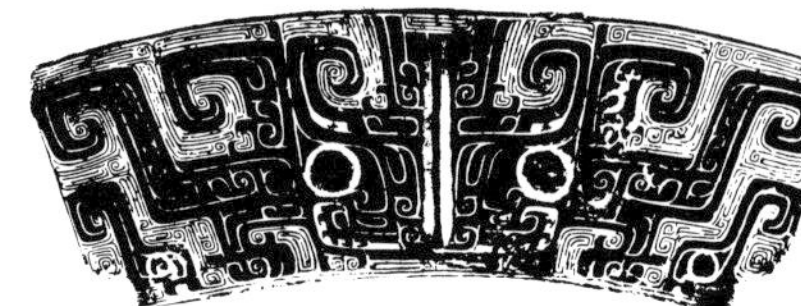

Fig. 42. *Xian hu* vessel, detail.
Yinxu II-III.

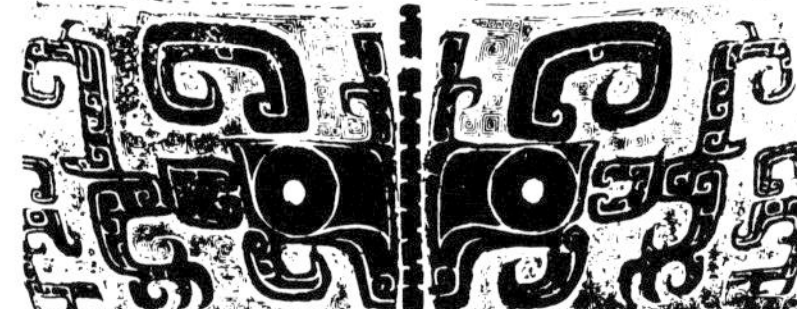

Fig. 43. *You* vessel, detail.
Yinxu IV.

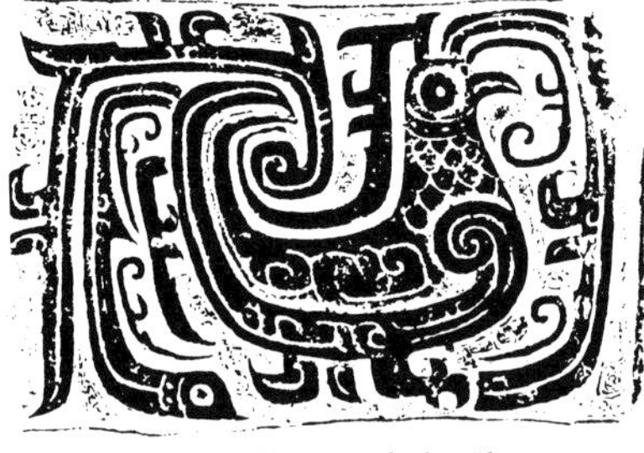

Fig. 45. *Gui* vessel, detail.
Early tenth century B.C.

Fig. 46. *Gui* vessel, detail.
Early tenth century B.C.

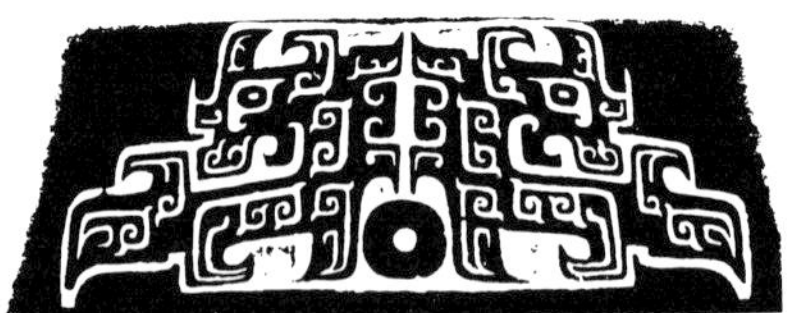

Fig. 44. *Zhong* bell, detail.
Fifth century B.C.

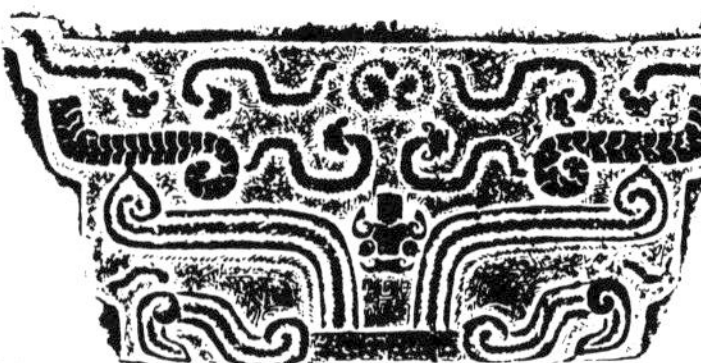

Fig. 47. *Zhong* bell, detail.
Fifth century B.C.

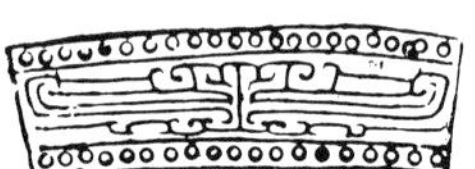

Fig. 48. *Jue* vessel, detail.
Erligang.

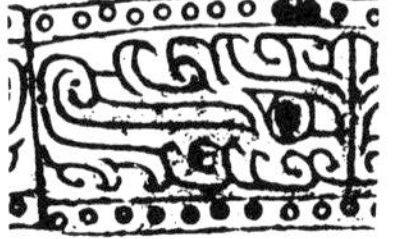

Fig. 49. *Jue* vessel, detail.
Erligang.

times and clearly marked as the last resolution of this pattern in its long history.

I realize that this is a small sampling, but such an analysis can be extended to innumerable examples, always bringing the same results. From these comparisons and interpretations, I reiterate that all this decor is graphic. Next, I conclude that the patterns are not only variants of a rather limited basic pictorial vocabulary but that they are the primary feature of all this decor, dominating all other considerations. In order further to substantiate this conclusion, I have gathered some additional examples in figures 40 through 49. These ten images are broadly representative of part of the standard repertoire of Shang and Zhou bronze decor, covering a period of about a thousand years, from the fifteenth or fourteenth century B.C. till about the middle of the first millennium B.C. Among these illustrations, some four separate groupings and transitions can be observed. The first group includes the bands of decor in figure 40 and in the double-image details in figures 48 and 49. All three are products of the Erligang phase of Shang bronze decor, and are characterized by symmetrically arranged bands, spirals, and triangular extensions on either side of a central axis. The symmetry extends from this mirror reflection between left and right to the echo of upper and lower edges on either side of the central bands.

At this point, questions of identification can be raised. Is it legitimate to call figures 40 and 49 masks? And what about figure 48? I have already committed myself in earlier comments on figures 28 and 29, and I would follow the same principle in these instances. Thus I would at least identify the central parts of the two with eyes as masks, since they have so much in common with the mask images normally identified as *taotie*. Figure 48, however, remains ambiguous because of the absence of anything that can be identified as eyes. Still, this figure has the same intentional symmetry and directions, and obviously is in the same framework as its companions with eyes. There are other difficulties with the reading of these images. Nothing is accidental in any of these representations. Every line and curve is precisely intended to be in its specific place; there are no uncertainties in the execution. Is there then an ambivalence towards meaning? With the center so easily recognized and the left and right seemingly eluding recognition, one is tempted to place the image in a double mode of existence—one mode leading to analogy with things we know, the other referring to an unquestioned existence for which we have no equivalent experience.

Another point that has sometimes given cause to further differentiation between 40 and 48 is that one reads black (surface) and the other as line (groove or ridge). On several occasions this question has already been mentioned and, again, I think that it is artificial to suggest differences between a positive and negative image, or whatever name one attaches to it, since both are structured from identical patterns. Positive and negative imagery can occur on the same vessel, and I suggest further that dense and widely spaced pattern modes are but another extension of this same principle.

The images in figures 41, 42, and 43 all follow the same layout. It does not take much practice to translate various shapes into frontal animal masks with eyes, horns, ears, and mouth and to see attachments of body, tail, and claws. Not all these features occur in all three images. Also, the images have a deceptive clarity since their shapes are set off against background patterns with dense linear textures that seem to refer to another mode of existence than the animal proper. Once again, the images are constructed of the same patterns of spiral-triangular extensions referred to repeatedly above. On that level of synonymy all parts of the mask and the animal are identical. The mouth forms are but a modification of the horns and ears; the same holds true for legs and tail. In other words, the procedure is the same as shown earlier in figures 6 and 8. All imagery is manipulated into existence from a basic set of autocratic patterns, as if a world can be magically brought into being using the same witchcraft formula. The controlled shape and appearance of the animal world, such as it exists in bronze decor, allows only a minimal view into that world. The very ambivalence of possible animal-power is made sacrosanct through the unchangeable and autonomous patterns. The animals live in a diagrammatic framework which prevents any discourse on their true physical nature or identity.

Here a question arises about the transition between the images in figures 40, 48, and 49 and those in figures 41 through 43. First of all, there seems to be a greater ambiguity in the earlier bands of decor since only the mask part of the decor can be identified. But that needs further consideration. The figures in 41, 42, and 43 are more clearly patterned and seem therefore less confusing. Or, in other words, the confusion is brilliantly masked by the deep intrusion of patterns into the shapes of reality. Another more critical difficulty is the greater ambiguity of whereabouts in the earlier images in figures 40, 48, and 49 versus the greater clarity of setting in figures 41 through 43. I would like to propose that the difference between these two sets of earlier and later images is not so much a matter of drastic change in attitude (towards greater specificity) but rather a somewhat different manner of dealing with essentially the same ambiguity.

Densely patterned images and broadly spaced patterns in the image itself have already been noticed to exist contemporaneously in separate images from the Fu Hao tomb, as described in figures 6 and 8. In tracing these images, I pointed out that the patterns in both are essentially the same and carry the same meaning. In addition, image making in which the surface and ridged outline are interchangeable is a longstanding tradition. Thus, whether one reads them in surface or outline, the patterns have equal shape, meaning, and intent. The result is that neither density of patterns or manner of readability make any difference in the basic visual language. These two points are, I think, the criteria by which one should judge the differences between the Erligang images and those of Yinxu, as exemplified in figures 40 through 49. Density of patterns does not alter function, and alternation between surface and outline does not change style. In figures 41 through 43, the dense smaller patterns conventionally seen as setting are made up of the same vocabulary as those in the images proper. If these units of vocabulary can at will mean leg, horn, mouth, or claw, then they should also be able to keep this intent and authority when they appear in dense arrangements not readily connected with the animal itself. The real problem is not that they have a function different from those in the image proper, but that their identity is so elusive and their intended meaning so difficult to define.

If the center parts of the Erligang-period images can in most cases be easily read as mask and the spirals and bands on either side of the mask as, vaguely, body and its whereabouts, there seems to be no reason this could not also be done for the Yinxu images in figures 41 through 43. The ambiguity in the earlier decor has in these later images found a more definite language, but it is in no way resolved. The patterns are more clearly distributed, but we do not know more about the representation. In all cases, the patterns are equally authoritative and all-pervading for what is animal and not animal. At best, the border between these modes of existence may be slightly less ambiguous in the one than in the other. In neither case are we clear about the patterns outside the animal, and the later traditional Chinese identification of these designs as thunder or cloud patterns (*leiwen*, *yunwen*), implying sky and the world above, may be as good as any other.

If, as I have shown, the dense patterns are the full equal of those in the more widely spaced manner, then there is no reason the one mode should be dominant over the other. The silent dialogue within the patterns themselves and their emergence into readable imagery is not determined by the dictates of some formal logic or meaning but by demands of ritual and the level of liturgical performance. Beautifully executed vessels covered with dense patterns are known at all times. In later Yinxu times, *gu*, *jue*, and *he* vessels seem to have been favored with densely patterned decor, both in the level and raised mode. Although I have paid attention mostly to the spiral-triangle (quill) pattern, one could present the same arguments for other spiral patterns, since most if not all of these derive from the spiral-triangle pattern in the first place. Especially in the decor of vessels from the Fu Hao tomb, the relationships among dense and widely spaced patterns of all kinds take on a complex development, and it seems that the neat side-by-side existence of these two modes begins to take shape already at that time. The fully developed and clean formula in these precise and finely regulated patterns appears in a great variety of execution. One is seen, for instance, in a later version in figure 42, and all of them are later than the vessels found in the Fu Hao tomb.

Figures 45 and 46 are the third set in need of some comments. It is easy to see that these images interrelate through similarities of pattern and that these patterns can again be viewed like those on figures 6 and 8. Within the bird image, the visual vocabulary is especially homogeneous, made up of bands, hooks, and spirals that seem more closely related to those in figure 40 than any other in this whole group. One may read the bird itself, with wing and claw, rather easily. For the other parts of the decor, one must assume crest, streamers, and fancy plumage if every detail is to function as bird image. An analogy to this ambiguous function can be found in the early image of figure 40 and in the patterns in and around the elephant of figure 46. Here the patterns are mostly reduced to their minimal make-up, thereby not necessarily introducing new ideas but simply referring to earlier forms as seen, for instance, in figure 11A. It is, in general, quite obvious that the patterns in these two Western Zhou images have changed from those of slightly earlier times, and it is surprising that they are closer to the earliest forms rather than to those seen in the mainstream of late Shang decor. The point would be difficult to demonstrate, but a comparison between some early Zhou decor and earlier Shang pieces generates a sense of archaism. This is not only true of the examples mentioned here, but similar instances occur, especially in the neatly arranged small quill patterns so well known in friezes of late Shang and early Zhou *you* and *ding* vessels. These later quill patterns relate closely to those seen in the decor of the later Erligang phase, exemplified on vessels from Panlongcheng.[27]

The relationship between the images in figures 45 and 46 and those in figures 41, 42, and 43 is instructive. Figure 41 from the Fu Hao tomb shows a lively and versatile use of the standard patterns already familiar from the comments made on figures 36 through 39. Figure 42 is, in comparison, much neater and more regulated in patterns that are, as a consequence, very similar and repetitious. The same observation holds true of the dense patterns of the *taotie*'s homeground. All these are neatly arranged to fit the broader patterns of the animal motif itself. In figure 43, the patterns are further simplified and a formulaic outcome is clear. There is a routine quality in this example and the patterns appear to liberate themselves from the image as I have pointed out earlier in figures 36 through 39. The image seems to yield in importance to ritual formalities. The patterns then expand further into festoonlike swirls in the bird image and somewhat less conspicuously in the elephant decor. These florid and gracefully curving scroll-like extensions of the spiral-triangle fill the surface they occupy. Often in these vessels the spirals take on their own life, irrespective of the function they might have in articulating part of the animal image. A good example can be seen in the extensions on the elephant in figure 46. This is typical of early Western Zhou imagery, where the patterns are clearly much more self-evident and thereby self-serving than they are respectful mediators, in the old manner, between the world of power and ritual and the world in its physical presence. In fact, much of the early Zhou bronze decor follows in the footsteps of figures 45 and 46. Whether that decor follows late Shang mannerisms or goes off into melodramatic and ponderous posturing, as in regional variants like those of Shaanxi, one is aware that the earlier meanings no longer have the same power. Instead, the patterns take over most of the action. Whereas in earlier times the patterns are themselves the very image and the embodiment of power, here they are only a graceful and illustrative memory.

Two more images, seen in figures 42 and 44, require some comment in terms of their relationship to the enduring patterns. Figure 44 begins to look like an upside-down *taotie*, though it is really made of two half-addorsed animal forms. The old pattern formula, readily recognizable throughout this decor, is remarkably tenacious. However, at this late date, in the middle of the first millennium B.C., there is only an echo of the earlier cohesiveness and authority of the patterns. Now they are used as floating ornaments, evenly distributed in a disconnected array over the standard animal image. Similarly, in figure 42 reminiscences occur of early forms.

These last two ornamental images are part of a large and very mixed group of decoratively arranged patterns and animal imagery. In the early and mid Western Zhou, well into the ninth century B.C., the old spiral-triangle vocabulary still had a commanding presence in its complex derivations from Shang elements and in regional adaptations. But by the middle of the first millennium B.C., the meandering, overlapping, and fanciful bands and sometimes heaped-up comma patterns, without sense of articulation, loose their meaning in free associations over the surface of the vessel. Inlay, a variety of materials, and rich overlays of color in late Zhou times replace earlier meanings with completely new associations. The old patterns are eventually separated into different categories, some serving the cosmos and others the needs of this world, the round and the square respectively.

A few closing remarks are in order. Many questions on dating remain. Archaeological evidence has provided a fairly clear picture of the earliest styles of Chinese bronze decor; I have used the general indication Erligang for that phase. Various problems concerning a possible transitional style between the later Erligang and early Yinxu phase have already been addressed by Thorp.[28] From the results of his painstaking analysis, it is clear that we should not expect an exact definition of a transitional period based on presently known archaeological evidence. Such decor as exists on vessels from sites now broadly assigned to Yinxu I seems conservative and rather closely related to late Erligang. The decor on some vessels from tombs assigned to Yinxu II relates well enough to that of the Fu Hao tomb, but that is of little direct help in setting up a transitional style.[29] Louise Huber's precise sequential dating of vessels by use and shape of dense spiral and quill patterns would seem more convincing, both in terms of date and elements of style, if it were argued proceeding from the vessels of the Fu Hao tomb rather than towards them.[30]

The style of the decor on vessels attested by excavation to belong to Yinxu I shows an already clear articulation of the im-

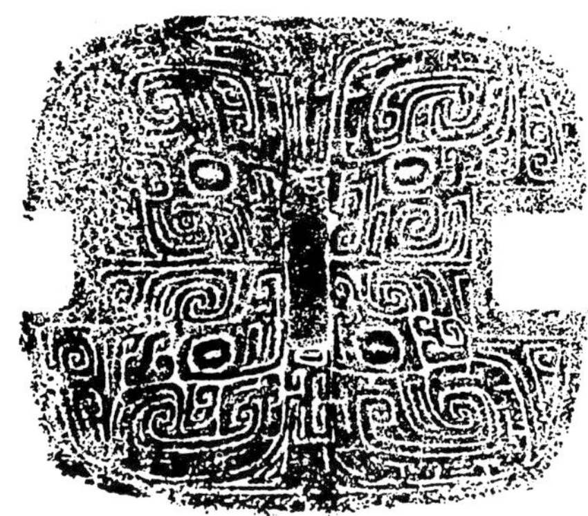

Fig. 50. *Jia* cover, detail. Fu Hao tomb, no. 845.

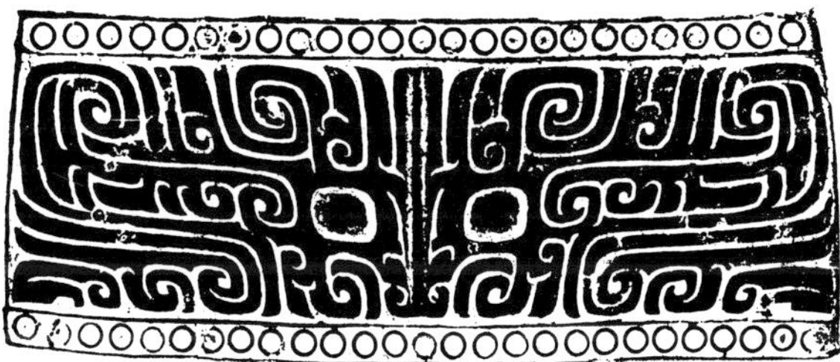

Fig. 51. *Hu* vessel, detail. Late Erligang.

portance of the patterns and a dominance of the quill form. The decor from tombs assigned to Yinxu II and especially those from Dasikongcun (SM539) is more closely related to that of the Fu Hao tomb. These vessels show a rich variety in the treatment of the standard vocabulary and as well as a more expanded repertory of imagery. In the Fu Hao tomb itself, there are vessels in a style that still relates well to late Erligang. The cover of the *jia* pictured in figure 50 is, among several others, a good example of that relationship and it compares closely with the Erligang decor on a *gui* vessel from Panlongcheng[31] and with the detail of the *hu* vessel in figure 51, of the same period. Other examples could be cited.

There is, of course, no question that the Fu Hao tomb decor in all its variety of materials and application remains startling. I suggest we credit a long and well-established use of patterns which, under the power of an extraordinary creative impulse (well attested under Wu Ding in other rituals), served the most unusual demands of new rituals and elaborate liturgical performances. And once again, great importance should be given to equivalence of patterns, as I have argued throughout this essay—whether they appear in dense or widely spaced modes, negative or positive, ridge or surface—and thereby to the predominantly graphic character of all decor.[32] The identical meaning of dense and widely spaced modes of decor is of paramount importance, since it contradicts any significant division between "background" and "image."

There remains little room for detailed discussion of the style of Yinxu I-III. Good points can be made for an early phase of Erligang and a later one. Patterns evolve from the bold, constantly changing, and lively aspects of spirals and triangular extensions, as seen in figure 14, to the later clearly established and dominant quill form in figure 51 from later Erligang. The freer and more open use of these same patterns, for instance in figure 8 from the Fu Hao tomb, is part of a later development. For the dating of vessels after the Fu Hao tomb till the beginning of Zhou, it is essential to see how Shang patterns appear in early dated Zhou vessels. In addition, some supporting evidence can be used from vessels excavated from Yinxu III-IV tombs, though that evidence is surprisingly sparse. I have pointed out earlier in figures 14 through 49 how changes in patterns take place. The dynamic decor of the Fu Hao tomb then becomes all the more clear and there is a tendency in later Shang style towards evenness of rhythms, simple and neat patterning,[33] and emphasis on plain and heightened clarity of contrasts. These then lead to a new role of the patterns themselves as indicated above.

Finally, the decor on Shang and Zhou bronzes remains fascinating and enigmatic. Its uniformity is constantly challenged by its own traditions and demands for adaptations by presumably changing rituals. The language of pattern establishes a vocabulary that signifies equally well various parts of any image, a vocabulary in which a leg is the same as an ear, horn, or mouth. This indiscriminate vocabulary is not fussy; a spoken or written word could not be used so broadly. I also suggest that there is no exact meaning in the pattern vocabulary or in the image it signifies. In that respect, the visual vocabulary resembles the cracks on oracle bones, which are in need of shamanic interpretation or at least confirmation. And maybe there is a parallel between the extremely well-prepared and controlled lines of the cracks on oracle bones and the patterns on the bronze decor. In both cases, the forms confirm that the power invoked is in agreement with the proposed rituals. In the oracle bones, the written word is confirmed in the rituals it prescribes. In the bronze image, the patterns assure that the powers of the animal world have been correctly ritualized. No matter where one turns, the correct answers are hard to come by.

NOTES

1. Bernhard Karlgren, "Notes on the Grammar of Early Bronze Decor," *Bulletin, The Museum of Far Eastern Antiquities, Stockholm* 23 (1951): 32.
2. Ibid., figs. 13a–n.
3. Karlgren, "Marginalia on Some Bronze Albums," *Bulletin, The Museum of Far Eastern Antiquities, Stockholm* 31 (1959): 328.
4. For the various types of bronze vessels and their respective functions, see Ma Chengyuan, "The Splendor of Ancient Chinese Bronzes," in Wen Fong, ed., *The Great Bronze Age of China: An Exhibition from the People's Republic of China* (exh. cat.) (New York: Metropolitan Museum of Art, 1980), 4–5, fig. 1. The *ding* and *liding*, like the *li*, *fang ding*, and *xian*, were used for cooking; the *gui*, *dou*, and *you* for serving and holding food; the *jue*, *jia*, and *he* for warming wine; and the *gu* and *zun* for holding and drinking wine. Other types include the *guang*, *hu*, and *pou*. See also Helmut Brinker, *Bronzen aus dem alten China* (exh. cat.) (Zurich: Museum Rietberg Zürich, 1975), 22–23.
5. Karlgren, "Marginalia," 330.
6. Ibid., 331.
7. Max Loehr, "The Bronze Styles of the Anyang Period," *Archives of the Chinese Art Society of America* 7 (1953): 42–53.
8. Ibid., 42; Karlgren, "Marginalia," 290, fn. 2.
9. Karlgren, "Marginalia," 328, fn. 2.
10. Ludwig Bachhofer, *A Short History of Chinese Art* (New York: Pantheon, 1946), 26–27.
11. Ibid., 26–27.

12. Loehr, "Bronze Styles," 52, n. 17.

13. See Alexander C. Soper, "Early, Middle and Late Shang: A Note," *Artibus Asiae* 28 (1966): 6–7; Robert W. Bagley, catalogue entries in Wen Fong, *Great Bronze Age*, 182 and passim; idem., *Shang Ritual Bronzes in the Arthur M. Sackler Collections* (Cambridge, Mass., and London: Harvard University Press, 1987), 20–24, 38–40, and numerous catalogue entries; Louise G. Fitzgerald Huber, "Some Anyang Royal Bronzes: Remarks on Shang Bronze Decor," in *The Great Bronze Age of China: A Symposium*, ed. George Kuwayama (Los Angeles: Los Angeles County Museum of Art, 1983), 16–43, passim; Robert L. Thorp, "The Archaeology of Style at Anyang: Tomb 5 in Context," *Archives of Asian Art* 41 (1988): 54ff.; idem., "The Growth of Early Shang Civilization: New Data from Ritual Vessels," *Harvard Journal of Asiatic Studies* 45 (1985): 5–75, passim. Other opinions on the validity of the sequence of five styles range from non-committal references (John A. Pope et al., *The Freer Chinese Bronzes,* Vol. I, *Catalogue* [Washington, D.C.: Smithsonian Institution, 1967]), to serious doubts (Kwang-chih Chang, *Art, Myth and Ritual: The Path to Political Authority in Ancient China* [Cambridge, Mass., and London: Harvard University Press, 1983], 61ff. and elsewhere), and, finally, to neglect by Chinese and Japanese scholars of early Chinese art.

14. For information on the Tomb of Fu Hao, see, among others, Thorp, "Archaeology of Style," 47–69, and Huber, "Some Anyang Royal Bronzes," 16–43.

15. See also Nancy T. Price, "Notes: Once Again on Loehr's Bronze Styles," *Early China* 3 (1973): 97, for comments on the reassessment of relative chronology in preconquest Zhou bronze styles based on the relief style V.

16. Virginia C. Kane, "The Chronological Significance of the Inscribed Ancestor Dedication in the Periodization of Shang Dynasty Bronze Vessels," *Artibus Asiae* 35 (1973): 355.

17. Thorp, "Archaeology of Style," 48. I follow Thorp's suggested periodization: Yinxu I-II, Pan Geng-early Wu Ding; Yinxu III, Lin Xin-Wen Ding; Yinxu IV, Di Yi-Di Xin. See also David N. Keightley, "The Late Shang State: When, Where, and What," in *The Origins of Chinese Civilization*, ed. Keightley (Berkeley, Calif., Los Angeles, and London: University of California Press, 1983), 524–526. For indications of any sequences of style used in this essay, whether implied or explicit, I am using these same periods. I am not using any numbered sequences. At the end of this essay appear more detailed remarks on the sequence of style in the Yinxu period and any periodization follows Yinxu I-IV.

18. Thorp, "Growth of Early Shang," 45–51 and figs. 6 and 7.

19. Ibid., 46, 48; Bagley, *Shang Ritual Bronzes*, 201, fn. 54. See also Kwang-chih Chang, "The Animal in Shang and Chou Bronze Art," *Harvard Journal of Asiatic Studies* 41 (1981): passim. Already in 1936 Herrlee G. Creel made the still valid observation that one could, for instance, use the name *taotie* for the sake of convenience, provided that one remembers that it is a motif and not a variety of animal; Creel, *The Birth of China* (New York: Frederick Ungar Publishing Co., 1954), 115.

20. Karlgren, "Marginalia," 330.

21. Thorp, "Growth of Early Shang," 16, 19, and 24. In the last, he notes that in some instances early bronze casters seem to have assembled the final product from several parts.

22. Robert J. Poor, "The Master of the 'Metropolis'-Emblem Ku," *Archives of Asian Art* 41 (1988): 70–89.

23. For assemblages and functional classes of Shang ritual vessels, see Thorp, "Growth of Early Shang," 29–37.

24. Early examples of vessels with a decor closely resembling this pattern are the Freer *hu* vessel (Pope et al., *Freer Chinese Bronzes*, pl. 4); a *ding* vessel reproduced in Seiichi Mizuno, *Bronzes and Jades of Ancient China*, trans. J. O. Gauntlett (Tokyo: Nihon Keizei, 1959), pl. 6; and an ax and *gui* shown in Wen Fong, *Great Bronze Age*, pls. 7 and 8, respectively.

25. For some of the chronology used here see Institute of Archaeology, Archaeologia Sinica, *Yinxu qingtongqi*, Yi series no. 24 (Beijing: Wenwu chubanshe, 1985), 27–72.

26. Ibid., pl. 233.

27. An excellent example of Yinxu IV is the Fu Ding *li* of tomb GM1102, illustrated in Institute of Archaeology, *Yinxu qingtongqi*, pl. 217. See also Thorp, "Archaeology of Style," fig. 18.

28. Thorp, "Growth of Early Shang," especially 40–51 and figs. 7A and B. See also idem., "Archaeology of Style," 56–58.

29. For vessels with a decor assigned to Yinxu I, see Institute of Archaeology, *Yinxu qingtongqi*, pls. 1 and 2; for possibly slightly later evidence see, among others, some of the better vessels from Tomb SM539 from Dasikongcun and from Tomb 18 Locus North. Both these tombs are likely from Yinxu II; for illustrations see ibid., pls. 61–63, 167, and 173–174; for tomb 18, see pls. 57–60, 150, and 155–159. See also Thorp, "Archaeology of Style," 48, table 1.

30. Huber, "Some Anyang Royal Bronzes," 18–19.

31. Illustrated in Wen Fong, *Great Bronze Age*, pl. 8.

32. See also Thorp, "Archaeology of Style," 57, who argues for a common goal for the earliest contrasts between ridge and surface decor as expressed in Loehr I and II.

33. A good example is the *ding* vessel of Tomb 2065, dated to Yinxu IV and illustrated in Institute of Archaeology, *Yinxu qingtongqi*, pl. 79. Much of the late Shang decor in applied plastic bands and layers is equally formulaic and placid in its rhythms, though it retains in the best pieces a strong dignity of conformance to established righteousness.

CATALOGUE OF RITUAL BRONZES, WEAPONRY, AND DOMESTIC ARTICLES

Dimensions are given in inches, followed by centimeters in parentheses. The following abbreviations are used: H. = height, W. = width, L. = length, DP. = depth, DIAM. = diameter. The maximum dimension is provided in all cases.

Abbreviated citations under PUBLICATIONS within entries are:

Bulletin: David and Alfred Smart Gallery, University of Chicago. *Bulletin of The David and Alfred Smart Gallery, The University of Chicago* 1 (1987–88).

Creel, *Birth of China*: Creel, Herrlee Glessner. *The Birth of China: A Survey of the Formative Period of Chinese Civilization*. London: Jonathan Cape, 1936; New York: John Day, 1937, Frederick Ungar Publishing Co., 1954, 1964.

Creel, "Origins": Creel, Herrlee Glessner. "On the Origins of the Manufacture and Decoration of Bronze in the Shang Period." *Monumenta Serica* 1, fasc. 1 (October 1935): 39–69.

All catalogue entries in this section have been prepared by Professor Robert J. Poor.

Neolithic and Bronze-Age Pottery

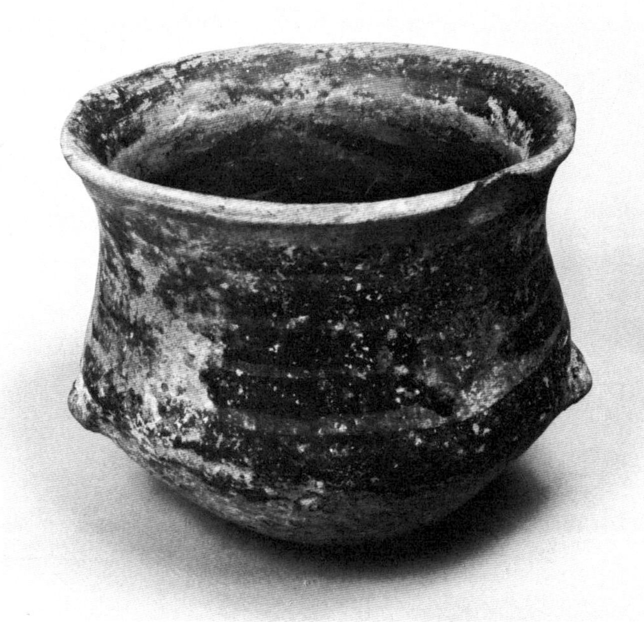

1

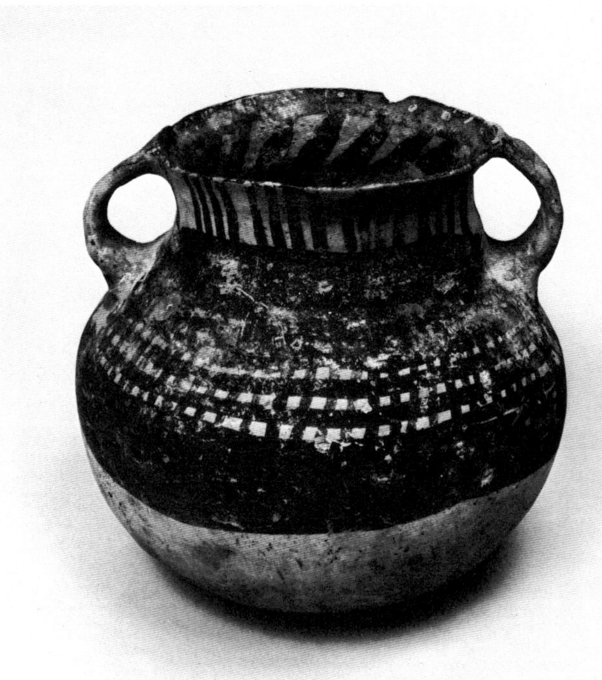

2

1 **Neolithic era**, Yangshao phase
Bowl, circa 2200 B.C.
Unglazed earthenware, with slip-painted decoration, H. 4 1/4 (10.8), DIAM. (mouth) 5 3/8 (13.7)
Gift of Geraldine Schmitt-Poor and Dr. Robert J. Poor
Acc. no. 1989.2

2 **Neolithic era**, Yangshao phase
Bowl with Handles, circa 2200 B.C.
Unglazed earthenware, with slip-painted decoration, H. 5 (12.7), DIAM. (belly) 5 5/8 (14.3)
Gift of Geraldine Schmitt-Poor and Dr. Robert J. Poor
Acc. no. 1989.3

3 **Shang dynasty**
Fragment of a Vessel
Unglazed light gray earthenware (grayware), with combed and coiled decoration, H. 2 15/16 (7.5), W. 7 1/2 (19)
Gift of Prof. and Mrs. Herrlee G. Creel
Acc. no. 1986.377
PUBLICATIONS *Bulletin*, 35.

4 **Shang dynasty**, Anyang period, found at Houjiazhuang
Fragment of a Vessel
Unglazed light gray earthenware (grayware), with incised decoration, H. 3 1/16 (7.6), W. 3 1/2 (8.8)
Gift of Prof. and Mrs. Herrlee G. Creel
Acc. no. 1986.378
PUBLICATIONS *Bulletin*, 35.

5 **Shang dynasty**, Anyang period, found at Houjiazhuang
Fragment of a Vessel
Unglazed dark gray earthenware (grayware), with incised and applied decoration, H. 2 1/2 (6.5), W. 4 9/16 (11.6)
Gift of Prof. and Mrs. Herrlee G. Creel
Acc. no. 1986.379
PUBLICATIONS *Bulletin*, 35.

6 **Shang dynasty**, Anyang period, found at Xiaotun
Fragment of a Vessel
Unglazed red earthenware (redware), with beaten paddle decoration, H. 4 (10.2), W. 5 1/8 (13)
Gift of Prof. and Mrs. Herrlee G. Creel
Acc. no. 1986.380
PUBLICATIONS *Bulletin*, 35.

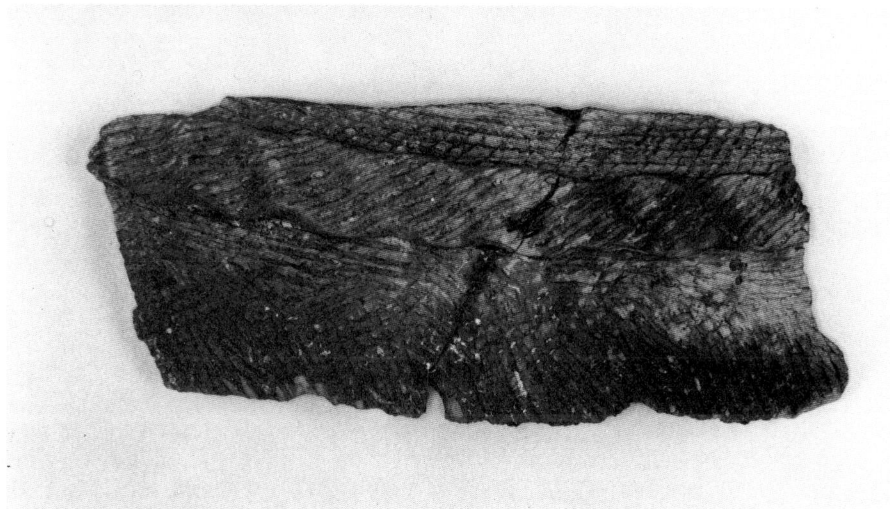
3

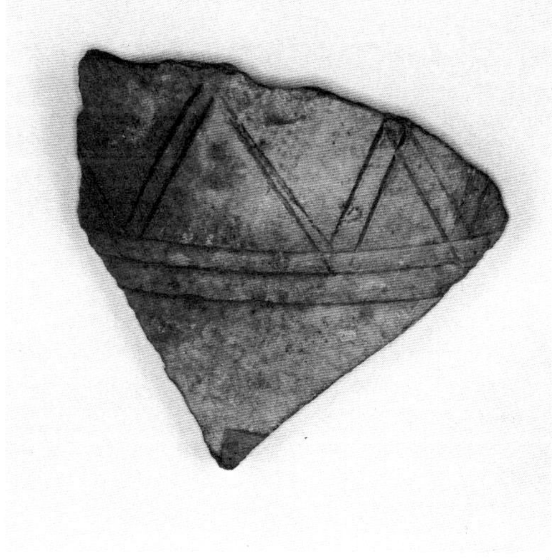
4

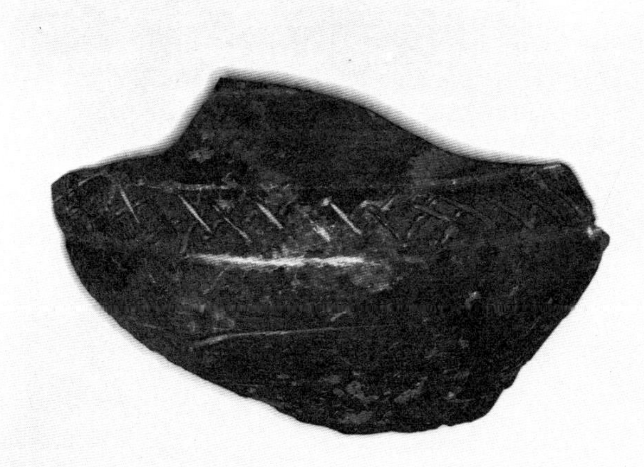
5

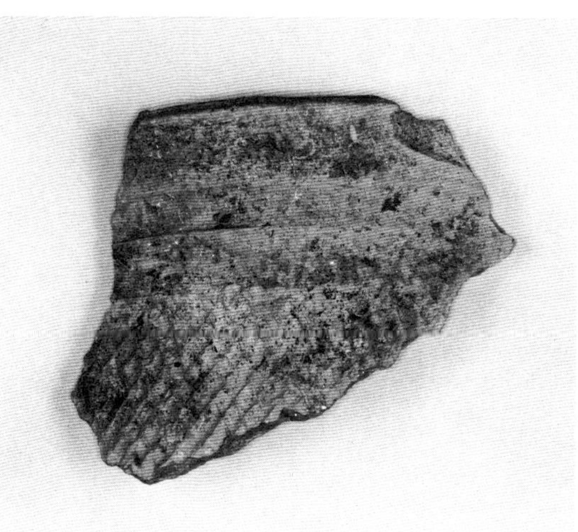
6

7 **Shang dynasty**, Anyang period
Fragment of a Vessel
Unglazed red earthenware (redware), with beaten paddle decoration, H. 3⅜ (8.6), W. 3½ (9)
Gift of Prof. and Mrs. Herrlee G. Creel
Acc. no. 1986.381
PUBLICATIONS *Bulletin*, 35.

8 **Shang dynasty**, Anyang period
Fragment of a Vessel
Unglazed red earthenware (redware), with beaten paddle decoration, H. 4⅜ (11.1), W. 6 (15.2)
Gift of Prof. and Mrs. Herrlee G. Creel
Acc. no. 1986.382
PUBLICATIONS *Bulletin*, 35.

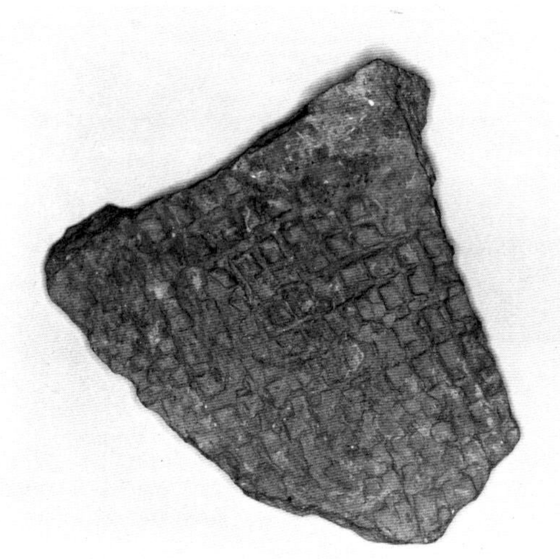

7

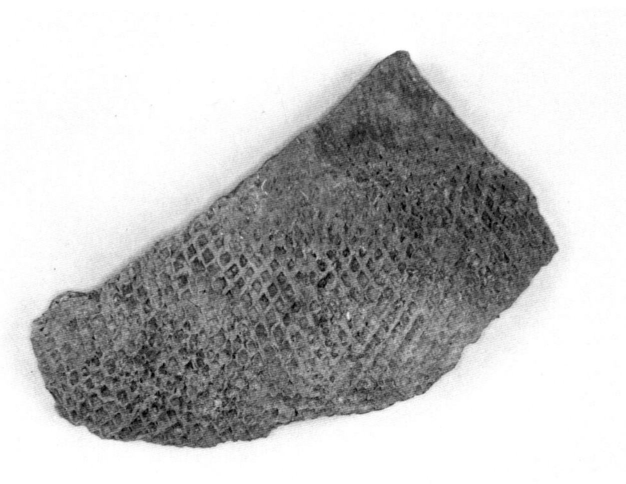

8

9

9 **Shang dynasty**, Anyang period, found at Houjiazhuang
Fragment of a Vessel
Unglazed red earthenware (redware), with combed decoration, H. 3 11/16 (9.4), W. 6 (15.2)
Gift of Prof. and Mrs. Herrlee G. Creel
Acc. no. 1986.383
PUBLICATIONS *Bulletin*, 35.

10 **Late Shang/Western Zhou dynasty**
Li, tripod cooking vessel, circa 1000 B.C.
Unglazed buff earthenware, with combed decoration, H. 5 5/8 (14.3), DIAM. (mouth) 5 15/16 (15.1)
Anonymous Gift in honor of the Divine Word Missionaries
Acc. no. 1989.1

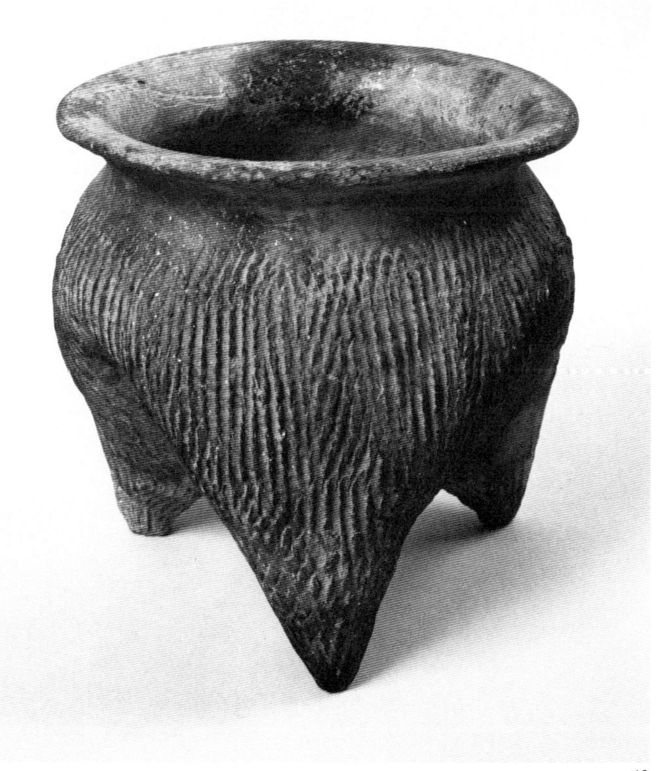

10

The two vases with painted decoration are representative of the kind of ware produced in northwest China during the Yangshao phase of Neolithic culture. The small pot with a wide mouth (cat. no. 1) is the color of red tile. A broad, dark-red band runs around the body on the ridge that marks the juncture of the upper and lower parts of the pot. Above that, there is a simple repeat pattern of four horizontal bars. On the inside of the lip, a garland pattern is framed by two more broad lines. In some places one can see where the pigment dripped; in other spots, the paint, which was thinly applied, has worn off.

In the Neolithic era, pottery was used for both common and special purposes. This pot is surprisingly heavy for its size, which suggests a humble use, but at one point it attained ceremonial stature: a hole in the bottom of this piece was deliberately drilled from the outside with a tubular drill bit that caused the inside of the pot to chip. No matter, for the intent was to render the vessel useless in everyday life. The second Yangshao vessel is made of a more finely prepared clay, and it is lighter in both weight and color (cat. no. 2).

Pottery is more durable than metal, it will not rust or decompose like wood or leather, and, even if it is broken, the fragments still give us a good idea of what the original looked like and how it was made. The fragments of Shang gray- or redware exhibit a considerable range of technique. Two pieces of unglazed redware (cat. nos. 7 and 8) demonstrate the consequence of beating the outside of the vessel with a paddle covered with string. This is a familiar hand-building technique, employed to get the proper thickness of the clay and, in China as elsewhere, it led to a spontaneous decorative effect. There is no doubt that the Shang potters were aware of this. The fragment of unglazed light grayware is a little essay in textures (cat. no. 3). Combining both coil and comb techniques, it represents just the kind of exercise featured in the Bauhaus.

The full potential of manipulating texture in this way is apparent in the complete *li* tripod (cat. no. 10). Here, the striations in the buff clay follow the contour of the body and, in a curious fashion, lend a sense of movement to the surface. At the same time, the very absence of these lines sets off the smooth surface of the mouth and rim, adding emphasis to those parts of the vessel. Because the *li* tripod is an ancient and tenacious type, it is especially difficult to date a piece of this sort. This example is no earlier than Shang and may well be much later.

There need be no doubt, however, about the remaining pieces. Three were found at Houjiazhuang and one at Xiaotun, the classic Anyang sites. The Xiaotun piece (cat. no. 6) effects a nice contrast between the beaten pattern and the smooth wall of the vessel at what looks like a rim. One of the pieces from Houjiazhuang (cat. no. 9) achieves a similar result. The two other pieces from this site (cat. nos. 4 and 5) seem more sophisticated and obviously were made on the wheel. The clay is finer, with a smooth luster that is inviting to the eye and fingers. Pieces like this presage the history of Chinese ceramics, but that development had to wait until the end of the Bronze Age. R.J.P.

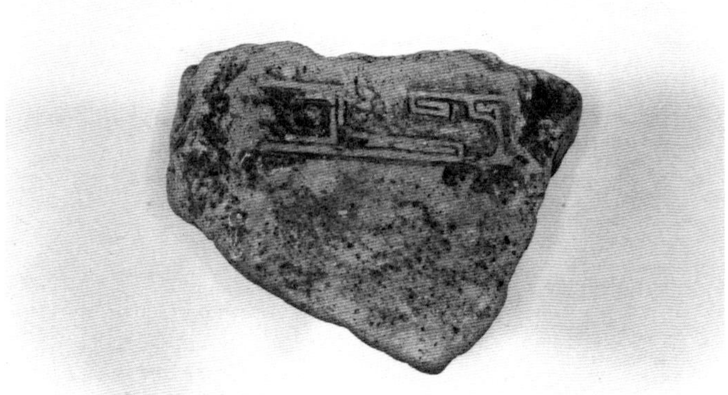

11

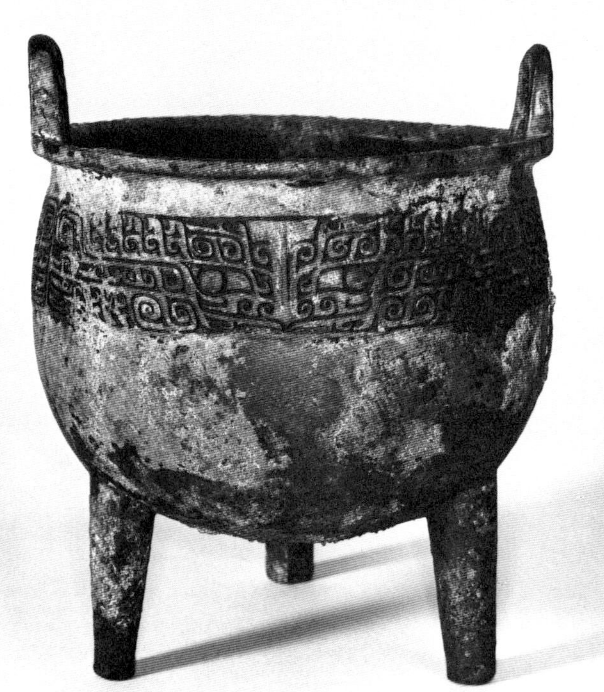

12

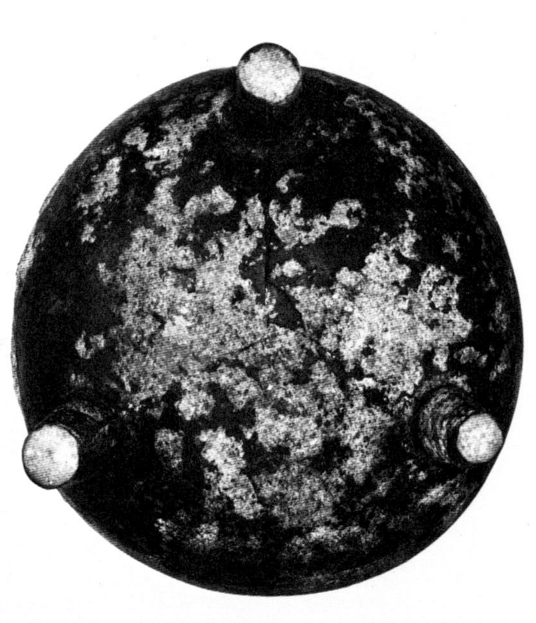

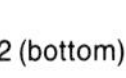

12 (bottom)

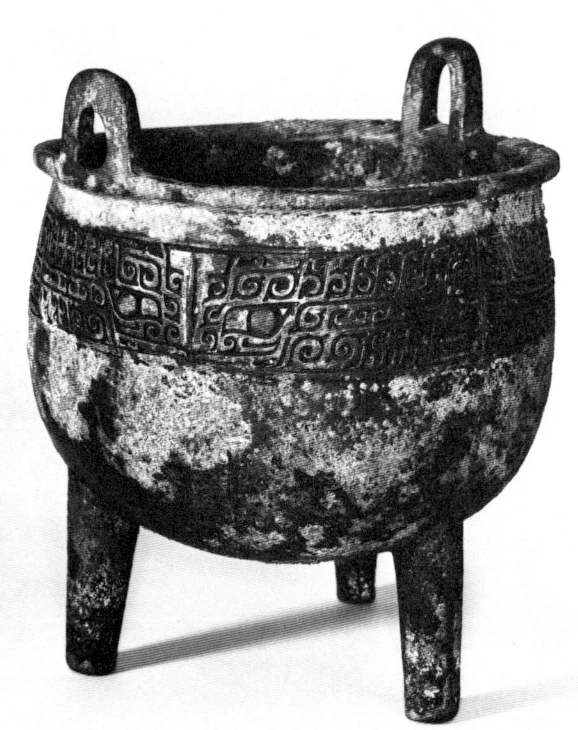

12

11 **Shang dynasty**, Anyang period

Fragment of a Mold for a Bronze Ritual Vessel

Unglazed buff earthenware, H. $1\frac{5}{8}$ (4.1), W. $2\frac{1}{16}$ (5.3)
Gift of Prof. and Mrs. Herrlee G. Creel
Acc. no. 1986.375
PUBLICATIONS *Bulletin*, 34.

Because the designs that appear in relief or in dense intaglio on the surface of Chinese bronzes were cast, the crispness of a line, or the sculptured quality of an animal motif, is due to the exact preparation of the inner faces of the molds in which these objects were made. Once the molten metal had been poured into the mold assembly, there was little the bronze master could do but wait anxiously to see the result. For, after the initial casting, only a bit of cosmetic filing or polishing could improve the general appearance.[1] Molds make the bronze.

A flat bronze blade was cast with just two mold pieces (see cat. nos. 19–23). A *ding* tripod required three sections, with the seams coming over the legs (see cat. nos. 12 and 13). The more complex shape of the *jue* was broken down into several mold segments for the bowl-shaped body and additional ones for the curving area of the spout and tail (see cat. no. 14). The seemingly simple structure of the *gu* was quartered along the vertical axis into four sections, and divided above and below the waist into three separate divisions, so that it took twelve pieces to make the complete mold assembly (and two more for the cores) (see cat. nos. 15 and 16). This elaborate sub-division of vessels of all shapes into so many parts was neither necessary nor efficient. Something else prompted that complicated procedure; the age-old procedure of dividing a complex shape into easily constructed parts. First seen in the manufacture of the neolithic wares of the Yangshao era (see cat. no. 2), the process of sectionalism prevailed into the Bronze Age.

One cannot tell from this small mold fragment what the shape of the final cast object might have been; the design suggests a border for a flat object or one with a curve of considerable dimensions. The extraordinarily fine lines that appear in delicate relief on the mold piece would have registered as sunken ones on the actual bronze. Herrlee Creel commented on the "delicate traceries [which] look quite sharp and clear even through a magnifying-glass. Its corners are corners; if a projection was intended, even for the tiniest fraction of an inch, it projects."[2] Creel noted that even lines that are less than one thirty-second of an inch in width have straight side walls and sharp corners. I can only add that the detail seems even more amazing under a microscope. The role of the mold maker is invisible, like that of a modern tool and die maker, or the person who designs the computer chip. Yet, ironically, it was the person working in clay, producing molds, who determined the final appearance of the object cast in bronze. R.J.P.

NOTES

1. Herrlee Glessner Creel, "On the Origins of the Manufacture and Decoration of Bronze in the Shang Period," *Monumenta Serica*, 1, fasc. 1 (October 1935): 67–68, pl. IV A and B, noted traces of postcast filing on the Smart Gallery *gu* (cat. no. 16). He also commented on the general absence of evidence of work of this sort on Chinese bronzes. See Creel, *The Birth of China* (New York: Frederick Ungar Publishing Co., 1964), 112.

2. Creel, *Birth of China*, 113.

12 **Shang dynasty**, late Erligang–early Anyang period

Ding, ritual cooking vessel, 14th–13th century B.C.

Bronze, H. with handles $6\frac{5}{8}$ (16.8), H. without handles $5\frac{9}{16}$ (14.1), DIAM. (mouth) $5\frac{11}{16}$ (14.4)
Inscribed, inside bowl: Xiu[1]
Gift of Mr. and Mrs. Isaac S. Goldman
Acc. no. 1976.163

All tripods are classified as *ding*. Those with a full, rounded shape like this one are called *guan ding*, meaning "pot-shaped." The deep, continuous curve of the bowl is characteristic of all types of such early-Shang vessels. The way the legs were placed low on the body, well under the bowl, and the straight vertical form of the arching handles are two additional symptoms of an early stage in the typology of the *ding*.[2]

The style of the decoration points in the same direction. Ornament is limited to a single broad *taotie* band on the shoulder, which is repeated three times. A low flange, flanked by two large eyes, centers the motif and serves as a facial shield. Just below this "nose" there is something that resembles a mouth, complete with tiny fangs. Above and to each side of the eyes, an assortment of geometric figures suggests an array of burgeoning body parts. The realization of the mask, and the rest of the imagined creature, depends on the conversion of these hooks, quills, and T-shaped devices into images—most especially the T. It recurs throughout the composition in varying sizes, both upright and inverted, to form a horn, body , or anything else that is needed. This is the early version of the animal mask.

This *ding* belongs to a special moment in the development of the bronze art of the Shang dynasty. The animated shape of the vessel, and even the slightly awkward placement of the legs, represents a significant step beyond the splayed-legged versions of the *ding* made in previous generations towards a more solid type. The *taotie* motif is richer in content and more complex in construction. Newly introduced elements, such as a jaw, will remain a permanent part of the bronze master's vocabulary until the end of the dynasty and beyond. More importantly, geometric figures like the T will be used as building blocks in the formation of the images of all the creatures, real or imagined, that appear in Shang art.

This vessel illustrates a style art historians like to call transitional, representing the last efflorescence of an old ideal and the first indications of a new set of artistic values. Seen in this way, our vessel can be dated to the late Erligang or early Anyang phase of Shang dynasty art. However, the historical judgment should not obscure the unique qualities of this dainty vessel as an independent work of art. R.J.P.

NOTES

1. I am pleased to acknowledge Professor Edward L. Shaughnessy for his expert advice in deciphering the graphs on the ritual bronze vessels and weapons (cat. nos. 12, 14, 15, and 18) in the Smart Gallery's collection.

2. Ursula Lienert, *Typology of the Ting in the Shang Dynasty: A Tentative Chronology of the Yin-hsü Period,* 2 vols., Publication the Asian Department of the Kunst historisches Institut der Universität Köln, no. 3 (Wiesbaden: Franz Steiner Verlag, 1979), provides a comprehensive discussion of the *ding*.

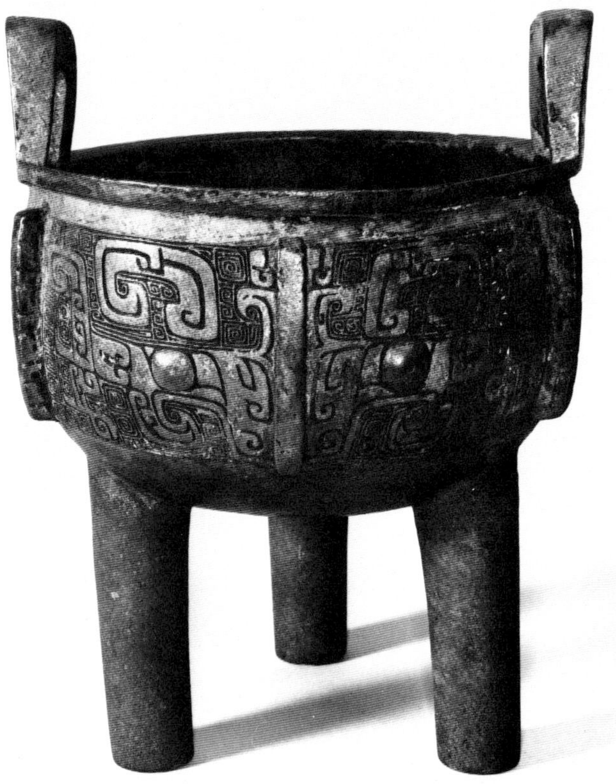

13

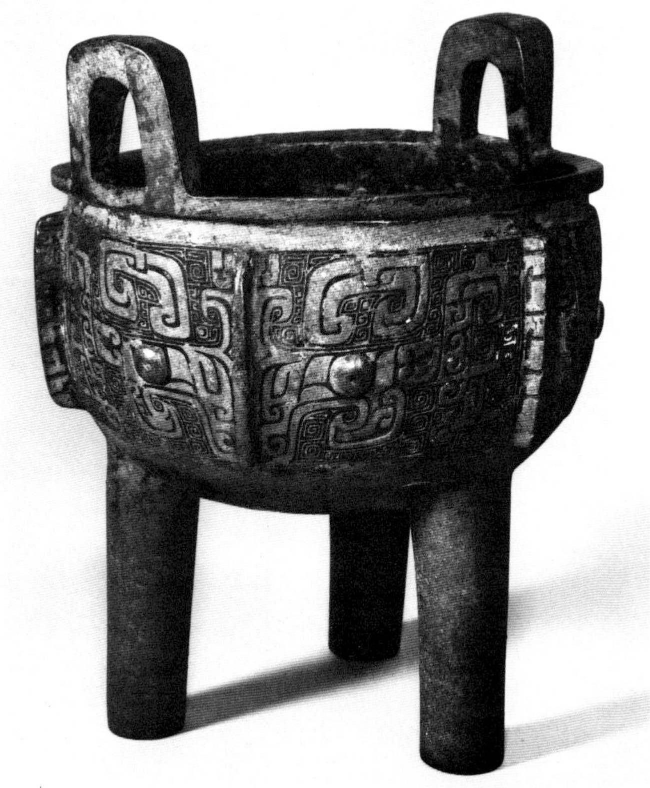

13

13 **Shang dynasty**, Anyang period

Ding, ritual cooking vessel, 13th–12th century B.C.
Bronze, H. with handles 8 (20.3), H. without handles 6 9/16 (16.7), DIAM. (mouth) 6 1/4 (15.9)
Uninscribed
Gift of Prof. and Mrs. Herrlee G. Creel
Acc. no. 1986.328
PUBLICATIONS *Bulletin*, 32.

The classic mask motif on this very fine *ding* is simply stated and boldly contrasted to the fine lines of the background. Two large eyes, set to either side of the prominent flange, form the nucleus of the design. The mask effect imparts special meaning to all of the other shapes within the field of decoration. Thus the curving forms above the eyes become horns and the leaf-shaped devices beside the eyes are easily read as ears. Of course, none of these geometric figures look like the body parts of real animals. A flange, for example, can be read as a nose only because of its position. This is an art of conventions, unconcerned with what we call naturalism. That does not diminish the power of these images: they exert a compelling presence, evoking a sense of the spiritual powers associated with these ceremonial vessels.

Masks of this sort are traditionally called *taotie*, an anachronistic term which translates roughly as "ogre." Although it has been the object of considerable attention and interpretation, the meaning of the mask to the Shang has eluded modern scholars. This is the mature version of the mask which, in this instance, dominates the side wall of the vessel. Both features point to a date in the Yinxu II–III period.

The robust shape of this piece is a perfect vehicle for its forceful decoration. The stout legs and handles (called "ears" in older Chinese texts) sound an emphatic note of stability echoed by the thickness of the bronze itself. One might expect that the Anyang foundry masters, who were by then in full control of bronze casting techniques, would have made their objects thin to conserve metal resources, but just the opposite is the case. Vessels like this one illustrate the social value of bronze; the thicker the casting the better, for expensive casting meant prestige.

The *ding* type has special significance in Chinese culture. A passage in *Zuo zhuan*, one of the classics dating from the end of the Bronze Age, relates the fable of Yu the Great, the founder of the Xia dynasty, and his famous cauldrons.[1] Yu was said to have collected tribute metal from distant quarters, metal which was used to cast bronzes that somehow replicated the spirits of those lands. These spirits, once revealed, were rendered harmless, and people could then venture to the remote places without fear. By the advent of the Qin dynasty, Nine Cauldrons had become the legendary symbol of the right to rule. Artists of the later Han dynasty frequently illustrated the futile attempts of the short-lived founder of the Qin to recover the lost tripods.

Vessels of this general shape were made in both bronze and ceramic throughout the succeeding centuries, and were decorated with various kinds of archaistic designs which are still popular. *Ding* often appear among the antiques in the backgrounds of paintings depicting scholars' studies, and *ding* of huge size still stand in the courtyards of the Forbidden City. The *ding*, like the jade *bi* disk (see cat. no. 57) or the dragon, is one of China's most enduring symbols. R.J.P.

NOTES

1. *Zuo zhuan*, *xuan* 3, 21:15b–16b. See James Legge, *The Ch'un Ts'ew, with the Tso Chuen*, vol. 5 of *The Chinese Classics* (Oxford: Clarendon Press, 1872), 293.

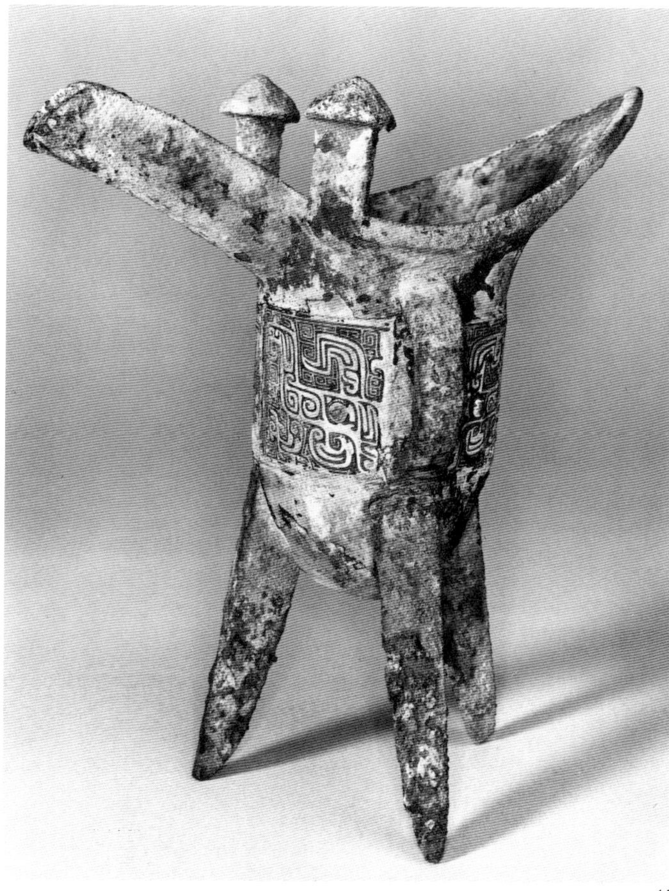

14

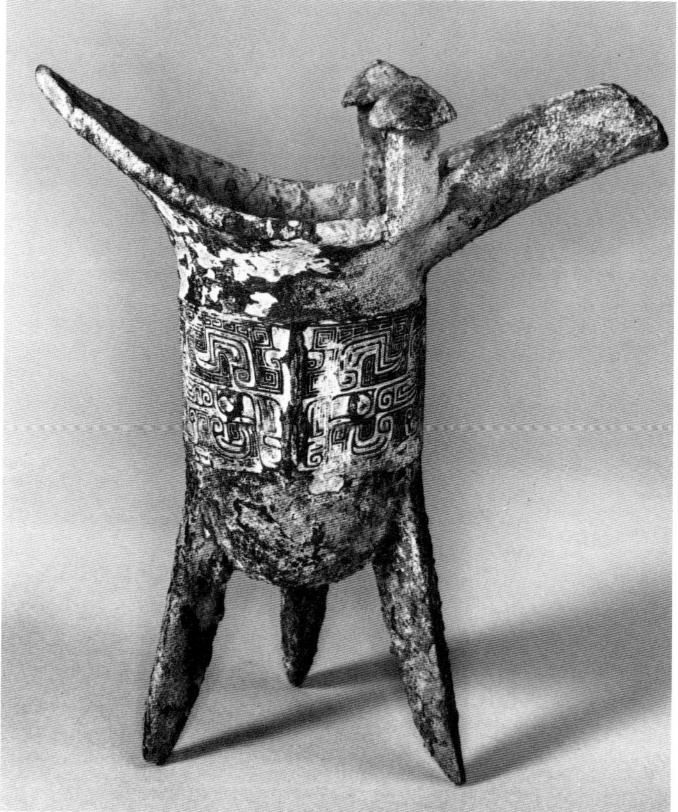

14

14 **Shang dynasty**, Anyang period
Jue, ritual wine vessel, late 13th-early 12th century B.C.

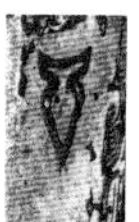

Bronze, H. 6⅝ (16.8)
Inscribed, under handle: undeciphered graph
Gift of Prof. and Mrs. Herrlee G. Creel
Acc. no. 1986.329
PUBLICATIONS Creel, "Origins," pl. XI A and B; Creel, *Birth of China*, pl. VI; *Bulletin*, 32.

Professor Creel published this vessel in 1935 in the inaugural issue of *Monumenta Serica* and again the following year in his famous *Birth of China*.[1] In the earlier article, he noted that the single character of the inscription "is probably a pictograph of a jar used to contain liquor, and may denote the pouring of a libation."[2] He pursued that idea in his book, commenting that it would be difficult to drink from this vessel but that the spout was "suited admirably" for pouring.[3] The questionable stories of the origin of this type—that its shape derived from an inverted helmet to which horns had been attached, or that the vessel was fashioned after a bird whose cry sounded like the Chinese phrase "temperance, temperance, enough, enough"—are, as he says, tales that have "more color . . . than plausibility". Creel made two other observations that bear directly on the archaeology of the type, namely, that the size of the *jue* is related to the size of a *gu* and they are "the commonest Shang vessels found today." That is still the case. In fact, the *jue* may actually have been the first kind of vessel made in metal.[4]

Our example illustrates the general features common to most *jue*. The handle is set over a leg, at an awkward right angle to the spout. Two posts with caps rise from the rim just at the base of the spout. An elongated tail balances the body on the opposite side. On later examples of the *jue* type, such as this one, the walls of the body are straight and the bottom may be either round or flat. The decoration, if there is just a single band, is as it appears here, filling the side wall and bridged by the handle. In more elaborately ornamented vessels, the decoration continues under the lip, spout, and tail. The complicated shape of the *jue* required that legs, handles, and even the little caps on the rim-posts be cast separately and later placed in the mold assembly. The molten metal of the body fused around them during the final casting. This *jue* was made according to strict mathematical rules which governed its shape, proportions, positioning of parts, and decoration—in short, every aspect of its design.[5]

The decoration on this vessel offers an excellent example of the kind of ambiguous imagery that can be read both as a powerful animal mask and as two animals seen in profile. The mask effect predominates on the uninterrupted side of the body. There, the small vertical fin serves as a nasal ridge which helps to complete the animal conceit. But on the handle side, where we can see only half the motif, the animal in profile is most apparent. The motifs are set off against the background with authority, conviction, and an exceptional clarity. This is characteristic of many of the vessels found at Anyang which are assigned to the Yinxu II phase of Shang art. And, this *jue* may be dated to that general period, the late-thirteenth or early-twelfth century B.C. R.J.P.

NOTES

1. Herrlee Glessner Creel, "On the Origins of the Manufacture and Decoration of Bronze in the Shang Period," *Monumenta Serica* 1, fasc. 1 (October 1935): 39–69, and *The Birth of China* (New York: Frederick Ungar Publishing Co., 1964).
2. Creel, "Origins," 69, pl. XI A and B.
3. Creel, *Birth of China*, 118, pl. VI.
4. Robert W. Bagley, "The Beginnings of the Bronze Age: The Erlitou Culture Period," in Wen Fong, ed., *The Great Bronze Age of China: An Exhibition from the People's Republic of China* (exh. cat.) (New York: Metropolitan Museum of Art, 1980) 74, figs. 17–18, and 79, pl. 1, provide some very fine photographs of the early *jue* from Erlitou.
5. I am preparing an extended manuscript dealing with specifics of this procedure as it applies to this vessel.

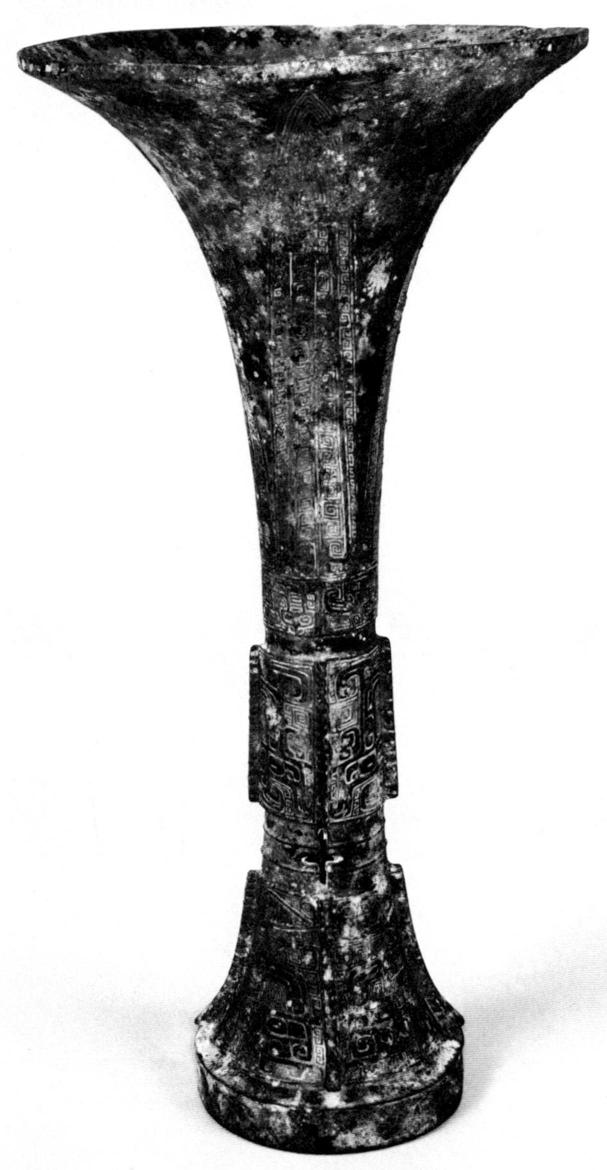

15

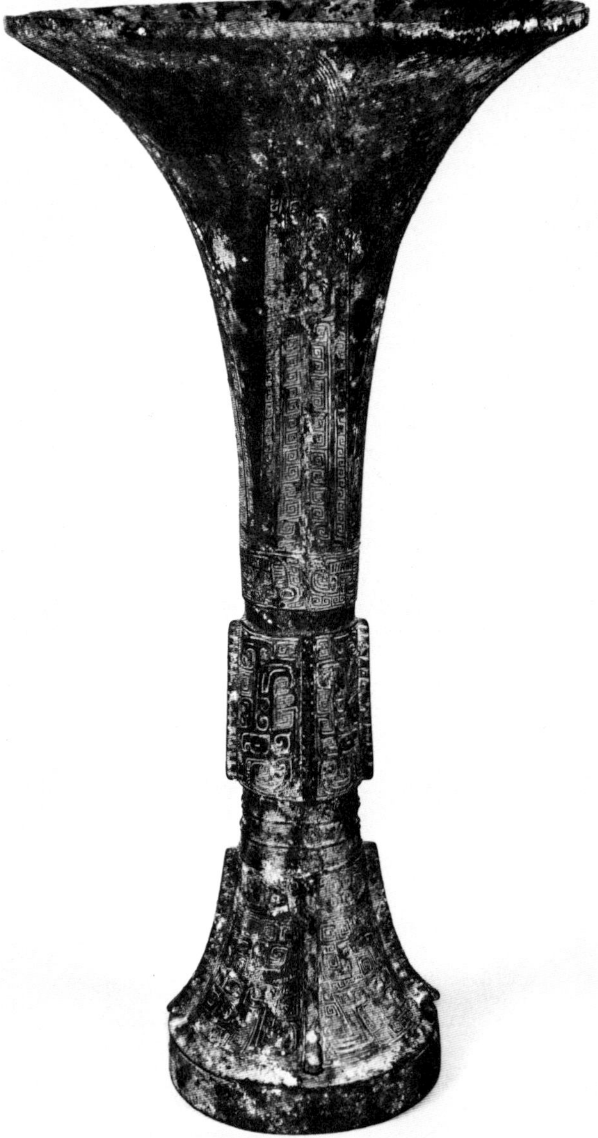

15

15 **Shang dynasty**, Anyang period

Gu, ritual wine beaker, late 13th–early 12th century B.C.

Bronze, H. 12 (30.5), DIAM. (mouth) 6 1/4 (15.9)
Inscribed, inside foot: Jing
Gift of Prof. and Mrs. Herrlee G. Creel
Acc. no. 1986.330
PUBLICATIONS *Bulletin*, 32 (illus.).

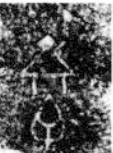

Although the ancient name of this type of vessel is not known, it has been called a *gu* since the eleventh century A.D., when scholars of the Northern Song dynasty published the first systematic studies of Chinese bronzes. Known as a wine beaker, the *gu* may well have been used to pour wine libations. The form of this particular vessel is characteristic of the mature *gu*: the long bell of the neck fits into the socket of the short tubular waist section, and the floor of the vessel is at the lowest point of the waist, just above the cross-shaped opening on the hollow foot.

This architectonic structure reflects the way the piece was cast. Using piece-molds, the bronze master did nothing to hide the traces of the process. Instead, low flanges actually mark the junctures between mold sections on the foot and waist assemblies. Often seen on later vessels, seldom on earlier ones, these flanges never exist out of technical necessity but because bronze masters of the Anyang period, like their neolithic predecessors in the Yangshao era, delighted in celebrating structure despite their complicated and risky procedures. They had first to produce clay molds which could be carved or impressed with the delicate designs that would appear in reverse on the finished object (see cat. no. 11). A vessel like this one required twelve mold pieces, four each for the foot, waist, and neck. Next, all these molds had to be bound around two cores shaped like the interior of the vessel. Finally, the whole assembly had to remain stable when the molten metal was poured into the narrow cavity between the mold sections and the cores.

In 1936, Herrlee Creel marveled at the precision of the cast decoration on a *gu* similar to this one, noting that the Shang standard had yet to be equalled in modern times.[1] His remarks still hold true. An important feature of the decoration on this vessel is that all decorative motifs are confined to distinct fields. Each zone, whether large or small, enjoys a quasi-independent status while simultaneously contributing to the overall composition. Thus, the animal mask on the foot can be read alone, or with its complementary cicada band, or as part of the total design. But no figure ever spreads beyond its borders. The snakes at the base of the neck zone, like the cicada at the top of the foot, are anchored in their assigned bands within a single mold section, and they do not intrude on the adjacent designs. Of course, the snakes and cicada could trade places; their relative positions are not absolute. The appeal of the decoration depends on the cumulative effect of these arrangements, one element added to another like motifs in a musical composition. The immediate charm of the piece is in its tall and slender shape.

Several excavated *gu*, all from Anyang, have the exact sequence of motifs found on this vessel.[2] The decoration on them is rendered in prominent relief and the different parts of the animal mask—horns, eyebrows, etc.—float unattached on the fine lines of the background. Prominent relief and the so-called dissolved form of the *taotie* are symptoms of a late date. Neither trait is apparent in our vessel. Moreover, the snakes and cicada, which are arranged in strict bisymmetrical formality on the other pieces, occur in serial order on this *gu*. Our vessel seems somewhat earlier than the excavated ones. It can be placed in the Yinxu II-III phase of Shang art, that is, the late thirteenth or earlier twelfth century B.C.

R.J.P.

NOTES

1. When Creel's *Birth of China* was first published in 1936, "common knowledge" had it that bronzes were made by the lost-wax process. Creel, however, had a very fine insight regarding the use of molds for casting and technical procedures in general: "Yet there is other evidence which makes it seem that vessels were certainly sometimes cast directly from sectional molds." See Creel, *The Birth of China* (New York: Frederick Ungar Publishing Co., 1964), 113.

2. The *gu* found in the western-zone tomb GM198 exhibits a mask effect in both the waist and foot zones and emphasizes frontality throughout. Chinese archaeologists assign this tomb to the Yinxu III phase (*Yinxu qingtongqi*, Yi series no. 24 [Beijing: Wenwu chubanshe, 1985], 472, pl. 201 [incorrectly captioned GM907], figs. 68.3, 69, and 73.8). A *gu* from another western-zone tomb, GM907, also dated to the Yinxu III phase, has more reserved plasticity, like our vessel, and a similar decor in the waist zone. But GM907 was very much a mixed find. Another *gu* from that tomb looks like a pre-Anyang vessel (*Yinxu qingtongqi*, 474, pl. 193 [incorrectly identified as GM198:3], figs. 71.3, 73.6; the earlier-looking piece, pl. 202). A pair of vessels found in M2006, R1043 and R1044, are so close to the first example GM198:3 that I attribute them to the same workshop (Li Chi and Wan Chia-pao, *Studies of the Bronze Ku-Beaker*, edited by Li Chi, Shih Chang-ju, and Kao Ch'ü-hsün, Archaeologia Sinica, n.s. no. 1 [Nankang, Taiwan: Institute of History and Philology Academia Sinica, 1964], 50, pl. XXIX–XXX, figs. 35–37). By a strange coincidence, Creel illustrated a vessel in the collection of Huang Po-ch'uan which could also belong to this group (Creel, *Birth of China*, pl. IX).

Scale 1cm = 1cm
mm
64
48
32
16
0
224
208
192
176
160
144
128
112
96
80
64
48
32
16
0
143mm
78mm
77mm
4mm
Fig. 1

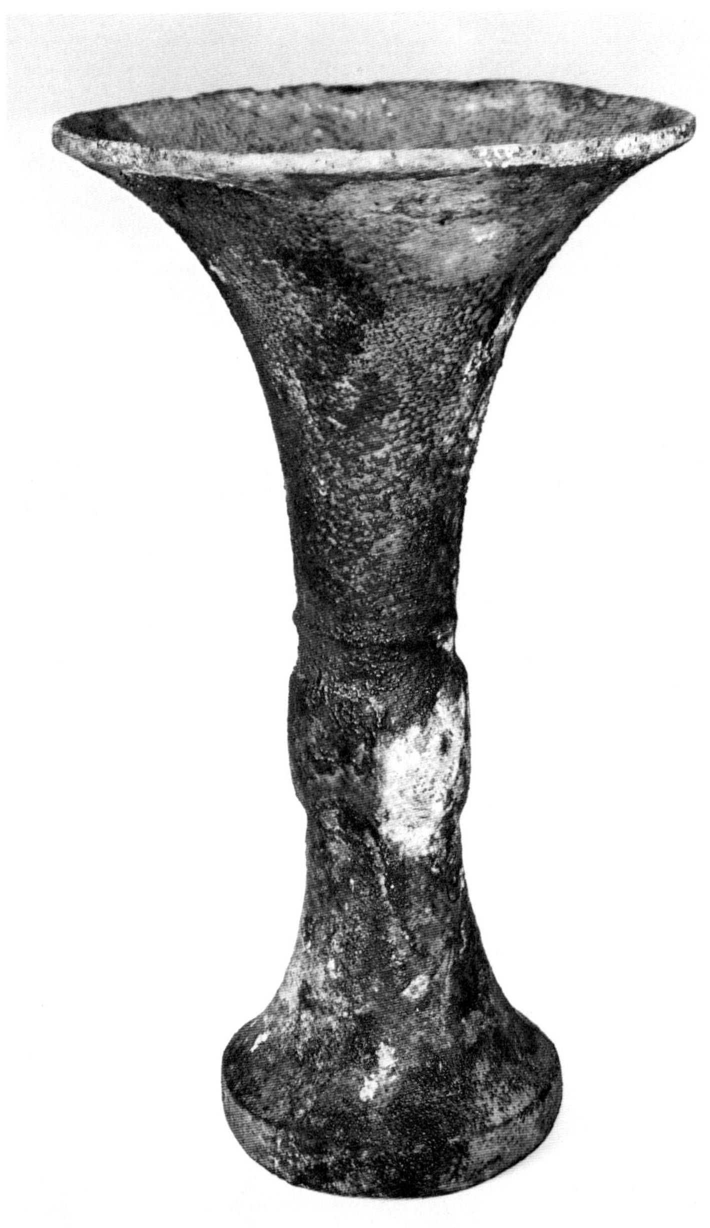

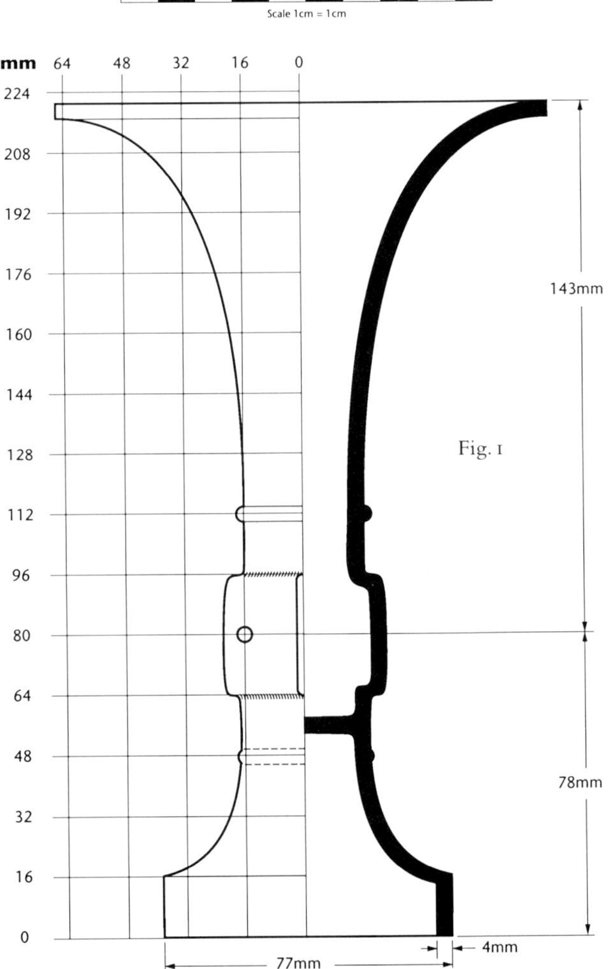

16

16 **Late Shang dynasty**, Anyang period

Gu, wine beaker, late 13th–12th century B.C.

Bronze, H. 8 11/16 (22.1), DIAM. (mouth) 5 1/4 (13.3)
Uninscribed
Gift of Prof. and Mrs. Herrlee G. Creel
Acc. no. 1986.331
PUBLICATIONS Creel, "Origins," 67–68, pl. IV A and B; *Bulletin*, 32.

The decoration of this vessel is obscured by a thick layer of minerals leached from the original bronze during its prolonged burial in the soil of north China. The blue-green patina creates a jadelike effect greatly admired by connoisseurs of bronzes. In the past, scholars regarded this patina as evidence of the age and even the provenance of an ancient piece; today, scientific examination of an object's physical properties, including the patina, has become an important part of bronze studies.[1]

Relatively plain vessels such as this one may have served some special purpose in antiquity. One possibility is that they were *mingqi*, inexpensive vessels made specifically for burial which presumably did not require decoration. Another prospect is that they were practical drinking vessels, utilitarian counterparts of the fully ornamented ceremonial pieces that may have been used to pour libations but not for drinking (see cat. no. 15). Whatever their use, plain vessels, and even sets of them, are often found alongside decorated ones in Shang burials.

There are many examples of plain *gu*; their proportions parallel those of decorated vessels. In a sense, plain pieces are simply abbreviated versions of their more elaborate mates. The decoration on the waist of this vessel, for example, which consists of two small dots and a short vertical fin, is an attenuated animal mask framed above and below by horizontal bowstring lines. Both kinds of *gu*, plain and ornamented, were made throughout the Shang and early Western Zhou dynasties. The plain ones are rarely taller than the others and, by the end of the Shang period, they are almost always shorter than the decorated pieces.

The shape of this vessel provides a clue to the date of its manufacture. The articulation of the foot, waist, and neck into a tightly structured whole is characteristic of a late phase in the development of the *gu*. So is the obvious emphasis given to the raised foot-rim, the edge of the mouth, and the pronounced bulge in the waist. In fact, this *gu*—like the *jue* (cat. no. 14) discussed previously—was designed according to a very precise mathematical canon which dictated every aspect of its shape and proportions. Underlying its form and the relationship of its parts is a module manifested in the following dimensions (see fig. 1).[2]

The thickness of the bronze is 4 millimeters throughout. That is also the approximate width of the bowstring ornaments above and below the waist, the gauge of the flanges, and the diameter of the eyes on the waist section. These eyes are set 16 millimeters to either side of the central vertical flange and the same distance from the top and bottom of the waist section. The flange itself is 16 millimeters long, which is also the distance between the bowstring ornament and the waist section, and the height of the foot-rim. Incidentally, the break in the curvature of the bell begins just 16 millimeters up the bell of the vessel.

The distance between the eyes (excluding the 4-millimeter fin) is the same as the height of the waist section and almost the same as the diameter of the waist. The whole bulging waist section is a 32-millimeter square. The diameter of the mouth is the same as the distance from the line of the eyes on the waist to the rim of the mouth. Thus, the entire upper half of the *gu* fits into an imaginary square measuring 132 millimeters. The distance from eye-line to foot-rim is the same as the diameter of the foot, 78 millimeters, another square comprising the lower half of the vessel. The distance from the foot to the bottom of the waist zone (64 millimeters) is twice the height of the waist zone.[3]

While all this is typical of late-Shang vessel design, it is difficult to date a plain vessel with much precision. This *gu* greatly resembles another plain one found at Anyang.[4] It seems likely, for the reasons given above, that our piece was made in the late-thirteenth or twelfth century B.C. R.J.P.

NOTES

1. Herrlee Glessner Creel noted the instance of mold slippage along the vertical axis of this piece and illustrated some abrasions on the inner bell which are the result of postcast tooling done to clean up rough edges and other imperfections; Creel, "On the Origins of the Manufacture and Decoration of Bronze in the Shang Period," *Monumenta Serica* 1, fasc. 1 (October 1935): 67–68, pl. IV A and B. I have discussed the different kinds of problems that can arise during the various stages of casting a vessel and the defects that result. See Robert J. Poor, "The Master of the 'Metropolis'-Emblem Ku," *Archives of Asian Art* 41 (1988): 74–75.

2. The gridded chart demonstrating the modular system has been kindly prepared by Jonathan Poor.

3. I made reference to the use of such modular systems in Poor, " 'Metropolis'-Emblem Ku," 76–77, 88, and am preparing a comprehensive study on the subject which will appear shortly.

4. The *gu* WH8, published in the original reports of the Anyang excavations, has the same decoration and general proportions as our vessel. See Li Chi and Wan Chia-pao, *Studies of the Bronze Ku-Beaker*, edited by Li Chi, Shih Chang-ju, and Kao Ch'ü-hsün, Archaeologia Sinica, no. 1 (Nankang, Taiwan: Institute of History and Philology Academia Sinica, 1964), 14, 51, pl. XXXIX. The dimensions of the two pieces are so similar that I am tempted to view them as a pair.

The Arts of Warfare: The *Ge* Dagger-Axe

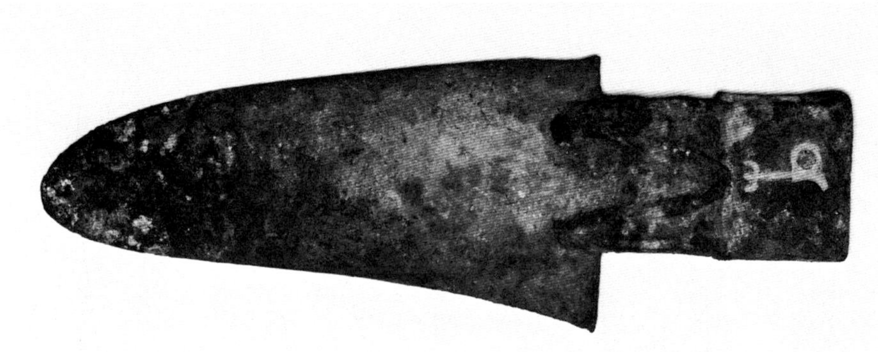

17

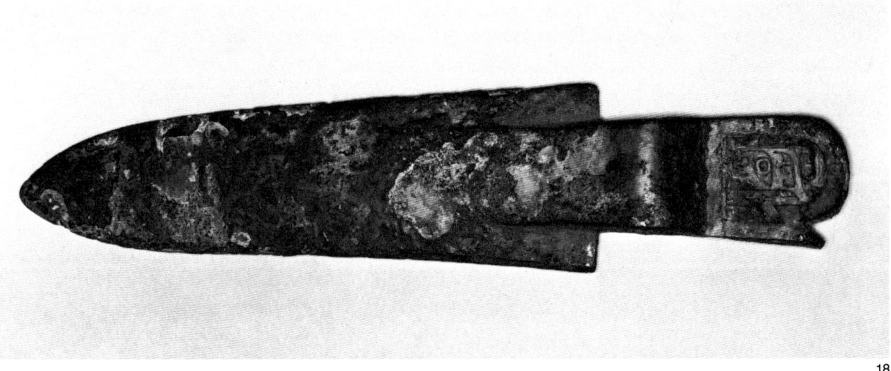

18

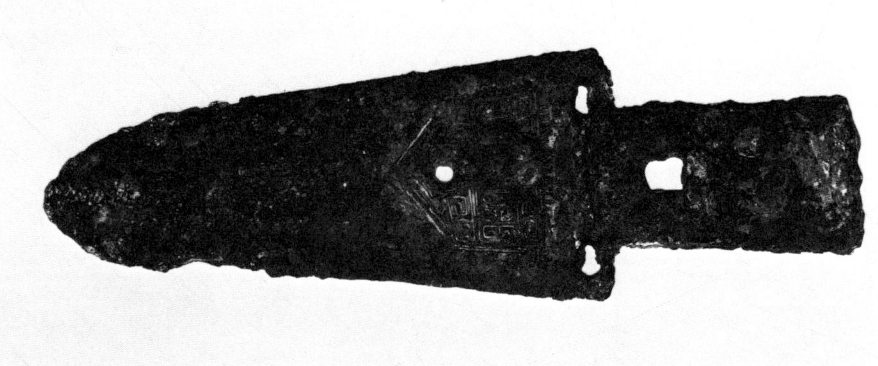

19

17 **Shang dynasty**
Ge, socketed dagger-axe
Bronze, L. 8 (20.3), W. 2⅝ (6.7)
Inscribed on tang: Yue
Gift of Prof. and Mrs. Herrlee G. Creel
Acc. no. 1986.332
PUBLICATIONS Creel, "Origins," 68, pl. V A; Creel, *Birth of China*, pl. XII; James Mellon Menzies, *The Shang Ko: A Study of the Characteristic Weapon of the Bronze Age in China during the Period 1311–1039 B.C.* (Toronto: Far Eastern Department of the Royal Ontario Museum, University of Toronto, 1965), 156, 185–189, no. 136, pl. LXIII; *Bulletin*, 32.

18 **Shang dynasty**
Ge, socketed dagger-axe
Bronze, L. 9⅜ (23.8), W. 2 (5.1)
Gift of Prof. and Mrs. Herrlee G. Creel
Acc. no. 1986.333
PUBLICATIONS *Bulletin*, 32.

19 **Shang dynasty**
Ge, dagger-axe
Bronze, L. 8½ (21.6), W. 2½ (6.3)
Gift of Prof. and Mrs. Herrlee G. Creel
Acc. no. 1986.334
PUBLICATIONS *Bulletin*, 32.

17

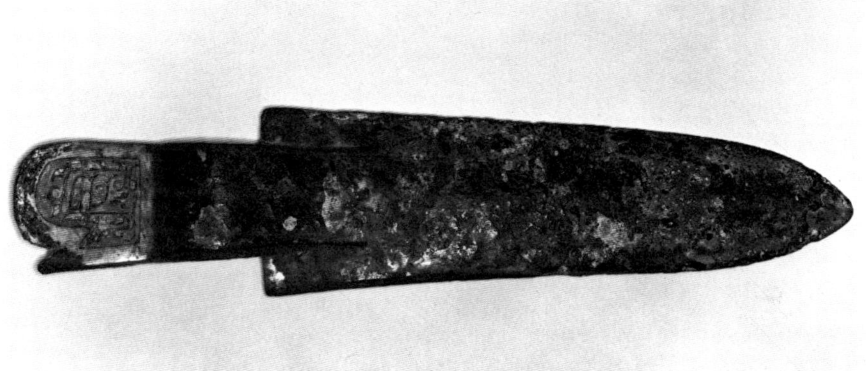
18

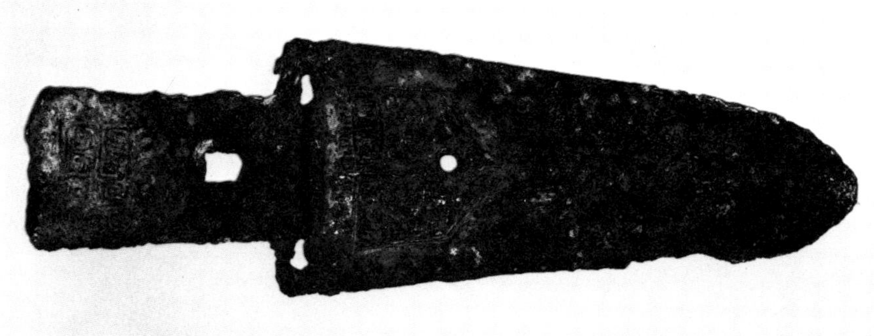
19

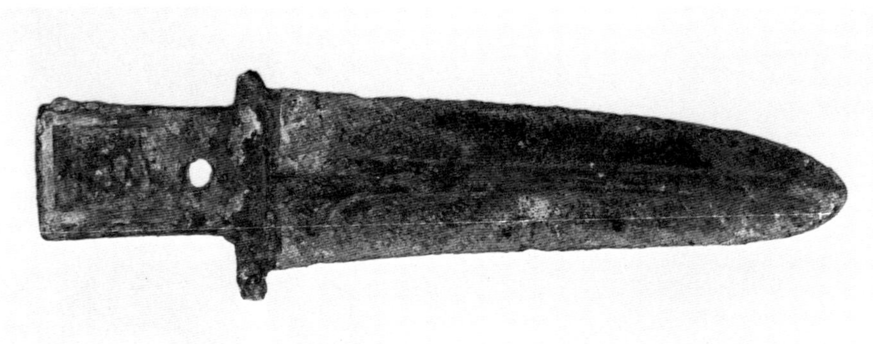

20

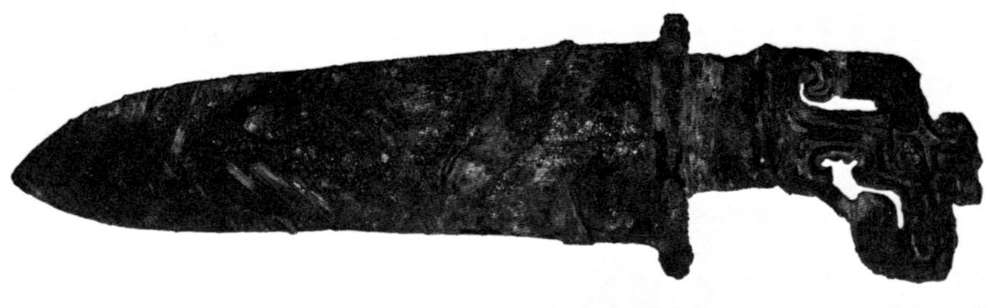

21

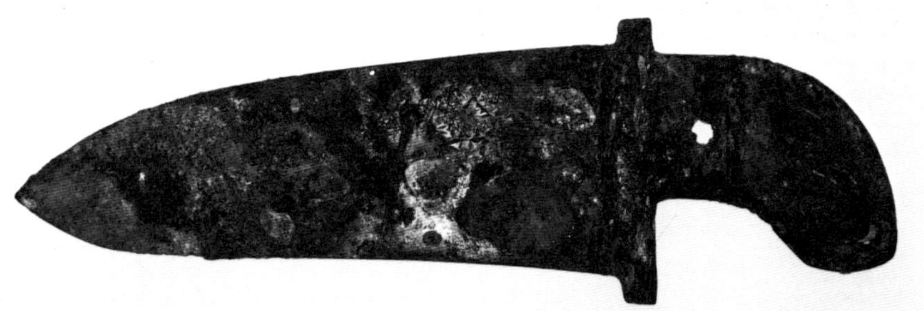

22

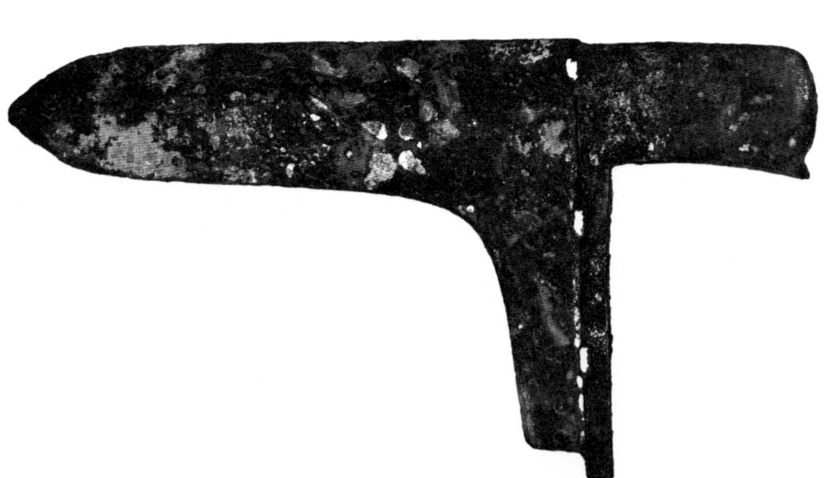

23

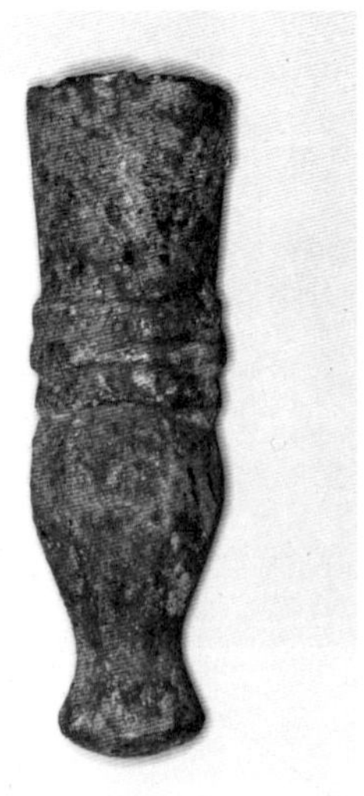

24

20 **Shang dynasty**
Ge, dagger-axe
Bronze, L. 10 (25.4), W. 2¾ (7)
Gift of Prof. and Mrs. Herrlee G. Creel
Acc. no. 1986.335
PUBLICATIONS *Bulletin*, 32.

21 **Shang dynasty**
Ge, dagger-axe
Bronze, L. 11⅜ (28.9), W. 3 (7.6)
Gift of Prof. and Mrs. Herrlee G. Creel
Acc. no. 1986.336
PUBLICATIONS *Bulletin*, 32.

22 **Shang dynasty**
Ge, dagger-axe
Bronze, L. 9½ (24.1), W. 3 (7.6)
Gift of Prof. and Mrs. Herrlee G. Creel
Acc. no. 1986.337
PUBLICATIONS *Bulletin*, 32.

23 **Late Shang dynasty**
Ge, dagger-axe
Bronze, L. 10 1/16 (25.5), W. 5 5/16 (13.5)
Gift of Prof. and Mrs. Herrlee G. Creel
Acc. no. 1986.338
PUBLICATIONS *Bulletin*, 32.

24 **Eastern Zhou dynasty**
Tun, ferrule
Bronze, L. 3⅞ (9.9), DIAM. (max. dim. oval mouth) 1 3/16 (3)
Gift of Prof. and Mrs. Herrlee G. Creel
Acc. no. 1986.346
PUBLICATIONS *Bulletin*, 33.

The dagger-axe was the premier weapon of the Shang army, having the stabbing potential of a dagger but delivering a thrust with the force of a blow from an axe. The weapon is also replicated in jade, or it may have a jade blade set in a bronze mount.[1] Sometimes, even metal *ge* are so thinly cast as to be of no practical use.[2] Apparently then, this weapon was so important to the Shang that it enjoyed both a symbolic and practical status. It must have been desirable to have as many *ge* as possible in a burial; they could be ceremonial implements, inexpensive imitations, or the real thing.

This type of weapon has a very long history in China. Occasionally, the written character "battle-axe" occurs on an actual weapon, as on one example in this collection previously published by Professor Creel (cat. no. 17).[3] He described the three feet at the bottom of the character as depicting "a stand to hold it erect." A four-clawed object that looks like a stand of this sort has since been found in Tomb 5 at Anyang, and another is known from a private collection.[4] (The plain shaft mounting in the Creel collection [cat. no. 24] illustrates an Eastern Zhou handle type). James Menzies, in his discussion of this piece, implied a date in the era of King Wu Ding, which is the presumed date of Tomb 5.[5]

The raised, ropelike ridges on the socket of this axe are an uncommon feature. They might help to strengthen the piece, but I think it is more likely that they are a decorative imitation of the heavy lashing used to secure the blade to the shaft.[6] A genuine instance of a reinforced blade is provided by another socketed *ge* in the collection (cat. no. 18). In this instance, the narrow tang was brought down into the blade, making it look as though one part had been welded to the other. But that is not the case; the weapon is a single piece, a normal bivalve casting. The delicate tracery on the tang, outlining a large eye and claw pattern, was probably originally inlaid with turquoise. The contrast between the vibrant blue of the stone inset and the once rich, golden color of the bronze must have been stunning. Clearly, the warriors of ancient China did not consider it inappropriate to decorate their weapons, even with the most delicate inlays. Indeed, we know that gifts made by the king to worthy retainers in the Western Zhou epoch often consisted of fancy military equipment.[7]

Five remaining Shang blades in the collection, all hafted like tomahawks, illustrate some of the less lavish forms of ornament. The curving tang of one (cat. no. 22) has some simple, recessed, geometric patterns. Designs of this sort could even be carried on the shoulder of the blade itself (cat. no. 19). In another example (cat. no. 21), the whole tang is treated like an animal in silhouette; nearly a dozen pieces closely resembling this piece were found in Tomb 5.[8] Of course, numerous *ge* are quite plain (cat. no. 20), and thus it follows that although some of these dagger-axes, especially those with jade blades, should be considered ceremonial, there must have been many weapons, modestly decorated or inscribed, that were still functioning tools of war.

The remaining *ge* in the collection, though still a Shang piece, is shaped differently than all the others and was attached to the shaft in a different way (cat. no. 23).[9] The throat of the blade has been pulled down until it runs parallel to the handle, and the butt end of the axe does the same. The piece slid into a slot in the shaft and was then lashed to it by passing leather thongs through the three perforations provided for this purpose.

The dagger-axe was a popular weapon throughout the Bronze Age. Battle scenes on bronze wine vessels dating from the later Zhou dynasty illustrate the use of the *ge* in close combat.[10] The latest form of the weapon was clearly derived from the curved Shang type. R.J.P.

NOTES

1. See Institute of Archaeology, Archaeologia Sinica, *Yinxu Fu Hao mu*, Ding series no. 23 (Beijing: Wenwu chubanshe, 1980), pls. CVII–CXIV, for illustrations of nearly three dozen jade *ge*; pl. LXXI for an exceptionally long jade blade set in a bronze mount; and pls. XVII'–XVIII' (sic) for appealing color illustrations of both variations.

2. Herrlee Glessner Creel, *The Birth of China* (New York: Frederick Ungar Publishing Co., 1964), 145–146, made the important observation that many of the very thinly cast *ge* are elaborately decorated and thus are not simply cheap imitations of real weapons. The same could be said of the *ge* with jade blades and turquoise inlays. He decided, quite correctly, that "if they were not designed for use in battle, the only alternative is that these weapons were made for purely ceremonial use." Jessica Rawson, *Ancient China: Art and Archaeology* (New York: Harper & Row, 1980), 48, fig. 34, states the same opinion and illustrates the three basic variations on the standard military model.

3. Creel, *Birth of China*, 250, pl. XII; the piece was then in the collection of Huang Po-ch'uan.

4. Institute of Archaeology, *Yinxu Fu Hao mu*, 110, item 847, pl. LXXIV, 6. The claw-shaped object is 13.8 cm. (5⁷⁄₁₆ in.) tall; the diameter of the hollow "bird-leg," which is called the "eye of the axe-hole," is 2.8 cm. (1³⁄₃₂ in.). The weight, 0.35 kilograms (a little better than three-quarters of a pound), and the spread of the legs are sufficient to provide stability. Max Loehr, *Chinese Bronze Age Weapons: The Werner Jannings Collection in the Chinese National Palace Museum, Peking* (Ann Arbor, Mich.: University of Michigan Press, 1956), 175, no. 84, fig. 95, pl. XXXIV, provides an example with "three long prongs . . . short, hooked clutch and a spur" dated as "probably Shang."

5. James Mellon Menzies, *The Shang Ko: A Study of the Characteristic Weapon of the Bronze Age in China during the Period 1311–1039 B.C.* (Toronto: Far Eastern Department of the Royal Ontario Museum, University of Toronto, 1965), 185–189, item no. 136, pl. LXIII (type VIID), interprets the inscriptional evidence as indicating a date in the era of King Wu Ding.

6. Ibid., 185.

7. Edward L. Shaughnessy, "Historical Perspectives on the Introduction of the Chariot into China," *Harvard Journal of Asiatic Studies* 48, no. 1 (June 1988): 222, discusses royal conferrals in association with the history of the chariot.

8. Institute of Archaeology, *Yinxu Fu Hao mu*, pls. LXXII–LXXIII, illustrates ten or more that are quite similar. For better illustrations of these, and two in color of additional pieces with different designs, all from the same tomb, see Institute of Archaeology, *Yinxu qingtongqi*, Yi series no. 24 (Beijing: Wenwu chubanshe, 1985), pl. 56, fig. 29:1–2.

9. Institute of Archaeology, *Yinxu qingtongqi*, 481–482; found in HGH10, this late-Shang assemblage includes another such example, related in shape but with a pole cap in the form of a recumbent animal, as well as a ring-handled knife, a *you* wine bucket (missing its lid), and a *jue*, illustrated in pls. 239–241 and figs. 89–90.

10. Jenny F. So, "The Inlaid Bronzes of the Warring States Period," in Wen Fong, ed., *The Great Bronze Age of China: An Exhibition from the People's Republic of China* (New York: Metropolitan Museum of Art, 1980), 309, 316 (color plates, pp. 290–292; fig. 107, p. 317), discusses a piece excavated in Chengdu, Sichuan Province, which illustrates the use of the *ge* in an attack on a walled fortification, and again in a naval engagement. So properly compares this vessel with the famous "Jannings *hu*." Her statement that the two vessels are identical should be understood as meaning only that they illustrate the same general themes. The Jannings vessel is discussed in Eleanor von Erdberg, "A Hu with Pictorial Decoration," *Archives of the Chinese Art Society of America* 6 (1952): 18; Charles D. Weber, *Chinese Pictorial Bronze Vessels of the Late Chou Period* (Ascona, Switz.: Artibus Asiae Publishers, 1968), 183–206, figs. 54–55, 68; see also Robert J. Poor, "Evolution of a Secular Vessel Type," *Oriental Art* 14, no. 2 (1968): 98–106. For a nearly identical vessel in Beijing, see Rawson, *Chinese Bronzes: Art and Ritual* (London: British Museum Publications, 1987), fig. 28e.

Shang Weapons and Tools

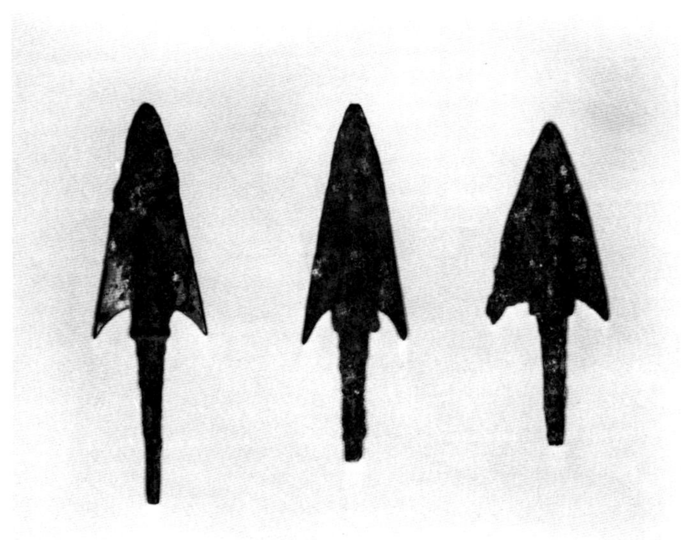

25, 26, 27

25 **Shang dynasty**
Arrowhead
Bronze, L. 2 13/16 (7.1), W. 13/16 (2)
Gift of Prof. and Mrs. Herrlee G. Creel
Acc. no. 1986.343
PUBLICATIONS Creel, "Origins," 68, pl. V C; Creel, *Birth of China*, pl. VII; *Bulletin*, 33.

26 **Shang dynasty**
Arrowhead
Bronze, L. 2 1/2 (6.4), W. 3/4 (1.9)
Gift of Prof. and Mrs. Herrlee G. Creel
Acc. no. 1986.344
PUBLICATIONS Creel, "Origins," 68, pl. V E; Creel, *Birth of China*, pl. VII; *Bulletin*, 33.

27 **Shang dynasty**
Arrowhead
Bronze, L. 2 3/16 (5.6), W. 7/8 (2.2)
Gift of Prof. and Mrs. Herrlee G. Creel
Acc. no. 1986.345
PUBLICATIONS Creel, *Birth of China*, pl. VII; *Bulletin*, 33.

28 **Shang dynasty**
Spearhead
Bronze, L. 9 5/8 (24.5), W. 1 7/8 (4.7)
Gift of Prof. and Mrs. Herrlee G. Creel
Acc. no. 1986.342
PUBLICATIONS *Bulletin*, 33.

29 **Shang dynasty**
Knife
Bronze, L. 10 3/4 (27.3), W. 1 15/16 (4.9)
Gift of Prof. and Mrs. Herrlee G. Creel
Acc. no. 1986.340
PUBLICATIONS *Bulletin*, 33.

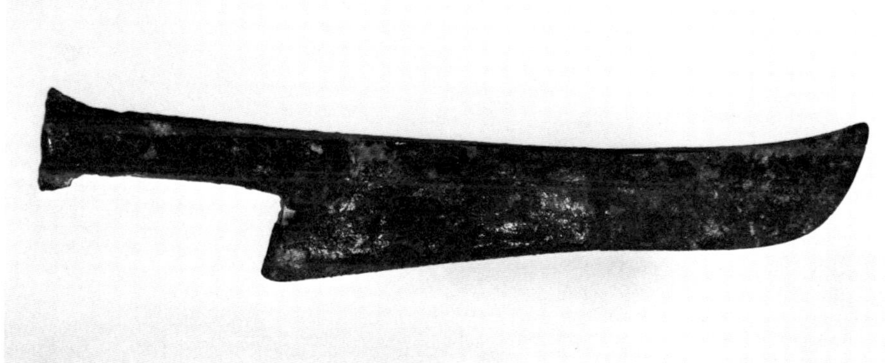

29

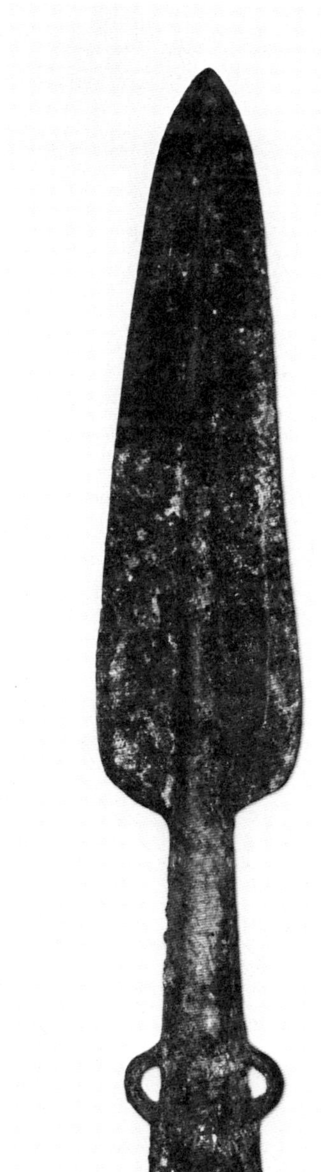

28

30 **Shang dynasty**
Knife

Bronze, L. 13⅞ (35.3), W. 2¼ (5.7)
Gift of Prof. and Mrs. Herrlee G. Creel
Acc. no. 1986.341
PUBLICATIONS Creel, "Origins," 68, pl. VI; *Bulletin*, 33.

31 **Shang dynasty**
Socketed Axe Head

Bronze, L. 5 (12.7), W. 1⅞ (4.7)
Gift of Prof. and Mrs. Herrlee G. Creel
Acc. no. 1986.339
PUBLICATIONS *Bulletin*, 33.

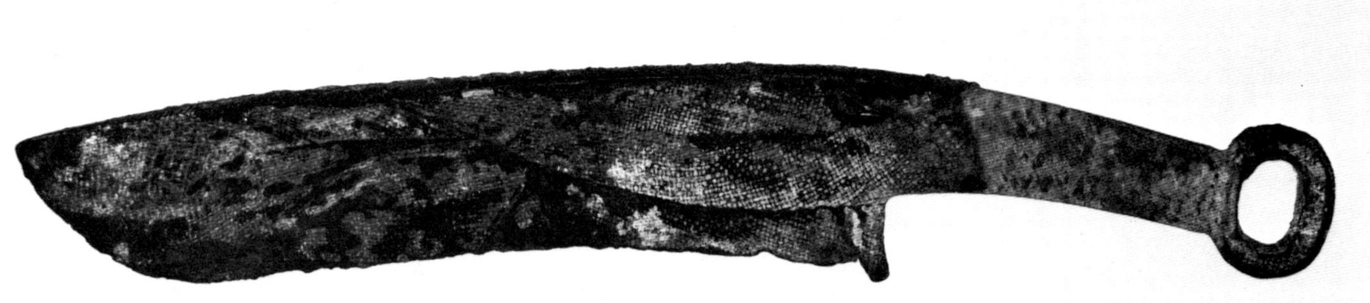

30

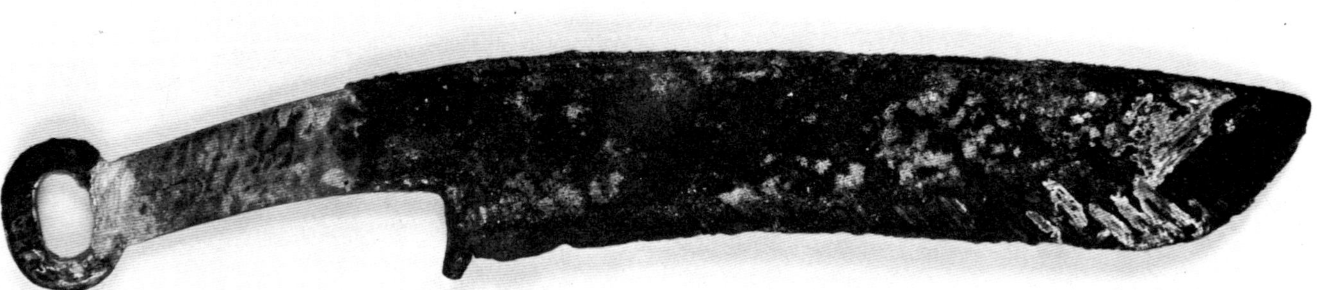

30

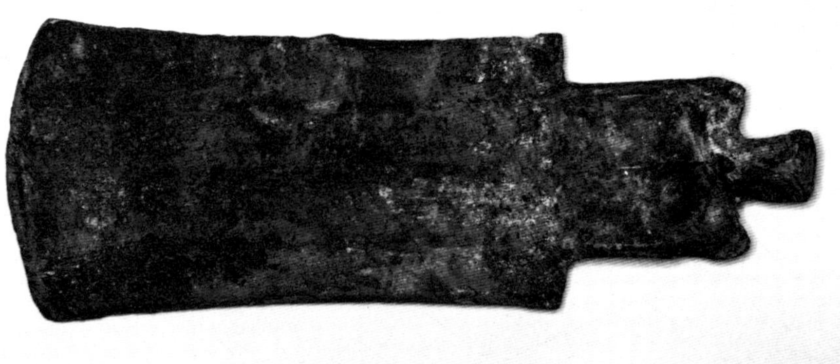

31

Tools and weapons like these are well represented among the materials discovered at Anyang, excavated for example from Tomb 5, associated with Lady Fu Hao, consort to King Wu Ding. The three arrowheads in our collection (cat. nos. 25–27) have the same broad, tapering, wing shape as those from the Fu Hao burial.[1] Arrowheads made in later centuries have a minimal wing and are much smaller, a modification that increases their armor-piercing potential and renders them more deadly.[2] In fact, the Shang arrowhead is like the kind usually seen on a hunting arrow, something designed to pierce skin or hide rather than bamboo, bone, or leather armor. Nonetheless, the impact of one these missiles must have been devastating, for the Chinese used a composite bow, shaped like our "Cupid's bow," probably made of horn and sinew with a framework of wood and a "pull" that may have been well over a hundred pounds. This composite bow was capable of delivering a bronze-tipped bamboo arrow with deadly force at a far greater distance than the more cumbersome long bow.[3]

The spearhead is also a Shang type, characterized by the simple leaf-shaped blade and the tubular socket for hafting the head onto a piece of wood (cat. no. 28). The two loops for binding are an optional feature. Although arrowheads are well known from prehistoric sites, the spear is not. This raises the question of origins, all the more so since there is an intriguing similarity between the Shang spear and a close counterpart found in modern-day southern Russia. Possibly, the spear, like the chariot, was imported (see cat. nos. 32–34).[4]

A similar discussion is prompted by the typology of the curved knife associated with chariot burials (cat. no. 30). Here, however, the suggestion is that the semilunar knife was exported from China to foreign lands, or that there was a reciprocal interchange of influences in both directions, the Chinese contributing the shape, and non-Chinese regions introducing the realistic animal heads that appear on the handles of some of these knives.[5] Irrespective of its origins, the knife is not a weapon but a tool, designed for cutting rather than stabbing or slashing, and was, on occasion, used in the sacrifice of animals.[6] Some ritual function is implied by the fact that knives of the plain-handled variety were also made in jade and are found in tombs alongside the metal ones. Knives of this kind must have had some special significance for the Shang. As if to corroborate this special ritual association, the ring-handled metal blade in our collection was wrapped in cloth and matting at the time of burial, just like a ritual vessel. Through time, both wrapping materials have hardened onto the blade, and are so well preserved as part of the patina that one can actually count the threads and reconstruct the weave.[7]

The small socketed axe provides another example of an ancient tool (cat. no. 31).[8] Three low ridges run the length of the blade and the edges all around are slightly raised. The parallel lines and small hammerlike lug also occur on other examples of this kind of axe, all of which are as poorly cast as this one. Thus, the lack of finish in our example and the somewhat haphazard treatment of the contour of the socket may be symptomatic of an early date. Indeed, this may be the earliest of the entire group of bronze tools and weapons. R.J.P.

NOTES

1. Institute of Archaeology, Archaeologia Sinica, *Yinxu Fu Hao mu*, Ding series no. 23 (Beijing: Wenwu chubanshe, 1980), pl. LXXIV, illustrates several dozen arrowheads of this sort.

2. Jessica Rawson, *Ancient China: Art and Archaeology* (New York: Harper & Row, 1980), 48, fig. 35, provides a good assembly of arrowheads showing the general development of the type. Max Loehr, *Chinese Bronze Age Weapons: The Werner Jannings Collection in the Chinese National Palace Museum, Peking* (Ann Arbor, Mich.: University of Michigan Press, 1956), 132–134, pl. XLVI, reproduces a collection that better illustrates the variety among single types.

3. Herrlee Glessner Creel, *The Birth of China* (New York: Frederick Ungar Publishing Co., 1964), 142, commented on the power of the bows used in the military examination system during the Qing dynasty. He estimated the pull on the bows he saw in curio shops at about 160 pounds—about the same as the modern pulley-bow, which is much like the composite-bow used in ancient China.

4. Loehr, *Chinese Bronze Age Weapons*, 239–248, provides an illustrated introduction to the subject.

5. Ibid., 65–71, illustrates knives much like ours including some with animal heads. See Institute of Archaeology, *Yinxu Fu Hao mu*, pl. LXVI, for a group of ring-handled knives and one specimen with animal head.

6. Creel, "On the Origins of the Manufacture and Decoration of Bronze in the Shang Period," *Monumenta Serica* 1, fasc. 1 (October 1935): 68, refers to inscriptional evidence which indicates "that knives something like this were used in sacrificing animals."

7. Ibid. Creel drew attention to the fact that just like the blade, "Shang corpses seemed to have been wrapped in matting."

8. Loehr, *Chinese Bronze Age Weapons*, 10–11, 130–131, pl. XIII, illustrates a piece much like ours and concludes his discussion with the following: "This type seems to belong to a sphere quite different from that of the Shang weapons with their inextricable relations to the ritual bronzes of the Anyang stage. Thus, a date earlier than 'Anyang' might be considered." Nonetheless, the date provided in the introductory paragraph of the catalogue entry reads: "Chou (?)."

The Arts of Warfare: The Chariot and Its Outfitting

32 **Shang dynasty**
Horse Trappings for a Chariot
a. *Two-part Bit (Snaffle)*
Bronze, L. (each unit) 4¼ (10.7), 4³⁄16 (10.6), W. (each unit) 1⅝ (4.2), 1⅝ (4.2)
Acc. no. 1986.347a
b. *Cheek-Piece (for a Snaffle)*
Bronze, L. 3³⁄16 (8.1), W. 2⅛ (5.4)
Acc. no. 1986.347b
Gift of Prof. and Mrs. Herrlee G. Creel
Acc. nos. 1986.347a–b
PUBLICATIONS *Bulletin*, 33.

33 **Shang dynasty**
Horse Trappings for a Chariot
a. *Harness Decoration: Cross Tube*
Bronze, L. 2 (5.2), W. 15⁄16 (2.4)
Acc. no. 1986.347c
b. *Harness Decoration: Cross Tube*
Bronze, L. 1⅝ (4.1), W. 1³⁄16 (2.9)
Acc. no. 1986.347d
c. *Harness Decoration: Boss*
Bronze, DIAM. 1¹¹⁄16 (4.3)
Acc. no. 1986.347e
d. *Harness Decoration: Pair of Bosses*
Bronze, DIAM. 1⅛ (2.8), DIAM. 1⅛ (2.8)
Acc. nos. 1986.347f–g
Gift of Prof. and Mrs. Herrlee G. Creel
Acc. nos. 1986.347c–g
PUBLICATIONS *Bulletin*, 33.

34 **Late Western Zhou dynasty/Western Han dynasty**
Luan, chariot jingle
Bronze, H. 7 (17.8), W. 4 (10.3), DP. 1⅞ (4.7)
Gift of Prof. and Mrs. Herrlee G. Creel
Acc. no. 1987.348
PUBLICATIONS *Bulletin*, 33.

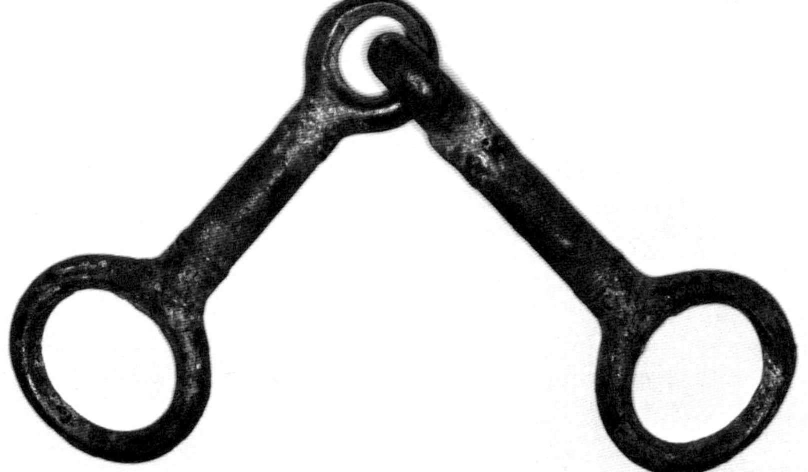

32a

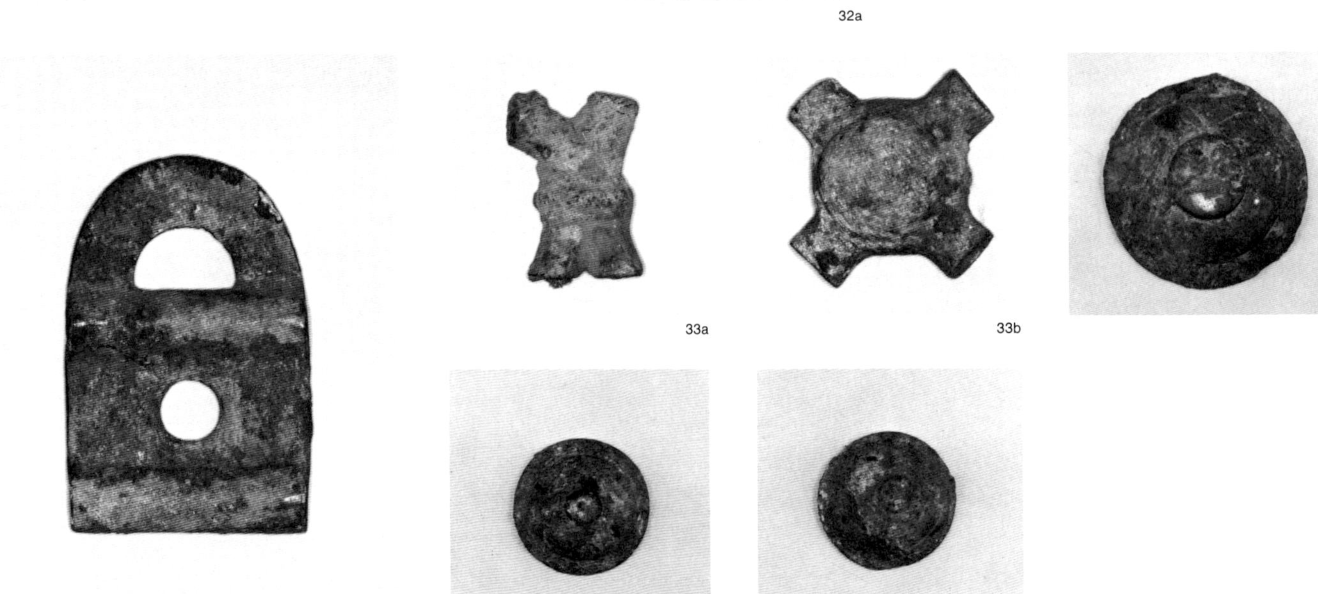

32b 33a 33b 33c 33d 33d

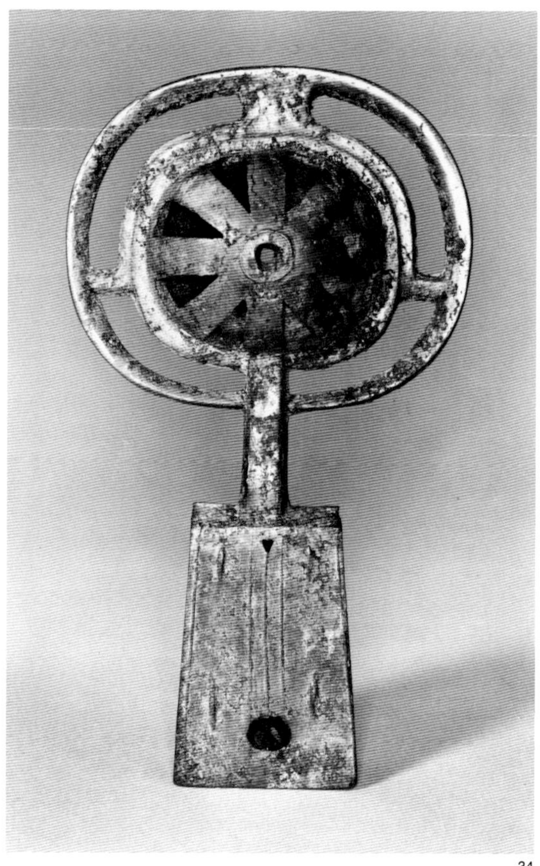

34

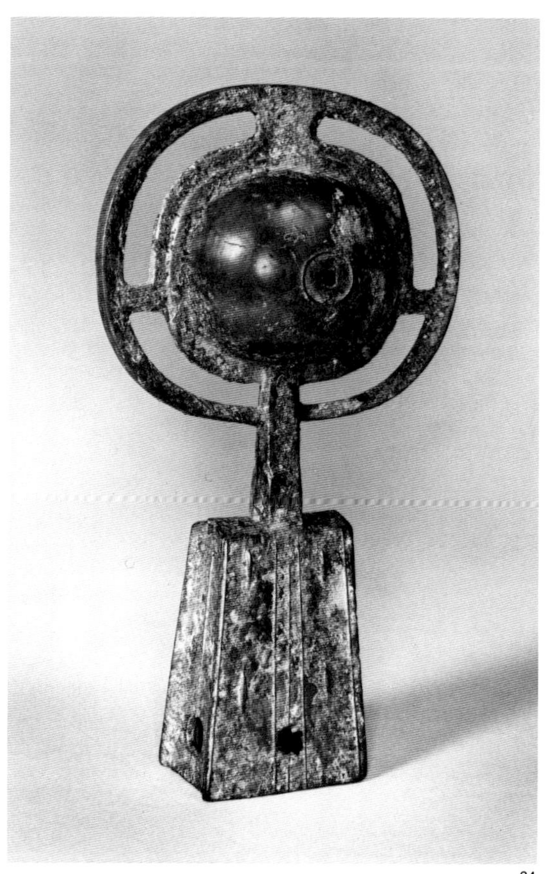

34

These trappings illustrate a small part of the equipment required to outfit a Chinese chariot and horses. The plain object joined by rings is a snaffle bit (cat. no. 32a), which slips between the gap in the horse's teeth at the corners of the mouth, and is connected to the cheek-piece (cat. no. 32b) and bridle. Bit and bridle are the minimum needed to guide these powerful animals; additional straps or lines would attach the horses as a team to the yoke of the chariot. The four-horse chariot, which was the prevailing model according to the evidence of the chariot burials discovered in the royal cemetery at Anyang, demanded a great many reins and strapping. The cross-shaped fittings (cat. nos. 33a and 33b) served to keep the tack orderly and also as decoration.

None of this equipment looks very ancient or particularly Chinese—for good reason. The chariot was a foreign import, arriving late in the Shang dynasty in a fully developed form. Indeed, the single most distinguishing feature of the Chinese chariot is the number of spokes in the wheel, and even this detail is not uniquely Chinese.[1] The case of the chariot illustrates the universal acceptance of a common design with only modest local adaptations.[2] As far as the tack is concerned, there is no appreciable difference between a modern bit and an ancient one, regardless of their place of origin.

Although chariot technology had already stabilized by the time the invention reached China, the use of the chariot, and its manufacture, remained local issues. For the Shang, the chariot seems to have been a parade vehicle or a mobile command post; its use as a weapon came later, in the Zhou dynasty. Eventually, the chariot was replaced by the mounted horseman, which prompted the introduction of the stirrup and saddle. But regardless of how or when the chariot was used, the Chinese themselves must have made the parts, for there is nothing to suggest foreign manufacture of chariot equipment or horse trappings or the engagement of foreign drivers. Quite the contrary: when items like these are decorated, the ornament is always in the style of the period and not much different from what could be found on contemporary weapons or ritual vessels. Moreover, skeletal remains indicate that the driver and the two weapons experts that made up the assault team were Chinese. The chariot, and all that went with it, was fully integrated into ancient Chinese culture.

The bronze rattle (cat. no. 34) is the only chariot fitting proper in the collection. As many as half a dozen such rattles were attached to the yoke of the vehicle, adding a jaunty note to its passage. Designed to maintain the clarity of the sound, the ring suspension is a later but persistent trait. The date proposed for rattles of this type ranges from the late Western Zhou down to the Western Han dynasty.[3] R.J.P.

NOTES

1. For a comprehensive survey of the chariot literature and an interpretation of chariot use, see Edward L. Shaughnessy, "Historical Perspectives on the Introduction of the Chariot into China," *Harvard Journal of Asiatic Studies* 48, no. 1 (June 1988): 189–238; for remarks on the number of spokes, see 193–194; for ancient drawings depicting the chariot, fig. 3. See also Jessica Rawson, *Ancient China: Art and Archaeology* (New York: Harper & Row, 1980), 49–52.

2. The late Ludwig Bachhofer was fond of quoting a conversation with Bishop White who had witnessed the opening of a Shang chariot burial. White noted that the Chinese chariot looked just like an Etruscan one he had seen in a museum, down to many of its details. The Etruscan chariot would have had fewer spokes.

3. See Eleanor von Erdberg, *Chinese Bronzes from the Collection of Chester Dale and Dolly Carter* (Ascona, Switz.: Artibus Asiae Publishers, 1978), no. 95, for a similar specimen attributed to "Late Western Chou through Ch'un-Ch'iu to Warring States." Another example in Edmund Capon and William MacQuitty, *The Princess of Jade* (London: Thomas Nelson and Sons, 1973), 133–134, is identified as "Western Han."

The Arts of Archery and The Hunt

35 **Shang dynasty**
Arrowhead
Bone, L. 4½ (11.5)
Gift of Prof. and Mrs. Herrlee G. Creel
Acc. no. 1986.350
PUBLICATIONS Creel, *Birth of China*, pl. VII; *Bulletin*, 33.

36 **Shang dynasty**
Arrowhead
Bone, L. 3⅝ (9.2)
Gift of Prof. and Mrs. Herrlee G. Creel
Acc. no. 1986.351
PUBLICATIONS Creel, *Birth of China*, pl. VII; *Bulletin*, 33.

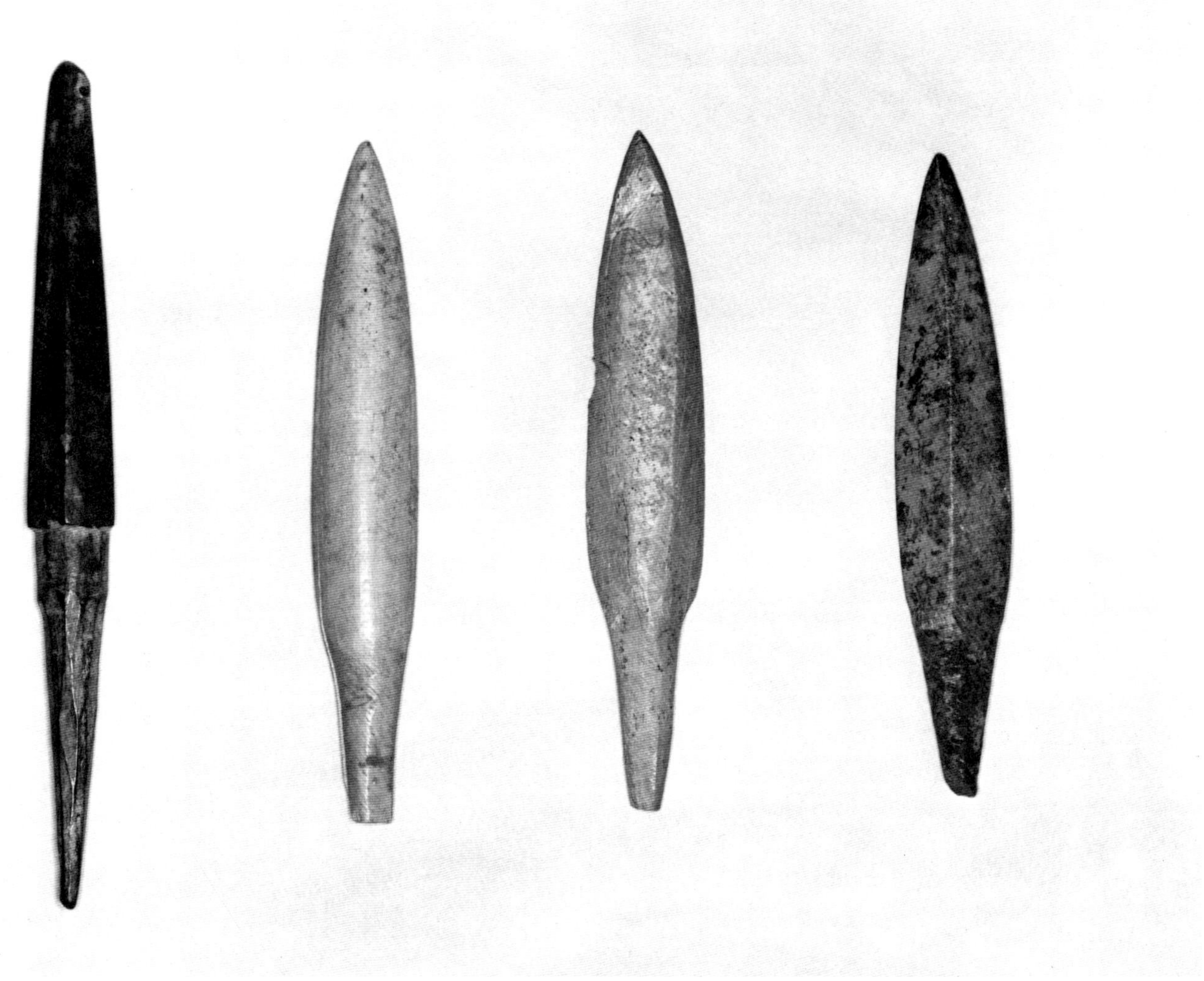

35, 36, 37, 38

37 **Shang dynasty**
Arrowhead
Bone, L. 3⅝ (9.2)
Gift of Prof. and Mrs. Herrlee G. Creel
Acc. no. 1986.352
PUBLICATIONS *Bulletin*, 33.

38 **Shang dynasty**
Arrowhead
Bone, L. 3 7/16 (8.7)
Gift of Prof. and Mrs. Herrlee G. Creel
Acc. no. 1986.353
PUBLICATIONS Creel, *Birth of China*, pl. VII; *Bulletin*, 33.

39 **Shang dynasty**
Arrowhead
Bone, L. 2⅞ (7.4)
Gift of Prof. and Mrs. Herrlee G. Creel
Acc. no. 1986.354
PUBLICATIONS Creel, *Birth of China*, pl. VII; *Bulletin*, 33.

40 **Shang dynasty**
Arrowhead
Bone, L. 2 (5.1)
Gift of Prof. and Mrs. Herrlee G. Creel
Acc. no. 1986.355
PUBLICATIONS Creel, *Birth of China*, pl. VII; *Bulletin*, 33.

During the Bronze Age, the Shang continued to use natural materials for ordinary tools and weapons. Bone, for example, was fashioned into needles, awls, fish hooks, ornaments, armor plate, bow tips, and arrowheads. In fact, bone arrowheads seem to outnumber those made of bronze. W. C. White classified them into three groups depending on their use for hunting, archery practice, or ceremonial purposes.[1] The shapes of the various types differ principally in the tips, which can be either round or flat, in the presence of a central rib, and barbs. All of them have tangs. Professor Creel interpreted this as an indication that the stem was fashioned to slip into a bamboo shaft.[2]

Four of our arrowheads are without barbs. One of these (cat. no. 36) closely resembles a piece discovered at Zhengzhou, which has been described as suitable for hunting birds.[3] The two examples with midrib and sharp point (cat. nos. 37 and 38) are also apparently for hunting, whereas the one with a rounded tip (cat. no. 35) seems more appropriate to archery.

The two remaining examples are barbed. One of these is an obvious imitation of the typical Shang bronze type (cat. no. 40, cf. cat. nos. 25–27). The single concession to the fact that it was carved from bone, rather than cast in bronze, is seen in the deep curve of the barb which looks almost as though it were drilled.[4] R.J.P.

NOTES

1. William Charles White, *Bone Culture of Ancient China*, Museum Studies 4 (Toronto: University of Toronto Press, 1945), 38, identifies the hunting and archery types, but not the ceremonial one.
2. Herrlee Glessner Creel, *The Birth of China* (New York: Frederick Ungar Publishing Co., 1964), 97–98, 143, notes that the tang seen on Chinese stone arrowheads does not make sense in functional terms.
3. See Royal Ontario Museum, *The Chinese Exhibition* (exh. cat.), rev. ed. (Toronto: Royal Ontario Museum in cooperation with Times Newspapers, 1974), 66, no. 65.
4. See White, *Bone Culture*, 202, no. NB. 2936, pl. XCVII B, for a close parallel with a better preserved tang.

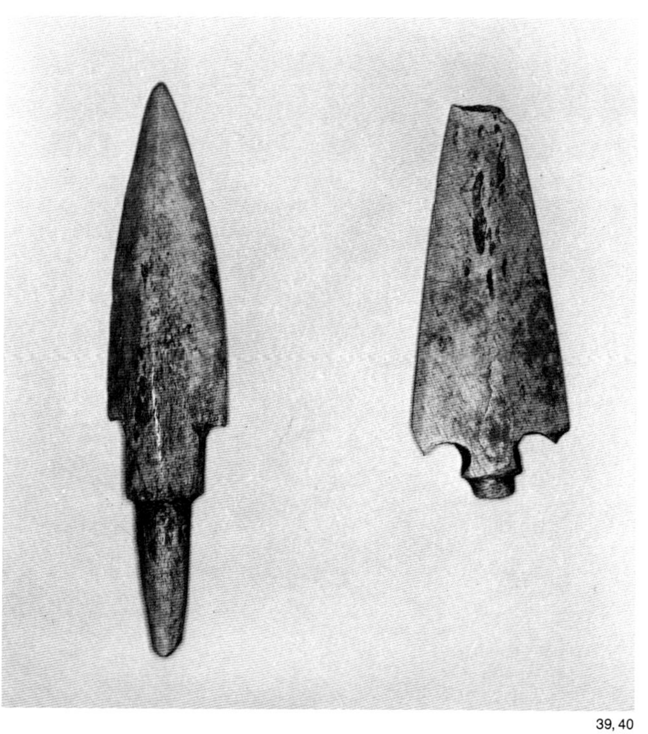

39, 40

Objects for Personal Adornment: The Hairpin

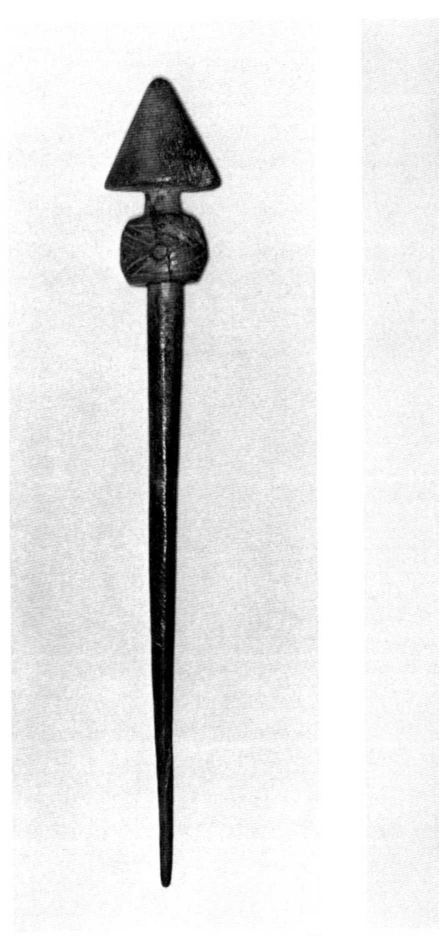

41

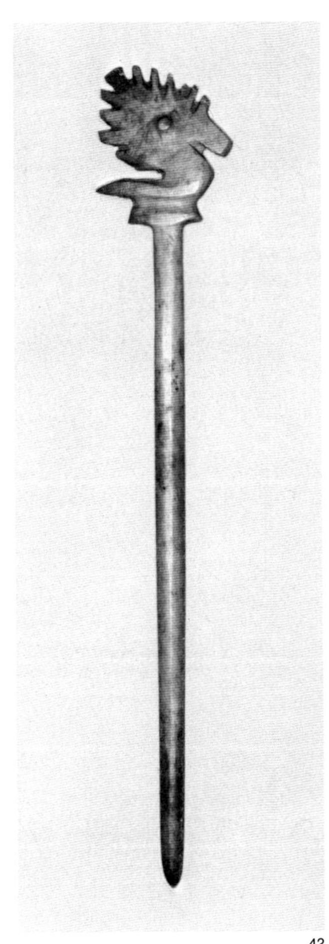

42

41 **Shang dynasty**
Hairpin
Bone, L. 5 1/16 (12.9)
Gift of Prof. and Mrs. Herrlee G. Creel
Acc. no. 1986.356
PUBLICATIONS *Bulletin*, 34.

42 **Shang dynasty**
Hairpin
Bone, L. 4 15/16 (12.6)
Gift of Prof. and Mrs. Herrlee G. Creel
Acc. no. 1986.357
PUBLICATIONS *Bulletin*, 34.

43 **Shang dynasty**
Hairpin
Bone, L. 3 1/2 (8.9)
Gift of Prof. and Mrs. Herrlee G. Creel
Acc. no. 1986.358
PUBLICATIONS *Bulletin*, 34.

44 **Shang dynasty**
Hairpin
Bone, L. 3 3/16 (8.1)
Gift of Prof. and Mrs. Herrlee G. Creel
Acc. no. 1986.359
PUBLICATIONS *Bulletin*, 34.

45 **Shang dynasty**
Hairpin Finial
Bone, L. 2 9/16 (6.5)
Gift of Prof. and Mrs. Herrlee G. Creel
Acc. no. 1986.360
PUBLICATIONS *Bulletin*, 34.

A great number of hairpins have been found in Shang burials, but none that are made of bronze. Indeed, there is a strange absence of metal body ornaments of any sort in the Shang finds. Why this is so is not clear. Perhaps metal was reserved for ritual implements, weapons, or emblems of state power. Whatever the reason, jade and bone were the favored materials for making objects of personal adornment, whether for men, women, or children.

The hairpins in our collection are of long, tapered pieces of bone with decoration at one end. Professor Creel noted that some bone hairpins are "polished so highly that persons seeing them for the first time refuse to believe that they are bone, or any other substance but jade."[1] That was the idea. Jade hairpins, such as those found in Tomb 5 at Anyang, were difficult to make, fragile, and expensive.[2] A bone hairpin, whether worn by a man to secure a ceremonial cap (if the Shang observed this practice), or by a woman as an ornament, would satisfy the purpose, be less costly, and look almost the same. Surprisingly, however, none of the small statuettes found in Shang tombs show a hairpin or comb of any kind, even in the most elaborate coiffure.[3]

Both Professor Creel and Bishop White commented on the common occurrence of a cock-head motif as decoration on these pins. However, the animals on the pieces published by White are unmistakably caricatures of a Mandarin duck, teal, or some bird like the merganser.[4] Using a motif drawn from nature as a personal ornament is a typically Chinese trait that persisted down to the end of the Qing dynasty.[5]

Li Ji (Li Chi), one of the original excavators of Anyang, proposed a typology of bone hairpins; our piece (cat. no. 44), with the well articulated roof-shaped cap, would be a mature example of this type according to his developmental scheme.[6] The hairpin with the cone-shaped terminal is unusual because of the barrel-shaped element at the top of the shaft (cat. no. 41). Both of the bird-finial pins are mature types. In one (cat. no. 43), the image of the fowl is reduced to a head, marked only by a few notches for a feathered crest, a thinly incised line on the bill, and the small plastic eye. The swelling of the chest and the spreading notched base give the appearance of a bird swimming among lily pads. The pin with multiple notches around the head supposedly represents a further step along the path of stylization (cat. no. 42). More than a dozen hairpins like this one were found in Tomb 5, but the disproportionately large size of the head on our example, the general elongation of its skull, and the absence of a downward-turning hook just beneath the tail, suggest that this is a later Shang piece.[7] The remaining piece (cat. no. 45) appears to be unfinished. R.J.P.

NOTES

1. Herrlee Glessner Creel, *The Birth of China* (New York: Frederick Ungar Publishing Co., 1964), 99.

2. See Institute of Archaeology, Archaeologia Sinica, *Yinxu Fu Hao mu*, Ding series no. 23 (Beijing: Wenwu chubanshe, 1980), pl. XXXV' (sic) for five hairpins attractively reproduced in color; 209–215, figs. 104–107, and pls. CLXXX–CLXXXI for nearly three dozen examples of different types; 166–167, figs. 86–87, and pls. XXXII'–XXXIII' (color) and CXLI–CXLV for a variety of bird plaques. Jade combs worn in the hair are also decorated with bird finials, as shown in 149, fig. 78, and pl. CSSVIII:2.

3. Ibid., figs. 79–80, pls. CXXIX–CXXXI, and color plates XXII'–XXV'.

4. Ibid., and William Charles White, *Bone Culture of Ancient China*, Museum Studies 4 (Toronto: University of Toronto Press, 1945), 189, pls. LXXXIX–XCI (bird-headed specimens are illustrated in the last two plates).

5. The bird motifs on these hairpins recall the elaborate "phoenix" hair ornaments popular in the Tang, Ming, and Qing dynasties. Some Tang examples from the collection of the Minneapolis Institute of the Arts are reproduced in Los Angeles County Museum, *The Arts of the Tang Dynasty* (exh. cat.) (Los Angeles: Los Angeles County Museum, 1957), 110, nos. 298 (gold phoenix ornament) and 300 (gold crown with butterfly set on a spring). A spectacular Ming crown of the Wanli Empress is reproduced in color in Wan-go Weng and Yang Boda, *The Palace Museum: Peking. Treasures of the Forbidden City* (New York: Harry N. Abrams, 1982), pl. 207; see also fig. 121 for a Song phoenix ornament.

6. For a very close parallel, see Li Chi, "Eight Types of Hairpins and the Evolution of Their Decorative Patterns," *Bulletin of the Institute of History and Philology* 30 (1959): 54, fig. 4:6 (B2226), pl. 9, no. 74. The comparable examples from Tomb 5 have a shorter and squatter "roof"; see Institute of Archaeology, *Yinxu Fu Hao mu*, 213–214, figs. 106–107, pl. CLXXXII:1.

7. Institute of Archaeology, *Yinxu Fu Hao mu*, 211, fig. 105, pl. CLXXXI; ibid., 59, fig. 5:7 (B2274: with notch). For an example without the hook, see White, *Bone Culture*, XCI:C (NB. 4299), which is perhaps unfinished.

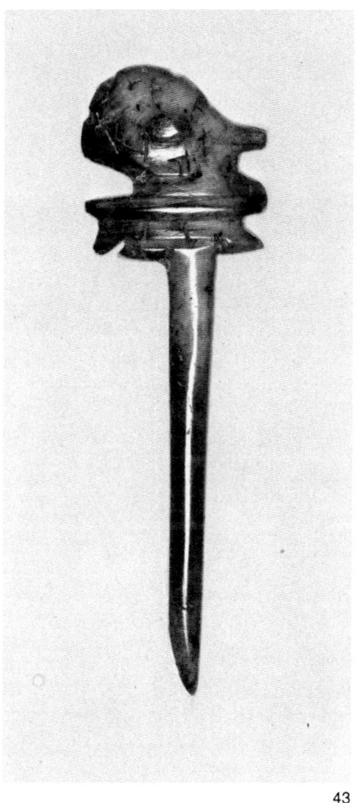

43

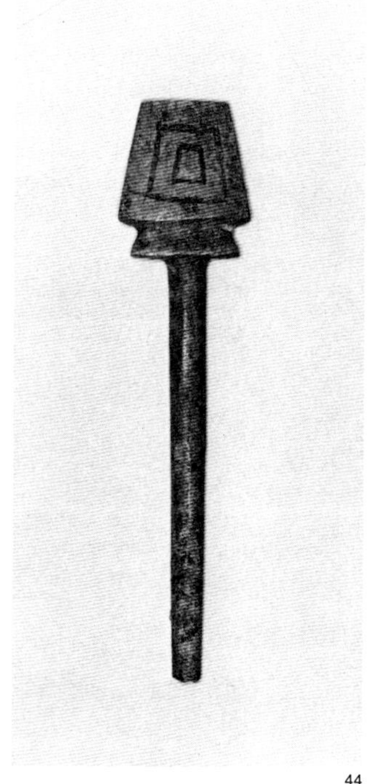

44

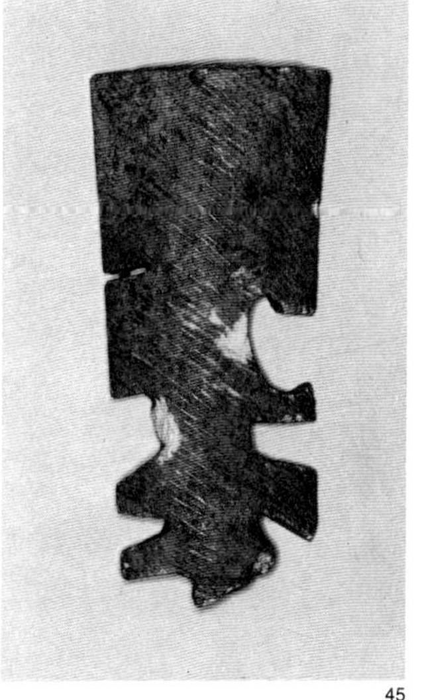

45

Ceremonial and Ornamental Objects in Bone, Shell, and Stone

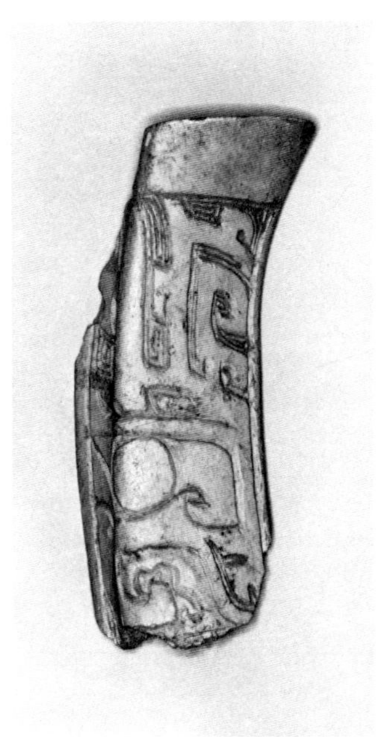
46

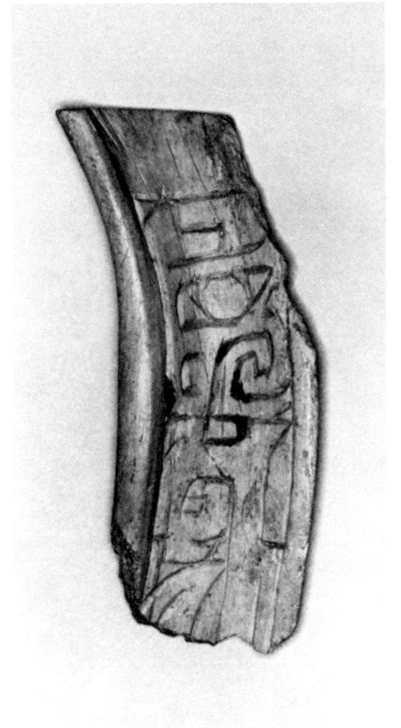
46

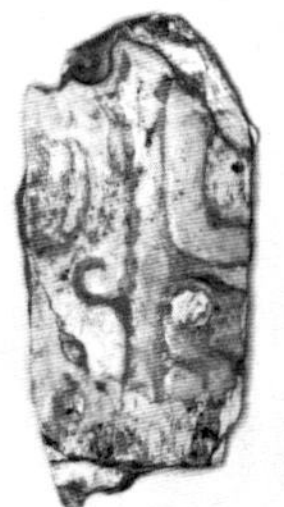
47

46 **Shang dynasty**, Anyang period
Fragment of a Spatula with Carved Taotie Decoration, 13th–11th century B.C.
Bone, L. 2⁹⁄₁₆ (6.5)
Gift of Prof. and Mrs. Herrlee G. Creel
Acc. no. 1986.361
PUBLICATIONS *Bulletin*, 33.

47 **Shang dynasty**
Fragment from a Carved and Inlaid Vessel (?)
Bone or ivory, inlaid with turquoise, L. 1¼ (3.2), W. ⅝ (1.6)
Gift of Prof. and Mrs. Herrlee G. Creel
Acc. no. 1986.362
PUBLICATIONS *Bulletin*, 34.

48 **Shang dynasty**
Fragment of a Spatula with Drilled Decoration
Bone, L. 2¾ (7.1)
Gift of Prof. and Mrs. Herrlee G. Creel
Acc. no. 1986.364
PUBLICATIONS *Bulletin*, 34.

49 **Shang dynasty**
Fragment of a Handle or Pendant with Incised Decoration
Bone, L. 1⅝ (4.2)
Gift of Prof. and Mrs. Herrlee G. Creel
Acc. no. 1986.365
PUBLICATIONS *Bulletin*, 34.

50 **Shang dynasty**
Pendant
Bone, L. 5 (12.8)
Gift of Prof. and Mrs. Herrlee G. Creel
Acc. no. 1986.363
PUBLICATIONS *Bulletin*, 34.

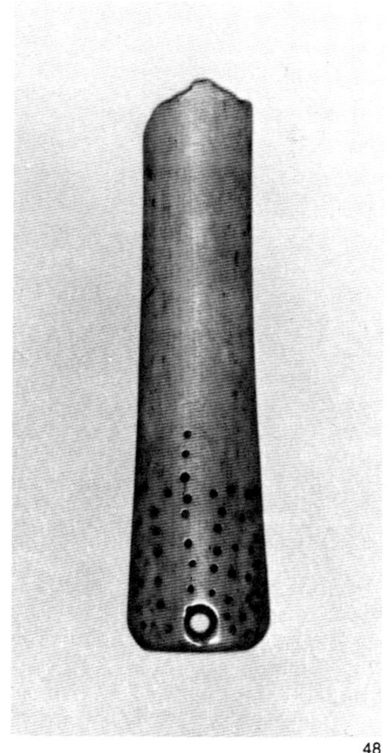
48

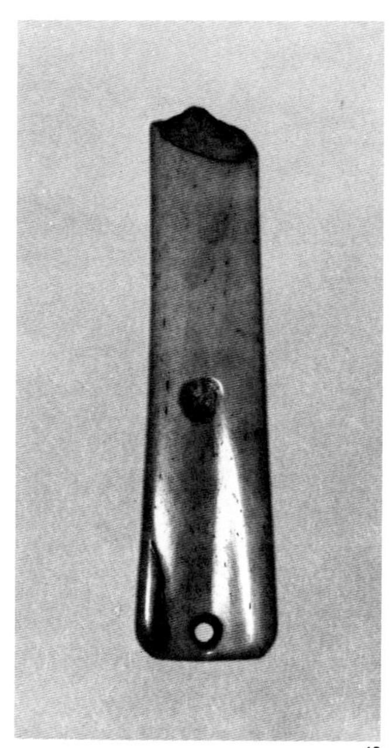
48

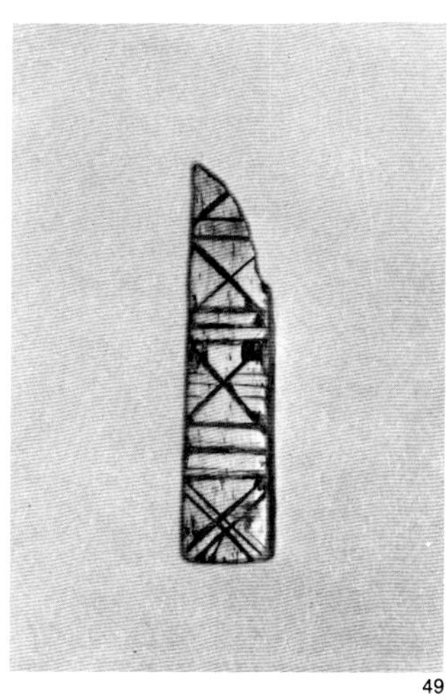
49

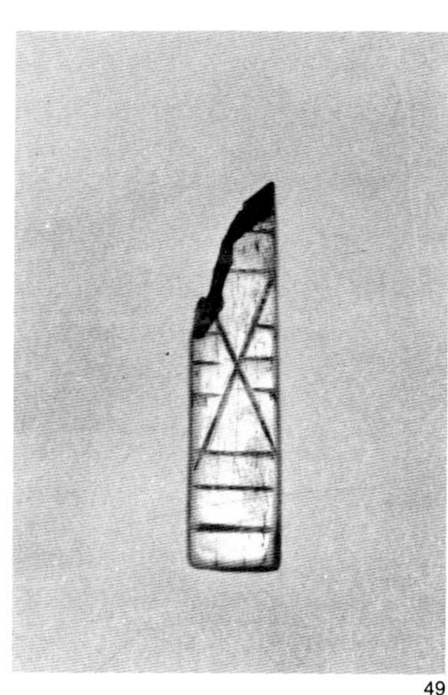
49

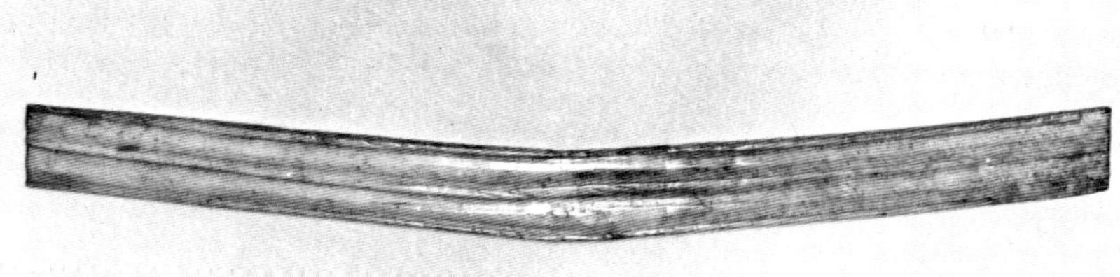
50

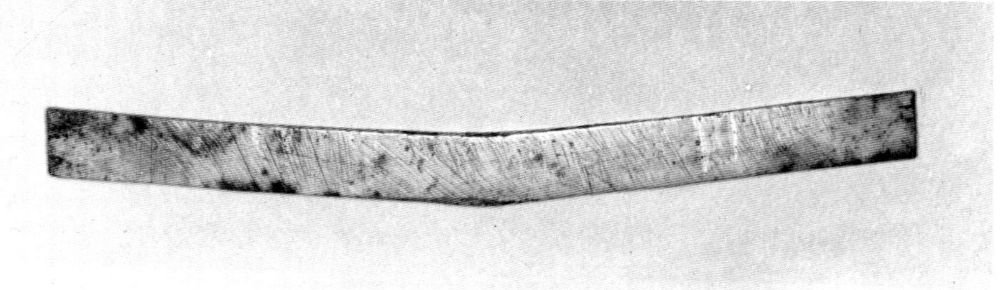
50

51 **Shang dynasty**
Carved Inlay (Teeth)
Shell, H. 11/16 (1.7), W. 7/8 (2.3)
Gift of Prof. and Mrs. Herrlee G. Creel
Acc. no. 1986.368
PUBLICATIONS Creel, *Birth of China*, pl. VII; *Bulletin*, 34.

52 **Shang dynasty**
Carved Inlay (Flange?)
Shell, H. 5/8 (1.6), W. 1 1/4 (3.1)
Gift of Prof. and Mrs. Herrlee G. Creel
Acc. no. 1986.370
PUBLICATIONS Creel, *Birth of China*, pl. VII; *Bulletin*, 34.

53 **Shang dynasty**
Carved Inlay
Shell, H. 13/16 (2.1), W. 1 1/4 (3.1)
Gift of Prof. and Mrs. Herrlee G. Creel
Acc. no. 1986.369
PUBLICATIONS Creel, *Birth of China*, pl. VII; *Bulletin*, 34.

54 **Shang dynasty**
Carved Inlay (Eye and Brow?)
Shell, H. 11/16 (1.7), W. 7/8 (2.3)
Gift of Prof. and Mrs. Herrlee G. Creel
Acc. no. 1986.371
PUBLICATIONS Creel, *Birth of China*, pl. VII; *Bulletin*, 34.

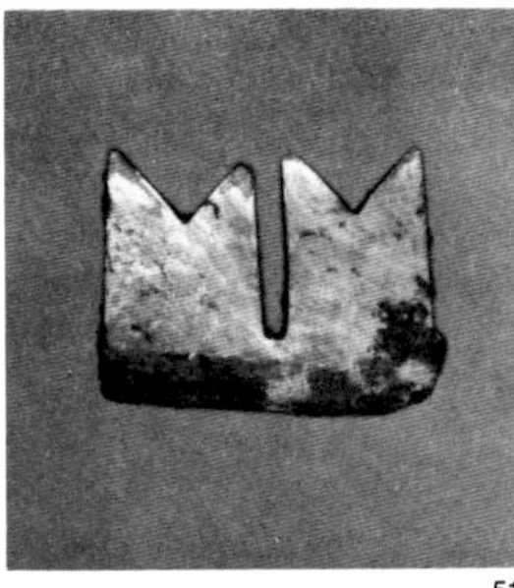
51

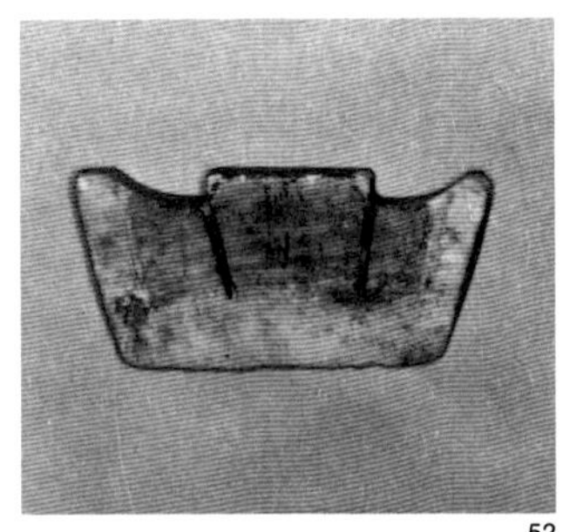
52

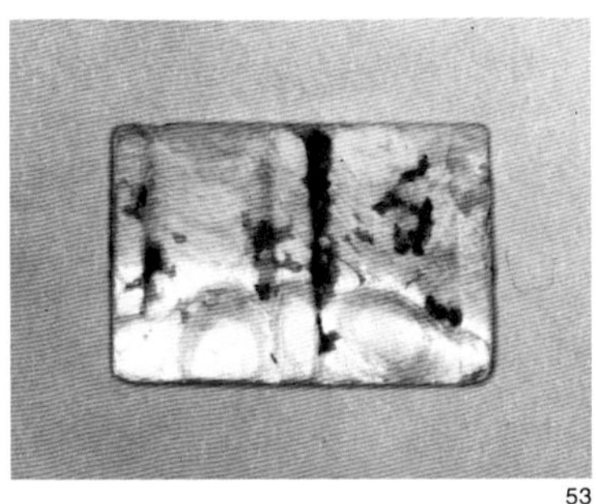
53

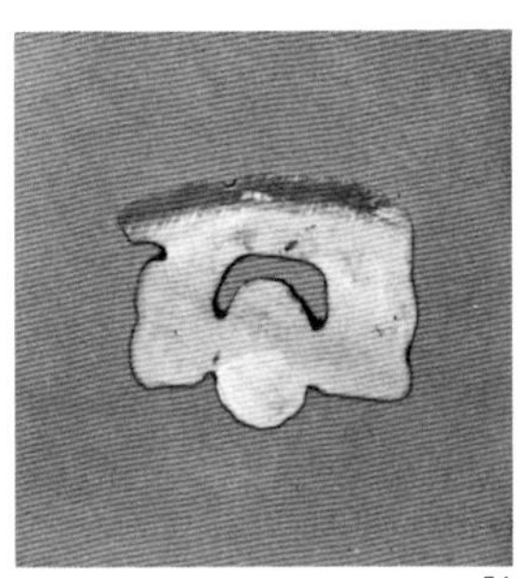
54

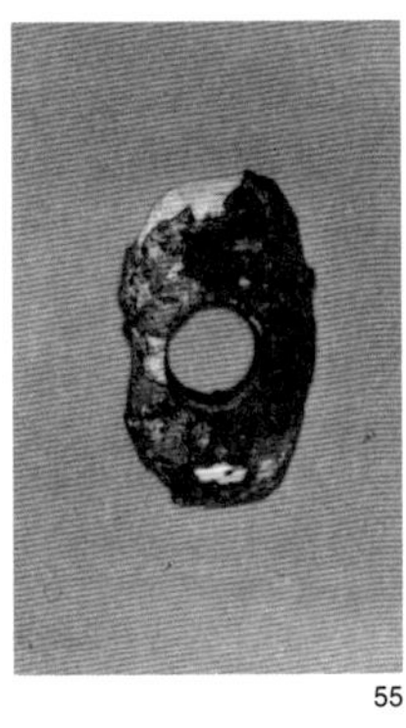
55

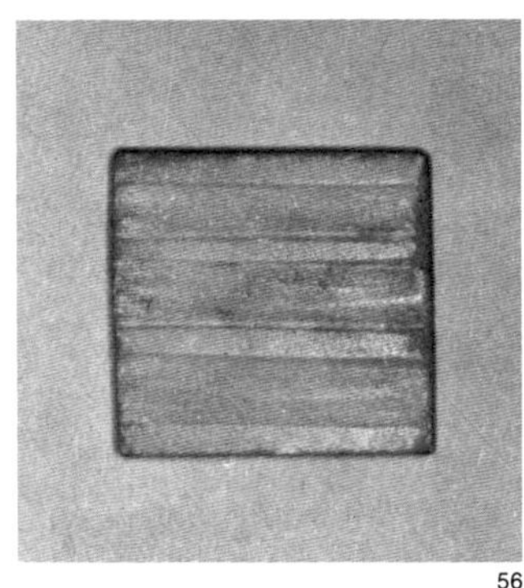
56

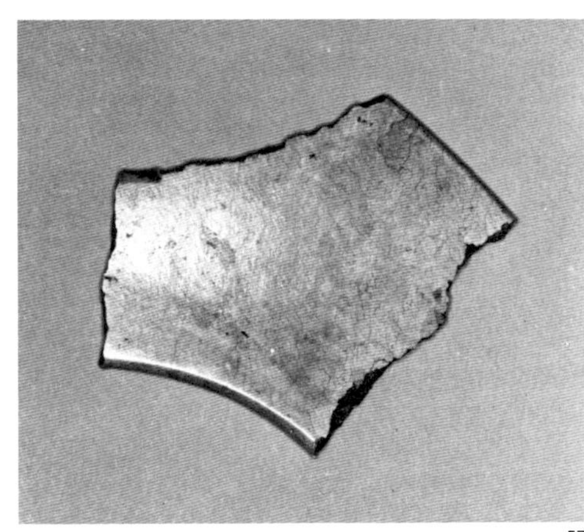
57

55 **Shang dynasty**
Carved Ornament (*Eye* or *Bead?*)
Shell, H. 7/8 (2.3), W. 9/16 (1.4)
Gift of Prof. and Mrs. Herrlee G. Creel
Acc. no. 1986.372
PUBLICATIONS *Bulletin*, 34.

56 **Shang dynasty**
Carved Inlay
Jade, H. 1 (2.5 cm.), W. 1 1/16 (2.8)
Gift of Prof. and Mrs. Herrlee G. Creel
Acc. no. 1986.373
PUBLICATIONS Creel, *Birth of China*, pl. VII; *Bulletin*, 34.

57 **Shang dynasty**
Fragment of a Bi *Disk*
Jade, H. (max. dim.) 1 3/4 (4.5),
W. (max. dim.) 1 1/2 (3.8 cm.), DP. 3/16–1/4 (0.5–0.6),
DIAM. (reconstruction of inner ring) 1 1/2 (3.8)
Gift of Prof. and Mrs. Herrlee G. Creel
Acc. no. 1986.374
PUBLICATIONS *Bulletin*, 34.

58 **Shang dynasty**
Spindle Whorl Ornament
Shell, DIAM. 1 1/2 (3.8)
Gift of Prof. and Mrs. Herrlee G. Creel
Acc. no. 1986.366
PUBLICATIONS Creel, *Birth of China*, pl. VII; *Bulletin*, 34.

59 **Shang dynasty**
Spindle Whorl Ornament or *Button*
Shell, DIAM. 3/4 (1.9)
Gift of Prof. and Mrs. Herrlee G. Creel
Acc. no. 1986.367
PUBLICATIONS Creel, *Birth of China*, pl. VII; *Bulletin*, 34.

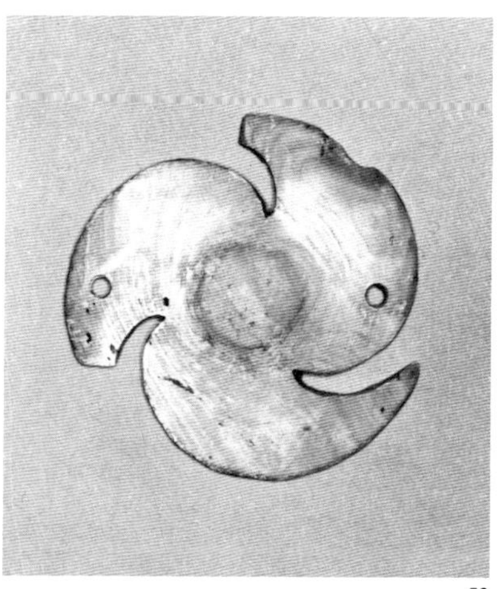
58

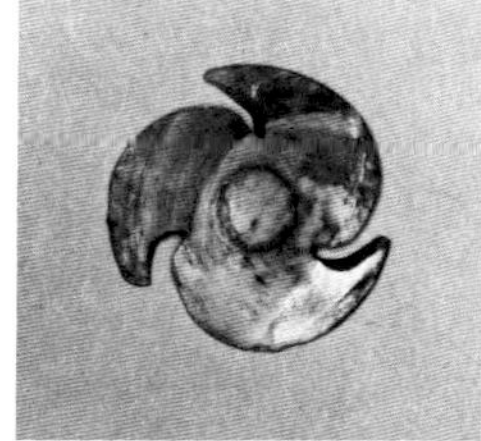
59

The objects illustrated here are made from raw materials, such as jade or shell, that are intrinsically appealing. In each case, the object has been shaped or carved, and the surface polished to enhance its natural appearance. The small drill holes in one of the shell spindle whorls (cat. no. 59) shows that this article,[1] like almost every one of these objects, was originally part of a larger composition. The saw-toothed fragment, for instance, was almost certainly part of a mask (cat. no. 51). Tooth-like forms, just like this one, are known from the materials scientifically excavated at Anyang.[2] Masks made of bronze or shell decorated chariots and horse trappings, and this tooth fragment must have been part of one such mask.

One can only guess at the use of the other fragments. They can be arranged, like buttons in a child's game, into innumerable patterns which cannot be reconstructed out of context. The shell mask was like a drawing, that is, the mother-of-pearl pieces were inlaid or attached to some backing material to make a linear design which was, in a broad sense, representational. As Shih Hsio-yen put it, the exaggerated eyes and teeth give a demonic cast to the image.[3] Indeed, this mask differs from those carved on the bone spatula and bone vessel fragment (cat. nos. 46 and 47) precisely because it exhibits "largely human characteristics [with] some animal traits," whereas the bone works "reveal the unity of stylization and design used on ancient Chinese works irrespective of media."[4] The carved bones look like bronzes.

The spindle whorl may involve a different kind of symbolism, one that strives to illustrate a concept, such as the brightness of fire or the movement of the sun, rather than to picture a thing (see cat. nos. 58 and 59).[5] This is most certainly so in the case of the fragmentary *bi* disk in the collection (cat. no. 57). The much discussed symbolism of this object is still unresolved. It may be a symbol of the heavens, of the female principle, or both. In any case, the *bi* provides an example of a non-representational mode of expressing ideas. This non-objective "representation of principles" is in remarkable contrast to the animal-oriented vocabulary of ancient Chinese art.[6]

A third alternative is exemplified by the pendant with a criss-cross design (cat. no. 49), the bone spatula with drill decoration (cat. no. 48), and the pieces in shell and jade with grooved lines (cat. nos. 53 and 56). In these instances, we encounter pure ornament, motifs that have no meaning beyond the rhythm of the design—or at least no meaning that can be deduced from these out-of-context fragments of the whole.

R.J.P.

NOTES

1. William Charles White, *Bone Culture of Ancient China*, Museum Studies 4 (Toronto: University of Toronto Press, 1945), 222, pl. CXII, illustrates a piece much like this one.

2. Ibid., 210, pls. XCIX–CV, illustrates shell pieces and reconstructed masks; see especially pl. CIII for tooth forms.

3. Shih Hsio-yen, "A Chinese Shell Inlay Motif," *Annual* [Art and Archaeology Division, Royal Ontario Museum, University of Toronto] (1962): 48; also illustrated is an extraordinarily different reconstruction of the shell mask in the Royal Ontario Museum.

4. Ibid., 47–48.

5. See Wen Fong, "The Study of Chinese Bronze Age Arts: Methods and Approaches," in Wen Fong, ed., *The Great Bronze Age of China: An Exhibition from the People's Republic of China* (exh. cat.) (New York: Metropolitan Museum of Art, 1980), 29–30, for an introduction to the question of these differing forms of symbolism. Ma Chengyuan, "The Splendor of Ancient Chinese Bronzes," ibid., 8, describes a whorl design on the waist of an early Shang *jia* vessel just below a *taotie* band: "Circular forms in bronze decoration were formerly called 'whorls,' but they are actually a pictorialization of the graph . . . meaning 'brightness of fire.' " Ma goes on to explain that when the "whorl" character was spoken rapidly it sounded like the name of the fire spirit. The vessel is cat. no. 6, illustrated in fig. 5, p. 30, and pl. 6, p. 85. See also White, *Bone Culture*, pl. CIX, for a shell whorl similar to the bronze one.

6. Wen Fong, "Study of Bronze Age Arts," 29–30.

SHANG ORACLE-BONE INSCRIPTIONS

Edward L. Shaughnessy

The story of the chance discovery of inscribed "oracle bones" has by now, ninety years after the fact, entered into the folklore of modern Chinese intellectual history. In 1899, a respected scholar and antiquarian by the name of Wang Yirong, apparently suffering from malaria, sent a servant to an apothecary in Peking for traditional Chinese drugs. Since, in addition to his knowledge of ancient China, Wang also prided himself on his knowledge of medicine, he instructed his servant to buy the ingredients, but that he would grind them himself at home. One of these ingredients was popularly known as "dragon bones." When Wang, together with his houseguest Liu Tieyun, also a noted collector of antiquities as well as one of the foremost novelists of the age, inspected these dragon bones, which included both bovine scapula bones and turtle plastrons, they discovered inscribed on them archaic graphs similar to those they knew from inscriptions on ancient bronze vessels. Their curiosity piqued, the two men immediately made the rounds of all of Peking's apothecaries, purchasing the capital's entire supply of dragon bones. While this initial collection of bones seems to have been no remedy for Wang Yirong's malaria, it did form the nucleus of Liu Tieyun's collection, which, upon its publication in 1903 under the title *Tieyun cang gui* (*[Liu] Tieyun's Treasured Turtles*), introduced their inscriptions to the scholarly world.

In his narrative of this discovery and the subsequent initial publications of oracle-bone inscriptions, Li Ji (Li Chi), longtime director of the Institute of History and Philology of Academia Sinica, made the astute observation that advances in scholarly learning, like mechanical inventions, require a sufficiently developed context before they can be recognized and effectively adopted.[1] In the case of oracle-bone inscriptions, the prerequisites were both technical and psychological. Recognition and eventual deciphering of the archaic script on the bones had been made possible in large part by the philological studies of the preceding two centuries. While the primary focus of these studies was to explicate the Confucian classics, by the nineteenth century scholars' interests had broadened to encompass an array of linguistic and paleographic concerns and data. But, perhaps even more important than the philological skills acquired by these scholars, their rigorous methodology also led them to question the traditional history of ancient China, which had been based exclusively on classical texts. This iconoclasm manifested itself in several ways, with some scholars demonstrating the spurious nature of parts of the classical texts while others attempted to reconstitute ancient texts that had long been lost. Still others endeavored for the first time to integrate the inscriptions on ancient bronze vessels into their corpus of historical documents.

It was in this context that inscriptions on oracle bones quickly attracted the attention of scholars as well as collectors. Indeed, before long these inscriptions provoked an even more pronounced iconoclastic empiricism. After two and a half decades of continued informal discovery and publication, during which time the exact source—the village of Xiaotun, just outside of Anyang, Henan—and the proximate date—the late Shang dynasty, circa 1200–1050 B.C.—of the oracle bones had become known, the expansion of this new field of learning led directly to the establishment in 1927 of the archaeologically inclined Academia Sinica. The institute's first and most important project was the excavation of Xiaotun village, beginning in late 1928 and proceeding through fifteen expeditions over the next nine years. Learning the new discipline as they worked, the individuals engaged in these excavations included, in addition to Li Ji, Dong Zuobin, Guo Baojun, Liang Siyong, Shi Zhangru, and, in the last seasons, Gao Quxun, Xia Nai, and Hu Houxuan, all scholars ranking in the top tier of twentieth-century Chinese scholarship. They demonstrated that Xiaotun was the site of the last capital city of the Shang dynasty, China's first historical dynasty. They also developed the archaeological skills that have continued to inform Chinese historical scholarship to the present day.

The Anyang excavations had an immediate impact on the way scholars in all disciplines would view the history of ancient China. The excavations coincided almost exactly with a series of publications by the comprehensive title of *Gushi bian* (*Debates on Ancient History*, 1926–1941), under the general editorship of Gu Jiegang, now regarded as the father of modern Chinese historiography.[2] Scholars from throughout China contributed essays in which they consciously adapted the technical rigor and, in some cases, even the terminology of archaeology (so the "stratigraphic" technique of Gu Jiegang) to textual and historical studies. In addition to these new studies, *Gushi bian* included, in the form of letters and rejoinders, the record of remarkably enthusiastic discussions among the most prominent historians of the time. Indeed, readers today are still moved with envy at the energy with which scholars of this period considered new evidence and debated new ideas.

Western sinologists were also quick to notice the importance of oracle-bone inscriptions and the challenges they posed for China's classical tradition. For a time after the first appearance of the oracle bones, it seemed in fact as if this might become a field dominated by foreign scholars, with important collections formed by missionaries and expatriates such as Frank H. Chalfant, Samuel Couling, and James M. Menzies.[3] Even before the Anyang excavations, Henri Maspero became the first scholar of any nationality to incorporate the new evidence into a synthetic revision of ancient Chinese history.[4] Nevertheless, with the first archaeological reports from Anyang and the first volumes of *Gushi bian*, it became clear that China itself was both the geographical and intellectual center for the study of ancient China. Thus it was that in 1932 Herrlee G. Creel, having just three years before received a Ph.D. from the University of Chicago, went to Peking to begin several years of on-site study. Out of his research, leavened with weekly dinner parties attended by the scholarly community of Peking and occasional trips to Anyang to observe the ongoing excavations firsthand, Creel produced his now classic *The Birth of China*.[5] Since he has recently described the context in which that book was written,[6] it seems appropriate here only to mention that in addition to his knowledge and memories, Creel left China in 1935 with a small collection of oracle bones bought chiefly from curio dealers in Peking. During his forty years of teaching at the University of Chicago, to which he returned in 1936, he used these oracle bones to share with his students some of the sense of discovery that was his in Peking. After his retirement, he donated the collection to the university's Smart Gallery, and it is this collection that is here exhibited and published in its entirety for the first time.[7]

While the initial discoveries at Anyang are well described in *The Birth of China*, they are by no means the end of the story of Chinese archaeological finds, for just after Creel's departure from China came the greatest discovery of oracle bones ever made at Anyang. On the last scheduled day of excavations in the thirteenth season, 12 June 1936, a pit, YH127, was found filled with 17,096 pieces (all but eight of which were of turtleshell). This event is noteworthy not only because of the great number of pieces uncovered but also because the pit had apparently been intentionally sealed during the Shang dynasty, suggesting that it comprised an integrated archive. Over the next twenty years, these pieces were more travelled than studied, being sent first *en masse* to the Academia Sinica offices in Nanjing, where they were cleaned. In 1937, when the Japanese army invaded China, the pieces were shipped for safekeeping to the southwestern province of Yunnan. After the war, they were returned briefly to Nanjing, where they were photographed and published (see fig. 1).[8] But, with the fall of the Republican government in 1949, the collection was evacuated once again, this time to Taiwan. There, during the 1950s and 1960s, scholars of Academia Sinica, now deprived of access to Anyang, undertook the painstaking task of piecing together the thousands of fragments of turtleshell. Eventually some four hundred complete plastrons were reconstructed, representing perhaps two-thirds of the original total in the pit (see fig. 2).[9] From these complete plastrons, it is possible to see how the inscriptions are related, showing the positive-negative duality of divination during the period spanned by the contents of this pit (the last part of the reign of King Wu Ding), the contemporaneity of individuals mentioned, the immediate sequence of events in military campaigns, and so on. Even though subsequent publication projects have tended to supersede the original publication of these reconstructions,[10] the three-volume catalogue remains almost certainly the most important single corpus of oracle-bone inscriptions.

The same political events that had twice forced the evacuation of the oracle bones found in pit YH127 also temporarily interrupted further excavations at Anyang. However, the new government of the People's Republic of China also took an active interest in archaeology, and Xiaotun village was the first site to be accorded the status of a National Historical Treasure. Excavations resumed there in the 1950s, with another significant group of oracle bones being discovered in 1972. This corpus, amounting to 5,023 pieces, was discovered at a site to the south of Xiaotun village, and is thus referred to as Xiaotun *nandi* (Xiaotun, Locus South). Unlike the single pit YH127, the oracle bones of Xiaotun *nandi* were found in a context that was dispersed both laterally and stratigraphically. Their stratigraphic relationships, in particular, have led scholars to propose resolutions to several important historiographical issues, especially those concerning the periodization of different types of oracle-bone inscriptions. Perhaps most important, the stratigraphy shows that it was possible for two or more types of inscriptions to exist simultaneously, thus undercutting a basic assumption that a given period was represented by only one type of inscription.[11]

It seems appropriate here to focus on just two of the many insights regarding Shang history and divination practice that have resulted from the nearly century-long study of the Xiaotun oracle-bone inscriptions. First, from the advances in periodization made possible by the Xiaotun *nandi* discovery, I believe that it is now possible to integrate political developments with the broader cultural context of the late Shang state. The traditional historical record suggests that prior to the establishment of Xiaotun as the capital in the mid-thirteenth century B.C., the Shang court had suffered through several generations of weak rulers and even fraternal battles for the kingship. Indeed, it appears that the evacuation to Xiaotun came at a particularly low point of Shang power, the site of the new capital probably being chosen for the protection afforded by the Taihang Mountains just to the west. This situation seems to be corroborated by the earliest oracle bones found at Anyang, those of the Dui group, dating roughly to the beginning or middle of Wu Ding's reign, perhaps about 1225 B.C. These inscriptions show the Shang court to be in a defensive posture militarily, with numerous enemy attacks reaching as far as the Shang capital region. Shortly thereafter, however, Wu Ding, known in traditional historical sources as a "restorationist" king, launched a series of military campaigns westward into the area of southern Shanxi province bordered roughly by the Yellow River to the south and west, the Fen River to the north, and the Taihang Mountains to the east (see maps, p. 142). There is considerable evidence from the inscriptions found in YH127 that Wu Ding conquered most of the independent states of this region and established Shang hegemony throughout. Thus, states that appeared as enemies in the earliest inscriptions appear in later inscriptions as allies of the Shang, receiving visits from the Shang king, entering into marital relations with the nobility, and engaging in trade with the capital region.[12]

The significance of these western relations is well illustrated by yet another recent archaeological discovery at Anyang. The excavation in 1975 of Tomb M5 did not include any oracle bones, but did contain several inscribed bronze vessels that suggest it was the tomb of one Fu Hao, known from oracle-bone inscriptions as the most prominent of Wu Ding's consorts. In the brief time that this so-called Fu Hao tomb has been known, scholars have acknowledged the almost revolutionary nature of the styles and types of its bronzeware and other artifacts.[13] For instance, there are several examples of the most mature form of Shang bronze decor, a decor that before this discovery would have been dated at least a century later. But more important, in my opinion, are the jade pieces and bronze mirrors found in the tomb. Neither of these has any precedent in the Shang cultural inventory, and both seem to have been introduced from areas to the distant north and/or west of its capital area. There is some indication that the jade may have been quarried as far west as

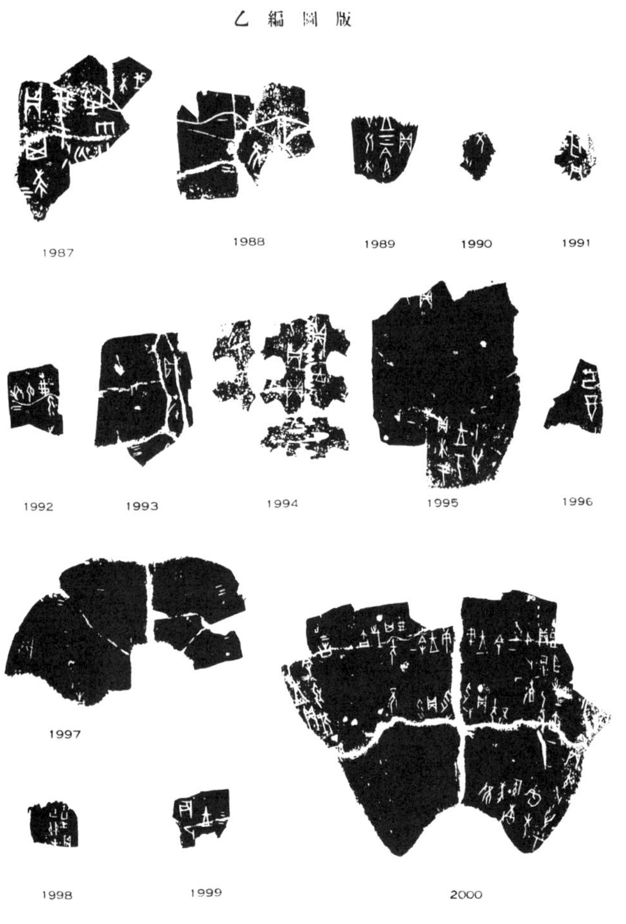

Fig. 1. Some of the 17,096 pieces of inscribed turtleshell found in 1936 in pit YH127. Note especially that piece no. 2000 (13.0.4149) comprises the bottom portion of the complete plastron illustrated in fig. 2.

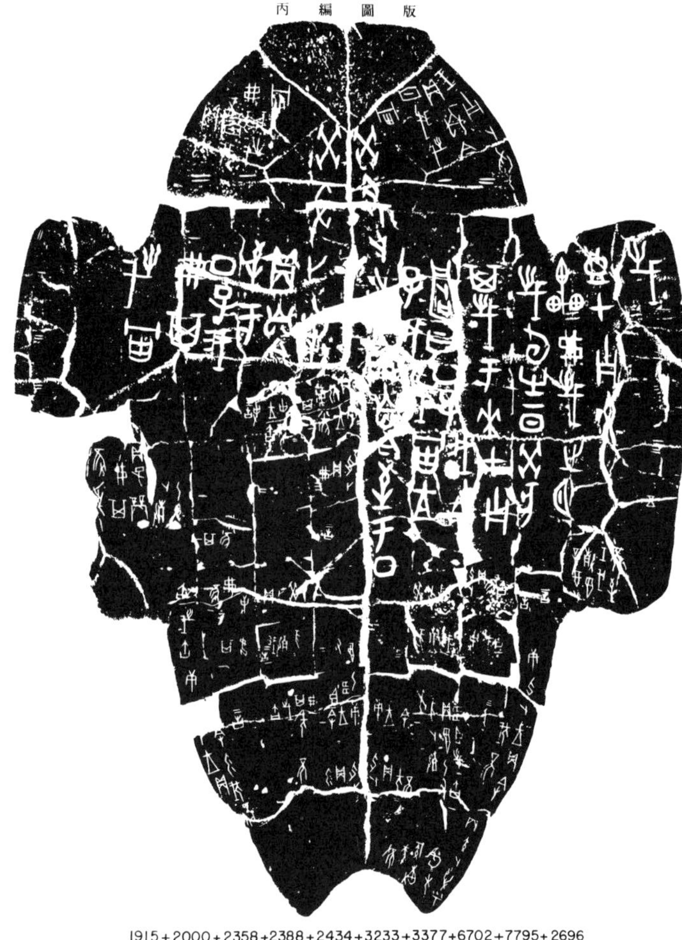

Fig. 2. Complete turtle plastron reconstructed from pieces found in pit YH127.

present-day Xinjiang province in Chinese Turkistan, and there are clear precedents for the type of mirror found in the tomb in the Karasuk culture of the Lake Baikal region of Soviet Siberia.[14] Indeed, these innovations seem to be part of a wave of (north-)western imports, led perhaps by the chariot, that entered China at about this time.[15]

I suspect that the avenue by which these innovations entered the Shang cultural sphere was the steppe zone along the northern reaches of the Yellow River, generally known in the West as the Ordos. This region in turn borders on the area of southern Shanxi that had been conquered by Wu Ding a few decades before the death of Fu Hao. In short, I would suggest that Wu Ding's hegemony in this area had greater implications for Shang cultural history than just the expansion of the territory under its control. While the Taihang Mountains protected the Shang capital, they also effectively isolated it from the trade in goods and ideas that was conducted all across the Central Asian and south Siberian steppe. But, when Wu Ding expanded into southern Shanxi, and thus to the west of the mountains, the Shang suddenly came into contact with this cultural continuum, enriching their own cultural inventory with many of its features.

Despite the obvious riches that this western hegemony brought, such as those seen in the tomb of Fu Hao, the caution that had originally caused the Shang to settle at Xiaotun was, in the end, apparently well founded. If I am not mistaken, Fu Hao, and perhaps even Wu Ding himself, met their deaths in the course of a war that resulted in the loss of the Shang western hegemony. Divinations concerning the outbreak of this war appear among the very latest found in YH127. These concern Shang campaigns against several western states known as Bafang, Xia Wei, and Ren. Many more inscriptions, very closely contemporary but not included among those found in YH127 (suggesting that they date to immediately after the closing of that pit), concern attacks against Shang and its allies by yet two other western states, Tufang and Gongfang, both probably located along the upper north-south stretch of the Yellow River. Since divinations were conducted before the event to which they refer, it is of course difficult to determine the outcome of the event from these inscriptions. However, in the case of inscriptions concerning attacks against other states, it is sometimes possible to infer a result from inscriptions of later periods. For instance, in the case of Wu Ding's westward expansion, many of the states he had initially attacked appear in somewhat later inscriptions as allies of the Shang. From this it is clear that they must have been conquered and brought under Shang control. In the case of the Shang war with Gongfang, the same principle indicates the reverse result. Several of the Shang western allies that were attacked by Gongfang reappear in inscriptions of later reigns as enemies of the Shang. It seems likely that they were overrun in the course of this war. Indeed, charting the geographical progress of the Gongfang attacks suggests that they carried as far as the final Shang defense perimeter along the Qin River, anchored in the Taihang Mountains to the north and the Yellow River to the south. There the attack was repulsed and the Shang capital was saved,[16] but it appears that the western hegemony of Wu Ding, who may well have died before the final battle of this war, was never reestablished. Shang remained safe behind its mountainous defense, but it also became increasingly isolated. This, I suspect, is one reason why the Fu Hao tomb seems to mark the cultural apogee of the dynasty, with its final century and a half showing relatively little cultural development.

Although there were few striking material innovations after this time, an important ritual change was introduced, perhaps, in a sense, as a reaction against the geopolitical losses sustained in the Gongfang War. During the reign of Zu Jia, the second of Wu Ding's sons to reign, the ancestral sacrifices were systematized into an annual cycle. Whereas ancestor sacrifices in Wu Ding's reign were more or less ad hoc, from the reign of Zu Jia on they were highly structured; an individual ancestor would receive one of five major sacrifices at one, and only one, time in the ritual year. While these ancestor sacrifices were being systematized, many of the other rituals and impromptu sacrifices, to nature spirits and non-royal ancestors, for instance, were discarded completely. And because the performance of these ad hoc rites had theretofore frequently been the topics of divination, with their abandonment the inscriptional record becomes increasingly impoverished. Divination seems to have become a routine means of confirming the ancestors' continued approbation of the ritual cycle. But one searches in vain for the sort of probing of the ancestors' will that had characterized the divination of the preceding period.

This theological development forms an important part of one of the most important ongoing scholarly debates in the field of oracle-bone studies. From the time that oracle-bone inscriptions were first recognized to be records of ancient divinations, it was assumed that they must have concerned future activities and that they must have been phrased in the form of questions. Support for this assumption was found in the earliest definition of the word *zhen* (inscriptional [illegible]), which occurs formulaically in virtually every oracle-bone inscription: "to inquire by crack-making" (*zhen: bu wen ye*). Therefore, scholars routinely translated the inscriptions as questions. However, in the early 1970s two Western scholars, David N. Keightley and Fr. Paul L.-M. Serruys, began independently to challenge this traditional assumption.[17] They noted, among other points, that neither divination nor inquiry conceptually requires interrogative phrasing, that *zhen* has other than interrogative uses in classical Chinese texts, and that most Shang oracle-bone inscriptions show no explicit interrogative grammar and, indeed, many make no sense understood as questions. In place of the traditional interpretation, these scholars proposed that the inscriptions should be interpreted as declarative statements.

Since the initial formulation of this argument, it has been accepted and refined by many Western scholars working in the field. More recently, Chinese scholars have also entered into the debate.[18] While a consensus has by no means yet been reached on this point, it does seem that a broad developmental outline of Shang divination practices can be discerned. The earliest inscriptions, those of the Dui group at the beginning or middle of Wu Ding's reign, were probably phrased in the form of actual grammatical questions. The grammar, if not the conception, was then revised in later inscriptions from Wu Ding's reign, as, for example, those found in pit YH127. These divinations were phrased in the form of grammatically declarative positive and negative pairs (*dui zhen*), the entirety of which seems still to have comprised a sort of conceptual question. With the systematization of the ancestor sacrifices during the reign of Zu Jia, however, the inquisitive intent of divination was for the most part replaced by a desire for confirmation. Thus it becomes quite rare to find even the positive-negative pairs so ubiquitous during the reign of Wu Ding. In their stead, we now routinely encounter such conceptually positive statements as "in the [next] ten-day week, there will be no misfortune" (*xun wang huo*) or "going and coming, [the king] will have no calamity" (*wang lai wang zai*). By this time, the rite of divination seems to have evolved into a sort of prayer, beseeching the aid of ancestors in realizing the favorable outcome of a future event. In fact, during the subsequent Zhou dynasty, divinations came to be phrased in exactly the same terms as prayers.[19]

The developments in political and intellectual history discussed above are, of course, but two of many insights into the cultural history of the Shang dynasty that have been gleaned from the all too often very fragmentary oracle-bone inscriptions. Much has also been learned, for instance, about the detailed performance of Shang religion, the structure of Shang government, and the nature of the Shang language. Some of these points of detail will be discussed in the following catalogue entries. Others, for which there is no evidence in the collection of inscribed oracle bones Professor Creel has presented to the Smart Gallery, are discussed in the numerous studies produced in the ninety years since Wang Yirong's first chance discovery of inscribed "dragon bones."[20] Whatever efficacy these bones might have had, or still have, in the cure of malaria or other ailments, I think their preservation in collections such as this marks a positive gain in the quest to understand how humankind has coped, and will continue to cope, with an uncertain future.

NOTES

1. Li Chi, *Anyang* (Seattle: University of Washington Press, 1977), 4.
2. *Gushi bian*, 7 vols., eds. Gu Jiegang (vols. 1–3, 5), Luo Genze (vols. 4, 6), Lu Simian and Tong Shuye (vol. 7) (1926–1941; reprint, Shanghai: Shanghai guji chubanshe, 1982).
3. For their collections, see *Ku-Fang ershi cang jiagu buci (The Couling-Chalfant Collection of Inscribed Oracle Bone)*, ed. Fang Falian (Frank H. Chalfant) and Bo Ruihua (Roswell S. Britton) (1935; reprint, Taipei, Taiwan: Yiwen yinshuguan, 1966); and *The Menzies Collection of Shang Dynasty Oracle Bones*, 2 vols., ed. Hsu Chin-hsiung (Toronto: Royal Ontario Museum, 1972, 1977). Note, however, that these collections are marred by numerous forgeries, for which, see David N. Keightley, *Sources of Shang History: The Oracle-Bone Inscriptions of Bronze Age China* (Berkeley, Calif., Los Angeles, and London: University of California Press, 1978), 142, n. 35.
4. Henri Maspero, *La Chine antique* (Paris: E. de Boccard, 1927).
5. Herrlee Glessner Creel, *The Birth of China: A Survey of the Formative Period of Chinese Civilization* (London: Jonathan Cape, 1936).
6. Creel, "On the Birth of *The Birth of China*," *Early China* 11–12 (1985–87): 1–5.
7. There are forty-three pieces in the collection. Photographs of six were published, identified as belonging to "a private collection," in Creel, *Birth of China*, facing p. 22 (these pieces have been given accession numbers 1986.388, 391, 392, 395, 397, 398; cat. nos. 67, 69, 74, 77, 78). One piece (1986.388) was therein acknowledged to be a forgery, deliberately acquired to illustrate this genre of spurious inscription. There are two other forgeries in the collection (1986.389, 390), which are not included in this exhibition or catalogue. The six pieces reproduced by Creel are mentioned again as in "a private collection" in Hung-hsiang Chou, *Oracle Bone Collections in the United States* (Berkeley, Calif., Los Angeles, and London: University of California Press, 1976), 23.
8. *Xiaotun: Yinxu wenzi, Yibian*, ed. Dong Zuobin (Nanjing: Academia Sinica, 1948).
9. *Xiaotun: Yinxu wenzi, Bingbian*, 3 vols., ed. Zhang Bingquan (Taipei, Taiwan: Academia Sinica, 1957–72).
10. Scholars, particularly those in mainland China, now generally cite inscriptions as they appear in *Jiaguwen heji*, 13 vols., ed. Hu Houxuan (Shanghai: Zhonghua shuju, 1978–82).
11. For a brief discussion of the implications of this discovery, see Edward L. Shaughnessy, "Recent Approaches to Oracle-Bone Periodization: A Review," *Early China* 8 (1982–83): 1–13. There are also numerous other points of detail, not possible to consider here, deriving from this discovery. For a discussion of these points, as well as references to relevant secondary literature, see Cai Fangpei, Edward L. Shaughnessy, and James F. Shaughnessy, Jr., *A Concordance of the Xiaotun Nandi Oracle-Bone Inscriptions* (Chicago: Early China Special Monograph Series, Number 1, 1988), iii–vii.
12. For a brief demonstration of this periodization technique and some of its geopolitical implications for the reign of King Wu Ding, see Xia Hanyi (Edward L. Shaughnessy), "Zaoqi Shang-Zhou guanxi ji qi dui Wu Ding yihou Yin Shang wangshi shili fanwei de yiyi," *Jiuzhou xuekan* 2, no. 1 (Autumn 1987): 19–32.
13. The preliminary report of this discovery is given in Zhongguo shehui kexueyuan kaogu yanjiusuo Anyang gongzuodui, "Anyang Yinxu wuhao mu de fajue," *Kaogu xuebao* 1977, no. 2, 57–96. This report has been translated into English as "Excavation of Tomb No. 5 at Yinxu, Anyang," ed. Elizabeth Childs-Johnson, *Chinese Sociology and Anthropology* 15, no. 3 (Spring 1983). A more fully illustrated monographic report is Institute of Archaeology, Archaeologia Sinica, *Yinxu Fu Hao mu* (Beijing: Wenwu chubanshe, 1980). For further discussion in English, together with excellent illustrations of many of the finest pieces from the Fu Hao tomb, see Wen Fong, ed., *The Great Bronze Age of China: An Exhibition from the People's Republic of China* (exh. cat.) (New York: Metropolitan Museum of Art, 1980), 177–189, and pls. 28–40. For a concise review of the periodization of the tomb, see Robert L. Thorp, "The Date of Tomb 5 at Yinxu, Anyang: A Review Article," *Artibus Asiae* 43, no. 3 (1982): 239–246.
14. Evidence substantiating a Xinjiang provenance for the jade found in the Fu Hao tomb was presented by Shen Min in a paper, "Fu Hao mu yuqi laiyuan de kaocha," presented at the International Conference on China's Yin-Shang Culture, Anyang, September 1987. For northern precedents for the mirrors found in this tomb, see Lin Yun, "A Reexamination of the Relationship between Bronzes of the Shang Culture and of the Northern Zone," in *Studies of Shang Archaeology: Selected Papers from the International Conference on Shang Civilization*, ed. Kwang-chih Chang (New Haven, Conn., and London: Yale University Press, 1986), 237–273, esp. 251–254.
15. See Edward L. Shaughnessy, "Historical Perspectives on the Introduction of the Chariot into China," *Harvard Journal of Asiatic Studies* 48, no. 1 (June 1988): 189–238.
16. I recently presented a detailed discussion of the inscriptions pertaining to this war, in "The Life and Death of Fu Hao: With Comments on the Sequence of the Shang Campaigns against Bafang, Tufang and Gongfang," at the Fortieth Annual Meeting of the Association for Asian Studies, San Francisco, 26 March 1988.
17. David N. Keightley, "*Shih cheng*: A New Hypothesis about the Nature of Shang Divination," paper presented to the conference of Asian Studies on the Pacific Coast, Monterey, California, 17 June 1972; Paul L.-M. Serruys, "Studies in the Language of the Shang Oracle Inscriptions," *T'oung Pao* 60, no. 1–3 (1974): 12–120, esp. 21ff.
18. See Qiu Xigui, "An Examination of Whether the Charges of Shang Oracle-Bone Inscriptions Are Questions," and discussions by Fan Yuzhou, David N. Keightley, Jean A. Lefeuvre, Li Xueqin, David S. Nivison, Rao Zongyi, Edward L. Shaughnessy, and Wang Yuxin in *Early China* 14 (1989), in press.
19. For a discussion of this aspect of Zhou divination, see Xia Hanyi (Edward L. Shaughnessy), "Shi lun Zhouyuan buci xin zi—jianlun Zhoudai zhenbu zhi xingzhi," *Guwenzi yanjiu* 16, in press.
20. For surveys of the field, see Hu Houxuan, *Wushi nian jiaguxue lunzhumu* (Shanghai: Zhonghua shuju, 1952); Dong Zuobin, *Jiaguxue liushi nian* (Taipei, Taiwan: Yiwen yinshuguan, 1965); and Wang Yuxin, *Jianguo yilai jiaguwen yanjiu* (Beijing: Zhongguo shehui kexue chubanshe, 1981). For the best overview of the field, see Keightley, *Sources of Shang History* (cited above, n. 3).

CATALOGUE OF ORACLE BONES

In the following entries, (S) indicates shell (turtle plastron) and (B) indicates bone (the scapula bone of an ox). The periodization of the shell, when ascertainable, is given using "I" or "II" to indicate the reign according to Dong Zuobin's sequence, with the diviner group indicated after the decimal. In the transcriptions proper, the following conventions of paleography are employed: [ ], indicates a graph or graphs only partially visible or that can be supplied on the basis of other information; (:), indicates that a graph is to be read as; . . indicates one graph missing; . . . indicates an indeterminate number of graphs missing.

Dimensions are given in inches, followed by centimeters in parentheses. The abbreviation H. = maximum height of the object described.

All oracle bones and plastrons in the catalogue are the gift of Prof. and Mrs. Herrlee G. Creel.

Catalogue entries and oracle-bone transcriptions in this section have been prepared by Professor Edward L. Shaughnessy and the oracle-bone transcriptions have been prepared for publication by Mr. Cai Fangpei.

The Preparation and Use of the Divination Shell

Shang divination generally employed scapula bones of oxen or turtle plastrons. In either case, an involved preparation process was required before the bone or shell could actually be used in the divination rite. Although there are certain natural differences in the ways in which these two media were prepared, in general the process was similar for both.[1]

In the case of plastrons, such as catalogue number 60 pictured here, most of the turtles (and it is important to note that almost invariably turtles and not tortoises were used) probably came from the vicinity of Anyang, although there are notations on many plastrons indicating that they were contributed by outlying states. Once the turtle had been killed, the plastron, i.e., the relatively soft and smooth ventral shell, was separated from the carapace, the distinctively humped dorsal shell, which is comparatively thick and rough. The plastron's outer circumference was then smoothed and the twelve epidermal scutes on its surface were removed, exposing (as the line drawings in fig. 3 show) the nine-sectioned plastron proper. The only further preparation of this front or recto side of the plastron involved polishing, presumably for the functional benefit of enhancing the visibility of the surface and also for aesthetic purposes — many of the pieces, such as catalogue number 60 here, having an almost jadelike luminosity. However, much more remained to be done to the back or verso side of the shell.

At this stage, initial notations indicating the source of the shell and/or the divination official responsible for its preparation might be incised on the back of the shell on the rectangular "bridge" where it had been connected to the carapace (for which reason these notations are usually referred to as "bridge notations"). Then, a number of holes or hollows were made, almost completely penetrating the shell, usually coming within 0.2 and 0.5 millimeters of the front surface. These hollows, clearly visible on the back of catalogue number 60, were designed to facilitate the creation of cracks on the front side of the shell, the portent on which the prognostication of the divination rite was based. The hollows consist of two parts: a chiseled oblong parallel to the central fissure of the plastron, and a drilled semicircle extending out from the middle of the oblong on the side facing the plastron's central fissure, the overall shape somewhat resembling an acorn or butternut. While there is no pattern to the number of such hollows that would be made into the back of the shell — some plastrons have over a hundred while others of similar size have as few as ten — they were generally arranged symmetrically about the central fissure.

With the making of the hollows, the shell was finally ready for the divination proper. Presumably part of a solemn ceremony,[2] the topic of the divination was first announced or "commanded" to the turtle (*ling* or *ming gui*). Then a red-hot brand was applied to the hollows in the back of the shell, the heat causing the shell to crack, with the crack lines appearing on the corresponding front surface. Owing to the peculiar butternut shape of the hollows, the cracks had a characteristic two-part ├ configuration, the vertical crack caused by the chiseled oblong and the branching horizontal crack by the drilled semicircle. It

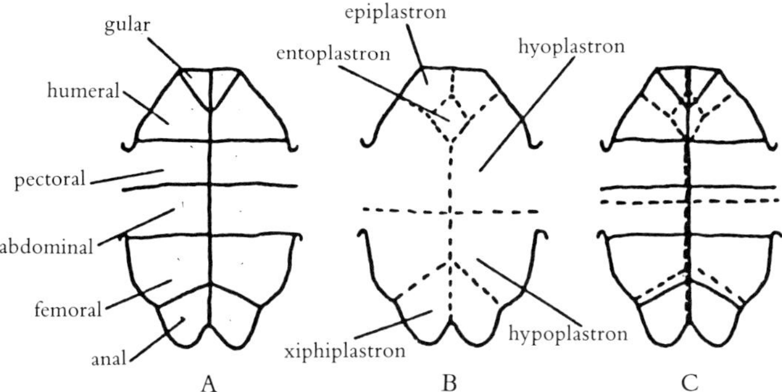

Fig. 3. Technical nomenclature of the turtle plastron. A) epidermal scutes, B) bony shell, C) epidermal scutes (unbroken line) and bony shell (dotted line) superimposed.

was the shape of the cracks that gave rise to the graph 卜 for the word *bu* meaning "to divine," referring specifically to pyromantic divination. Numerous such cracks are clearly apparent on catalogue number 60, as well as on catalogue numbers 61 and 62, both of which are also turtle plastrons.

Next, the crack was interpreted, usually by the king himself. Although there are later divination manuals that prescribe prognostications based on the shape of the crack (and particularly on whether the branching crack turned up or down), there seems to be no pattern to the way the Shang interpreted their cracks. It is therefore thought that there may have been a prior oral agreement, similar to the case in flipping coins of first agreeing "heads we go, tails we stay." The divination could be repeated a number of times—there is a distinct but not invariable preference throughout the Shang for divination in sets of five—using either the same shell or different shells. Moreover, a single shell could be and normally was used for several different divinations. Whether the divinations for which a single shell was employed were intrinsically related remains open to interpretation.[3] At this stage, two different types of notations could be inscribed into the front of the shell: a "crack number" (an example of which can be seen on cat. no. 65), usually placed beside the top of the vertical crack on the same side as the branch crack and indicating the sequence in which the crack had been produced; and a "crack notation" (examples of which include the "approval" [*ruo*] of cat. nos. 63 and 66 and the problematic "do not again use the turtle" [*bu zai ming*] of cat. no. 64[4]), perhaps indicating the preliminary interpretation of the presiding divination official.

Finally, after the divination had been completed, a record of it could be engraved on the front of the shell, presumably alongside the related crack. However, as in the case of catalogue number 60, which has very clear cracks but which is completely uninscribed, such records were by no means automatically made. When engraved, the inscriptions could consist of several discrete portions (the terminology being that used conventionally by modern scholars): a preface, often (as in cat. no. 67 below) in the form of "crack on *guimao* (day forty), Xiong divining," in which "*guimao*" is one day in a recurring cycle of sixty days and "Xiong" is the name of the official who presided over this particular divination; the charge, the one essential portion of all inscriptions, usually stated as a declarative sentence and often (especially towards the end of the dynasty) indicating the result the Shang desired to obtain (as in the charge of cat. no. 67: "In the [next] ten-day week there will be no misfortune"); a prognostication (no examples in the Creel collection), differing from the preliminary crack notation by being addressed specifically to the topic of the divination and almost always representing the king's personal interpretation of the crack; a verification (also not represented in the Creel collection), indicating at some later date what really did happen; and a "month notation" (such as the notation "first month" in cat. no. 67), usually somewhat separate from the other elements of the inscription proper.

It is well known that Shang oracle-bone inscriptions are the earliest examples of writing in China, coming a full millennium before Qin Shi huangdi, the first emperor of China (r. 246/221–210 B.C.), unified writing styles throughout the nation. For this reason, a specialized field of study, *jiaguxue* (oracle-bone studies), has developed within the general field of Chinese paleography to decipher the inscriptions. However, it should also be said that the millennium between the time of the oracle-bone inscriptions and Qin Shi huangdi's unification of the script was witness to an unbroken literary tradition, with various kinds of texts inscribed on such media as bronze, jade and other stones, bamboo, wood, and silk. It is their position at the head of this tradition, more than anything else, that has enabled oracle-bone inscriptions to be understood and, through them, the history of the Shang dynasty to be better known.

E.L.S.

NOTES

1. The best description of this preparation process is to be found in David N. Keightley, *Sources of Shang History: The Oracle-Bone Inscriptions of Bronze Age China* (Berkeley, Calif., Los Angeles, and London: University of California Press, 1978), 6–27, from which most of the following discussion is drawn. For more details based on personal experiments in preparing and cracking bones and shells, see Chang Kuang-yuan, "Late-Shang Divination: An Experimental Reconstruction of Methods of Preparation, Use and Inscription of Oracle Bone Materials," *National Palace Museum Bulletin* 18, no. 1–2 (March-April/May-June 1983): 1–25; 18, no. 3–4 (July-August/September-October 1983): 1–25.

2. A complete description of such a ceremony is included in the *Shiji* (*Historical Records*) of Sima Qian (circa 145–89 B.C.) (Beijing: Zhonghua shuju, 1959), 128.3239–40. For a survey of divination practices contemporary with those described in the *Shiji*, see Michael Loewe, "Divination by Shells, Bones and Stalks during the Han Period," *T'oung Pao* 74, no. 1–3 (1988): 81–118.

3. For a detailed interpretation of all of the divinations for which one set of shells (*Bingbian* 12–20) was used, including the suggestion that divinations regarding an aching tooth may have been related to other divinations about military attacks on enemy states, see Keightley, *Sources of Shang History*, 76–90.

4. For a succinct review of the scholarship concerning this enigmatic notation, see Keightley, *Sources of Shang History*, 121, n. 134.

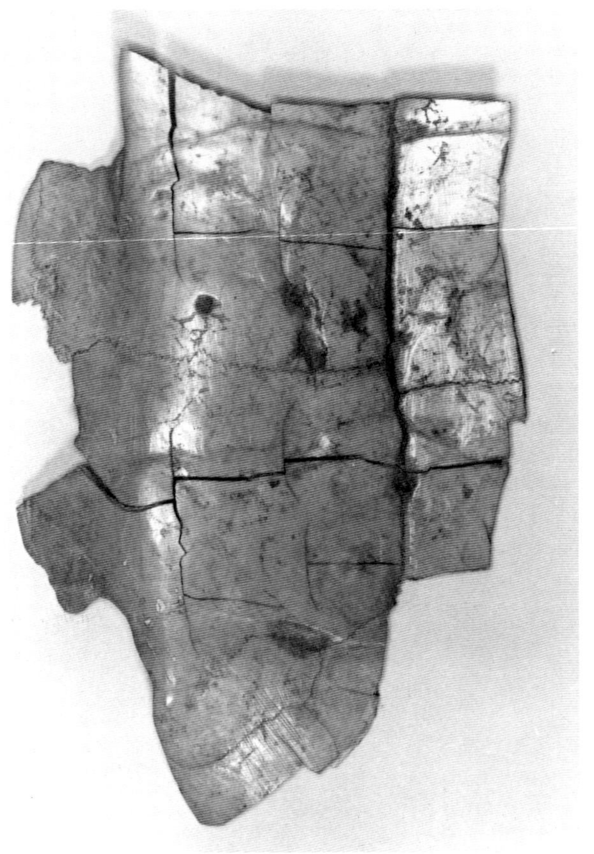

60

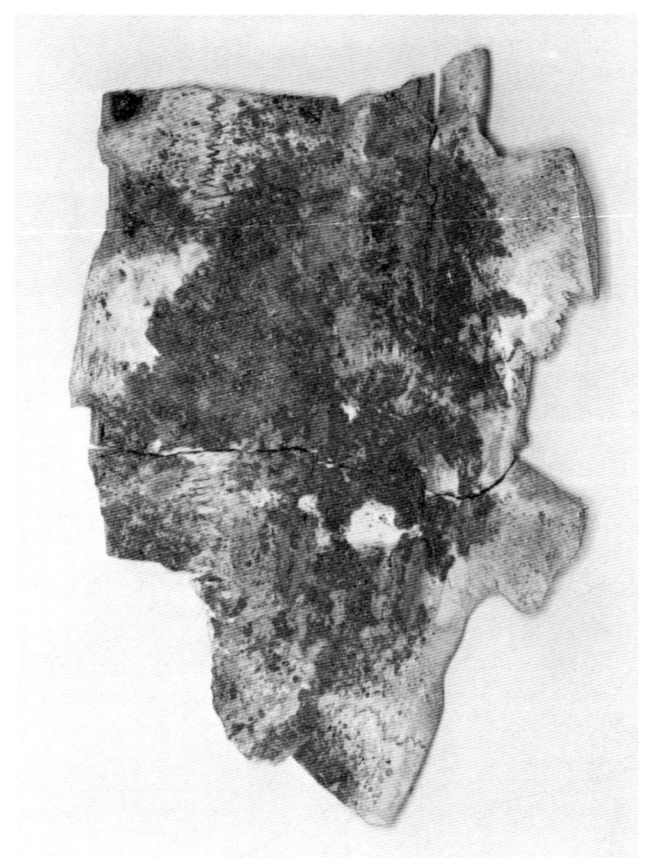

60 (reverse)

60 **Late Shang dynasty**
Oracle Plastron
H. 4 1/16 (10.3)
Acc. no. 1986.385
(S)
Uninscribed.

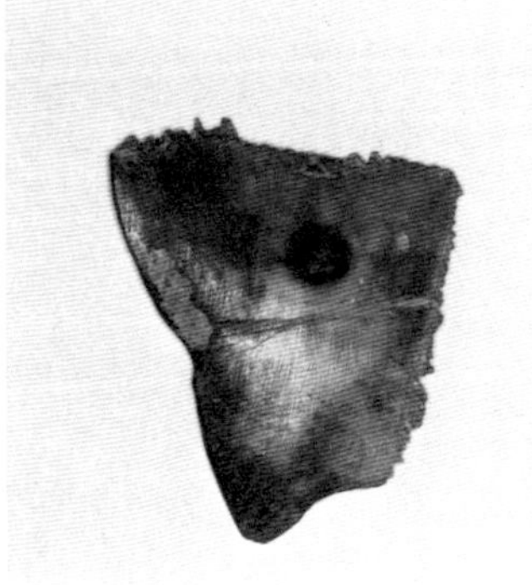

62

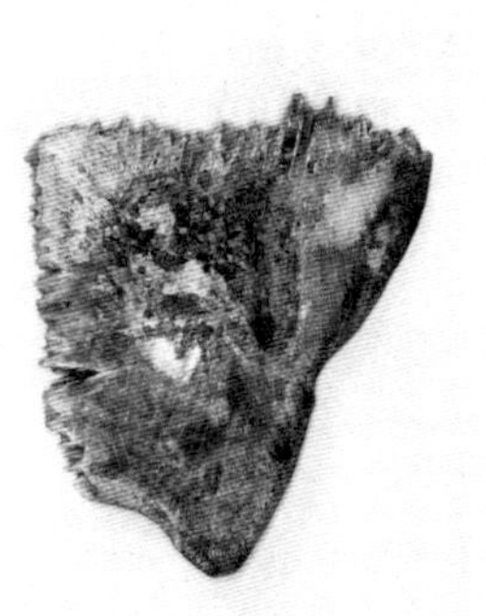

62 (reverse)

62 **Late Shang dynasty**
Oracle Plastron
H. 1 5/16 (3.3)
Acc. no. 1986.387
(S)
𠀠(太?:) 王
. . . king . . .

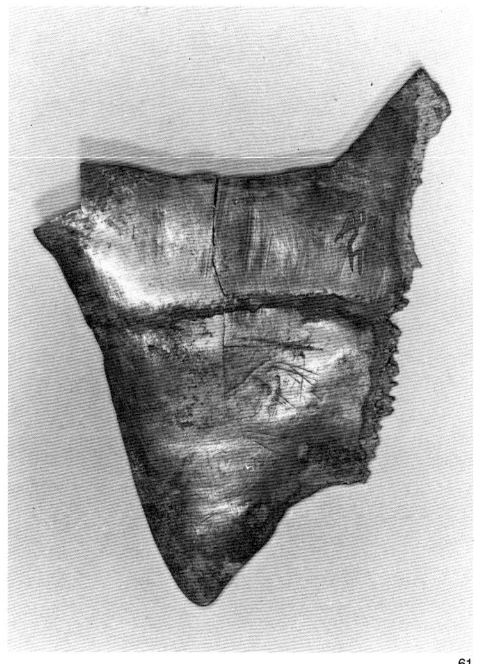

61

61 (reverse)

61 **Late Shang dynasty**
Oracle Plastron
H. 2¾ (7)
Acc. no. 1986.386
(S); I.Bin.
[illegible] (:每?)
Mei(?).

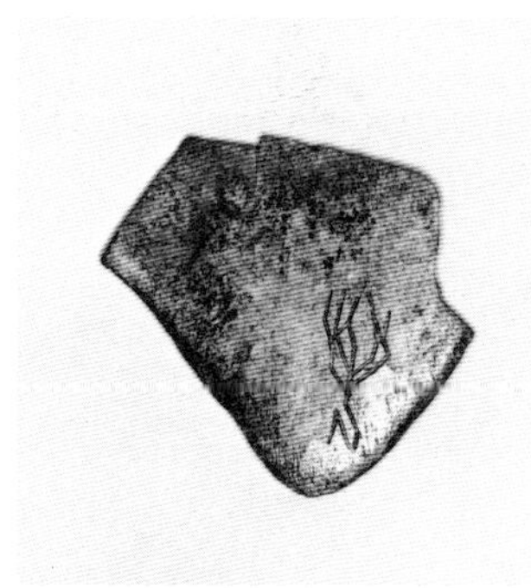

63

63 **Late Shang dynasty**
Oracle Plastron
H. 1⅛ (2.9)
Acc. no. 1986.404
(S); I.Bin.
若
Approval.

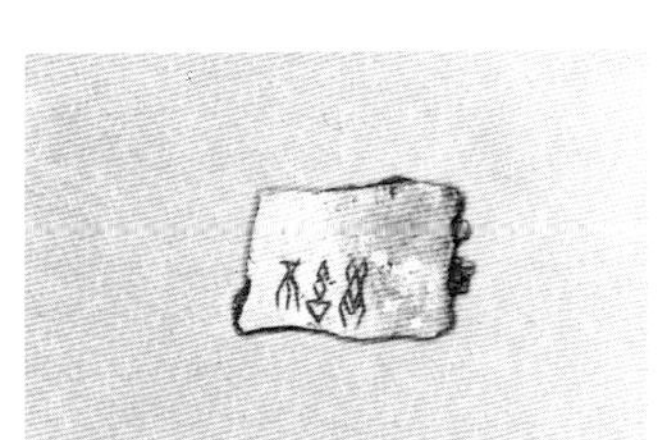

64

64 **Late Shang dynasty**
Oracle Plastron
H. ⅜ (1)
Acc. no. 1986.411
(S); I.Bin.
[illegible][illegible][illegible] (:不再黽?)
Do not again (use) the turtle.

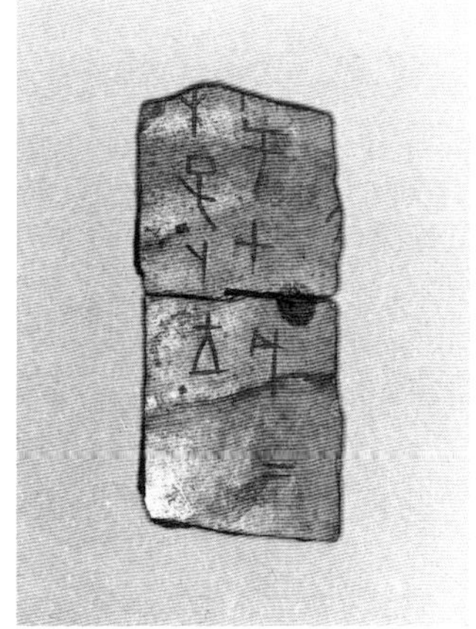

65

65 **Late Shang dynasty**
Oracle Plastron
H. 1⅝ (4.1)
Acc. no. 1986.412
(S); I.Dui-Bin.
辛子(:巳)卜王... 于甲戌... 二
Crack on *xinsi* (day eighteen), the king (divining): "On *jiaxu* (day eleven), ..." Two.

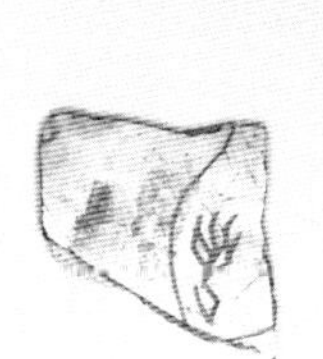

66

66 **Late Shang dynasty**
Oracle Plastron
H. ⅝ (1.6)
Acc. no. 1986.418
(S); I.Bin.
若
Approval.

Periodization According to Diviners

With the discovery of the long-buried oracle bones, the task of "working" the bones and shells has now been handed to modern historians. After deciphering the inscriptions, a process obviously too involved for brief explication here, the most important step in the treatment of the oracle bones as historical documents is the determination of their dates. It is known from their archaeological context that the oracle bones derive from the late Shang dynasty, and particularly from the time after the relocation of the capital to Xiaotun (i.e., Anyang), traditionally believed to have taken place during the reign of Pan Geng, the eighteenth king of the dynasty. It has been possible on the basis of evidence contained in the inscriptions themselves to go considerably further than this and to date most of them to individual reigns within this period. This too entails an involved process, but it is possible to sketch at least the broad outlines of the methodology used in this periodization.

As can be seen from the inscriptions in the Creel collection (e.g., cat. nos. 68 and 77, as well as 69 and, less specifically, 71 and 74), many of the inscriptions pertain to sacrifices to be offered to Shang royal ancestors, who were referred to posthumously by an ancestor title, such as *fu* (father) or *zu* (grandfather or ancestor), and by the name of the day in the Shang ten-day week on which they normally received cult.[1] For example, one divination on catalogue number 68 proposes that the king make offering to Zu Yi, perhaps a reference to the twelfth king of the dynasty who reigned three generations prior to the move of the capital to Xiaotun: "The king will offer the *sui*-sacrifice of a penned cow to Ancestor Yi." But the possibility that the title *zu* could refer either specifically to an ancestor of the "grandfather's" generation or, more generally, to any "ancestor" renders this particular inscription somewhat ambiguous for dating purposes.[2]

There is less ambiguity in cases of *fu* or "father" (unfortunately not represented in the Creel collection), which can only refer to an ancestor of the immediately preceding generation, although not necessarily one's biological father. However, because of the Shang predilection for offering cult on only a few, presumably lucky days of their week (especially *jia*, *yi*, and *ding*), and thus for assigning the same day-name to ancestors of different generations, even references to sacrifices offered to a father can be ambiguous. For instance, among the eleven or twelve kings who reigned at Xiaotun, there were three who had the day-name *yi* as part of their posthumous temple name: Xiao Yi (K20, i.e., the twentieth king of the dynasty), Wu Yi (K26), and Di Yi (K28).[3] Sacrifices would have been offered to a "Father Yi" during all three generations ruled by their respective sons, Wu Ding (K21), Wen Ding (K27), and Di Xin (K29). Thus, while it is possible to use a single ancestor title to narrow the range of reigns during which a divination could have been performed, it is rarely sufficient in itself to pinpoint a particular reign.

This deficiency was decisively answered in a 1933 article entitled "Studies in Oracle-Bone Periodization" by Dong Zuobin, a leading member of the first Academia Sinica excavations at Xiaotun.[4] Having discovered in the course of those excavations several complete turtle plastrons (similar to *Bingbian* 1 [see fig. 2, p. 70] but differing in that they had never broken apart), Dong recognized that words such as *Xiong* in the formulaic preface to the inscription on catalogue number 67 represent the proper names of the divination officials presiding over the divination. He further surmised that all of the inscriptions recorded on a single plastron must have been very closely contemporary. Given this assumption, he concluded that if the names of two or more divination officials appear on a single shell or bone, they must also be presumed to have been contemporaries. To illustrate this point, we might notice that on the reconstructed plastron *Bingbian* 1, divinations are about evenly divided between diviners Que and Zheng, suggesting that these two officials must have served at the Shang court at the same time. (Both are represented, albeit fragmentarily, in the Creel collection: Que in the fragmentary preface on cat. no. 70, and Zheng in the single graph on cat. nos. 72 and 73.) To take another example, *Yizhu* 620 contains three separate inscriptions:

a. 辛丑卜㱿貞：婦好有子．三月．
Crack on *xinchou* (day thirty-eight), Que divining: "Fu Hao will have a son." Third month.

b. 辛丑卜亘貞：... 王固曰：好其有子．
Crack on *xinchou* (day thirty-eight), Xuan divining: . . . The king prognosticated and said, "Hao will have a son."

c. 乙卯卜宊貞：乎婦好㞢𠬝于比癸．
Crack on *yimao* (day fifty-two), Bin divining: "Fu Hao will offer [a] captive to Bi Gui."

Yizhu 620; I.Bin

Given this same premise, Que must have served at the same time as both Xuan and Bin. Moreover, by logical extension, if Zheng were contemporary with Que then he probably was also contemporary with Xuan and Bin. In this way, it is possible to obtain a set of four contemporary diviner officials. Dong Zuobin thoroughly developed this methodology, demonstrating various more or less extensive sets of diviner officials who shared such associations.[5]

This allowed Dong to take two further steps in his study. First, having a relatively large sample of inscriptions known to be contemporary, he could relate a number of different ancestor titles and thereby pinpoint particular reigns. For instance, in the case of the inscriptions we have discussed so far (the set including diviners Zheng, Que, Xuan, Bin, and so on, generally known as the "Bin-group"), in addition to sacrifices to a "Father Yi," which as we have already seen might characterize any of three different generations, the names of three other "fathers" also appear: Father Jia, Father Geng, and Father Xin. Comparison of these records with the genealogy of the Shang royal house shows without question that these inscriptions must date to the reign of Wu Ding, a king who was preceded by, in addition to his father, Xiao Yi, three uncles: Xiang Jia (K17), Pan Geng (K18), and Xiao Xin (K19). Remembering that the title "father" could also be used with respect to uncles, it is easy to see that Father Yi corresponds to Xiao Yi, Father Jia to Xiang Jia, Father Geng to Pan Geng, and Father Xin to Xiao Xin. Since no other generation would have this same set of "fatherly" ancestors, the Bin-group inscriptions, which encompass more than half of all Shang inscriptions so far discovered, are certain to have dated from the reign of Wu Ding and serve as a foundation against which all other inscription groups can be evaluated.

Given this basis, Dong then went on to determine the regnal periods of other inscriptions grouped into independent sets of diviners. For instance, the set of inscriptions associated with the diviner Chu contains examples of sacrifices to Father Ding, Brother (Xiong) Ji, and Brother Geng. A "Father Ding" could be the recipient of sacrifices in three of the eight generations of Xiaotun kings: the reigns of Zu Geng (K22) and Zu Jia (K23), both sons of Wu Ding, the reign of Wu Yi (K26), son of Kang Ding (K25), and the reign of Di Yi (K28), son of Wen Ding (K27). The appearance of sacrifices to Brothers Ji and Geng allows this group to be further specified: Brother Ji refers to Xiao Ji, known from later texts to have been the eldest son of Wu Ding, but who predeceased his notably long-lived father and thus did not reign in his own right; and Brother Geng is Zu Jia's appellation for his elder brother Zu Geng. The Chu-group inscriptions can therefore be dated generally to the generation immediately following the Bin-group inscriptions.

It is possible to use this same method to periodize inscriptions throughout the remaining generations of kings at Xiaotun; indeed, because of the increasingly formulaic nature of the ancestral cult conducted during these reigns, it is often easier to date these later inscriptions. But since none of the pieces in the Creel collection seems to derive from these later reigns, it will not be necessary here to continue this description of Dong's methodology. However, at least one issue involving inscriptions Dong assigned to this later period, those of the Dui- and Li-groups, which *are* represented in the Creel collection, has been hotly debated in the fifty-some years since he first proposed his periodization. This issue will be the topic of the next entry.

E.L.S.

NOTES

1. The days of the Shang week were *jia*, *yi*, *bing*, *ding*, *wu*, *ji*, *geng*, *xin*, *ren*, and *gui*.

2. It is also possible that the "*Zu*" of this title should be construed more narrowly to mean "Grandfather," in which case this Zu Yi or Grandfather Yi would have to refer to a later Yi ancestor, such as Xiao Yi, the twentieth king and grandfather (at least generationally) of the kings Zu Geng and Zu Jia.

3. For a convenient chart of the Shang royal genealogy, see David N. Keightley, *Sources of Shang History: The Oracle-Bone Inscriptions of Bronze Age China* (Berkeley, Calif., Los Angeles, and London: University of California Press, 1978), 185–187, table 1.

4. Dong Zuobin, "Jiaguwen duandai yanjiu li," *Zhongyang yanjiusuo jikan waibian* 1, no. 1 (1933): 323–424.

5. For a convenient list of the major diviners and their periods, see Keightley, *Sources of Shang History*, 195, table 6.

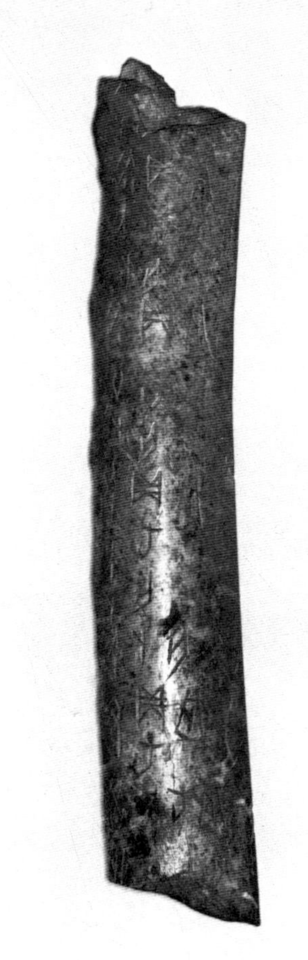

67

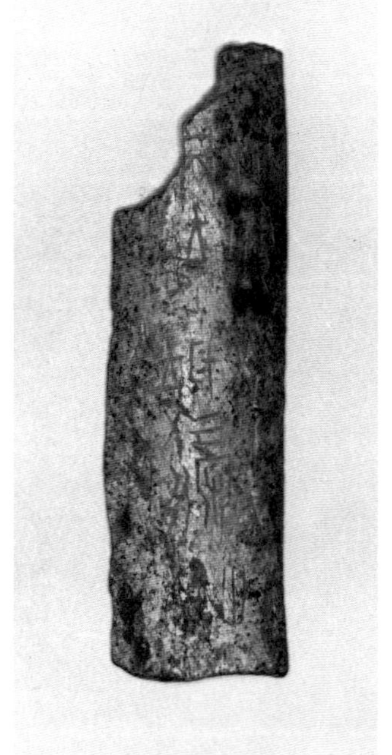

68

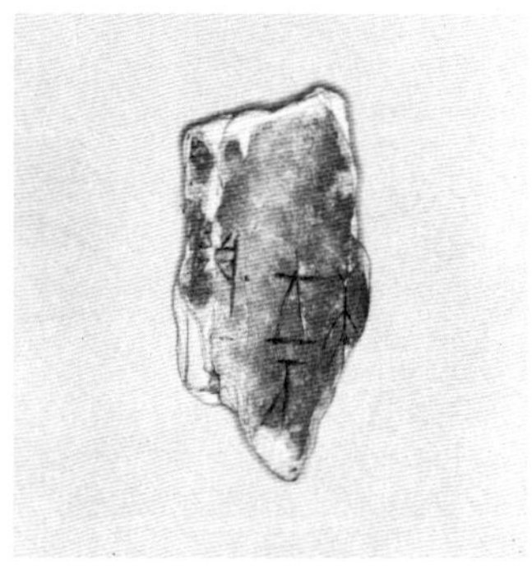

69

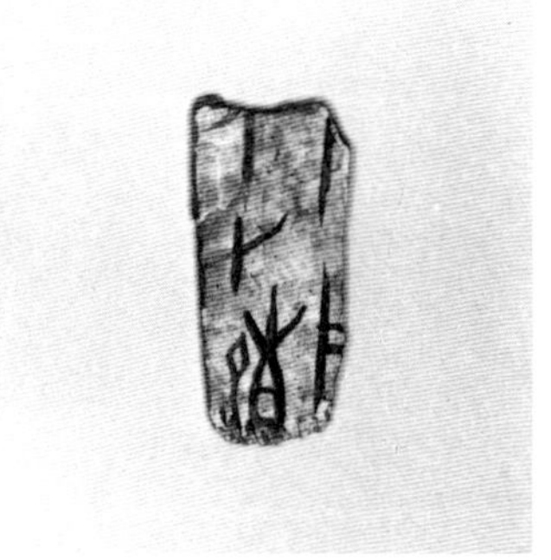

70

67 **Late Shang dynasty**
Oracle Bone

H. 4 5/16 (10.9)
Acc. no. 1986.391
(B); II.Chu.

癸卯[卜]，兄貞：旬王囚．一月．
Crack on *guimao* (day forty), Xiong divining: "In the (next) ten-day week there will be no misfortune." First month.

癸丑卜，貞：旬亡囚．
Crack on *guichou* (day fifty), divining: "In the (next) ten-day week there will be no misfortune."

癸亥卜，貞：旬亡囚．
Crack on *guihai* (day sixty), divining: "In the (next) ten-day week there will be no misfortune."

癸酉卜，貞：旬亡囚．
Crack on *guiyou* (day ten), divining: "In the (next) ten-day week there will be no misfortune."

癸亥卜，貞：旬亡囚．
Crack on *guihai* (day sixty), divining: "In the (next) ten-day week there will be no misfortune."

..[亥]卜... [旬]...
Crack on [*gui*]-*hai* (day sixty)... "In the (next) ten-day week..."

68 **Late Shang dynasty**
Oracle Bone

H. 2 3/4 (7)
Acc. no. 1986.394
(B); I.Bin.

... 卅...
... thirty ...

癸卯貞：王又彳歲三牢羌十五．
Divining on *guimao* (day forty): "The king will offer and elevate *sui*-sacrifice of three penned cows and fifteen Qiang."

貞：王又歲于且(:祖)乙牢．
Divining: "The king will offer *sui*-sacrifice of a penned cow to Ancestor Yi."

69 **Late Shang dynasty**
Oracle Bone

H. 1 1/4 (3.2)
Acc. no. 1986.395
(B); I.Bin.

貞：[于]王亥桒...
Divining: "(To) Wang Hai make ritual-entreaty ..."

70 **Late Shang dynasty**
Oracle Plastron

H. 1 1/16 (2.7)
Acc. no. 1986.402
(S); I.Bin.

... [亥]卜殻...
Crack on . .-*hai*, Que ...

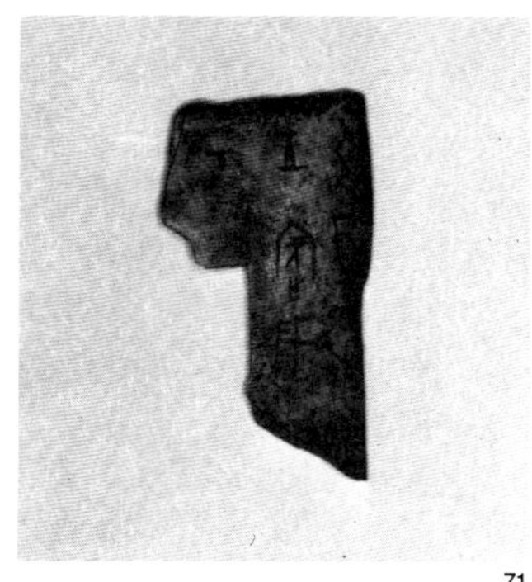

71

71 **Late Shang dynasty**
Oracle Plastron

H. 1¼ (3.2)
Acc. no. 1986.407
(S); I.Bin.

. . . 冎

. . . bone.

乙酉卜王賓歲

Crack on *yiyou* (day twenty-two): "The king will entertain and *sui*-sacrifice."

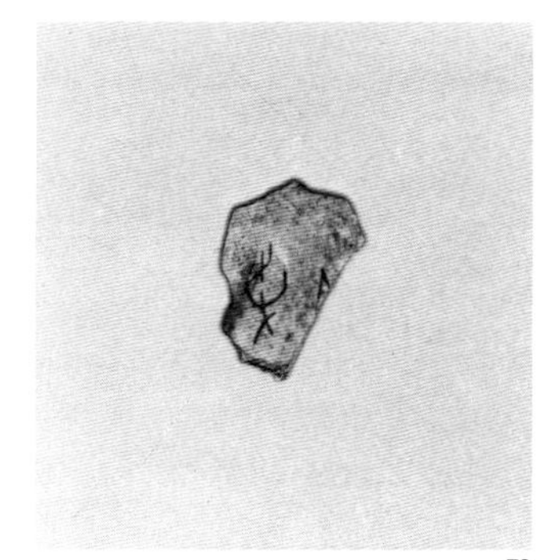

72

72 **Late Shang dynasty**
Oracle Plastron

H. ⅝ (1.6)
Acc. no. 1986.420
(S); I.Bin.

. . . 爭[貞] . . .

. . . Zheng divining . . .

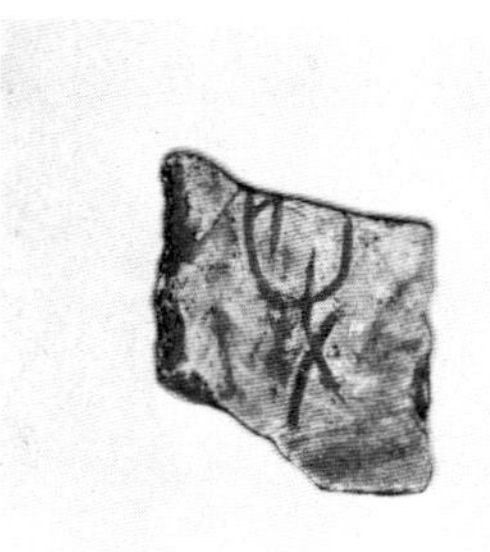

73

73 **Late Shang dynasty**
Oracle Plastron

H. ⅞ (2.2)
Acc. no. 1986.423
(S); I.Bin.

. . . 爭 . . .

. . . Zheng . . .

Periodization of the Dui and Li Groups

Dong Zuobin convincingly assigned inscriptions associated with the Bin, Chu, He, and Huang groups of diviners to the respective reigns of Wu Ding (K21), Zu Geng (K22) and Zu Jia (K23), Lin Xin (K24) and Kang Ding (K25), and Di Yi (K28) and Di Xin (K29), which he termed Periods I, II, III, and V. However, he found remaining a few isolated but typologically similar groups of inscriptions, associated with the diviners Dui and Li and, less numerous, with Wu and Zi, which together referred to sacrifices to a "Father Yi" and a "Father Ding." As already discussed in the preceding entry, in the case of inscriptions containing just the ancestor title "Father Yi," three different reigns during the Anyang period could be indicated: Wu Ding's with respect to his father, Xiao Yi (K20); Wen Ding's (K27) with respect to his father, Wu Yi (K26); or Di Xin's with respect to his father, Di Yi. And in the case of "Father Ding," three more generations could be indicated: Zu Geng's and Zu Jia's with respect to their father, Wu Ding; Wu Yi's with respect to his father, Kang Ding; and Di Yi's with respect to his father, Wen Ding. In all three cases, the correlation of these two ancestor titles could produce a period of two contiguous generations: the first would include Wu Ding and Zu Geng and Zu Jia, the second Wu Yi and Wen Ding, and the third Di Yi and Di Xin. Despite these three possibilities, Dong reckoned that since inscriptions from the reigns of Wu Ding (Period I), Zu Geng and Zu Jia (Period II), and Di Yi and Di Xin (Period V) had already been identified with certitude, by process of elimination the remaining more or less contemporary diviner groups must date to the reigns of Wu Yi and Wen Ding. He designated these two reigns, the only reigns among the last kings at Xiaotun for which he had not previously identified any inscriptions, as Period IV.

After having deduced this periodization scheme, Dong discovered in the course of examining inscriptions from YH127, the important pit whose discovery in 1936 was described in the introductory essay to this section, that while the overwhelming majority of inscriptions belonged to the Bin group (his Period I), there were also inscriptions associated with the diviners Dui, Wu, and Zi, inscription types that he had previously dated to the much later Period IV. Instead of reconsidering the periodization of these inscriptions in light of this new archaeological evidence, Dong constructed a theory of alternating "schools" of divination officials to explain their anachronistic context. According to this theory, the diviners active during the reigns of Wu Ding and Zu Geng, whose tradition could best be characterized as ad hoc, lost favor during the reign of Zu Jia and were replaced by diviners from a completely different tradition of divination, one that was extremely structured.

This tradition, which Dong termed the "New School" in distinction to the "Old School" of Wu Ding, retained favor throughout the following reigns of Lin Xin and Kang Ding. Then, according to Dong, the similarity between inscriptions of the diviners Dui, Li, Zi, and Wu and those of the Bin group, even to the point of taking up many of the same divination topics and referring to individuals of identical or nearly identical names, was evidence that the "Old School" of divination had once again found favor with the following kings, Wu Yi and Wen Ding. Finally, the reversion to a highly structured divination style in what Dong termed the Period V inscriptions of Kings Di Yi and Di Xin suggested that the "Old School" had once again lost favor and had been supplanted.

Not a few scholars, however, disputed this logic, arguing that the coincidence of a great number of names in inscriptions of these two groups (a coincidence that is not found with inscriptions of any other groups) could only indicate their contemporaneity.[1] What is more, these scholars argued that considering these inscriptions as belonging to Period I rather than to Period IV would greatly simplify our view of Shang historical development. They also recognized the change from an Old School to a New School during the reign of Zu Jia, but, if all the various Old School inscriptions could be dated to the reigns of Wu Ding and Zu Geng, then the change to the New School would continue without further reversion until the end of the dynasty.

This debate over the correct periodization of the Dui and Li groups continued for more than a generation until 1973, when, as noted briefly in the introductory oracle-bone essay, more than five thousand pieces of inscribed oracle bone were excavated at Xiaotun *nandi* under controlled conditions by archaeologists of the Institute of Archaeology, Chinese Academy of Sciences. One of the most important aspects of this discovery is that the earliest stratum contained exclusively bones with Dui-group inscriptions, showing beyond doubt that this type of inscription not only dates to the reign of Wu Ding but that it is also earlier than the standard Bin-group inscriptions of the same reign.[2] Moreover, the discovery also suggests that the other contested groups of inscriptions probably also date roughly to the reign of Wu Ding, a suggestion that has subsequently been demonstrated by several scholars.[3]

Although none of the inscriptions in the Creel collection mentions diviners Dui or Li (or Wu or Zi, for that matter), there are a few pieces (e.g., cat. nos. 68, 74, 77, and 79) that can be assigned to these groups on the basis of typological evidence, especially their calligraphy. Of these, the most interesting is catalogue number 77, a scapula bone fragment that still contains all or portions of four different inscriptions, including two virtually identical divinations regarding the announcement of the sacrifice of a lamb, one to the ancestor Da Jia and the other to Da Yi:

> Divining on *xinwei* (day eight): "To Da Jia announce a shepherded lamb."
> Divining on *xinwei*: "To Da Yi announce a shepherded lamb."

The first of these inscriptions is also identical to one on another Li-group scapula bone discovered at Xiaotun *nandi*. Moreover, that bone, *Tunnan* 1024, contains another inscription mentioning a sacrifice to a "Father Ding," showing that it (and, by implication, cat. no. 77 as well) must date to the reign of Zu Geng, the son of Wu Ding.[4] The cross-regnal periodization of the Li-group inscriptions, in which some inscriptions (those referring to "Father Ding") date to Zu Geng's reign, while others (referring to "Father Yi," i.e., Xiao Yi) date to the reign of Wu Ding himself, has implications that go far beyond just the internal periodization of this one group of inscriptions. As we shall see in the next entry, it also suggests ways in which the Bin-group inscriptions, far and away the most numerous of all of the different types of inscriptions, can also be internally periodized. This final step (at least for the purposes of this catalogue) in the periodization of Shang oracle-bone inscriptions will demonstrate how the historical developments described in the introductory essay were reconstructed. E.L.S.

NOTES

1. See, for example, Chen Mengjia, *Yinxu buci zongshu* (Beijing: Kexue chubanshe, 1956), 145–167, and Kaizuka Shigeki and Itō Michiharu, "Kōkotsubun dandai kenkyūhō no saikento—Dōshi no Bunbutei jidai bokuji o chūshin to shite," *Tōhō gakuhō* 23 (1953): 1–78. For a complete survey of this debate, tending generally to side with the views of Chen and Kaizuka and Itō, see David N. Keightley, *Sources of Shang History: The Oracle-Bone Inscriptions of Bronze Age China* (Berkeley, Calif., Los Angeles, and London: University of California, 1978), 91–133.

2. For this stratigraphy, see Xiao Nan, "Anyang Xiaotun nandi faxian de Duizu buci—jianlun Duizu buci de shidai ji qi xiangguan wenti," *Kaogu* 1976.4, 234–241; and *Xiaotun nandi jiagu* (Shanghai: Zhonghua shuju, 1980), vol. 1, 17.

3. See, for example, Li Xueqin, "Xiaotun nandi jiagu yu jiagu fenqi," *Wenwu* 1981.5, 27–33; Qiu Xigui, "Lun Lizu buci de shidai," *Guwenzi yanjiu* 6 (1981): 262–320, and Lin Yun, "Xiaotun nandi fajue yu Yinxu jiagu duandai" *Guwenzi yanjiu* 9 (1984): 111–154. For an English-language resume of these studies, see Edward L. Shaughnessy, "Recent Approaches to Oracle-Bone Periodization: A Review," *Early China* 8 (1982–83): 1–13.

4. I am particularly grateful to Professor Qiu Xigui for calling my attention to this parallel.

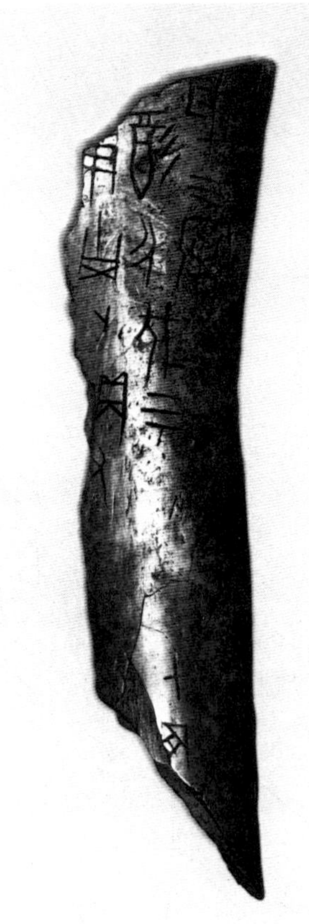

74

74 Late Shang dynasty
Oracle Bone

H. 3 7/8 (9.8)
Acc. no. 1986.392
(B); I.Dui-Li.

庚子卜，貞：又酒升伐三歲三牢.

Crack on *gengzi* (day thirty), divining: "Offer wine, elevate three decapitants, and *sui*-sacrifice three penned cows."

[癸]... 甲辰...

. . . [*gui-*] . . . *jiachen* (day forty-one) . . .

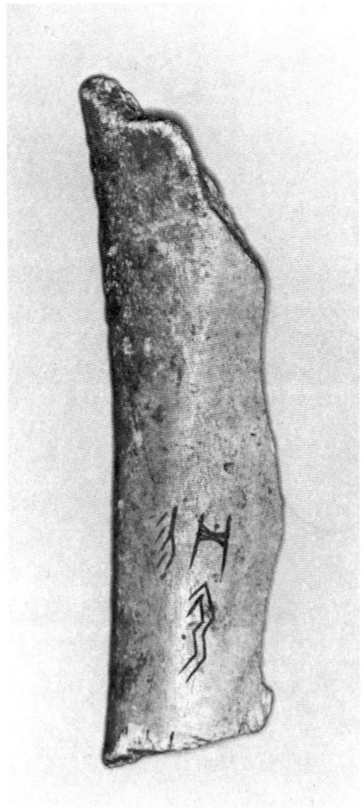

75

75 Late Shang dynasty
Oracle Bone

H. 3 1/16 (7.8)
Acc. no. 1986.393
(B); II.Chu.

貞：弜勿.

Divining: "Wu ought not."

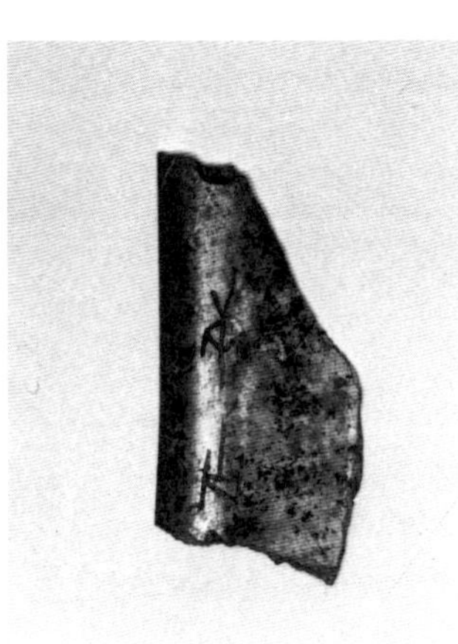

76

76 Late Shang dynasty
Oracle Bone

H. 1 1/2 (3.8)
Acc. no. 1986.396
(B); II.Li.

庚子

On *gengzi* (day thirty-seven) . . .

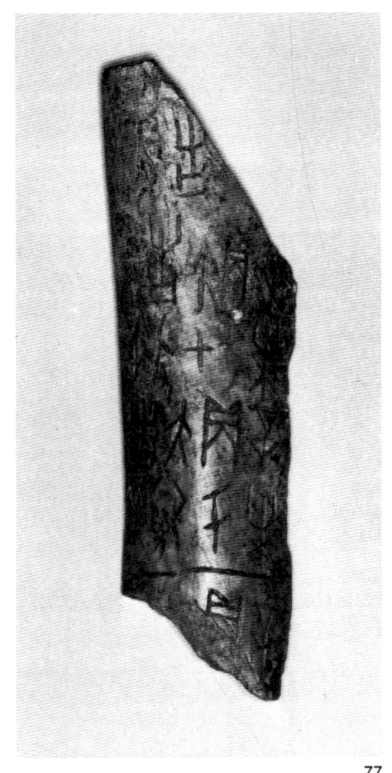

77

77 Late Shang dynasty
Oracle Bone

H. 2 3/4 (7)
Acc. no. 1986.397
(B); II.Li.

辛... 貞...

Divining on *xin-* . . .

辛未貞：于大乙告羖.

Divining on *xinwei* (day eight): "To Da Yi announce a shepherded lamb."

辛未貞：于大甲告羖.

Divining on *xinwei* (day eight): "To Da Jia announce a shepherded lamb."

... 告[羖].

. . . announce a (shepherded) lamb.

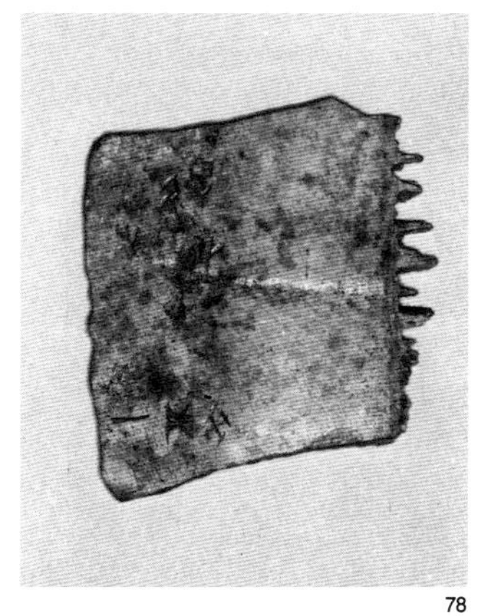

78

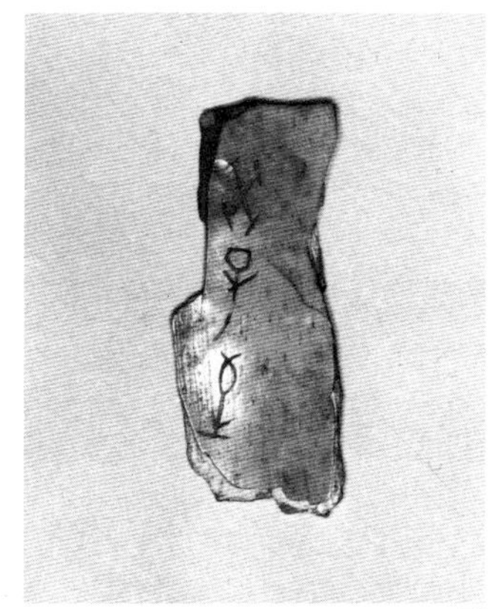

79

78 **Late Shang dynasty**
Oracle Plastron
H. 1$\frac{3}{8}$ (3.5)
Acc. no. 1986.398
(S); II.Bin-Chu.
癸 . . . 貞 . . .
. . . on *gui* . . . , divining . . .
子(:巳)卜 . . . 勿 . . . 步
Crack on . . -*si*, . . . do not . . . walk.

79 **Late Shang dynasty**
Oracle Plastron
H. 1$\frac{7}{16}$ (3.7)
Acc. no. 1986.399
(S); I.Dui.
. . . 癸子(:巳)至 . . .
. . . *guisi* (day thirty) until . . .

The Date and Implications of the Gongfang War

Because of the fragmentary nature of many of its pieces, the Creel collection of oracle bones does not greatly add to our knowledge of Shang history. Nevertheless, several pieces are plausibly related to an event that apparently played a pivotal role in the fortunes of the late Shang state—the war with a state known as Gongfang. This enemy state, which was located to the west of Shang, in or near the area generally known as the Ordos, is mentioned in the inscription on catalogue number 93: ". . . Gong . . . catch . . . " While this inscription is so fragmentary that it is impossible to determine even if it concerns a Shang or Gongfang attack, the presence of the verb *ji* 及/及(to catch), rendered pictographically as a hand grasping a man from behind, does indicate at least a divination concerning hostilities between the two states. Other inscriptions may also be related to this war. Catalogue number 81, for example, mentions Guo, the personal name of the leader of the state of Zhi (and thus usually referred to as Zhi Guo), an important ally of Shang throughout the reign of King Wu Ding and especially during the Gongfang War. Another inscription, on catalogue number 89, contains the word *wang*, which, among other uses, serves as the name of a state allied to Shang at this time, the leader of which, Wang Cheng, led troops against enemies of the Shang. Finally, catalogue number 85 mentions Yue, yet another state allied to Shang, and, as we will see, one which was very much involved in the fighting with Gongfang.

The Shang war with Gongfang, just barely hinted at in these inscriptions, is without a doubt the single most frequently divined event in the entire corpus of Shang oracle-bone inscriptions, with upwards of five hundred different inscriptions available in collections published to date.[1] Almost all these derive from the Bin group of diviners, which, as we have seen, Dong Zuobin dated to the reign of King Wu Ding. Because Wu Ding is known in traditional Chinese histories as a "restorationist" king, most scholars have assumed that the fighting between the two states came in the course of a major expansion of the territory under his control and that the result must have been a crushing defeat for Gongfang (indeed, according to some scholars, its virtual extermination);[2] for with the exception of one Chu-group inscription (Dong Zuobin's Period II), Gongfang never again serves as the topic of Shang divinations.

Reasonable though this assumption might seem, it is not directly substantiated by any inscriptional evidence. In fact, there is some evidence, equally indirect to be sure, that suggests quite the opposite conclusion. For instance, the state Yue, mentioned on catalogue number 85, was a very close ally of the Shang during much of Wu Ding's reign, as the following inscriptions show:

己丑卜賓貞：戉受又.

Crack on *jichou* (day twenty-six), Bin divining: "Yue will receive aid."

Shiduo 1.382; I.Bin

貞：戉其乎來.

Divining: "Yue is expected to be called to come."

Yicun 16; I.Bin

However, in later reigns, this state, like Gongfang, is almost never the topic of Shang divinations, and on the few occasions when it is, it is clearly as an enemy of the Shang:

乙丑王... 伐西戉... 余其比... 于余受...
On *yichou* (day two) "the king . . . attacks west Yue . . . I will ally . . . in my receiving . . ."

(V.Huang)[3]

This radical shift in Yue's status, from ally to enemy, implies that the Shang must have suffered some setback in their western alliance. In this regard, it might be important to note that Yue was apparently attacked by Gongfang:

己巳卜㱿貞：𢀛方弗允𢦏戉．十月．
Crack on *jisi* (day six), Que divining: "Gongfang will not really harm Yue." Tenth month.

Heji 6371; I-II.Bin

If Yue were not only "harmed" but actually overrun at this time,[4] its defeat would explain well how and why its alliance with Shang was severed. Nor is Yue an isolated example. Several other western states, not represented in the inscriptions of the Creel collection, show precisely the same pattern in their relations with the Shang court: first allies of Wu Ding, then attacked by Gongfang, and finally enemies of Shang.[5] These developments suggest that whatever the final outcome of the direct fighting between Shang and Gongfang, the result of the war must have been something less than a resounding Shang victory.

Because of the ambiguity of most oracle-bone inscriptions, which as records of divination preserve only predictions concerning future events and very rarely indicate their actual outcome (and even then only in cases that display the prognosticatory prescience of the Shang king), it has been difficult to choose between the two scenarios presented above regarding the Gongfang War. However, with the recent developments in historiographical method described in the preceding entry, and especially the archaeological proof that inscriptions of the Dui group are the earliest of all inscriptions, and the recognition that the Li-group inscriptions overlap the reigns of Wu Ding and Zu Geng, it is now possible to know more precisely the temporal context of the Gongfang inscriptions and, therefore, to interpret their place in the geopolitical developments of the Shang state.

Heretofore, inscriptions of the Bin group, to which almost all the Gongfang inscriptions belong and which account for roughly half of all Shang inscriptions, had been amorphously dated to the reign of Wu Ding, with little attempt to periodize them in relation to each other. Now, however, it is a relatively simple matter to show that those examples of the Bin group that share traits such as calligraphy, personal names, and divination format with the earlier Dui-group inscriptions must date close to the beginning of the Bin group. (These inscriptions are indicated as "I.Dui-Bin" in this catalogue; see, for example, cat. no. 65). On the other hand, those that share characteristics with the later portion of the Li group (that portion containing the ancestor title "Father Ding") or with the Chu group of Zu Geng's reign, can be seen as the latest of the Bin group (indicated in this catalogue as "II.Bin-Chu"; e.g., cat. nos. 83, 87, 92, and 99). Between these two extremes can be discerned a third typological group, which might be termed "Standard Bin-group" inscriptions (or simply "I.Bin" as in this catalogue) and presumably date to the final years of Wu Ding's reign.[6]

Among other uses, this internal periodization of the Bin-group inscriptions can help to resolve the dynamics of Wu Ding's relations with the western lands. While, as mentioned in the introductory essay to this section, the Dui-group inscriptions suggest a weak and embattled Shang state, fighting just to defend its own capital region, the earliest of the Bin-group inscriptions show a much more powerful state, with Shang forces attacking, and presumably conquering, as many as twenty-five different western states. That these states were conquered is apparent from their allied (and doubtless subservient) relationship with the Shang court in the slightly later Standard Bin-group inscriptions. To this extent, this new periodization confirms the traditional view of King Wu Ding as a restorer of Shang strength. However, it is now also clear that the inscriptions pertaining to the Gongfang War derive from a still later period; indeed, it seems likely that the war was not concluded until after Wu Ding's death. From this perspective, it seems that this war was not so much an aspect of Wu Ding's initial expansion as it was a precursor to (and perhaps even the cause of) the territorially reduced Shang state of subsequent reigns. Thus can be seen the importance that the methodology of periodization holds for the study not only of Shang oracle-bone inscriptions but also of all Shang history.

E.L.S.

NOTES

1. For a convenient listing of these inscriptions, see Hu Houxuan, "Yindai Gongfang kao," in *Jiaguxue Shangshi luncong chuji* (Chengdu: Qilu daxue, 1944), inconsecutively paginated. I should note that by "event" here, I intend only historically individuated events, and not such divination topics as the "week," royal travels, and so on, which were divined about regularly throughout the dynasty.

2. See, for example, Luo Kun, "Gaozong fa Guifang shiji kaobian," in *Jiaguwen yu Yin-Shang shi*, ed. Hu Houxuan (Shanghai: Guji chubanshe, 1983), 106–107.

3. Chen Mengjia, *Yinxu buci zongshu* (Beijing: Kexue chubanshe, 1956), pl. 3.

4. In a paper titled "The Life and Death of Fu Hao: With Comments on the Sequence of the Shang Campaigns against Bafang, Tufang, and Gongfang," presented to the Fortieth Annual Meeting of the Association for Asian Studies, San Francisco, 26 March 1988, which I expect to publish in due course, I have attempted to show the sequential relationships among inscriptions pertaining to the Gongfang War.

5. For a brief study of these states and the implications of their changing relationships with Shang, see Xia Hanyi, "Zaoqi Shang-Zhou guanxi ji qi dui Wu Ding yihou Yin-Shang wangshi shili fanwei de yiyi," *Jiuzhou xuekan* 2, no. 1 (Autumn 1987): 19–32.

6. I am particularly grateful to Professor Qiu Xigui for his advice in the periodization of these inscriptions.

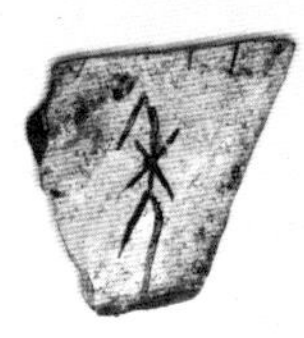

80

80 **Late Shang dynasty**
Oracle Bone
H. ¾ (1.9)
Acc. no. 1986.400
(B); I.Bin(?).
. . . 年 . . .
. . . harvest . . .

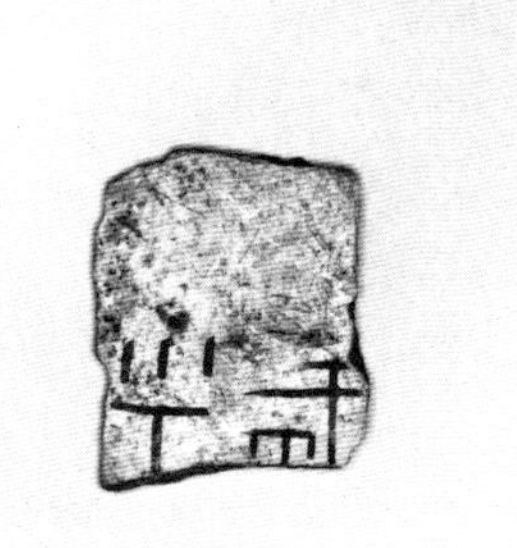

81

81 **Late Shang dynasty**
Oracle Plastron
H. ⅞ (2.2)
Acc. no. 1986.401
(S); I.Bin.
. . . 乎 . . . 戠 . . .
. . . call . . . Guo . . .

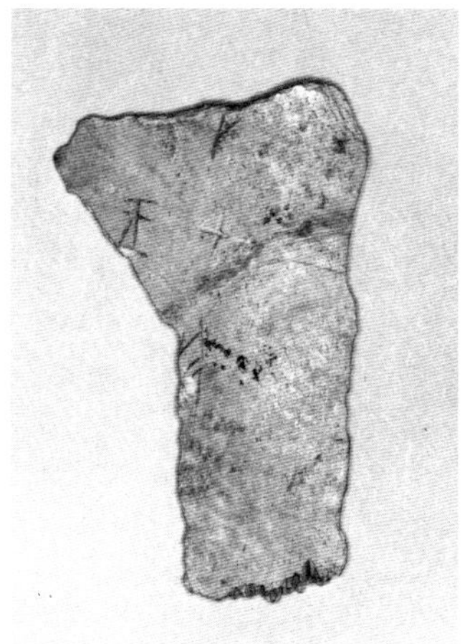

82

82 **Late Shang dynasty**
Oracle Plastron
H. 1⅞ (4.8)
Acc. no. 1986.403
(S); II.Chu.
甲申卜: 王 . . .
Crack on *jiashen* (day twenty-one): "The king. . . ."

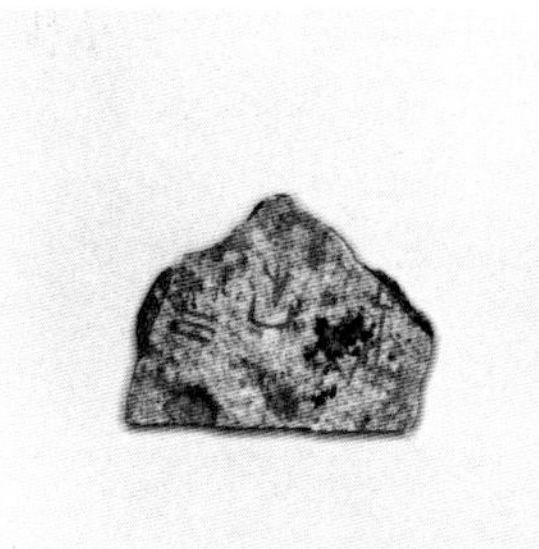

83

83 **Late Shang dynasty**
Oracle Plastron
H. ⅝ (1.6)
Acc. no. 1986.405
(S); II.Bin-Chu.
子(:巳) . . . 出 . . . 三
. . -*si* . . . go out . . . three . . .

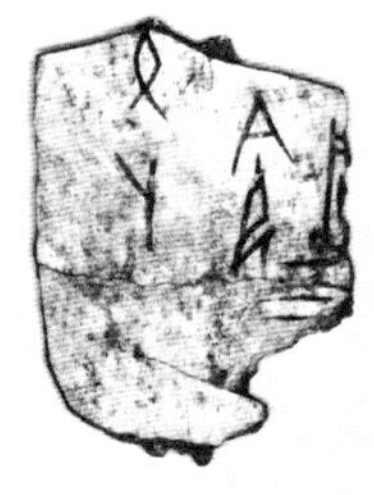

84

84 **Late Shang dynasty**
Oracle Plastron
H. 1⅛ (2.9)
Acc. no. 1986.406
(S); I.Bin.
. . . 寅卜 . . . 令 . . .
Crack on . . -*yin*, . . . command . . .

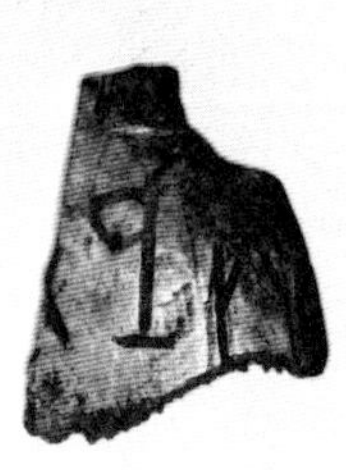

85

85 **Late Shang dynasty**
Oracle Plastron
H. 1 (2.5)
Acc. no. 1986.408
(S); I.Bin.
丙 . . . 戉
. . *bing*- . . . Yue . . .

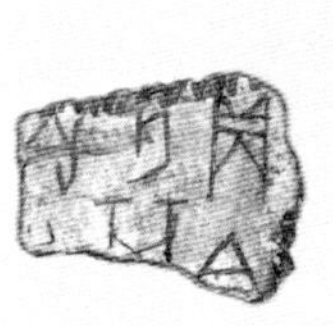

86

86 **Late Shang dynasty**
Oracle Plastron
H. ⅝ (1.6)
Acc. no. 1986.409
(S); I.Bin.
. . . 貞今 . . . 亡其 . . . 自
. . . divining: "This . . . will not expect to . . . from. . . ."

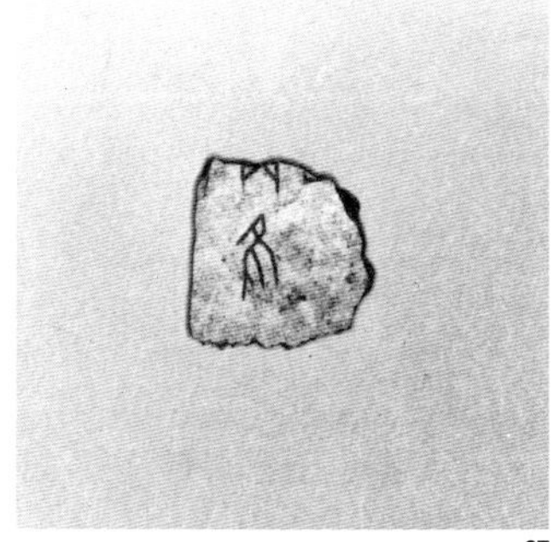

87

87 **Late Shang dynasty**
Oracle Plastron
H. 9/16 (1.4)
Acc. no. 1986.410
(S); II.Bin-Chu.
. . . 貞隹 . . .
. . . divining: "Let it be . . . . "

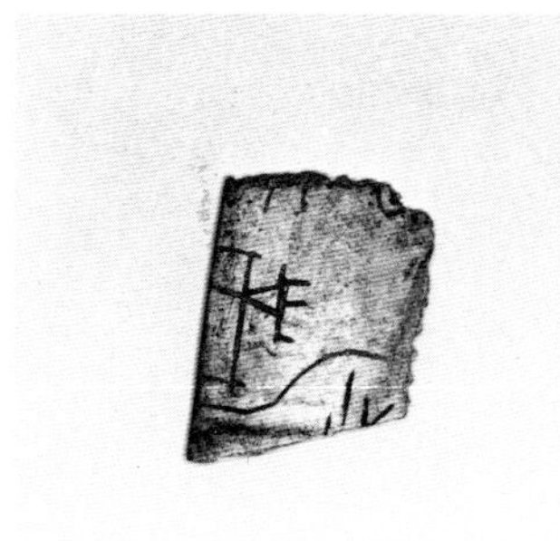

88

88 Late Shang dynasty
Oracle Plastron
H. 7/8 (2.2)
Acc. no. 1986.413
(S); I.Bin.
... 我 ...
... we ...

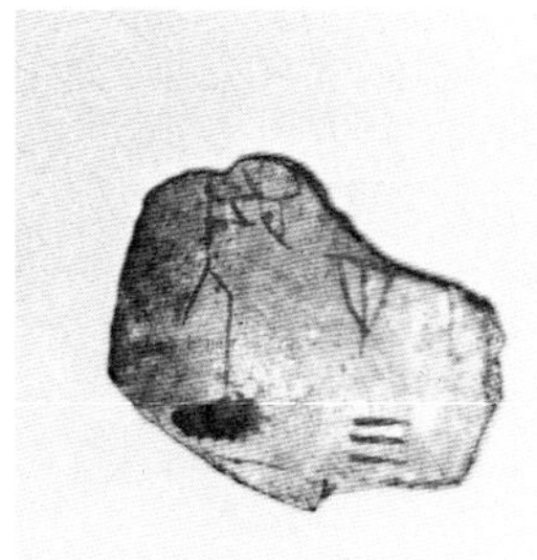

89

89 Late Shang dynasty
Oracle Plastron
H. 15/16 (2.4)
Acc. no. 1986.414
(S); I.Bin.
... 朢(:望)... 才... 三
... Wang ... at ... three ...

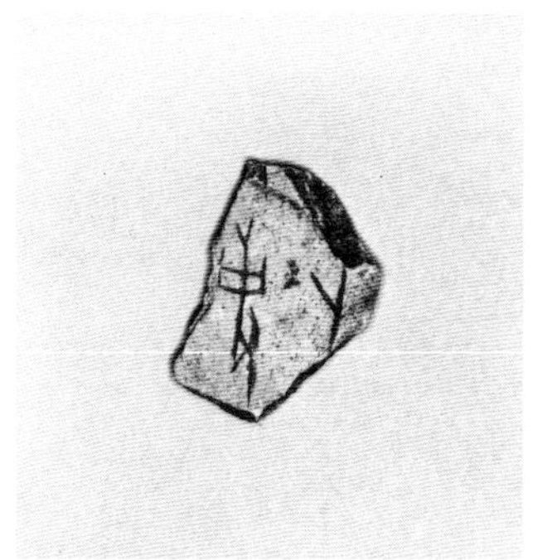

90

90 Late Shang dynasty
Oracle Plastron
H. 13/16 (2.1)
Acc. no. 1986.415
(S); I.Bin.
... 卜... 事...
Crack ... serve ...

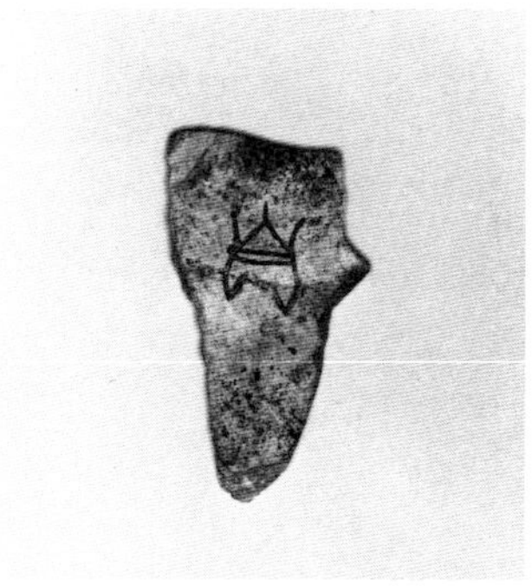

91

91 Late Shang dynasty
Oracle Plastron
H. 1 1/8 (2.9)
Acc. no. 1986.416
(S); I.Bin.
... 自...
... from ...

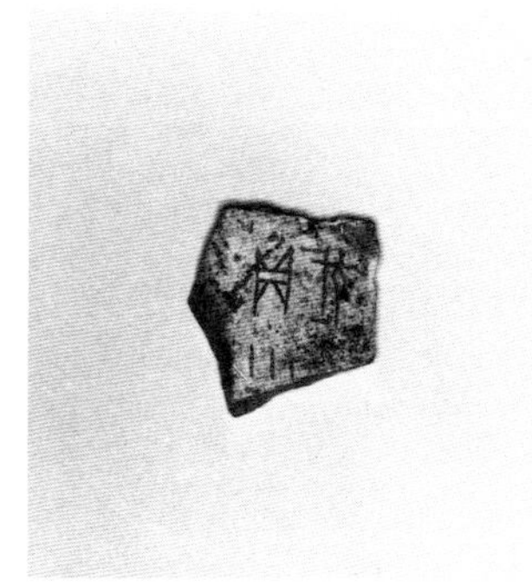

92

92 Late Shang dynasty
Oracle Bone
H. 5/8 (1.6)
Acc. no. 1986.417
(?); II.Bin-Chu.
貞屮(?)伐...
Divining: "Offer decapitants. . . ."

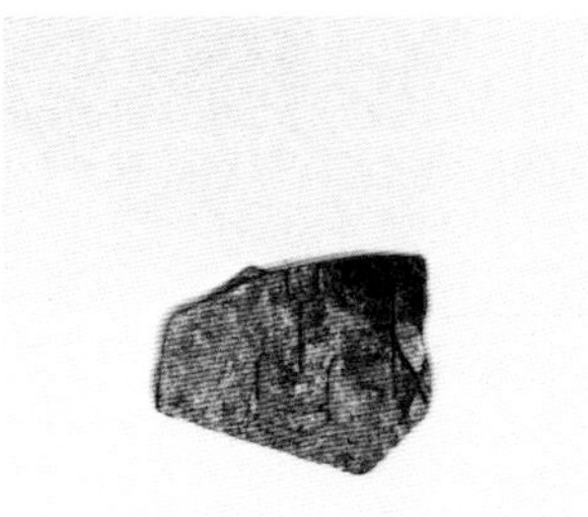

93

93 Late Shang dynasty
Oracle Plastron
H. 9/16 (1.4)
Acc. no. 1986.419
(S); I-II.Bin.
... 𠙵... 及
... Gong ... catch ...

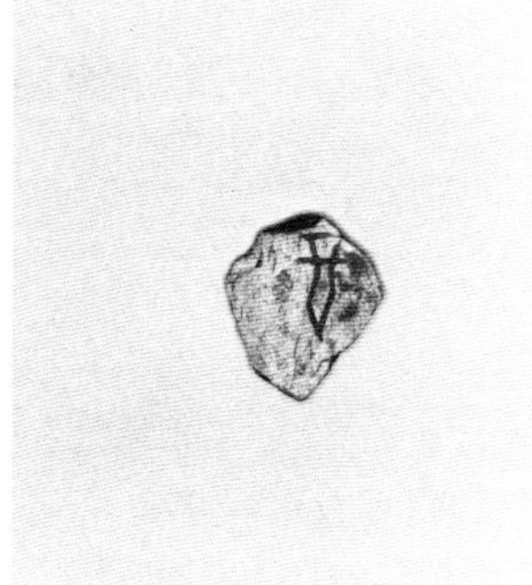

94

94 Late Shang dynasty
Oracle Plastron
H. 1/2 (1.3)
Acc. no. 1986.421
(S); I.Bin.
... 酉...
. . -*you* . . .

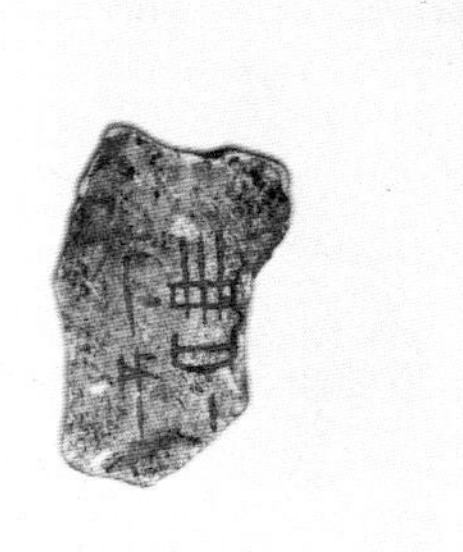

95

95 Late Shang dynasty
Oracle Bone
H. 15/16 (2.4)
Acc. no. 1986.422
(?); I.Bin.
戊戌... 冊
. . on *wuxu* (day thirty-five), . . . *ce*-(promissory)-sacrifice . . .

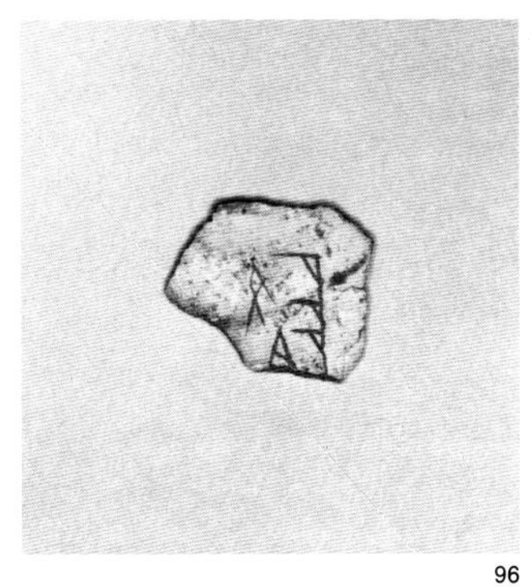

96

96 **Late Shang dynasty**
Oracle Plastron
H. 9/16 (1.4)
Acc. no. 1986.424
(S); I.Bin.
. . . 降 . . .
. . . send down . . .

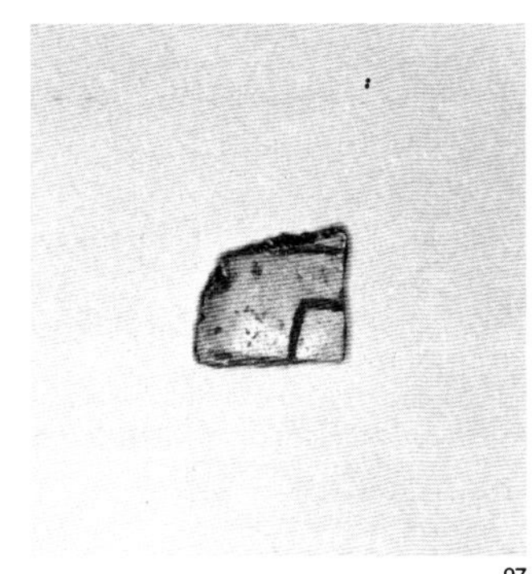

97

97 **Late Shang dynasty**
Oracle Plastron
H. 7/16 (1.1)
Acc. no. 1986.425
(S); I.Bin.
己 . . .
Ji . . .

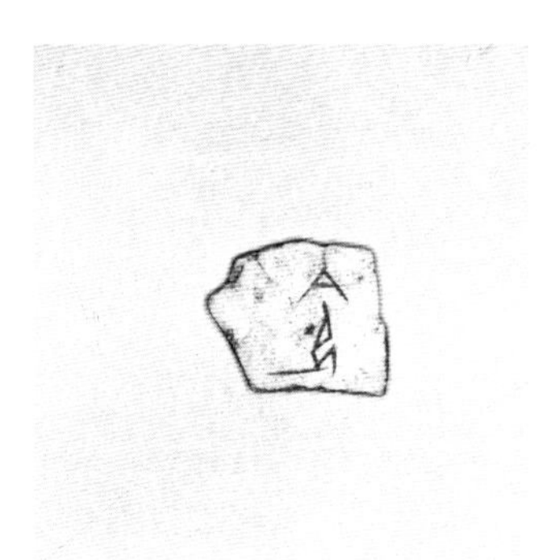

98

98 **Late Shang dynasty**
Oracle Plastron
H. 1/2 (1.3)
Acc. no. 1986.426
(S); I.?
. . . 令 . . .
. . . command . . .

99

99 **Late Shang dynasty**
Oracle Plastron
H. 5/8 (1.6)
Acc. no. 1986.427
(S); II.Bin-Chu.
. . . 今夕 . . . 雨
. . . "This evening . . . rain."

PAINTINGS OF THE MING AND QING DYNASTIES

LATER TRADITIONS OF CHINESE PAINTING

Harrie A. Vanderstappen

In addition to ancient bronze vessels and oracle bones, Chinese art in the Smart Gallery collection incorporates a sampling of paintings from the middle Ming through the middle Qing dynasties. As a group, these handscrolls (*juan*) and hanging scrolls (*zhou*) on silk, satin, or paper represent in a small way the many traditions of painting and cultural trends that are part of the total intellectual and artistic milieu of China from the sixteenth to the nineteenth century. The reassessment by Ming and Qing artists and critics of the meaning and development of Chinese painting is evident in both the great variety of extant work and in the claims each of them makes for the validity of the particular lineages to which their paintings or writings refer. Underlying these often contradictory claims, however, is the constant presence of a deeply honored and well-maintained craft, to which all these artists—no matter what tradition—must pay respect. This craft is evident in works by lesser artists as well as in the more standard or even routine works by artists renown for their aesthetic innovations.

There is an emphasis in the collection on the academic and professional aspects of China's artistic heritage. It is for this reason that one finds paintings by well-known artists—varying from the scholar-amateur or statesman-artist to the nonconformist and eccentric—next to works by professional artist-craftsmen, called *huagong*, a term scholar-gentry critics used to denigrate professional and court academy painters. Three paintings in the collection represent the first great self-proclaimed literati or scholar-amateur tradition (*shidafu hua*) in Chinese painting, associated with the Northern Song painter, eccentric, and critic Mi Fu (1051–1107). The earliest of these is Mi Wanzhong's hanging scroll *Among the Fragrant Snowy Mountains of Lan Garden* painted in 1621 (cat. no. 106). In the tall cone-shaped mountain peaks executed in broad dots and washes, the late-Ming official and gentleman painter refers at once to Mi Fu, his family ancestor, and to the Mi painting tradition: such conical mountains, minimally rendered houses among misty, rainy, or drifting clouds, and shaded foliage on bare tree trunks are hallmarks of the Mi tradition. About a century later, following this same tradition, the middle-Qing artist Huang Ding painted *Clouded Mountains* (1724, cat. no. 114). Instead of referring directly to Mi Fu, however, Huang mentions in his inscription that he painted this landscape in the manner of Gao Kegong (1248–circa 1310), who was himself a distant follower of the Mi style. In *Clouded Mountains*, Huang modified the traditional, generalized cloud-covered countryside into an explicitly outlined and textured fisherman's retreat. In the landscape *Rain View* (cat. no. 119), painted around 1810, Gu Haoqing restates the original intent of the Mi-style cone-shaped mountain tops, dotted ink mannerisms, and naked tree trunks. The bluntly textured and watery strokes in the mountains and elsewhere clearly identify the Mi manner in its basic elements. Although the quality of these paintings varies, they show how the same tradition takes on its own peculiarities depending on the artist and time of execution.

Lan Ying is another seventeenth-century artist who, like Mi Wanzhong, restated and crystallized ancient painting traditions. Stylistically, in measured and edged strokes, Lan brings a lively and attractive presence to ancient formulas. In contrast to the works discussed above, however, which emulate literati traditions (*wenren hua*), Lan's paintings carry on academic and professional traditions, especially those of the so-called blue-and-green manner. Without much visual evidence, Lan is also identified in Qing critical writings as the last of the Zhe School, an early-Ming academic and professional school of painting begun, according to tradition, by the court painter Dai Wenjing (1388–1462). Of the three works by Lan Ying in the Smart Gallery collection, the best known is the monumental handscroll *Landscape (after Huang Gongwang)* (circa 1637–38, cat. no. 108). This painting shows the professional strength of Lan's hand as well as his ambition—professed in his claim to be in the lineage of one of China's most outstanding literati painters—for a place in the history of Chinese painting. The scroll also demonstrates the peculiar attitude of the connoisseurs who refer in the numerous inscriptions on the painting to Lan's talent while hinting at his lack of proper background by exaggerating his ability to emulate Huang Gongwang, an archetype of literati traditions. The force of Lan's brush is again well represented in the rocks and water depicted in a collaborative painting (undated, cat. no. 110), in which the bamboo was executed by Sun Di. This hanging scroll is a good example of a counterpart in monochrome ink to the colored handscroll in the manner of Huang Gongwang. Lan is well known in the history of Chinese painting, and it is obvious from these works that he was a master of brush, ink, and color and that he could maintain a high degree of skill in a complex, demanding, and very long handscroll. The scrolls represent the efforts of a professional artist who wants to paint and at the same time to express, in his choice of a literatus model, cultural aspirations not necessarily in tune with the opinions of the critical community. These same points are at present still part of the evaluation of Lan's work.

Allusions to an alternative blue-and-green manner also appear in Wu Da's *Summer Pavilion (after Zhao Danian)*, dated 1675, and Hua Yan's *Paths and Cliffs Beautiful under Clouds* of 1746 (cat. nos. 112, 116). The color in these two paintings is similar to that used by Lan in his handscroll, but the soft and graded tones refer to a gentler and more elegant manner, cleverly identified with eighth-century mid-Tang traditions by the late-Ming artist and critic Dong Qichang (1555–1636): "I once saw," he wrote, "a genuine work by Yang Sheng [active during the first half of the eighth century]. . . . From this one realizes the striking impact of the ancient spontaneous brush, that, like the fleeting glow of vermilion clouds, is something rarely seen in this world."[1] The same subtle shades of blue, green, and orange in the hanging scroll that bears this inscription by Dong also characterize the paintings by Wu Da and Hua Yan. Wu claims as a model Zhao Danian (active circa 1070–1100), a member of the imperial family well-known for his gentle river scenes employing light ink tones and subtle coloring, and these two paintings in the collection are good representatives of this ancient courtly manner. The references in Wu's painting to a summer retreat, to withdrawal from officialdom to a life of pleasure in retirement match well the elegance of the "boneless manner" of painting represented in the scrolls by Wu and Hua. In this manner, the *mogu* technique, the artist eschews outlines or contours, building forms with inks and color washes alone.

A famous school of Song painting in the twelfth and thirteenth centuries is often called the Ma-Xia School after two of its best-known representatives, Ma Yuan and Xia Gui, who worked at the imperial court around 1200. In paintings of the Ma-Xia School, haze-filled vistas and figures of appropriate fame are executed in articulated sets of strokes, dots, and ink washes, following the limited options set by academic rules. Though clearly definable in the early and middle Ming periods, as for instance in the anonymous Zhe School scroll in the Smart Gallery collection (circa 1500–50, cat. no. 100), the influence of the Ma-Xia School is less conspicuous in later Ming and Qing times. *Storing Garments of the Husband in Far Away Territory* by Guo Xu (circa 1500–30, cat. no. 101) is an excellent example of this tradition in the early sixteenth century. The bold strokes and the haze in the foliage and distance are reminiscences of this Southern Song court tradition. Similarly, the strong ink and textures in the landscape by Zhu Qizhen of 1633 (cat. no. 111) may well be indebted to the same tradition, although in this late-Ming painting other academic traditions going back to the eleventh-century Northern Song master Guo Xi may also play a role.

In the fourteenth century, the town of Suzhou near Shanghai emerged as a center of culture, expanding after the middle of the fifteenth century into a focus of aesthetic activity that had a lasting impact on a variety of subsequent artistic expressions in China. The arts of calligraphy, poetry, garden architecture, and painting of later Ming and Qing times branched out into various schools and regional developments, each in some degree always indebted to the genius of Suzhou artists of mid-Ming times. A few paintings in the collection reflect this very important development; the earliest, a landscape by Wen Jia (1561, cat. no. 102). The weave of textures and dotted outlines in the cluster of hills and rocks in this painting on silk are typical of the Wu School, the main school associated with the town of Suzhou.[2] The angular character of the trees and the compartmental accumulation, from the bottom to the top of the painting, of foreground, middle ground, and background constitute an authoritative mid sixteenth-century interpretation of late fourteenth-century devices. The delineated, curvilinear cloud patterns are part of the same repertory, and are well-established references to the classical form of landscape frequently encountered in paintings by Wen and other later Ming artists.

The Red Cliff (1575, cat. no. 103) by Qian Gu is also beholden to the Wu School of Suzhou. Interpreted in this short handscroll in color on silk is a well-known Song description in two odes of the poet Su Shi (1037–1101) and some of his friends visiting the Red Cliff, boating on the Yangzi River, and reciting poetry while drunk. The boat with Su and his friends figures prominently on the water in front of a stretch of a rocky shoreline identified as the Red Cliff. Qian's brisk use of dark ink and gentle colors and textures highlights this very representative painting of a distinctive color tradition, associated with famous illustrations of paradisiacal lands and idyllic encounters. The early seventeenth-century landscape by Chen Guan (circa 1620, cat. no. 107) belongs to the later Wu School, and exemplifies the way in which the fourteenth-century tradition of Ni Zan was carried out in the late Ming period: here the pale and subtle textures only dimly recall, in an unassertive memory, the once grand inventions of Ni, a principal Yuan model of the Wu School. If Chen's painting is an update of Ni, Song Xu claims in the inscription on his *Drifting Mountains in Fog* (1603, cat. no. 105) to rework Wu Zhen, another fourteenth-century artist and frequent Yuan exemplar for the painters of the Wu School. Sometimes it is difficult at this late date to determine what the artist had in mind from claims made in his own inscriptions for a painting, but it is interesting to see how Song's painting refers to an easily readable image of nature which is well in tune with works by his model Wu Zhen. The Wu School's varied approaches to painting of the past is clearly a matter of much wider scope than these few paintings can suggest. Still, they are enough to challenge the student of Chinese art to come to grips with the complexities of originality, style, and reverence for traditions inherent in Chinese painting.

Three paintings of plum blossoms and of the fragrant orchid should finally be mentioned, since their subjects partake of a thousand-year Chinese tradition. In his austere undated plum-blossom painting (cat. no. 117), the eighteenth-century scholar-amateur artist Tong Yu follows an ancient tradition said to have originated with the early twelfth-century painter Zhongren. Contrasted against a painted dark background, the blossoms are like pale spots reflected on translucent paper windows on a moonlit night. Enhanced by the lyricism of the inscription, the painting exhibits a mixture of literary references and visual metaphor perfected over centuries of practice, resulting in an impeccably tasteful performance. A later example of this same theme is the painting of 1819 by Zhu Xuan (cat. no. 120). Again the light plum blossoms drift against the darker background, like stars in a moonlit sky. In the inscription, Zhu mentions that the natural sheen of the blossom has no need of color and its life is secure on the sturdy tree trunk. This poetic sentiment is part of the standard metaphor of the plum blossom, which appears in early spring from a seemingly dead, old and hoary tree trunk. The blossoms are witnesses to new life and survival from the cold and stormy winter, and they became symbols of life especially in times of oppression, tyranny, or disaster. Another painting of great charm and interest is the handscroll of orchids (1824, cat. no. 121) by the only woman artist represented in the collection, Yun Xiang. Blossoming and spreading its fragrance unappreciated in lonely places in the faraway countryside, the orchid came to stand for the unrecognized scholar and forgotten talent. The references to the fragility of physical beauty and the fleeting importance of literary flourishes are also part of the metaphor expressed in the painting by Yun, a lady of charm and many talents, dependent on uncertain loyalties of friends and admirers and the fickleness of her own commitment. In their ephemeral beauty and brittle quickness of execution, the images in this scroll are a true reflection of the ritual of the richly felt but casual spontaneity of the passing glory of fame and fortune, which is at the heart of the metaphor of the orchid.

NOTES

1. Dong Qichang's inscription, which appears on his painting *Boneless Landscape in the Manner of Yang Sheng* (1615), is cited in Wai-Kam Ho et al., *Eight Dynasties of Chinese Painting: The Collections of the Nelson Gallery-Atkins Museum, Kansas City, and The Cleveland Museum of Art* (exh. cat.) (Cleveland: Cleveland Museum of Art in cooperation with Indiana University Press, 1980), 243 (cat. no. 190).

2. See *Min Shin no kaiga* (Tokyo: Kokuritsu Hakubutsukan, 1964), pls. 42, 46, and Jiang Zhaoshan, *Wen Zhengming hua xinian* (Taipei, Taiwan: National Palace Museum, 1976), pl. 26.

CATALOGUE OF PAINTINGS

All dimensions are given in inches, followed by centimeters in parentheses. Height precedes width. Dimensions are for paintings only, exclusive of mountings.

Abbreviated citations under PUBLICATIONS within entries are:

Bulletin: David and Alfred Smart Gallery, University of Chicago. *Bulletin of The David and Alfred Smart Gallery, The University of Chicago* 1 (1987–88).

Hamburg, *Chinesische Malerei*: Museum für Kunst und Gewerbe. *Chinesische Malerie der letzten vier Jahrhunderte* (exh. cat.). Hamburg: Museum für Kunst und Gewerbe, 1949.

Sirén, *Leading Masters*: Sirén, Osvald. *Chinese Painting: Leading Masters and Principles*. 7 vols. London: Lund Humphries and Co., 1956–58.

Suzuki, *Catalog*: Suzuki Kei. *Comprehensive Illustrated Catalog of Chinese Paintings*. 5 vols. Tokyo: University of Tokyo Press, 1982–83.

Catalogue entries in this section have been prepared by the following authors:

P.B. Paula Berger
R.A.B. Richard A. Born
A.B. Professor Anne Burkus
D.A.D. Daphne Anderson Deeds
S.K. Sandy Kita
M.L. Professor Mary Lawton
R.L. Rob Linrothe
K.L. Professor Kathlyn Liscomb
A.M. Amy McNair
H.M. Hoshikawa Masanobu
S.M. Stanley Murashige
K.R.T. Katherine R. Tsiang
H.A.V. Professor Harrie A. Vanderstappen

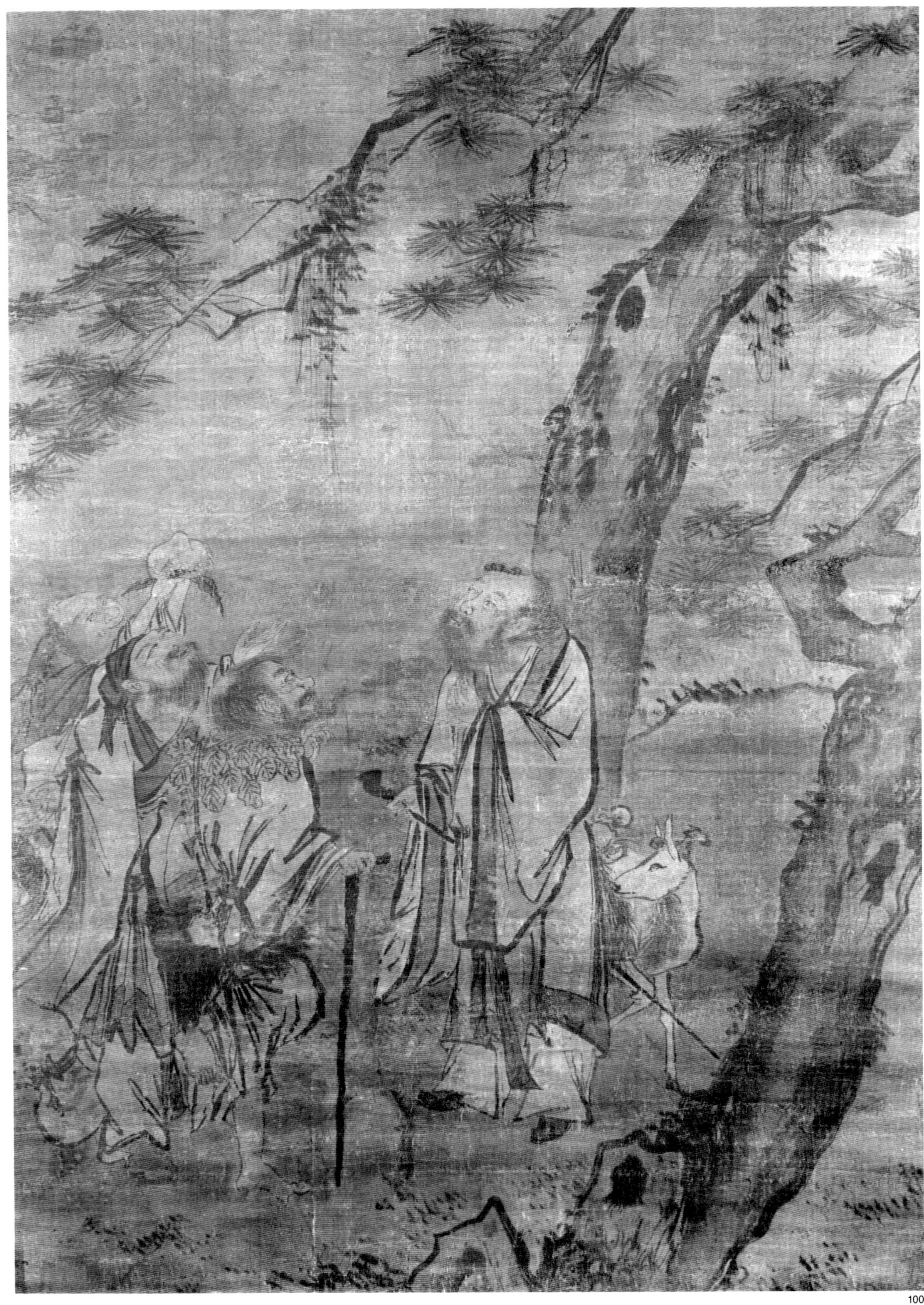

100

100 **Artist Unknown, Zhe School**, Ming dynasty
The God of Longevity and Three Immortals under Pine Trees, circa 1500–50

Hanging scroll, ink and light color on silk, 51 3/16 x 37 1/2 (130 x 95.3)
Purchase, Gift of Mr. and Mrs. Gaylord Donnelley
Acc. no. 1974.103

INSCRIPTIONS
Unsigned and uninscribed.

SEALS
No seals.

PROVENANCE
Yamanaka and Co., Kyoto (1974).

This unsigned and uninscribed painting of *The God of Longevity and Three Immortals under a Pine Tree* can be assigned on the basis of style and composition to a painter of the Zhe School of the middle Ming dynasty. In addition to the dramatic use of ink and brush that emphasizes fluctuating line and contrasts of lights and darks, one notices the boldly calligraphic brushwork in the drapery and tree and the fine, controlled linear definition of facial features overlaying pale colored washes. This combination of blunt and refined brushstrokes with subtle washes, as well as the large silk format, are hallmarks of the professional and court academy painters of the Zhe School, in particular the fifteenth- and sixteenth-century masters derogatorily termed the "Wild and Heterodox" School in late-Ming and Qing art criticism.[1] The composition, concentrating on a limited number of foreground figures in an intimate setting, harks back to the one-corner compositions of the Southern Song painters Ma Yuan and Xia Gui, with the tree in the lower center and right-hand portion of the painting acting as a repoussoir element and then reappearing at the top of the painting as an enclosure for the immortals. The asymmetrical Ma-Xia format was a favorite of the Zhe School, whose members frequently employed figures with boldly foreshortened heads — often gazing up into misty panoramas — and complicated poses from the back, as seen in the present painting.[2]

The legend of the Eight Immortals or *Ba xian* of Daoism appears as early as the Song dynasty and in art by the time of the Yuan dynasty.[3] The pantheon of popular immortals forms the largest single group of identifiable images in figure paintings by several of the principal masters of the "Wild and Heterodox" School, many of whom took sobriquets referring to individual immortals. They represent a superior class of human beings, who after canonization retain their bodily form and dwell in remote mountains and hills. From scholars to lunatics, the immortals led a carefree life, unstinted in drinking and festivity, and they generally acted in an irresponsible manner.

Three immortals and Shoulao, the Daoist god of longevity, are depicted in the Smart Gallery painting. The god of longevity stands apart, to the right of the group of three immortals. Traditionally, he is of happy mien, with a high forehead, and accompanied by his stag. His attributes include a long staff, gourd, and scroll, as well as a large peach from the fabulous *pantao* tree, which blossoms every three thousand years and yields peaches only three thousand years thereafter. The staff and stag are present here, and Shoulao may with his left hand cradle a peach in the folds of his garment.[4] Closest to the god of longevity is Li Tieguai, leaning on his iron crutch with his gourd of magic medicines on his back. Li was originally of commanding stature and dignified disposition. When summoned by the first sage of Daoism, Laozi, his soul left his body on an astral journey to the sacred Mount Hua, and when he returned to find his own moribund body cremated, Li was forced to take refuge in the body of a recently deceased lame beggar.[5] The Smart Gallery painting is faithful to traditional descriptions of his beggar's blackened face, woolly and disheveled beard and hair, and gigantic eyes.[6] The garland of leaves around his neck and the matted girdle of animal hair or grasses are familiar garb of the immortals. Directly behind Li stands Cao Guoqiu, in court headdress and official robes as befits the brother of Empress Cao Hou (wife of the Song Emperor Ren Cung).[7] Both Cao Guoqiu's hands are raised empty, and because the painting appears to have been trimmed at the left edge, it is impossible to determine whether his attributes, a pair of castanets and the tablet of admission to court, were once present. The figure bringing up the rear is Zhongli Quan, Chief of the Immortals, easily identified by his stoutness and bare midriff.[8] Zhongli holds up one of his attributes, a large peach still attached to its leaf (or phoenix feather), as if making an offering to the god of longevity; but the usual fan for reviving souls of the dead is missing. The pines and fungi are common references to longevity and immortality in Chinese art.

The artist of the Smart Gallery painting was familiar with works by leading masters of the Zhe School, such as Wu Wei and Zhang Lu (circa 1464–circa 1538), judging by his use of a broad, fluid stroke, thick in the outlines of garments but sharp and angled in the inner folds. Because the strokes are wider and blunter than those generally used by Wu, there is a greater affinity to Zhang. A comparison between this painting and *Shide Laughing at the Moon* (Washington, D.C., Freer Gallery of Art) attributed to Zhang confirms this affinity.[9] The pose of Shide, for instance, in its overall conception and especially in the mannerism of the foreshortened right arm is close to that of Cao Guoqiu in the Smart Gallery painting. Although the painter of *The God of Longevity and Three Immortals* emulated Zhang's figure style, he did not possess the same understanding of the construction of the body and the natural fall of garments over it. He emphasized instead the calligraphic outlines and inner folds of the clothing, producing flattened forms rather than round volumes and their enveloping robes. P.B./R.A.B.

NOTES

1. For the Zhe School, see Roderick Whitfield, "Che School Paintings in the British Museum," *Burlington Magazine* 114, no. 830 (May 1962): 285–294. On the "Wild and Heterodox" School, see Richard Barnhart, "The 'Wild and Heterodox School' of Ming Painting," in *Theories of the Arts in China*, ed. Susan Bush and Christian F. Murck (Princeton, N.J.: Princeton University Press, 1983), 365–396.

2. Compare, for example, the foreshortened, three-quarter view heads of the immortals Shoulao, Cao Guoqiu, and Zhongli Quan in the Smart Gallery scroll with similar heads in paintings of immortals and scholars by Zhang Lu and Zhu Bang reproduced in James Cahill, *Parting at the Shore: Chinese Painting of the Early and Middle Ming Dynasty, 1368–1580* (New York and Tokyo: John Weatherhill, 1978), pl. 56, and Barnhart, "Wild and Heterodox School," pl. 8. For the pose of the beggar immortal, Li Tieguai, in the Chicago painting, see the fisherman in Zhang Lu's hanging scroll in the Kokoku-ji, Tokyo, reproduced in Cahill, *Parting at the Shore*, pl. 55, and the boy assistant in Zhu Bang's painting in the Art Museum, Princeton University referred to above.

3. On the Eight Immortals, see E. T. Chalmers Werner, *Myths and Legends of China* (London: George G. Harrap and Co., 1922), 288–289; C. A. S. Williams, *Outlines of Chinese Symbolism* (Beijing: Customs College Press, 1931), 124; William F. Mayers, *Chinese Reader's Manual* (Shanghai: American Presbyterian Mission Press, and London: Trubner and Co., 1874), vol. 2, no. 251; V. R. Burkhardt, *Chinese Creeds and Customs* (Hong Kong: South China Morning Post, 1953), 158. For the theme of the Eight Immortals in the visual arts, see Stephen Little, *Realm of the Immortals: Daoism in the Arts of China* (exh. cat.) (Cleveland: Cleveland Museum of Art in association with Indiana University Press, 1988), 10–12.

4. Williams, *Outlines of Chinese Symbolism*, 174; Werner, *Myths and Legends*, 171–172.

5. Burkhardt, *Chinese Creeds*, 159–160; Williams, *Outlines of Chinese Symbolism*, 127; Mayers, *Chinese Reader's Manual*, vol. 1, no. 718; Werner, *Myths and Legends*, 289–291.

6. Behind Li Tieguai is a large cinctured object tied in the middle with a bow, probably the pilgrim's gourd often associated with this transcendent.

7. Burkhardt, *Chinese Creeds*, 159; Williams, *Outlines of Chinese Symbolism*, 126; Mayers, *Chinese Reader's Manual*, vol. 1, no. 763; Werner, *Myths and Legends*, 300–303.

8. Burkhardt, *Chinese Creeds*, 159; Williams, *Outlines of Chinese Symbolism*, 125; Mayers, *Chinese Reader's Manual*, vol. 1, no. 90; Werner, *Myths and Legends*, 291–292.

9. Published in Thomas Lawton, *Chinese Figure Painting* (exh. cat.) (Washington, D.C.: Freer Gallery of Art, 1973), cat. no. 29.

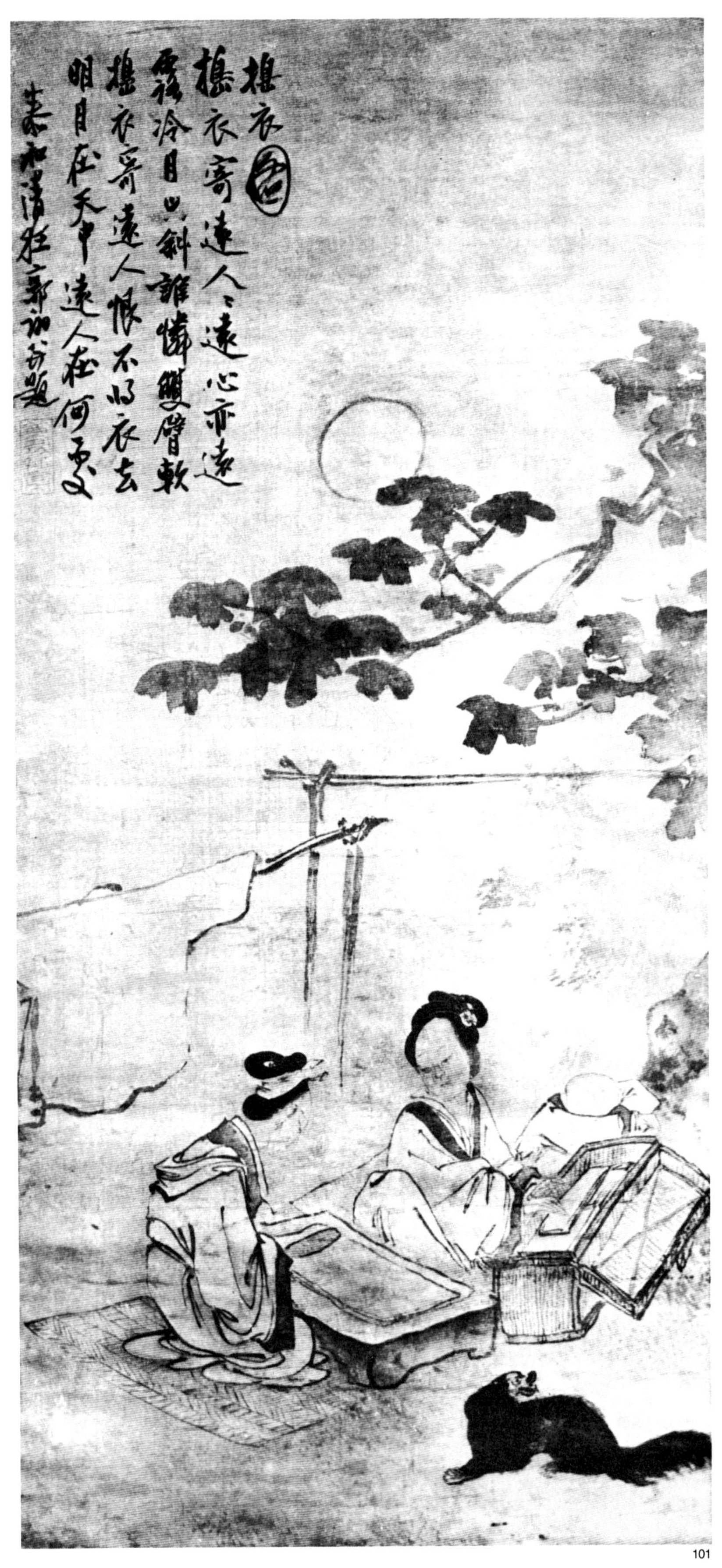

101

101 **Guo Xu**, 1465–circa 1530
Storing Garments of the Husband in Far Away Territory, 1500–30

Hanging scroll, ink and color on silk, 45 3/16 x 22 (115.3 x 55.9)
Purchase, Anonymous Gift
Acc. no. 1974.84

INSCRIPTIONS
Artist's poem:
Beating a garment makes me feel close to a person living in a distant place
Even if a person is in a distant place, my soul is always with the person's soul.
The fog becomes chilly and the moon rises behind a mountain
But nobody knows why I am working so hard.
Beating a garment makes me feel close to a person living in a distant place
I wish I could send these garments to him.
The moon shines and goes up higher
I wonder where he is at this time of the night.
[signed] "Pure and Wild/Crazy" [Guo Xu's *hao*[1]].

SEALS
To left of artist's poem, artist's seal: Qing Kuang Weng.
After artist's signature: [undeciphered character] Xu Ding.
At lower left, three collectors' seals: Tian Chuan Ge, Ji Shui Wan Shi, Lu Xi Shan Zhuang Kao Cang zhi yin.

PROVENANCE
Nü Wa Chai Collection [Victoria Contag von Winterfeldt]; C. C. Wang, New York (1968).

PUBLICATIONS
Suzuki, *Catalog*, no. A 2-003, 1:28, 424 and 5:177; National Palace Museum, *Hai-wai Yi-chen (Chinese Art in Overseas Collections: Paintings [II])* (Taipei, Taiwan: National Palace Museum, 1988), no. 52.

Born in Taihe, Jiangxi province, Guo Xu is reported to have been as famous by the 1490s as his contemporaries Wu Wei, Shen Zhou, and Du Jin. Such was his stature that the great philosopher-statesman Wang Yangming (1472–1528) inscribed one of Guo's paintings and presented it as a gift to the emperor.[2] Recommended by Wang, Guo was summoned during the Hongzhi era to the capital city of Beijing by the powerful eunuch Xiao Jing, who offered to arrange an administrative appointment for him in the Embroidered Uniform Guard (*Jinyiwei*), the emperor's honorary personal bodyguard. Guo, however, rejected the official post and the opportunity to work as a painter-in-attendance at court. During the second decade of the sixteenth century, the Prince of Ning, Zhu Chenhao, requested Guo's presence again at court in Beijing. But the artist soon left and was thus not implicated in the abortive coup of 1519 staged in the Jiangxi city of Nanchang by this rebellious member of the imperial clan.[3]

Guo Xu gave up all ambition for a bureaucratic post. Instead, following a peripatetic artist's life, he practiced a style of painting outside the conventions of the contemporary Zhe and Wu Schools.[4] For this reason, he is counted today among the "nonconformist" painters of the early to middle Ming period.[5] Late sixteenth-century critics, however, vilified Guo as one of the "Wild and Heterodox" painters associated with the Zhe School of court academy and professional painters. These artists, including Wu Wei (1459–1508) and his pupil Zhang Lu (circa 1464–circa 1538), were judged to have developed a pretentious and flashy, and therefore vulgar, brushwork out of the Southern Song academic painting styles of Ma Yuan and Xia Gui. Like other painters associated with the "Wild and Heterodox" School, Guo apparently cultivated an aura of eccentricity, choosing the sobriquet, "Qingkuang" (Pure and Wild).[6] James Cahill argues that Guo was an eclectic painter without a clearly recognizable style of his own.[7] However, his artistic identity (at least in figurative painting) can be discovered in certain similarities between the Smart Gallery hanging scroll and his *Woman and Child in a Garden*, a leaf in an undated album in the Shanghai Museum.[8]

In *Storing Garments of the Husband in Far Away Territory*, attention is focused on the foreground group of two simply dressed, elegantly coifed women. The woman at the left, kneeling on a mat, is beating a garment with a stick on a wooden table. Her companion sits calmly behind this table, in a complex cross-legged pose, her head turned back toward the beating action and her hands resting in front of her on the rim of a bamboo chest. It is as though she has just finished folding and storing the garment visible in the open basket. To her right, a child sleeps with head down in his arms; behind him one sees the base of a tree. Moving along this receding diagonal, specificity and descriptive detail diminish as individual, rich-black ink strokes become gray wash, reinforcing the primacy of the foreground activity of the two women.

The group centered around the low table is bracketed by the dog in the foreground and the two hanging clothes poles behind. The pole with the suspended shirt reiterates the recession of the tilted basket, while the empty pole establishes a pronounced parallel to the surface of the painting, forming a spatial cell around the figurative group. Several leafy branches emerge from the right, spreading out above the women through a series of diagonal twists and forks. Distant foliage, which fills the space between branches and figures, is brushed in with dark- to pale-gray washes suggesting forms enveloped in mist. From behind the uppermost branches, the full moon shines, centered over the activity of the two women.

Except for the prominent inscription in the bold cursive "grass" script, *caoshu*, almost the entire upper third of the painting is blank, while branches, pole, basket, and figures establish a strong diagonal composition below. This is also a prominent feature in the above-mentioned *Woman and Child in a Garden* by Guo, in which the right side of the painting is dominated by a grotesque boulder before patterns of leaves and dots in the mist that trail off to the left. Guo's compositional format is based ultimately on the Ma-Xia tradition of the Southern Song one-corner composition, which enjoyed popularity among the Zhe School painters of the fifteenth and sixteenth centuries (see cat. no. 100).

Despite its indebtedness to Southern Song academic formulation, possibly transmitted through contemporary Zhe School practice, the Smart Gallery composition emphasizes human life over nature. There is a definite shift from the Southern Song concern for balanced depictions of human beings in harmony with vast natural forces; the simplified forms and diffused washes of the trees and bushes in Guo's painting act as a foil for the prominent domestic activity of the women. This is a creative exploration of the Ma-Xia one-sided configuration of prominent boulder and woman in *Woman and Child in a Garden*, which is in turn linked compositionally to Wu Wei's *Scholar Seated under a Tree* (Boston, Museum of Fine Arts). However, the Smart Gallery painting seems closer psychologically to the painting *Laozi Riding on a Water-Buffalo* (Taipei, Taiwan, National Palace Museum) by Zhang Lu, in which the emotional interplay between the old sage and his beast similarly occurs between the women in *Storing Garments of the Husband in Far Away Territory*. Both of Guo's paintings depend on the same brush techniques, for example, in coiffures, cheeks, and garment folds, that characterize the sensitive curving lines of his masterly calligraphy, freed from any descriptive function. It was the boldness and spontaneity of such virtuoso brushwork that offended late-Ming and Qing critics of the "Wild and Heterodox" painters, who had, they argued, "not the slightest affiliation with correct traditions, merely recklessly smearing and rubbing away. . . ."[9]

The inscription, signed by Guo using his nickname "Pure and Wild," recalls the Japanese Muromachi-period play *Kinuta* (*Beating Silk*), written by the great master of Noh drama, Zeami (1363–1443).[10] The play concerns a housewife waiting for her husband who is living in a faraway land. Whenever she misses him, she beats a cloth, for she believes that the sound of *kinuta* echoes her husband's sentiment. Sadly, she dies without seeing him again. Such feelings of absence and longing are also expressed in the poem "Pounding Cloth" by the great Tang dynasty poet Du Fu (712–770):

> That her man can not come back she knows.
> But with autumn she brushes the pounding-stone
> Since the long, cold months are drawing on
> And he has been gone so long, so long—
>
> She does not tire of pounding the clothes.
> She will send them to him wherever he is.
> Can't you hear through the cold clear autumn's reverberant air?[11]

According to He Qiaoyuan (fl. 1586) in his biography of Ming painters, *Mingshan Cang*, Guo worked simultaneously in poetry and painting, as though they were interchangeable: "He thereupon impressed his hand to make a painting. When he was done painting he inscribed a poem, but before he had written the poem completely he let himself go in painting, but before the painting was done he again exhausted himself in poetry."[12] In the Smart Gallery painting, the sophisticated combination of text and image and the similarity between assured calligraphy and brushwork confirm Guo's literary and artistic ease, and with his innovative use of the sanctioned one-corner composition they belie late-Ming and Qing moralistic dismissals of Guo Xu as an uncouth artisan lacking a proper painting lineage. H.M./R.A.B.

NOTES

1. In China the surname (*xing*) comes first, followed by the given name (*ming*). This is the formal name given at birth and is used by parents. *Hao* is one of several informal, often fanciful, studio names chosen by an artist, used in signatures and seals on works. In addition to these literary names or sobriquets, the adult individual assumes a courtesy name (*zi*) for social use.
2. James Cahill, *Parting at the Shore: Chinese Painting of the Early and Middle Ming Dynasty, 1368–1580* (New York and Tokyo: John Weatherhill, 1978), 154.
3. Howard Rogers and Sherman E. Lee, *Masterworks of Ming and Qing Painting from the Forbidden City* (exh. cat.) (Lansdale, Pa.: International Arts Council, 1988), 126.
4. For a discussion of the differences between these two schools of painting see Yoshino Yonezawa, *Painting in the Ming Dynasty* (Tokyo: Maruyama and Co., 1956), 13–16.
5. Cahill, *Parting at the Shore*, 154.
6. On the "Wild and Heterodox" School and late Ming-Qing criticism, see Richard Barnhart, "The 'Wild and Heterodox School' of Ming Painting," in *Theories of the Arts in China*, ed. Susan Bush and Christian F. Murck (Princeton, N.J.: Princeton University Press, 1983), 365–396, esp. 365–373.
7. Cahill, *Parting at the Shore*, 154.
8. Ibid., 154 and pl. 71.
9. Quoted in Barnhart, "Wild and Heterodox School," 378, from He Liangqun's (1506–1573) notes on painting, *Siyouzhai hualun* (*Theories of Painting from the Studio of Four Friends*).
10. See Izuru Nishimura, *Kohjien* (Tokyo: Iwanami Shoten, 1974), 543. Also see Ryusaku Tsunoda, "The Vocabulary of Japanese Aesthetics II," in *Sources of Japanese Tradition* (New York: Columbia University Press, 1958), 277–297.
11. Translated in *Tu Fu: Wanderer and Minstrel under Moons of Cathay*, trans. Edna Worthley Underwood and Chi Hwang Chu (Portland, Me.: Mosher Press, 1929), 37.
12. Cited in Rogers and Lee, *Masterworks*, 126.

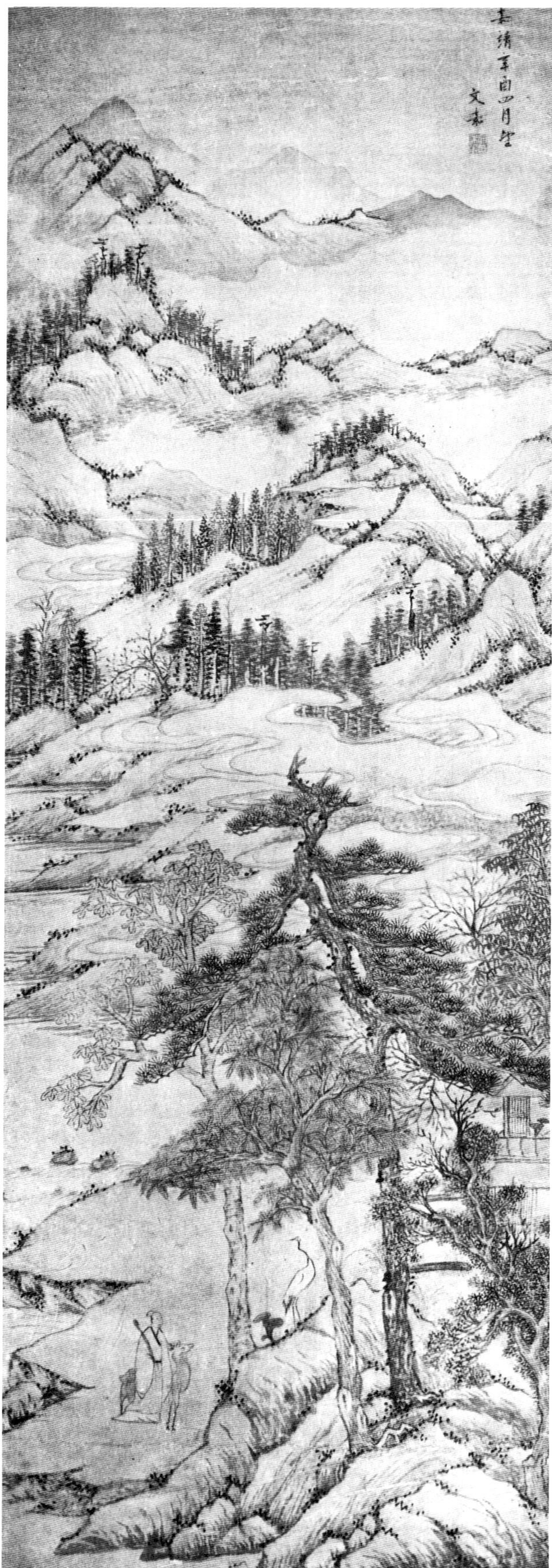

102

102 **Wen Jia**, 1501–1583

Landscape, 1561

Hanging scroll, ink and color on silk, 46 15/16 x 17 3/8 (119.2 x 44.1)
Purchase, Anonymous Gift
Acc. no. 1974.82

INSCRIPTIONS
Artist's inscription:
Painted in the fourth month of the *Yinyu* year of the Jiajing reign [1561]. [signed] Wen Jia.

SEALS
After artist's signature: Wen Shi Xiucheng.
At lower left, collector's seal: Ceng Zai Wei Qi Zhan Jia.

PROVENANCE
Nü Wa Chai Collection [Victoria Contag von Winterfeldt]; C. C. Wang, New York (1968).

PUBLICATIONS
Hamburg, *Chinesische Malerie*, cat. no. 8; Sirén, *Leading Masters*, 7:263; Suzuki, *Catalog*, no. A 2-005, 1:28, 424 and 5:177.

As the second son of Wen Zhengming (1470–1559), Wen Jia was part of the painting establishment of Suzhou. Following the Wen family heritage of classical literary study and connoisseurship, Wen Jia wrote books on art, including an important biography of his famous father. In his own right he is one of the few of the Wen family, other than Wen Zhengming the founder, who established themselves as painters of note.[1]

In this landscape, well-defined, rolling clouds separate the shoreline in the foreground from the cumulative clusters of background hills. The trees in the foreground, accentuated by the picturesque pine, are a standard eye-catching arrangement in many sixteenth-century landscapes produced by Suzhou painters in the circle of Wen Zhengming and his Wu School followers. But there is special interest in the gentleman, and the deer, fungus, and crane, which signify longevity (see cat. no. 100). The painting may celebrate the gentleman, who himself seems of venerable age.

Although the surface of this hanging scroll is rather brown, obscuring the true quality of the work, one can still see the firmly executed dotted and textured outlines and the cohesive structure of the elements, especially in the background hills. All features of the composition, texture, and inventiveness of layering in rocks and hills are indications of the Wen tradition of painting. There is a fan painting of 1558 by Wen Jia in the Musée Guimet, Paris, that shows very similar features of style.[2] Compositional devices and textured outlines in the accumulated background hills in Wen's scroll *Peach Blossom Spring* (Asian Art Museum of San Francisco, Avery Brundage Collection) recall forms in the Smart Gallery painting, and other similarities may be seen in the album by Wen Jia titled *Landscape and Poems* in the Wan-go H. C. Weng Collection.[3] H.A.V.

NOTES

1. For further information on Wen Jia, see Alice R. Merrill, "Wen Chia (1501–1583): Derivation and Innovation" (Ph.D. diss., University of Michigan, Ann Arbor), 1981.
2. Published in Jean Pierre Dubosc, *Arte Cínese (Chinese Art)* (exh. cat.) (Venice: Alfieri Editore, 1954), cat. no. 821.
3. Both works are reproduced in Alice R. M. Hyland, *The Literati Vision: Sixteenth-Century Wu School Painting and Calligraphy* (exh. cat.) (Memphis, Tenn.: Memphis Brooks Museum of Art, 1984), pl. V, figs. 24a–c.

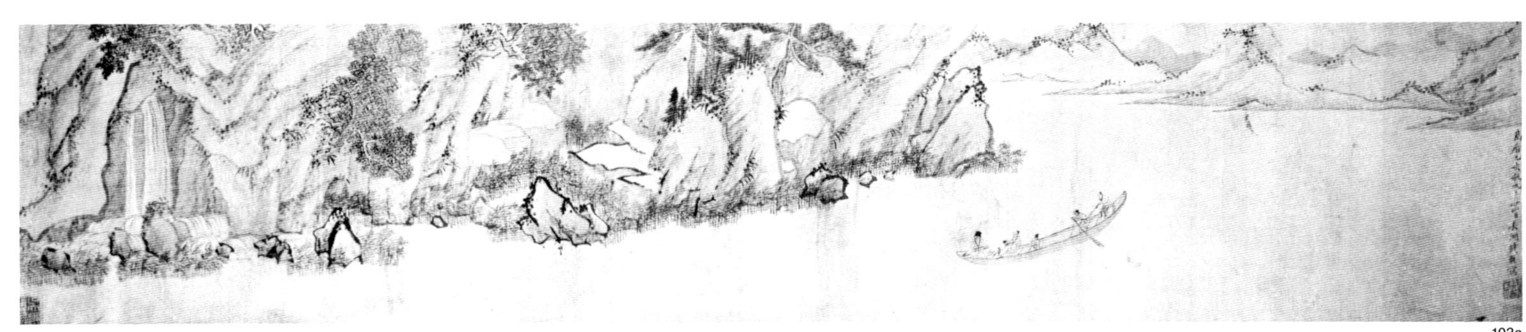

103a

103b

103 **Qian Gu**, 1508–after 1578
The Red Cliff, 1575

Handscroll, ink and color on silk, painting panel: 10 1/16 x 49 1/16 (25.6 x 124.6); text panel: 10 5/8 x 53 5/8 (27 x 136.2)
Purchase, Anonymous Gift
Acc. no. 1974.90

INSCRIPTIONS
At the right edge, artist's inscription:
Qian Gu of Changzhou painted this on the twenty-fourth day in the ninth month of the *Yihai* year of the Wanli reign [1575].

On second panel, transcription of the two prose-poems, "Odes on the Red Cliff," by the Song author Su Shi (1037–1101).[1]

SEALS
After artist's inscription, two seals: Shu Bao, Xuan Qing Shi.
At left edge of painting panel, artist's seal: Wuyue Wang Sun.
On text panel, at beginning of prose-poems: Gan Qing Yun Er Zhi Shang.
On text panel, after prose-poems, two seals: Yin Tang, Zhuang Rong.

PROVENANCE
Nü Wa Chai Collection [Victoria Contag von Winterfeldt]; C. C. Wang, New York (1968).

PUBLICATIONS
Hamburg, *Chinesische Malerei*, cat. no. 11; Sirén, *Leading Masters*, 7:172; Suzuki, *Catalog*, no. A 2-006, 1:28, 29, 424 and 5:177; Kenneth S. Ganza, *Journeys of the Spirit: Landscape Portraits of Places in China* (exh. cat.) (Memphis, Tenn.: Memphis State Department of Art, 1987), cat. no. 18.

The poet and painter Qian Gu studied under Wen Zhengming (1470–1559), the dominant creative force in sixteenth-century Suzhou painting of the Wu School. This association gave the ardent bibliophile Qian access to Wen's personal library, where he spent much of his time copying, annotating, and collating old texts.

At the opening of the *Red Cliff* handscroll, distant rolling hills and mountains on the closer shore unfold across a peaceful scene around a bend of the Yangzi River. A proportionately large boat rowed by two people carries three passengers in front of the far shore marked by jagged rocks, a waterfall, and clinging trees. The scene illustrates the second of a two-part ode in which the Song poet Su Shi describes his visit to the Red Cliff, his midnight reveries to the accompaniment of drinks, and the flight of the single crane. At the end of the second poem, crane and immortality are linked, and this reference joins Qian's scene and the encounter of friends to the metaphor of an otherworldly existence.

References to ideal places of existence abound in Chinese literature, and they tend to be represented in appropriate traditional modes of painting. This scroll in light colors and textured outlines, mixed with jagged contrasting ink strokes defining the rocks along the waterline, is typical of a number of paintings in the manner of Song representations. These Song paintings were reinterpreted in Ming times, and the most representative of them were done by Wen Zhengming.[2] The Smart Gallery handscroll is a good, slightly later example of that elegant manner. H.A.V.

NOTES

1. Translated in English in *Su Tung-p'o: Selections from a Sung Dynasty Poet*, trans. Burton Watson (New York and London: Columbia University Press, 1965), 87–93.
2. Several of Wen Zhengming's handscrolls, as well as a fan and hanging scroll, on this theme are discussed in Richard Edwards et. al., *The Art of Wen Cheng-ming (1470–1559)* (exh. cat.) (Ann Arbor, Mich.: University of Michigan Museum of Art, 1976), cat. nos. 25, 52, 58, 62 and fig. 12. Wen Zhengming's nephew, Wen Boren (1502–1575), also used this subject on a fan; see Tseng Yu-ho Ecke, *Poetry on the Wind: The Art of Chinese Folding Fans from the Ming and Ch'ing Dynasties* (exh. cat.) (Honolulu: Honolulu Academy of Arts, 1981), cat. no. 24. Among Wen Zhengming's contemporaries, the Suzhou poet, calligrapher, and painter Chen Shun (1483–1544) executed a handscroll inspired by the first ode on the Red Cliff; this scroll is published in Torao Miyagawa, ed., *Chinese Painting* (New York, Tokyo, and Kyoto: John Weatherhill and Tankosha, 1983), 197, pl. 88.

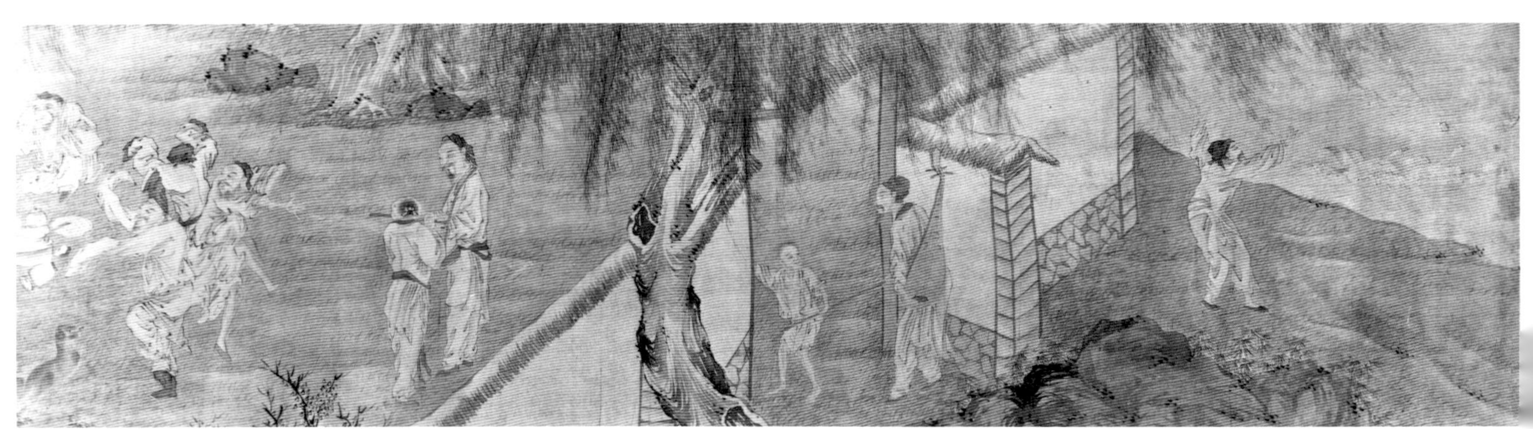

104a

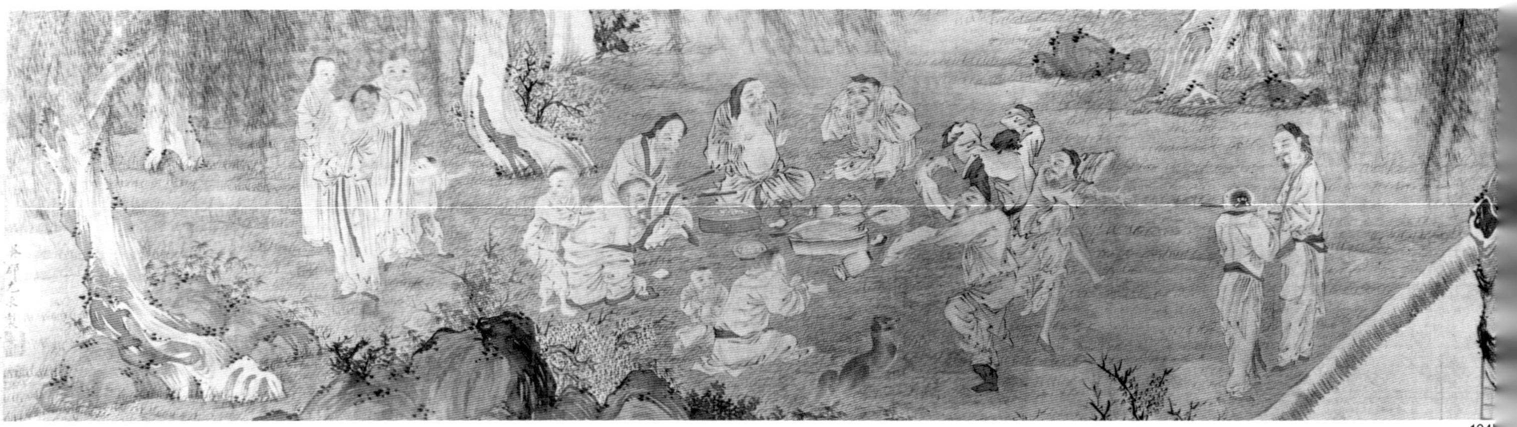

104b

104 **You Qiu**, active 1560–1590
The Immortals, 2nd half of 16th century

Handscroll, ink and light color on paper, 9 31/32 x 57 11/16 (25.3 x 146.5)
Purchase, Anonymous Gift
Acc. no. 1974.86

INSCRIPTIONS
Artist's inscription at left:
Made by You Qiu from Suzhou.

SEALS
After artist's inscription, two seals: Chang zhou You Qiu, Feng Qiu.

PROVENANCE
Nü Wa Chai Collection [Victoria Contag von Winterfeldt]; C. C. Wang, New York (1968).

PUBLICATIONS
Sirén, *Leading Masters*, 7:274; Suzuki, *Catalog*, no. A 2-007, 1:29, 424 and 5:177.

You Qiu is recorded as a painter of figures and landscapes. Living in Taicang, Jiangsu province, he painted Buddhist wall paintings in the Guandi Miao and in other locations in the city. Though You is not recorded as a pupil of Qiu Ying (circa 1495–1552), documents do indicate that the two artists together illustrated the story of the Changmen palace. You's extant paintings are dated to the second half of the sixteenth century.

The Smart Gallery handscroll begins at the right with geese chased about in the water by a wildly gesturing man on the shore.[1] This scene is followed immediately by a wall with a gate through which a boy leads a blind musician into an area seemingly enclosed by the wall. In the center of this garden setting is a group of eight men in a circle engaged in a wild dance, drumming, clapping hands, and making merry. Two children and a dog are also part of this circle. To the left are three women and two children; to the right, a man and a boy playing a flute. The subject has been variously identified as dancing peasants,[2] the land of the immortals, or at least of people acting out similarly remote transcendent existence. The interpretation as immortals (see cat. no. 100) seems more likely because of the long-sleeved garments, shoes, and boots worn by the men, the long garments of the women, and the neatly dressed children. The nervous and choppy, twisting line used for the garments is frequently associated with otherworldly beings. H.A.V.

NOTES

1. It is evident that prior to its acquisition in the present mounting, the scroll had been cut down at the right; a thin vertical strip of an aquatic scene was incorrectly remounted at the left edge of the painting, out of context, after the garden setting.

2. Osvald Sirén, *Chinese Painting: Leading Masters and Principles* (London: Lund Humphries and Co., 1956–58), 7:274.

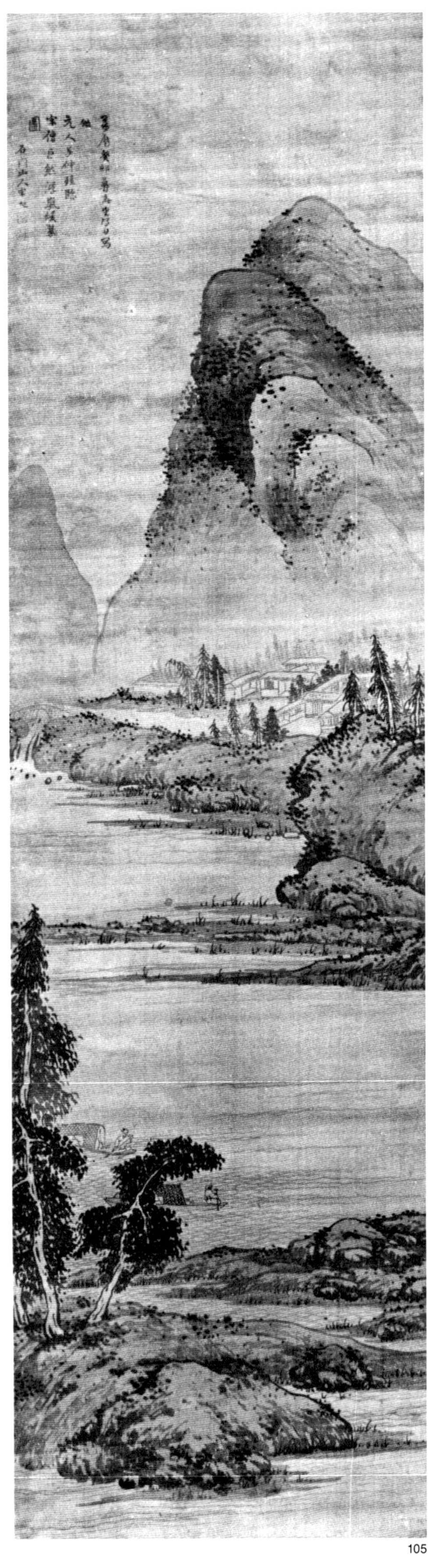

105

105 **Song Xu**, 1525–after 1605
Drifting Mountains in Fog (after Wu Zhen), 1603

Hanging scroll, ink on silk, 62⅜ x 17⁹⁄₁₆ (158.4 x 44.6)
Purchase, Gift of Mr. and Mrs. Gaylord Donnelley
Acc. no. 1974.94

INSCRIPTIONS
Artist's inscription:
Painted in the *Guimao* year of the Wanli reign [1603], after a copy by Wu Zhen which he did after the painting *Balmy Floating Mountain Mist* by the Song monk-painter Juran.

SEALS
After the inscription, two artist's seals: Song Xu zhi yin, Shi Men Shan Ren. Lower right: [partially cut, undecipherable collector's seal].

PROVENANCE
Yabumoto (1971).

PUBLICATIONS
Suzuki *Catalog*, no. A 2-008, 1:29, 424 and 5:177.

Song Xu was born in Jiaxing in 1525. Although Yoko Woodson states that Song was "active during his early years in the region of northern Zhejiang province,"[1] suggesting that his style was shaped by the Zhe School of professional painters (see cat. nos. 100 and 101), the artist is usually regarded as a follower of Shen Zhou, working in the tradition of the Wu School (see cat. nos. 102 and 103). Song was part of the social circle of Songjiang in southern Kiangsu province, which included Gu Zhengyi and Mo Shilong, close associates of the late-Ming painter, calligrapher, poet, and theoretician Dong Qichang. Song's study of Yuan masters such as Huang Gongwang late in life possibly was the result of Dong's influence. Despite a few pupils, including Song Moujin and Zhao Zuo, Song Xu did not attract any sizable following. His style is judged today as a different current in the mainstream Orthodoxy defined by Dong Qichang.

Song Xu's oeuvre represents an odd mixture of styles and painting lineages. His technical skill, interest in the decorative, and adaptation of Song painting forms reveal Zhe School influence; but his flowing brushstroke, curling texture lines derived from Shen Zhou, and elongated vertical compositions show a debt to the Wu School. Song's personal solution to the impasse in late-Ming painting consisted of flattened compositions enlivened by decorous cloud patterns. The importance of vaporous mists as an active formal element inevitably led him to the concept of solids and voids propounded by Dong Qichang:

> By "insubstantiality" and "substantiality" one means the varying degree of using the brush in a detailed or summary manner in each part of the painting. A detailed area must be followed by a summary passage. The "insubstantiality" and the "substantiality" must complement each other. If a painting is too sparse, the landscape will lack depth and distance. If it is too dense, it will loose spirit and resonance. Only when the painter weighs the "insubstantiality" against the "substantiality" will his painting naturally become extraordinary.[2]

As discussed in Professor Vanderstappen's introductory painting essay, it is not clear what the artist meant when he wrote that the landscape is after the Yuan painter Wu Zhen (1280–1354), who himself was copying a Song landscape of mist-filled mountains by the monk Juran (active 960–980). Nonetheless, the scene is coherent and believable, conceived with the spacial clarity of the traditions invoked, although lacking their implied depth. The surface of the painting is reinforced and pictorial recession inhibited, for example, through the equivalent modulation of ink tones in close-up river bank or distant mountains. Or again, the lichen dots (*dian*), despite their dispersal throughout the landscape, are rendered everywhere with the same brushstroke and moderate inkiness. Precisely drawn, detailed terrain alternates with blank sections of silk in the development of an abstract, instead of organic, structure. The overall effect is of an airless river valley, in which stock trees, rocks, mountains, boats, and houses are evoked by the refined, even rarified, vision of the scholar's studio and its cultivated reminiscences of revered earlier masters. S.K./H.A.V./R.A.B.

NOTES

1. Woodson, "The Sung-chiang (Yü-chien) Painters, I: Sung Hsü and His Followers," in James Cahill, ed., *The Restless Landscape: Chinese Painting of the Late Ming Period* (exh. cat.) (Berkeley, Calif.: University Art Museum, 1971), 75.
2. Mae Anna Quan Pang, "The Sung-chiang (Hua-t'ing) Painters II: Tung Ch'i-ch'ang and His Circle," in Cahill, ed., *Restless Landscape*, 91.

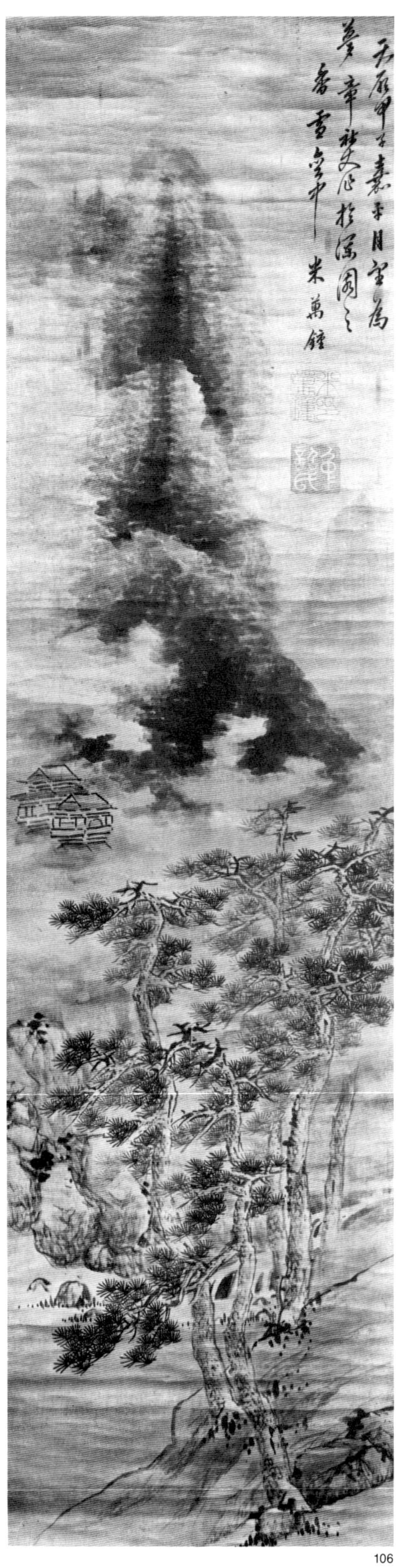

106

106 **Mi Wanzhong**, circa 1570–1628
Among the Fragrant Snowy Mountains of Lan Garden, 1621

Hanging scroll, ink on satin, 73 11/16 x 19 1/8 (187.2 x 48.6)
Purchase, Gift of Mr. and Mrs. Gaylord Donnelley
Acc. no. 1974.92

INSCRIPTIONS
Artist's inscription:
Inscribed on the fifteenth day of the twelfth lunar month of 1621 for Ming Zhang [Fan Jingwen] among the fragrant snowy mountains of Lan Garden. [signed] Mi Wanzhong.

SEALS
After artist's signature, two seals: Mi Wanzhong, Zhong Zhao.

PROVENANCE
Mayuyama, Tokyo (1971).

PUBLICATIONS
Suzuki, *Catalog*, no. A 2-001, 1:28, 424 and 5:177; David and Alfred Smart Gallery, University of Chicago, *Handbook of the Collection* (Chicago: David and Alfred Smart Gallery, University of Chicago), forthcoming, entry by Stanley Murashige.

Mi Wanzhong was originally from Shaanxi province, Chang An prefecture, but spent much of his life in Beijing, serving in a number of official posts. He was famous as a calligrapher, working in the style of his ancestor Mi Fu, the eleventh-century painter, calligrapher, and literatus. Mi Wanzhong was also known for his landscapes and flower paintings. It is said he was fond of collecting strange rocks, and his sobriquet "You Shi" or "Befriender of Stones" recalls Mi Fu's eccentric appreciation of bizarre rocks, one of which, according to legend, he addressed as "Shixiong," "Elder Brother Stone." [1]

Among the Fragrant Snowy Mountains of Lan Garden bears an inscription by Mi Wanzhong and two of his seals. The inscription, which dedicates the painting to the Ming dynasty official Fan Jingwen, indicates that the work was perhaps a gift or an exchange, to commemorate an occasion such as a wedding or birth, or possibly a gesture of inspired friendship. Not a depiction of a particular landscape, the work is instead a kind of aesthetic demonstration piece in the literati painting tradition. Through style more than subject matter, Mi's picture addresses the knowing collector or connoisseur about the non-professional statesman-artist's personal way of viewing nature.

In the upper half of the image, Mi paints a sequence of three cone-shaped mountain peaks in wet, rounded brushstrokes. The blotches of ink, lighter at the mountain's edges, build up into darker areas along the core of each shape. To the lower right of these mountains, Mi renders the upper stories of two buildings as they emerge from surrounding mists. In the lower half of the painting, five gnarled pines near a stream stretch upward, their branches twisting and turning under the force of Mi's sharp, inky brushwork. The lively facture, startling in its contrasts, contributes to the energy established by Mi's use of exaggerated proportions. Throughout, one feels the vertical elongation of shapes. The mountains rise heavenward, their ascendant longing accented by the vertical alignment of dark and light tones and the rhyming of simple rounded shapes; the trees below grow into the mists, setting off a curious juxtaposition of near and far, of upper and lower zones of the painting. Mi also plays on the slight eccentricity of shapes, the peculiarity of their orientation and placement. There is an oddness, too, in the exaggeration of the pines' branches and needles and in the strange configurations of the mists.

Such idiosyncracies constitute Mi's personal adaptation of a highly traditional aesthetic. For neither the motifs nor the essential visual language of the work are new or unusual. The manner in which Mi paints mountains and mists is rooted in the Northern Song traditions of his ancestor Mi Fu, and the pines have precedents in the tenth- and eleventh-century monumental landscape paintings by Li Cheng and Guo Xi. What is new, and characteristic of Mi's work and Ming dynasty painting in general, is the recollection and reworking of these earlier landscape traditions, in a shift away from the realism still lingering in the refined literati paintings of the scholar-amateur Wu School (see cat. no. 103). This shift reflects a new understanding of nature and its representation in art. For Mi and a number of his contemporaries—Li Shida, Wang Jianzhang, Song Xu (cat. no. 105) and Zhang Hong, for example—it was the vivacity not the appearance of nature that was significant. They discovered the being of a mountain, with its retinue of trees and streams, in the idiosyncratic presentation of its shapes and their relationships. From this point of view, nature has presence and life only by virtue of its underlying exuberance, expressed outwardly by the exotic rather than the routine features of landscape. S.M.

NOTES

1. The event is often depicted in Chinese painting from the seventeenth century onwards. Mi Fu's rock connoisseurship and its place in later Chinese art is treated in John Hay, *Kernels of Energy, Bones of Earth: The Rock in Chinese Art* (exh. cat.) (New York: China Institute in America and China House Gallery, 1985), 27–34, cat. nos. 48–50.

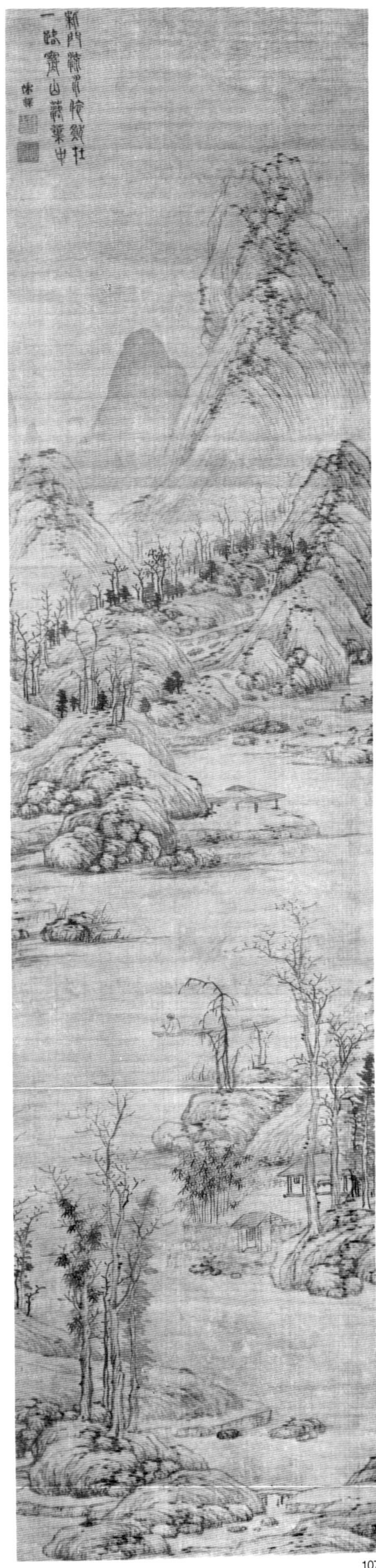
107

107 **Chen Guan**, b. 1563, active 1610–1640[1]
Landscape, circa 1620

Hanging scroll, ink on silk, 71 9/16 x 17 1/2 in.
Purchase, Gift of Mr. and Mrs. Gaylord Donnelley
Acc. no. 1974.93

INSCRIPTIONS
Artist's inscription:
The river flows slowly past the brushwood gate,
Leaves are falling on the cold mountain road.
[signed] Chen Guan.

SEALS
After artist's signature, two seals: Chen Guan zhi yin, Po Shi [Chen Guan's *hao*].

PROVENANCE
Yabumoto, Amagasaki, Hyōgo (1971).

Chen Guan is considered a native of Suzhou, although he is sometimes mentioned as a native of nearby Yunqian, Songjiang prefecture, possibly because of his friendship with Chen Jiru and Dong Qichang.[2] Details of Chen Guan's life are scarce,[3] but he was probably a professional painter, for it is reported that there was great competition for his paintings on silk.[4] However, Chen emulated literati practice, giving his own works to comrades and executing collaborative paintings with colleagues, including Cheng Jiasui (1565–1644), Wen Congjian (1574–1648), Sheng Maoye (active circa 1625–1640), and Bian Wenyu (active circa 1620–1670). He painted at times for recreation and enjoyed poetry; his calligraphy, particularly his "running" and "standard" scripts, was especially admired. In the fashion of a literatus, he retired late in life to Tiger Hill just outside the walls of Suzhou and composed poetry. A collection of his writings was published as *Qujie ji* (*Poems Understood by an Old Woman*).

According to standard biographic anthologies, Chen Guan was a painter of landscapes in the manner of Southern Song and Yuan masters, especially Zhao Boju, Zhao Mengfu, and the early Wu School master Wen Zhengming. Chen's immediate model has been identified as the Suzhou professional painter Qiu Ying (d. 1552), who collaborated for a time with the literatus Wen Zhengming. Chen Guan counted the scholar, critic, and artist Li Rihua (1565–1635) among his friends and in 1609 is reported to have sent Li a scroll by the Yuan master Huang Gongwang. Extant paintings bear out Chen's affinity for a sometimes slightly archaizing late-Wu style, but they also include works that have more in common with the landscapes of the seventeenth-century Anhui School.[5]

The Smart Gallery scroll exemplifies the conservative vision of the late Wu School. While the late-Wu painter never abandoned his roots in thirteenth- and fourteenth-century literati traditions, there was a tendency to refer to recent interpretations of Yuan masterpieces by Wu School intermediaries rather than to the Yuan originals. In addition, exposure to professional tendencies of the Ming court academy and the unavoidable presence of the theorist-painter Dong Qichang created diverse relationships among artisans and scholar-amateur artists. The traditional distinctions between professional and literati painters were obscured by the seventeenth century,[6] and Suzhou artists who lived from the sale of their work painted in the manner of Yuan and early Wu School masters sanctified in Dong's Southern school lineage. Often exhibiting admirable talent, these secondary artists seldom professed radical formal concerns, preferring instead to reiterate questions posed by their predecessors.

Chen's painting depicts a river with its source in a distant mountain range, flowing by a scholar's pavilion in the middle ground, past a fenced house with a boat and fisherman nearby, and finally bending around a land mass in the foreground. The composition is closely bound to Yuan antecedents. But there is a distinction between the upper and lower parts of the painting: whereas Chen's four distinct zones imitate the reserved compositions of Ni Zan's tripartite "one river, two banks" scheme, the serpentine mountains with their rounded boulders and diminutive trees are familiar from paintings by Huang Gongwang. Moreover, although a unified setting is implied by the reserved brushwork and tranquil mood reminiscent of Yuan literati painting, the seemingly logical landscape lacks coherency. In spite of the lucid mountain range, the upper part of the painting is unconnected to the rest of the composition, without the kind of subtle transitions used by Ni Zan such as the tangency of tips of close-up trees with distant mountains. Chen's elongated trees and precipitously angled mountain slopes echo the narrow proportions of the scroll and manifest the exaggerated verticality frequently encountered in late Wu School hanging scrolls.

Unlike Ni's distilled compositions, Chen's painting is full of unessential minutiae, betraying professional training. Although the brushwork is accomplished, the artist belabors each shape and object, until every area of the painting is busy with reiterated forms. Details initially look like ardent attempts at recreating the scene, but in his methodical enthusiasm Chen has allowed ostensibly descriptive brushstrokes near autonomy. His facture develops into a rhythmic cadence of light and dark, determined by the application of wet and dry brush, thick and thin stroke. This alternation—recalling similar use of the brush in Huang Gongwang's handscroll *Dwelling in the Fuchun Mountains* (Taipei, Taiwan, National Palace Museum)—results in a random texture that unifies the surface and overshadows any concern for overt realism or spatial recession. Chen's use of *cun* (interior brushstrokes that model outlined forms) and *dian* or dots is almost a literal transcription of Huang's boulders and trees and their placement in the mountains. The dark clusters of thick ink *dian*, shorthand indications of trees, serve more to activate the surface than to recreate the specifics of nature.

In the Smart Gallery landscape, the balance between expressive brushwork and natural forms found in Yuan and early Wu School painting is redefined in late-Ming terms. The execution is detached, devoid of strong emotion in either the physical act of painting or the interpretation of the subject. Because the basic format of the painting is relatively simple—and patterned after sanctioned models—the studied application of ink and plethora of details seem superficial, more a demonstration of learned mannerisms than a heartfelt response to nature experienced firsthand and expressed on a personal level through the evocation of earlier styles. The somewhat arid quality of the painting recalls the eminent scholar Fan Yunlin's (1558–1641) comment on the followers of Wen Zhengming: "They manage a slight resemblance. But with all their copying, they only capture the 'skin' of [Wen's] eternal form, without getting anything of his spirit and principle."[7]

D.A.D./M.L./R.A.B.

NOTES

1. On the basis of an inscription on a lost album leaf, Chen's birthdate has been postulated by Ellen Johnston Laing, "Biographical Notes on Three Seventeenth-Century Chinese Painters," in *The Translation of Art: Essays on Chinese Painting and Poetry*, ed. James C. Y. Watt, Renditions 6, (Hong Kong: Centre for Translation Projects, Chinese University of Hong Kong, 1976), 109. This is in accord with some sources that mention Chen as a man of the Jiajing period (1522–66); see Chu-Tsing Li, *A Thousand Peaks and Myriad Ravines: Chinese Paintings in the Charles A. Drenowatz Collection* (Ascona, Switz.: Artibus Asiae Publishers, 1974), 1:78.

2. Li, *Thousand Peaks*, 1:84.

3. Sources for the standard composite biography of the artist are gathered together in Laing, "Biographical Notes," 107–109. See also Osvald Sirén, *Chinese Painting: Leading Masters and Principles* (London: Lund Humphries and Co., 1956–58), 5:28, 7:165–166.

4. Cited by Marsha Smith, "The Wu School in Late Ming, I: Conservative Masters," in James Cahill, ed., *The Restless Landscape: Chinese Painting of the Late Ming Period* (exh. cat.) (Berkeley, Calif.: University Art Museum, 1971), 45. Paper was the preferred medium of the amateur literatus, whereas silk was more suitable for the professional artisan because of the technical difficulties of painting on this intractable medium.

5. See Ju-hsi Chou and Claudia Brown, *Heritage of the Brush: The Roy and Marilyn Papp Collection of Chinese Painting* (exh. cat.) (Phoenix: Phoenix Art Museum, 1989), 53.

6. On the question of professional and amateur painting in late-Ming Suzhou and Chen's place in the late Wu School, see James Cahill, *The Distant Mountains: Chinese Painting of the Late Ming Dynasty, 1570–1644* (New York and Tokyo: John Weatherhill, 1982), 32–33.

7. Quoted by Mae Anna Quan Pang, "Late Ming Painting Theory," in Cahill, ed., *Restless Landscape*, 22.

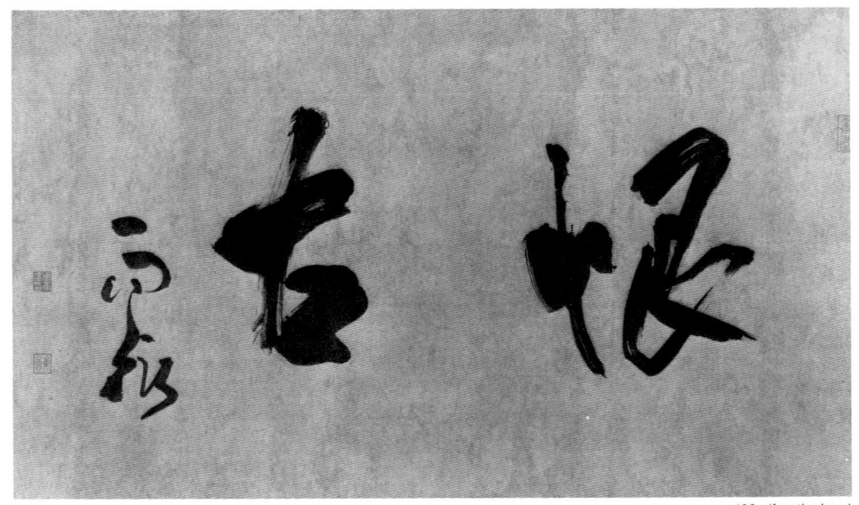
108a (frontispiece)

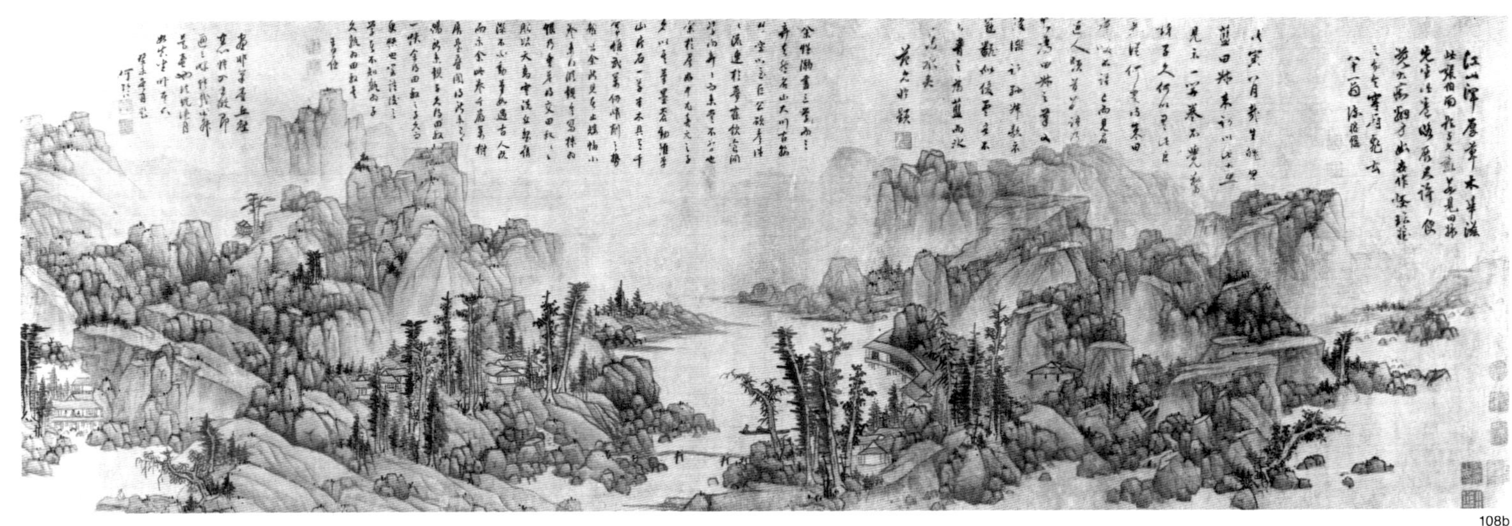
108b

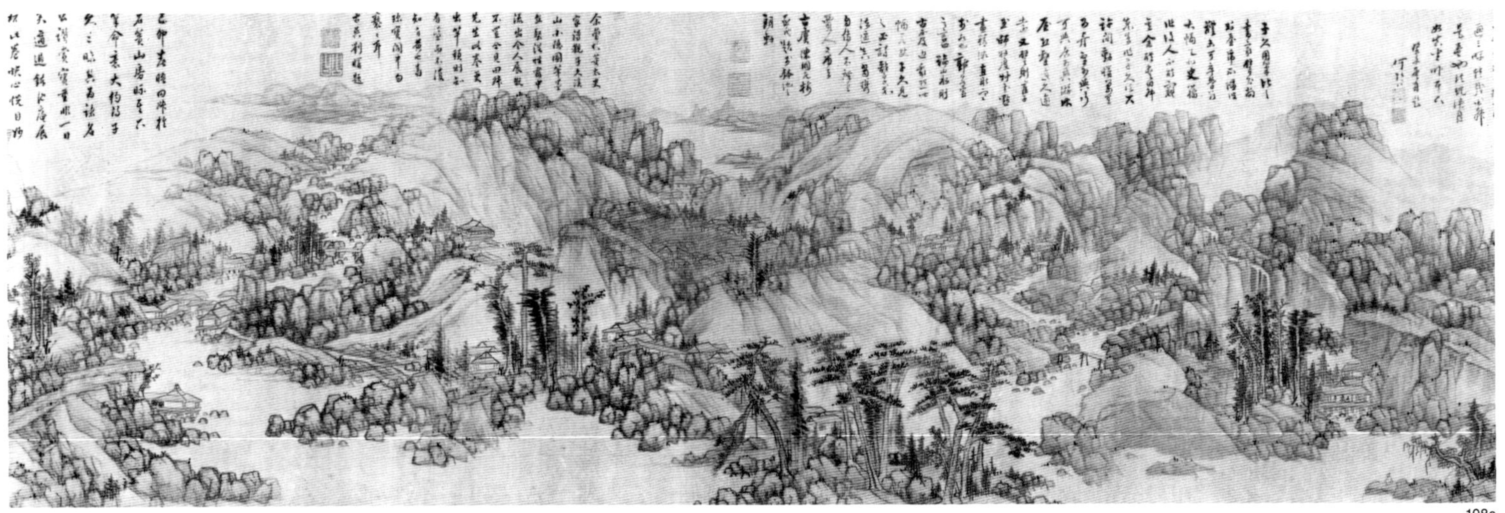
108c

108 **Lan Ying**, 1585–after 1664
Landscape (after Huang Gongwang), circa 1637–38

Handscroll, ink on paper (frontispiece), and ink and color on silk (painting and colophons), frontispiece panel: 23 1/16 x 40 5/16 (58.7 x 102.4); painting and colophon panel: 23 1/16 x 379 1/8 (58.7 x 1014.7)
Gift of Jeannette Shambaugh Elliott in honor of Prof. Harrie Vanderstappen
Acc. no. 1987.56

INSCRIPTIONS
Artist's inscription at end of painting:
Of all the extant scrolls by Huang Gongwang, I have had a chance to see more than half the treasures in the empire. My thirty years of research and study of the masters have come to this. If the Four Yuan Masters could see this scroll of mine, they certainly would allow me to enter their groves. Connoisseurs, what is your opinion? [signed] Xihu waishi, Lan Ying.[1]

There are seven inscriptions on the painting and six appended colophons following, the last two on a separate piece of silk.[2]

SEALS
The painting and inscriptions include forty-six seals by the artist, collectors, and connoisseurs.[3]

PROVENANCE
Mi Fu Gallery, New York (1973).

PUBLICATIONS
Yang Enshou, *Yanfubian*, preface 1885, vol. 3, part 2, *juan* 15:36a–41b, in *Danyuan chuanji*; reprint: Taipei, Taiwan: Wenshizhe chubanshe, 1971; Fu Shen and Marilyn Fu, *Studies in Connoisseurship: Chinese Paintings from the Arthur M. Sackler Collection in New York and Princeton* (exh. cat.) (Princeton, N.J.: Princeton University Press, 1973), 112–113; Yen Chuan-ying, "Lan Ying yü fang-ku hui-hua" ("Lan Ying and the imitation of old painting styles") (Master's thesis, Taiwan National University, Taipei, 1977), 14–15; James Cahill, *The Distant Mountains: Chinese Painting of the Late Ming Dynasty, 1570–1644* (New York and Tokyo: John Weatherhill, 1982), 183; Suzuki, *Catalog*, no. A 2-011, 1:30–31, 5:177; *Bulletin*, 35 (illus.); David and Alfred Smart Gallery, University of Chicago, *Handbook of the Collection* (Chicago: David and Alfred Smart Gallery, University of Chicago), forthcoming, entry by Katherine R. Tsiang.

Lan Ying was a late-Ming professional painter, who sold his work for a living, not a "scholar-artist" for whom painting was an avocation, primarily serving personal enjoyment, self-expression, and communication with like-minded friends, scholars, and collectors. Nonetheless, Lan was well versed in the painting styles of great artists of the past and couched his own works in the manners of earlier literati painters. He could, for example, execute strikingly good landscapes in the monumental Northern Song tradition, such as his *Listening to a Waterfall in a Pavilion in Spring in the Manner of Li Cheng* (1622; see also cat. no. 109).[4] Because Lan Ying displayed talent at an early age, he gained the esteem of well-known contemporary literati such as Dong Qichang (1555–1636), Chen Jiru (1558–1639), and Sun Kehong (1532–1610). After his introduction to their scholarly ideals—their concern with brushwork and formal issues and their prejudice against court academic and professional painters—he turned to the emulation of artists approved by Dong Qichang in his formulation of the Southern school lineage of Chinese painting, including the Four Masters of the Yuan dynasty—Huang Gongwang, Ni Zan, Wang Meng, and Wu Zhen. In so doing, Lan Ying combined the technical competence of the professional painter with the artistic aspiration of the scholar-amateur. Nonetheless, by the eighteenth century critics disparagingly associated Lan with the academicism and "bad taste" of the Zhe School (see cat. nos. 100, 101), citing his professionalism and his birthplace—Qiantang [Hangzhou], Zhejiang province, the original center of the Zhe School in the fifteenth and sixteenth centuries and the place after which the school was called.

Lan's inscription towards the end of the Smart Gallery handscroll indicates that the artist considered this work one of his finest. It is a landscape painting of monumental conception, both unusually large in size and grandiose in the endlessly changing mountains and vistas revealed when the scroll is unrolled section by section. Lan is recorded to have traveled widely and observed the scenery of many regions of China, and although retrospective in style, the handscroll achieves some of its impact from the attention given the specifics of each imaginary site.

An early album of 1622, *Following Ancient Masters*, includes a leaf in the manner of Huang Gongwang (1269–1354) that demonstrates a close adherence to the soft texture strokes and mountain forms in Huang's painting titled *Nine Pearllike Verdant Peaks*.[5] Lan clearly developed a special affinity for the style of this Yuan master. His works in the manner of Huang Gongwang are numerous and include several dated hanging scrolls, handscrolls, and album leaves. The handscroll in the Art Museum at Princeton University, dated 1624, is based on Huang's greatest surviving painting, *Dwelling in the Fuchun Mountains*.[6] Another, in the National Palace Museum in Taipei, dated 1639, has veined and steeply sloping mountains with squarish rocks clustered around the range's base.[7] Recalling elements of the Smart Gallery handscroll, the Taipei scroll appears to be a closely contemporary, but less successful work, and Lan's own inscription on the painting is less confident: "[Huang Gongwang's] scholarship and disposition were truly marvelous. His character was not only lofty and rustic, but he was able to perceive the nature of the universe through meditation and achieved fame for a thousand years. I have revered him as a teacher for thirty years but I understand him only superficially. The connoisseurs will certainly decide."[8]

The mountains in the Smart Gallery landscape resemble, too, those in a hanging scroll from 1640 also in the National Palace Museum[9]. Another scroll from 1650 in the Kohata Collection, Tokyo, exhibits similar texture strokes but employs harder outlines, transforming the tightly clustered rocks into blocklike forms from which the picture is constructed.[10] The effect is repetitious and more artificial, although these tendencies were already emerging in Lan's works from 1639 to 1640. An album dated 1642 in the Sackler Collection contains a leaf after Huang which combines an appealing textural roughness with a relaxed, expansive composition closer in character to that of the Smart Gallery handscroll.[11]

The stylistic similarities between the Smart Gallery painting and dated works from the late 1630s and early forties are supported by the inscriptions on the painting, which are dated from 1638 to 1646.[12] The work is therefore likely to have been executed in or shortly before 1638. Seven colophons are written on the painting along with the artist's own inscription. Among these the first, in order of appearance on the scroll, is signed by Chen Jiru, a well-known scholar, collector, and calligrapher and close friend of Dong Qichang, in his eighty-first year (1638). Chen expresses the highest praise for Lan's painting, saying that viewing it gave him a strange feeling that Huang Gongwang had reappeared. The second inscription, by Fan Yunlin (1558–1641), a scholar and official who excelled at calligraphy and landscape painting, is also dated 1638. Fan confesses that when Lan showed him the scroll, he thought that he was looking at a real work by Huang, until he noticed the inscription by Chen. The third colophon is signed Wang Siren (1576–1646), an official, poet, and calligrapher from Shaoxing. Lan's own inscription, close to the end of the painting, is undated.

Appended to the painting are six additional colophons, the first by Yang Wencong (1597–1646). Although written in 1638—the same year as Chen's and Fan's inscriptions at the beginning of the scroll—Yang's comments are modestly placed after the painting instead of on it, prob-

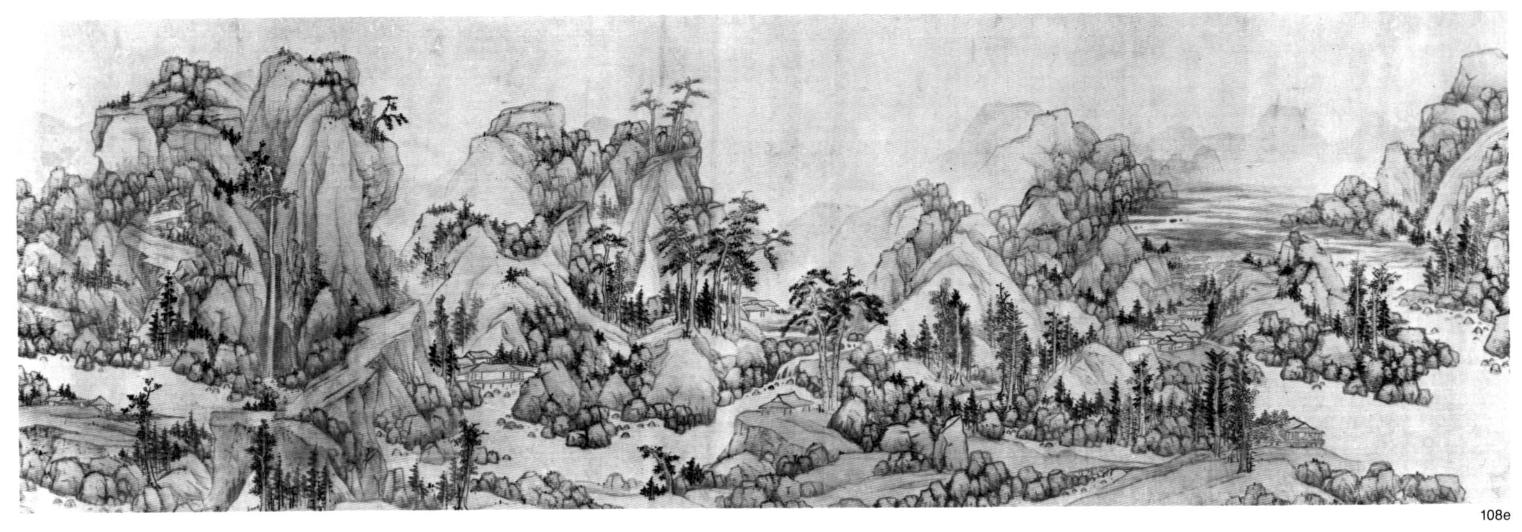

108e

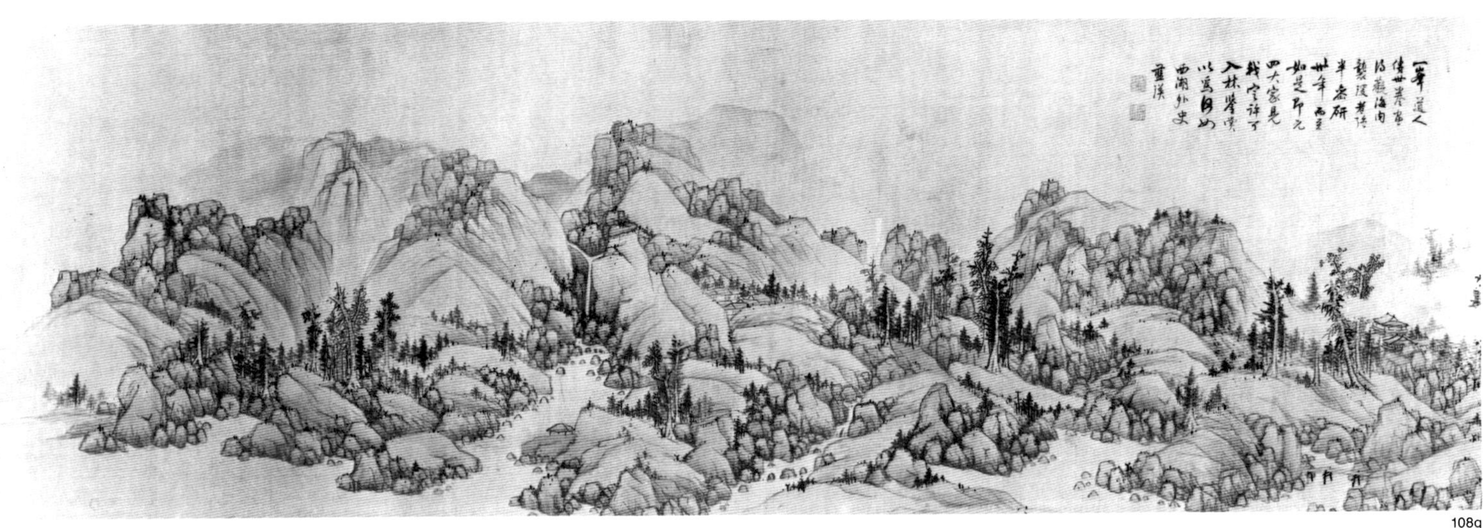

108g

一峯老人畫神韻秀逸體
勢夭矯錯奇所作平岡淺岫
皆兼疊嶂層巒滃渤次之多
者也今春自吾友田畊筆端
傳寫神似展卷一覽恍如置
身在千巖萬壑中至乎青峰
插天怪石林立烟雲杳靄山
水變幻又處處引人著勝地乃
今子久提筆來忍見斯大觀也
然此全卷可以出田子胸中丘
壑矣
任林澤拜秋題

余嘗聞子久畫世不多見
即有得其片楮者寶之兄
其所長尚以為至寶今觀
田畊先生此卷真得子久曾
中逸氣姿態不凡為藏家
秀動脫盡畫家陋習深
入古人之堂奧也董太史云
子久畫法得虞山與天池
山原可為師矣曩歲遊山
陰訪朱氏觀風出江藏子久
畫有卷題云千山萬山
青入眼大樹小樹如遊龍
井西道人出神之處過
筆第一峰 余味此
詩恍然置田畊前身
矣
丙戌夏茂苑曹自光跋

109i

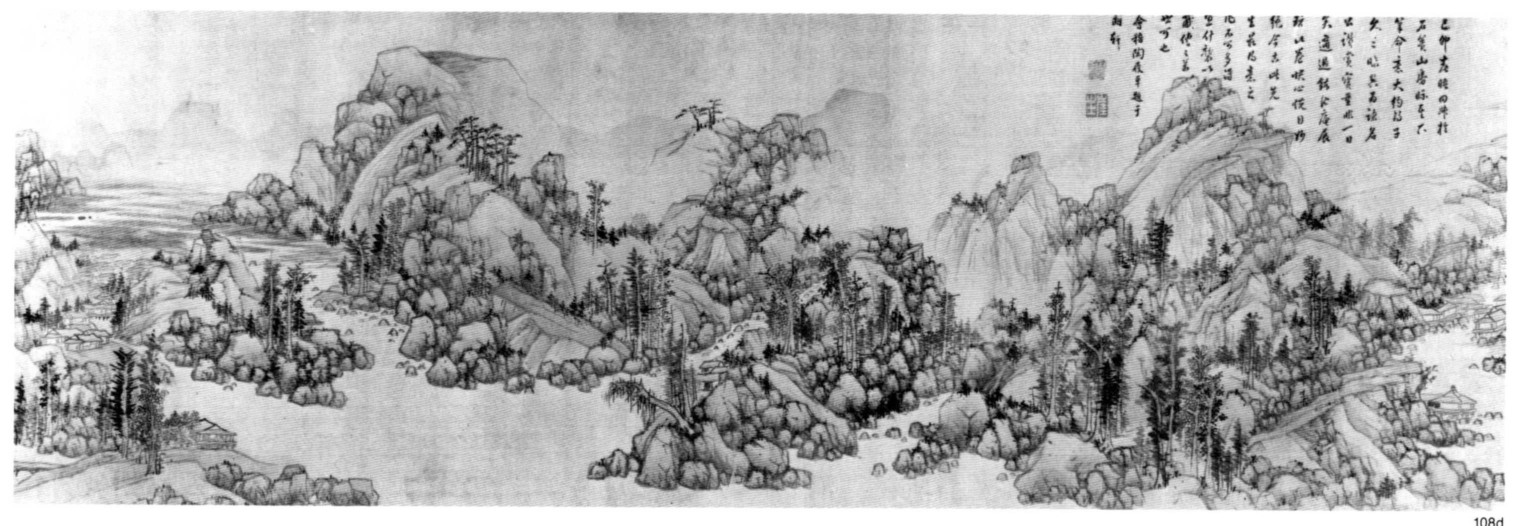

108d

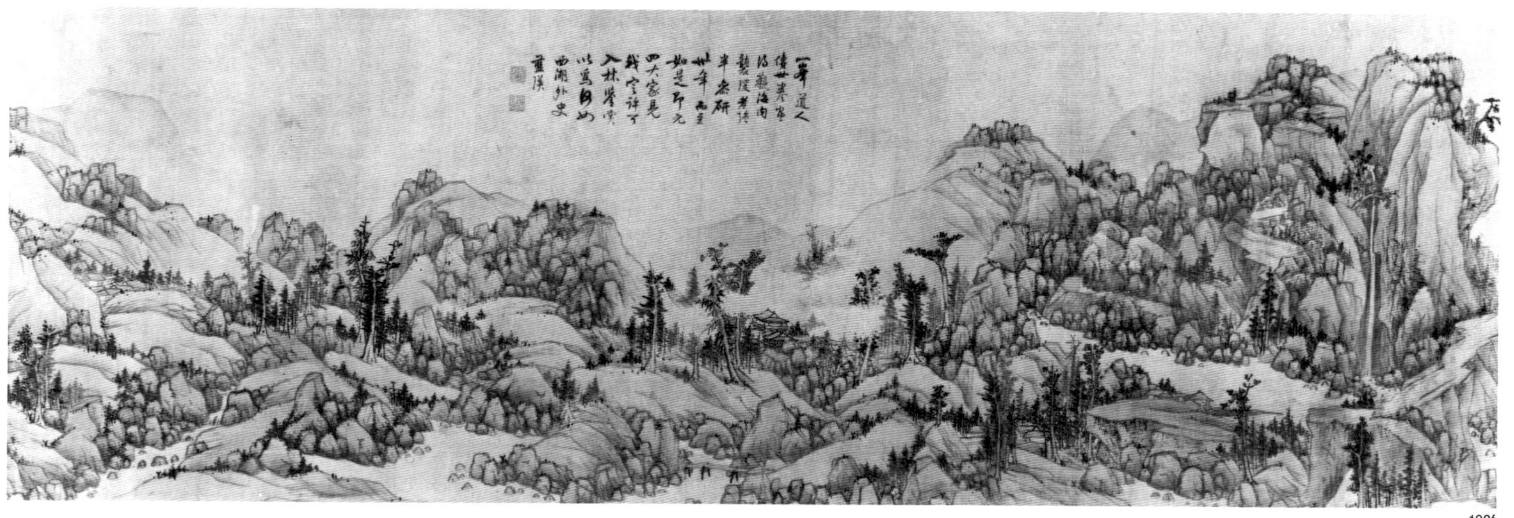

108f

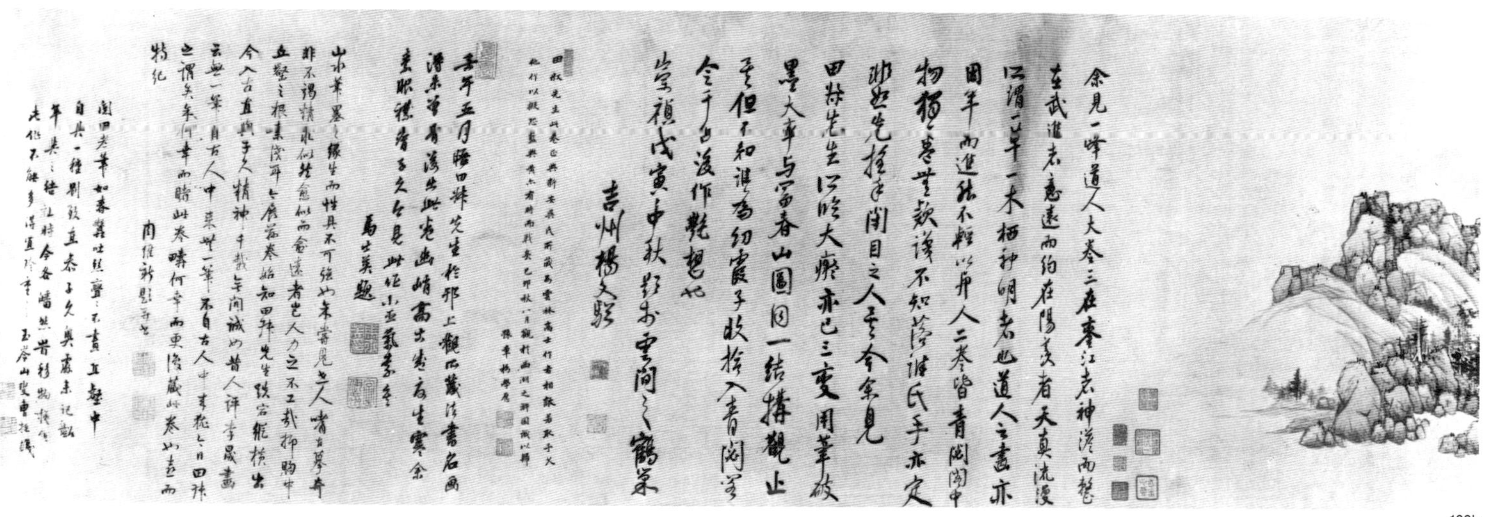

108h

ably because of their author's comparative youth. The third appended inscription, by Ma Shiying (1591–1646), is dated 1642. Ma was to become chief Grand Secretary of the scandalous Southern Ming court of the Hongguang Emperor, Zhu Yousong (d. 1646), and is considered one of the most treacherous villains of Ming history. Yang was criticized for his connections with his brother-in-law Ma. It is possible that Lan's reputation also suffered from his association with Ma, for scholarly opinion after his death reflects almost none of the admiration evident in the inscriptions on the Smart Gallery handscroll. Zhang Geng (1685–1760) in the *Guochao huazhenglu* records, for example, that in his youth he heard his elders speak of Lan with disdain.[13] Yang Enshou, in whose late nineteenth-century catalogue the scroll is described and its inscriptions recorded (after an earlier nineteenth-century publication), wrote that Lan lived for a time on Ma's estate.[14] While there is no historical corroboration for this, both Ma and Lan appear as characters in the famous 1699 drama by Kong Shangren (1648–1719), *Taohua shan* (*The Peach Blossom Fan*).[15] The Smart Gallery painting provides further evidence of an association between them and perhaps of the underlying reason for the decline of Lan Ying's prestige in his later years and following his death, when he was derogatorily labelled as the last of the Zhe School painters. K.R.T.

NOTES

1. Translated in part by Shen Fu and Marilyn Fu, in *Studies in Connoisseurship: Chinese Paintings from the Arthur M. Sackler Collection in New York and Princeton* (exh. cat.) (Princeton, N.J.: Princeton University Press, 1973), 112, from Yang Enshou's *Yanfubian*. In Yang's recording of inscriptions in this late-nineteenth-century catalogue, there are some errors. For example, the artist's signature appears as "Xilin waishi, Lan Ying" instead of "Xihu waishi, Lan Ying."

2. Transcriptions of the texts by Wan-go H. C. Weng are included in the documentary files of the Smart Gallery.

3. Transcriptions of the seals by Wan-go H. C. Weng are on file at the Smart Gallery.

4. The painting, in the Liaoning Provincial Museum, Shenyang, is reproduced in James Cahill, *The Distant Mountains: Chinese Painting of the Late Ming Dynasty, 1570–1644* (New York and Tokyo: John Weatherhill, 1982), pl. 98.

5. Both these works are in the National Palace Museum, Taipei, Taiwan.

6. See Wen Fong et al., *Images of the Mind: Selections from the Edward L. Elliott Family and John B. Elliott Collections of Chinese Calligraphy and Painting at the Art Museum* (exh. cat.) (Princeton, N.J.: Art Museum, Princeton University, 1984), cat. no. 30.

7. National Palace Museum, *Wanming bianxing zhuyi huajia zuopin zhan* (*Style Transformed: A Special Exhibition of Works by Five Late Ming Artists*) (exh. cat.) (Taipei, Taiwan: National Palace Museum, 1977), cat. no. 049.

8. Ibid., 88.

9. Ibid., cat. no. 050.

10. See Cahill, *Distant Mountains*, pl. 102.

11. See Fu and Fu, *Studies in Connoisseurship*, pl. VIIG.

12. While the inscriptions have been discredited by some scholars, this has not been demonstrated by historical evidence. The date 1638, correctly indicated in the Yang Wencong inscription itself, is erroneously recorded in Yang Enshou (*Yanfubian*, preface 1885, vol. 3, part 2, *juan* 15:36a–41b) as 1608 or 1668, both impossible in the historical context of the painting (see Cahill, *Distant Mountains*, 183 and 278, n. 19).

13. Zhang Geng, *Guochao huazhenglu*, preface 1735, part 1:13. See also Fu and Fu, *Studies in Connoisseurship*, 113.

14. Yang Enshou, *Yanfubian*, vol. 3, part 1, *juan* 12.

15. Yang Wencong's name features prominently in the play as the artist who painted the fan by converting bloodstains into peach blossoms.

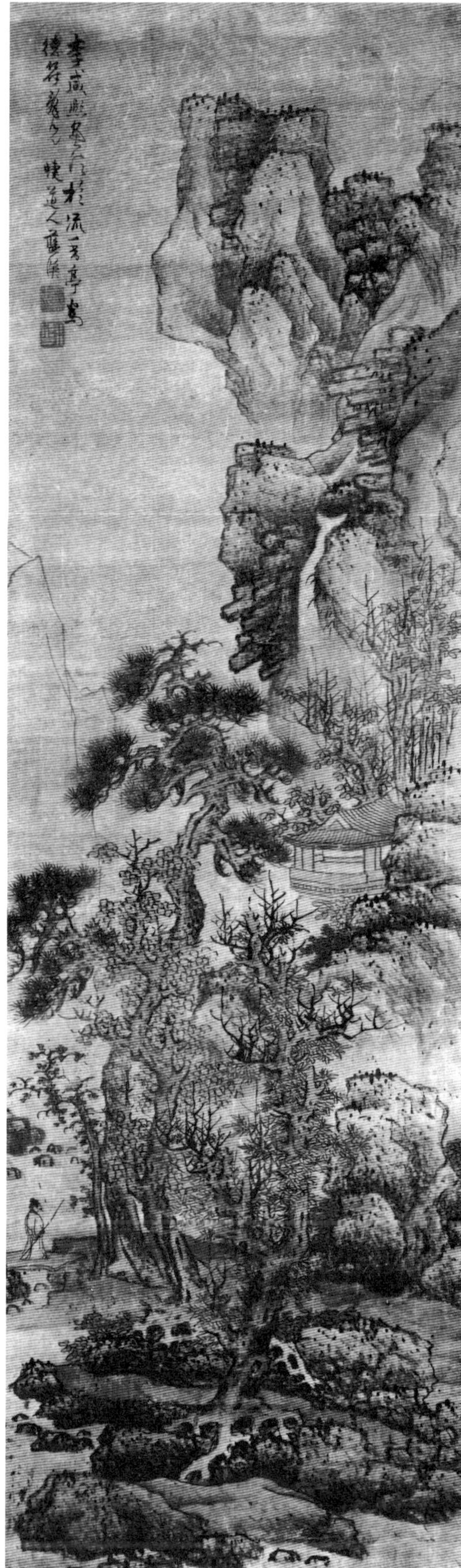
109

109 **Lan Ying**, 1585–after 1664
Landscape (after Li Cheng), circa 1630–50

Hanging scroll, ink and color on silk, 62 1/16 x 19 1/4 (158.1 x 48.9)
Purchase, Anonymous Gift
Acc. no. 1974.83

INSCRIPTIONS
Artist's inscription:
Respectfully painted for De Fu, after Li Cheng, in the Liufang Pavilion. [signed] The Butterfly Daoist Lan Ying.

SEALS
After artist's signature, two seals: Lan Ying zhi yin, Shu Tian.

PROVENANCE
Nü Wa Chai Collection [Victoria Contag von Winterfeldt]; C. C. Wang, New York (1968).

PUBLICATIONS
Hamburg, *Chinesische Malerei*, cat. no. 24; Sirén, *Leading Masters*, 7:205.

Lan Ying's biography and activities remain difficult to interpret.[1] His surviving oeuvre shows him to have been a superb craftsman with a subtle understanding of line, color, and composition. But this feeling for the physical appearance of things, coupled with his lack of proper literary background, is the source of ambiguities surrounding Lan's stature in traditional Chinese evaluations, in which excellence is predicated on literary accomplishment rather than technical proficency. Lan seems, then, to belie that principle, affecting all assessments by contemporary and later commentators. Interestingly, Japanese artists, collectors, and connoisseurs avidly sought his work, and Lan had a tremendous impact on the eighteenth-century literati Nanga (Southern Painting) School.[2]

In *Landscape (after Li Cheng)*, three tall trees of different species overshadow a gentleman with a staff crossing a stone bridge beyond a rocky river bank. Massive boulders and layered rocks rise above the treetops to the right, forming a backdrop to the pavilion nestled at the foot of a waterfall. Faintly outlined mountains rise up in the distance at the left. A connection is clearly established between the scholar and the pavilion, based on the convention of such scenes in traditional landscape painting and underscored by the inscription that mentions the execution of the painting in the Liufang Pavilion. The reference in the colophon to the painter Li Cheng (919–circa 967) is, at best, traditional: the prominent tall trees, stratified rocks, and the short, round, choppy brushstrokes are part of the Li Cheng heritage. For instance, the trees are in the manner of those found in early Li-style paintings such as *The Crooked Trees*, attributed to the eleventh century, in the National Palace Museum in Taipei.[3]

The recipient of the painting, De Fu, might be the minor author Zhang Xicung, from Ningbo in Zhejiang province, who is remembered for his collection of writings, *Yunshan ji* (*Cloud Mountain Record*). Since Zhang is not well recorded and his life and possible connections with Lan are not mentioned, it is difficult to verify that he is the Mr. Zhang referred to in the inscription. H.A.V.

NOTES

1. For the most recent short biography of Lan Ying, see Howard Rogers and Sherman E. Lee, *Masterworks of Ming and Qing Painting from the Forbidden City* (exh. cat.) (Lansdale, Pa.: International Arts Council, 1988), 147–149.
2. For a discussion of Lan's relation to the Nanga School and Japanese literati painting, see Stephen Addiss et al., *Japanese Quest for a New Vision: The Impact of Visiting Chinese Painters, 1600–1900* (exh. cat.) (Lawrence, Kans.: Spencer Museum of Art, University of Kansas, 1986), 95.
3. Illustrated in Max Loehr, *The Great Painters of China* (New York: Harper and Row, 1980), fig. 69.

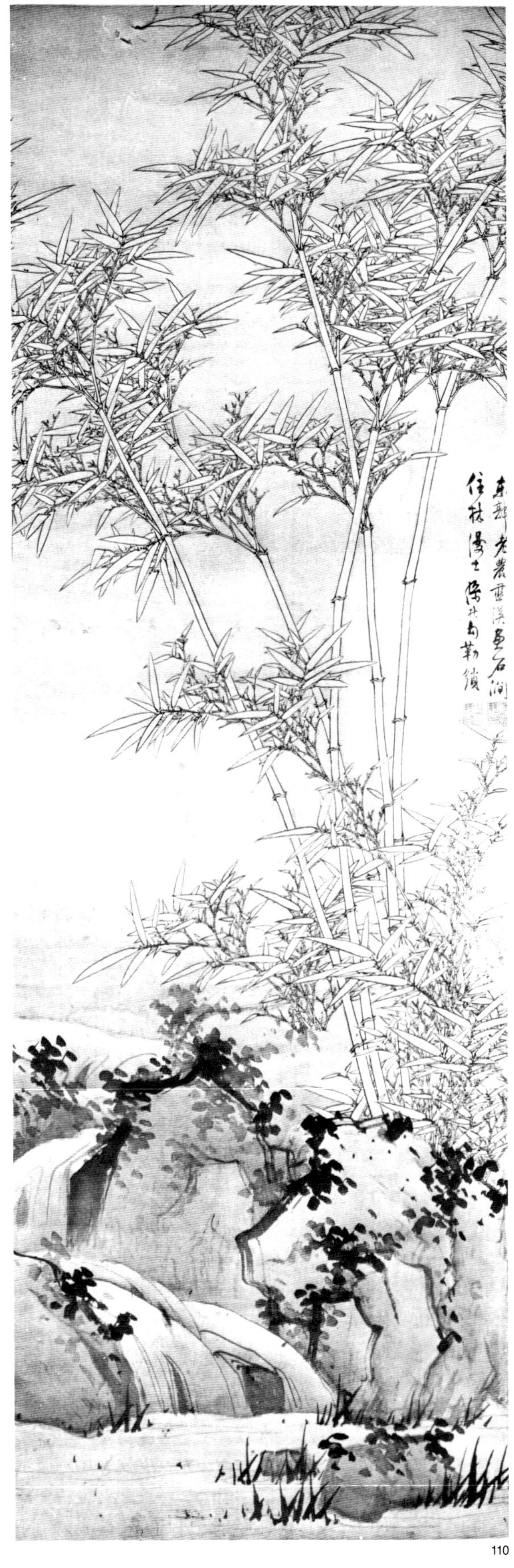

110

110 **Lan Ying**, 1585–after 1664
Sun Di, d. 1651[1]
Bamboo and Rocks, circa 1640–50

Hanging scroll, ink on silk, 64⅞ x 22⁹⁄₁₆ (164.8 x 57.3)
Purchase, Anonymous Gift
Acc. no. 1974.89

INSCRIPTIONS
Artist's inscription:
Lan Ying, the "Old Farmer from the Eastern Outskirts of Town," painted the rocky brook.
Artist's inscription:
Sun Di, the "Unfettered Gentleman Who Dwells in the Forest," outlined [undeciphered character].

SEALS
After Lan Ying's inscription: Lan Ying zhi yin.
After Sun Di's inscription: Sun Di zhi yin.

PROVENANCE
Nü Wa Chai Collection [Victoria Contag von Winterfeldt]; C. C. Wang, New York (1968).

PUBLICATIONS
Hamburg, *Chinesische Malerei*, cat. no. 22, pl. 12; Sirén, *Leading Masters*, 7:205, 398; Suzuki, *Catalog*, no. A 2-002, 1:28, 424 and 5:177; Anne Burkus, "The Artefacts of Biography in Ch'en Hung-shou's *Pao-lun-t'ang chi*" (Ph.D. diss., University of California, Berkeley, 1987), 318–321; National Palace Museum, *Hai-wai Yi-chen (Chinese Art in Overseas Collections: Painting III)* (Taipei, Taiwan: National Palace Museum), forthcoming.

Scant historical evidence confirms the social acquaintance of the painters Lan Ying and Sun Di, both of whom spent their careers in the southern district of Qiantang and its fabled city Hangzhou.[2] *Bamboo and Rocks*, a solitary record of their artistic collaboration, indicates that their relationship may even have become occasionally a professional one. Lan Ying is today by far the better known of the two painters (see cat. nos. 108, 109). But among seventeenth-century critics Sun Di had established a reputation of his own, notably in the genres of bamboo and bird-and-flower painting; the presence of a small local following also affords proof of his status.[3] Critical description of Sun's work focuses on its coloring and sharp delineation of form, characteristics associated with the old masters Huang Quan (903–968) and Zhao Chang (circa 960–after 1016). Referring to this archaistic aspect of Sun's style, one contemporary observer explained that since the "brushwork is forceful and strong, the application of color heavy and voluptuous, [Sun Di] obtains the correct school of the ancients — this is not the lightly drawn and blandly stained [product] of a seductive era."[4] However, surviving examples of Sun's large floral compositions, which feature a complex netting of branch and foliage stretched taut across the picture plane, owe as much to Ming academy works in this genre.

The flourishing plant Sun Di contributed to *Bamboo and Rocks* also shows his preference for old-fashioned drawing techniques, in this case the so-called *goule* method for which late-Ming critics specially commended him. Ordinarily translated as "outline," the term *goule* more literally renders the act of using a brush as the carving of words or images into a surface with a hooked point. The technical term *shuanggou* or "double hook," sometimes used as a synonym for *goule*, denotes the shape assumed by the forefinger and middle finger as they hold the brush securely against the thumb in order to execute fine, even delineations, which might appear to have been engraved. Sun did not color the stark forms of leaf or joint in *Bamboo and Rocks*, eliminating the final step in the traditional procedure of "outlining" bamboo. Rather, he concentrated on the more subtle tonal contrast between the color of the plain silk contained within the plant forms and the pale gray wash of ink that stains the silk around them. Sun thus allies his work with the separate genre of ink bamboo, or *mozhu*, which had flourished among educated men since the eleventh century.

The broader and more relaxed application of the brush, which produces the black leaves that characterize this genre, is more expressly represented, however, in the rocky brook Lan Ying depicted to accompany Sun Di's bamboo. In these rocks, which only roughly suggest the shape of what they represent, Lan exemplifies the techniques of ink play to which fourteenth-century specialists in ink bamboo were committed. The strokes of a slanted brush, partially loaded with dry ink and dragged quickly across the silk, draw attention to themselves; moss dots that hover in scattered groups along the path of these strokes signal the restlessness of the brush that produced them. Lan, who as a landscapist also preferred the idioms of amateur painting, thus provides a foil to the restrained calculation of Sun's outlined bamboo. Like his acquaintance Chen Hongshou, Sun Di was inclined toward a more archaic and courtly tradition.

The stylistic tensions that inform *Bamboo and Rocks* make it a splendid and unusual example of its genre. Popular among Chinese painters, images of bamboo and rock, like the related subject of old trees and rocks, symbolize human character refined by austerity and difficulty. The distinct components of the image, ordinarily shown in isolation, encouraged collaboration by allowing a convenient separation of labor. Although in some instances painters who worked together to paint a bamboo and rock intended to make a memorial of their artistic encounter, it was not uncommon for painters who had joined together for other purposes to execute their work apart and at different times. Unfortunately, only the signatures of Lan Ying and Sun Di are recorded on the Smart Gallery painting; nothing is known of the circumstances under which they were brought together to paint.[5] A.B.

NOTES

1. There is some confusion about Sun Di's dates of activity. It is not known when he was born, but the painter Chen Hongshou (1598–1652), with whom he was acquainted, writes in 1651 about mourning his death. See "Author's Preface to Jiang (Tinggan) Qiji's Handwritten Manuscript *Chen Laolian shi* (*Chen [Hongshou] Old Lotus's poems*)" in Chen Hongshou, *Baoluntang ji* (*Collected Writings from Hall for the Cherishment of Silken Cords*), comp. Chen Zi (late seventeenth–early eighteenth century); reprint, Dong Jinjian, ed., 1888, ch. 1:8b. Leaves from an album of flower paintings that Sun Di made between 1650 and 1651 indicate that he must have died in 1651 (*Gugong zhoukan* 140 [11 May 1932]: 38; 150 [15 June 1932]: 78). The editors of *Tuhui bao jian xu zuan* (*Supplement to Precious Speculum on Painting*) assert, moreover, that Sun Di died at an early age (late seventeenth century; reprint, Yu Anlan, ed., *Huashi congshu* [*Compendium of Art-Historical Texts*] [Shanghai: Shanghai renmin meishu chubanshe, 1962; Taipei, Taiwan: Wenshizhe chubanshe, 1974], ch. 2, 15).

2. Yen Chüan-ying recounts what little is known about the association of Lan Ying and Sun Di in *Lan Ying yu fanggu huihua* (*Lan Ying and Archaistic Painting*) (Taipei, Taiwan: National Palace Museum, 1980), 7. Both men, moreover, attended the funeral of Chen Hongshou's mother in 1615 and wrote poems to mourn the death of Chen Hongshou's father in 1606. See Chen Yuchao, *Zhuluoshan gao* (*Manuscript from Zhuluo Mountain*) (1615), appendix of "pall-bearers' poems": 2a–3a; 14b.

3. See Xu Chin, *Ming hua lu* (*Record of Ming Painters*) (seventeenth century; reprint, Yu Anlan, ed., *Huashi congshu*), ch. 6, 87; *Tuhui bao jian xu zuan*, ch. 2, 15; *Zhejiang tong zhi* (*Comprehensive Record of Zhejiang Province*) (1684), ch. 42, 13a–b. The editors of *Tuhui bao jian xu zuan* identify Sun Di's followers, who included his son (ch. 2, pp. 15, 26, 39). See also Yu Jianhua, comp., *Zhongguo meishujia renming cidian* (*Dictionary of Chinese Artists' Names*) (Shanghai: Shanghai renmin meishu chubanshe, 1980), 682.

4. *Tuhui bao jian xu zuan*, ch. 2, 15.

5. Sun Di's signature as "Zhulin," one "Who Dwells in the Forest," is unusual. Typically, he only signed his paintings with the sobriquet "Manshi," the "Unfettered Gentleman." The addition of these two extra characters to his name may have been motivated by a desire to make his signature structurally parallel with the four-character signature of Lan Ying. Another collaborative painting, between Lan Ying and Xie Bin (active mid-seventeenth century), is a handscroll titled *Landscape with Scholars*, dated 1648, and published in James Cahill, ed., *The Restless Landscape: Chinese Painting of the Late Ming Period* (exh. cat.) (Berkeley, Calif.: University Art Museum, 1971), cat. no. 81.

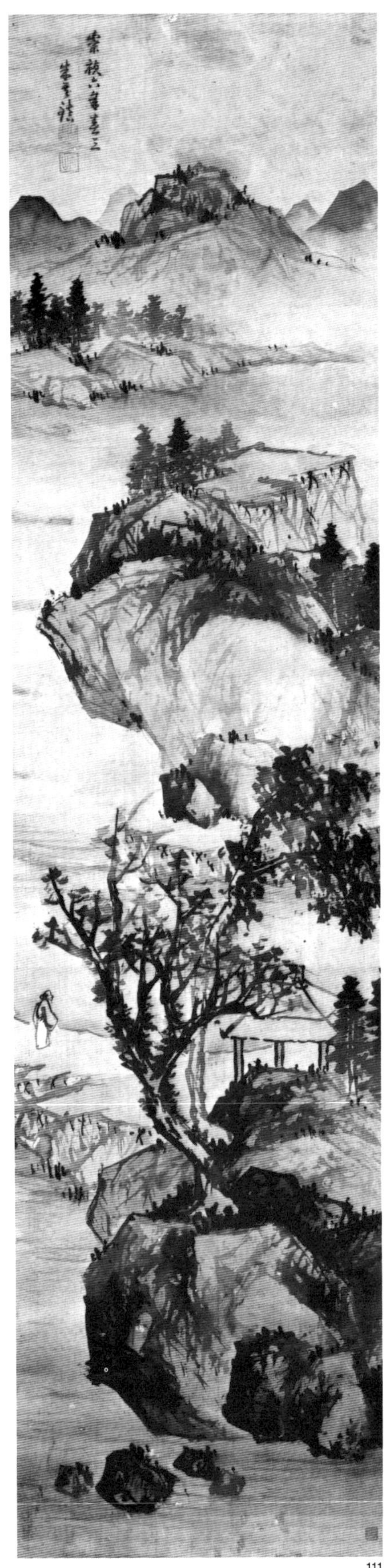

111

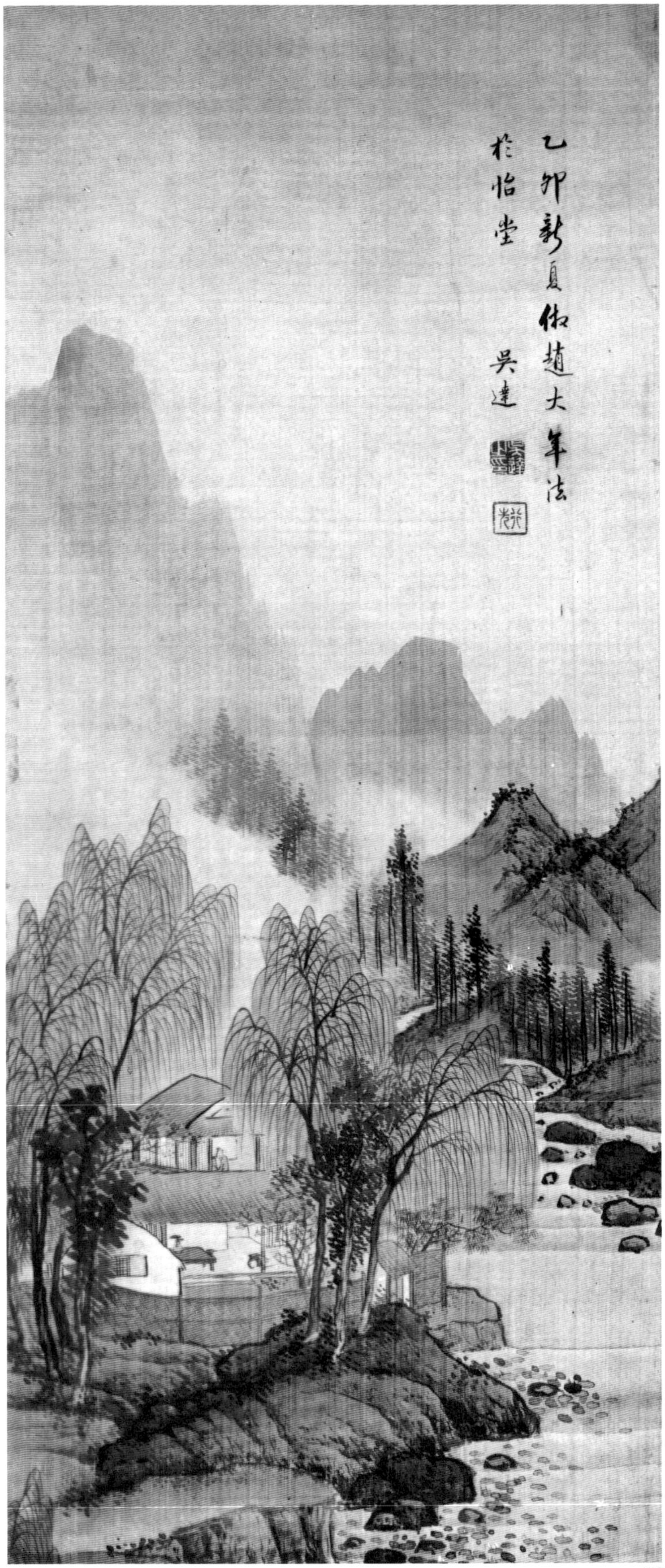

112

111 **Zhu Qizhen**, active mid-seventeenth century
Landscape, 1633

Hanging scroll, ink and light color on silk, 67 13/16 x 17 1/8 (172.2 x 43.5)
Gift of Jeannette Shambaugh Elliott
Acc. no. 1987.12

INSCRIPTIONS
Artist's inscription:
In the third month of spring of the sixth year of the Chongzhen reign [1633].

SEALS
After artist's inscription, two seals: Zhu Qizhen yin, Jiu Shan.
Lower left, collector's seal: Tong Yin Guan.
Lower right, three seals: [uppermost seal is unreadable], Yi Zhi Chan, Zeng Gui Mo Ge.

PUBLICATIONS
Bulletin, 36.

The painter Zhu Qizhen is not mentioned in any of the standard biographic anthologies. An artist-calligrapher by the same name from Zhejiang province, who was also known as Jiu Shan and who received his *jinshi* degree in 1829, is mentioned. However, there is no indication that these two artists have anything to do with each other, unless one assumes that the date on the Smart Gallery painting is a later interpolation, for which there is no evidence.

In this landscape with a far shore of trees and a mountain range, there is, standing on a walkway behind large rounded boulders with two slightly gruff trees and a pavilion, a person viewing the boulders and cliffs of the middle distance. The execution of this painting is marked by unusually bold brushwork, which refers to paintings—seldom quoted in the late Ming period—of the early-Ming Zhe School, which in turn depends on the Northern Song style of the court academy artist Guo Xi (active in the early eleventh century) and late Song academic styles of the thirteenth century. The bold use of ink and abrupt stroke endings remind one of paintings executed with finger and fingernail techniques, largely associated with the individualist painters of the early to middle Qing dynasty,[1] and the label on the outside of the scroll also identifies the work as a finger painting. H.A.V.

NOTES

1. See, for example, Shih Hsio-yen and Henry S. Trubner, *Individualists and Eccentrics: The Mr. and Mrs. R. W. Finlayson Collection of Chinese Paintings* (exh. cat.) (Toronto: University of Toronto Press, 1963), xi–xii, 35–36, and cat. no. 10. The use of finger painting techniques in landscape painting is described as early as the Tang dynasty; see Susan Bush and Shih Hsio-yen, eds., *Early Chinese Texts on Painting* (Cambridge, Mass., and London: Harvard University Press, 1985), 65, 67.

112 **Wu Da**, active circa 1675
Summer Pavilion (after Zhao Danian), 1675

Hanging scroll, ink and color on satin, 42 1/8 x 18 3/16 (107 x 46.2)
Purchase, Gift of Mr. and Mrs. Gaylord Donnelley
Acc. no. 1974.91

INSCRIPTIONS
Artist's inscription:
In the *Yimao* year [1675], in the early summer, in the style of Zhao Danian, made in the Yitang [Hall of Harmony]. [signed] Wu Da.

SEALS
After artist's signature, two seals: Wu Da zhi yin, Xing Sheng.

PROVENANCE
Yamanaka, Kyoto (1971).

The specifics of Wu Da's life are unknown. He is briefly recorded as a painter from Shaoxing in Zhejiang province. His *hao*, or style name, was Xing Sheng and an additional name was Mo Zhuang. He is listed in *Tuhui bao jian xu zuan (Supplement to Precious Speculum on Painting)* without entry,[1] but his dates cannot be verified from that information. Judging from the style of the Smart Gallery scroll, it seems likely that the cyclical date in the inscription might be 1675, rather than later.[2]

The painting features a rather broadly conceived foreground setting with a compound that possibly represents the Yitang (Hall of Harmony) referred to in the inscription. The willows, faint color, and rounded, lightly textured rocks with hazy mountains above the clouds can be remotely linked to what we know of the Song paintings of Zhao Danian (active 1070–1100), a member of the imperial family, mentioned in Wu's inscription. Aspects of Wu's use of color are reminiscent of similar techniques employed in paintings by the late-Ming artist Lan Ying (see cat. no. 108), but in this case the gentle fading of color and emphasis on ease of tone may have been borrowed from the *mogu* or boneless manner of painting, in which ink or color washes alone, without a bounding outline, define form. H.A.V.

NOTES

1. Composed by Xia Wenyan with a foreword dated 1365, this book was updated in 1519 by Wang Ang and in the seventeenth century by Lan Ying and Xie Bin.
2. The Chinese system of dating is based on a revolving cycle of sixty years that matches the combination of ten Stems and twelve Branches (references to the zodiac). Each year in the cycle is identified by a combination of Stem and Branch, which is repeated every sixty years. Without additional information of a reign date or biographical data, a cyclical date cannot be matched to a year in the western calendar.

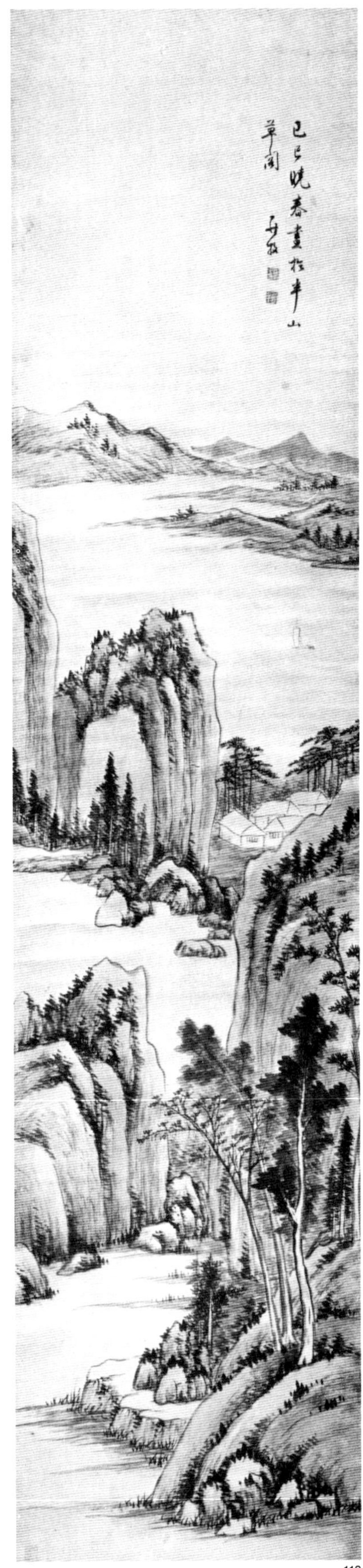

113

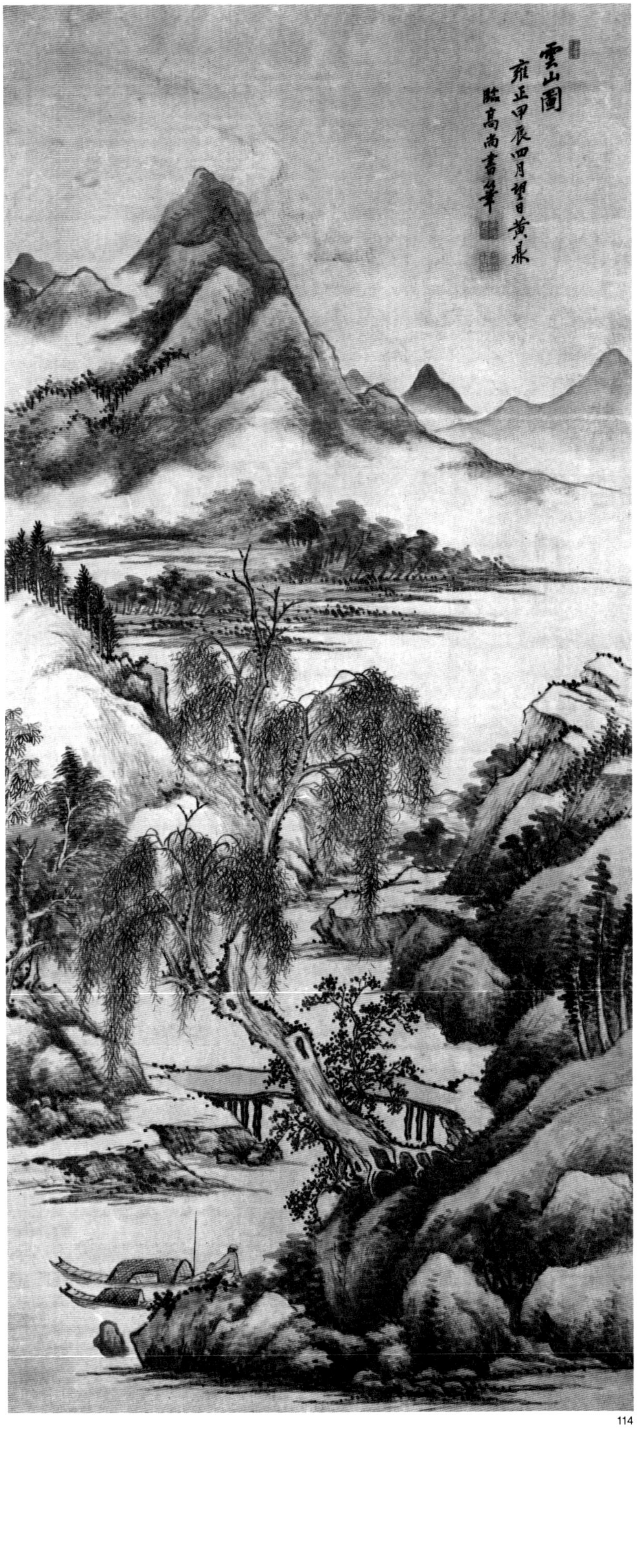

雲山圖
雍正甲辰四月望日黃鼎
臨高尚書筆

114

113 **Luo Mu**, 1622–after 1706
Landscape, 1689

Hanging scroll, ink on satin, 79³⁄₁₆ x 19⅛ (201.1 x 48.6)
Purchase, Anonymous Gift
Acc. no. 1974.87

INSCRIPTIONS
Artist's inscription:
Painted in the *Jisi* year [1689], in the early spring, in a thatched pavilion in Banshan [Jiangsu]. [signed] Luo Mu.

SEALS
After artist's signature, two seals: Luo Mu zhi yin, Fan Niu.
Lower left, collector's seal: Xiao Zhan Guo Yan.
Lower right, two collectors' seals: Zi [undeciphered character] Yan Fu, Hui Xiang Guan Cang (round seal).

PROVENANCE
Nü Wa Chai Collection [Victoria Contag von Winterfeldt]; C. C. Wang, New York (1968).

PUBLICATIONS
Hamburg, *Chinesische Malerie*, cat. no. 102; Sirén, *Leading Masters*, 7:379; Suzuki, *Catalog*, no. A 2-010, 1:29, 424 and 5:177.

Luo Mu worked in Jiangxi, mainly in the province's capital, Nanchang. Often called the head of the Jiangxi School of painting in the seventeenth century, he was also a calligrapher, poet, and tea connoisseur. The Smart Gallery hanging scroll bears a seal with his *hao*, or style name, Fan Niu, but he also went under the name of Yunan.

A good number of Luo's paintings are known, and his style followed Dong Qichang's Orthodox approach of creative regeneration of earlier traditions. The brushwork in this scroll can be interpreted as an adaptation of the hemp-fiber stroke (*pima cun*) of the tenth-century painter Dong Yuan. Luo is particularly known for this brush style, and another painting in this manner, but in an even broader rendition, is the 1693 painting of a pavilion under cedars in the Art Institute of Chicago.[1] In its uniformly upward-directed composition, the Smart Gallery landscape is like a vertically extended panorama. The long, firmly delineated strokes add to the sense of uniformity and to the easily identified manner. Luo was sought after possibly for this readily identifiable composition, long-established in Chinese traditions of landscape painting.

H.A.V.

NOTES
1. Suzuki Kei, *Comprehensive Illustrated Catalog of Chinese Paintings*, 5 vols. (Tokyo: University of Tokyo Press, 1982–83), no. A 3-003, 1:30 and 5:178.

114 **Huang Ding**, 1660–1730
Clouded Mountains, 1724

Hanging scroll, ink on silk, 48½ x 22⅜ (123.2 x 56.8)
Purchase, Anonymous Gift
Acc. no. 1974.80

INSCRIPTIONS
Artist's inscription:
In the fourth month, on full moon day, of the *Jiazhen* year, in the Yongzheng reign [1724], Huang Ding copied Gao Shangshu [Gao Kegong].

SEALS
Next to the beginning of artist's inscription: Du Zhu.
After artist's inscription, two seals: Huang Ding zhi yin, Zun Gu.

PROVENANCE
Nü Wa Chai Collection [Victoria Contag von Winterfeldt]; C. C. Wang, New York (1968).

PUBLICATIONS
Hamburg, *Chinesische Malerei*, cat. no. 58; Sirén, *Leading Masters*, 7:349–350.

Huang Ding came from Jiangsu province and studied with his townsman Wang Hui (1632–1717). While residing in the capital, Beijing, Huang also befriended the founder of the conservative Luodong School, Wang Yuanqi (1642–1715). Huang is said to have traveled much, hence his sobriquet, "Duwangke" or "Lonely Traveler"; his landscape paintings presumably reflect the things he saw during nearly thirty years of wandering. However, a look at his published oeuvre indicates that he emulated traditional masters, and there is little evidence of original interpretation. He followed instead in the footsteps of the Four Wangs—Wang Shimin, Wang Jian, Wang Yuanqi, and Wang Hui—and Wu Li and Yun Shouping, known as the Six Great Masters of the early Qing period, who worked according to the Orthodox theories of Dong Qichang, Wang Shimin's teacher. Huang himself never achieved the same level of recognition as the Six Masters.

The present painting is unusual within Huang's oeuvre in the intensity of ink and brushwork and the choice of antecedent. Huang renders hills and mountains in blunt brushstrokes and thickly dotted textures in a traditional landscape form, "copying" the Mi-style interpretation of the Southern Song painter Gao Kegong (1248–circa 1310), referred to in the inscription. The tones of lights and dark, and the distribution of trees, bridge, and water are convincing. Though much of Huang's other work—often referring to the styles of Yuan literati, including Ni Zan—is more ambitious and lighter in texture, one should note that he experimented with a variety of earlier forms of painting, and it seems safe to accept this painting as part of his repertoire.[1]

H.A.V.

NOTES
1. For comparison with a similar painting, although after a different artist, see *Shina nanga shūsei* (Tokyo, 1919), 1:9, pl. 8 and III:3, 11.

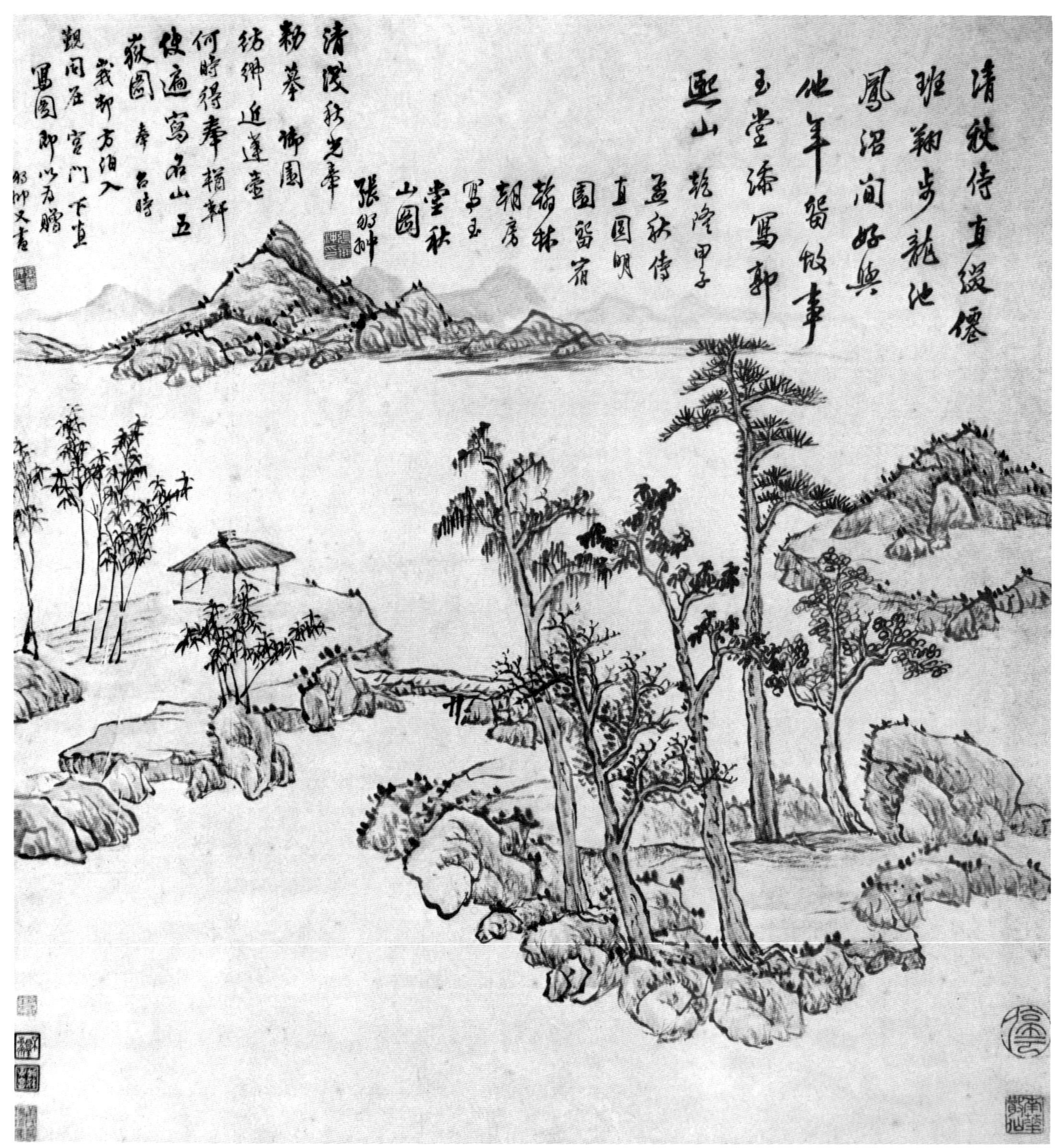

115

115 **Zhang Pengzhong**, 1688–1745
Jade Hall in Autumn Mountains, 1744

Hanging scroll, ink and color on paper, 26⅜ x 25 (67 x 63.5)
Gift of Mitchell Hutchinson
Acc. no. 1984.97

INSCRIPTIONS[1]

Artist's poem:

In pure autumn, attending the emperor overnight and thus numbering in the contingent of immortals [i.e. officials]
Roaming the Dragon's Pool and the Phoenix's Pond [i.e. palace]
The better in order to leave behind for later years a precedent.
To Jade Halls I have added in writing Guo Xi's mountains.

Artist's inscription:

In the *Jiazi* year of the Qianlong reign [1744–45], in the first month of autumn [8 August–6 September 1744], I was in attendance to the emperor and stayed overnight at the Yuan Ming Yuan. In the palace chambers in which the Hanlin Academy is received by the emperor, I "wrote" this painting of the Jade Hall in Autumn Mountains.

Artist's poem:

In the pure, clear autumn light I traced [paintings] with respect
Being in the imperial park is as if in Peng-hu [-lai] Paradise.
Yet when will I ever be appointed You Xuan Shi
So I can depict the famous mountains and Five Peaks?

Artist's inscription:

When I was summoned, the Provincial Administration Commissioner from my home province had come for an audience with the emperor.
As we came off duty together I wrote this painting to present as a gift.
[signed] Pengzhong has also written this.

SEALS

Following and adjacent to artist's first prose inscription: Zhang Pengzhong yin.
Following artist's second prose inscription: Zhang Pengzhong yin.
Lower right, upper seal: Tingyun [to stay in the clouds, to think of a friend].
Lower right, lower seal: Nanhua San Xian ["The Retired Immortal of Southern Mountain," one of the artist's *zi*].
Lower left, four unidentified collectors' seals, one reading: Ziqun Zhai [a studio name].

PUBLICATIONS

Tseng Yu-ho Ecke, *Wen-jen Hua: Chinese Literati Painting from the Collection of Mr. and Mrs. Mitchell Hutchinson* (exh. cat.) (Honolulu: Honolulu Academy of Arts), 1988, cat. no. 25.

Zhang Pengzhong was born on Chongming Island, at the mouth of the Yangzi, Jiangsu province, and later settled in nearby Jiading.[2] He received his *jinshi* degree—the highest level civil examination award based on literary ability and knowledge of the classics—in 1727[3] and was appointed to the Hanlin Academy following his success in the metropolitan exams. Little is known of his official career, except that in 1744, the year he painted the Smart Gallery scroll, he was promoted to supervisor of the Crown Prince's household. Zhang was also a poet, and two collections of his works survive, the *Nanhua shanren shichao* (*Poetic Transcriptions of the Mountain Recluse "Southern Blossom"*) in sixteen *juan*, and the *Cishi genghe ji* (*Collected Poesy*).

Sometime between the first week of August and the first week of September in 1744, Zhang was summoned to the newly rebuilt Summer Palace to stay overnight in attendance on the Qianlong Emperor, Gaozong. This was an event of great personal significance, for in traditional Chinese culture direct contact with the Son of Heaven fulfilled the greatest social, familial, and personal expectations of a literatus. Two aspects of the encounter engaged the poet and painter in Zhang: the imperial gardens and the paintings in the imperial collection. The gardens, called the Yuan Ming Yuan, situated about ten kilometers northwest of the capital of Beijing, had been founded by Gaozong's grandfather, the Kangxi Emperor, who ruled from 1662 to 1722. By 1744, the Qianlong Emperor had completed the initial building project, transforming the relatively modest gardens where he had spent his youth into a magnificent complex, unrivaled in its splendor. At least forty pleasure palaces were hidden from each other by artfully landscaped hillocks and copses, connected by ponds, pools, and watercourses. In summer, with Beijing sweltering, breezes wafting over the little lakes and through groves of perfuming trees provided cooling relief for the emperor and his retinue.[4]

However important for Zhang, his attendance upon Gaozong was not deemed of sufficient importance for inclusion in the record of the emperor's activities, the *Qing Shilu*, which does confirm, nonetheless, that the emperor was at the Yuan Ming Yuan during this period.[5] Zhang himself commemorated the event in poetic inscriptions on the Smart Gallery painting, which he presented to someone identified in the inscription as the Provincial Administration Commissioner (*fangbai*) from Zhang's home province, Jiangsu. This would have been the newly appointed Manchu official, Aibida, who had come for an imperial audience the day Zhang was in attendance.

Only a few of Zhang's paintings are known or published, all in Taiwan or Japan.[6] His two most ambitious surviving works, in the National Palace Museum, Taipei, include a long narrow painting titled *Kingfisher-Blue Peaks in the High Mountain*,[7] signed and dated to the ninth day of the ninth month, the ninth year of the Qianlong period (14 October 1744). The other painting is dated the same day and also shares the title but is a different composition. It too bears a dedication to the Qianlong Emperor, as well as a polite response and poem by the emperor himself, dated the same day.[8]

The composition of the Smart Gallery painting is immediately recognizable as a variation on a theme made famous by Ni Zan (1301–1374), one of the four great late-Yuan masters. Many famous Ming and Qing artists, including Shen Zhou, Wang Shimin, and Wang Yuanqi (1642–1715) made paintings that are conscious recollections of Ni's work. Ni himself frequently employed this basic tripartite configuration of a rocky foreground with trees and sometimes a pavilion, a middle ground of a plain expanse of water, and a background of soft mountain forms "not for any obsessive attachment to that scene, but rather for a detachment from it."[9] The repetition and plainness of this formula devalued representation without, however, severing the connection to nature; Ni attempted to bring the representation of nature into balance with other goals. The scenery is itself unexciting and rather ordinary but provided the artist a basic vocabulary with which to create a dry, crystalline surface structure and to display, without ostentation, the variety and artfulness of his brushwork.

Later artists used the same scheme with very different results, though not without a kind of homage to Ni, who seems to have been able to communicate his delicate, refined sensibilities and socially withdrawing tendencies through the airless, transparent quality of his rocks and trees. Almost four hundred years separated Zhang Pengzhong from his model in Ni Zan; intermediaries had as much an effect on the form of Zhang's painting as Ni himself. The scholar, writer, and artist Dong Qichang (1555–1636), for example, had a profound importance for literati painters of the late Ming and Qing periods. Perhaps without intending to, Dong set the stage for the increasing academicization of painting, for stiffening conventions, and for eliminating experimentation and exploration of natural and formal possibilities outside a narrow, sanctified tradition.

Osvald Sirén includes Zhang Pengzhong within a group of artists related to the Zhejiang artist Dong Bangda (1699–1769), "either by their manner of painting or personal associations."[10] In the case of Zhang, he must have intended the latter, for Zhang's paintings do not resemble the younger artist's work. Dong Bangda seems to have been primarily an imitator of Northern Song painters, without the intimacy or loose brush of Zhang. Zhang's immediate painterly roots seem much more firmly grounded in the work of Wang Shimin's grandson, Wang Yuanqi. The elder Wang, a famous painter of the early seventeenth century, had been a pupil of Dong Qichang. Wang Yuanqi learned painting from his grandfather and so was in a direct line of transmission from Dong. Zhang was already twenty-seven years old at Wang Yuanqi's death, but the latter's reputation at court and in literary circles must still have reverberated when Zhang was appointed to the Hanlin Academy in 1727. Jiading, where Zhang lived, was also the home of Wang Jingming, "a prominent scholar and Han-Lin [Hanlin] member" and one of Wang Yuanqi's pupils.[11] Thus, direct or indirect links between Wang Yuanqi and Zhang are possible.

A glance at Wang Yuanqi's paintings in the manner of famous Yuan literati, Ni or Huang Gongwang, for example, shows the relationship between the styles of Wang and Zhang Pengzhong.[12] Both make use of light, pastel ink washes in the same way in the same areas: pale blue for the background mountains and pale iron-ocher, sometimes blue, for the tree trunks and leaves. Both artists tend to build their forms with repeated applications of different types of brushstrokes. Moreover, Wang and Zhang employ some of the same brush techniques: wavering hemp-fiber strokes and dry, ragged strokes resulting from a brush dragged across the paper where a wetter line has already described a form. Empty space is an important component in their compositions, and Wang is one of the few who, like Zhang, regularly leaves a blank area at the bottom of the picture, lifting up the landforms. Both make use of the blank ground to set off the leaves of trees, which often similarly lean away from the perpendicular, and both favor flat-topped mesas as elements of the depicted terrain.

Wang's principal artistic concerns are conventionally described as compositional structure, spatial relationships, and volume. In the Smart Gallery painting, Zhang is also interested in such formal problems. The lofty pine stretching vertically all the way across the expanse of water to the distant mountains is an element intended to establish stability and surface unity, but the effect is rather a disconcerting uneasiness. Although the motif tends to connect the foreground and background, to unify the tripartite divisions, the landmass in the foreground seems to bob up and down: the water below tends to lift it up, floating, while the meeting of pine branches and upper horizontal of the mountain range constrains its rise.

Both Wang Yuanqi and Zhang Pengzhong use *dian*—dash-like marks or dots—at the edges of forms, but Zhang diverges from Wang in specific habits. Wang varies his *dian* within a single painting and from painting to painting; they are sometimes horizontal and other times vertical or rounded. Zhang, however, invariably strokes them at an angle just short of the vertical, so that they point, like many of his trees and rocks, toward the upper left. Further, his *dian* usually appear in pairs, as his hand dips, dabs twice, and moves on. Equally habitual is Zhang's concentration of *dian* on the left sides of forms. This is as true of his tree trunks as of his rocks and boulders.

Zhang's inability to free himself from repetitive patterns is not limited to his brushwork. One notes the same clumps of trees with the same leaners, the same variety of leaves and their placement on the Smart Gallery painting and on another inscribed by the Qianlong Emperor in the National Palace Museum, Taipei. These habits, unconsciously engaged, of brushwork and composition are indicative of Zhang's limited artistic resources and of learned, acquired manners invariably applied.

Zhang's dependence on Wang is clear from many of the latter's recommendations on painting techniques in his *Yu chuang man bi* (*Scattered Notes at a Rainy Window*).[13] Moreover, Wang's method is also preserved in an extraordinary description by a contemporary who, on a number of occasions, watched him work.[14] From these sources it is possible to follow Zhang's method as well. Wang worked from light to dark; he would also work and rework, adding to his original layout. These tendencies find counterparts in Zhang's painting. For instance, the cone-shaped mountain, though a relatively simple form, has been built up with several applications of the brush. Following Wang's procedure, Zhang first put down an even mid-gray outline, followed by darker gray interior modeling strokes or "wrinkles" done with an unevenly charged brush. Pale ocher washes were then applied as more interior modeling. After these had dried—perhaps with the ironing process—scumbly dark, very dry strokes were added. Some of these sit on top of the first outlines as well as inside the shapes. The dark, splotchy-wet *dian* were diagonally laid in, and finally the blue wash was added for the distant mountains.[15]

Zhang's use of color is quite delicate and important to the overall effect. He refrains from the vulgarity Wang describes in contemporary paintings, in which one "sees simply a blaze of red and green colours which are enough to make one disgusted and satiated,"[16] and instead applies subtle washes of blue, ocher, and rose-pink. But Wang's most emphatic instructions relate to the attitude and mental preparation of the artist before he begins a painting. "The idea must be conceived before the brush is grasped—such is the principal point in painting."[17] After sitting down in a tranquil frame of mind "silent before the white silk roll," the artist must "look at the high and the low, examine right and left, inside and outside the scroll, the road to enter and the road to leave"; only then should he "dip the brush and lick the tip."[18] It is this point that Zhang had in mind when he "wrote" the Smart Gallery painting.

Not unrelated to this approach is the notion that all the details had to work together to express the central theme. Zhang's inscription on the work naming the painting, *Jade Hall in Autumn Mountains*, identifies the season in which he painted and what he hoped to capture in the work. Autumn is immediately associated with the closing of the year and, metaphorically, with a life drawing to its conclusion. Perhaps the faintness of the rose wash is to be interpreted as suggesting the beginning of the end, the first hint that the leaves are changing. In fact, it was Zhang's final autumn.

Besides the title, there are two other clues to his intentions. One is the clear pictorial reference to Ni Zan, famous for his withdrawn, chilly landscapes. Yet, in the inscriptions, Zhang mentions not Ni, but the Northern Song painter Guo Xi. The combination of a composition indebted to Ni—through the lineage of Wang Yuanqi, Wang Shimin, and Dong Qichang—and an inscription that labels it a "Guo Xi mountain" requires explanation. The two references are contradictory in terms of the critical writing in the Orthodox painting tradition to which Zhang belonged, because Ni and Guo are paragons of the opposing Southern and Northern schools respectively. For Dong Qichang, the preeminent early articulator of this theory, Ni and other Southern school painters "present superior artistic qualities. . . . while the painters placed into the Northern school are denied all genius."[19] Zhang must have acquired similar biases against the "vulgar" Northern style, and he was too well-educated and well-exposed to art collections really to have considered that this painting echoed Guo's Northern Song monumental mountain landscapes, with their crab-claw trees looming up, silhouetted against mist-drenched "crumpled pillow" rocks. Nonetheless, Dong and his later followers, including Wang Yuanqi, reserved their strongest disdain for the sixteenth-century Zhe School (see cat. nos. 100, 101) and were not wholly without praise for the Northern Song masters. Guo Xi and Li Cheng overshadowed their followers, according to Dong, by "expressing much by little."[20] Most interestingly, Dong mentions Guo and Ni in the same passage, relating their painting styles: "Even Ni Tsan [Ni Zan] came out of Kuo Hsi [Guo Xi] and Li Ch'eng [Li Cheng], though he added softness and refinement [to their style]."[21]

Thus Zhang, even if painting in the Southern school manner, did not altogether reject the Northern school founders with their later followers. The reference to Guo is bound to Wang Yuanqi's dictum that "the idea must be conceived before the brush is grasped."[22] Since the landscape idiom was a given as the most proper subject for *wenren hua*, "literary man's painting," the innovation rested on the manner of portrayal of mountains and water. This invariably meant a season, usually spring, summer, or fall; winter was a less common choice, possibly because of its associations with Northern Song painting. In the Smart Gallery landscape, Zhang mentions *qing qiu*, "pure autumn," in the very first line of the inscription; in the prose inscription between the two poems, he does not give the day and month in numbers but uses a literary appellation that includes the word autumn, *meng qiu*. In the same text, he titles the painting *Yutang qiu shan* (*Jade Hall in Autumn Mountains*), and in the final inscription, he speaks of *qing qian qiu guang*, "the pure, clear autumn light."

The "theme" of the painting is clear, bright autumn mountains. Zhang would have found this idea discussed in the *Shan shui xun* (*Comments on Landscape*) section of Guo's *Lin quan gao zhi* (*The Lofty Message of Forests and Streams*), a treatise still in circulation in the Qing, in which Guo describes the appearance of mountains in each of the four seasons. "The autumn mountains," for instance, "are bright and clear, as if [adorned with] make-up (*Qiu shan ming jing er ru zhuang*)."[23] Although Guo uses *ming jing* rather than *qing*, in this context, Zhang's visual references to Ni and his literary reference of Guo are not as paradoxical as it first appears.

The first line of the second poem in the inscription refers to another of Zhang's activities in accord with Wang Yuanqi's injunctions. Apparently, while at the Yuan Ming Yuan, Zhang had the chance to look at and copy paintings in the emperor's collection. "In the pure, clear autumn light," he writes, "I traced [paintings] with respect." In his *Scattered Notes*, Wang refers to examining and copying old paintings, emphasizing these aesthetic exercises more than the study of nature itself.[24] Nonetheless, the expression of the creative force that unfolds in and through natural forms remained an important endeavor in early and mid-Ming painting. Harrie Vanderstappen has made a strong case that in seventeenth-century Orthodox painting, forms are ordained by the aspects of nature depicted while artists' inscriptions stress their debt to tradition; as the century progressed, however, artists began to experience "a general uneasiness about their competence to render nature on its own terms."[25] Artists began to rely on a visual language derived from traditionally sanctioned manners rather than from nature itself. Wang Yuanqi was still able to balance nature as a pictorial aim with traditional forms and brush vocabulary, but Zhang constructed his paintings from hallowed forms and habitual brush manners and not from experience with nature. This is confirmed, for instance, in the Smart Gallery landscape by the rocks in the water and boulders on the shore, which are not lapped gently by the still water and do not respond to their natural context.

Qing literati painters professed disdain for academic artists and professionalism, yet Zhang's reliance on learned manners or modes of painting is itself a kind of Orthodox academicism. In a sense it grew out of literary training for the *jinshi* examination, which was notorious for insistence on compliance with rigid restrictions, outward formality, and limited, narrow adherence to sanctified models and genres.

The Hanlin Academy received only those who were ranked first or second grade in the exam,[26] and although it is not known where Zhang placed when he passed the metropolitan exams, he was appointed to the Academy as a junior compiler, *bian xiu*. This appointment meant opportunity for professional advancement, since "it was usually these *hanlin* who held the highest positions in officialdom. . . . They formed the reservoir from which examiners for provincial examinations and provincial directors-of-studies were appointed."[27] Within the capital, they "did drafting and editing work in preparation of the more ceremonious imperial pronouncements and the compilation of imperially sponsored historical and other works."[28] Tenure of office for compilers in the Hanlin Academy was usually three years, after which they could be appointed as censors in the capital, circuit intendants, or prefects in the provinces.[29] In 1744, Zhang was appointed to *Zhanshi*, Supervisor of the Household of the Heir Apparent,[30] a nominal position under the Manchus for they usually did not designate an heir apparent. As he made clear in an edict in 1752, the Qianlong Emperor ascribed to this policy, but the title was retained "as a stepping stone for the promotion of members of the Academy of Letters [Hanlin]."[31] It was reserved for men of seniority and was an appointment made by the emperor himself.[32]

Although the *jinshi* degree and Hanlin Academy appointments were prestigious, those who achieved them during the Qing were "by no means the flowers of Chinese scholarship."[33] Such training was ill-suited for innovative artistic pursuits, either literary or visual. It reserved a place in the literatus' life for producing art, but the niche was institutionalized and transcended by only a few, such as Wang Yuanqi. Although Zhang Pengzhong does not count among the creative forefront of the middle Qing, the Smart Gallery landscape is a solid example of this elite tradition of painting by officials at court. R.L.

NOTES

1. I am grateful to Amy McNair for her many helpful suggestions in deciphering the Chinese characters on the painting. For making sense of the inscriptions and pointing out errors, I am indebted to Professor David Roy. The help of Ma Tai-loi, Chinese bibliographer of the East Asian library, The University of Chicago, is also acknowledged. Any errors that remain are solely the author's.

2. Sources for Zhang's life are the standard encyclopedic dictionaries of biographies, including Arthur W. Hummel, ed., *Eminent Chinese of the Ch'ing Period (1644–1912)* (Washington, D.C.: United States Government Printing Office, 1943); Kuo Wei-ch'u, *Song Yuan Ming Qing shu huajia nianbiao* (*Song, Yuan, Ming and Qing Painters' Chronology*) (Beijing, 1958); Shang Ch'eng-tso and Huang Hua, *Zhongguo lidai shuhua quanke jia zihao suoyin* (*Index of Alternate Names of Chinese Calligraphers, Painters and Seal Carvers*) (Beijing, 1960); Sun Tao-kung, *Zhongguo huajia renming da zidian* (*Biographical Dictionary of Chinese Painters*) (Shanghai, 1931).

3. Zhang was thirty-nine when he received his degree, perhaps slightly older than usual, but this was by no means exceptional; two artists who received their degrees the same year were even older than Zhang, having been born in 1683 and 1685 respectively, while a third, born in 1701, was a relative prodigy (see Kuo Wei-ch'u, *Song Yuan Ming Qing*, 331).

4. For the Yuan Ming Yuan, see Osvald Sirén, *Gardens of China* (New York: Ronald Press, 1949), 126; Carroll Brown Malone, *History of the Peking Summer Palaces under the Ch'ing Dynasty* (Ph.D. diss., University of Illinois, 1928), reprinted from *Illinois Studies in the Social Sciences* 19, nos. 1–2 (1934); and Committee of the Chinese Yuan Ming Yuan Institute, *Yuan Ming Yuan*, vol. 2 (Beijing, 1983).

5. *Da Qing Gaozong chun huangdi shilu: Qing Gaozong chun huangdi shilu* (*Veritable Records of the Successive Reigns of the Qing Dynasty: Veritable Records of the Qianlong Reign*) (Manchuria, 1937), Qianlong section, box 7; *juan* 220–222.

6. A painting of wintry trees and bamboo, signed and dated 1736, in the collection of the Kurokawa Institute of Ancient Cultures, Ashiya, Hyōgo prefecture, Japan, is published in Suzuki Kei, *Comprehensive Illustrated Catalog of Chinese Painting*, 5 vols. (Tokyo: Tokyo University Press, 1982–83), 3:no. JM 19-020; it also appears in the *Shen Zhou Guo Guang Ji* 2 (Shanghai, 1909). A fan painting of a landscape in the Yuzo Kanaoka Collection is published in Suzuki Kei, *Catalog* 4: no. JP 71. See also *Gugong shuhua lu*, 4 vols. (Taipei, Taiwan, 1965), 4:*juan* 8: 47, 105, 146.

7. *Gugong shuhua ji* (*Record of Painting and Calligraphy in the Palace Museum*), 45 vols. (Peking, 1930–36), vol. 9.

8. The description of this painting as a *Zhu-shou hua*, a painting of birthday congratulations to the emperor, is doubtful. The Qianlong Emperor's birthdate is the thirteenth day of the eighth month, which in 1744 fell on September 18; the inscription dates the work almost three weeks later. On the other hand, the ninth day of the ninth month, which fell on October 14 in 1744, was a day traditionally given to climbing a high hill looking down at the scenery, known as *Denggao*. It would have been appropriate on such a day to give a painting of a high mountain, one with the word *Gao* in its title. Within the Yuan Ming Yuan there was a hill, the Han Shan, which was used by the emperor on the *Denggao* days (see Malone, *Peking Summer Palaces*, 88).

9. James Cahill, *Hills Beyond a River: Chinese Painting of the Yuan Dynasty, 1279–1368* (New York and Tokyo: John Weatherhill, 1976), 119.

10. Sirén, *A History of Later Chinese Painting* (London: Medici Society, 1939; reprint, New York: Hacker, 1978), 2:197.

11. Osvald Sirén, *Chinese Painting: Leading Masters and Principles*, 7 vols. (London: Lund Humphries and Co., 1956–58), 5:202.

12. See, for example, Wang Yuanqi's hanging scroll, *Landscape in the Style of Dong Qichang* (1710), in the Franco Vannotti Collection, Muzzano (*Chinese Art in Western Collections* [Tokyo: Kōdansha, 1973], vol. 2,2:no. 65). Or compare a handscroll by Wang, *Pine and Mist on a Mountain Range in Spring* (1708), in the Asian Art Museum of San Francisco, Avery Brundage Collection, (ibid., no. 64). Other paintings by Wang are published in Jean Dubosc, *A Loan Exhibition: Great Chinese Paintings of the Ming and Ch'ing Dynasties* (exh. cat.) (New York: Wildenstein and Co., 1949), cat. nos. 49–53 and 55 (illustrated). Finally, see also Sirén, *Later Chinese Painting*, 2:pls. 218–219 and idem., *Leading Masters*, 6:pls. 421–430.

13. See Osvald Sirén, *The Chinese on the Art of Painting* (Beijing: H. Vetch, 1936; reprint, New York: Shocken Books, 1963), 203, 206, 207.

14. This lengthy report is reprinted in Sirén, *Leading Masters*, 5:204. Wang's visitor was the Manchu scholar Ke-da, who related it to his friend Zhang Geng, who wrote it down.

15. Ke-da, ibid., credits Wang with using "green" paint mixed with ink, while in Zhang's painting it is blue that is used to "emphasize lights and shadows." Besides the ambiguity of Chinese color words, it should be pointed out that Wang tends to use both blue and green.

16. Quoted in Sirén, *On the Art of Painting*, 207.

17. Ibid., 203.

18. Ibid.

19. Ibid., 131.

20. Ibid., 140.

21. Ibid., 143.

22. Ibid., 203.

23. Guo Xi in *Meishu Congshu* (*Collected Works on Fine Arts*), comp. Huang Binhong and Deng Shi (rev. ed., Shanghai, 1947), part B, 9:10.

24. See Wang, quoted in Sirén, *On the Art of Painting*, 205.

25. Harrie A. Vanderstappen, "The Style of Some Seventeenth-Century Chinese Paintings" in *Artists and Traditions: Uses of the Past in Chinese Culture*, ed. Christian F. Murck (Princeton, N.J.: Princeton University Press, 1976), 165.

26. Pao-chao Hsieh, *The Government of China (1644–1911)* (New York: Johns Hopkins Press, 1925; reprint: Octagon, 1966), 166.

27. Chung-li Chang, *The Chinese Gentry: Studies on Their Role in Nineteenth-Century Chinese Society* (Seattle: University of Washington Press, 1955), 122.

28. Charles O. Hucker, *A Dictionary of Official Titles in Imperial China* (Stanford, Calif.: Stanford University Press, 1985), 223.

29. Hsieh, *Government of China*, 278.

30. Title as translated by Hucker, *Dictionary of Titles*, 207.

31. Hsieh, *Government of China*, 281.

32. Ibid., 119.

33. Ibid., 275.

116 **Hua Yan**, 1682–1756

Paths and Cliffs Beautiful under Clouds, 1746

Hanging scroll, ink and color on silk, 49 9/16 x 24 1/2 (125.9 x 62.2)
Purchase, Anonymous Gift
Acc. no. 1974.79

INSCRIPTIONS

Artist's poem and inscription:

Paths and cliffs beautiful under clouds and sun; peaks and
 ranges gorgeous under leek and cyan.
Trailing vines follow bending branches; hollow grottoes pierce
 the brilliant sky.
For folio and scroll, a decadence of figured brocade; for
 pillow and mat, a plethora of florescent blooms.
Secluded torrents toss a lively music; cascade and zephyr
 harmonize with soughing pines.
Early bamboo sports rank new shoots; sunlit valley resounds
 with oriole song.
This prospect has so many virtues, you need but cast your gaze
 to satisfy intellect and emotion.
When joy is found in only this, sincerely may you decline a
 fleeting fame.

On a spring day in the *Bingyin* year of the Qianlong era [1746], sketched and inscribed [at] the Pavilion of Mountains and Clouds in Vernal Verdure by Xinluo shanren.

SEALS

Lower left: zhi yin.
Upper right: you xin ru wei.
After artist's inscription, two seals: Hua Yan, Qiuyue

PROVENANCE

Nü Wa Chai Collection [Victoria Contag von Winterfeldt]; C. C. Wang, New York (1968).

PUBLICATIONS

Hamburg, *Chinesische Malerei*, cat. no. 83; Sirén, *Leading Masters*, 7:343; Suzuki, *Catalog*, no. A 2-004, 1:28, 424 and 5:177; Shan Guolin, ed., *Hua Yan shu hua ji* (*Collection of Paintings and Calligraphy by Hua Yan*) (Beijing: Wenwu chubanshe, 1987), 118.

Hua Yan was born the second son of an impoverished farmer and papermaker in the southern province of Fujian. His earliest extant painting, a practiced depiction of cranes under pine trees, is dated to 1697, when he was fifteen years old. In 1703, Hua moved to Hangzhou, where he joined a prominent group of scholars who included him in their excursions to temples and scenic places, as well as their poetry competitions and literary discussions. Hua studied literature and martial arts, hoping to become a government official, while he continued to make his living as a professional painter.

Around 1715, Hua traveled to Beijing to take the imperial examinations for government office. Although he passed in the top rank, since he held no degree he was only eligible for a minor local post. Declining this, he visited the famous cities and mountains of the north, then returned to the south, where he toured through Zhejiang province. Hua settled his family on a small farm outside Hangzhou, but in 1724, he visited the distant wealthy metropolis of Yangzhou, the center of a flourishing art market and bold new stylistic currents in painting.

In Yangzhou, Hua Yan met many of the leading painters of the day, including Jin Nong, Gao Xiang, Li Shan, and Zheng Xie, today counted among the "Eight Eccentrics of Yangzhou." Around 1730, Hua came to know Yuan Guotang, the merchant who became his patron and furnished him with a studio; he also gained the friendship of the brothers Ma Riguan and Ma Rilu, wealthy bibliophiles and art collectors. Through the scholarly gatherings they sponsored, Hua was able to see many masterworks of Song and Yuan dynasty painting in the collections of the Ma brothers' social circle.

Hua's range of subjects and his knowledge of painting styles were extraordinarily broad, and his skill in the use of ink tonality and ap-

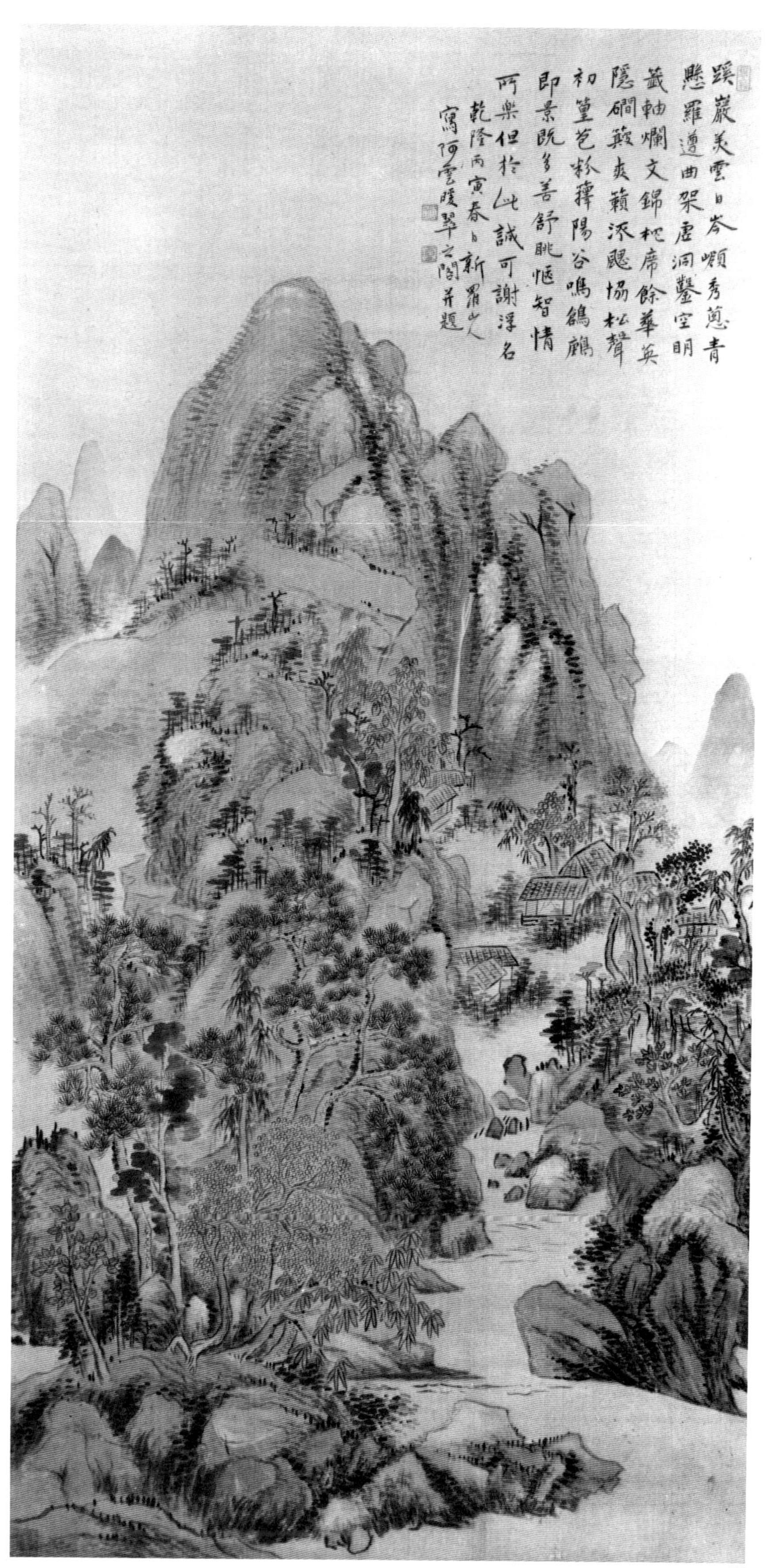

116

plication of color was matched by his sensitive control of the brush. In his own day, he was best known for bird-and-flower compositions which combined fine brushwork and luxuriant color with immediacy and whimsicality. He also found success as a figure painter, following the style of Chen Hongshou.

Hua's landscape paintings are more admired now than they were during his own time. Perhaps because he traveled so widely, his landscapes are quite varied, encompassing actual places, literary gatherings in landscape or garden settings, and imaginary scenes usually with references to the style of an earlier painter. The Smart Gallery painting is one of the latter. The composition harks back, ultimately, to a type of monumental landscape associated with the Northern Song painter Fan Kuan, and the rock forms, depicted with the hemp-fiber stroke (*pima cun*) and moss dots (*dian*), may be traced to sources in tenth-century landscapes by Dong Yuan and Juran.

The use of mineral blue and green also constitutes an evocation of the past, for even though strong colors had been revived among amateur painters during the middle of the Ming dynasty—professional painters had used them all along—blue-and-green landscape painting still held the connotation of extreme antiquity or the realm of the immortals. This evocation of other worlds is associated with escape or respite from mundane routine, especially pressures of office, echoing the sentiment of the poem inscribed on the painting, with its prescription for avoiding the stress of "fleeting fame." The theme of the Smart Gallery painting and the sentiment of the poem take on a particular poignancy when we remember Hua Yan's failed aspirations for a career as an official.

The authenticity of this painting, however, is not universally accepted. The wording of the inscription is somewhat jumbled, reversing two characters in the name of the pavilion—of Clouds and Mountains, not Mountains and Clouds—where the scroll was painted. The melting ink tone and delicate brushwork of many of Hua's other works are not in evidence here, nor any hint of the quirky or odd. Yet the composition has Hua's solidity of construction, the brushwork is assured and elegantly understated, and the calligraphy of the inscription is convincing. A.M.

117 **Tong Yu**, 1721–1782
Plum Blossom

Hanging scroll, ink on paper, 33½ x 10¾ (85.1 x 27.3)
Gift of Richard and Mali Edmonds
Acc. no. 1988.6

INSCRIPTIONS
Artist's poem:
Early sunlight falls on the curtain [bamboo, fence]
A dark fragrance drifts about
I am putting it in this painting
The Spring breeze cannot dispel it.
[signed] Tong Yu.[1]

SEALS
After artist's signature, two seals: Tong Yu zhi yin, Shujoshi.
Lower left, artist's seal: Wan Fu Mei Hua Wan Shou Shi.
Lower right, collector's seal: Yi Chuan Kao Cang hua yin.

PUBLICATIONS
Bulletin, 35–36 (illus.).

Born in Shaoxing, Zhejiang province, the literatus Tong Yu was active in Qiantu near Yangzhou in neighboring Kiangsu province. An amateur painter of landscapes as well as flowers but most highly regarded for his plum blossom paintings,[2] he was also a poet, seal carver, and collector of old seals. Although Tong's activity conforms to conventional descriptions found in biographies of mid-Qing gentlemen-scholars, his engagement with painting, poetry, and seal connoisseurship may also betray his origins near Hangzhou, the cultural center of Zhejiang renowned for seal carving in the antique manner in the eighteenth century.[3] Osvald Sirén identified Tong as one of "a number of younger painters who followed lines of expressionistic ink-painting similar to those of the Yangchou [Yangzhou] masters,"[4] individualist painters collectively known by the late nineteenth century as the "Eight Eccentrics of Yangzhou." These independent painters—most of whom were not native to Yangzhou but drawn there by the patronage of newly wealthy salt merchants and businessmen—were often penniless scholars or failed officials who earned their living through the sale of their paintings. They institutionalized nonconformity in defiance of the conventional values of life and art in the Qianlong Emperor's court.[5]

The Smart Gallery hanging scroll of flowering plum branches is painted in the monochrome ink-plum or *momei* genre, which stresses the expressive concerns of the painter over the faithful depiction of the subject.[6] The downgrading of the Song academy's representational virtuosity by the early practitioners of *momei*, the origins of which are traditionally ascribed to the Buddhist monk Zhongren (d. 1123), was accomplished through the elevation of brushwork and the "ink-play" idiom of calligraphy. In *Plum Blossom*, Tong Yu combines two venerable ink-plum techniques developed during the Southern Song: the "circled-petal" or *quanban* method and the reverse-saturation or *daoyun* method. He covers the entire surface of the painting with a pale-gray ink wash except for the petals, which are left in reserve and then further defined by flicks of a brush dipped in rich black ink and applied quickly to create modulated outlines and irregular blotches.

The calligraphic ink play in Tong's plum blossom painting varies from broad, wet, medium-gray to gray or black striated "flying white" (*feibai*) brushstrokes caused by the uneven discharge of ink during the drag of the partially loaded brush across the surface of the paper. The saturated, coal-black, blunt dabs and quick trailings that puddle and diffuse when set down on the dampened paper are overlaid by wet, diluted gray passages forming the stems of the branches. The dabs are suggestive—but not descriptive—of ancient fungal growth, old stubs, or new shoots. The brusk, linear type of stroke used for the austere branches blots at point of contact with the paper, thins as it is pulled over the surface, and then thickens when the brush is lifted off the scroll, all in one rapid gesture. The cursive script (*caoshu*) of the accompanying inscription is executed in much the same manner. Overall, the flux and flow of inkiness, dry and wet tracks of the brush, and swift, controlled consistency of the brushwork are the same in picture and text.

By the late Ming, ink-plum specialists in Zhejiang, such as Liu Shiru (active in the sixteenth century), had identified with the plum blossom lineage of Wang Mian (d. 1359) and Chen Lu (active 1436–49). Characterized by strong surface pattern, flattened forms, and formal rather than organic relations between branch and trunk or bud and stem, this continuing tradition further distanced the genre from naturalistic description during the early Qing period. Tong Yu's abbreviated format in *Plum Blossom*—the plum tree reduced to a pair of downward arching branches with abrupt tangential shoots, and the setting pared to a pale wash ground—was fully comprehensible to the connoisseur of the mid-Qing period precisely because of the ongoing transmission of the *momei* heritage; thus, it is not surprising to find a nearly identical composition in Liu Shiru's earlier undated scroll, *Plum in Snow* (New York, Metropolitan Museum of Art). Nonetheless, the immediate stylistic predecessors for Tong Yu are the individualist painters of the seventeenth century, in particular Daoji and Mei Qing, and the eccentric artists of his own day, gathered around Yangzhou.

The inclusion of a poetic inscription on the Smart Gallery painting is unexceptional within the ink-plum tradition, since after around 1200 artists recognized that the combination established a resonance beyond the capacity of image or words alone. What is new in the middle Qing period is the integration of ink-play painting, idiosyncratic calligraphy, and seals into a formal and expressive unity, as exemplified in the work of Jin Nong (1687–1763), one of the "eccentric painters" of Yangzhou. Tong also orchestrates such formal correspondences: between the calligraphic painting method and cursive script, in the tonal range of inks employed, by the placement of the text within the space of the plum branches, and through the subtle reiteration of the configuration of stems and branches by the unequal lines of compressed and elongated characters.

Equally significant is the expressive interplay between text and image. The moment evoked by the poem—when sun and warm spring breezes just begin to dispel wintry dampness—is also suggested by the tight blossoms' petals in the painting. Because the plum tree flowers at the end of winter, when cold and snow still threaten, the barely opened buds on stark branches are reminders of winter's lingering hold. In general, the plum blossom was seen from the Song as an emblem of both transience and longevity, since during the seasonal cycle it suffered damage but flowered anew before all other plants after the barren winter months. This symbolism, moreover, is expressed in the Smart Gallery painting by the well-established motif of snapped branches combined with new shoots and opening buds. By the eighteenth century, there had accumulated a rich five-hundred year literary tradition of lofty symbolism associated with the flowering plum, and the prunus had come to stand for the integrity of the recluse scholar and his resilient virtue. Particularly suited to literati painters and failed civil servants, it was a favorite literary and pictorial subject of the Yangzhou masters.

R.A.B.

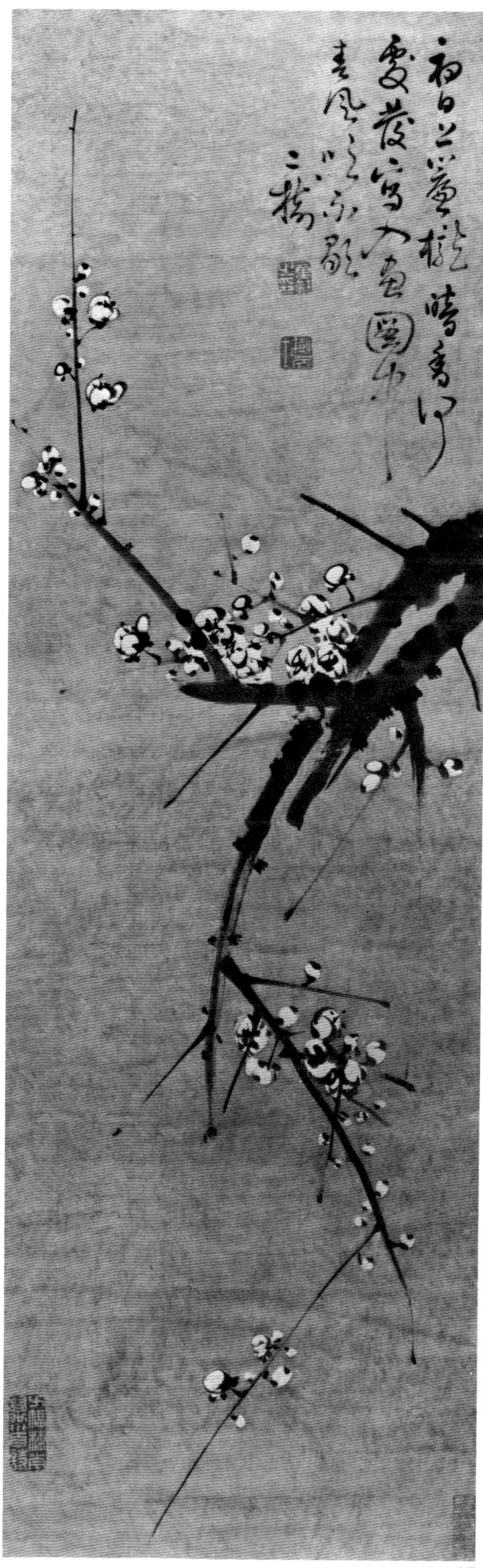

117

NOTES

1. Translation by Professor Harrie Vanderstappen.
2. Another of Tong Yu's ink-plum paintings, *Prunus Blossom and Moon*, a hanging scroll in ink on paper, is in the Montreal Museum of Fine Arts, Quebec; see Barry Till, *Chinese Paintings in Canadian Collections* (exh. cat.) (Victoria, B. C.: Art Gallery of Greater Victoria, 1982), cat. no. 32.
3. The center of Zhe School painting in the fifteenth and sixteenth centuries (see cat. no. 100), Hangzhou was the seat of an influential school of textual research, *kaoju*,

in the seventeenth century; by the eighteenth century the city's literati had directed their considerable knowledge of archaic texts carved in stone or cast in bronze toward the revival of the art of ancient seal carving, establishing the new "Zhe School" of superior seal carvers called the "Eight Xileng Masters," who, like Tong Yu, were also calligraphers and painters. See Jung Ying Tsao, *Chinese Paintings of the Middle Qing Dynasty* (San Francisco: San Francisco Graphic Society, 1987), 124.

4. Osvald Sirén, *Chinese Painting: Leading Masters and Principles*, 7 vols. (London: Lund Humphries and Co., 1956–58), 5:237.

5. On the Yangzhou masters, see Art Gallery, Institute of Chinese Studies, Chinese University of Hong Kong, *Paintings by Yangzhou Artists of the Qing Dynasty from the Palace Museum* (exh. cat.) (Hong Kong: Art Gallery, Institute of Chinese Studies, Chinese University of Hong Kong, 1984), 21–32. For the economic and social background of middle-Qing Yangzhou, see also Ho Ping-ti, "The Salt Merchants of Yangzhou: A Study of Commercial Capitalism in Eighteenth-Century China," *Harvard Journal of Asiatic Studies* 17 (1954): 130–168, and William Henry Scott, "Yangchow and Its Eight Eccentrics," *Asiatische Studien* 17 (1964): 1–19, esp. 1–5.

6. For a thorough account in English of the flowering plum tradition in literature and the visual arts, see Maggie Bickford, *Bones of Jade, Soul of Ice: The Flowering Plum in Chinese Art* (exh. cat.) (New Haven, Conn.: Yale University Art Gallery, 1985).

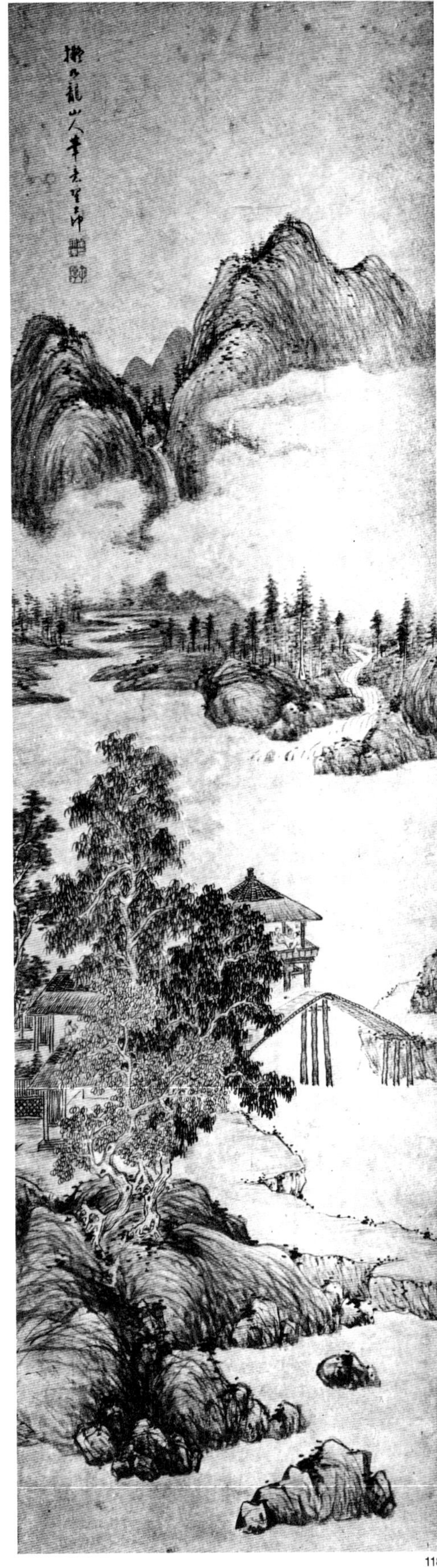

118

118 **Zhai Dakun**, d. 1804
Landscape (after Wang Fu), circa 1790–1800

Hanging scroll, ink on gold-flecked paper, 61⅝ x 18 (156.5 x 45.7)
Purchase, Anonymous Gift
Acc. no. 1974.85

INSCRIPTIONS
Artist's inscription:
An interpretation of the brush concept of Jiulongshanren [Wang Fu] by Zhai Dakun.

SEALS
After artist's inscription, two seals: Zhai Dakun yin, Zihou [Zai Dakun's *zi*].

PROVENANCE
Nü Wa Chai Collection [Victoria Contag von Winterfeldt]; C. C. Wang, New York (1968).

PUBLICATIONS
Hamburg, *Chinesische Malerei*, cat. no. 108; Sirén, *Leading Masters*, 7:285; Suzuki, *Catalog*, no. A 2-009, 1:29, 424 and 5:177.

Like many other Qing dynasty artists influenced by the Orthodox School, Zhai Dakun often copied earlier masterpieces from the Orthodox canon—paintings by Wang Wei (699–759), for example, Dong Yuan (d. 962), Juran (active circa 960–980), and famous Yuan literati including Gao Kegong (1248–1310), Huang Gongwang (1269–1354), Wang Meng (1308–1385), and Fang Congyi (d. 1393).[1] Zhai lived most of his life in Suzhou, Jiangsu province, where he absorbed the lingering influence of the earlier Ming dynasty Wu School. Qing dynasty authors such as Qin Zuyong indicate that Zhai followed Wu School painters Shen Zhou (1427–1509) and Chen Shun (1483–1544) in painting *xiesheng* or "sketches from life"—in this context a broad category of themes including plants, animals and insects—and that he was deeply influenced by Shen's landscapes.[2] Extant paintings reveal that Zhai also was drawn to the expressive landscapes of Tang Yin (1470–1524).[3]

The Smart Gallery landscape is a creative interpretation of the style or brush concept (*biyi*) of Wang Fu (1362–1416), a native of Wuxi, Jiangsu, who served at the Ming court as a draftsman in the Central Drafting Office. Wang Fu achieved fame during his lifetime for his dashing bamboo compositions and landscapes, the latter of which were often painted in the styles of his immediate predecessors Wang Meng and Ni Zan. Wang Fu's own personal style differs only subtly from such late Yuan models, and consequently few later artists attempted paintings "in his style." Though the path leading to the hermitage in this landscape invites us to enter the scene in imagination, Zhai's inscription suggests that he intends for us to move through time rather than space, exploring the ideas and sources for Wang Fu's landscapes. Overlaying the pleasant scenery is Zhai's interpretation of Wang Fu's adoption of Wang Meng's personal appropriation of the tradition established by Dong Yuan. Zhai notes the origins of this artistic lineage, using the dotting technique and hemp-fiber stroke (*pima cun*) associated with Dong Yuan. The particularly dense texturing and energetically posed trees recall Wang Meng's manner of depicting idyllic retreats. This much was fairly standard by the Qing dynasty. The challenge for Zhai was to articulate the special qualities of Wang Fu's interpretation of Wang Meng, since Wang Fu's personal style was less distinctive than that of his great predecessor and model. Zhai relied on his knowledge of Wang Fu's brush mannerisms to add this final layer of allusion. The Wang Fu "personal stamp" is particularly noticeable in the foreground, in the fluidly fluctuating contour lines of the large boulder protruding from the water, and in the expressively haphazard display of criss-crossing texture strokes that define the landmass near the trees.[4]

The influence of Shen Zhou noted by Qing authors is not especially obvious in this and many other surviving landscapes by Zhai Dakun. On reflection, however, it is apparent that like Shen, Zhai was drawn to earlier paintings celebrating a contented harmony with nature. Here Zhai expresses a nostalgic fondness for this enduring ideal and impresses the viewer with his extensive knowledge of earlier painting traditions.

K.L.

NOTES

1. Li Yufen, *Ouboloshi shuhua guomu kao*, pref. dated 1894, 3:31, describes a painting in the style of Fang Congyi. For the others, see Osvald Sirén, *Chinese Painting: Leading Masters and Principles* (London: Lund Humphries and Co., 1956–58), 7:285; Ju-hsi Chou and Claudia Brown, *The Elegant Brush: Chinese Painting under the Qianlong Emperor, 1735–1795* (exh. cat.) (Phoenix: Phoenix Art Museum, 1985), no. 85; and Tseng Yu-ho Ecke, *Wen-jen Hua: Chinese Literati Painting from the Collection of Mr. and Mrs. Mitchell Hutchinson* (exh. cat.) (Honolulu: Honolulu Academy of Arts, 1988), no. 48.
2. Qin Zuyong, *Tongyin lunhua*, pref. dated 1864, part 1, 1:23.
3. Chou and Brown, *The Elegant Brush*, no. 85, leaf E, and Ecke, *Wen-jen Hua*, no. 48, leaf 2.
4. For Wang Fu's painting style, see James Cahill, *Parting at the Shore: Chinese Painting of the Early and Middle Ming Dynasty, 1368–1580* (New York and Tokyo: John Weatherhill, 1978), 58–59 and pls. 22–23, and Kathlyn Liscomb, "Wang Fu's Contribution to the Formation of a New Painting Style in the Ming Dynasty," *Artibus Asiae* 47 (1987): 39–78.

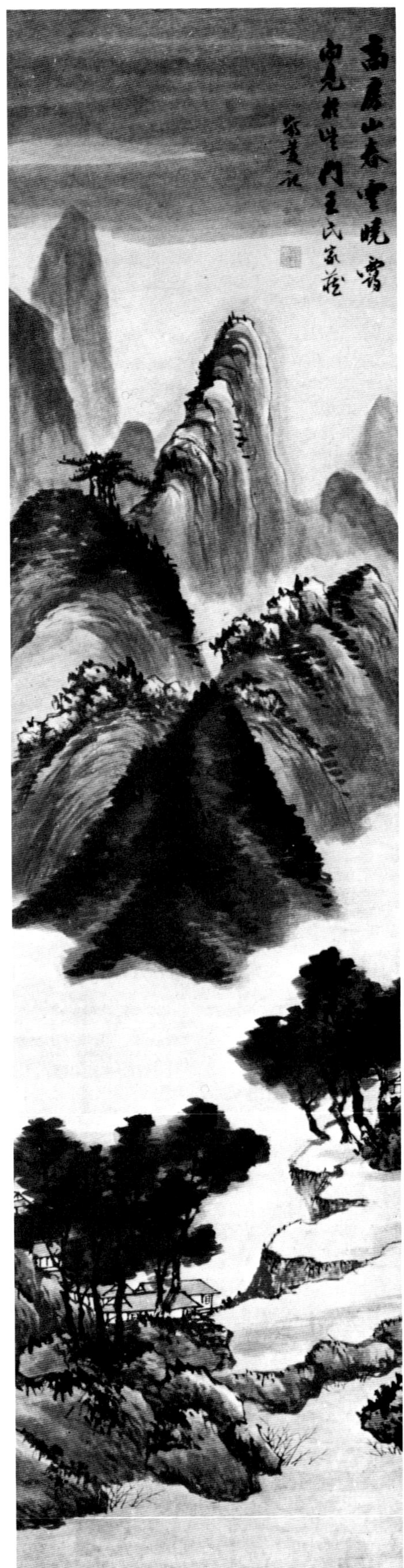

119

119 **Gu Haoqing**, 1766–circa 1830
Rain View, circa 1810

Hanging scroll, ink and color on paper, $55\frac{1}{4}$ x $14\frac{5}{16}$ (140.3 x 37.2)
Purchase, Anonymous Gift
Acc. no. 1974.81

INSCRIPTIONS
Artist's inscription:
Gao Fangshan's [Gao Kegong's] bright clouds in early spring, which I saw in the collection of the family estate of Mr. Wang. [signed] Gu Haoqing.

SEALS
After artist's signature, two seals: Taoan Hua Han, Gu Haoqing yin.

PROVENANCE
Nü Wa Chai Collection [Victoria Contag von Winterfeldt]; C. C. Wang, New York (1968).

PUBLICATIONS
Hamburg, *Chinesische Malerei*, cat. no. 111; Sirén, *Leading Masters*, 7:362.

Little is known about Gu Haoqing, whose other names include Ziyu, Taoan, and Gu Yiliu. He was from Dantu in Jiangsu province and is identified more as a poet-calligrapher than as a painter. Accordingly, he was considered locally a person of the "Three Accomplishments"—poetry, calligraphy, and painting.[1] He belonged to a society of poets called the "Seven Sons of Jingjiang," centered at the house of Wang Yu (Wang Yinhe, Liucun) in Dantu. Wang is undoubtedly the Mr. Wang in the inscription in whose collection Gu saw the painting by Gao Kegong (1248–circa 1310), to which the Smart Gallery landscape is a reprise.

As already mentioned in the introduction to this section of the catalogue, this painting reflects a well-known manner deriving from the Northern Song self-styled literatus Mi Fu (1051–1107) and handed down through the Southern Song painter Gao Kegong into later Chinese painting traditions. Here, the wet ink, repeated triangular shapes, and clearly defined clouds and trees—all part of the vocabulary of the Mi manner of painting—are directly and explicitly stated. H.A.V.

NOTES
1. For a concise discussion of the "Three Accomplishments," also called the "Three Perfections," see Michael Sullivan, *The Three Perfections: Chinese Painting and Poetry and Calligraphy* (London: Thames and Hudson, 1974).

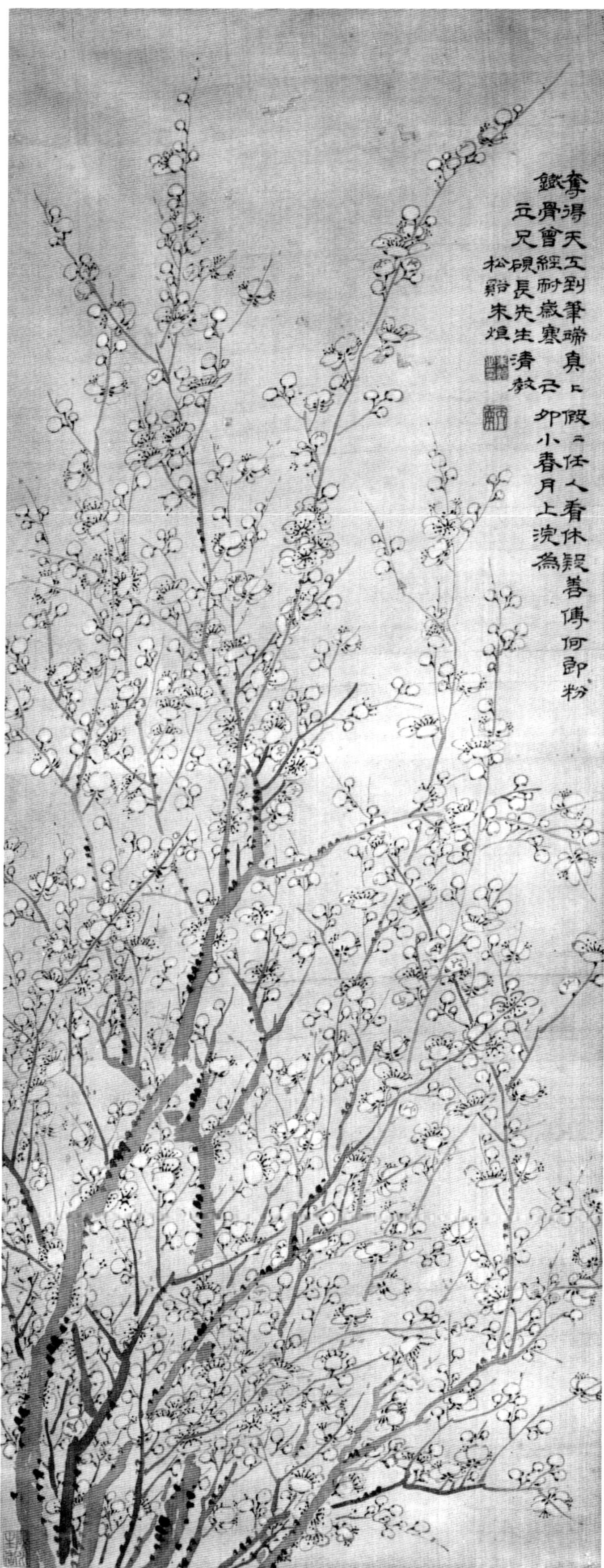

120

120 **Zhu Xuan**, active circa 1790–1820
Plum Blossoms, 1819

Hanging scroll, ink on silk, 34 15/16 x 13 11/16 (88.7 x 34.8)
Purchase, Gift of Mr. and Mrs. Gaylord Donnelley
Acc. no. 1974.96

INSCRIPTIONS
Artist's inscription:
Heavenly skills are secured in the tip of my brush,
Those who know will see if that is true or false.
All the beauty is in the sheen of the blossoms, why add color,
Like metal and bone they have withstood the season's cold.

In the *Jimao* year [1819], in the early spring, respectfully made for Mr. Yan Chang. [signed] Songxi Zhu Xuan.

SEALS
After artist's signature, two seals: Zhu Xuan zhi yin, Bing Nan.
Lower left, collector's seal: Yan Guang Sheng Xiang.

PROVENANCE
Nakanishi, Kyoto (1971).

Very little is known about Zhu Xuan. Coming from Hangxian in Zhejiang province, he is recorded to have painted landscapes, flowers, and plum blossoms. There is another plum blossom painting by Zhu, dated 1789,[1] which indicates that he was active for at least thirty years. No teacher is listed, but judging from the 1789 *Plum Blossoms*, he is clearly indebted to the "Yangzhou Eccentric" Jin Nong (1687–1763). If Zhu is a direct pupil of Jin, he would have been around seventy when he painted the Smart Gallery hanging scroll. How much the present painting depends on Jin is clear when it is compared, for example, with his *Flowering Plum Branches* of 1754 (Beijing, Palace Museum),[2] in which a rich and finely textured cloud of blossoms spreads over the surface of the painting from the lower left.

The Smart Gallery painting in the ink-plum (*momei*) tradition and its inscription correspond to the standard plum blossom metaphor. In its simplicity and fragrance, the prunus is the harbinger of new life growing from old, seemingly dead wood, barely waiting for winter to fade and snow to melt before sprouting its delicate blossoms. Without the trimmings of color and ornament, the blossoms are the life-breath of nature; even their shadows on moonlit paper windows are fully expressive of their inner life, in accordance with the *momei* reverse saturation (*daoyun*) method of ink wash ground evoking the prunus in moonlight. Contrasted in this painting in light tones against the gray wash background, the blossoming branches reverberate with the same meaning. H.A.V.

NOTES

1. See Wai-fong Anita Siu, *The Modern Spirit in Chinese Painting: Selections from the Jeannette Shambaugh Elliott Collection* (exh. cat.) (Phoenix: Phoenix Art Museum, 1985), 8–9 (illus.).
2. Published in François Fourcade, *Peking Museum: Paintings and Ceramics* (London: Thames and Hudson, 1965), 106–107, cat. no. 43.

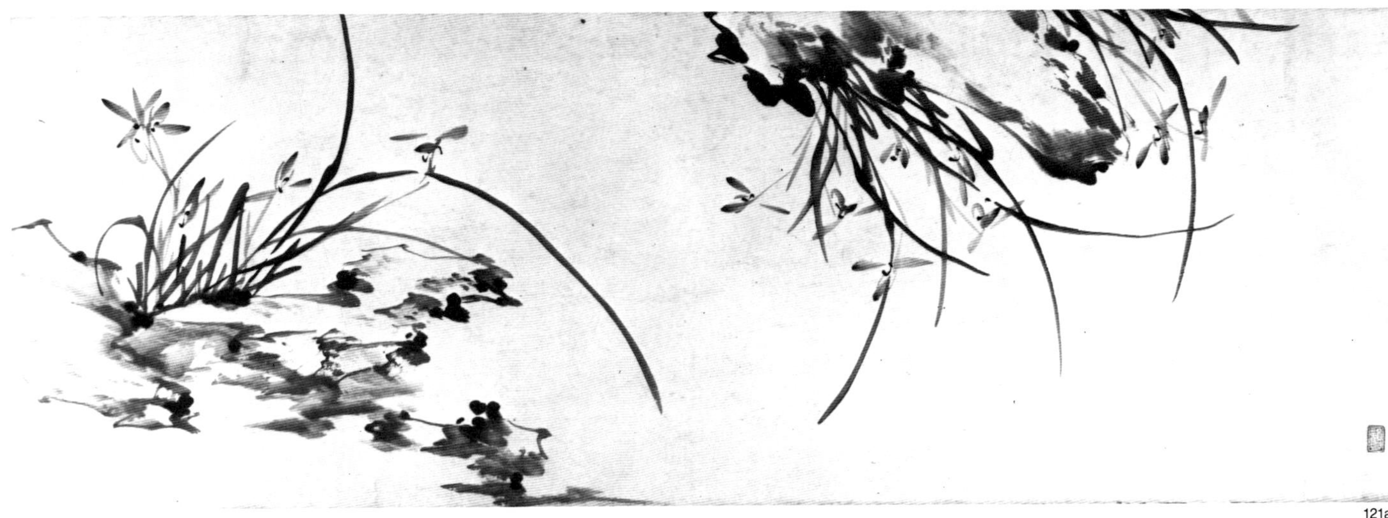

121a

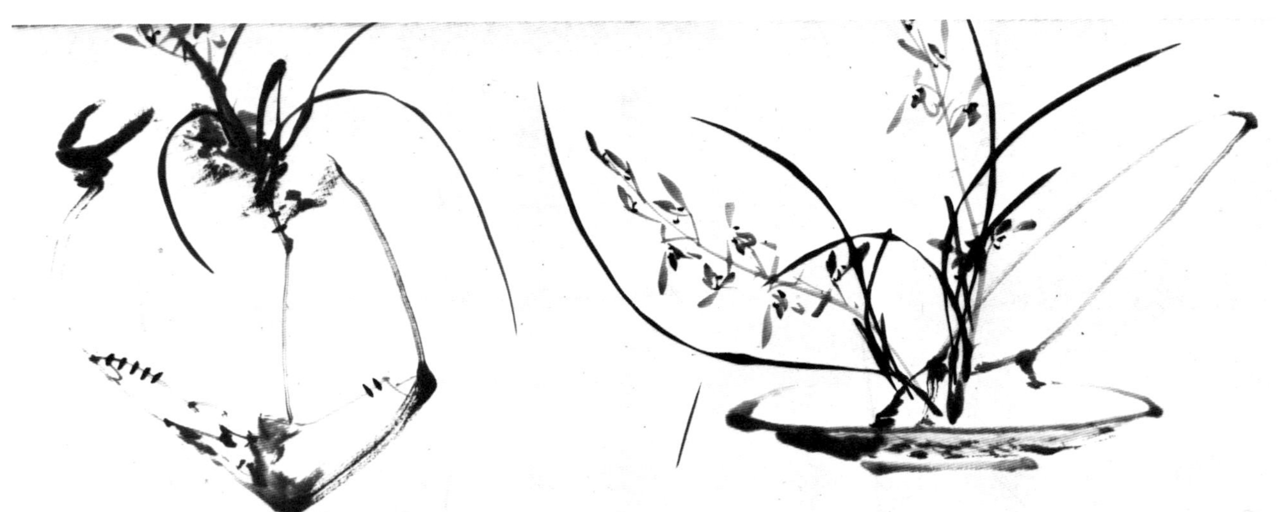

121b

121 **Yun Xiang**, d. 1827
Orchids, 1824

Handscroll, ink on paper, four painting panels: 13 1/4 x 37 11/16 (33.7 x 95.7), 13 1/4 x 37 3/4 (33.7 x 95.9), 13 1/4 x 37 3/4 (33.7 x 95.9), 13 1/4 x 37 3/8 (33.7 x 94.9); colophon panel: 13 1/4 x 107 1/2 (33.7 x 273.1)
Gift of Warren G. Moon, Ph.D. 1975, in behalf of Harrie Vanderstappen
Acc. no. 1983.9

INSCRIPTIONS

Artist's inscription, on fourth section of scroll:
I have heard that there is a field of flowers in Guangdong. This field is the capital where the flowers grow. The great retired scholar of the "Bamboo Tower" served as an official in Yue [Guangdong] for many years. The small grasses covered by the shade of the *tang* tree grow in splendor. With reverence, I have painted this scroll and offer it as a gift. Although I have not been able to convey the kindness and compassion of these plants in the flower field or been able to convey the beneficial influence one can receive through intimacy with them, I have been able closely to imbue the image with the deep veneration I have for them. Painted in the eighth month of Autumn, 1824. The sixth scroll of orchids. [signed] The Daoist nun Yun Xiang of Xi Shan.

Unidentified collector's colophon on fifth section of scroll:
This scroll was brought from the north back to the capital by a member of the family of Hu Cipu, the salt distribution commissioner. The scroll had inscriptions by many noteworthy men, but suddenly, the various sheets of paper with the inscriptions were lost. By chance, while perusing the *Qiangcun yishu*,[1] I found these two poems and I record them here, at the end of the scroll.[2] The scroll is in its original form. Her [Yun Xiang's] inscription and signature have not been altered, and the original needle holes and creases have not perished.

The salt distribution commissioner, [Hu] Cipu, had gathered up the sheets of inscriptions [that were appended to the painting] but has not yet had them mounted, wishing to preserve the scroll's state as it originally existed over one hundred years ago.

Written in 1944, during the last ten days of *liqiu* [the first fifteen days of autumn], in the *Chengguan tang*. From the time of [Yun Xiang's] original inscription, it is exactly one hundred-twenty years.

Collector's inscription by Ye Gongchuo on fifth section of scroll:
The story of "Qingwei Daoren" [Yun Xiang] has been told long before, so I shall not waste words by repeating it here. My family has long had in its possession her painting, *Kongshan tingyu tu* [*Listening to the Rain in the Empty Mountains*]. The inscriptions on it are as numerous as the trees in a forest. This painting was the favorite treasure of my ancestor, Nan Xue [Ye Yanlan]. Later, the painting passed into the hands of Xu Jiyu [also called] Naichang. I bargained with him for the painting, but he died before we could settle on a price. I do not know the whereabouts of a number of the things in his collection and for a long time had been anxious [about this painting]. Now, I, too, can no longer preserve my own collection, nor my own existence, and therefore have already entrusted these things to the mist and clouds that pass before one's eyes. This scroll is what I have harbored within my original feelings. Its style is soft, beautiful and graceful, truly of Yun Xiang's distinctive character. The mysteries of the cosmos remain as they have always been, and the person who has passed away is not far away. I do not know the surname of the "retired scholar of the 'Bamboo Tower.'" This scroll was given as a gift to him, who had gone to serve as an official in Yue [Guangdong]. Truly, fate has joined me with this official of Yue.[3] The thirty-seventh year of the Republic [1948]. [signed] Xiaweng [Ye Gongchuo].

SEALS

First panel, lower left: Yun Xiang.
Second panel, lower right: Qingwei nüdaoren shuhua zhi zhang.
Third panel, lower right: suxin zhuren.
Fourth panel, upper right, adjacent to artist's inscription: ming yue qian shen.
Fourth panel, after artist's inscription, two seals: Qingwei daoren, Yun Xiang.
Fifth panel, after unidentified collector's colophon, two seals of the writer: jialin xihu, shishi tianquan.
Fifth panel, after Ye Gongchuo's colophon: Gongchuo.

PROVENANCE

Collection of the unidentified writer of the first colophon (1944); Ye Gongchuo (1948); A. C. Scott (1948); Professor Warren G. Moon, Madison, Wisconsin.

The Smart Gallery scroll of orchids was painted in the autumn of 1824 by an artist from Wuxi, Jiangsu province, named Wang Jinglian.[4] Some biographical sources identify her as Wang Lian or Wang Yuelian.[5] Her *zi* was Yun Xiang, and her *hao* severally were Yujing Daoren, Qingwei Daoren, and Erquan. Yun herself mentions that when she was young her parents, following the advice of a fortune teller, placed her in a Buddhist convent.[6] At the age of nineteen, she left the convent to become a follower of Daoism.[7] She was skilled in calligraphy, painting, and poetry, and could sing and play the *qin* (Chinese zither). She was especially noted for her *xiaokai* style calligraphy, and for her paintings of orchids and bamboo. Two texts by her are recorded—the *Qingfen jingshe xiaoji* (*Small Record of the Fragrant Villa*) and the *Shuozhu* (*Explanations on Bamboo*).

Yun attracted the attention of numerous high officials and literati, many of whom wrote inscriptions on her paintings. One such painting, *Kongshan tingyu tu* (*Listening to the Rain in the Empty Mountains*), which was lost during her lifetime, possibly more than once, bore inscriptions by over five hundred people.[8] Deng Zhicheng claims that her relationships with these admirers were not always proper, and a contemporary source, written the year after her death and quoted by Ding Chuanjing, claims that her suicide by hanging resulted from relationships with three (unnamed) officials.[9] Marsha Weidner suggests that Yun might have been one of a number of Daoist nuns who lived as courtesans.[10] Other sources allude to some incident or incidents involving one of her visitors, and perhaps the painting *Kongshan tingyu tu*, which caused her to take her own life on the eve of her forty-ninth birthday (that is, on New Year's Eve, since birthdays were traditionally celebrated on New Year's Day). Yet, another source notes that when Yun entertained guests, she always sat off to the side and never improperly close.[11]

The Smart Gallery handscroll consists of four sections, depicting orchids sprouting among floating rocks, in a shallow pan, and from a broken pot. The fourth panel contains an inscription signed and dated by Yun. Appended to the end of the scroll is a fifth section bearing two inscriptions, the first written in 1944 by someone as yet unidentified and the second in 1948 by Ye Gongchuo (1880–1968), a prominent railway administrator.[12] Nothing suggests that the scroll was not always mounted in sections as it is now; and indeed the writer of the 1944 inscription, noting the creases and incised lines running vertically between the lines of Yun's inscription, and the needle holes she used as guides, states that the scroll was mounted as it had been originally. The ink blotches and brushstrokes that run beyond the edges of the paper and onto the backing further suggest the artist painted the orchids after the scroll had been mounted.

On the first section of the scroll, Yun depicts two groups of rocks and orchids, paired diagonally across a drifting space. The first cluster juts in from above, pulling the composition leftward across an angling space towards the second clump of flowers, which rises from the bottom of the panel and draws the eye into the next section. Like the opening section, this one splits along an angled space separating two orchid clusters. Here, the first group stretches out of a shallow pan and leans towards the second, which sprouts from a tipped, broken pot. The character and tempo of the movement change in the third panel, where orchids and rocks alternate in a horizontal staccato across the scroll. In the final section, orchids and a strangely shaped rock jut down to the right from the upper edge. From the center, orchids stretch towards the undulating contour of this rock, and also set off the low, drifting rocks that end the scroll. In the space at the upper left, framed by rocks below and orchids to the right, appears Yun's inscription.

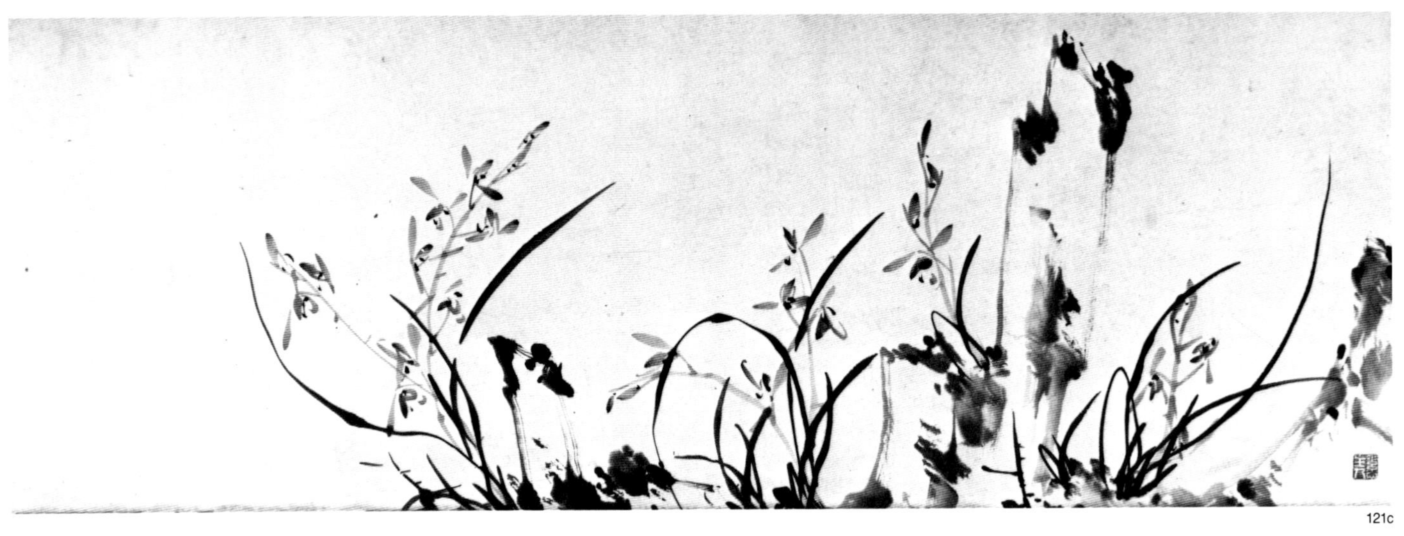

121c

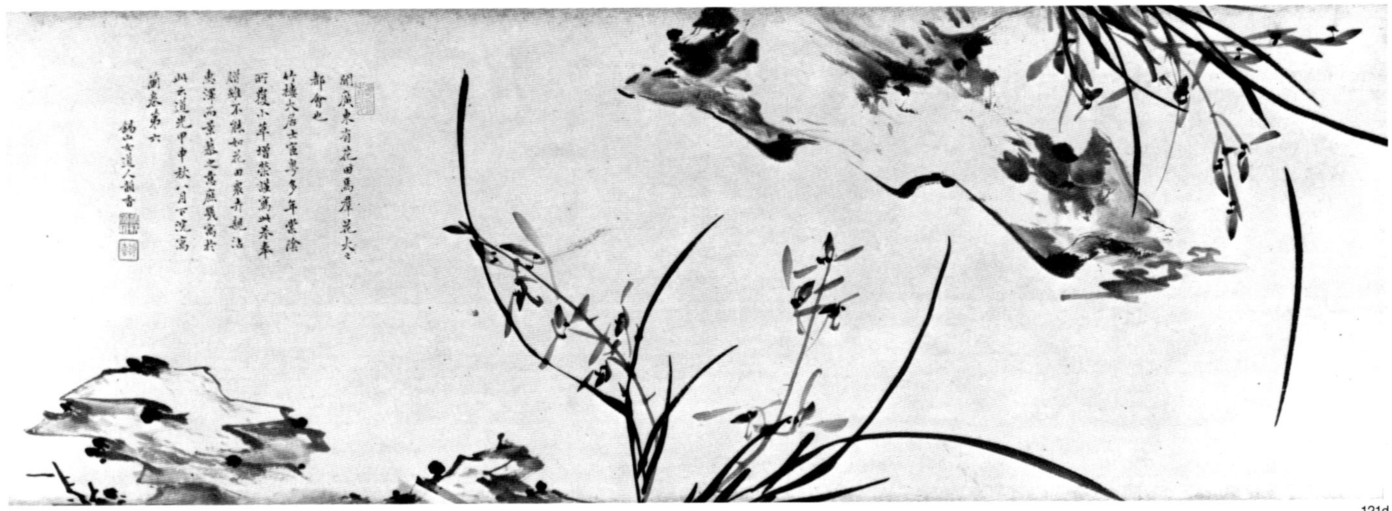

121d

121e

Yun's orchids belong to a long painting tradition that extends at least as far back as Zheng Sixiao (1241–1318). But whereas Zheng's lone, rootless orchid projects the depth and purity of Confucian virtue, Yun's orchids dance in capricious play. She delights in confounding our expectations: at the beginning of the scroll, what at first seems upside down is in fact right-side up. In the second section, the orchids appear to be both in front of the handle of the pan as well as behind it, while the handle itself alternates between a sidelong view and a frontal one. Further to the left, the broken pot, sketched in a few blotchy strokes and dry, diaphanous lines, is not readily recognizable. It tilts precariously on one corner, floating in space. Throughout the scroll, Yun manipulates ink blotches, washes, long and short curving brushstrokes, thin floating lines, and empty space in a perplexing fantasy. Her manner, swift and somewhat slick, and her fondness for ambiguity bring to mind paintings by Bada Shanren (1626–1705); Bada, however, used ambiguity of space, line, and border to vivify his images with the power of nature. Yun sees ambiguity as a kind of riddle. Her flowers confuse, tease, delight, and finally charm.

According to the *Guangzhou fuzhi*, the flower field Yun mentions in her inscription lay some three miles west of the prefectural seat, Guangzhou fu, and was planted with jasmine (*suxin*).[13] The *Nanzhenglu* says that during the Southern Han, in Liu Yin's time (874–911),[14] beautiful women were buried there, and subsequently the flowers gave off an exceptional fragrance, unequalled by flowers in other places.[15] Yun identifies the flower field as a capital, or seat of governance; hence, the flowers allude to officials who ruled in Guangzhou, such as the "retired scholar of the Bamboo Tower." Yun elaborates her metaphor by referring to the shade of the *tang* tree. The expression *tang yin* refers to the official Shao Gong, son of Zhou Wen Wang by a concubine. Shao, while on an inspection tour of the south, stopped beneath the shade of a *tang* tree to conduct administrative affairs. His governance, fair and just, earned him a reputation for wise rule, and after his death the *tang* tree came to signify his virtue.[16] Thus, the small grasses in Yun's inscription—a Confucian metaphor for the people—have flourished under the virtuous shade of the "retired scholar of the Bamboo Tower."

In the next lines, Yun states that she has painted these orchids as a gift and apologizes for her inability to evoke the benevolent influence—*qinzhan* and *huize*—of the flowers. The first character in *qinzhan* suggests intimacy, such as one has with a close relative or lover. The second character, *zhan*, means to moisten or soak and, by extension, to enrich or make prosperous. Therefore, *qinzhan* might mean something like "to be benefited or influenced by closeness or intimacy with another." *Hui*, the first character of the expression *huize*, means blessing, favor, kindness, or mercy. It can also act as a verb, "to render benevolence." The meaning of *ze*, a swamp or marsh, is close to that of *zhan*; *ze* can by extension also mean blessing or beneficence and, as a verb, "to bestow benevolence upon." Consequently, the expression *huize* might mean something like "the kindness, compassion, beneficence, or good influence bestowed upon one by another."

The orchids in Yun's painting, then, allude to the public character of "the retired scholar of the Bamboo Tower," and also to his personal virtue, felt intimately by the artist. As early as Han times, when the lore about Qu Yuan became an established Confucian tradition, orchids have been poetic images for moral probity. Qu was an official serving the southern state of Chu. When some ministers, envious of his close relationship with the king, convinced the latter that Qu was disloyal and unworthy of office, the king banished him to a remote region. During his exile, Qu wrote a long poem, the "Lisao" ("Encountering Sorrow"), deploring the wretchedness of his fate.[17] Because the irony of his situation was insufferable, and with no alternative to unwavering loyalty, he drowned himself in the Mi Le River. Qu's lament, the "Lisao," abounds in flower imagery; of the many kinds of flowers mentioned, it was the orchid that became the emblem of the "Lisao" and the personification of Qu himself.

But the symbolic aspect of the orchid reached beyond the legend of Qu to embody the virtue of the ideal Confucian gentleman, the *junzi*. Huang Tingjian observes that orchids were valued before Qu's time and likens the orchid to the *junzi*:

> Growing in a thicket of other plants or deep within mountains, the orchid releases its fragrance, whether or not there are people nearby. Despite the relentless onslaught of winter, an orchid will not waver from its true nature. . . . The orchid, concealing its fragrance, and maintaining its purity, will grow among weeds and seem no different from them, but when a pure breeze blows, it will release its lush perfume. When in a room, its fragrance will fill the room. When in a hall, its fragrance will fill the hall. This is what is called, "concealing one's beauty until the appropriate time."[18]

The orchid's fragrance is its most exceptional quality; pure and beautiful, it permeates and affects its surroundings. Likewise, given its proper time, the virtue of the *junzi* touches and affects the surrounding world. By Yun's time, the metaphorical significance of orchids had become a well-established tradition in both poetry and painting. As an invocation of this tradition, Yun's orchids recall the Confucian sage and the power and unwavering strength of his virtue. She claims these qualities for her friend, the scholar of the Bamboo Tower. He is the flower venerated in the inscription and whose benevolence she summons in her painting. S.M.

NOTES

1. *Qiancun yishu*, Zhu Xiaozang, ed.; Zhu changed his given name from Xiaozang to Zumou after the founding of the Republic in 1911.

2. The two poems are not translated here. The first poem is a *ci* on the tune "Zhegu Tian" written by Chen Cengshou and is in the *Qiangcun yishu*, "Canghai yiyinji," "Jiuyue yici," 22. The second is by Zhu Xiaozang himself in imitation of Li Fanxie to the tune "Liu Shao Qing" and is in the *Qiangcun yishu*, "Qiangcunji waici," 12.

3. The flower field mentioned in Yun's inscription was not far from Ye's home, which may account for this remark about his fateful relationship with the person to whom she addressed her inscription.

4. Two other paintings by Yun are known. One, a fan painting in the Chengxun tang Collection, Hong Kong, has been published in an entry by Marsha Weidner in Weidner et al., *Views from Jade Terrace: Chinese Women Artists, 1300–1912* (exh. cat.) (Indianapolis: Indianapolis Museum of Art, and New York: Rizzoli International Publications, 1988), 144, cat. no. 55; a hanging scroll of bamboo, orchids, and rock is also mentioned, ibid., 144, cat. no. 55, note 9.

5. Ye Yanlan, in his preface inscribed on what survived of Wang Jinglian's painting *Kongshan tingyu tu* (*Listening to the Rain in the Empty Mountains*), gives Wang Yuelian, as does the *Qing huajia shishi*. The *Guochao shuren jilüe* gives Wang Lian, and Yu Jianhua (as noted by Weidner in *Views from Jade Terrace*, 144) in his *Zhongguo meishujia renming cidian* lists her under two entries—Jing Lian and Wang Lian. I see no reason to favor one name over another and here would use Wang Jinglian, since Weidner has done so in her catalogue entry, but because most of the sources use her *zi*, Yun Xiang, or *hao* (as it is sometimes called), I will refer to her as Yun Xiang.

6. Yun, *Shuozhu* (*Explanations on Bamboo*), quoted in Ding Chuanjing, *Fuhui shuangxiuan xiaoji*, 2a, a collection of quotations with commentary by Ding from writings on and by Yun and from inscriptions on some of her paintings.

7. Ye in his preface, dated 1877, to her painting (or what survived of it), *Kongshan tingyu tu*, as recorded by Ding in *Fuhui shuangxiuan xiaoji*, 5b. Most sources refer to her as a Daoist, though there are at least two that identify her as a Buddhist nun.

8. Yun selected a number of these inscriptions, putting them together into two scrolls (Ye's 1877 preface to *Kongshan tingyu tu*, as recorded by Ding, *Fuhui shuangxiuan xiaoji*, 5b).

9. Deng Zhicheng, *Gudong suoji*, 1933, 7:25a, b and Zhang Jiliang, *Jintai canyuan ji*, quoted by Ding, *Fuhui shuangxiuan xiaoji*, 1b.

10. Weidner in *Views from Jade Terrace*, 144.

11. Gong Quangeng, *Yusuowen*, quoted by Ding, *Fuhui shuangxiuan xiaoji*, 1b.

12. Howard L. Boorman and Richard C. Howard, eds., *Biographical Dictionary of Republican China* (New York: Columbia University Press, 1971), 4:31–33.

13. *Guangzhou fuzhi*, 87:3b. Yun also uses *suxin* in one of her seals, *suxin zhuren*.

14. Liu Yin was a member of the royal family; his younger brother, Liu Yan, was founder of the Southern Han (917–971).

15. Quoted in the *Guangzhou fuzhi*, 87:3b.

16. Sima Qian, *Shiji*, 34, "Yan Shao Gong shijia," Zhonghua shuju, ed., 1959, 5:1550. For a translation of the story in French, see *Les Mémoires historiques de Se-ma Ts'ien*, trans. Edouard Chavannes (Paris: Librarie d'Amérique et d'Orient, 1967), 4:134–135.

17. For a translation and discussion of the "Lisao," see David Hawkes, *Ch'u Tz'u: The Songs of the South* (London: Clarendon Press, 1959).

18. Huang Tingjian, as quoted in the *Gujin tushu jicheng*, Zhonghua shuju, ed., *ce* 538, 22b.

MAPS, CHRONOLOGY, AND BIBLIOGRAPHY

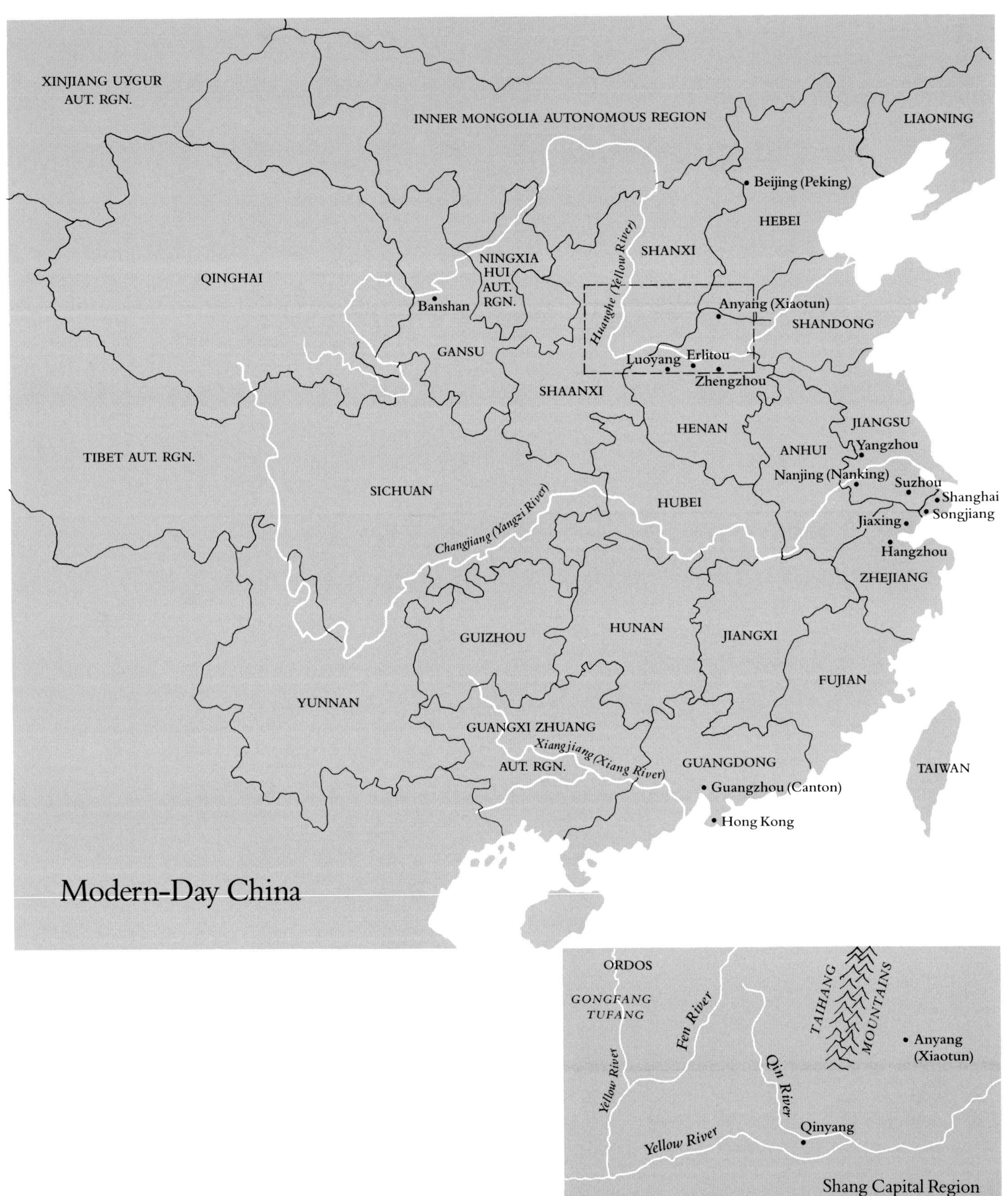
XINJIANG UYGUR
AUT. RGN.
INNER MONGOLIA AUTONOMOUS REGION
LIAONING
Beijing (Peking)
HEBEI
QINGHAI
NINGXIA
HUI
AUT.
RGN.
Huanghe (Yellow River)
SHANXI
Banshan
Anyang (Xiaotun)
SHANDONG
GANSU
Luoyang
Erlitou
Zhengzhou
SHAANXI
HENAN
JIANGSU
TIBET AUT. RGN.
ANHUI
Yangzhou
Nanjing (Nanking)
Suzhou
Shanghai
Songjiang
SICHUAN
HUBEI
Changjiang (Yangzi River)
Jiaxing
Hangzhou
ZHEJIANG
GUIZHOU
HUNAN
JIANGXI
FUJIAN
YUNNAN
GUANGXI ZHUANG
AUT. RGN.
Xiangjiang (Xiang River)
GUANGDONG
TAIWAN
Guangzhou (Canton)
Hong Kong
Modern-Day China
ORDOS
GONGFANG
TUFANG
Fen River
TAIHANG
MOUNTAINS
Anyang
(Xiaotun)
Yellow River
Qin River
Qinyang
Yellow River
Shang Capital Region

CHRONOLOGICAL TABLE

NEOLITHIC PERIOD
Yangshao Culture 5000–2000 B.C.
Longshan Culture 3000/2500–1500 B.C.

XIA 2000–1600 B.C.
Erlitou Culture (Erlitou I–IV, Xia/Early Shang ?) 2000–1500 B.C.

SHANG 1600–1045 B.C.
Erligang Phase (Early Shang) 1600–1200 B.C.
Anyang Period, Yinxu I–IV (Late Shang) 1300/1250–1045 B.C.

Xiang Jia	I*	
Pan Geng	I	
Xiao Xin	I	
Xiao Yi	I	
Wu Ding	I/II	I**
Zu Geng	II	II
Zu Jia	II	II
Lin Xin	III	III
Kang Ding	III	III
Wu Yi	III	IV
Wen Ding	III	IV
Di Yi	IV	V
Di Xin	IV	V

ZHOU 1045–221 B.C.
Western Zhou 1045–771 B.C.
Eastern Zhou 770–256 B.C.
Spring and Autumn Annals 770–476 B.C.
Warring States Period 475–221 B.C.

QIN 221–207 B.C.

HAN 206 B.C.–220 A.D.

THREE KINGDOMS 220–280

NORTHERN AND SOUTHERN DYNASTIES 386–581

SUI 581–618

TANG 618–907

FIVE DYNASTIES 907–960

LIAO 916–1125

SONG 960–1279
Northern Song 960–1127
Southern Song 1127–1279

JIN 1115–1234

YUAN 1271–1368

MING 1368–1644
Hongwu reign 1368–1398
Jianwen reign 1399–1402
Yongle reign 1403–1424
Hongxi reign 1425
Xuande reign 1426–1435
Zhengtong reign 1436–1449
Jingtai reign 1450–1456
Tianshun reign 1457–1464
Chenghua reign 1465–1487
Hongzhi reign 1488–1505
Zhengde reign 1506–1521
Jiajing reign 1522–1566
Longqing reign 1567–1572
Wanli reign 1573–1620
Taichang reign 1620
Tianqi reign 1621–1627
Chongzhen reign 1628–1644
Hongguang reign 1645
Longwu reign 1645–1646
Shaowu reign 1646
Yongli reign 1647

QING 1644–1911
Shunzhi reign 1644–1661
Kangxi reign 1662–1722
Yongzheng reign 1723–1735
Qianlong reign 1736–1795
Jiaqing reign 1796–1820
Daoguang reign 1821–1850
Xianfeng reign 1851–1861
Tongzhi reign 1862–1874
Guangxu reign 1875–1908
Yuantong reign 1909–1911
Hongxian reign 1912

*Archaeological Sequence
**Oracle-Bone Inscription Periodization

SELECTED BIBLIOGRAPHY

BRONZE AGE ART AND ARCHAEOLOGY

Bachhofer, Ludwig. "The Evolution of Shang and Early Chou Bronzes." *The Art Bulletin* 26 (June 1944): 107–116.

——. *A Short History of Chinese Art*. New York: Pantheon, 1946.

Bagley, Robert W. *Shang Ritual Bronzes in the Arthur M. Sackler Collections*. Cambridge, Mass., and London: Harvard University Press, 1987.

Barnard, Noel. "Records of Discoveries of Bronze Vessels in Literary Sources, and Some Pertinent Remarks on Aspects of Chinese Historiography." *Chung-wên-ta-hsüeh chung kuo wên hua yên chiu so hsüeh pao (Journal of the Institute of Chinese Studies of the Chinese University of Hong Kong)* 6, no. 2 (1973): 455–546.

Brinker, Helmut. *Bronzen aus dem alten China* (exh. cat.). Zurich: Museum Rietberg Zürich, 1975.

——. "The Decor Styles of Shang White Pottery." *Archives of Asian Art* 21 (1967–68): 39–62.

Cai Fangpei, Edward L. Shaughnessy, and James F. Shaughnessy, Jr. *A Concordance of the Xiaotun Nandi Oracle-Bone Inscriptions*. Chicago: Early China Special Monograph Series, no. 1, 1988.

Chang Kwang-chih. *The Archaeology of Ancient China*. 4th rev. ed. New Haven, Conn., and London: Yale University Press, 1986.

——. *Shang Civilization*. New Haven, Conn., and London: Yale University Press, 1980.

——. *Studies of Shang Archaeology: Selected Papers from the International Conference on Shang Civilization*. New Haven, Conn., and London: Yale University Press, 1986.

Childs-Johnson, Elizabeth. "The *Jue* and Its Ceremonial Use in the Ancestor Cult of China." *Artibus Asiae* 18, nos. 3-4 (1987): 171–196.

Chou Hung-hsiang. *Oracle Bone Collections in the United States*. Berkeley, Calif., Los Angeles, and London: University of California Press, 1976.

Creel, Herrlee Glessner. *The Birth of China: A Survey of the Formative Period of Chinese Civilization*. London: Jonathan Cape, 1936; New York: John Day, 1937, Frederick Ungar Publishing Co., 1954, 1964.

——. "Notes on Professor Karlgren's System for Dating Chinese Bronzes." *Journal of the Royal Asiatic Society* (1936): 463–473.

——. "On the Birth of *The Birth of China*." *Early China* 11–12 (1985–87): 1–5.

——. "On the Origins of the Manufacture and Decoration of Bronze in the Shang Period." *Monumenta Serica* 1, fasc. 1 (October 1935): 39–69.

——. *The Origins of Statecraft in China*. Vol. I, *The Western Chou Empire*. Chicago and London: University of Chicago Press, 1970.

Dewall, Magdalene von. *Pferd und Wagen in Frühen China*. Saarbrücker Beiträge zur Altertumskunde, vol. 1. Bonn: Rudolf Habelt Verlag, 1964.

Elkins, James. "Remarks on the Western Art Historical Study of Chinese Bronzes, 1930–1980." *Oriental Art* n.s. 33, no. 3 (Autumn 1987): 250–260.

Erdberg, Eleanor von. *Chinese Bronzes from the Collection of Chester Dale and Dolly Carter*. Ascona, Switz.: Artibus Asiae Publishers, 1978.

Fong Wen, ed. *The Great Bronze Age of China: An Exhibition from the People's Republic of China* (exh. cat.). New York: Metropolitan Museum of Art, 1980.

Hearn, Maxwell K. *Ancient Chinese Art: The Ernest Erickson Collection in the Metropolitan Museum of Art*. New York: Metropolitan Museum of Art, 1987.

Hochstadter, Walter. "Pottery and Stonewares of Shang, Chou and Han." *Bulletin, The Museum of Far Eastern Antiquities, Stockholm* 24 (1952): 81–108.

Hsu Chin-hsiung, ed. *The Menzies Collection of Shang Dynasty Oracle Bones*. 2 vols. Toronto: Royal Ontario Museum, 1972, 1977.

Kane, Virginia C. "The Independent Bronze Industries in the South of China Contemporary with the Shang and Western Chou Dynasties." *Archives of Asian Art* 28 (1974–5): 77–107.

Karlbeck, Orvar. "Anyang Moulds." *Bulletin, The Museum of Far Eastern Antiquities, Stockholm* 7 (1935): 39–60.

Karlgren, Bernhard. *A Catalogue of the Chinese Bronzes in the Alfred F. Pillsbury Collection*. Minneapolis: Minneapolis Institute of Arts, 1952.

——. "Marginalia on Some Bronze Albums." *Bulletin, The Museum of Far Eastern Antiquities, Stockholm* 31 (1959): 289–331.

——. "New Studies on Chinese Bronzes." *Bulletin, The Museum of Far Eastern Antiquities, Stockholm* 9 (1937): 1–117.

——. "Notes on the Grammar of Early Bronze Decor." *Bulletin, The Museum of Far Eastern Antiquities, Stockholm* 23 (1951): 1–37.

Keightley, David N. *Sources of Shang History: The Oracle-Bone Inscriptions of Bronze Age China*. Berkeley, Calif., Los Angeles, and London: University of California Press, 1978.

——, ed. *The Origins of Chinese Civilization*. Berkeley, Calif., Los Angeles, and London: University of California Press, 1983.

Kelley, Charles Fabens, and Ch'en Meng-chia. *Chinese Bronzes from the Buckingham Collection*. Chicago: Art Institute of Chicago, 1946.

Kidder, Jonathan Edward, Jr. *Early Chinese Bronzes in the City Art Museum of St. Louis*. St. Louis: City Art Museum of St. Louis, 1956.

Kuwayama, George. *Ancient Ritual Bronzes of China* (exh. cat.). Los Angeles: Los Angeles County Museum of Art, 1976.

——, ed. *The Great Bronze Age of China: A Symposium*. Los Angeles: Los Angeles County Museum of Art, 1983.

Lefebvre d'Argencé, René-Yvon. *Bronze Vessels of Ancient China in the Avery Brundage Collection*. San Francisco: Asian Art Museum of San Francisco, 1977.

Li Chi. "Studies of the Hsiao-t'un Pottery: Yin and Pre-Yin." *Annals of Academia Sinica* 2, no.1 (May 1955): 103–129.

Li Chi, and Wan Chia-pao. *Studies of Fifty-Three Ritual Bronzes*. Edited by Li Chi, Shih Chang-ju, and Kao Ch'ü-hsün. Archaeologia Sinica, n.s. no. 5. Nankang, Taiwan: Institute of History and Philology Academia Sinica, 1972.

——. *Studies of the Bronze Chia-Vessel*. Edited by Li Chi, Shih Chang-ju, and Kao Ch'ü-hsün. Archaeologia Sinica, n.s. no. 3. Nankang, Taiwan: Institute of History and Philology Academia Sinica, 1968.

——. *Studies of the Bronze Chüeh-Cup*. Edited by Li Chi, Shih Chang-ju, and Kao Ch'ü-hsün. Archaeologia Sinica, n.s. no. 2. Nankang, Taiwan: Institute of History and Philology Academia Sinica, 1966.

——. *Studies of the Bronze Ku-Beaker*. Edited by Li Chi, Shih Chang-ju, and Kao Ch'ü-hsün. Archaeologia Sinica, n.s. no. 1. Nankang, Taiwan: Institute of History and Philology Academia Sinica, 1964.

——. *Studies of the Bronze Ting-Cauldron*. Edited by Li Chi, Shih Chang-ju, and Kao Ch'ü-hsün. Archaeologia Sinica, n.s. no. 4. Nankang, Taiwan: Institute of History and Philology Academia Sinica, 1970.

Li Chi, and Kao Ch'ü-hsün, eds. *Hou Chia Chuang (The Yin-Shang Cemetery Site at Anyang, Honan)*. 8 vols. Archaeologia Sinica, no. 3. Taipei, Taiwan: Institute of History and Philology Academia Sinica, 1962–76.

Li Xueqin. *The Wonder of Chinese Bronzes*. Beijing: Waiwen chubanshe, 1980.

Lienert, Ursula. *Typology of the Ting in the Shang Dynasty: A Tentative Chronology of the Yin-hsü Period*. 2 vols. Publication the Asian Department of the Kunsthistorisches Institut der Universität Köln, no. 3. Wiesbaden: Franz Steiner Verlag, 1979.

Loehr, Max. "The Bronze Styles of the Anyang Period." *Archives of the Chinese Art Society of America* 7 (1953): 42–53.

——. *Chinese Bronze Age Weapons: The Werner Jannings Collection in the Chinese National Palace Museum, Peking*. Ann Arbor, Mich.: University of Michigan Press, 1956.

——. *Ritual Vessels of Bronze Age China* (exh. cat.). New York: Asia Society, 1968.

Ma Chengyuan. *Ancient Chinese Bronzes*. Edited by Hsio-yen Shih. Hong Kong, Oxford, and New York: Oxford University Press, 1986.

Menzies, James Mellon. *The Shang Ko: A Study of the Characteristic Weapon of the Bronze Age in China during the Period 1311–1039 B.C.* Toronto: Far Eastern Department of the Royal Ontario Museum, University of Toronto, 1965.

Mino Yutaka, and James Robinson. *Beauty and Tranquility: The Ely Lilly Collection of Chinese Art*. Indianapolis: Indianapolis Museum of Art, 1983.

Poor, Robert J. *Ancient Chinese Bronzes*. New York: Intercultural Arts, 1968.

——. *Ancient Chinese Bronzes, Ceramics and Jade in the Collection of the Honolulu Academy of Arts*. Honolulu: Honolulu Academy of Arts, 1979.

——. "The Master of the 'Metropolis'-Emblem Ku." *Archives of Asian Art* 41 (1988): 70–89.

——. "Notes on Sung Archaeological Catalogs." *Archives of the Chinese Art Society of America* 19 (1965): 33–40.

Pope, John Alexander, Rutherford John Gettens, James Cahill, and Noel Barnard. *The Freer Chinese Bronzes*. Vol. I, *Catalogue*. Washington, D.C.: Smithsonian Institution, 1967.

Rawson, Jessica. *Ancient China: Art and Archaeology*. London: British Museum Publications, 1980.

——. *Chinese Bronzes: Art and Ritual* (exh. cat.). London: British Museum Publications in association with Sainsbury Centre for Visual Arts, University of East Anglia, 1987.

Roy, David T., and Tsuen-hsuin Tsien, eds. *Ancient China: Studies in Early Civilization*. Hong Kong: Chinese University Press, 1978.

Royal Ontario Museum. *The Chinese Exhibition: The Exhibition of Archaeological Finds of the People's Republic of China* (exh. cat.). Rev. ed. Toronto: Royal Ontario Museum in cooperation with Times Newspapers, 1974.

Shangraw, Clarence F. *Origins of Chinese Ceramics* (exh. cat.). New York: China Institute in America and China House Gallery, 1978.

Shaughnessy, Edward L. "Historical Perspectives on the Introduction of the Chariot into China." *Harvard Journal of Asiatic Studies* 48, no. 1 (June 1988): 189–238.

——. "Recent Approaches to Oracle-Bone Periodization: A Review." *Early China* 8 (1982–83): 1–13.

Shih Hsio-yen. "A Chinese Shell-Inlay Motif." *Annual* [Art and Archaeology Division, Royal Ontario Museum, University of Toronto] (1962): 43–9.

——. "Painted Pottery in the Chinese Neolithic." *Bulletin of the Oriental Ceramic Society of Hong Kong* 7 (1984–86): 11–30.

Soper, Alexander C. "Early, Middle and Late Shang: A Note." *Artibus Asiae* 28 (1966): 5–38.

Thorp, Robert L. "The Archaeology of Style at Anyang: Tomb 5 in Context." *Archives of Asian Art* 41 (1988): 47–69.

——. "The Date of Tomb 5 at Yinxu, Anyang: A Review Article." *Artibus Asiae* 43, no. 3 (1982): 239–246.

——. "The Growth of Early Shang Civilization: New Data from Ritual Vessels." *Harvard Journal of Asiatic Studies* 45 (1985): 5–75.

Watson, William. *Ancient Chinese Bronzes*. London: Faber and Faber, 1962. Rev. ed., 1977.

White, William Charles. *Bone Culture of Ancient China*. Museum Studies 4. Toronto: University of Toronto Press, 1945.

MING AND QING PAINTING

Art Gallery, Chinese University of Hong Kong. *Paintings by Yangzhou Artists of the Qing Dynasty from the Palace Museum* (exh. cat.). Hong Kong: Art Gallery, Institute of Chinese Studies, Chinese University of Hong Kong, 1984.

Barnhart, Richard. "The 'Wild and Heterodox School' of Ming Painting." In *Theories of the Arts in China*, edited by Susan Bush and Christian F. Murck, 365–396. Princeton, N.J.: Princeton University Press, 1983.

Bickford, Maggie. *Bones of Jade, Soul of Ice: The Flowering Plum in Chinese Art* (exh. cat.). New Haven, Conn.: Yale University Art Gallery, 1985.

Bush, Susan, ed. *The Chinese Literati on Painting: Su Shi (1037–1101) to Tung Ch'i-Ch'ang (1555–1636)*. Cambridge, Mass.: Harvard University Press, 1971.

——, and Shih Hsio-yen, eds. *Early Chinese Texts on Painting*. Cambridge, Mass., and London: Harvard University Press, 1985.

Cahill, James. *The Compelling Image: Nature and Style in Seventeenth-Century Chinese Painting*. Cambridge, Mass., and London: Harvard University Press, 1982.

——. *The Distant Mountains: Chinese Painting of the Late Ming Dynasty, 1570–1644*. New York and Tokyo: John Weatherhill, 1982.

——. *Fantastics and Eccentrics in Chinese Painting* (exh. cat.). New York: Asia Society, 1967.

——. *Hills Beyond a River: Chinese Painting of the Yuan Dynasty, 1279–1368*. New York and Tokyo: John Weatherhill, 1976.

——. *Parting at the Shore: Chinese Painting of the Early and Middle Ming Dynasty, 1368–1580*. New York and Tokyo: John Weatherhill, 1978.

——. "Style as Idea in Ming-Qing Painting." In *The Mozartian Historian: Essays on the Works of Joseph R. Levenson*, edited by Maurice Meisner and Roads Murphey, 137–156. Berkeley, Calif.: University of California Press, 1976.

——, ed. *The Restless Landscape: Chinese Painting of the Late Ming Period* (exh. cat.). Berkeley, Calif.: University Art Museum, 1971.

——, ed. *Shadows of Mt. Huang: Chinese Painting and Printing of the Anhui School* (exh. cat.). Berkeley, Calif.: University Art Museum, 1981.

Capon, Edmund, and Mae Anna Pang. *Chinese Paintings of the Ming and Qing Dynasties: 14th–20th Centuries* (exh. cat.). N.p.: International Cultural Corporation of Australia, 1981.

Caswell, James O. *The Single Brushstroke: 600 Years of Chinese Painting from the Ching Yuan Chai Collection* (exh. cat.). Vancouver, B.C.: Vancouver Art Gallery, 1985.

Chou Ju-hsi, and Claudia Brown. *The Elegant Brush: Chinese Painting under the Qianlong Emperor, 1735–1795* (exh. cat.). Phoenix: Phoenix Art Museum, 1985.

——. *Heritage of the Brush: The Roy and Marilyn Papp Collection of Chinese Painting* (exh. cat.). Phoenix: Phoenix Art Museum, 1989.

Contag, Victoria, and Wang Chi-ch'üan. *Seals of Chinese Painters and Collectors of the Ming and Ch'ing Periods*. Rev. ed. Hong Kong: Hong Kong University Press, 1966.

Ecke, Tseng Yu-ho. *Poetry on the Wind: The Art of Chinese Folding Fans from the Ming and Ch'ing Dynasties* (exh. cat.). Honolulu: Honolulu Academy of Arts, 1981.

——. *Wen-jen Hua: Chinese Literati Painting from the Collection of Mr. and Mrs. Mitchell Hutchinson* (exh. cat.). Honolulu: Honolulu Academy of Arts, 1988.

Edwards, Richard, et al. *The Art of Wen Cheng-ming (1470–1559)* (exh. cat.). Ann Arbor,Mich.: University of Michigan Museum of Art, 1976.

Fong Wen. "Tung Ch'i-Ch'ang and the Orthodox Theory of Painting." *National Palace Museum Quarterly* 2, no. 3 (1969): 1–26.

——, and Maxwell K. Hearn. "Silent Poetry: Chinese Paintings in the Douglas Dillon Galleries." *The Metropolitan Museum of Art Bulletin* 39, no. 3 (Winter 1981–82).

——, Alfreda Murck, Shih Shou-chien, Ch'en Pao-chen, and Jan Stuart. *Images of the Mind: Selections from the Edward L. Elliott Family and John B. Elliott Collections of Chinese Calligraphy and Painting* (exh. cat.). Princeton, N.J.: Art Museum, Princeton University, 1984.

Fu Shen, and Marilyn Fu. *Studies in Connoisseurship: Chinese Paintings from the Arthur M. Sackler Collection in New York and Princeton* (exh. cat.). Princeton, N.J.: Princeton University Press, 1973.

Goodrich, L. Carrington, and Fang Chaoying, eds. *Dictionary of Ming Biography, 1368–1644*. 2 vols. London and New York: Columbia University Press, 1976.

Museum für Kunst und Gewerbe. *Chinesische Malerie der letzten vier Jahrhunderte* (exh. cat.). Hamburg: Museum für Kunst und Gewerbe, 1949.

Hay, John. *Kernels of Energy, Bones of Earth: The Rock in Chinese Art* (exh. cat.). New York: China Institute in America and China House Gallery, 1985.

Ho Wai-Kam. "Tung Ch'i-Ch'ang's New Orthodoxy and the Southern School Theory." In *Artists and Tradition: Uses of the Past in Chinese Culture*, edited by Christian F. Murck, 113–129. Princeton, N.J.: Princeton University Press, 1976.

——, Sherman E. Lee, Laurence Sickman, and Marc F. Wilson. *Eight Dynasties of Chinese Painting: The Collections of the Nelson Gallery-Atkins Museum, Kansas City, and The Cleveland Museum of Art* (exh. cat.). Cleveland: Cleveland Museum of Art in cooperation with Indiana University Press, 1980.

Hummel, Arthur W., ed. *Eminent Chinese of the Ch'ing Period (1644–1912)*. Washington, D.C.: United States Government Printing Office, 1943.

Hyland, Alice R. M. *Deities, Emperors, Ladies and Literati: Figure Painting of the Ming and Qing Dynasties* (exh. cat.). Birmingham, Ala.: Birmingham Museum of Art, 1987.

——. *The Literati Vision: Sixteenth-Century Wu School Painting and Calligraphy* (exh. cat.). Memphis, Tenn.: Memphis Brooks Museum of Art, 1984.

Laing, Ellen Johnston. "Biographical Notes on Three Seventeenth-Century Chinese Painters." In *The Translation of Art: Essays on Chinese Painting and Poetry*, edited by James C. Y. Watt, 107–110. Renditions 6. Hong Kong: Centre for Translation Projects, Chinese University of Hong Kong, 1976.

Lawton, Mary S. *Hsieh Shih-ch'ên: A Ming Dynasty Painter Reinterprets the Past* (exh. cat.). Chicago: David and Alfred Smart Gallery, University of Chicago, 1978.

Ledderose, Lothar, ed. *Im Schatten hoher Bäume: Malerei der Ming- und Qing-Dynastien (1368–1911) aus der Volksrepublik China* (exh. cat.). Baden-Baden: Staatliche Kunsthalle Baden-Baden in cooperation with Kunsthistorische Institut der Universität Heidelberg, 1985.

Lee, Sherman E. *The Colors of Ink: Chinese Paintings and Related Ceramics from The Cleveland Museum of Art* (exh. cat.). New York: Asia Society, 1974.

——. "Some Problems in Ming and Ch'ing Landscape Painting." *Ars Orientalis* 2 (1957): 471–485.

Li Chu-Tsing. *A Thousand Peaks and Myriad Ravines: Chinese Paintings in the Charles A. Drenowatz Collection*. 2 vols. Ascona, Switz.: Artibus Asiae Publishers, 1974.

——, and James C. Y. Watt, eds. *The Chinese Scholar's Studio: Artistic Life in the Late Ming Period* (exh. cat.). New York: Asia Society, 1987.

Little, Stephen. *Realm of the Immortals: Daoism in the Arts of China* (exh. cat.). Cleveland: Cleveland Museum of Art in cooperation with Indiana University Press, 1988.

National Palace Museum. *Hai-wai Yi-chen (Chinese Art in Overseas Collections: Painting [II])*. Taipei, Taiwan: National Palace Museum, 1988.

——. *Wu-pai hua chiu-shih nien (Ninety Years of Wu School Painting)* (exh. cat.). Taipei,Taiwan: National Palace Museum, 1975.

Owyoung, Steven D. "Chinese Painting." *The Bulletin of The Saint Louis Art Museum*, n.s. 17, no. 3 (Summer 1985).

Rogers, Howard, and Sherman E. Lee. *Masterworks of Ming and Qing Painting from the Forbidden City* (exh. cat.). Lansdale, Pa.: International Arts Council, 1988.

Shih Hsio-yen, and Henry S. Trubner. *Individualists and Eccentrics: The Mr. and Mrs. R. W. Finlayson Collection of Chinese Paintings* (exh. cat.). Toronto: University of Toronto Press, 1963.

Sickman, Laurence, and Alexander C. Soper. *The Art and Architecture of China*. Harmondsworth, Eng.: Penguin Books, 1971.

Sirén, Osvald. *The Chinese on the Art of Painting*. Beijing: H. Vetch, 1936. Reprint. New York: Shocken Books, 1963.

——. *Chinese Painting: Leading Masters and Principles*. 7 vols. London: Lund Humphries and Co., 1956–58.

Siu Wai-fong Anita. *The Modern Spirit in Chinese Painting: Selections from the Jeannette Shambaugh Elliott Collection* (exh. cat.). Phoenix: Phoenix Art Museum, 1985.

Sullivan, Michael. *Symbols of Eternity: The Art of Landscape Painting in China*. Oxford: Clarendon Press, 1979.

——. *The Three Perfections: Chinese Painting and Poetry and Calligraphy*. London: Thames and Hudson, 1974.

Suzuki Kei. *Comprehensive Illustrated Catalog of Chinese Paintings*. 5 vols. Tokyo: University of Tokyo Press, 1982–83.

Tsao Jung Ying. *Chinese Paintings of the Middle Qing Dynasty*. San Francisco: San Francisco Graphic Society, 1987.

Vanderstappen, Harrie A. "Late Ming Fans." *Journal* [Honolulu Academy of Arts] 2 (1977): 48–73.

——. "A Note on Minor Traditions in Late Ming Landscape Painting." *Oriental Art* 16, no. 1 (Spring 1970): 45–50.

——. "Paintings at the Early Ming Court (1368–1435) and the Problems of a Painting Academy." *Monumenta Serica* 15 (1956): 259–302; 16 (1957): 315–346.

——. "The Style of Some Seventeenth-Century Chinese Paintings." In *Arts and Traditions: Uses of the Past in Chinese Culture*, edited by Christian F. Murck, 149–168. Princeton, N.J.: Princeton University Press, 1976.

Weidner, Marsha, Ellen Johnston Laing, Irving Yucheng Lo, Christina Chu, and James Robinson. *Views from Jade Terrace: Chinese Women Artists, 1300–1912* (exh. cat.). Indianapolis: Indianapolis Museum of Art, and New York: Rizzoli International Publications, 1988.

Whitfield, Roderick. *In Pursuit of Antiquity: Chinese Paintings of the Ming and Ch'ing Dynasties from the Collection of Mr. and Mrs. Earle Morse* (exh. cat.). Princeton, N.J.: Art Museum, Princeton University, 1969.

Wong Kwan S., and Celeste Adams. "In the Way of the Master: Chinese and Japanese Painting and Calligraphy." *Bulletin* [The Museum of Fine Arts, Houston] n.s. 7, no. 3 (February 1981).

Wu, Nelson I. "Tung Ch'i-Ch'ang (1555–1636): Apathy in Government and Fervor in Art." In *Confucian Personalities*, edited by Arthur Wright and Denis Twitchett, 260–293. Stanford, Calif.: Stanford University Press, 1962.

PHOTOGRAPHY CREDITS

All photographs Jerry Kobylecky Museum Photography, with the following exceptions:

Pages 27–36:

Figs. 1, 2, 6, 8, 30, 41, 50. Reprinted from Institute of Archaeology, Archaeologia Sinica, *Yinxu Fu Hao mu*, Ding series no. 23 (Beijing: Wenwu chubanshe, 1980), figs. 14.1, 14.2, 14.3, 19.4, 14.3, 15.4, 45, respectively.

Figs. 3, 4, 5; 10; 12; 13; 31; 32; 33; 37; 38. Reprinted from Institute of Archaeology, Archaeologia Sinica, *Yinxu qingtongqi*, Yi series no. 24 (Beijing: Wenwu chubanshe, 1985), figs. 34, 35.7, 35.1, 33.4, 41.4, 87.5, 82.3, 90.2, 38.1, respectively.

Figs. 14, 15 and 16, 17–29, 34–36, 39, 40, 42–49, 51. Reprinted from Ma Chengwan, *Shang Zhou qingtongqi wenshi* (Beijing: Wenwu chubanshe, 1984), figs. 348; 360; 152, 360, 787, 154, 22, 245, 9, 28, 63, 490, 229, 153, 28; 181, 22, 606; 592; 153; 88, 31, 698, 530, 596, 232, 228, 63; 81, respectively.

Page 48:

Fig. 1. Courtesy of Jon Poor/Poor Design. © 1989 Robert Poor.

Pages 68–90:

Fig. 1. Reprinted from *Xiaotun: Yinxu wenzi, Yibian*, vol. 1, ed. Dong Zuobin (Nanjing: Academia Sinica, 1948), pl. 164.

Fig. 2. Reprinted from *Xiaotun: Yinxu wenzi, Bingbian*, vol. 1.1, ed. Zhang Bingquan (Taipei, Taiwan: Academia Sinica, 1957), pl. 1.

Fig. 3: Reprinted from David N. Keightley, *Sources of Shang History: The Oracle-Bone Inscriptions of Bronze Age China* (Berkeley, Calif., Los Angeles, and London: University of California Press, 1978), fig. 3.

DESIGN: Harvey Retzloff
TYPESETTING: RT Associates, Inc.
PRINTING: Congress Printing Company